2015
DRIVER'S ATLAS
BRITAIN
BRITAIN'S CLEAREST MAPPING

Atlas con

D0552809

Scale 1:250,000 or 3.95 r

Map pages south	inside front cover
Route planner	II–VII
Mileage chart	VIII
Atlas Symbols	1
Road maps 1:250,000 scale	2–237
Western Isles 1:700,000 scale	232–233
Orkney Islands 1:636,000 scale	234
Shetland Islands 1:636,000 scale	235
Channel Islands 1:150,000 scale	236
Isle of Man 1:317,000 scale	237
Restricted junctions	238–239
Index to place names	240–320
County, administrative area map	240–241
Place name index	242–320
Ireland	endpaper
Map pages north	inside back cover

13th edition June 2014

© AA Media Limited 2014

Cartography:

All cartography in this atlas edited, designed and produced by the Mapping Services Department of AA Publishing (A05183).

This atlas contains Ordnance Survey data © Crown copyright and database right 2014 and Royal Mail data © Royal Mail copyright and database right 2014.

Land & Property Services
Paper Map Licensed Partner
ORDNANCE SURVEY OF NORTHERN IRELAND

This atlas is based upon Crown Copyright and is reproduced with the permission of Land & Property Services under delegated authority from the Controller of Her Majesty's Stationery Office, © Crown copyright and database right 2014, PMLPA No. 100497

Ordnance Survey Ireland
Ireland's National Mapping Agency

© Ordnance Survey Ireland/ Government of Ireland. Copyright Permit No. MP0000314

Publisher's notes:
Published by AA Publishing (a trading name of AA Media Limited, whose registered office is Fanum House, Basing View, Basingstoke, Hampshire RG21 4EA, UK. Registered number 06112600).

All rights reserved. No part of this publication may be reproduced, stored in a retrieval system, or transmitted in any form or by any means – electronic, mechanical, photocopying, recording or otherwise – unless the permission of the publisher has been given beforehand.

ISBN: 978 0 7495 7606 6 (flexibound)

A CIP catalogue record for this book is available from The British Library.

Disclaimer:
The contents of this atlas are believed to be correct at the time of the latest revision, it will not contain any subsequent amended, new or temporary information including diversions and traffic control or enforcement systems. The publishers cannot be held responsible or liable for any loss or damage occasioned to any person acting or refraining from action as a result of any use or reliance on material in this atlas, nor for any errors, omissions or changes in such material. This does not affect your statutory rights.

The publishers would welcome information to correct any errors or omissions and to keep this atlas up to date. Please write to the Atlas Editor, AA Publishing, The Automobile Association, Fanum House, Basing View, Basingstoke, Hampshire RG21 4EA, UK.
E-mail: roadatlasfeedback@theaa.com

Acknowledgements:
AA Publishing would like to thank the following for their assistance in producing this atlas:

RoadPilot®

Information on fixed speed camera locations provided by and © 2014 RoadPilot® Driving Technology. Crematoria database provided by Cremation Society of Great Britain. Cadw, English Heritage, Forestry Commission, Historic Scotland, Johnsons, National Trust and National Trust for Scotland, RSPB, The Wildlife Trust, Scottish Natural Heritage, Natural England, The Countryside Council for Wales.

Printer:
1010 Printing International.

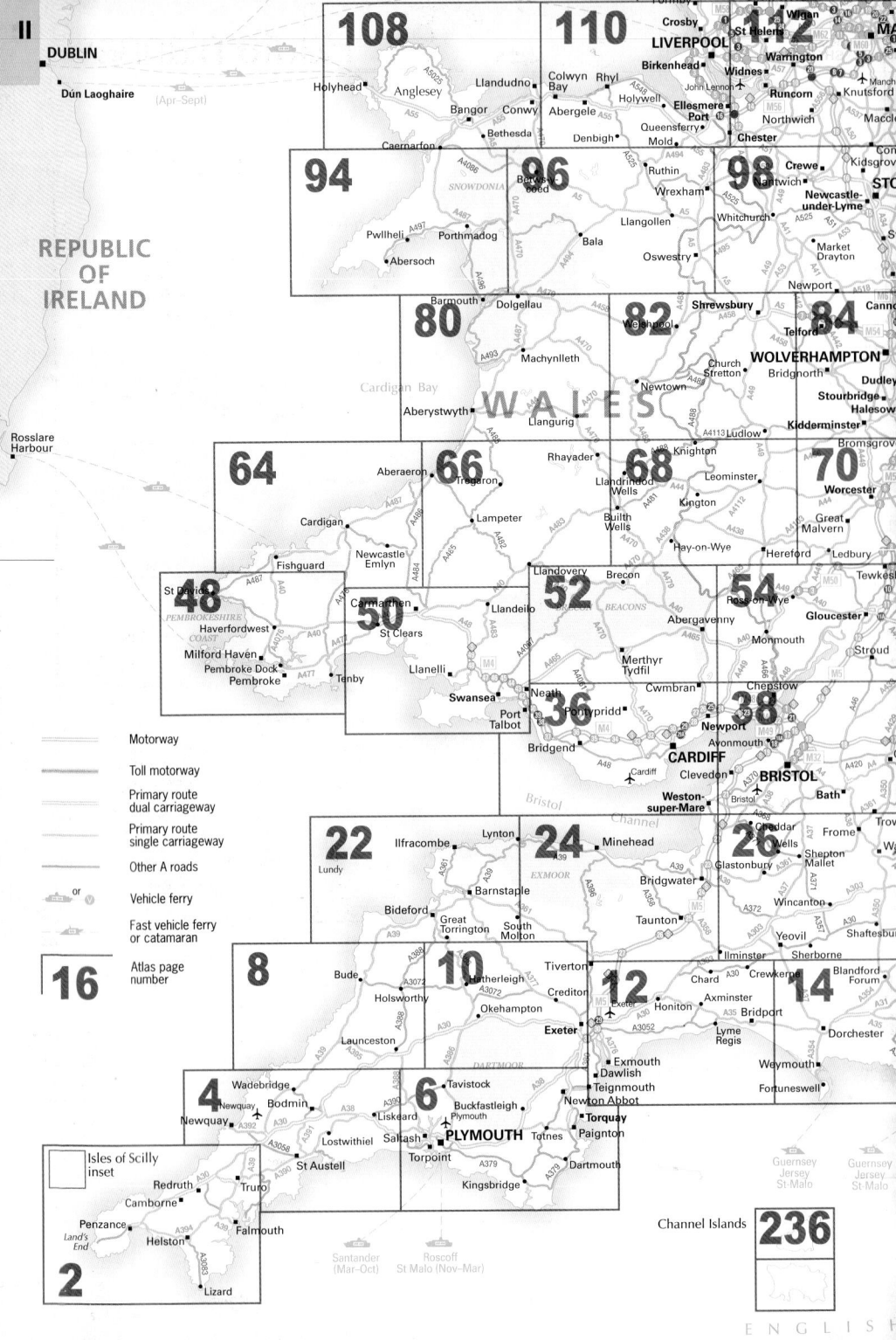

Route planner

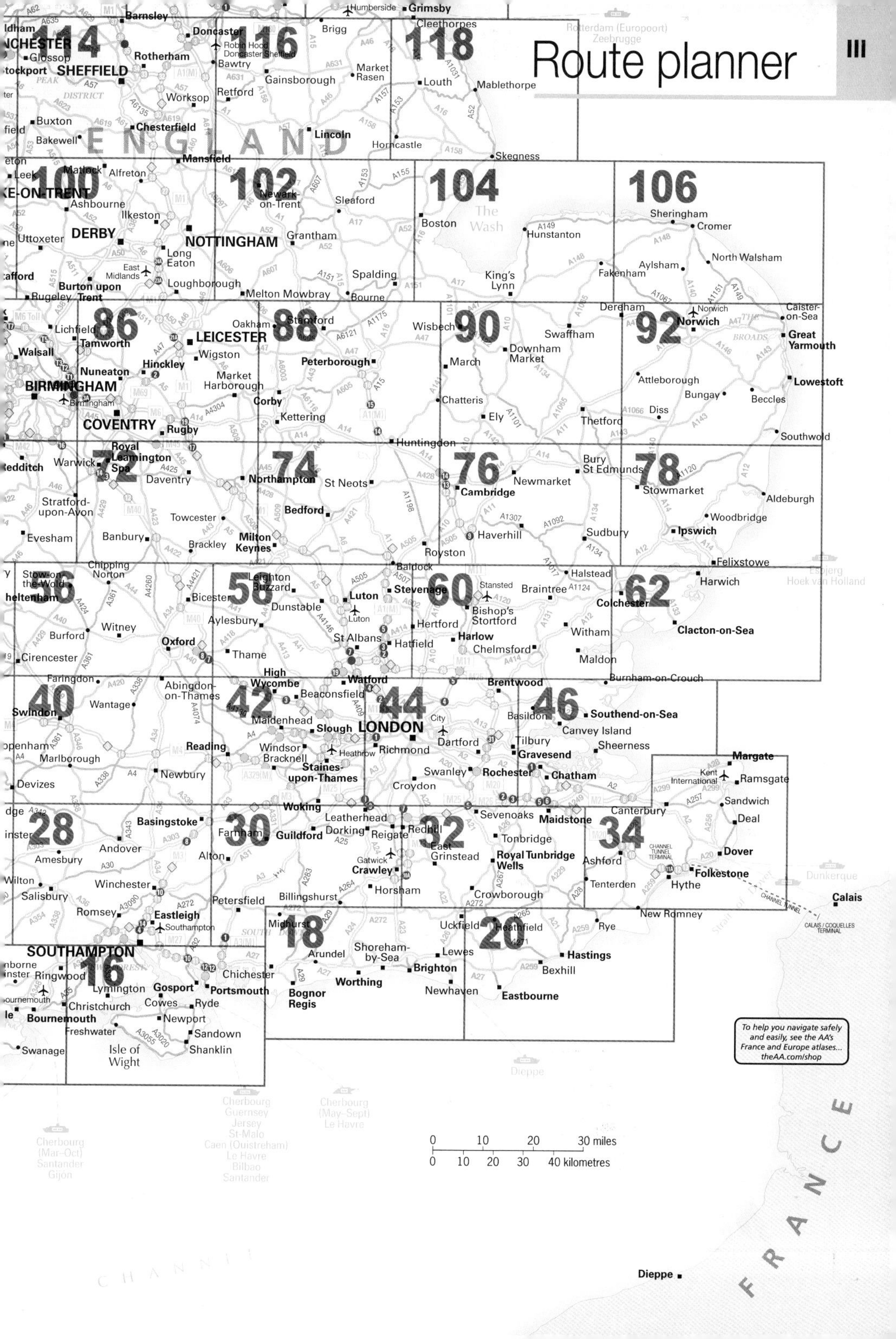

Grid numbers: 114, 116, 118, 100, 102, 104, 106, 86, 88, 90, 92, 72, 74, 76, 78, 6, 58, 60, 62, 40, 42, 44, 46, 28, 30, 32, 34, 16, 18, 20

Place names include:
Barnsley, Doncaster, Grimsby, Cleethorpes, Brigg, Humberside, MANCHESTER, Rotherham, SHEFFIELD, Stockport, Glossop, Oldham, Robin Hood Doncaster Sheffield, Bawtry, Market Rasen, Louth, Mablethorpe, Worksop, Retford, Gainsborough, Rotterdam (Europoort) Zeebrugge, Buxton, Chesterfield, Lincoln, Bakewell, Mansfield, Horncastle, Skegness, PEAK DISTRICT

STOKE-ON-TRENT, DERBY, NOTTINGHAM, Sleaford, Boston, The Wash, Sheringham, Cromer, North Walsham, Ashbourne, Ilkeston, Newark-on-Trent, Grantham, Hunstanton, Aylsham, Fakenham, King's Lynn, ENGLAND

Lichfield, Tamworth, LEICESTER, Wigston, Stamford, Wisbech, Swaffham, Downham Market, Norwich, Caister-on-Sea, Great Yarmouth, BROADS, Walsall, Hinckley, Market Harborough, Peterborough, Corby, March, Attleborough, Bungay, Beccles, Lowestoft, BIRMINGHAM, Nuneaton, Kettering, Chatteris, Ely, Thetford, Diss, Southwold, COVENTRY, Rugby, Huntingdon, Bury St Edmunds

Redditch, Royal Leamington Spa, Warwick, Daventry, Northampton, St Neots, Cambridge, Newmarket, Stowmarket, Aldeburgh, Stratford-upon-Avon, Towcester, Bedford, Haverhill, Sudbury, Woodbridge, Ipswich, Evesham, Banbury, Brackley, Milton Keynes, Royston, Felixstowe, Harwich, Hoek van Holland

Stow-on-the-Wold, Cheltenham, Chipping Norton, Bicester, Leighton Buzzard, Luton, Stevenage, Stansted, Braintree, Colchester, Witney, Dunstable, Bishop's Stortford, Harlow, Witham, Clacton-on-Sea, Burford, Oxford, Aylesbury, Thame, St Albans, Hertford, Hatfield, Chelmsford, Maldon, Cirencester, Faringdon, Abingdon-on-Thames, Burnham-on-Crouch, Halstead

Swindon, Wantage, High Wycombe, Watford, Brentwood, Marlborough, Maidenhead, Slough, LONDON, Basildon, Southend-on-Sea, Margate, Reading, Windsor, Bracknell, Richmond, Dartford, Tilbury, Canvey Island, Sheerness, Ramsgate, Newbury, Staines-upon-Thames, Heathrow, Swanley, Gravesend, Kent International, Sandwich, Devizes, Woking, Croydon, Rochester, Chatham, Canterbury, Deal, Leatherhead, Sevenoaks, Maidstone, Dover, Basingstoke, Farnham, Guildford, Dorking, Reigate, Redhill, Tonbridge, Ashford, Channel Tunnel Terminal, Folkestone, Andover, Alton, East Grinstead, Royal Tunbridge Wells, Tenterden, Hythe, Calais, Amesbury, Gatwick, Crawley, Crowborough, New Romney, Calais/Coquelles Terminal, Wilton, Salisbury, Petersfield, Billingshurst, Horsham, Rye, Dunkerque, Romsey, Eastleigh, Southampton, Midhurst, Shoreham-by-Sea, Uckfield, Heathfield, Hastings, SOUTHAMPTON, Chichester, Arundel, Lewes, Brighton, Bexhill, Ringwood, Lymington, Gosport, Portsmouth, Worthing, Newhaven, Eastbourne, Bournemouth, Christchurch, Cowes, Ryde, Bognor Regis, Newport, Sandown, Swanage, Freshwater, Shanklin, Isle of Wight, Dieppe, FRANCE, CHANNEL

Cherbourg (Mar–Oct), Santander, Gijón, Cherbourg, Guernsey, Jersey, St-Malo, Caen (Ouistreham), Le Havre, Bilbao, Santander, Cherbourg (May–Sept) Le Havre, Dieppe

Scale:
0   10   20   30 miles
0 10 20 30 40 kilometres

To help you navigate safely and easily, see the AA's France and Europe atlases... theAA.com/shop

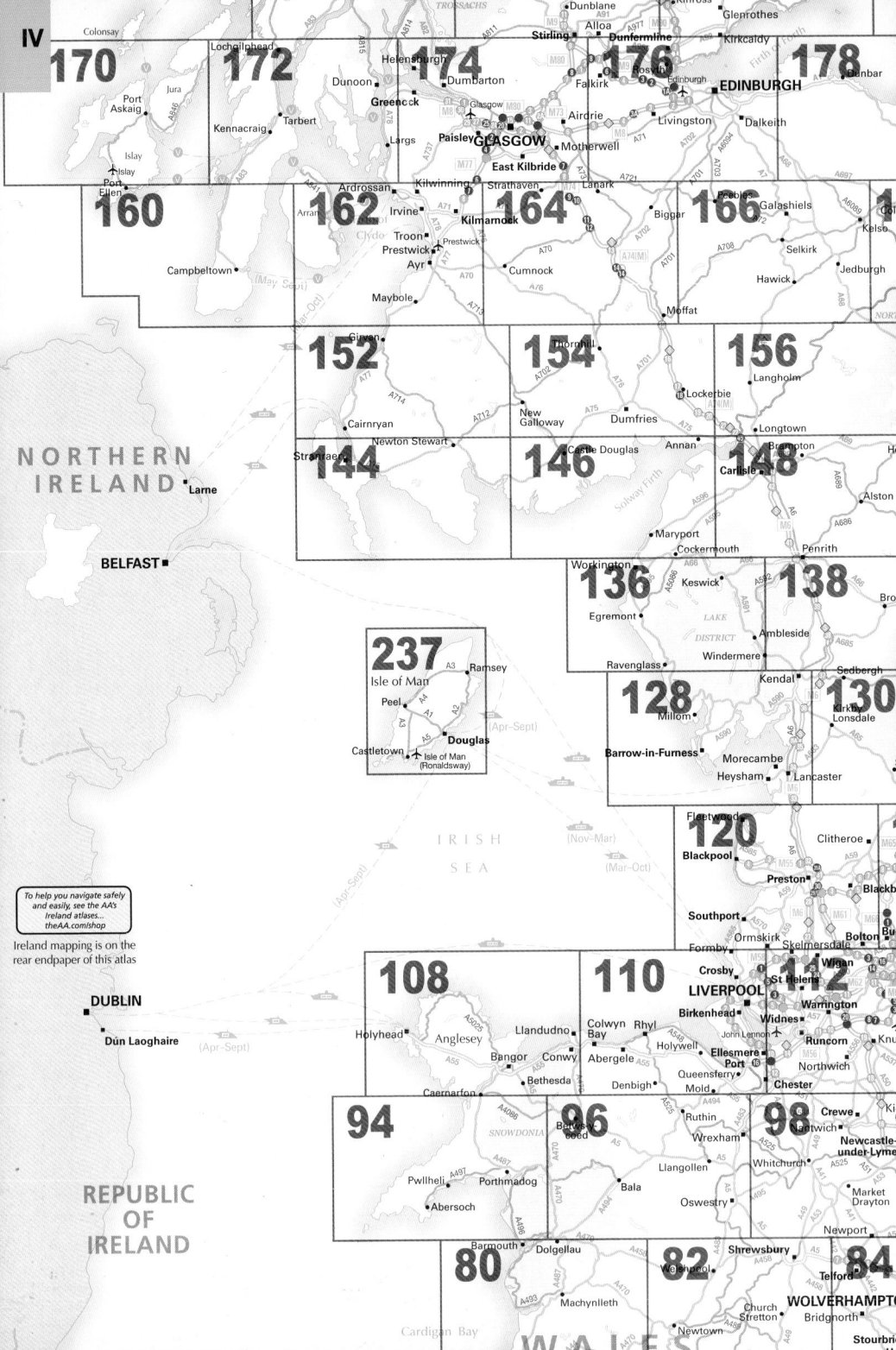

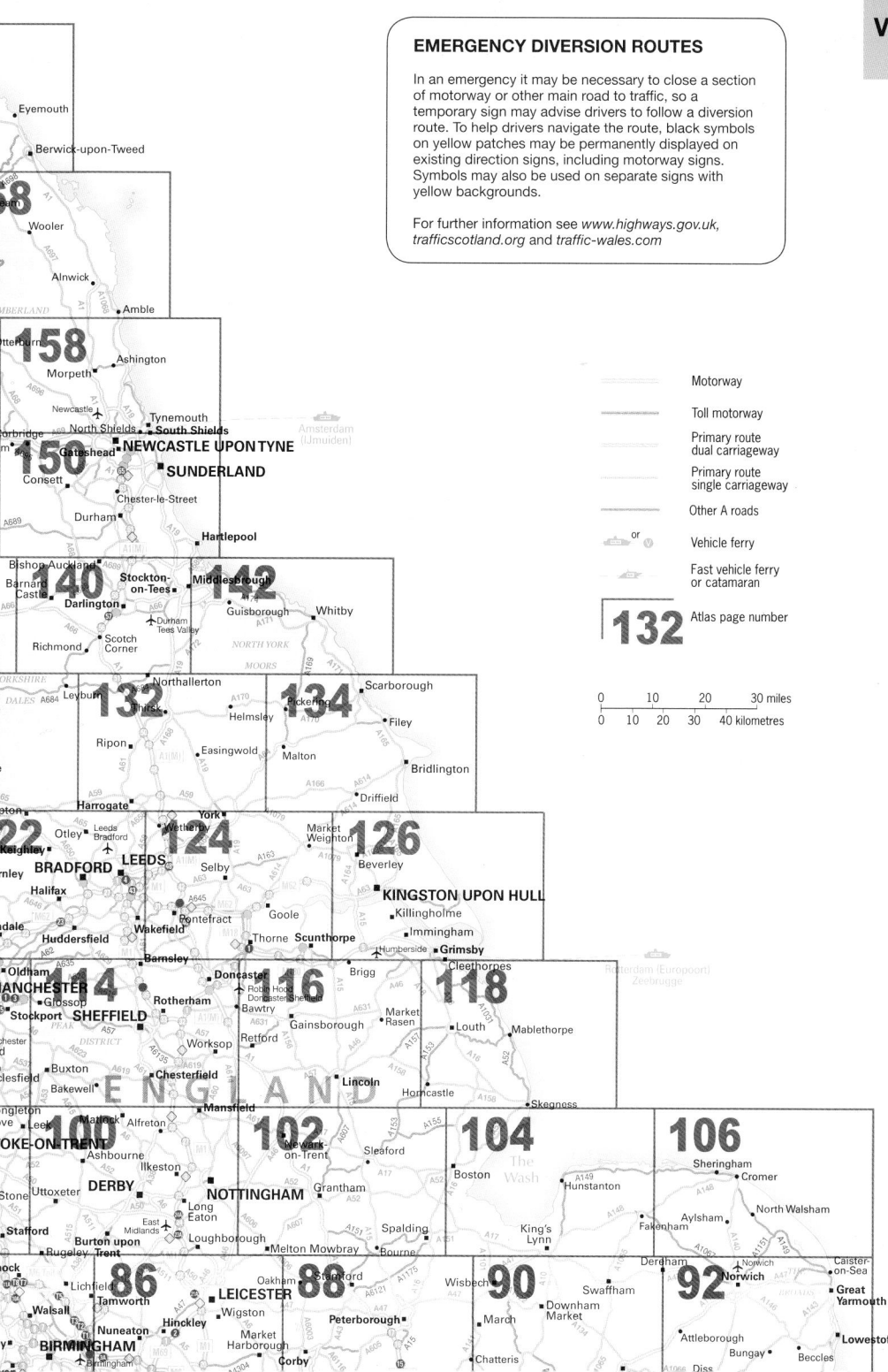

V

EMERGENCY DIVERSION ROUTES

In an emergency it may be necessary to close a section of motorway or other main road to traffic, so a temporary sign may advise drivers to follow a diversion route. To help drivers navigate the route, black symbols on yellow patches may be permanently displayed on existing direction signs, including motorway signs. Symbols may also be used on separate signs with yellow backgrounds.

For further information see *www.highways.gov.uk*, *trafficscotland.org* and *traffic-wales.com*

	Motorway
	Toll motorway
	Primary route dual carriageway
	Primary route single carriageway
	Other A roads
or V	Vehicle ferry
	Fast vehicle ferry or catamaran
132	Atlas page number

0   10   20   30 miles
0 10 20 30 40 kilometres

FERRY INFORMATION

Hebrides and west coast Scotland
calmac.co.uk   0800 066 5000
skyeferry.co.uk
western-ferries.co.uk   01369 704 452

Orkney and Shetland
northlinkferries.co.uk   0845 6000 449
pentlandferries.co.uk   0800 688 8998
orkneyferries.co.uk   01856 872 044
shetland.gov.uk/ferries   01595 743 970

Isle of Man
steam-packet.com   08722 992 992

Ireland
irishferries.com   08717 300 400
poferries.com   08716 642 121
stenaline.co.uk   08447 70 70 70

North Sea (Scandinavia and Benelux)
dfdsseaways.co.uk   08715 229 955
poferries.com   08716 642 121
stenaline.co.uk   08447 70 70 70

Isle of Wight
wightlink.co.uk   0871 376 1000
redfunnel.co.uk   0844 844 9988

Channel Islands
condorferries.co.uk   0845 609 1024

Channel hopping (France and Belgium)
brittany-ferries.co.uk   0871 244 0744
condorferries.co.uk   0845 609 1024
eurotunnel.com   08443 35 35 35
ldlines.co.uk   0844 576 8836
dfdsseaways.co.uk   08715 229 955
poferries.com   08716 642 121
myferrylink.com   0844 2482 100

Northern Spain
brittany-ferries.co.uk   0871 244 0744
ldlines.co.uk   0844 576 8836

Motorway
Toll motorway
Primary route dual carriageway
Primary route single carriageway
Other A roads
Vehicle ferry
Fast vehicle ferry or catamaran

192 Atlas page number

0 10 20 30 miles
0 10 20 30 40 kilometres

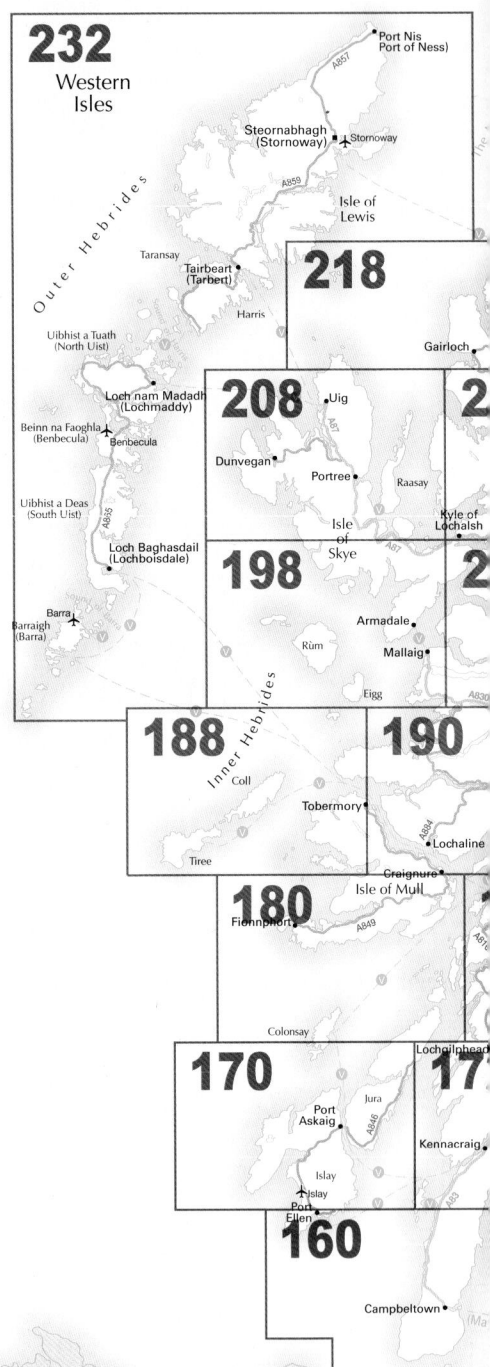

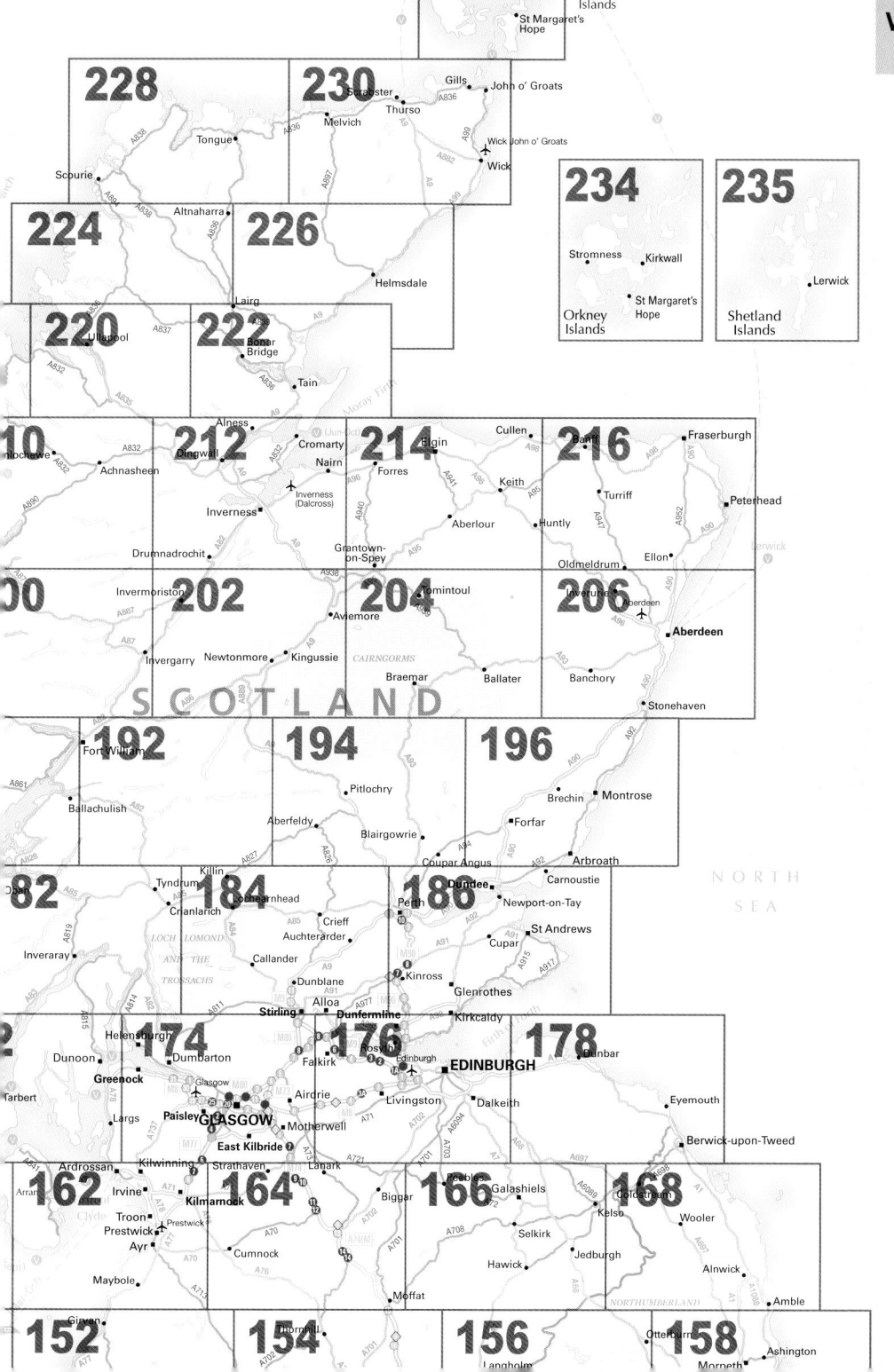

Mileage chart

The mileage chart shows distances in miles between two towns along AA-recommended routes. Using motorways and other main roads this is normally the fastest route, though not necessarily the shortest.

The journey times, shown in hours and minutes, are average off-peak driving times along AA-recommended routes. These times should be used as a guide only and do not allow for unforeseen traffic delays, rest breaks or fuel stops.

For example, the 378 miles (608 km) journey between Glasgow and Norwich should take approximately 7 hours 28 minutes.

Journey times

The following diagonal labels run through the chart, each representing a town:

Aberdeen
Aberystwyth
Barnstaple
Birmingham
Brighton
Bristol
Cambridge
Cardiff
Carlisle
Carmarthen
Dorchester
Dover
Edinburgh
Exeter
Fort William
Glasgow
Gloucester
Guildford
Hereford
Holyhead
Hull
Inverness
Kendal
Leeds
Lincoln
Liverpool
Maidstone
Manchester
Middlesbrough
Newcastle
Northampton
Norwich
Nottingham
Oxford
Penzance
Perth
Peterborough
Plymouth
Portsmouth
Preston
Salisbury
Sheffield
Shrewsbury
Southampton
Stoke-on-Trent
Stranraer
Taunton
Wick
York
LONDON

Distances in miles (one mile equals 1.6093 km)

Atlas symbols

Motorway with number	Minor road, more than 4 metres wide, less than 4 metres wide	Safety camera site (fixed location) with speed limit in mph
Toll motorway with toll station	Roundabout	Section of road with two or more fixed safety cameras, with speed limit in mph
Restricted motorway junctions	Interchange/junction	Average speed (SPECS™) camera system with speed limit in mph
Motorway service area	Narrow primary/other A/B road with passing places (Scotland)	Fixed safety camera site with variable speed limit
Motorway and junction under construction	Road under construction/approved	Vehicle ferry
Primary route single/dual carriageway	Road tunnel	Fast vehicle ferry or catamaran
Primary route junction with and without number	Road toll, steep gradient (arrows point downhill)	Airport, heliport, international freight terminal
Restricted primary route junctions	Distance in miles between symbols	24-hour Accident & Emergency hospital
Primary route service area	Railway line, in tunnel	Crematorium
Primary route destination	Railway station and level crossing	Park and Ride (at least 6 days per week)
Other A road single/dual carriageway	Tourist railway	City, town, village or other built-up area
B road single/dual carriageway	Height in metres, mountain pass	National boundary, county or administrative boundary

Scenic route	Aqueduct or viaduct	Forest drive	Horse racing, show jumping
Tourist Information Centre (all year/seasonal)	Garden, arboretum	National trail	Air show venue, motor-racing circuit
Visitor or heritage centre	Vineyard	Viewpoint	Ski slope (natural, artificial)
Picnic site	Country park	Hill-fort	National Trust property (England & Wales, Scotland)
Caravan site (AA inspected)	Agricultural showground	Prehistoric monument, Roman antiquity	English Heritage site
Camping site (AA inspected)	Theme park	Battle site with year	Historic Scotland site
Caravan & camping site (AA inspected)	Farm or animal centre	Steam railway centre	Cadw (Welsh heritage) site
Abbey, cathedral or priory	Zoological or wildlife collection	Cave	Major shopping centre, other place of interest
Ruined abbey, cathedral or priory	Bird collection, aquarium	Windmill, monument	Attraction within urban area
Castle	RSPB site	Golf course (AA listed)	World Heritage Site (UNESCO)
Historic house or building	National Nature Reserve (England, Scotland, Wales)	County cricket ground	National Park and National Scenic Area (Scotland)
Museum or art gallery	Local nature reserve	Rugby Union national stadium	Forest Park
Industrial interest	Wildlife Trust reserve	International athletics stadium	Heritage coast

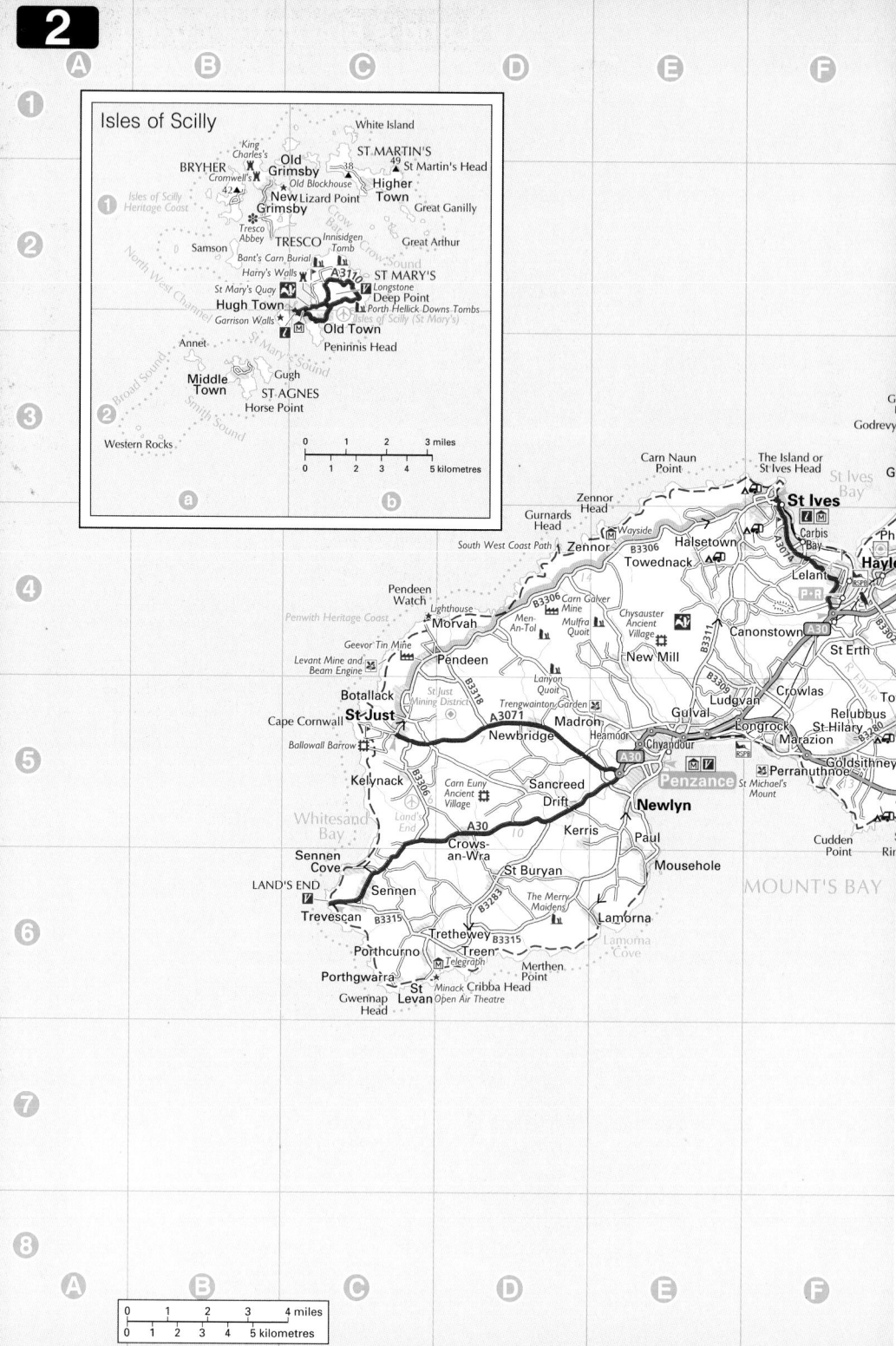

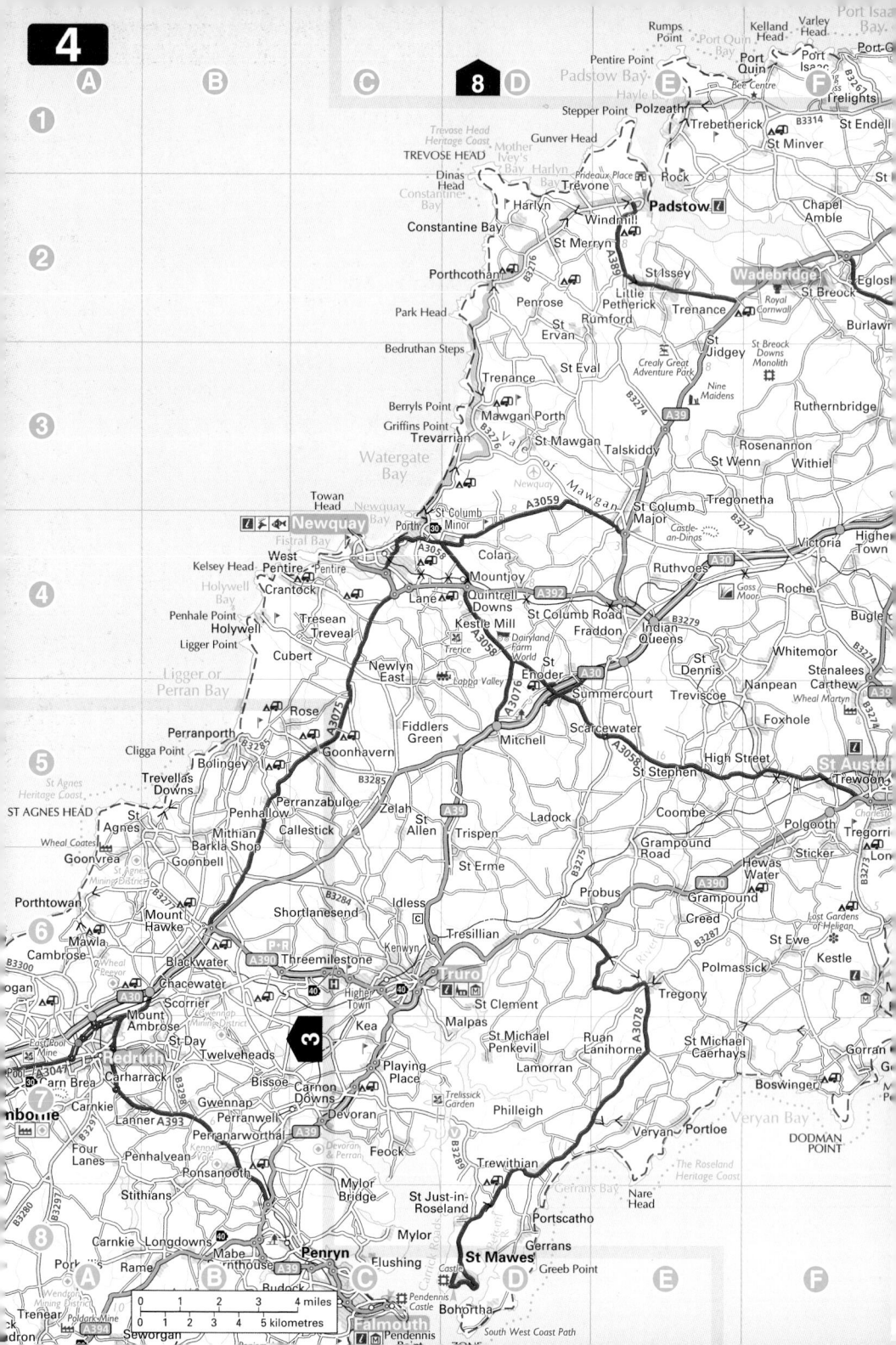

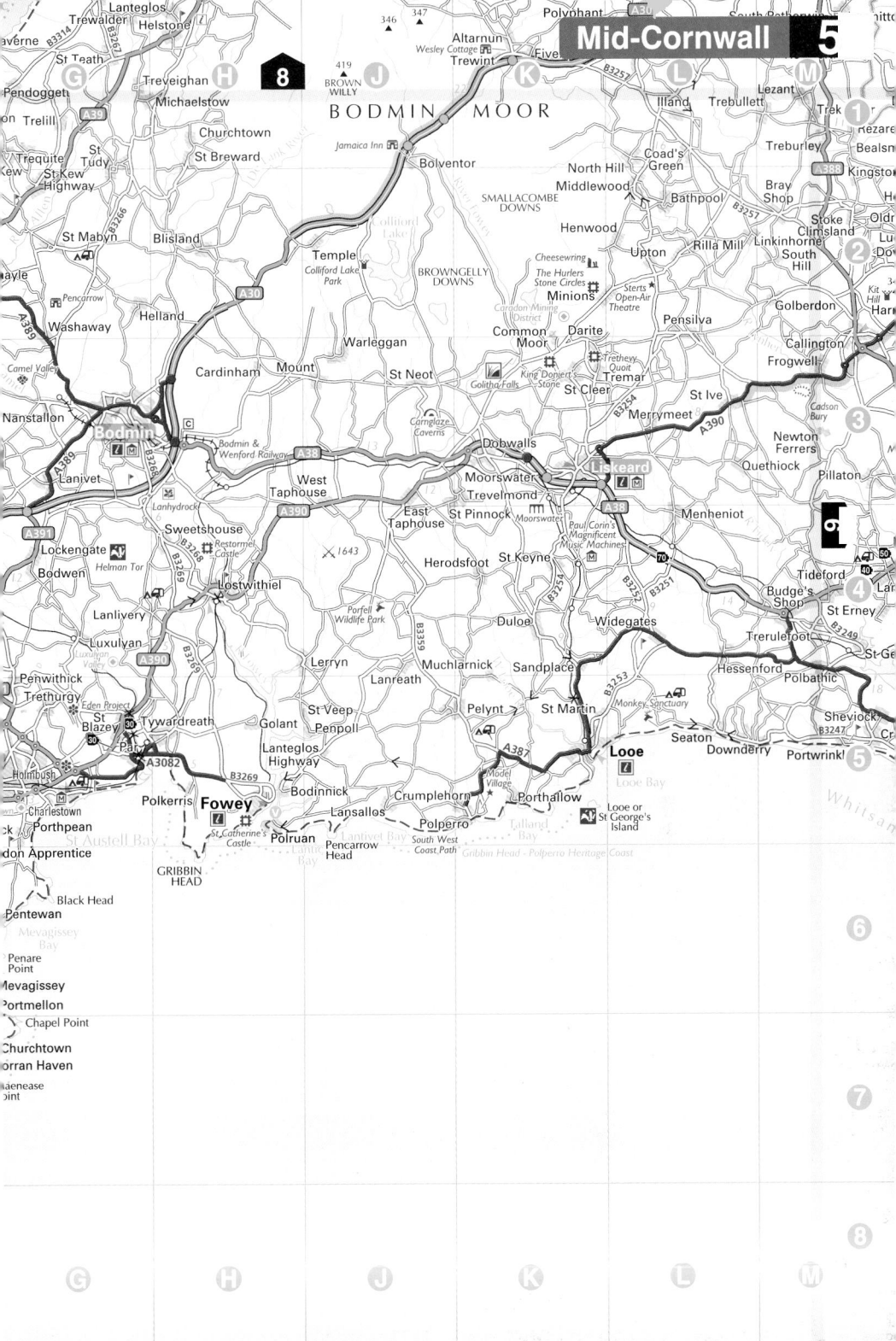

M

Higher Sharpno

Lower Sharpno

Ste

Bude
Bay

Wid

Dizzard Point   Po

St
Gennys

Crackington Haven   Coxfor
Cambeak

Sweets

Wainho
Corne

B3263

A39

Witchcraft   Marshgate

Pentire Point   Widemouth   Tresparrett
Heritage Coast

Boscastle   Lesnewth
Treyalga   Otterha

Castle   B3263
TINTAGEL HEAD   Trethevey
Tintagel   B3266
Old Post Office   Bossiney
Penhallic Point   Davidstow

Treknow   Trewarmett   B3262

Tremail
B3314

B3266

South West Coast Path   Delabole   Pengelly   Crow
Reservoir
Westdowns   Camelford

Rumps   Kelland   Varley   Lanteglos   34
Point   Port Quin   Head   Head   Port Isaac   Trewalder   Helstone
Pentire Point   Bay   Port   Bay   Port Gaverne   B3314
Padstow Bay   Quin   B3267
Bee Centre   Isaac   419
Long   BROWN
Stepper Point   Cross   Treveighan   WILLY
Polzeath   Trelights   Pendoggett   Michaelstow

Trevose   TREVOSE HEAD   Mother   St Minver   St Endelli   relill   A39   Churchtown   BODM
Heritage Coast   Ivey   St Teath
Bay   Treveighan   Jamaica Inn
Dinas   Trequite   St   St Breward
Head   Trevone   St Kew   Tudy
St Kew
Highway

0 1 2 3 4 miles
0 1 2 3 4 5 kilometres

4

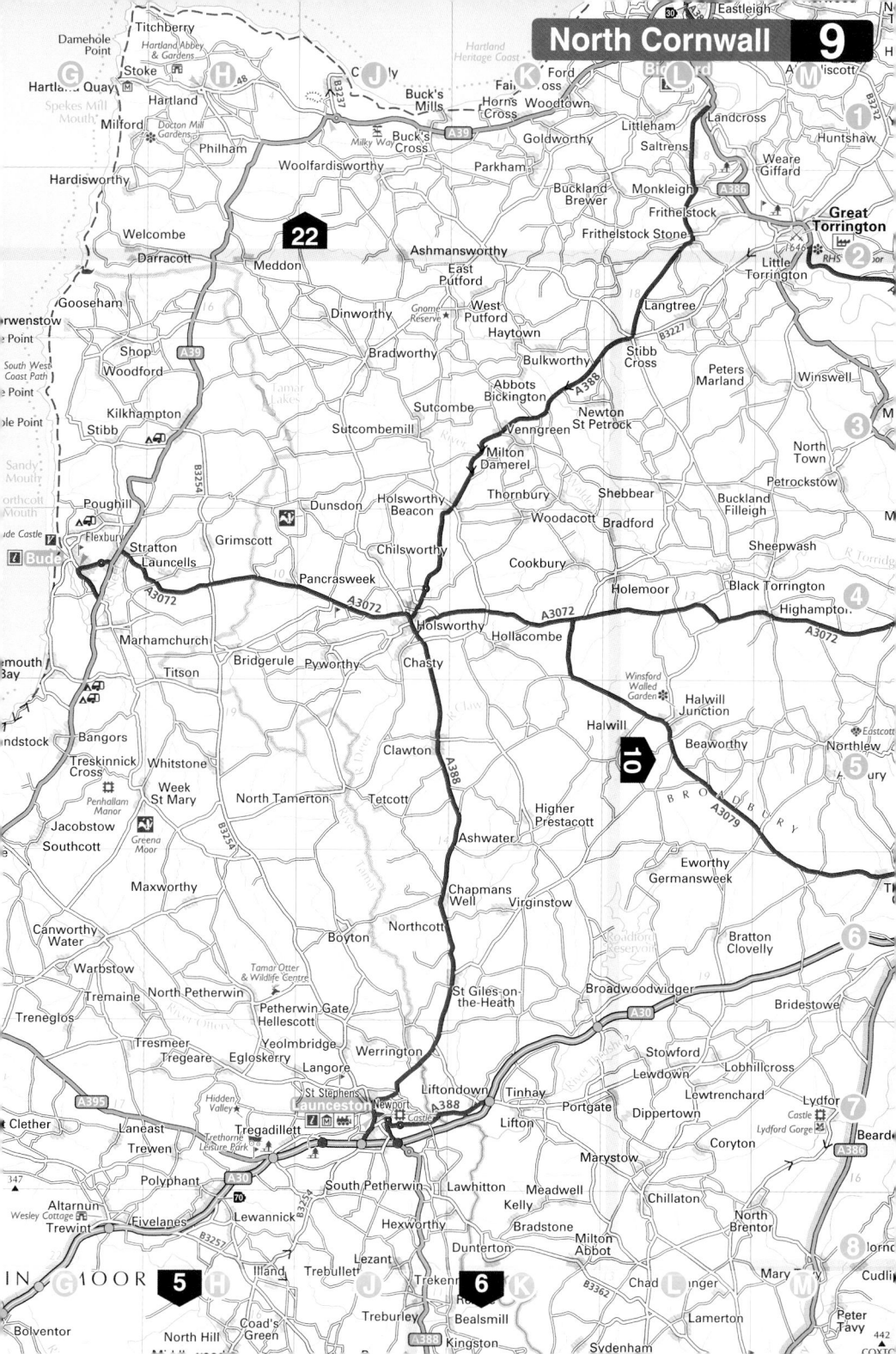

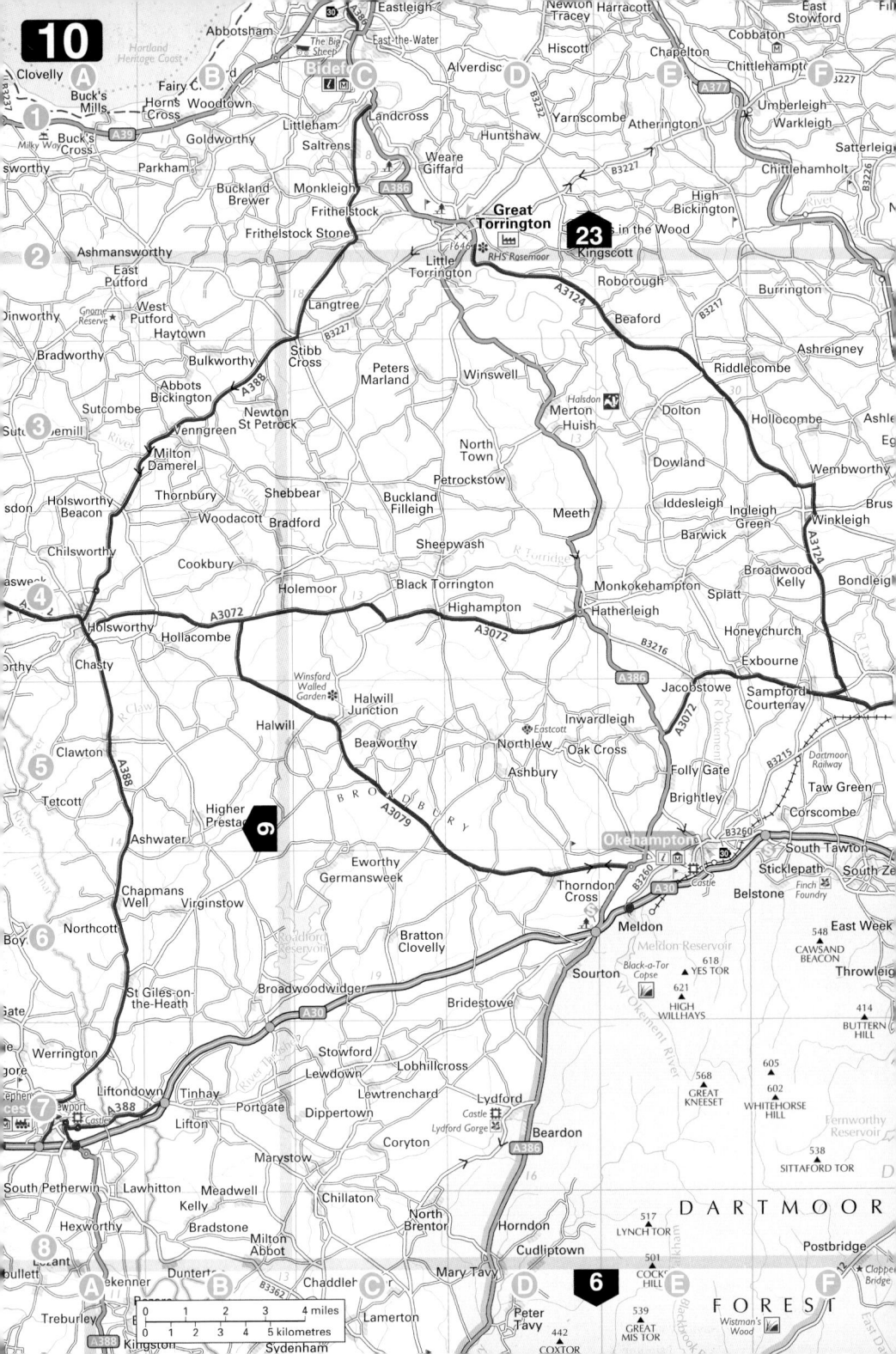

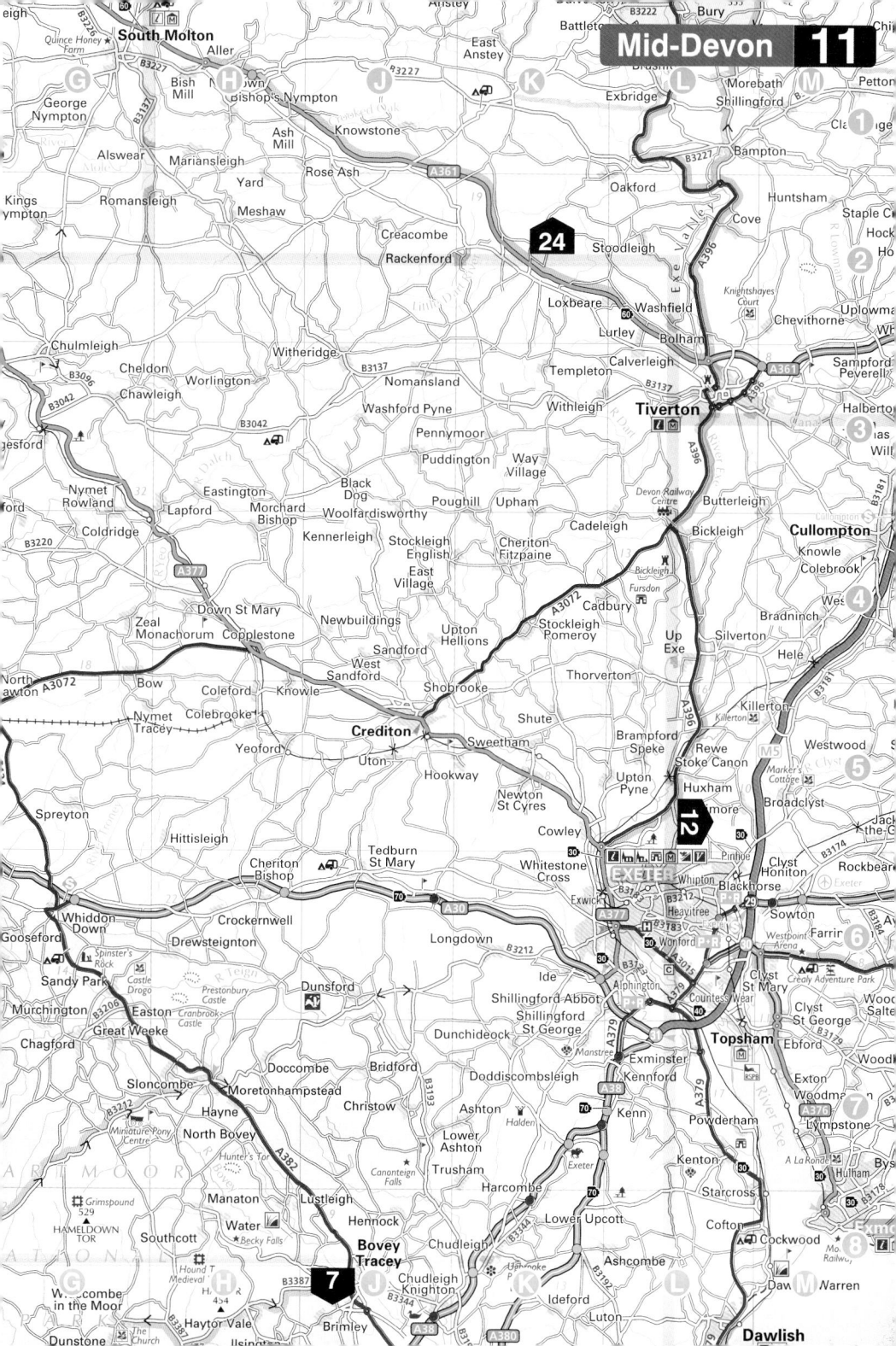

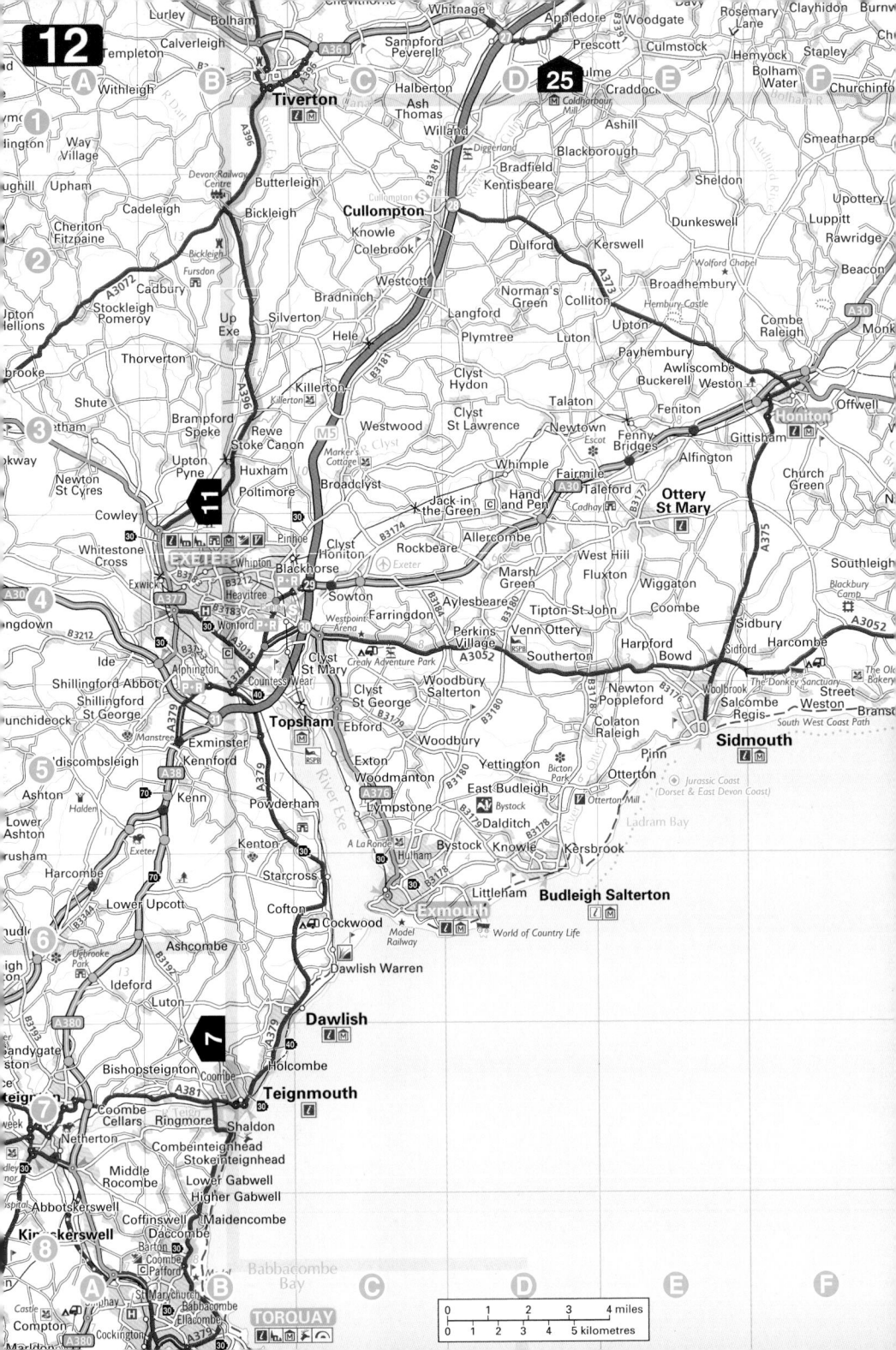

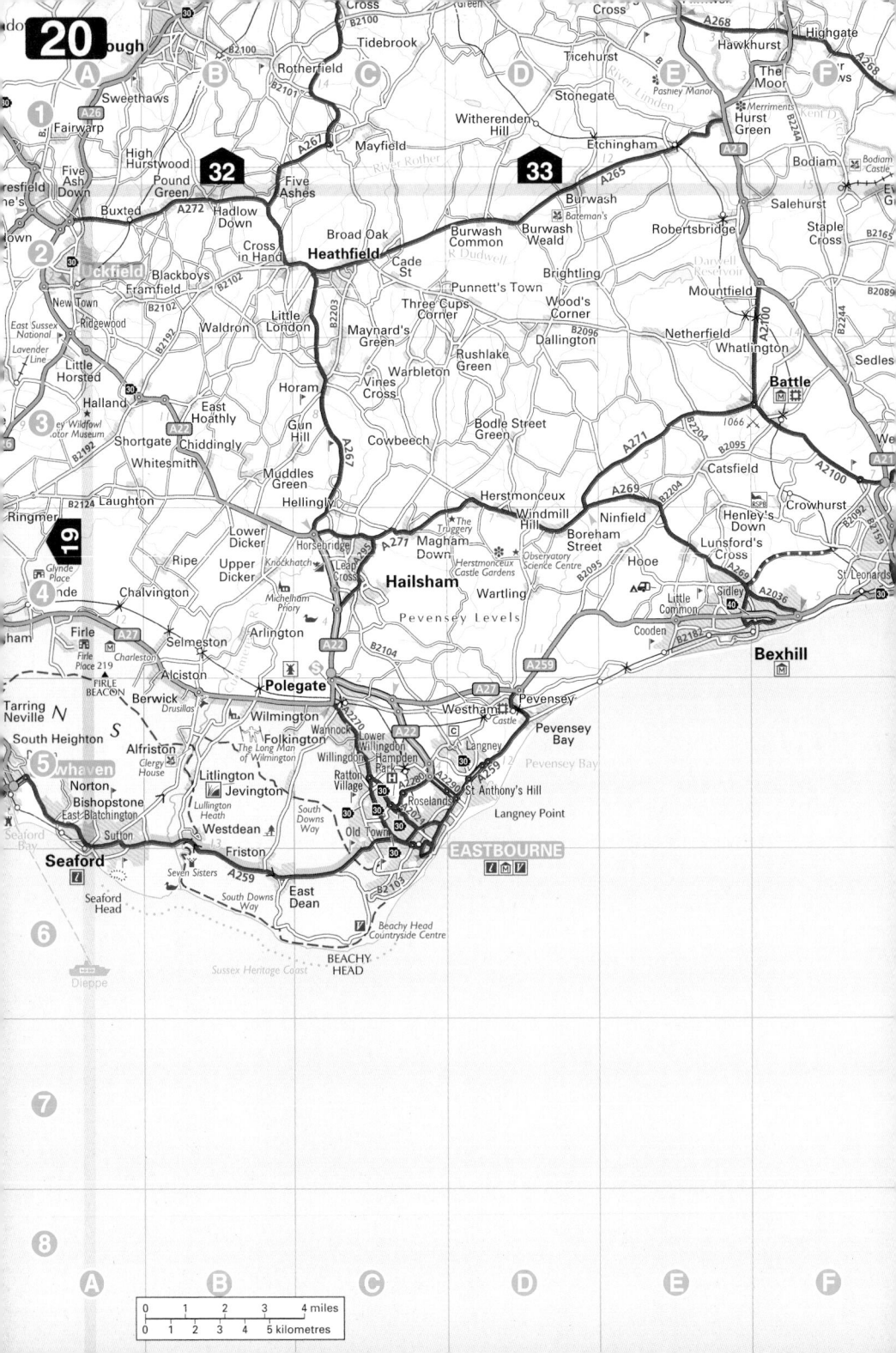

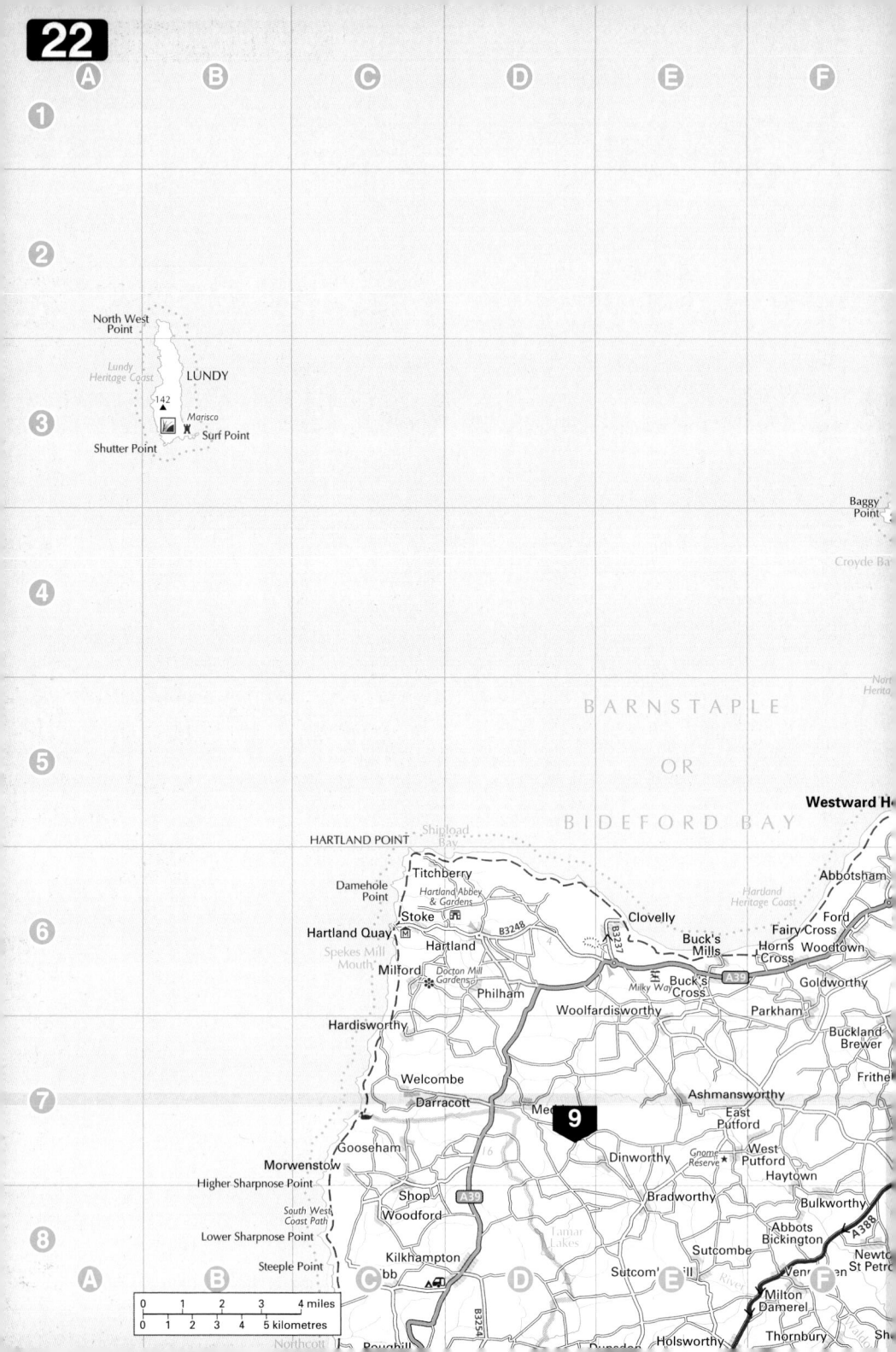

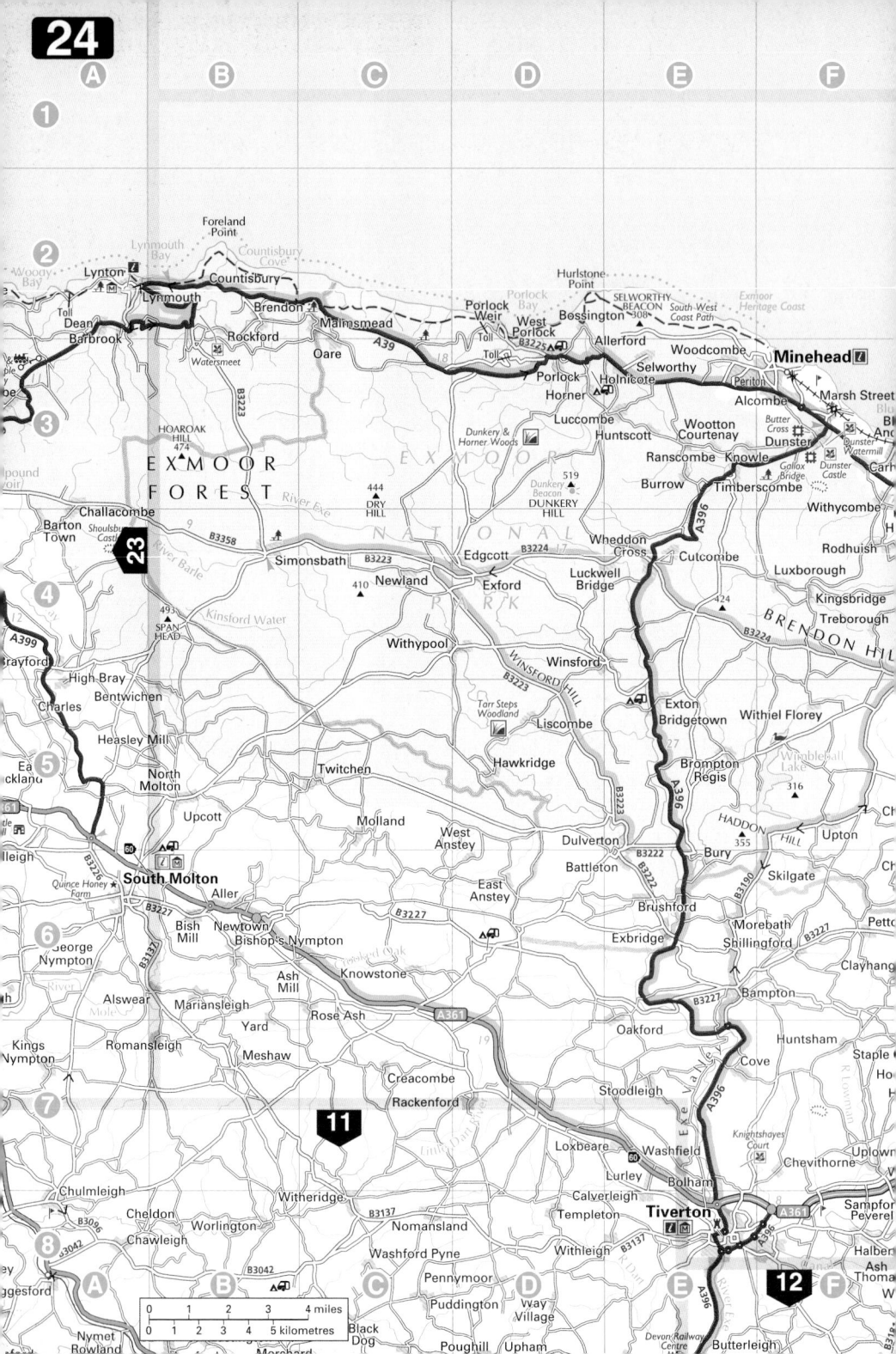

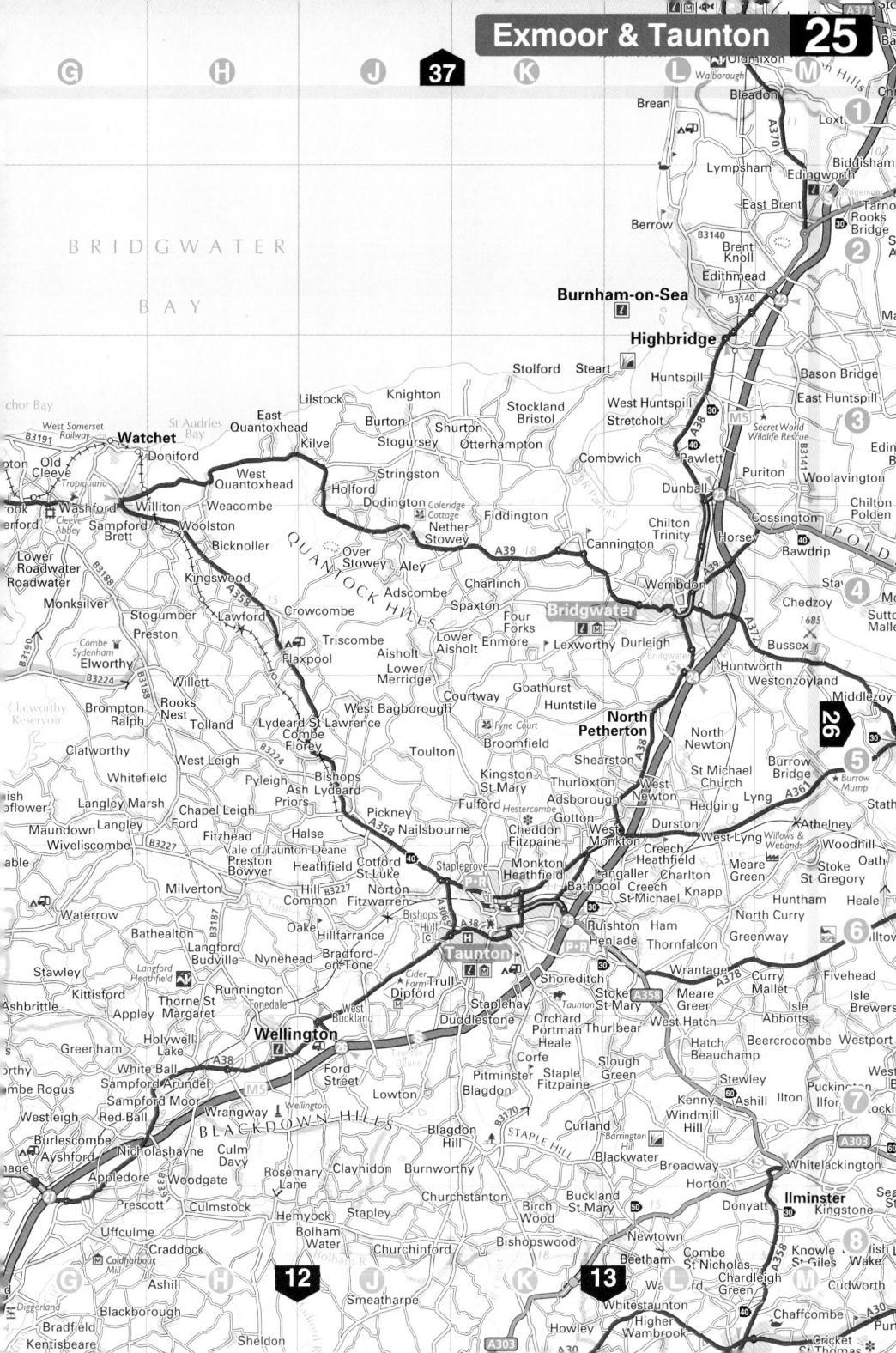

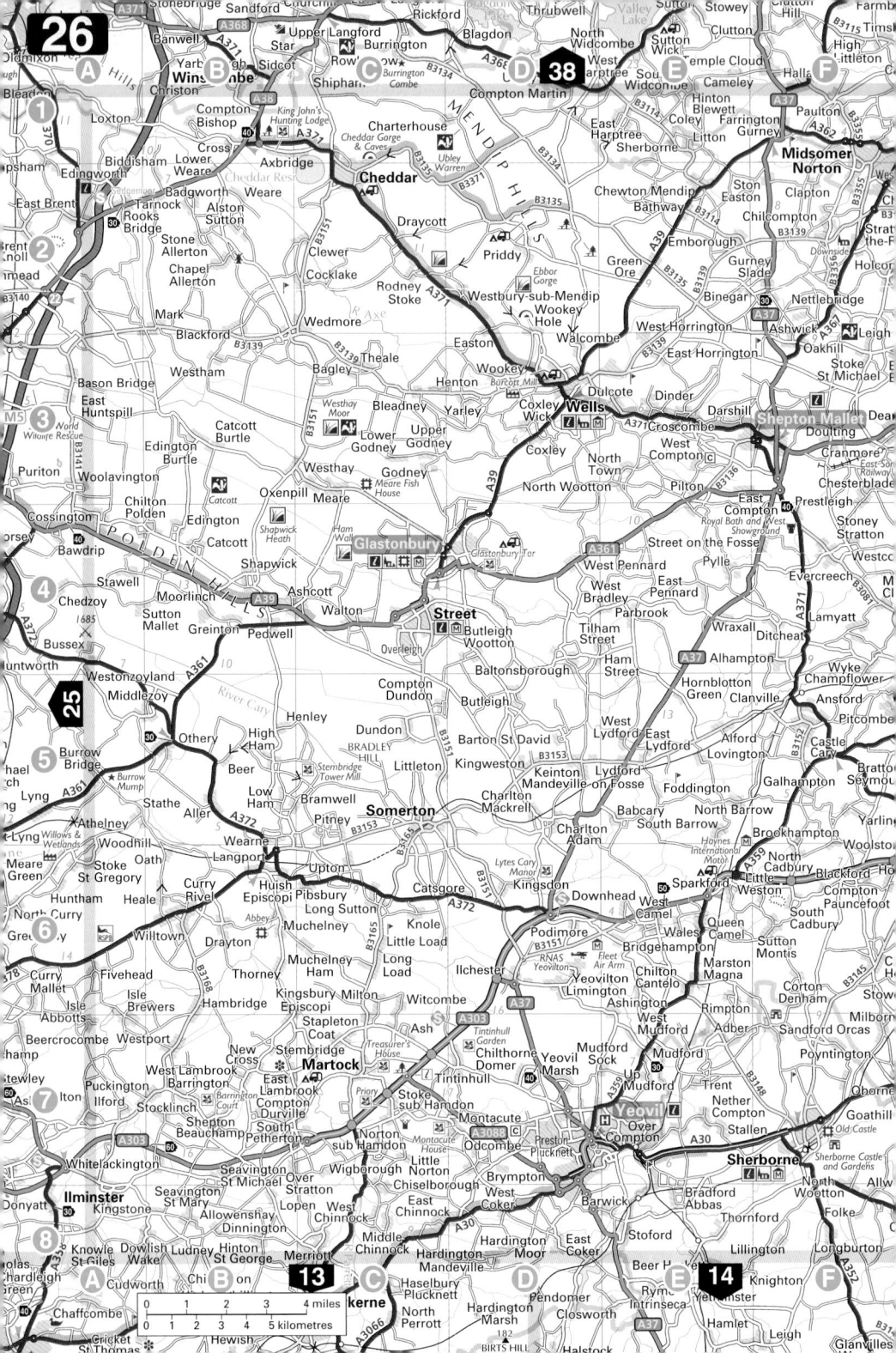

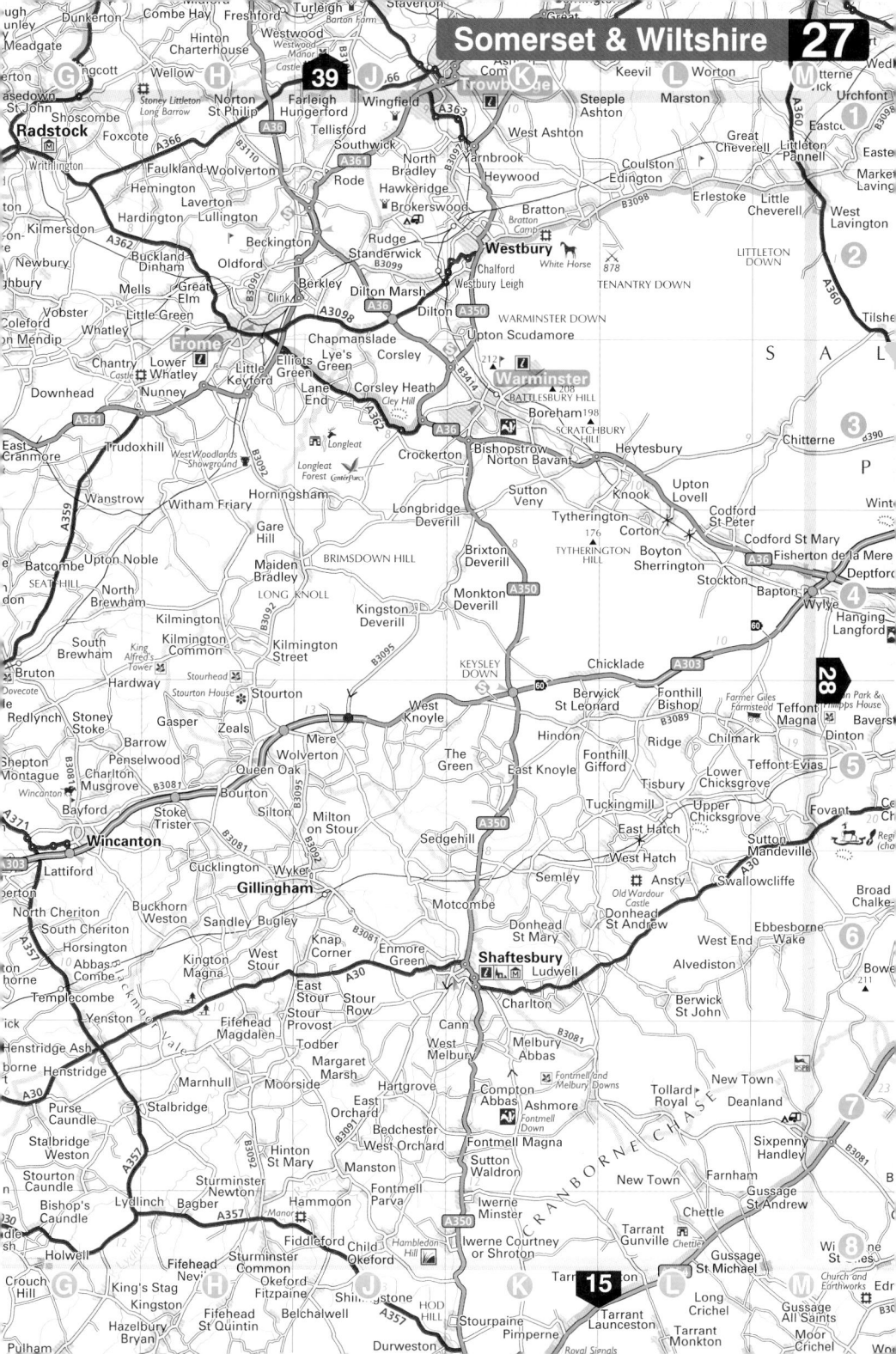

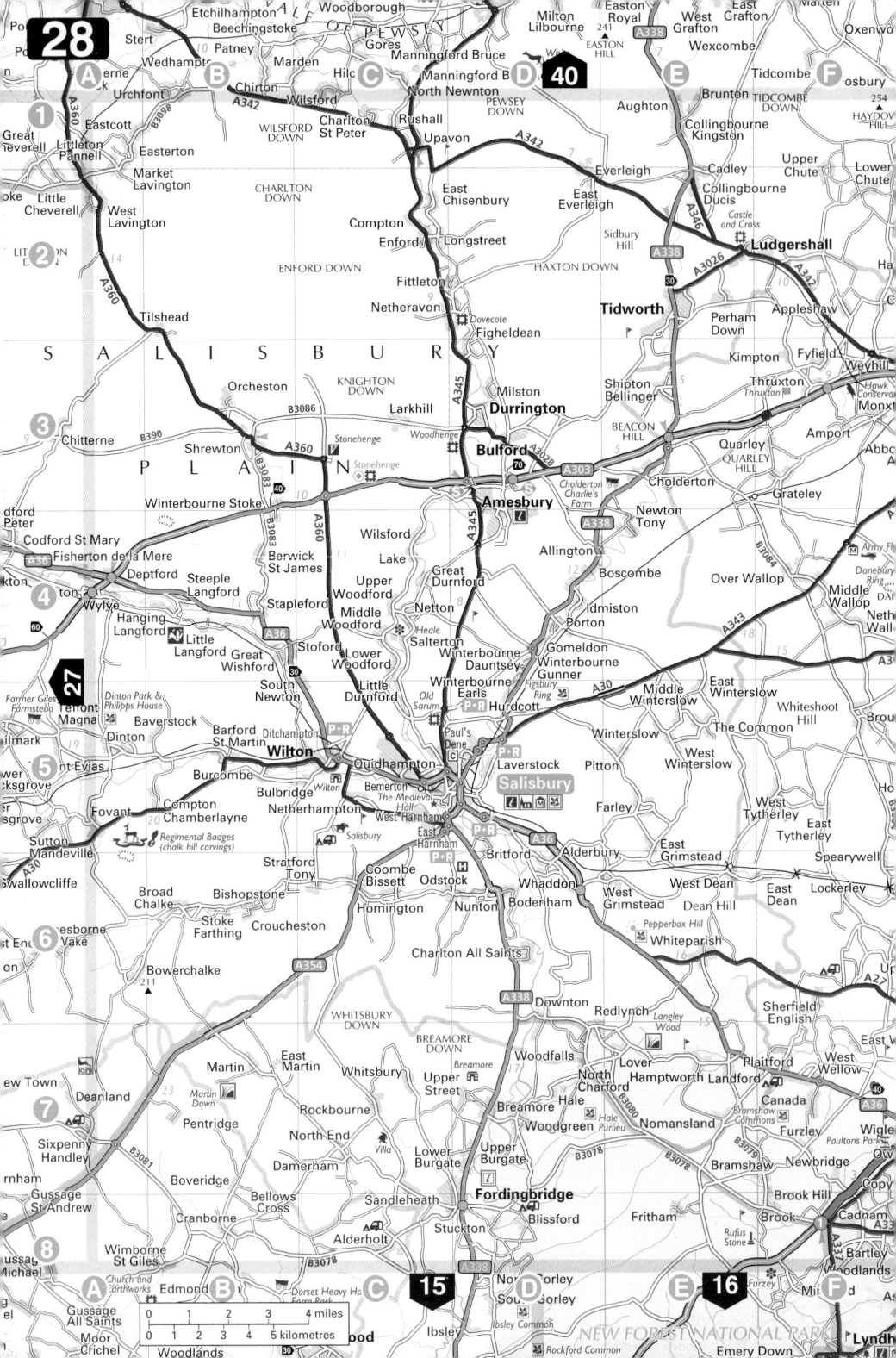

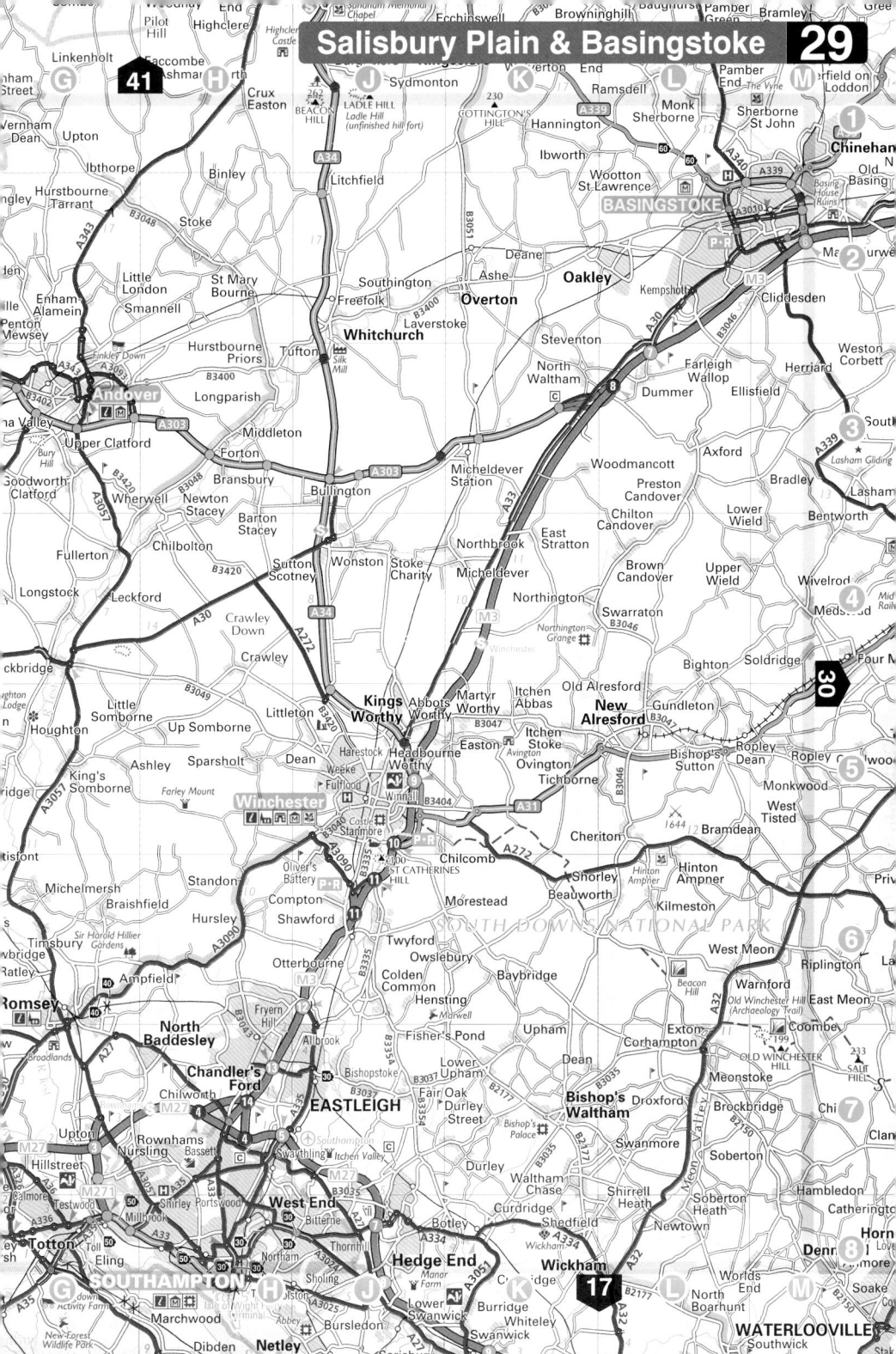
Salisbury Plain & Basingstoke **29**

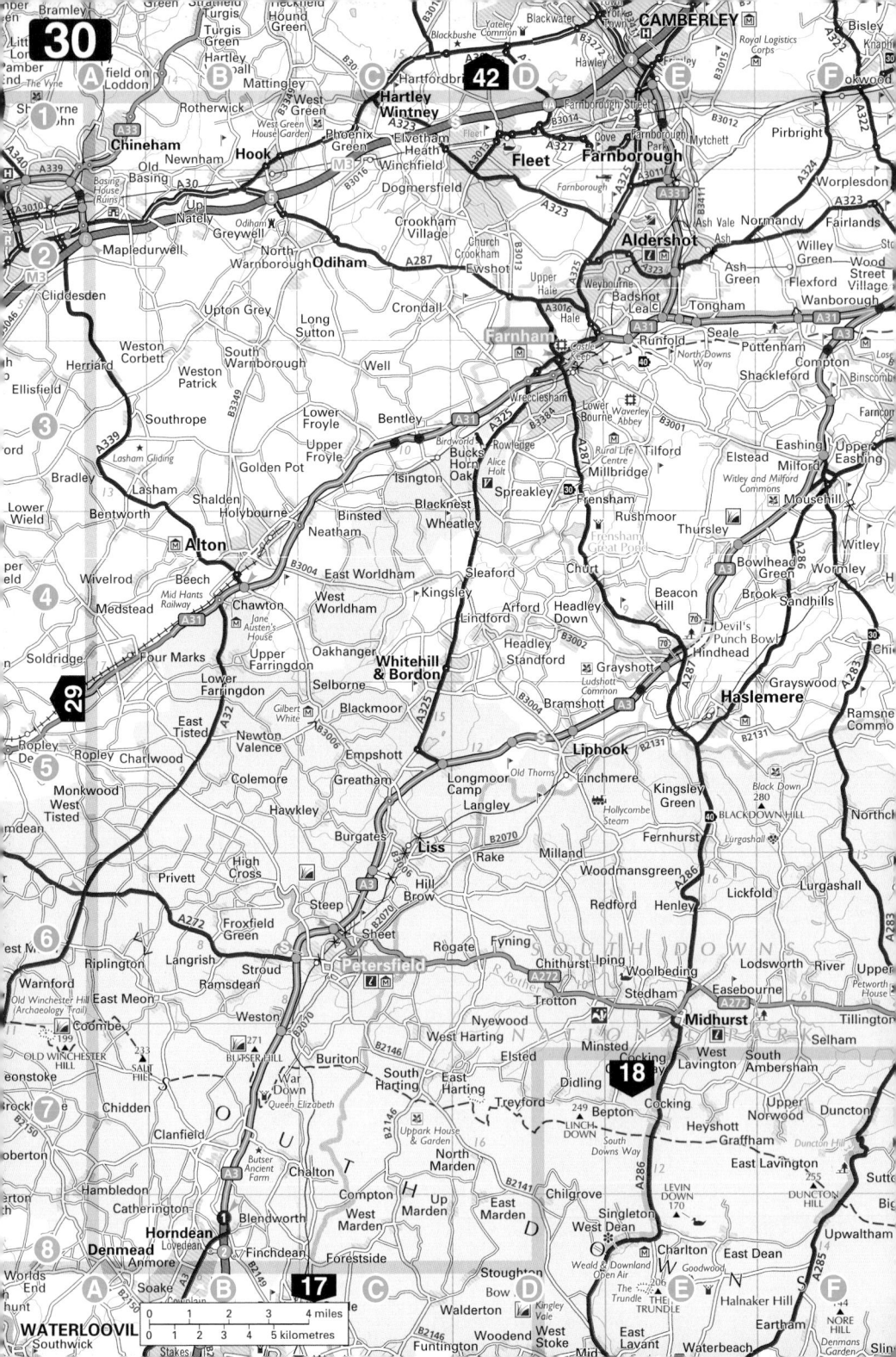

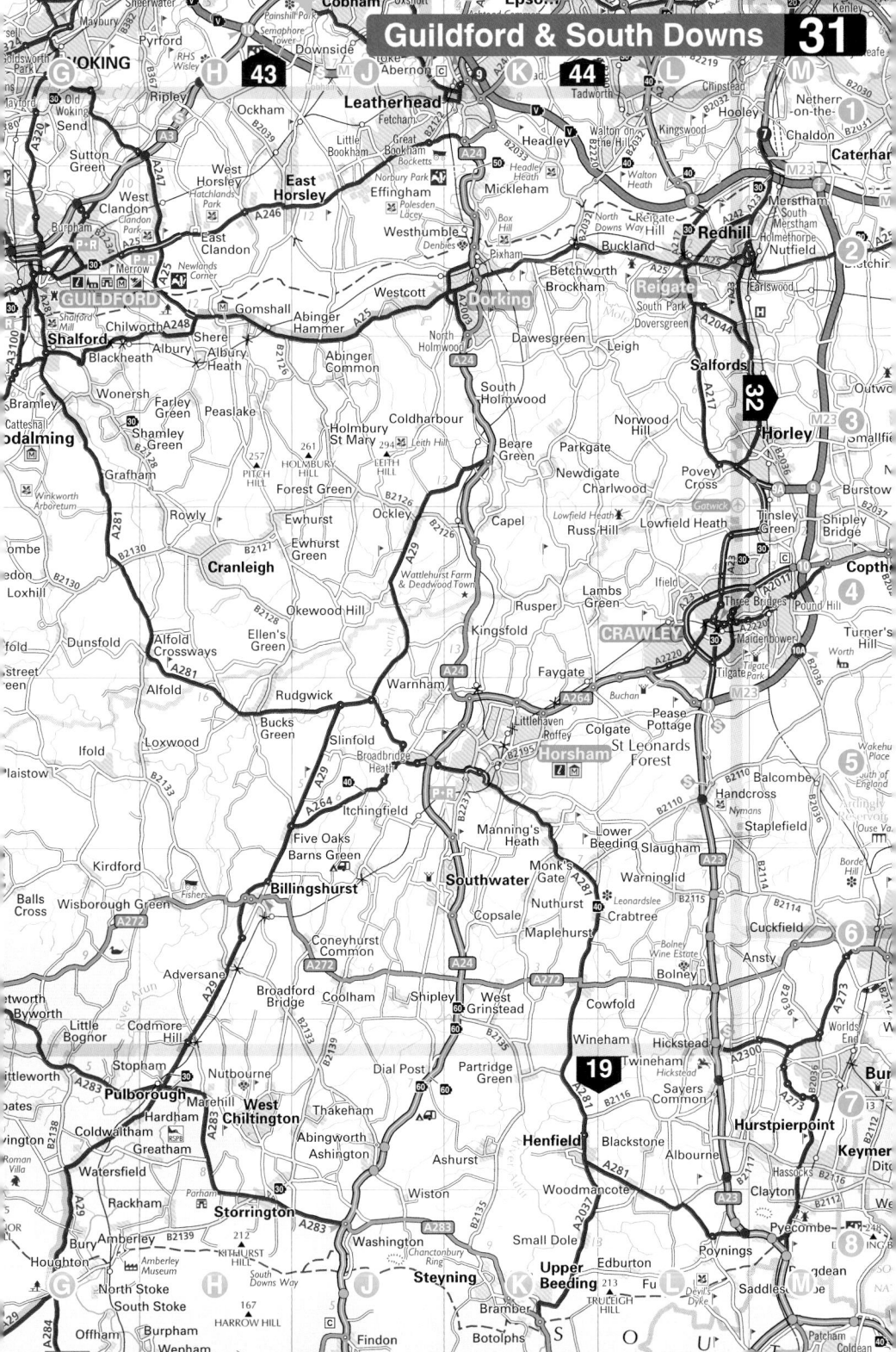

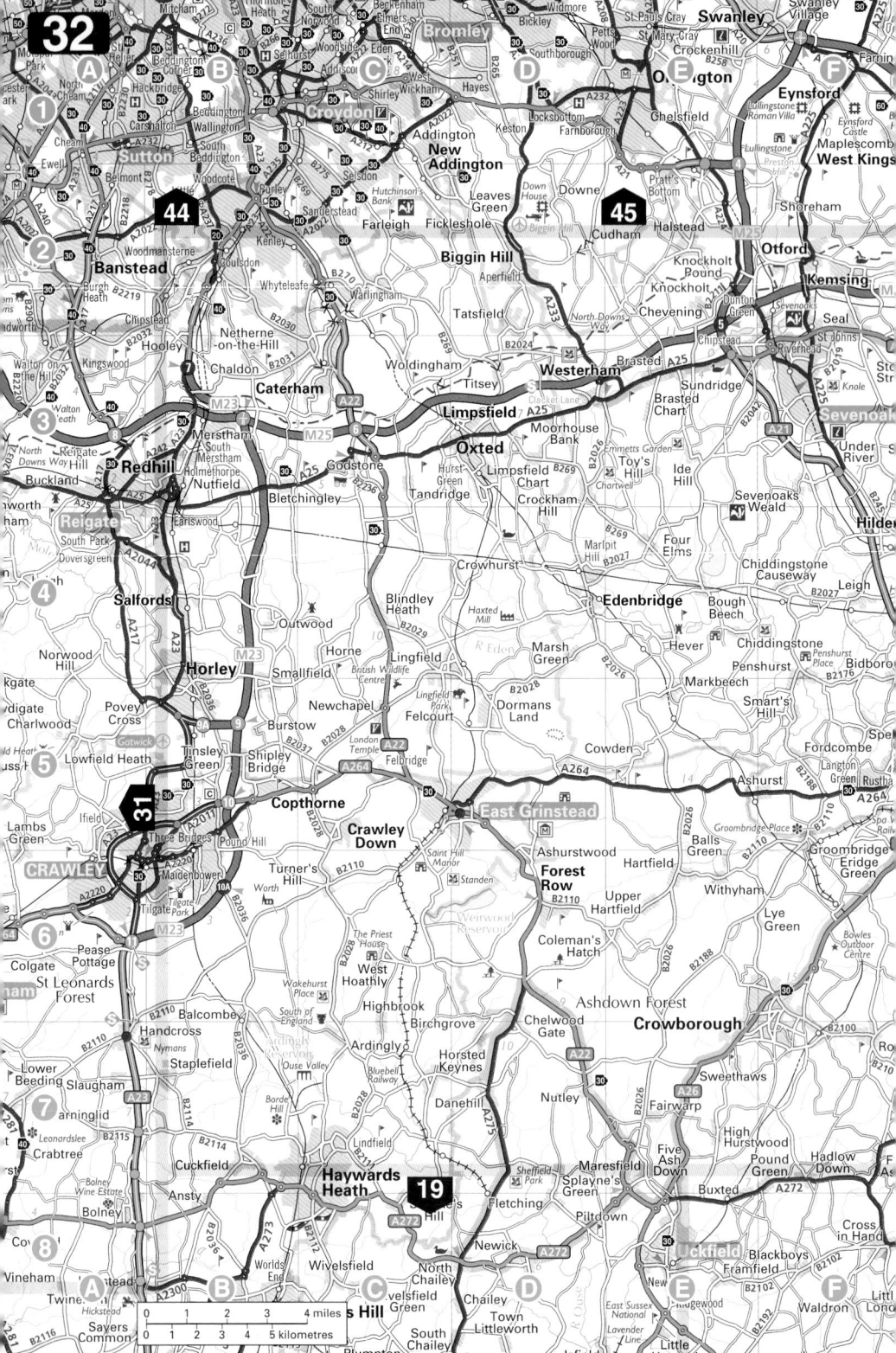

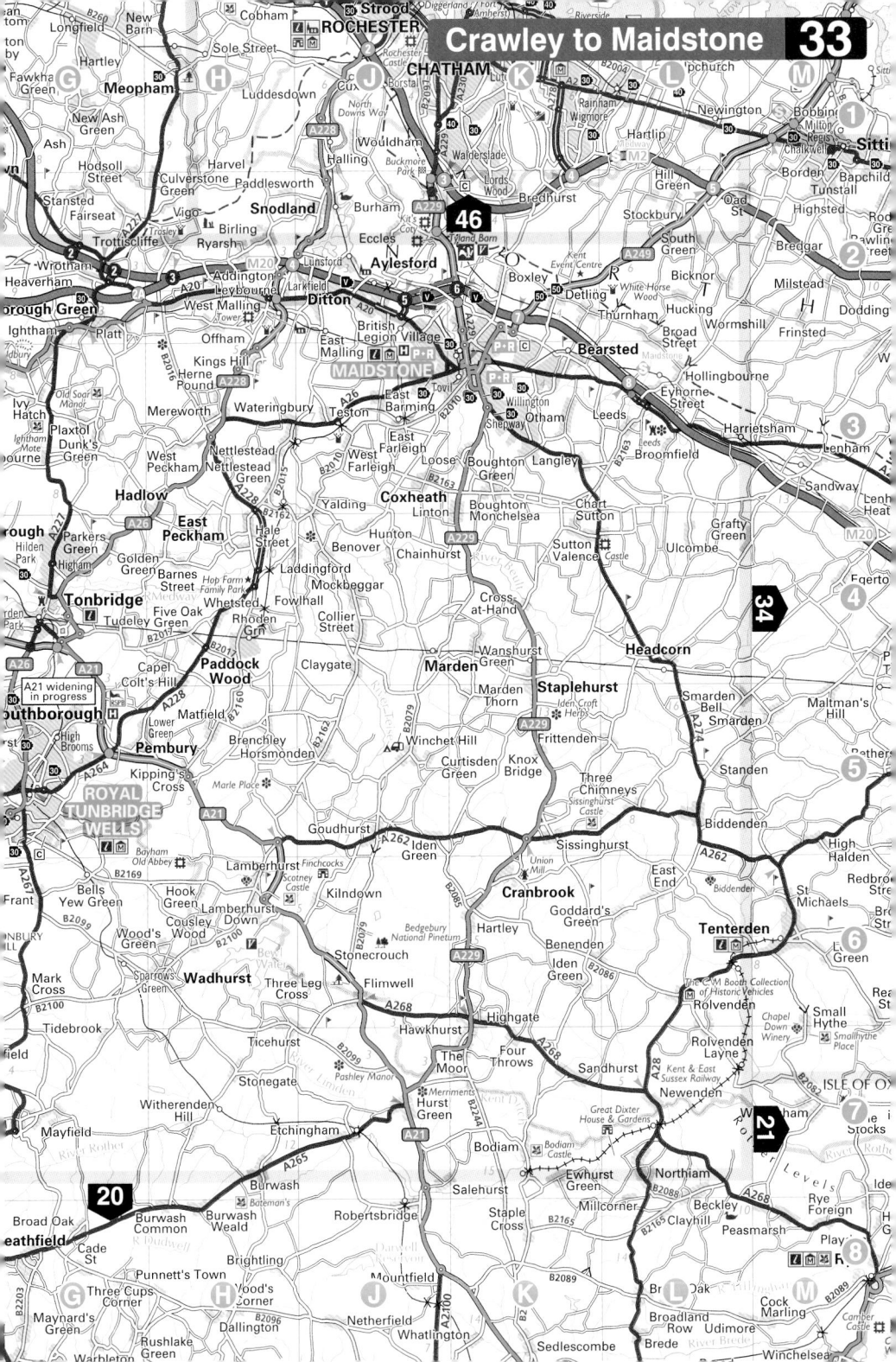

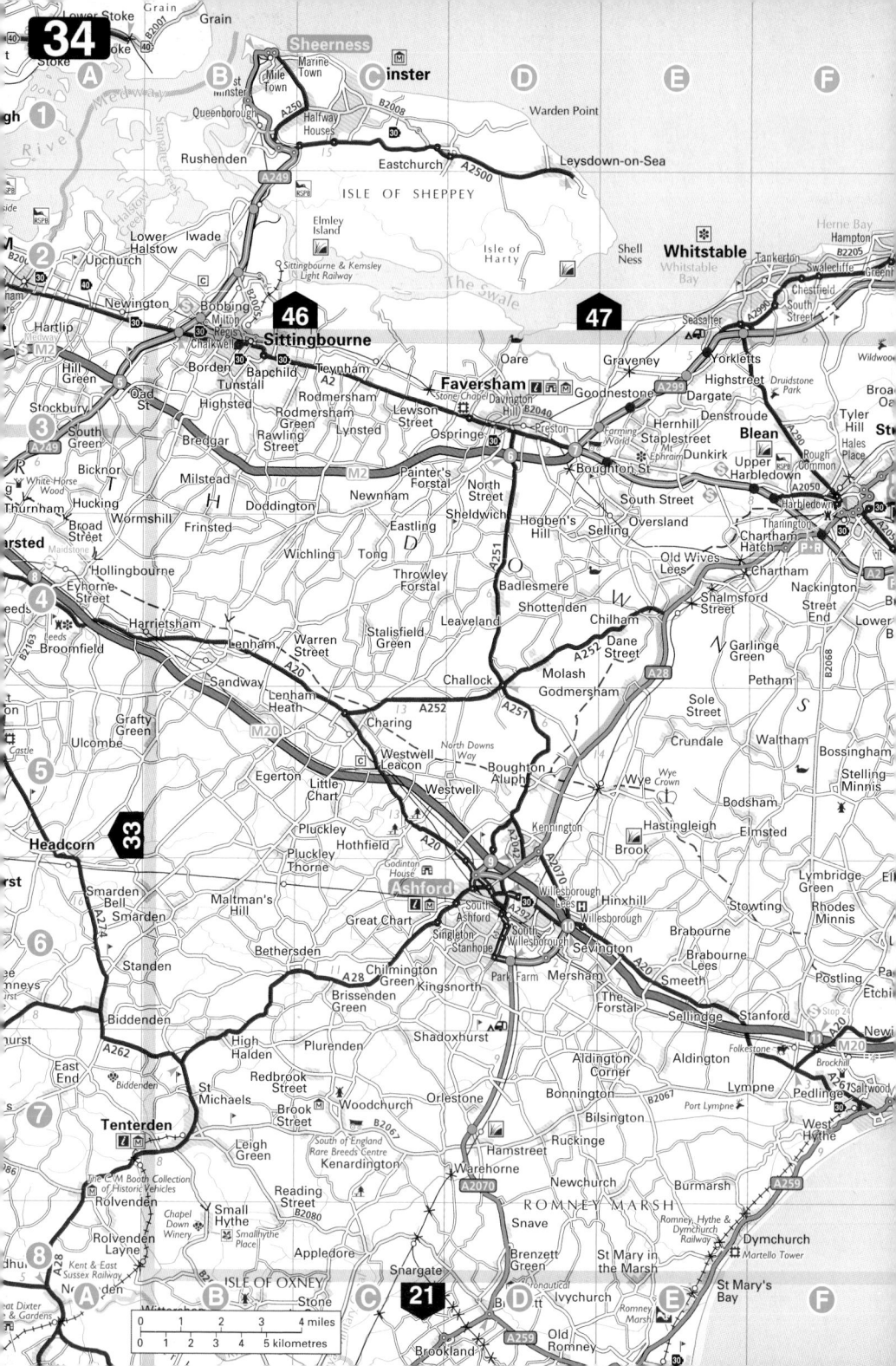

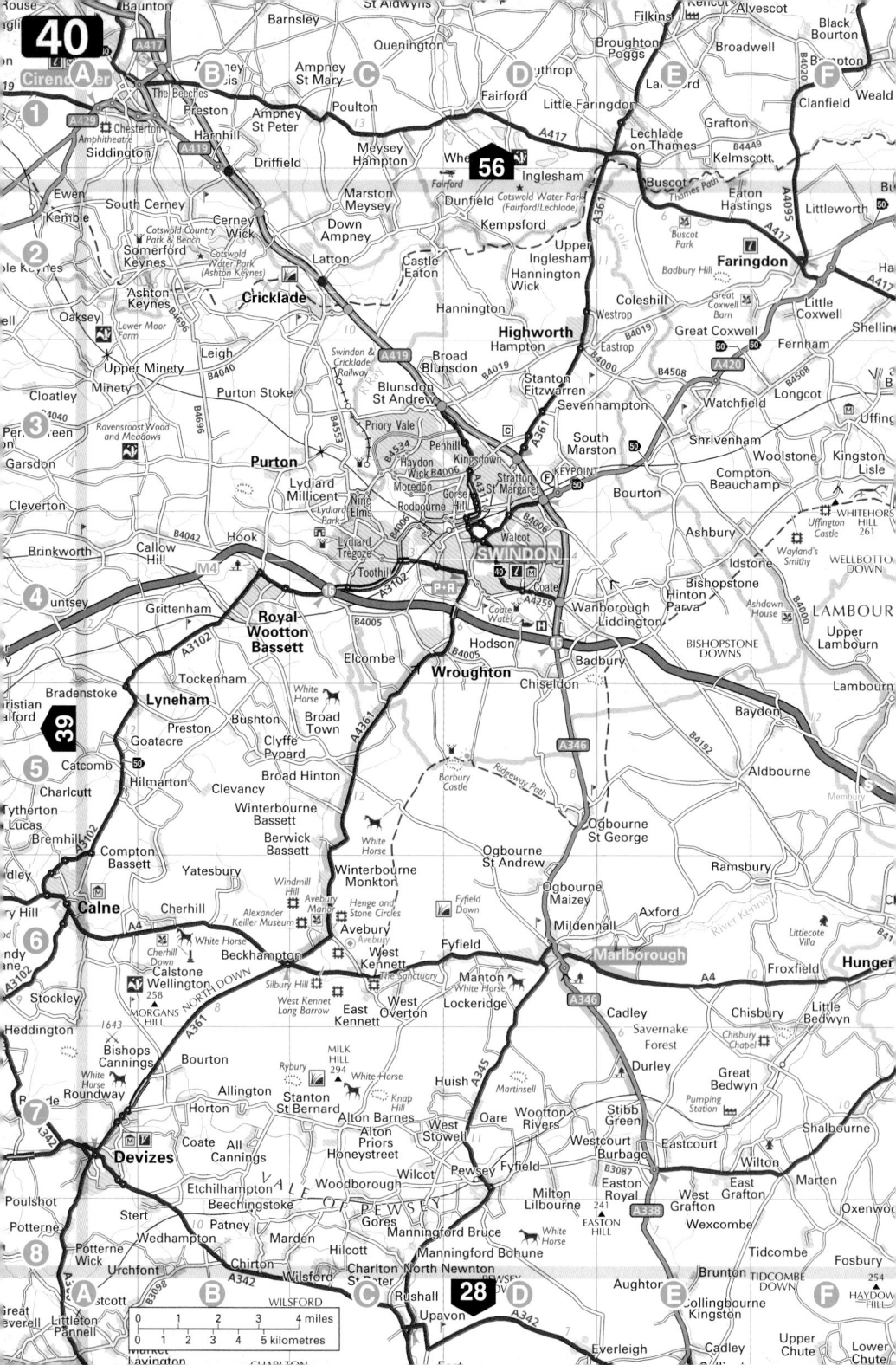

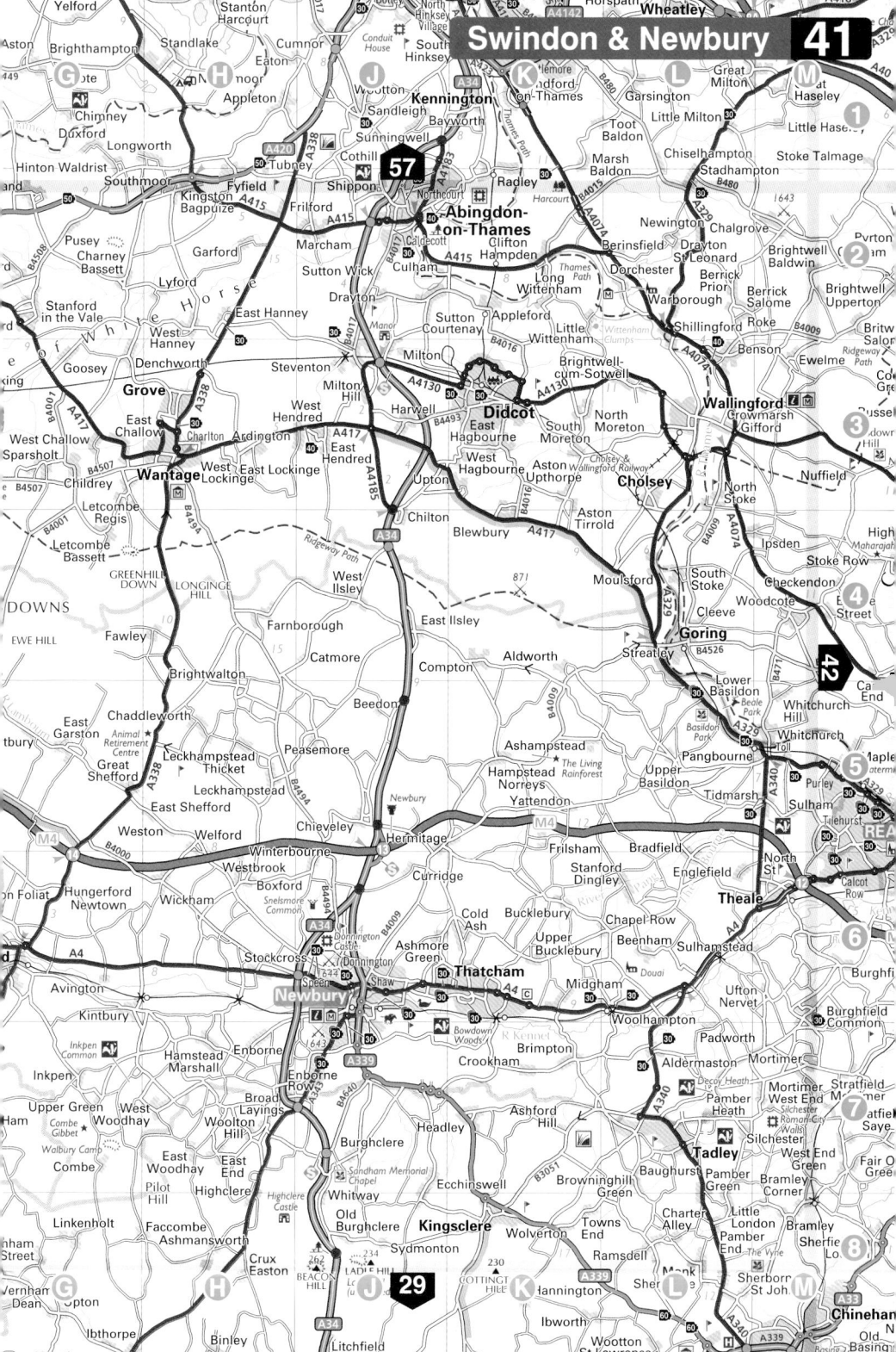

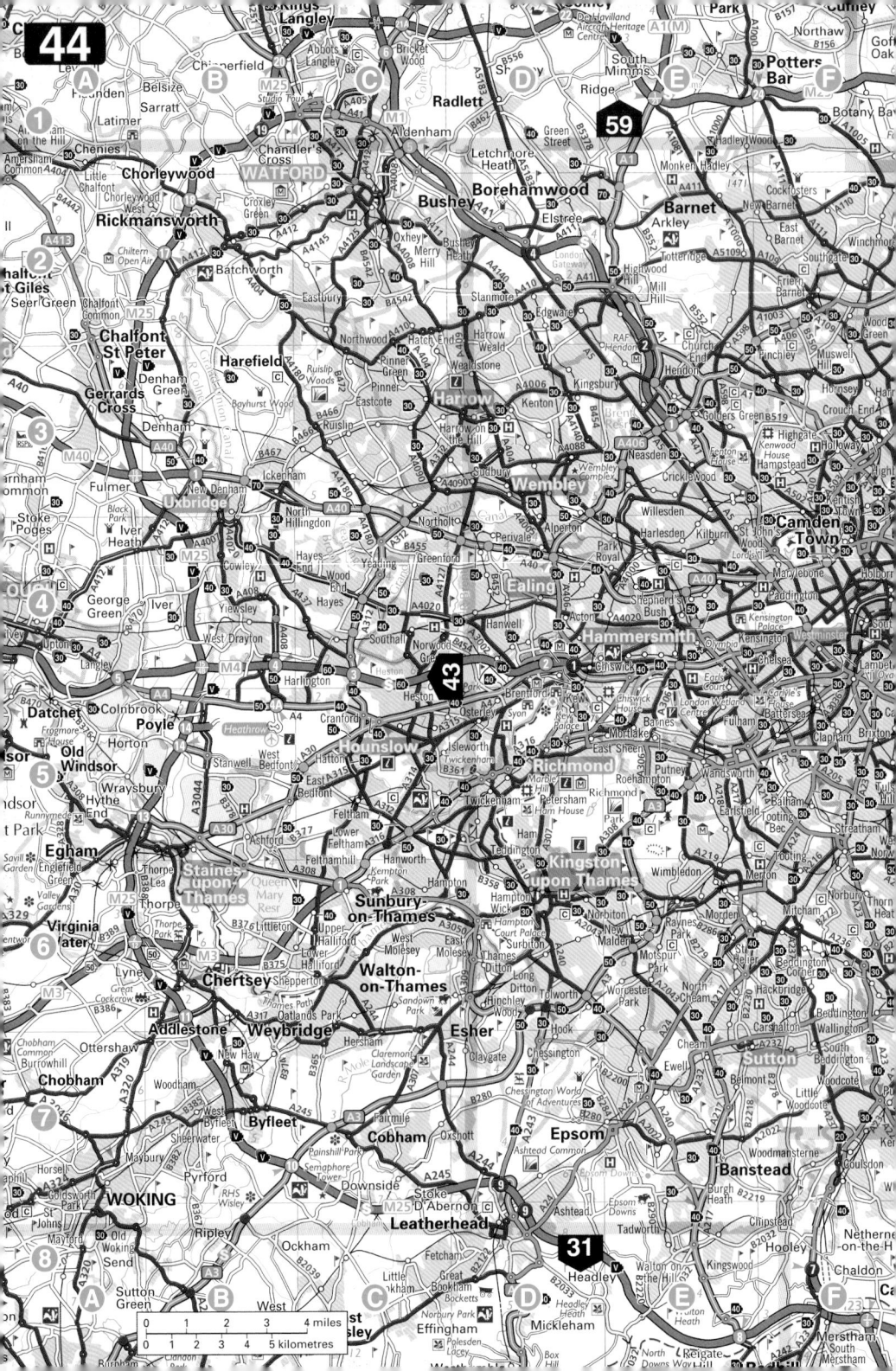

62

Dengie
eldham **G**
minster

Holliwell
Point
Foulness
Point

on-Crouch

Courtsend

Churchend

FOULNESS
ISLAND

Warden Point

Leysdown-on-Sea

35
Westgate
on Sea

Birchington

Shell
Ness

Whitstable

Whitstable
Bay

Herne Bay
Hampton
Tankerton
Swalecliffe
Chestfield
Greenhill
South
Street
Seasalter

Herne Bay

Beltinge

Reculver Towers
& Roman Fort
Reculver

Bishopstone

Minnis
Bay

St Nicholas
at Wade
Boyden
Gate
Sarre
Chislet

Broomfield

Herne

Monkton
Durlock

OF
NET

RAF Manston
Acol
B2190

35
Minster

SHEPPEY

Isle of
Harty

The Swale

Oare

34
ley
Yorkletts
Highstreet
Dargate
Denstroude

Goodnestone

Faversham

Stone/Chapel
Davington
Hill
Preston
Ospringe
North
Street
Sheldwich

Hernhill
Staplestreet
Dunkirk

Blean
Upper
Harbledown

Boughton St

South Street

Hogben's
Hill
Selling

Overland

Druidstone
Park

Tyler
Hill
Rough
Common

Harbledown

Wildwood

Broad
Oak
Hales
Place

Sturry

Fordwich

Hoath
Upstreet

Hersden

Westbere
Stodmarsh

West
Stourmouth

East Stourmouth
Westmarsh

Elmstone

Wickhambreaux
Ickham
Littlebourne

Preston

Cop
Street
Hoaden

Ash

Minster

Durlock

Richboro
oman

Stone
Cross
Woodnesbor

Canterbury

Bramling

Staple
Statenborou

Thanington
Chartham
Hatch

Old Wives
Lees

Chartham

Jackington
Street
End

Bridge

Bekesbourne
Patrixbourne

Wingham Marshborough

Goodnestone

Shalmsford
Street

Lower Hardres
Bishopsbourne

Adisham

Ra

Nonington

Eastry

Badlesmere

Shottenden
Chilham

Leaveland

Dane
Street

Garlinge
Green

North Downs
Way

Aylesham

Chillenden

Betteshanger

G **H** **J** **K** **L** **M**

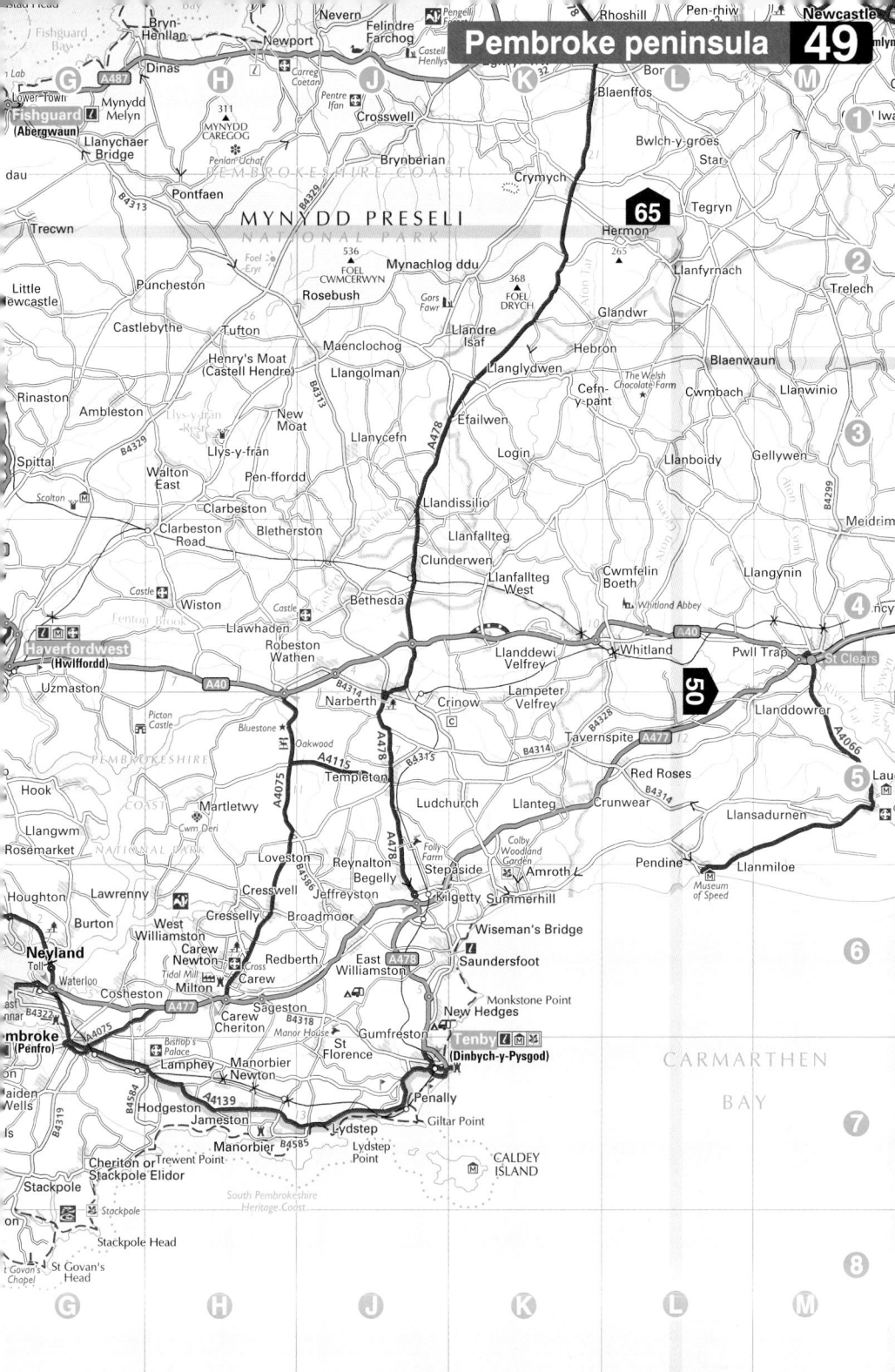

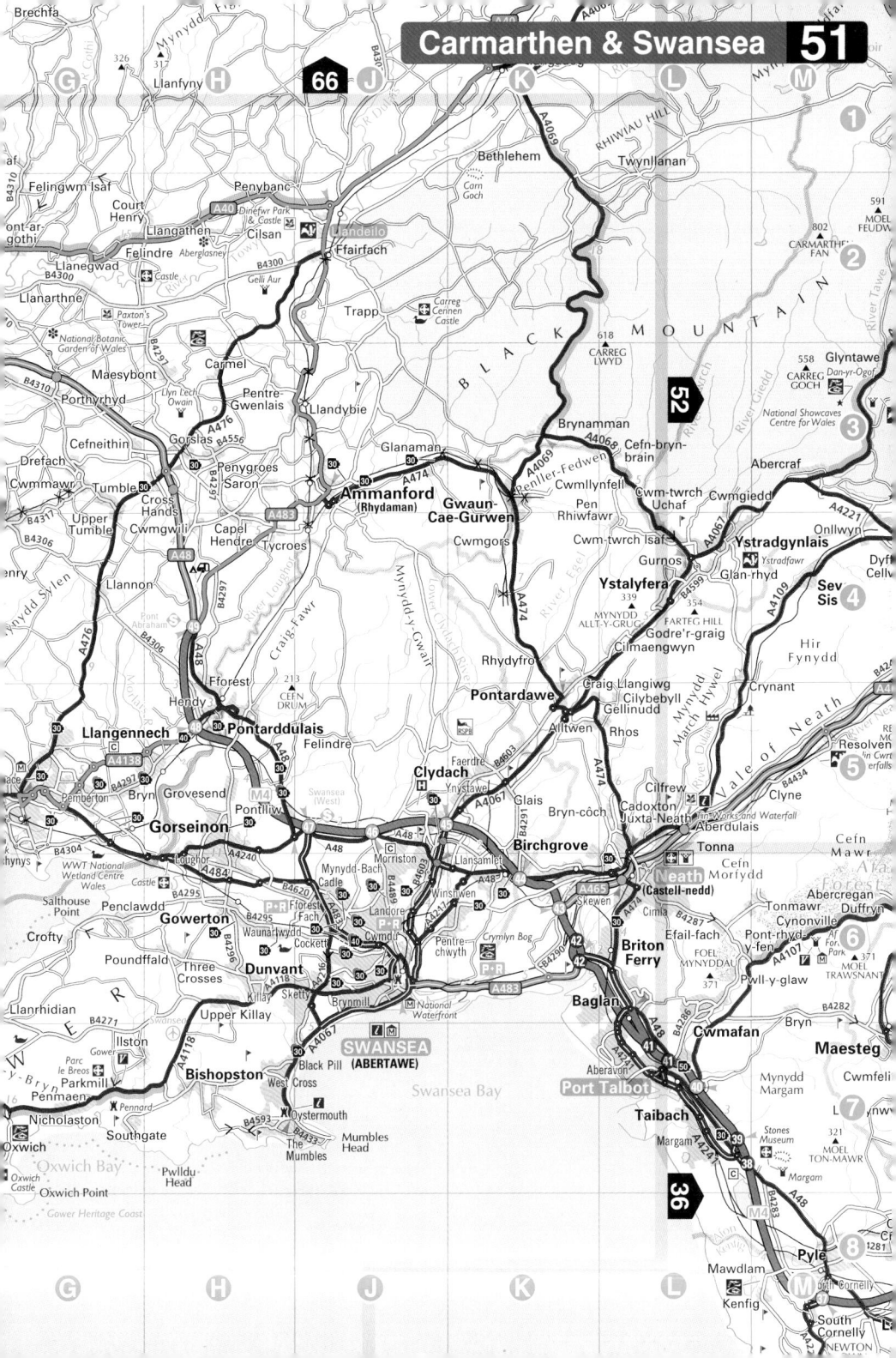

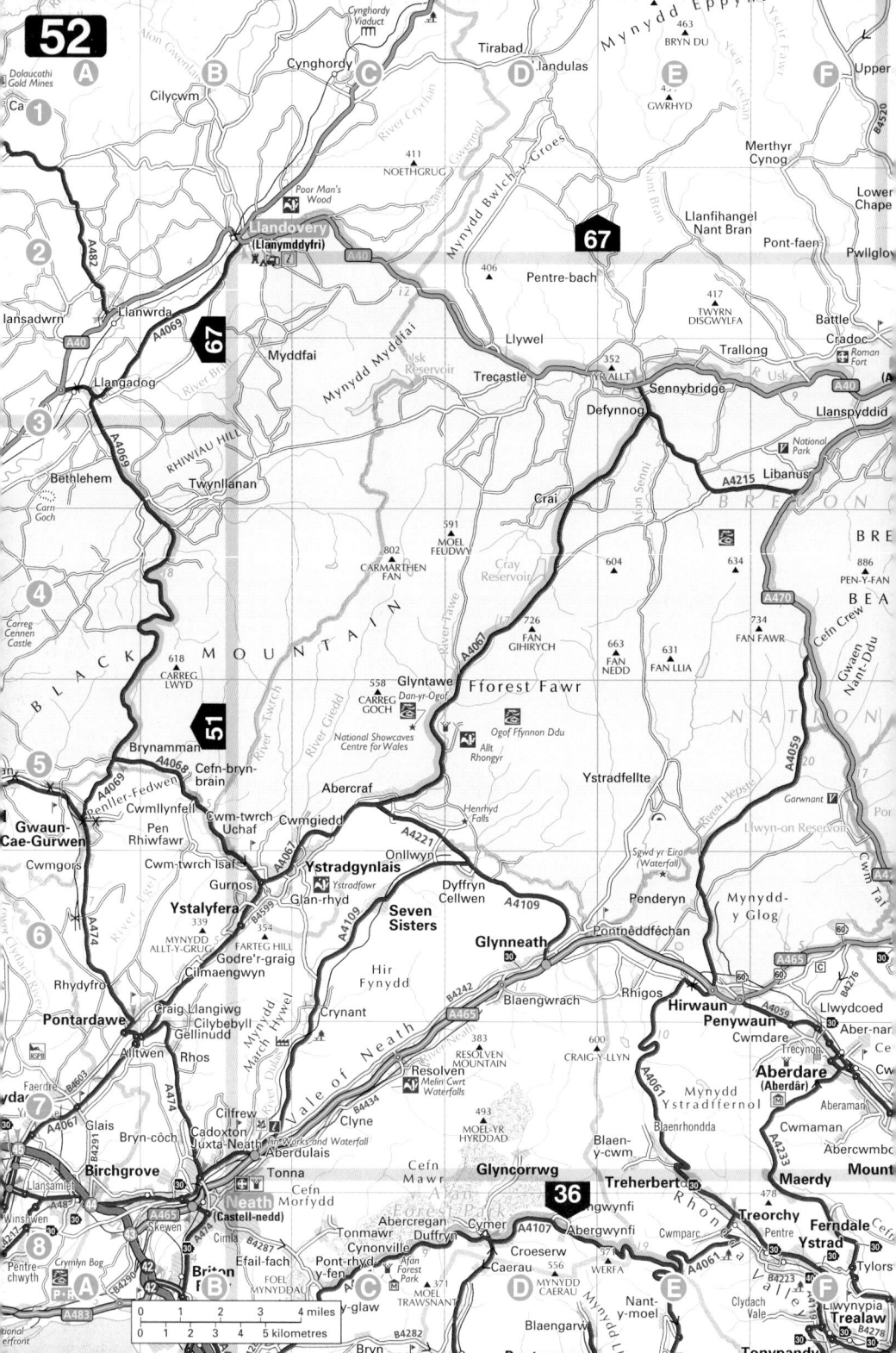

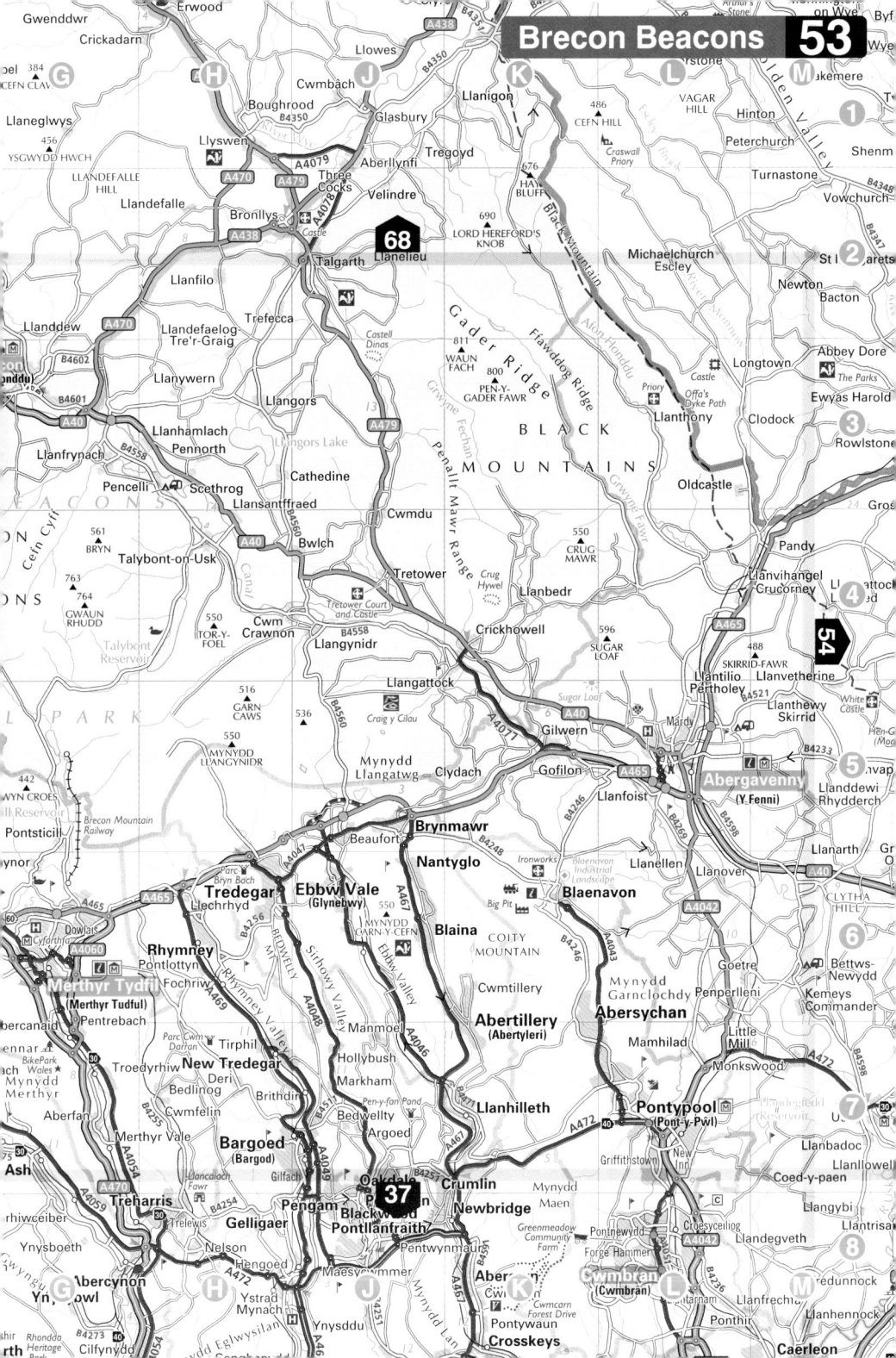

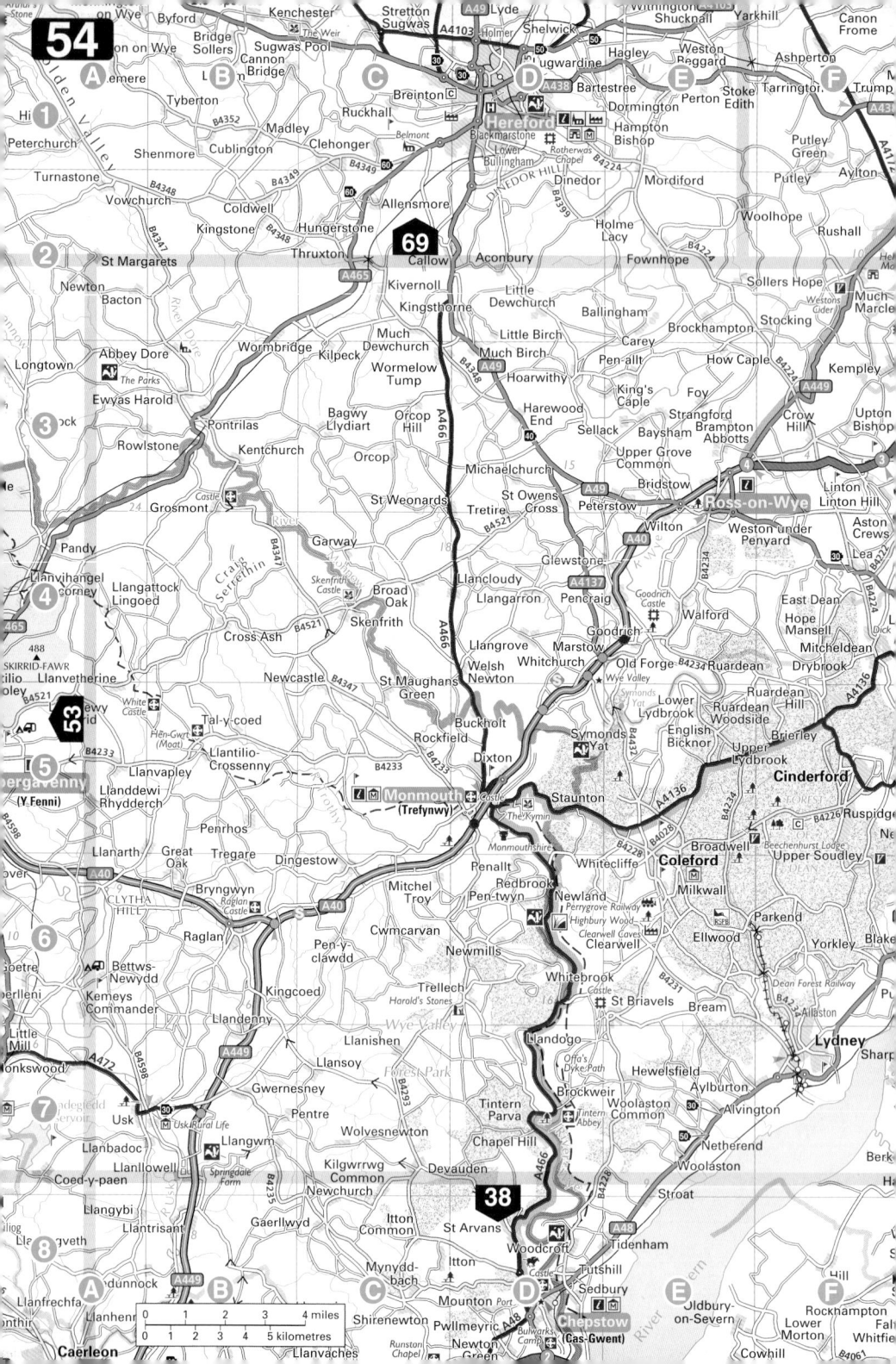

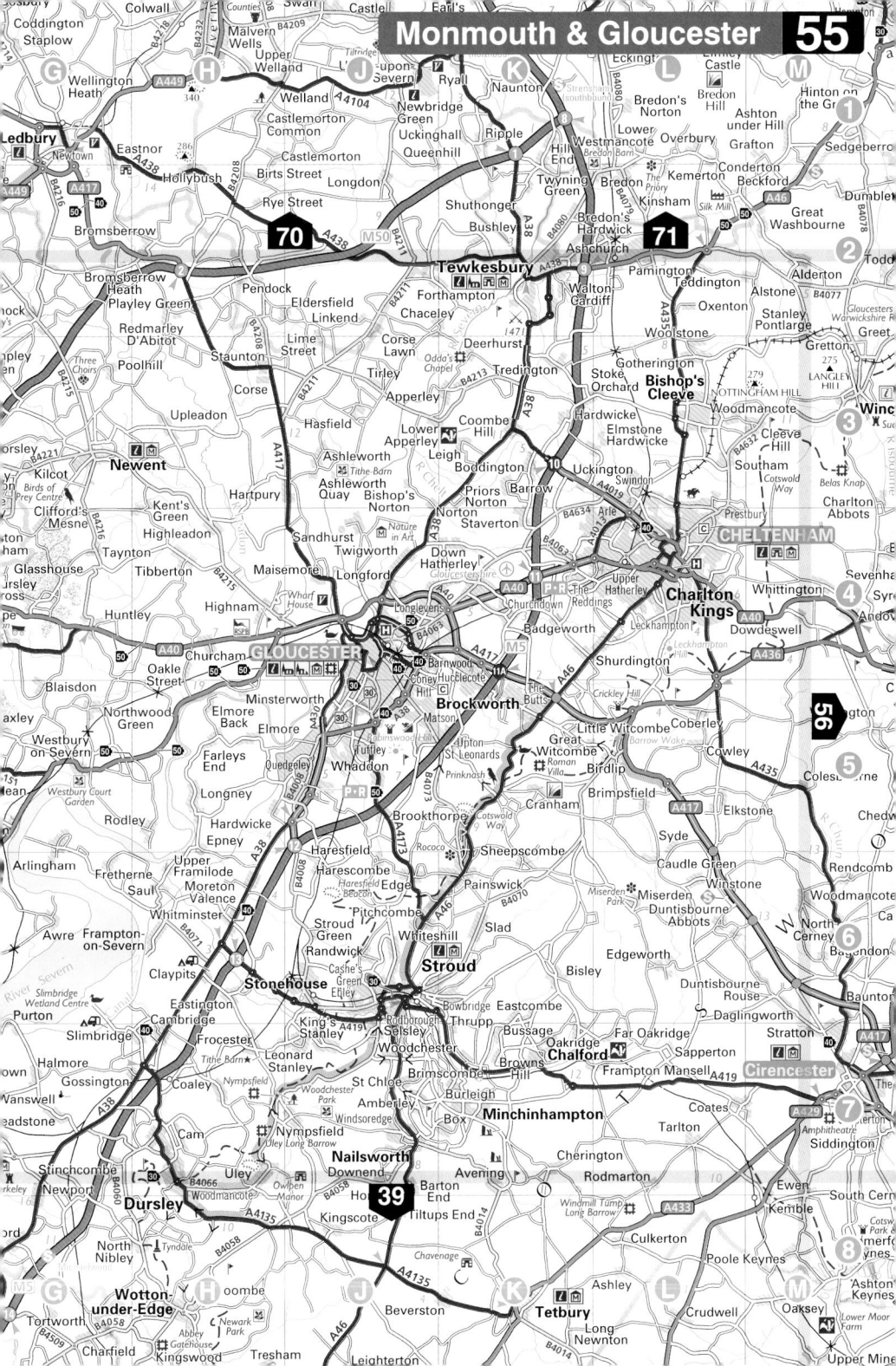

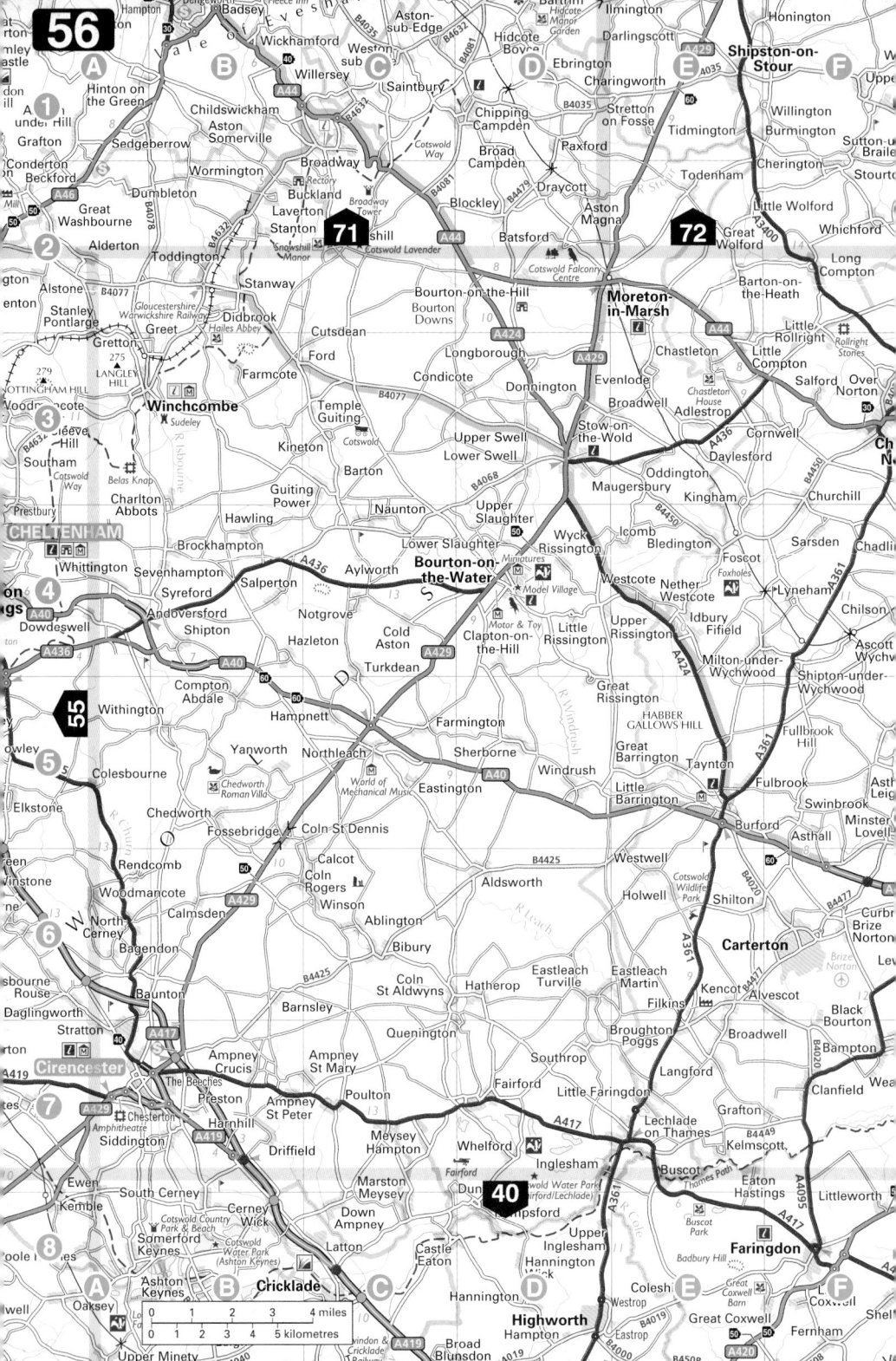

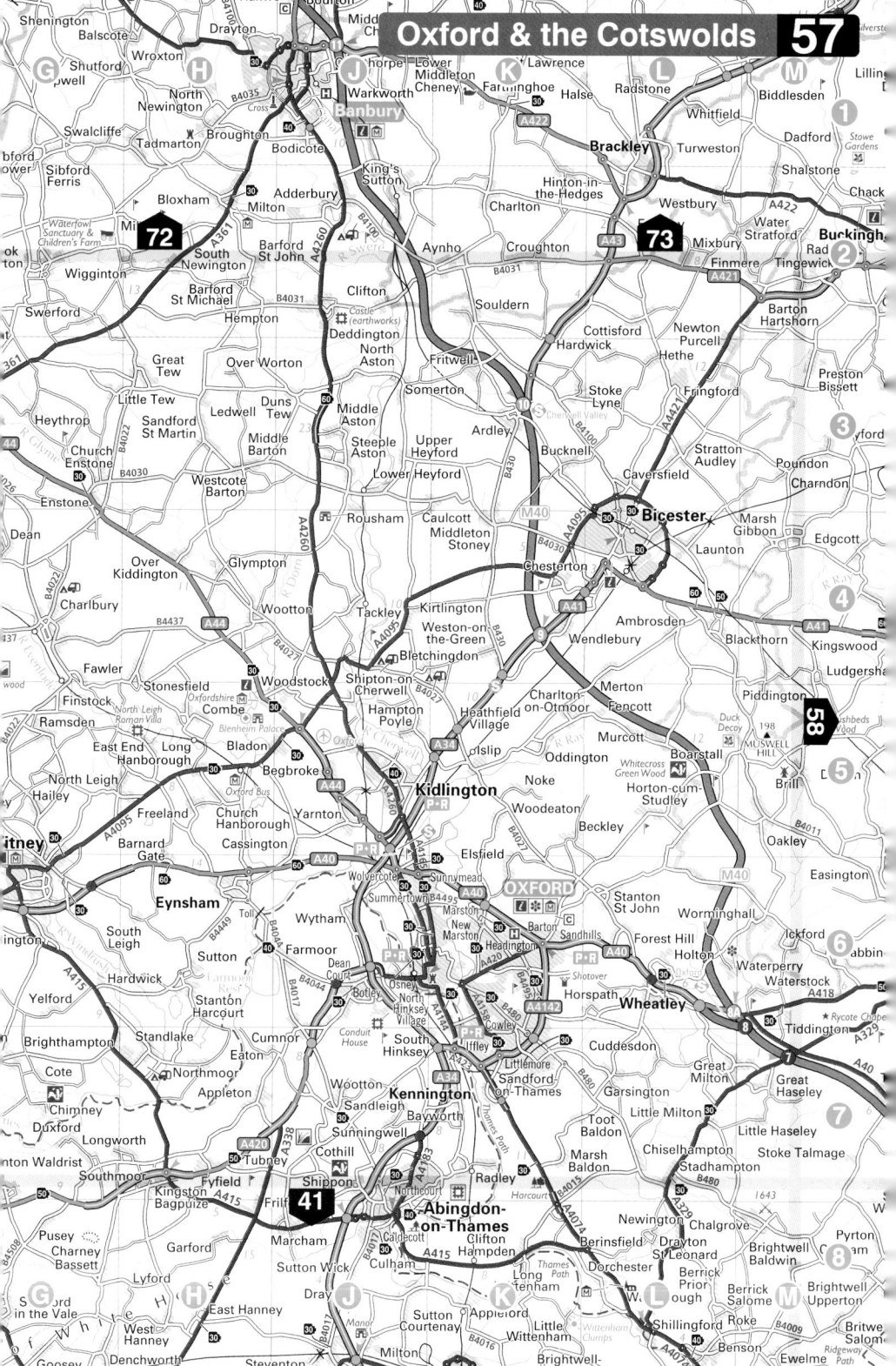

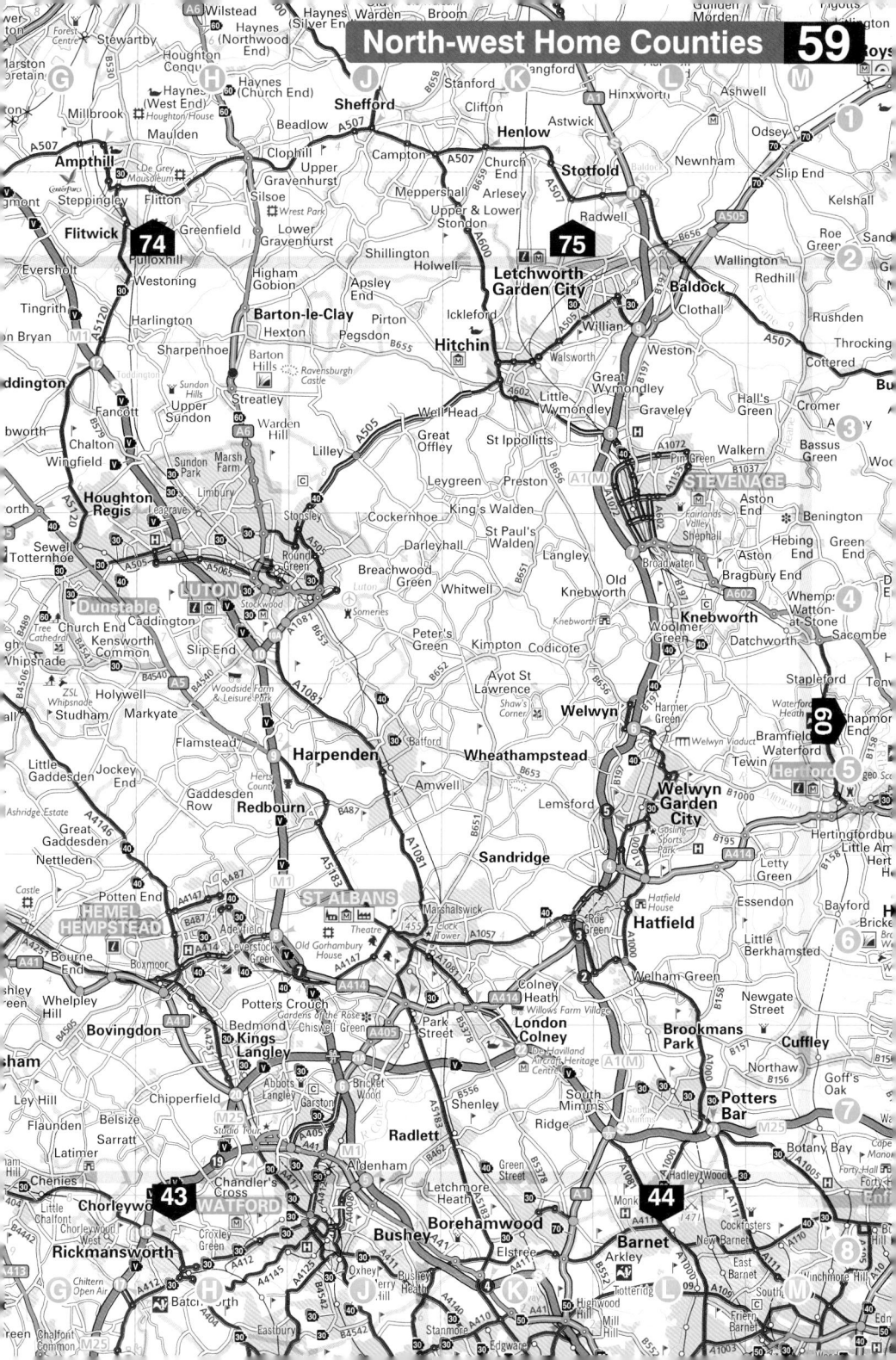

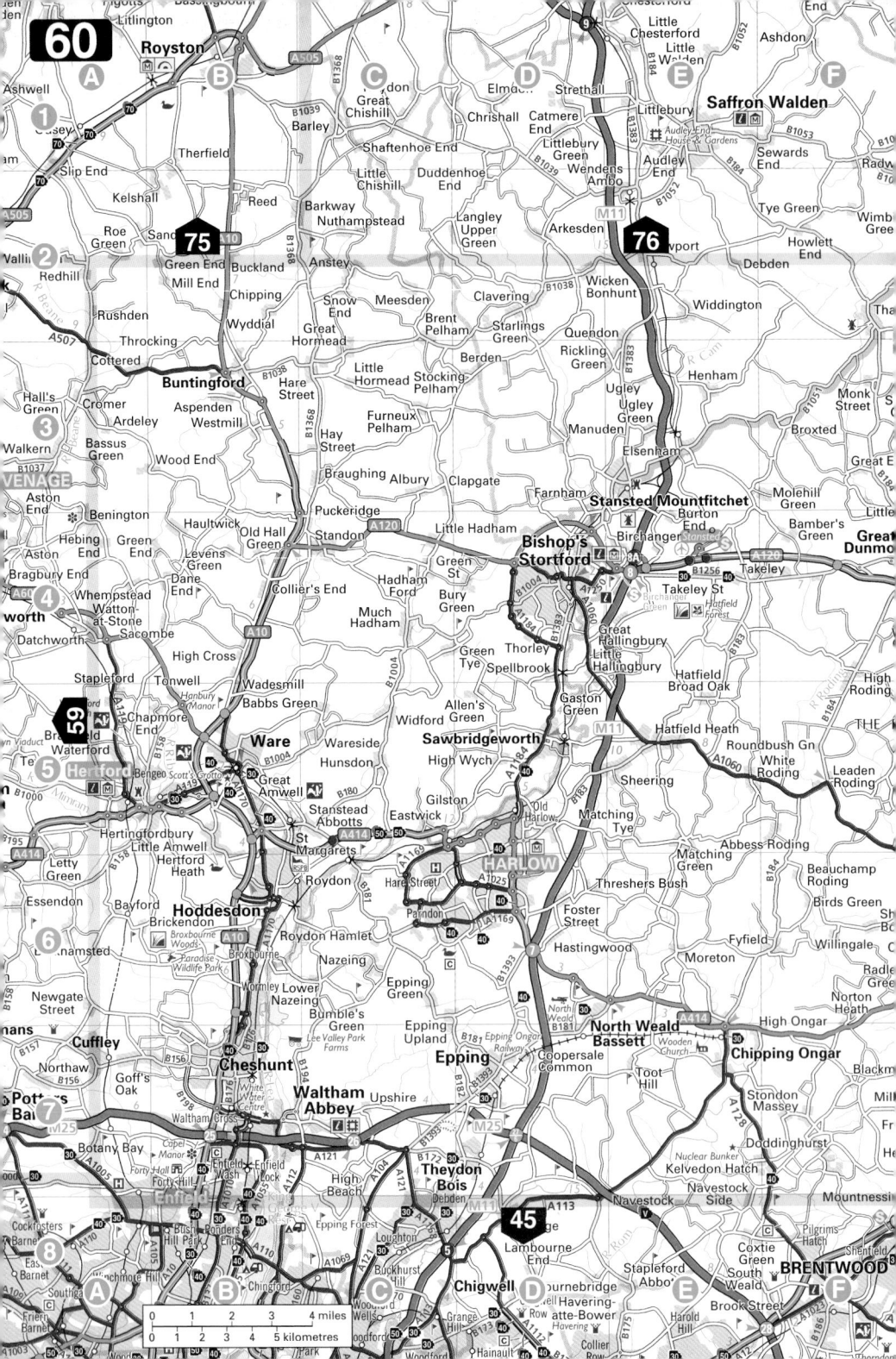

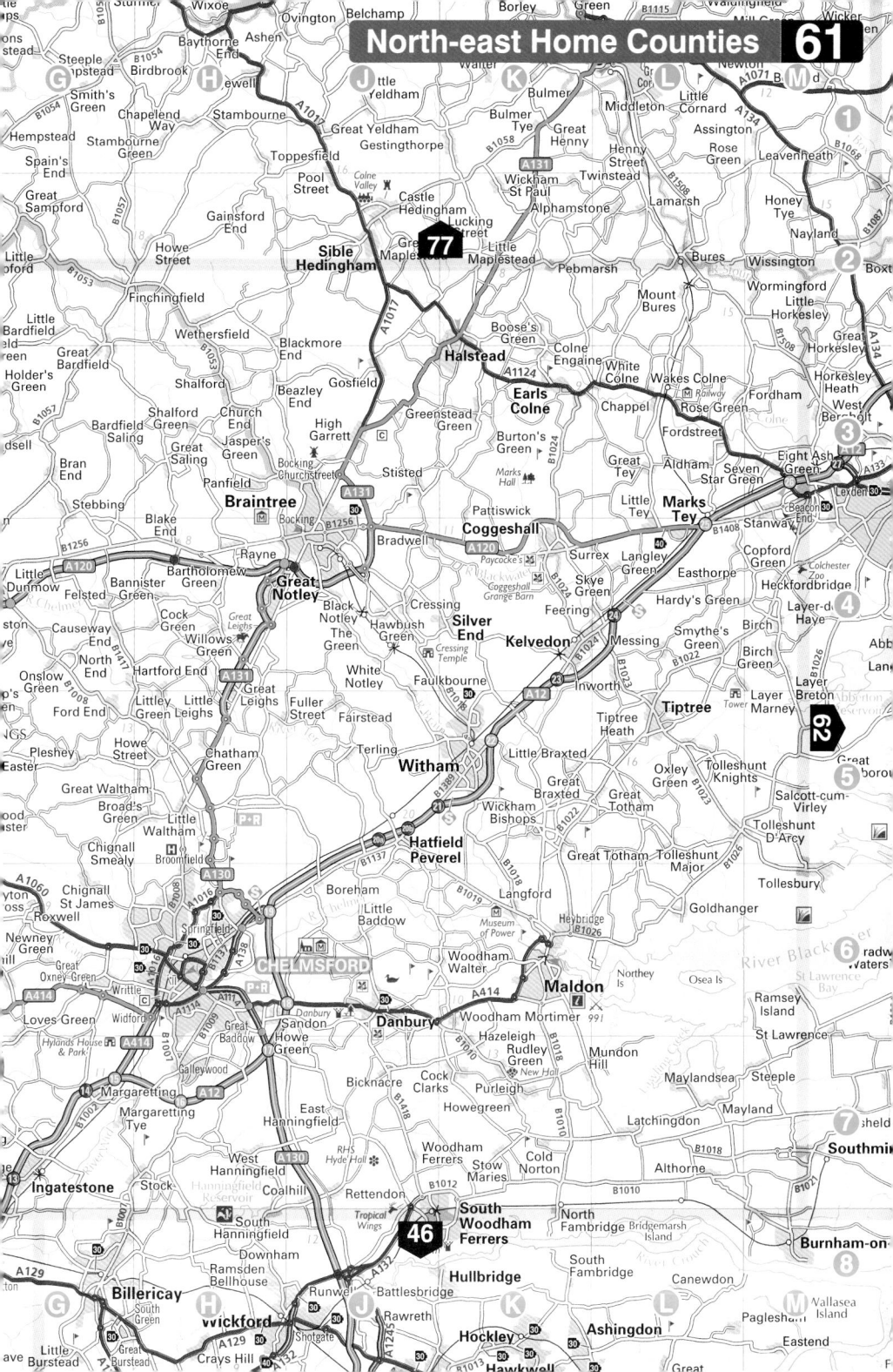

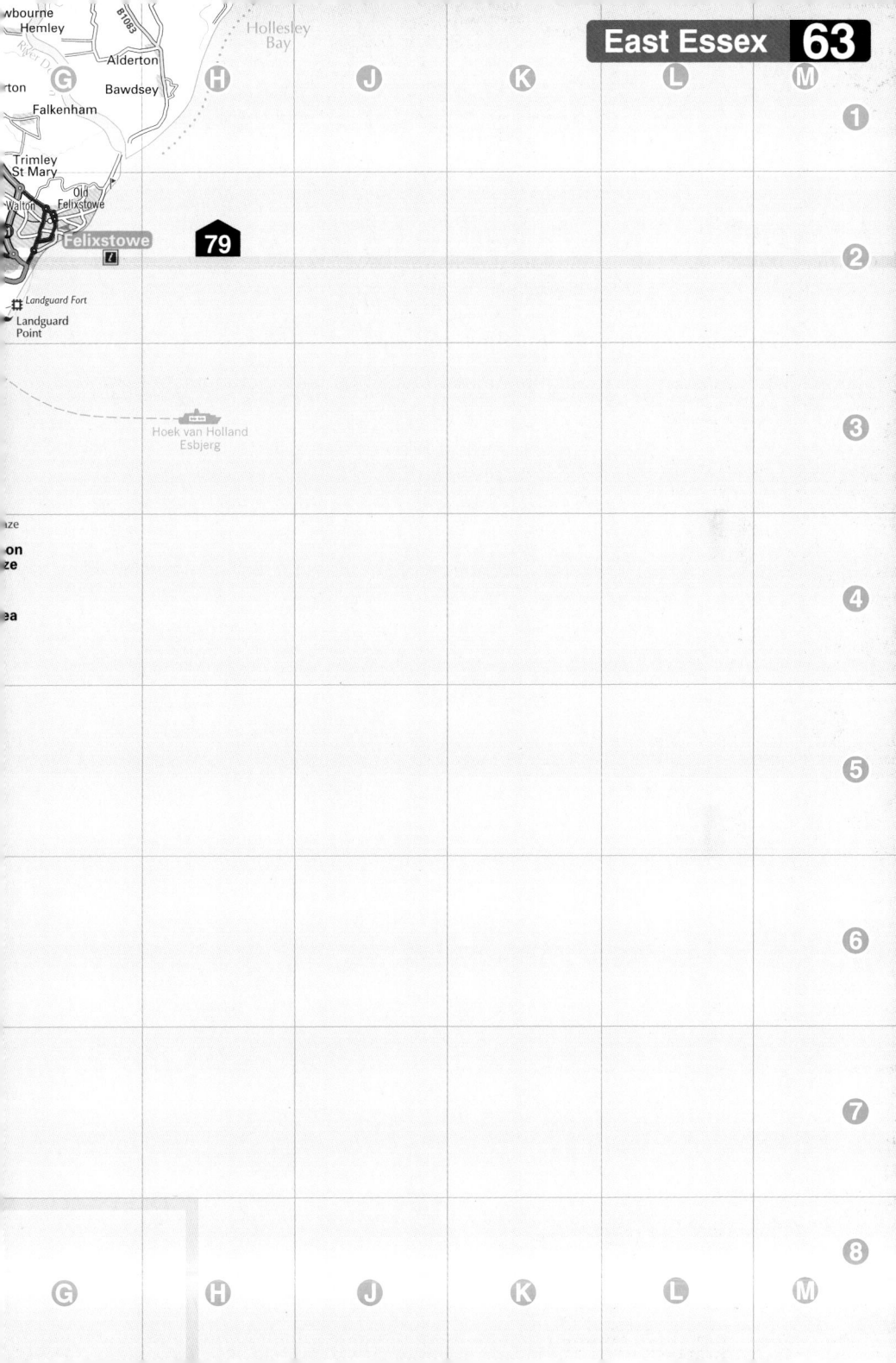

wbourne
Hemley

Hollesley
Bay

Alderton

Bawdsey

rton

Falkenham

Trimley
St Mary

Old
Felixstowe

Walton

Felixstowe **79**

✛ *Landguard Fort*

Landguard
Point

Hoek van Holland
Esbjerg

aze

on
ze

ea

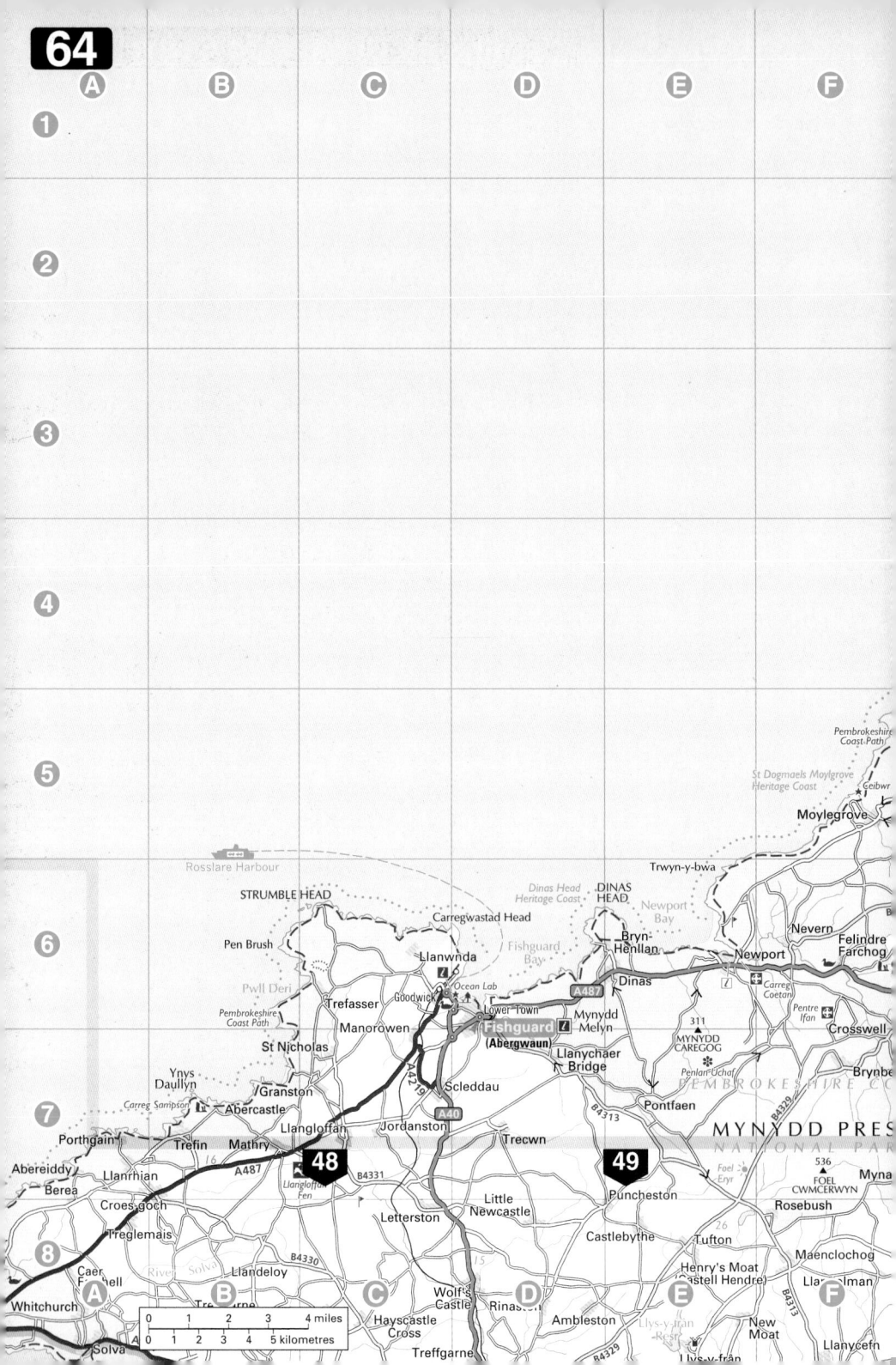

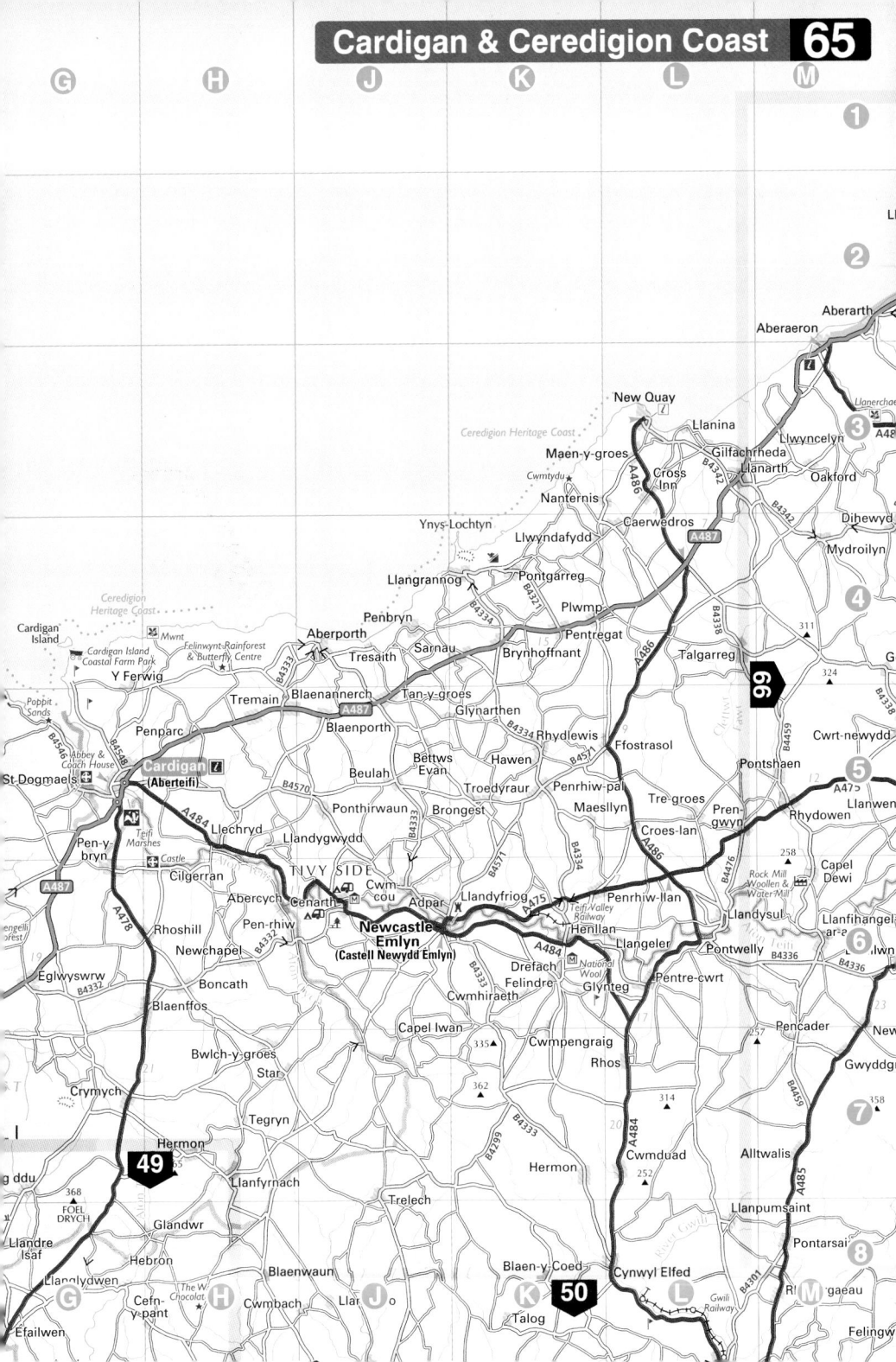

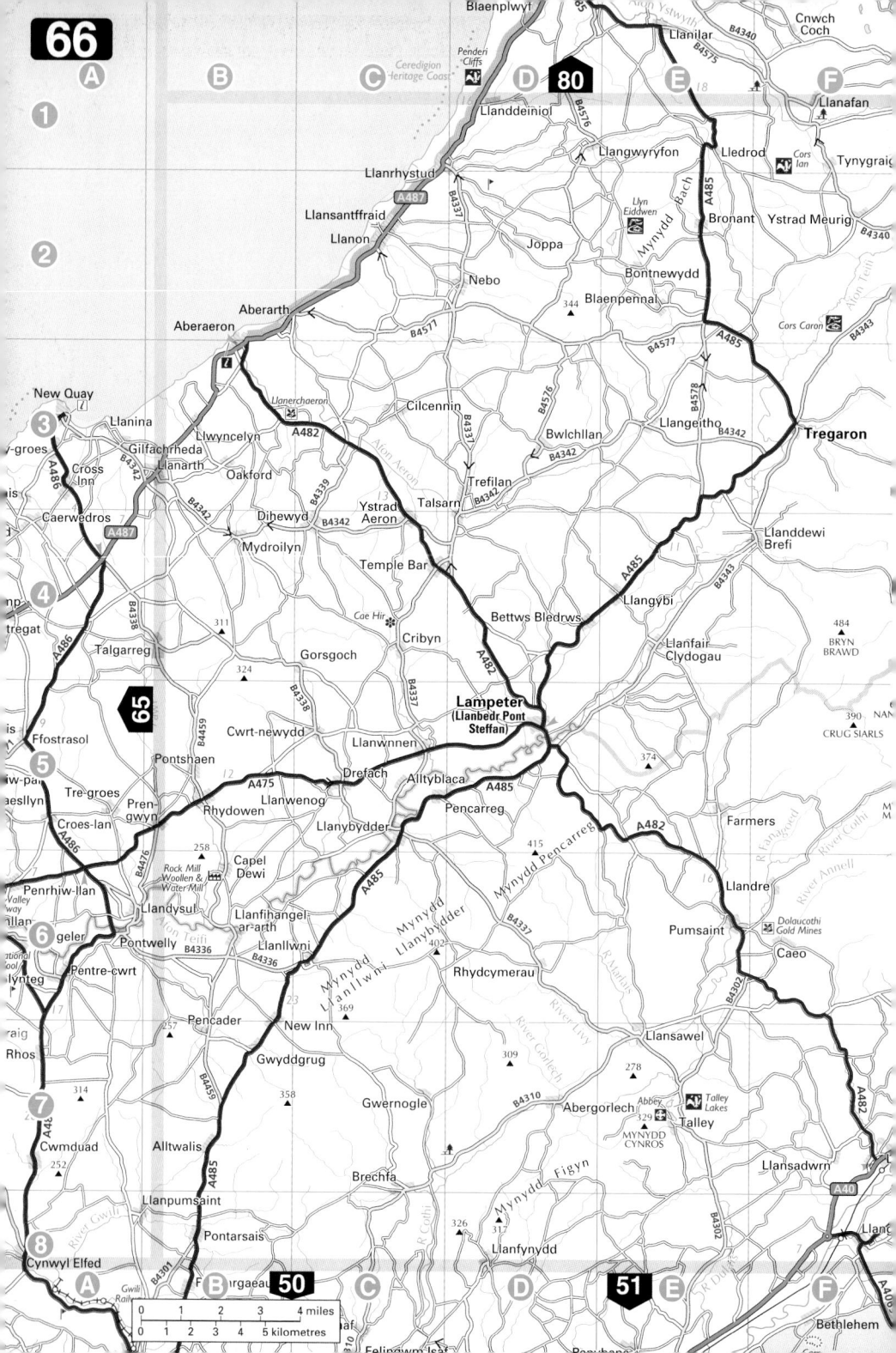

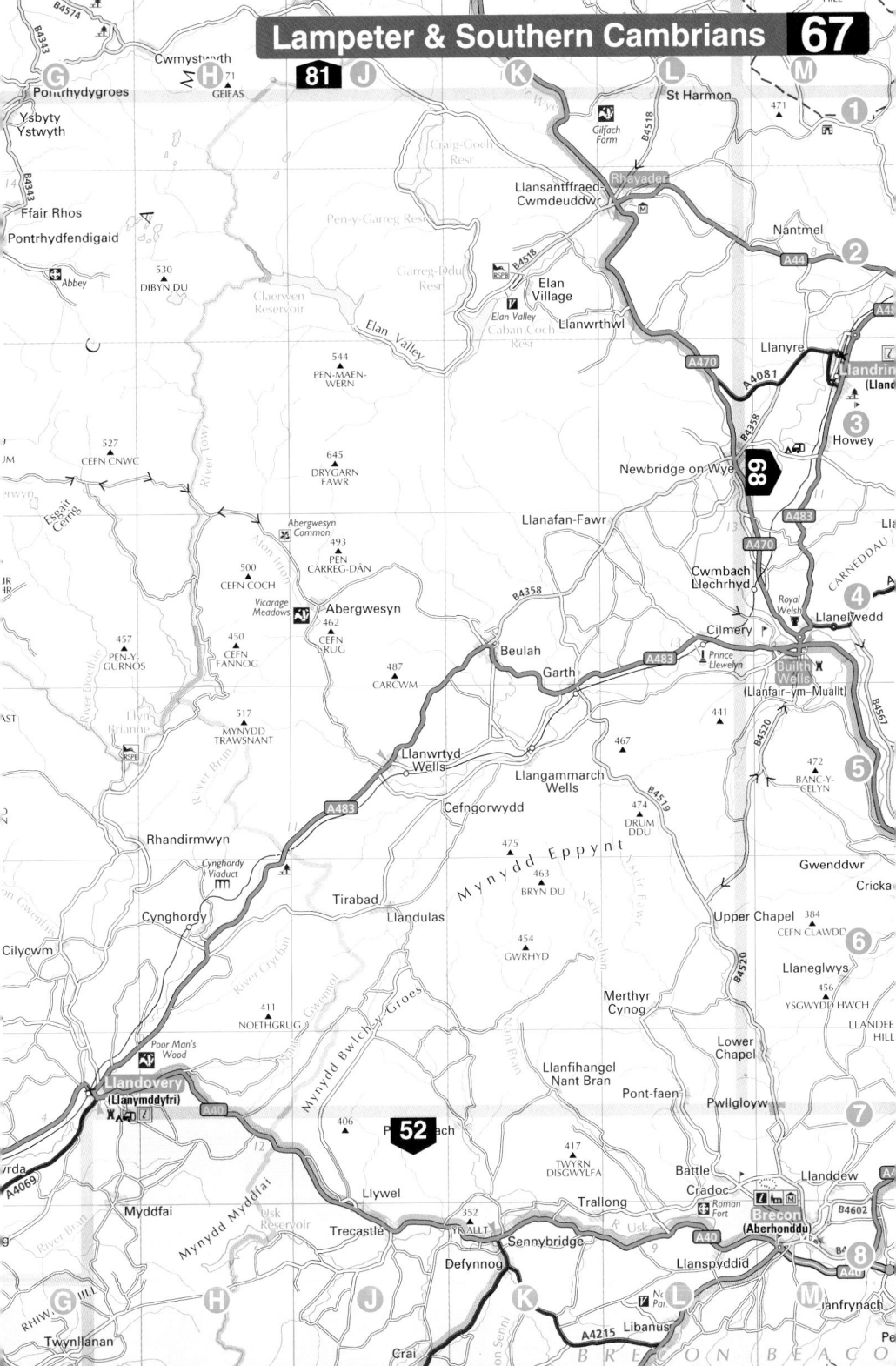

G **H** **81** **J** **K** **L** **M**

1

Cwmystwyth
71
GEIFAS

Pontrhydygroes

Ysbyty
Ystwyth

St Harmon

Gilfach
Farm

Rhayader

Llansantffraed-
Cwmdeuddwr

Nantmel

2

Ffair Rhos

Pontrhydfendigaid

Abbey
530
DIBYN DU

Pen-y-Garreg Resr

Caerwen
Reservoir

Garreg-Ddu
Resr

Elan
Village

Elan Valley

Caban-Coch
Resr

Llanwrthwl

Llanyre

Llandrin
(Lland

7

544
PEN-MAEN-
WERN

Elan Valley

A470

A4081

A470

B3358

Howey

3

CEFN CNWC
527

645
DRYGARN
FAWR

Newbridge on Wye

68

A483

Esgair
Cerrig

Abergwesyn
Common

493
PEN
CARREG-DÂN

Llanafan-Fawr

Cwmbach
Llechrhyd

Royal
Welsh

Llanelwedd

CARNEDDAU

4

500
CEFN COCH

Vicarage
Meadows

Abergwesyn

462
CEFN
GRUG

Beulah

Cilmery

Prince
Llewelyn

Builth
Wells
(Llanfair-ym-Muallt)

457
PEN-Y-
GURNOS

450
CEFN
FANNOG

487
CARCWM

Garth

A483

B4358

13

B4520

441

5

Llyn
Brianne

517
MYNYDD
TRAWSNANT

Llanwrtyd
Wells

Llangammarch
Wells

467

472
BANC-Y-
CELYN

Rhandirmwyn

Cynghordy
Viaduct

Cefngorwydd

A483

474
DRUM
DDU

B4519

Gwenddwr

Cricka

Cilycwm

Cynghordy

Tirabad

Llandulas

475

Mynydd Eppynt

463
BRYN DU

Upper Chapel

384
CEFN CLAWDD

6

411
NOETHGRUG

454
GWRHYD

Merthyr
Cynog

B4520

Llaneglwys

456
YSGWYDD HWCH

LLANDEF
HILL

Poor Man's
Wood

Llandovery
(Llanymddyfri)

A40

52

406

Llanfihangel
Nant Bran

Lower
Chapel

Pont-faen

Pwllgloyw

7

Myddfai

Usk
Reservoir

Llywel

Trecastle

YR ALLT
352

Trallong

417
TWRN
DISGWYLFA

Battle
Cradoc

Roman
Fort

Brecon
(Aberhonddu)

Llanddew

B4602

8

A4069

Mynydd Myddfai

Defynnog

Sennybridge

A40

Llanspyddid

anfrynach

A40

Twynllanan

G **H** **J** **K** **L** **M**

Libanus

Crai

A4215

BRECON BEACO

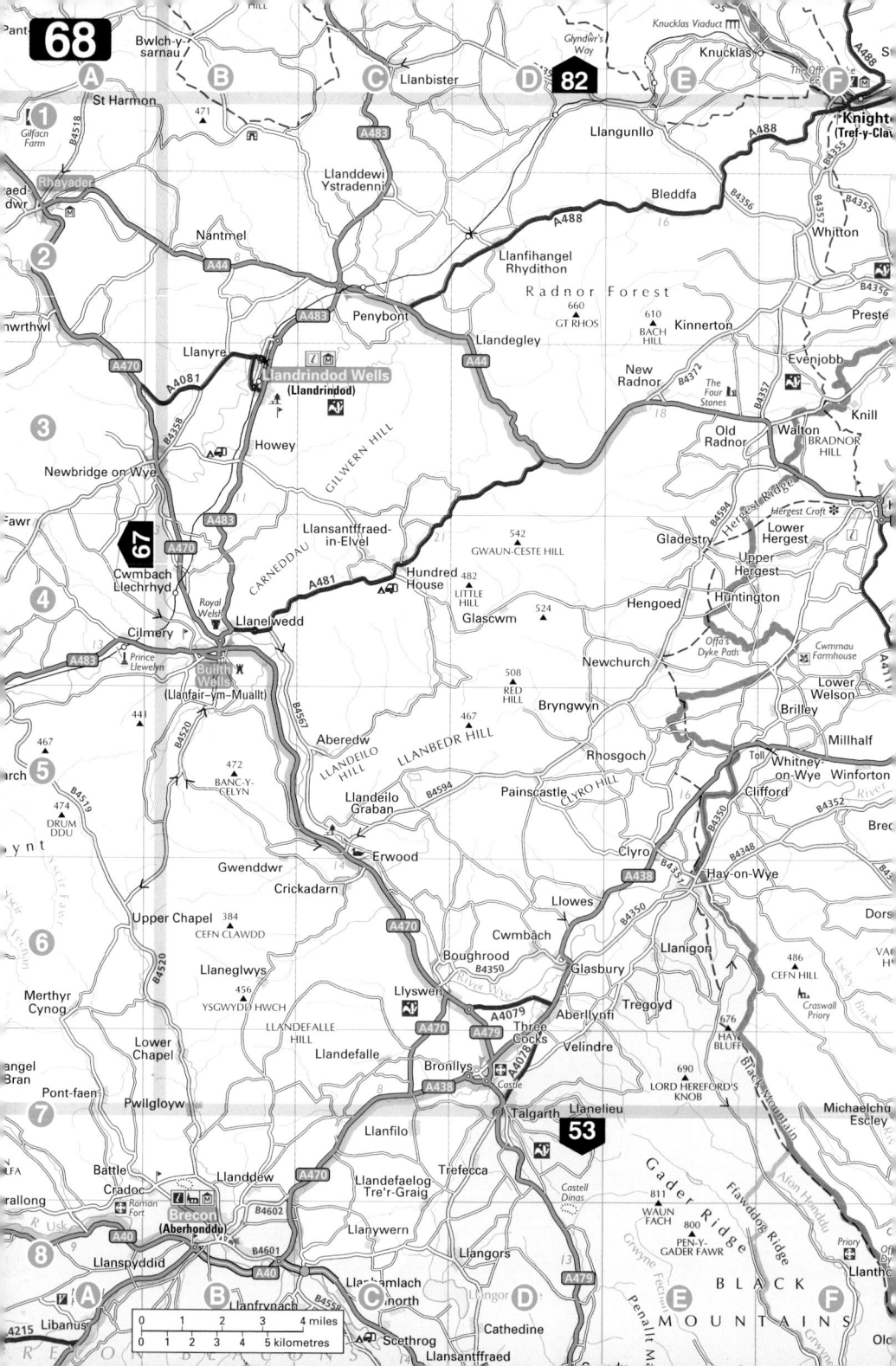

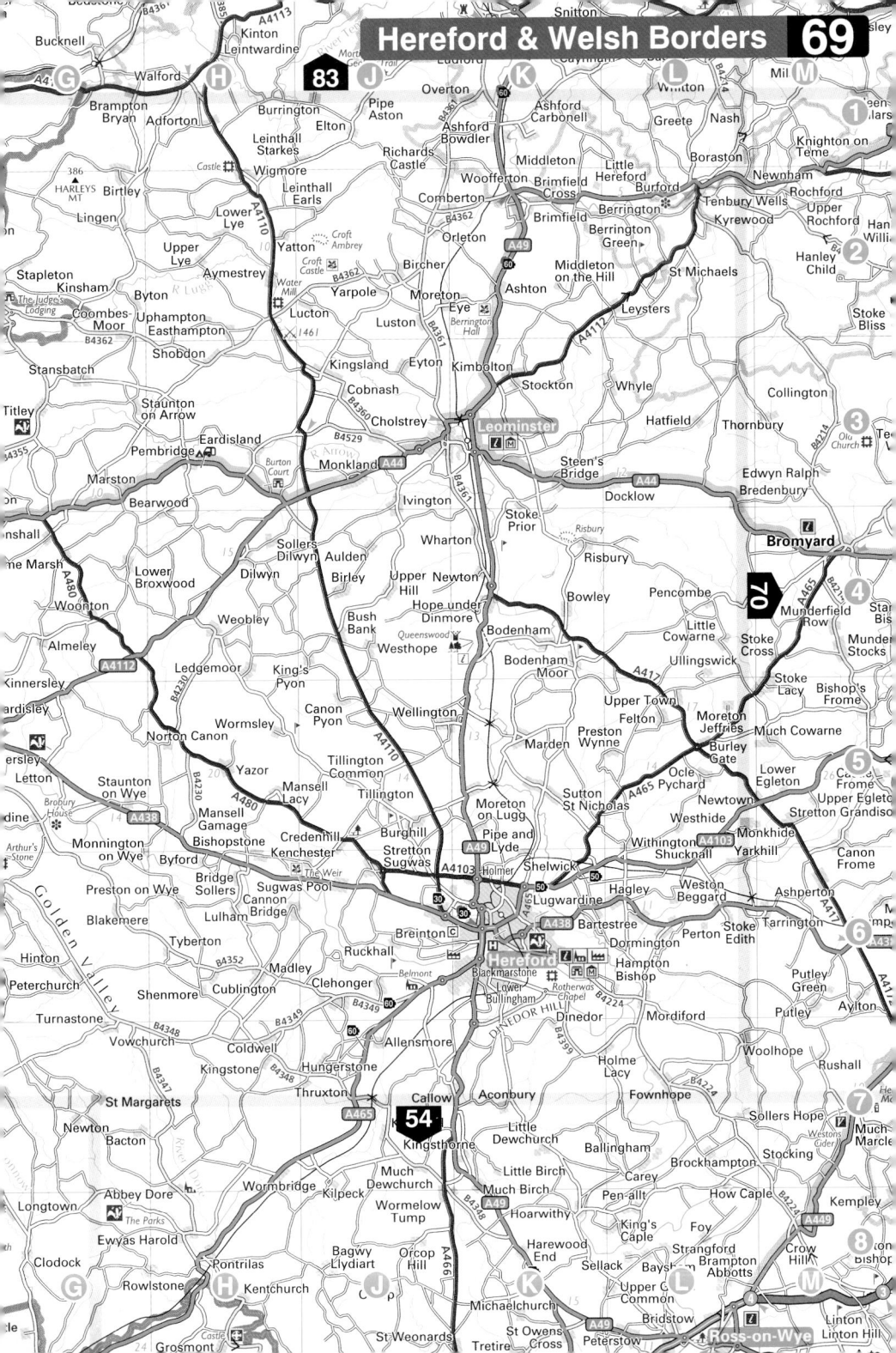

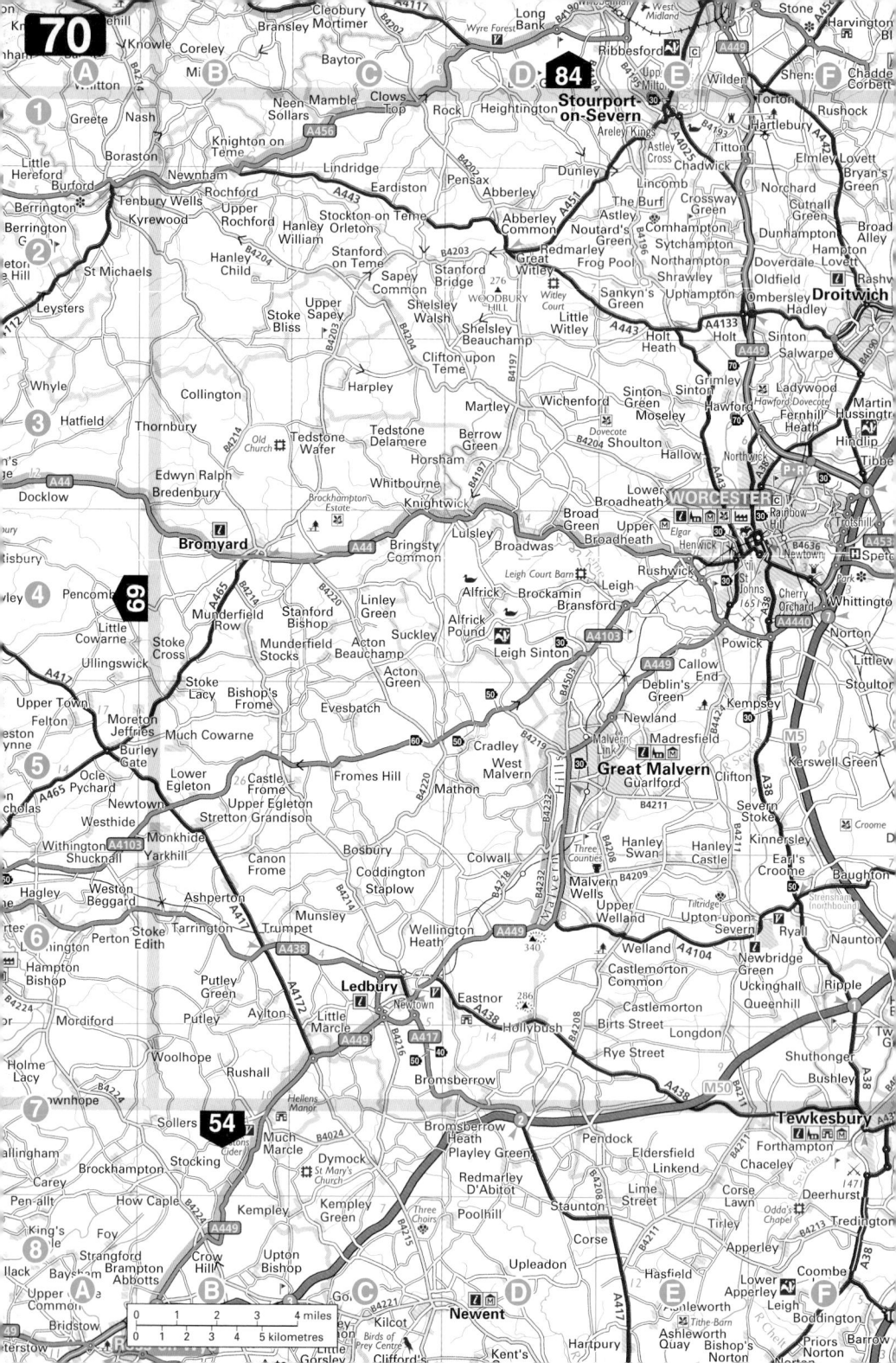

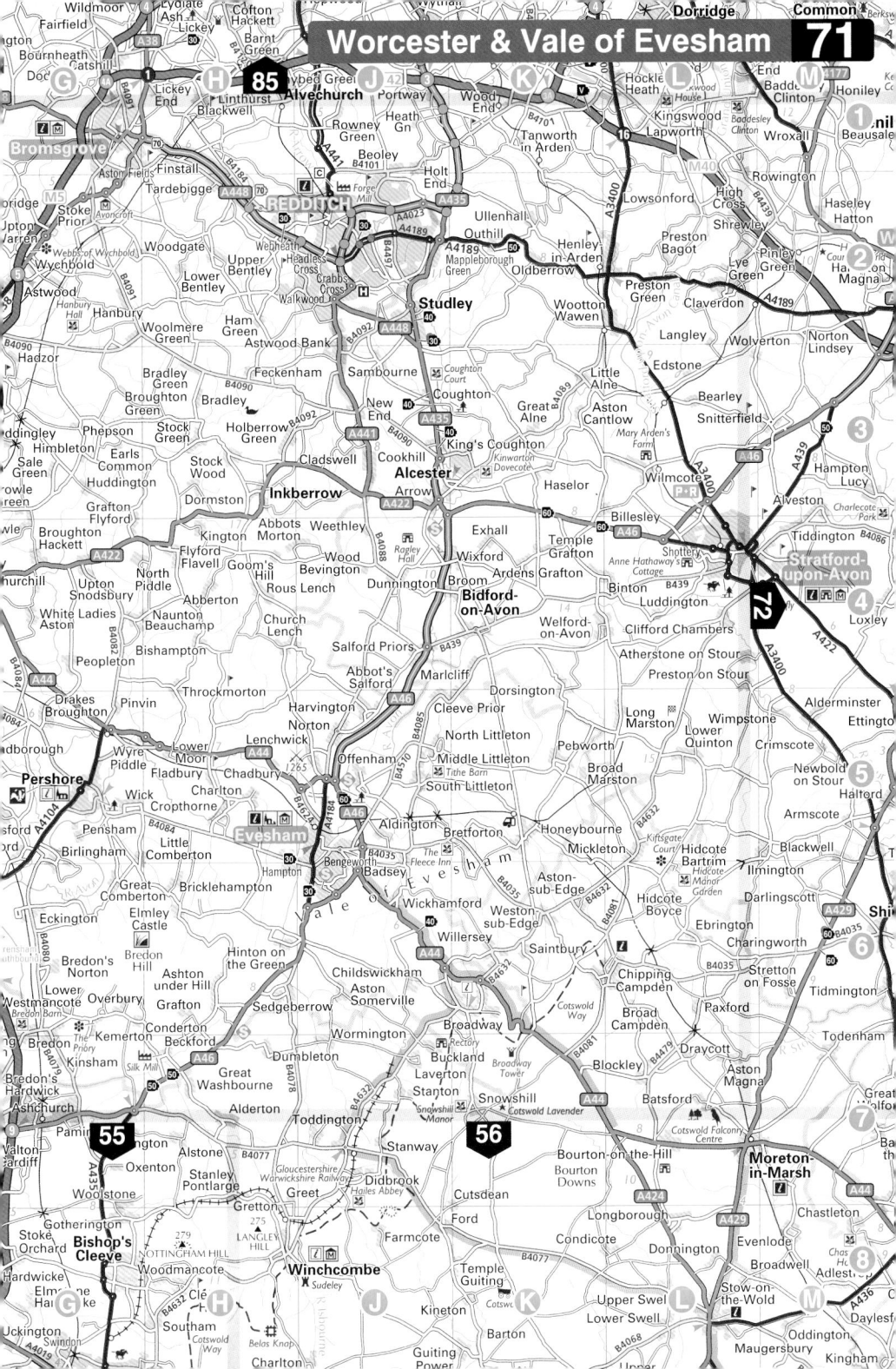

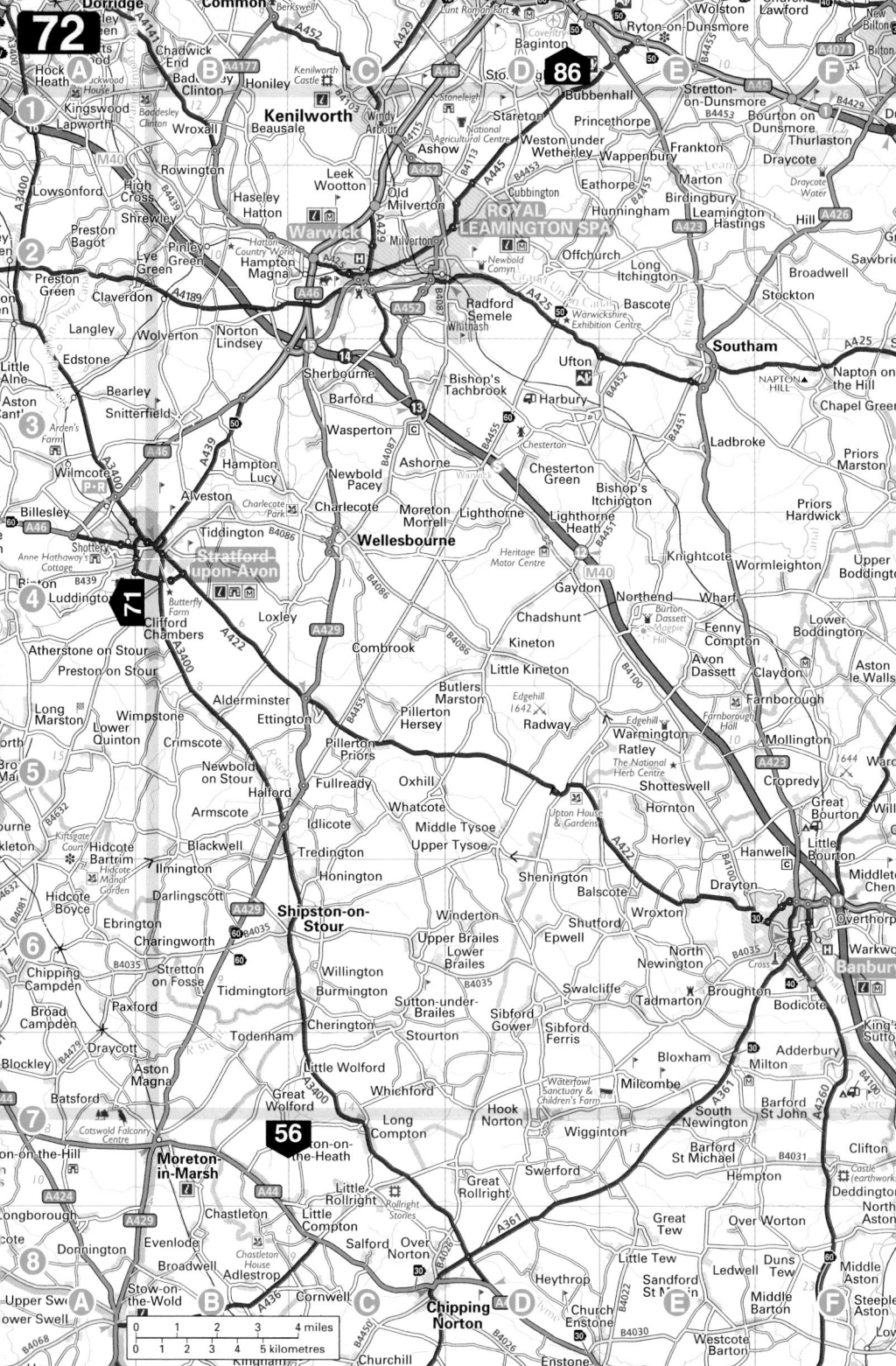

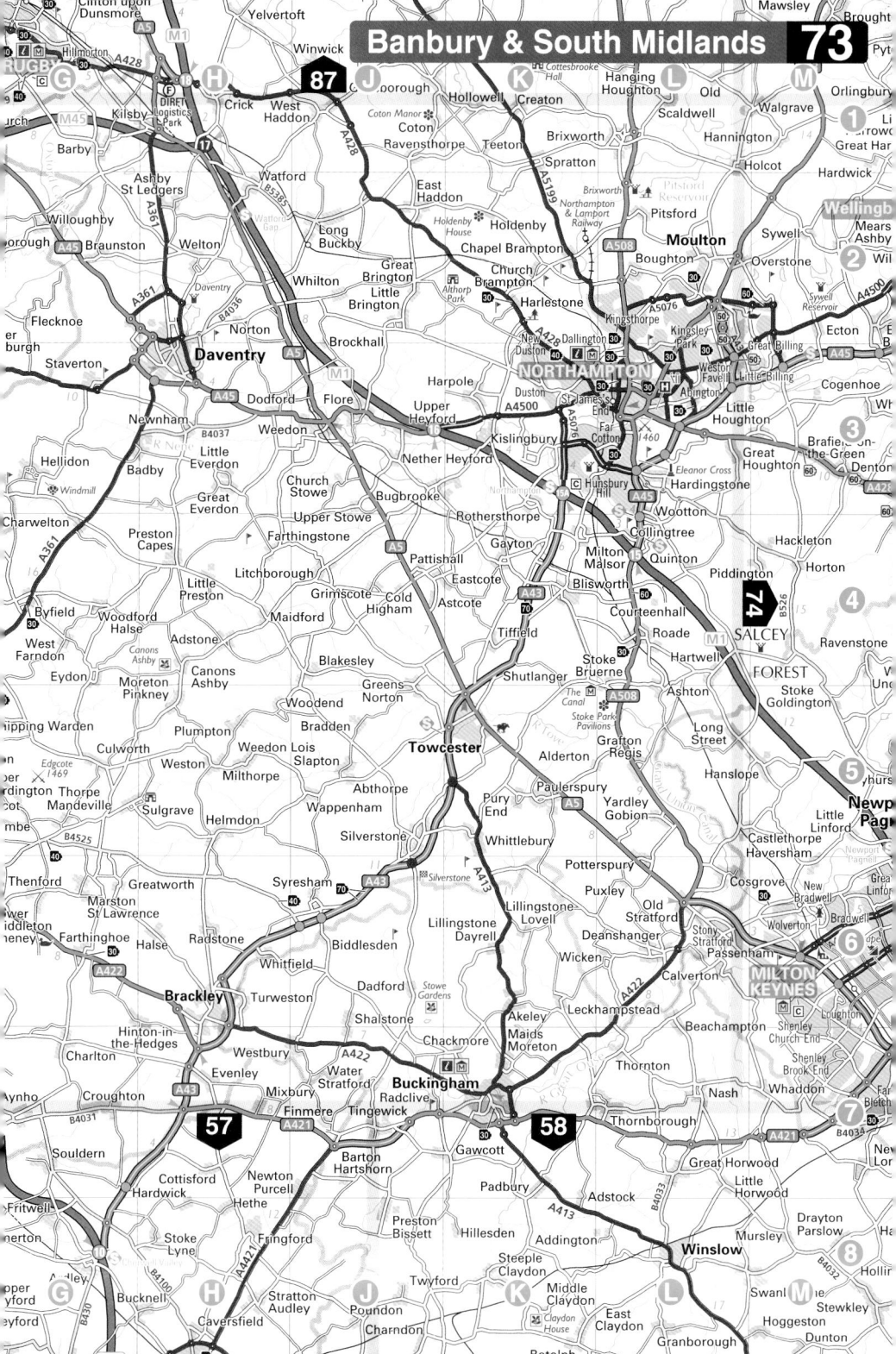

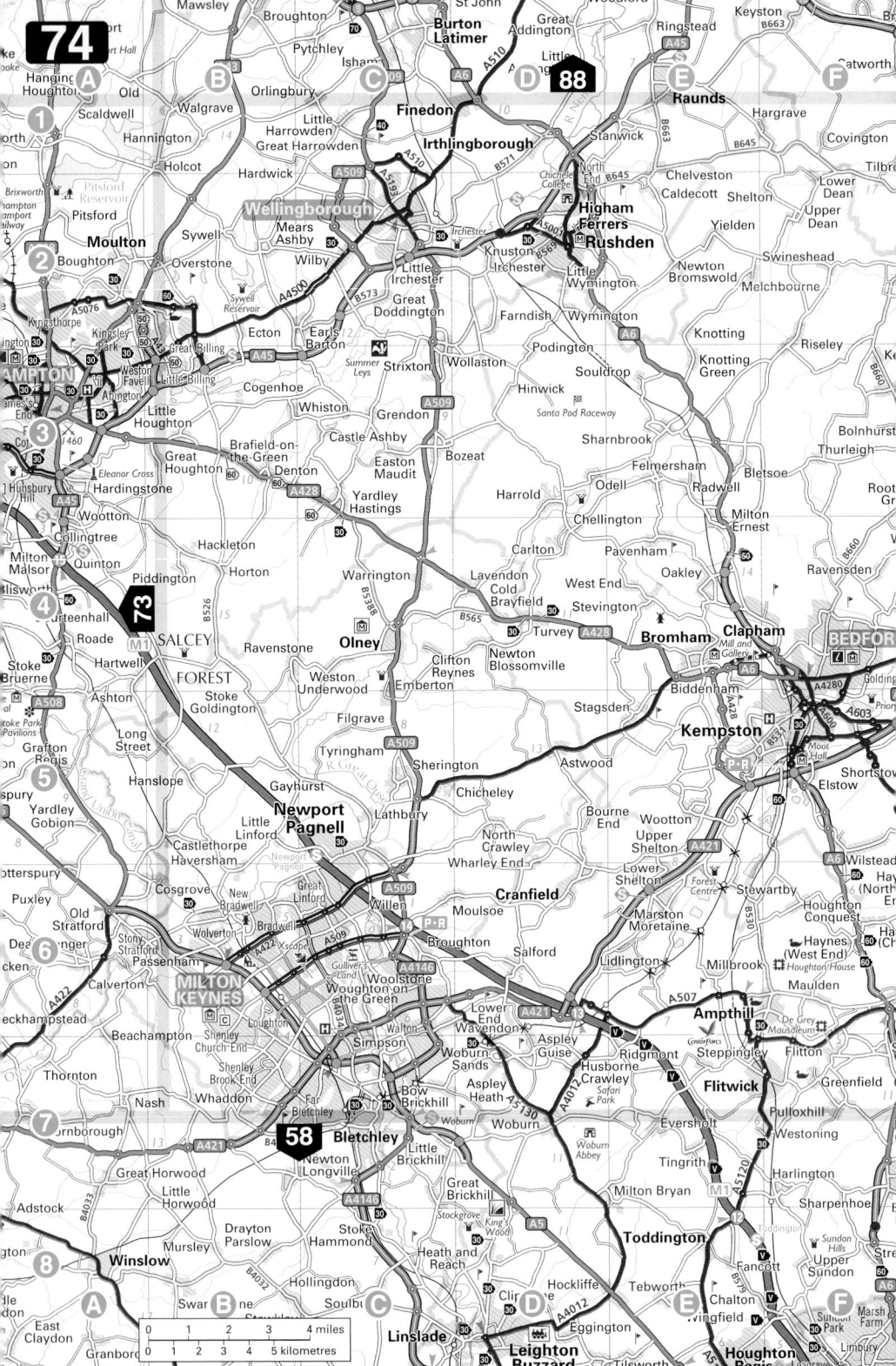

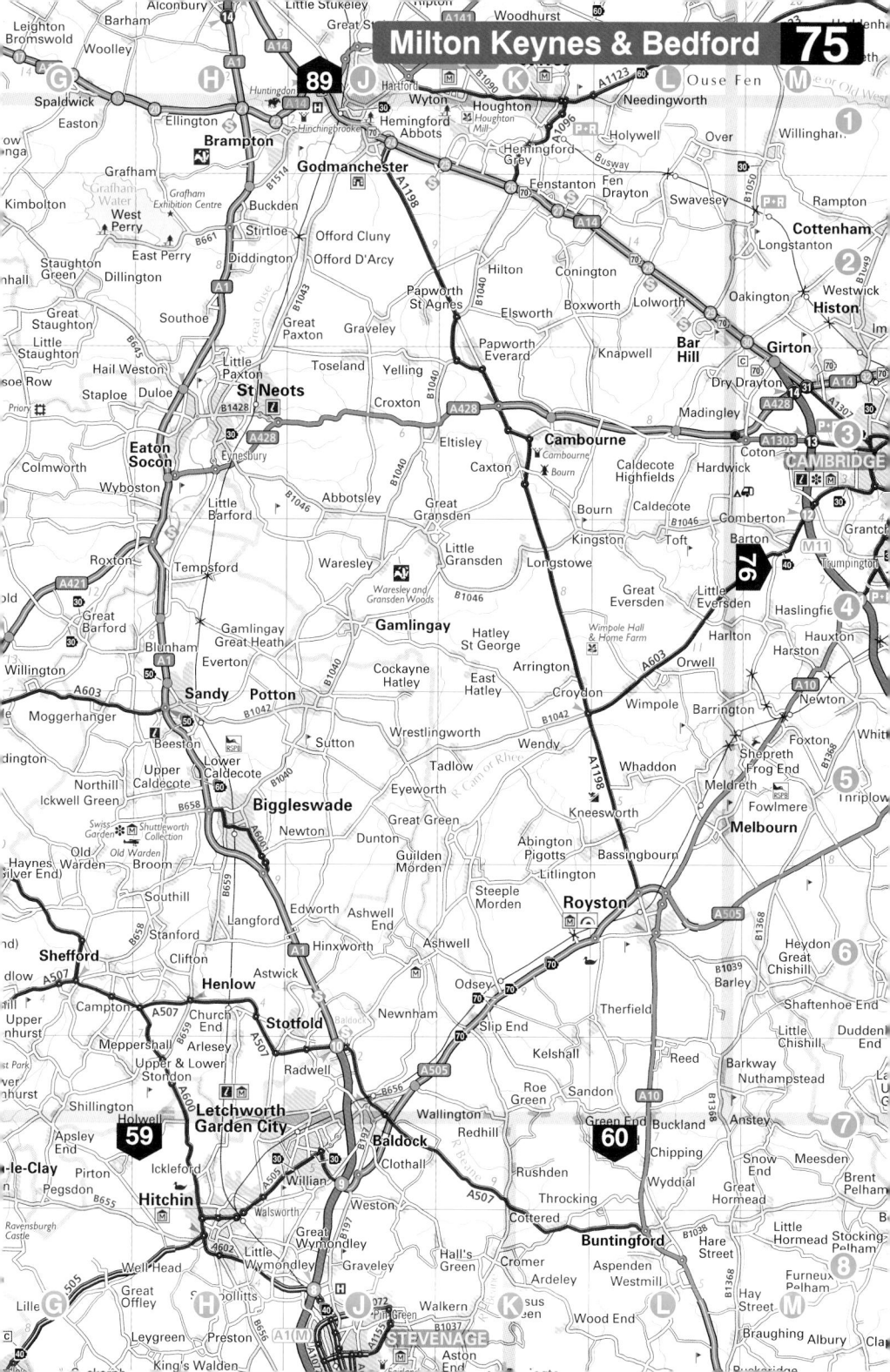

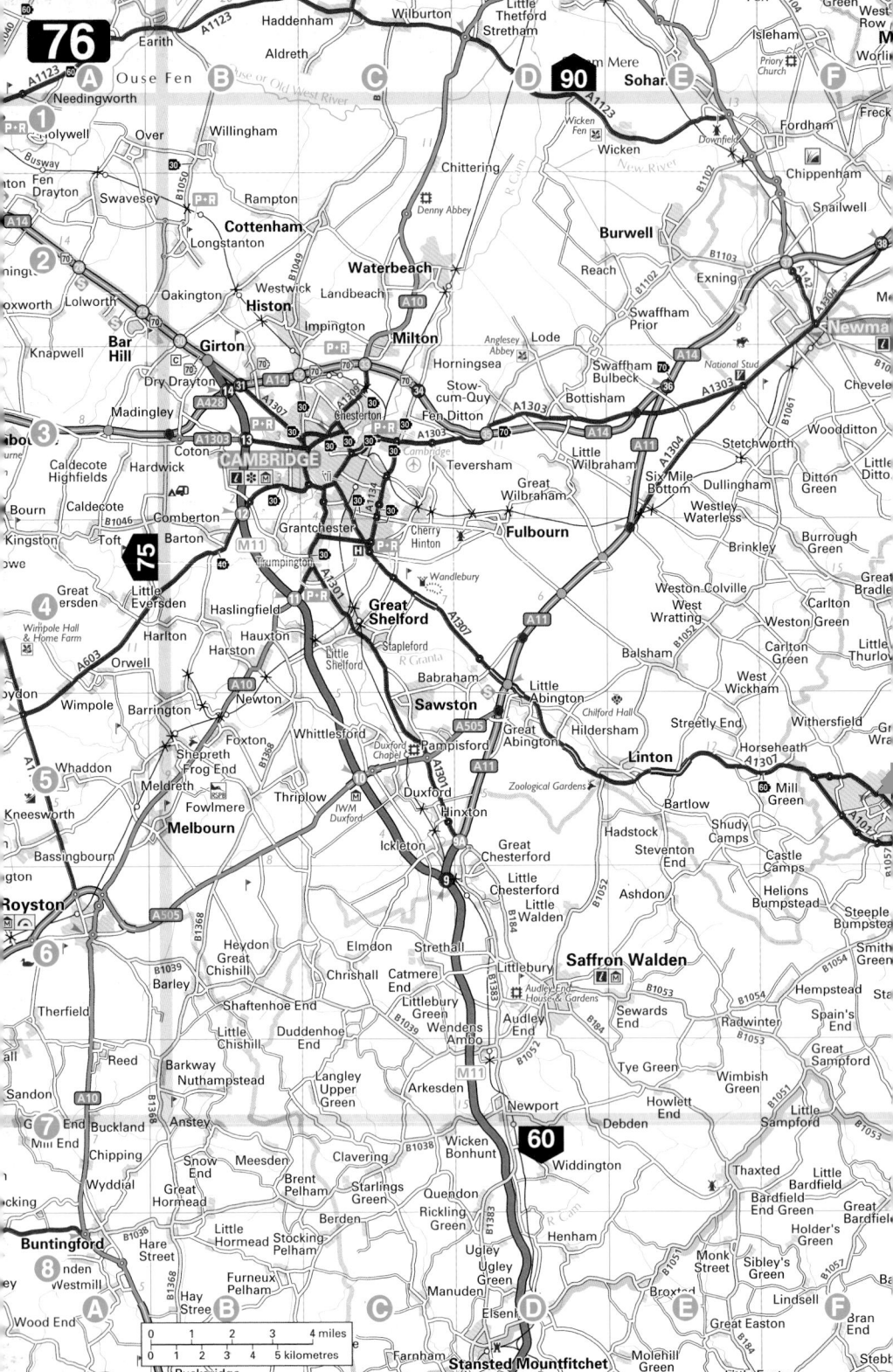

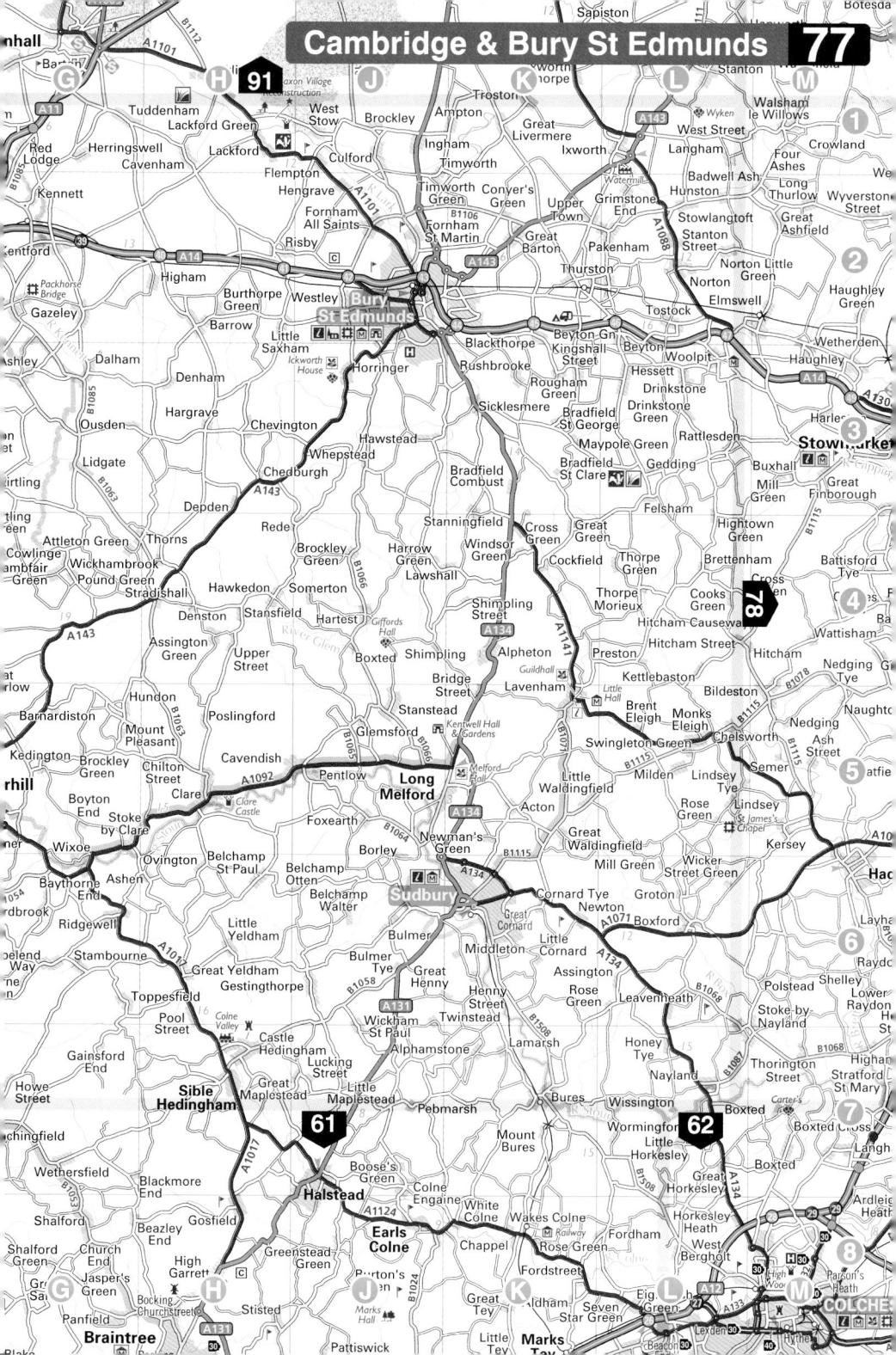

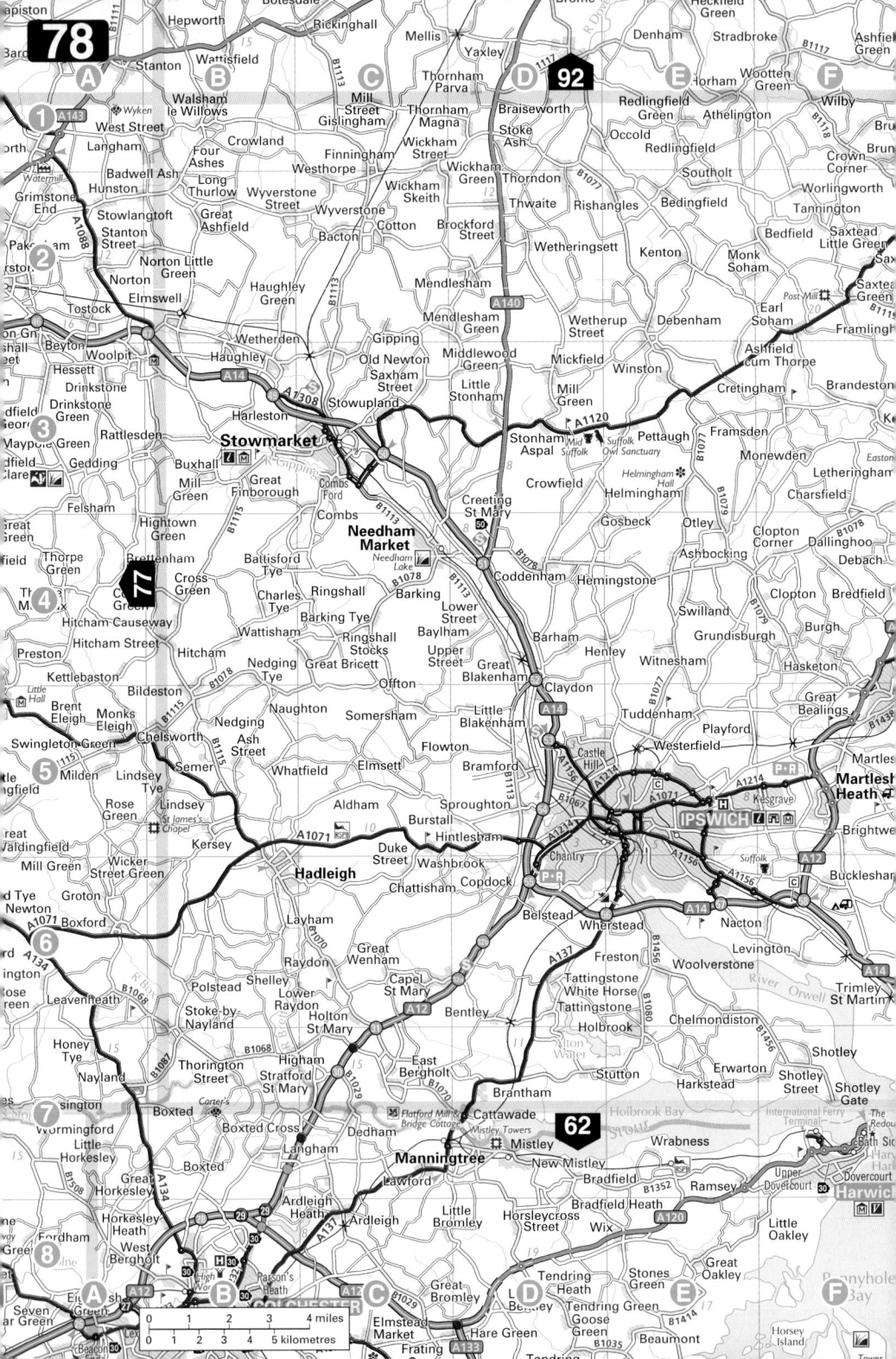

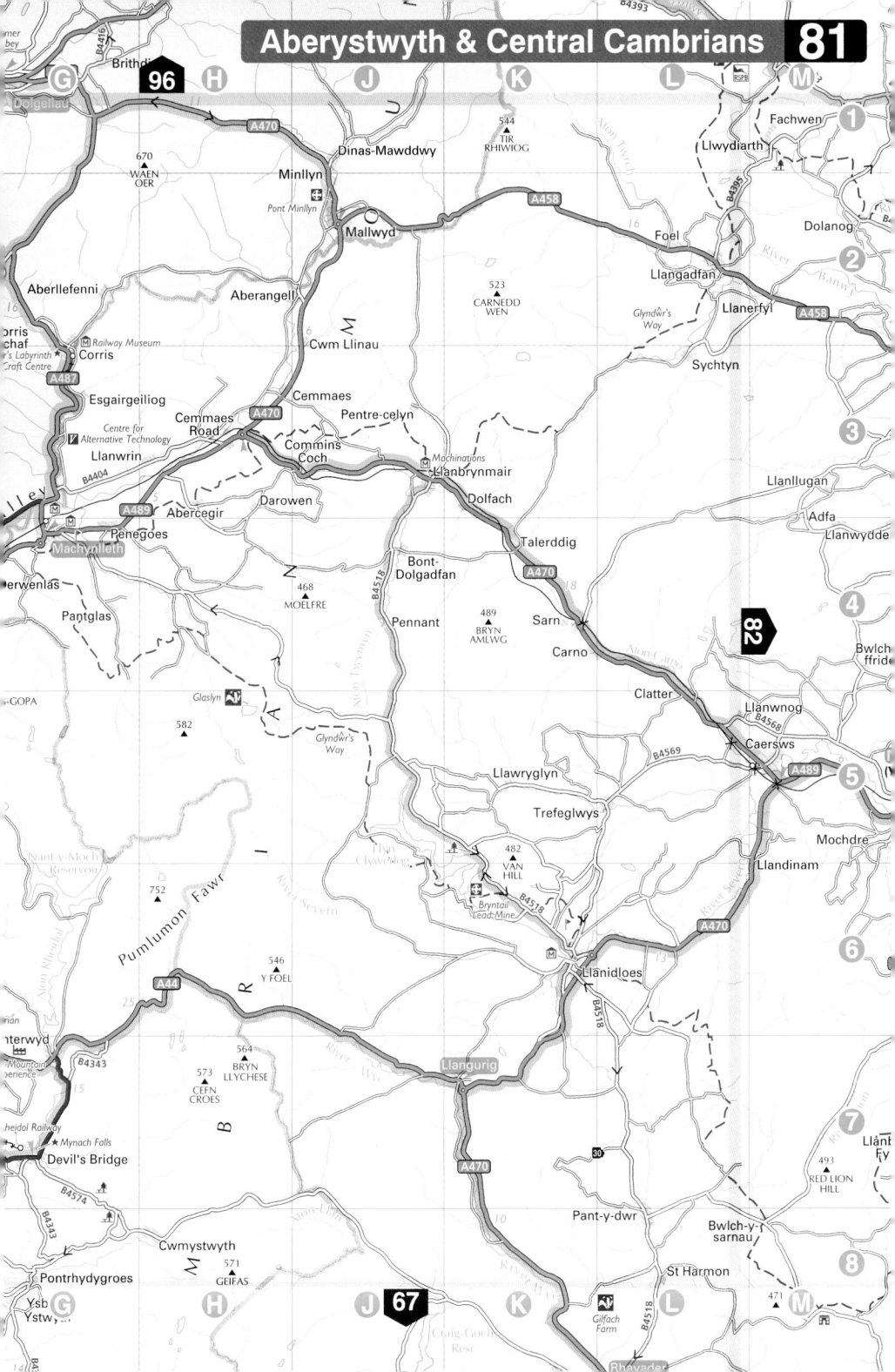

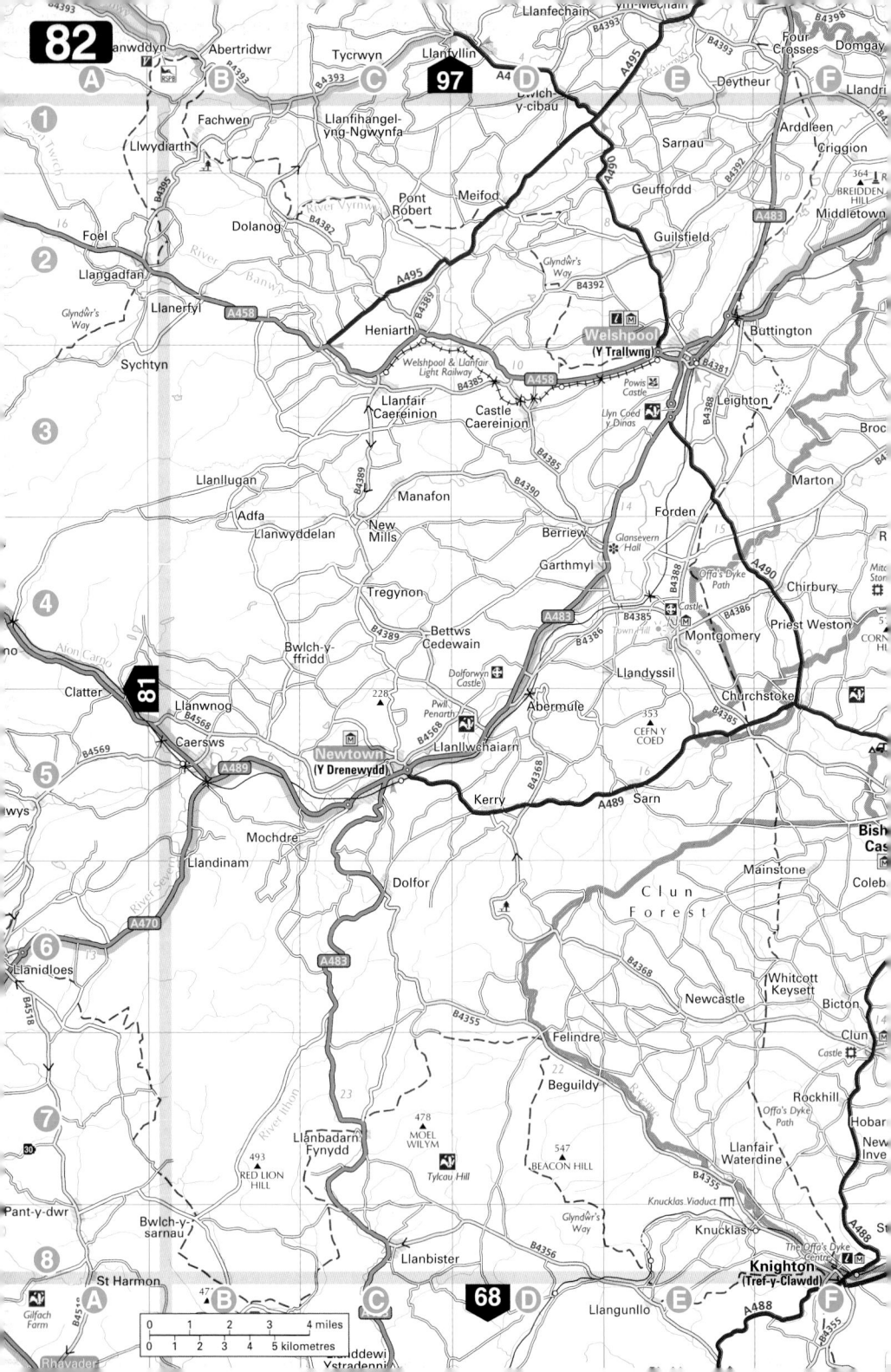

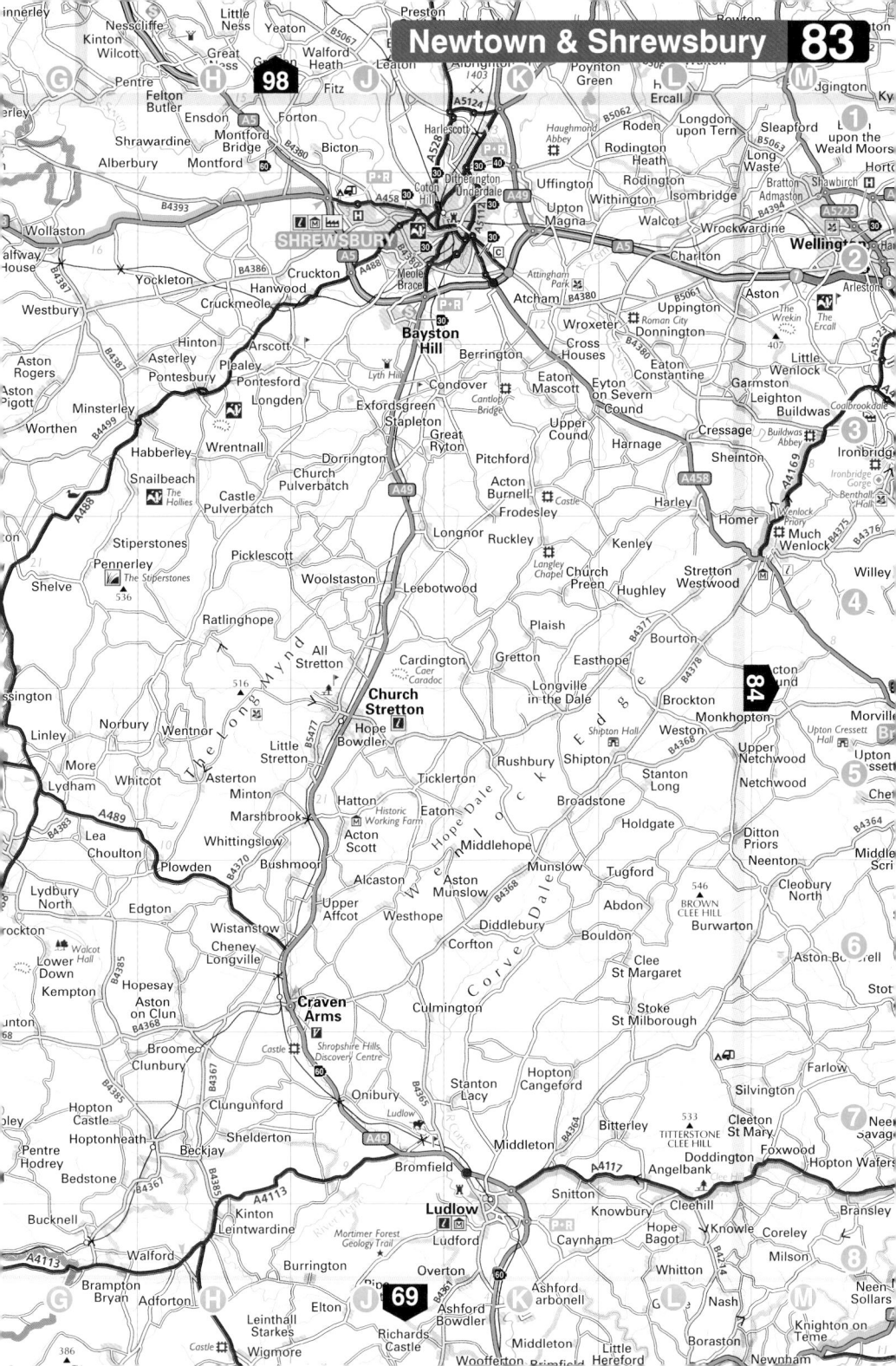

Newtown & Shrewsbury 83

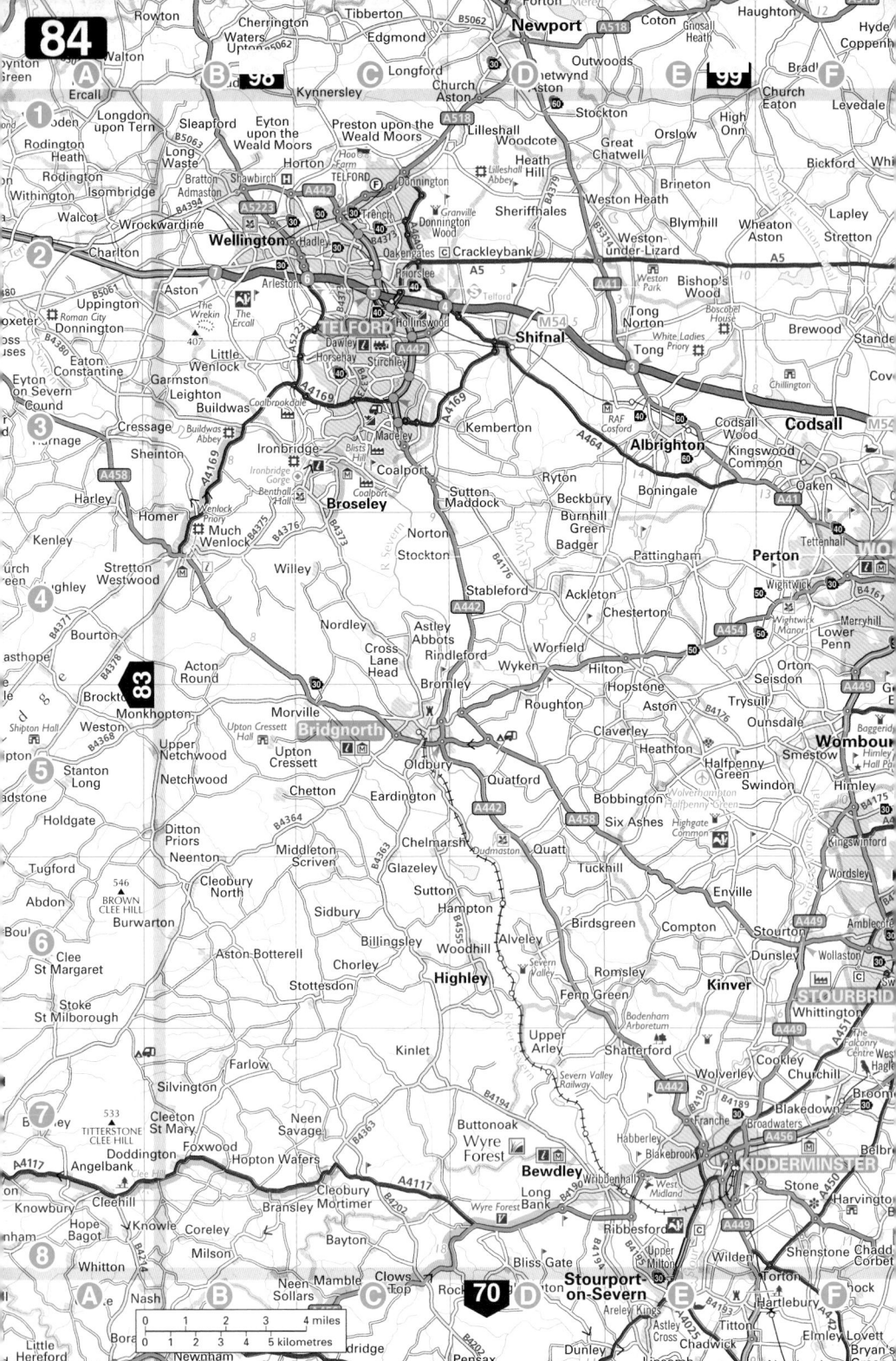

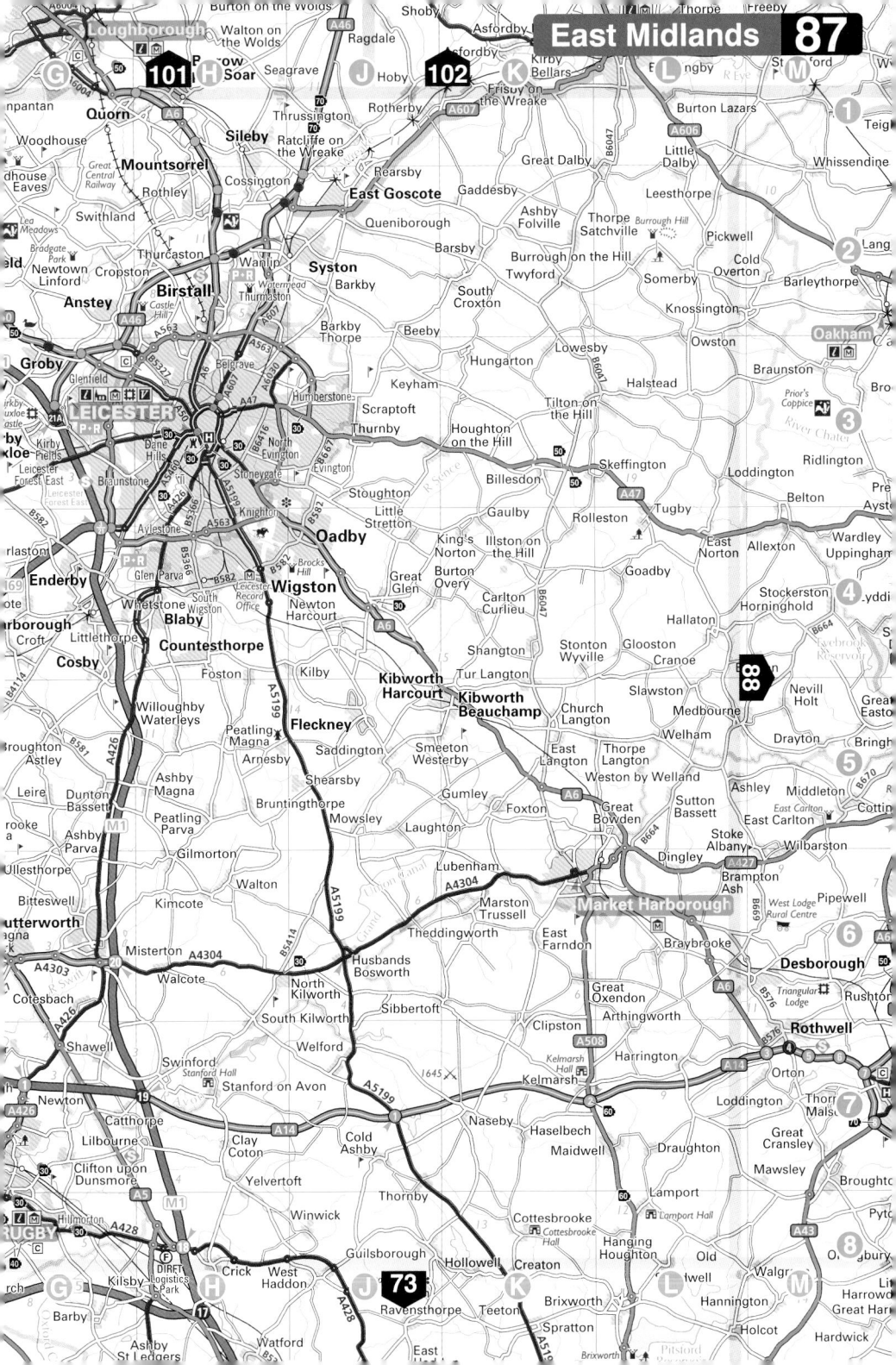

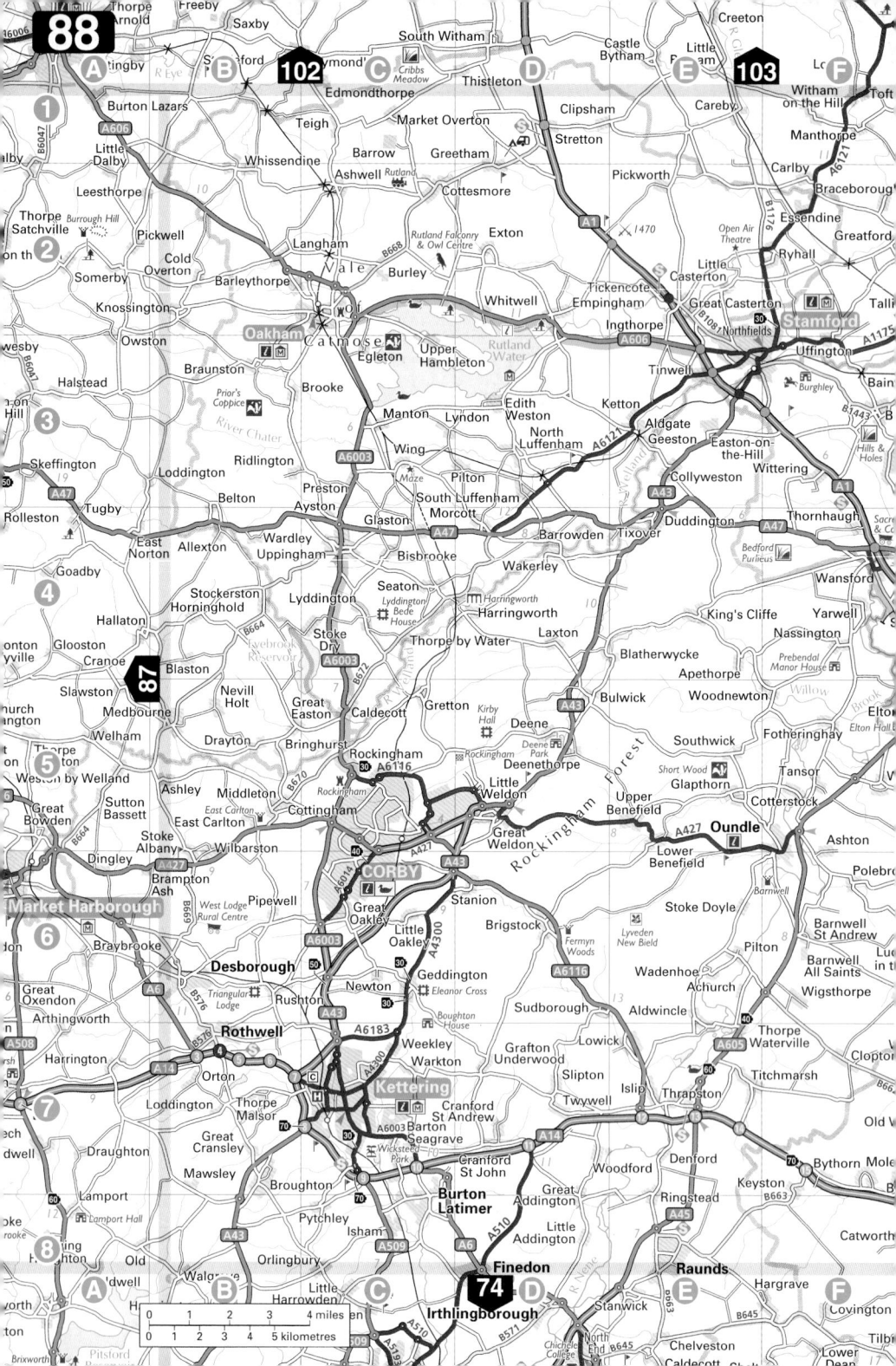

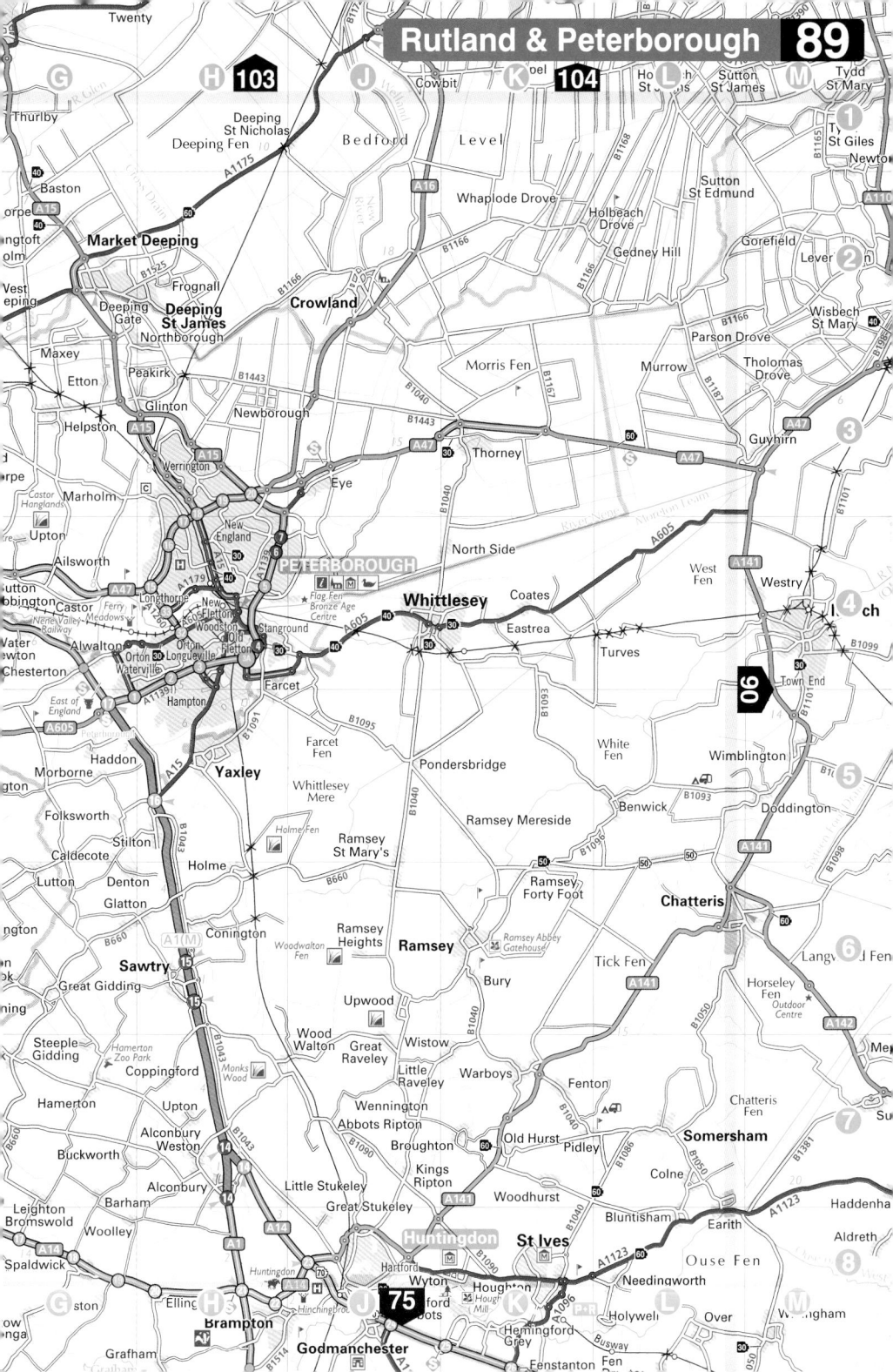

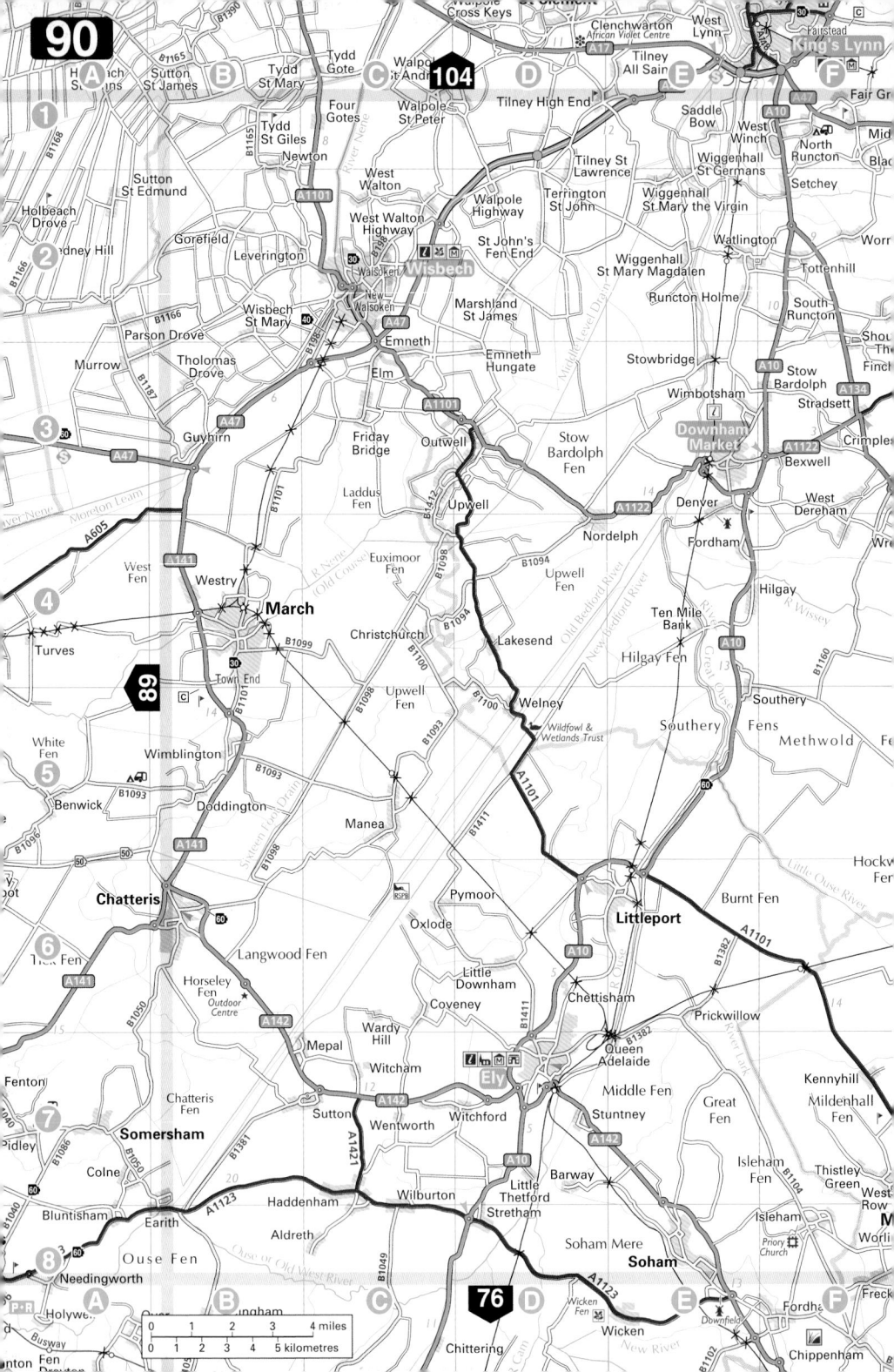

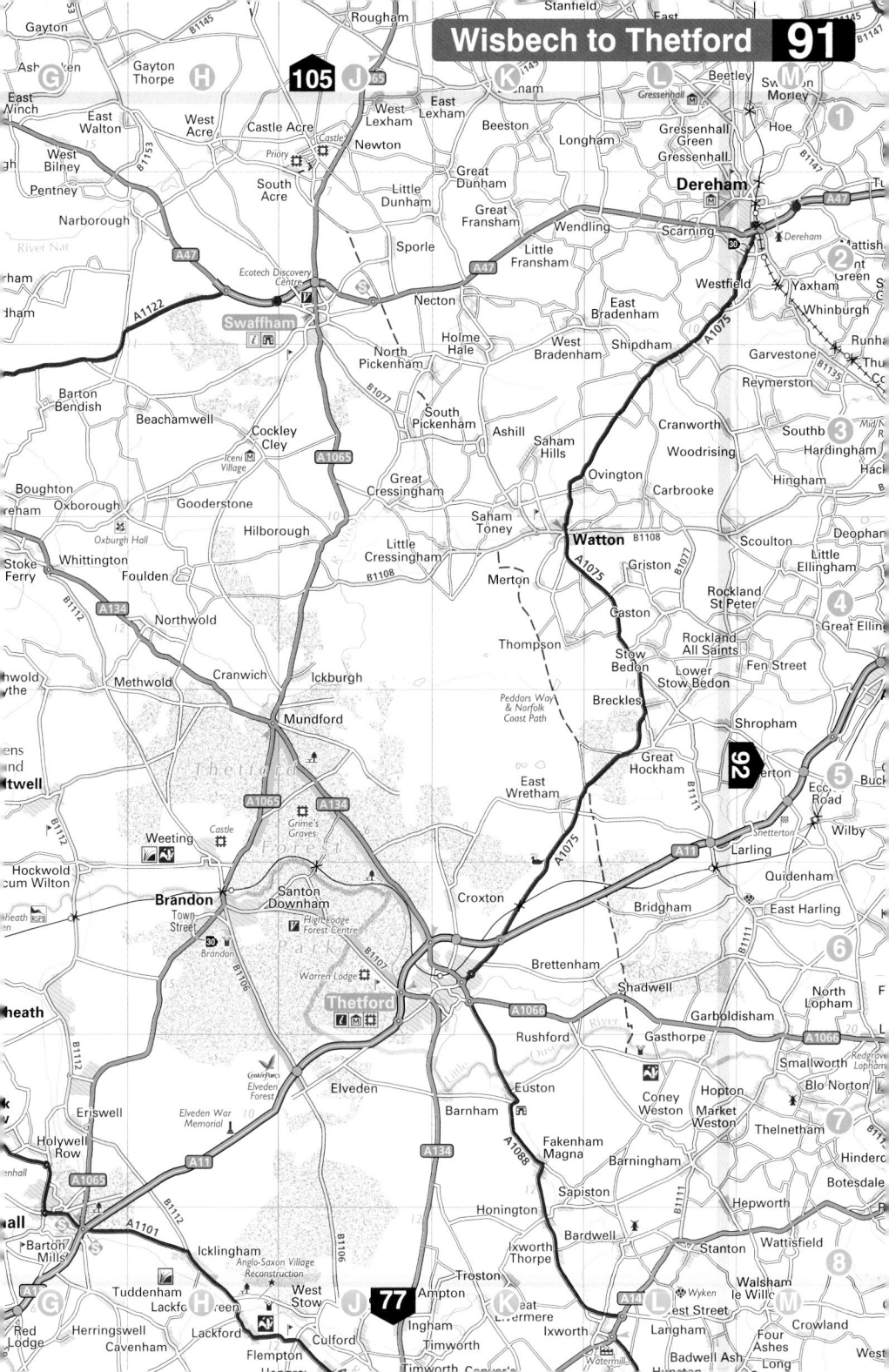

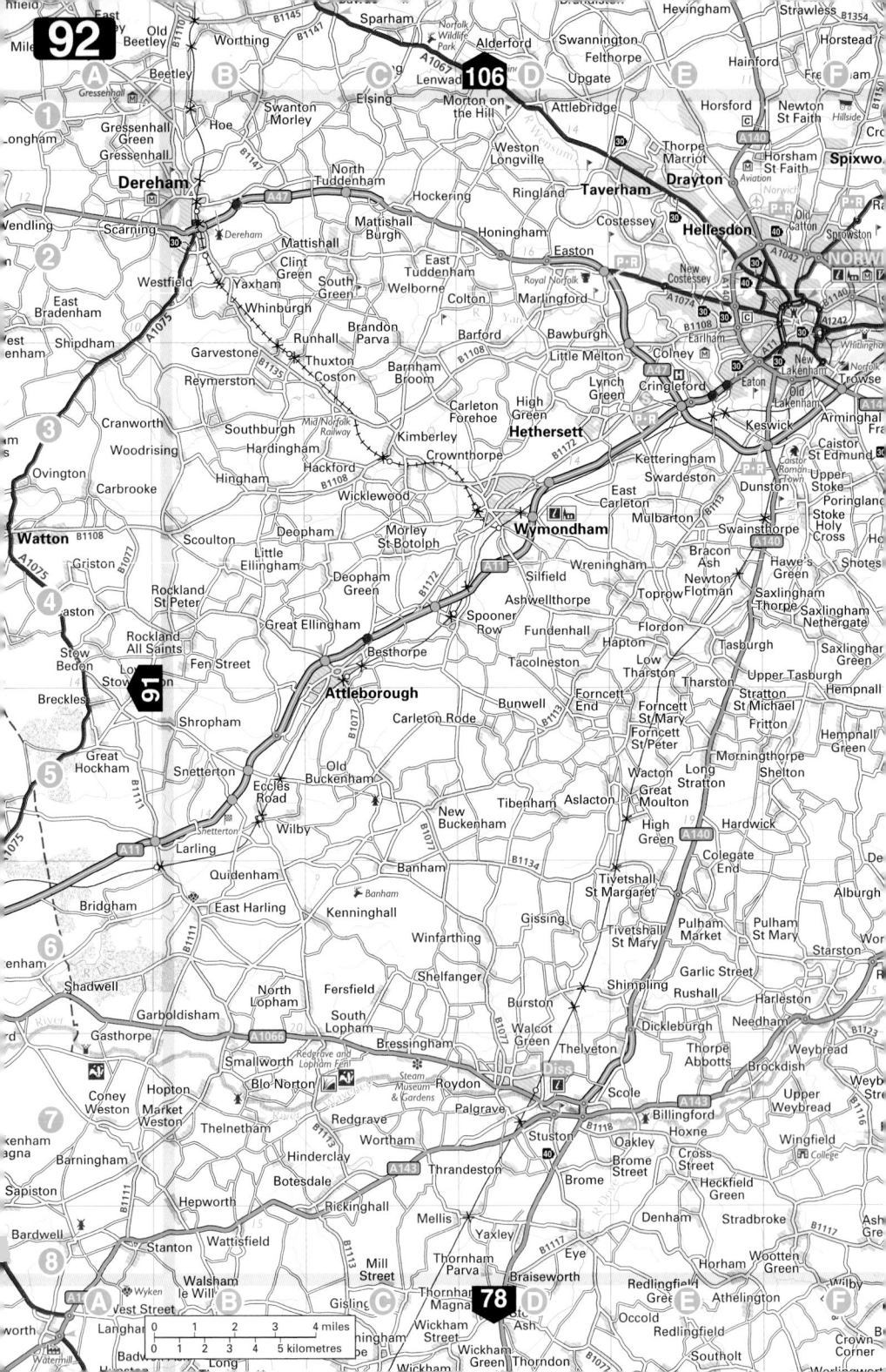

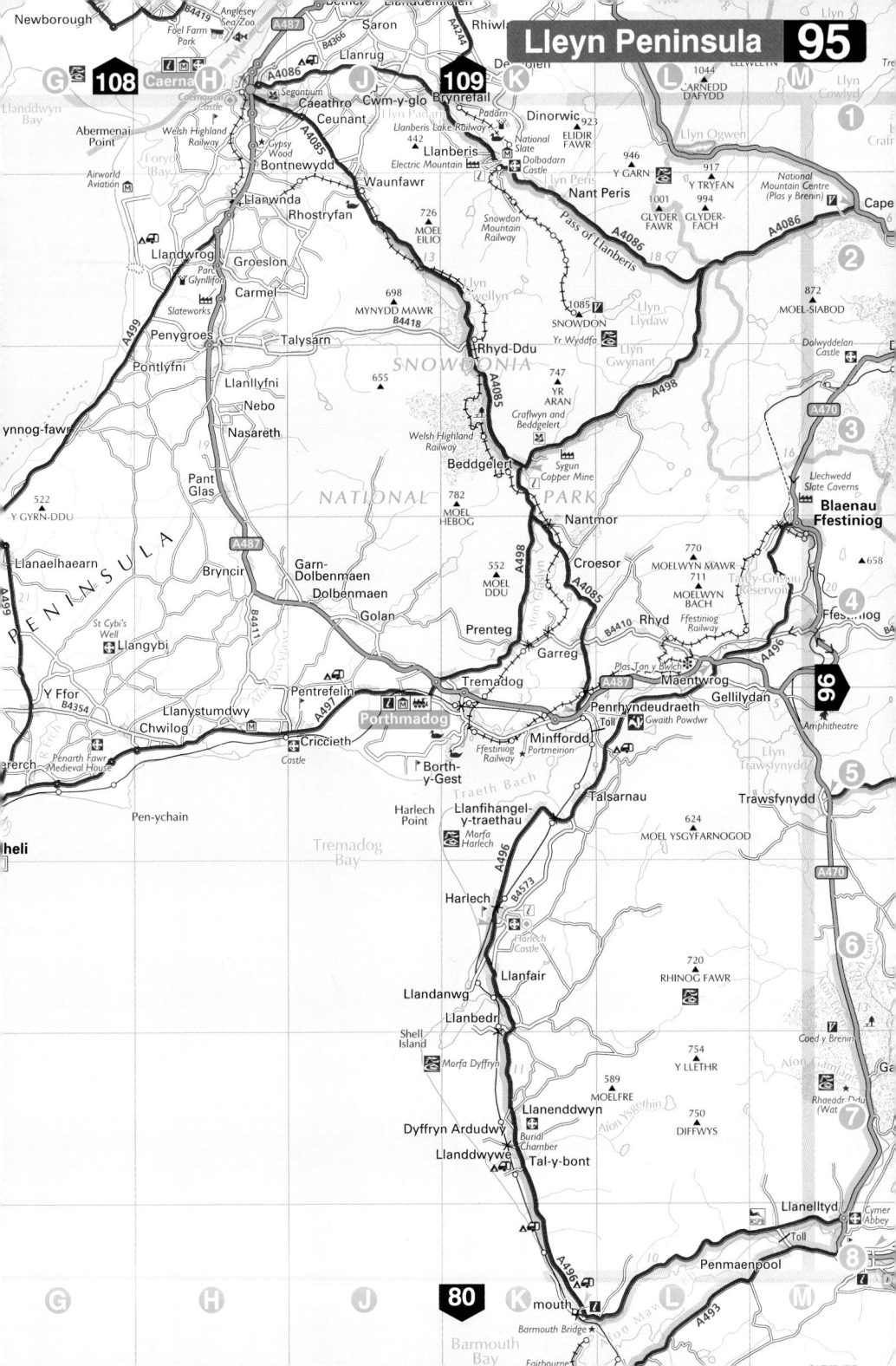

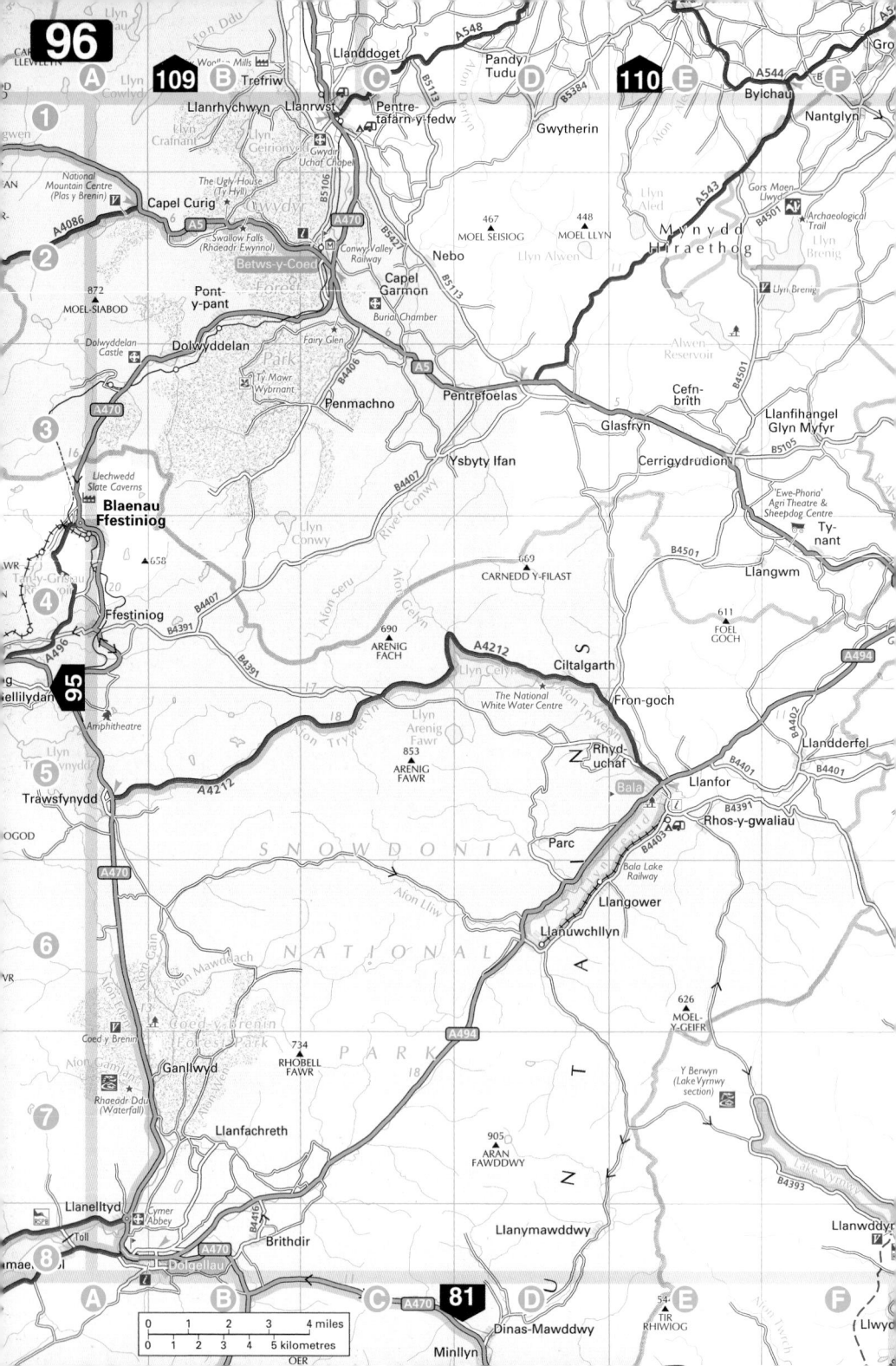

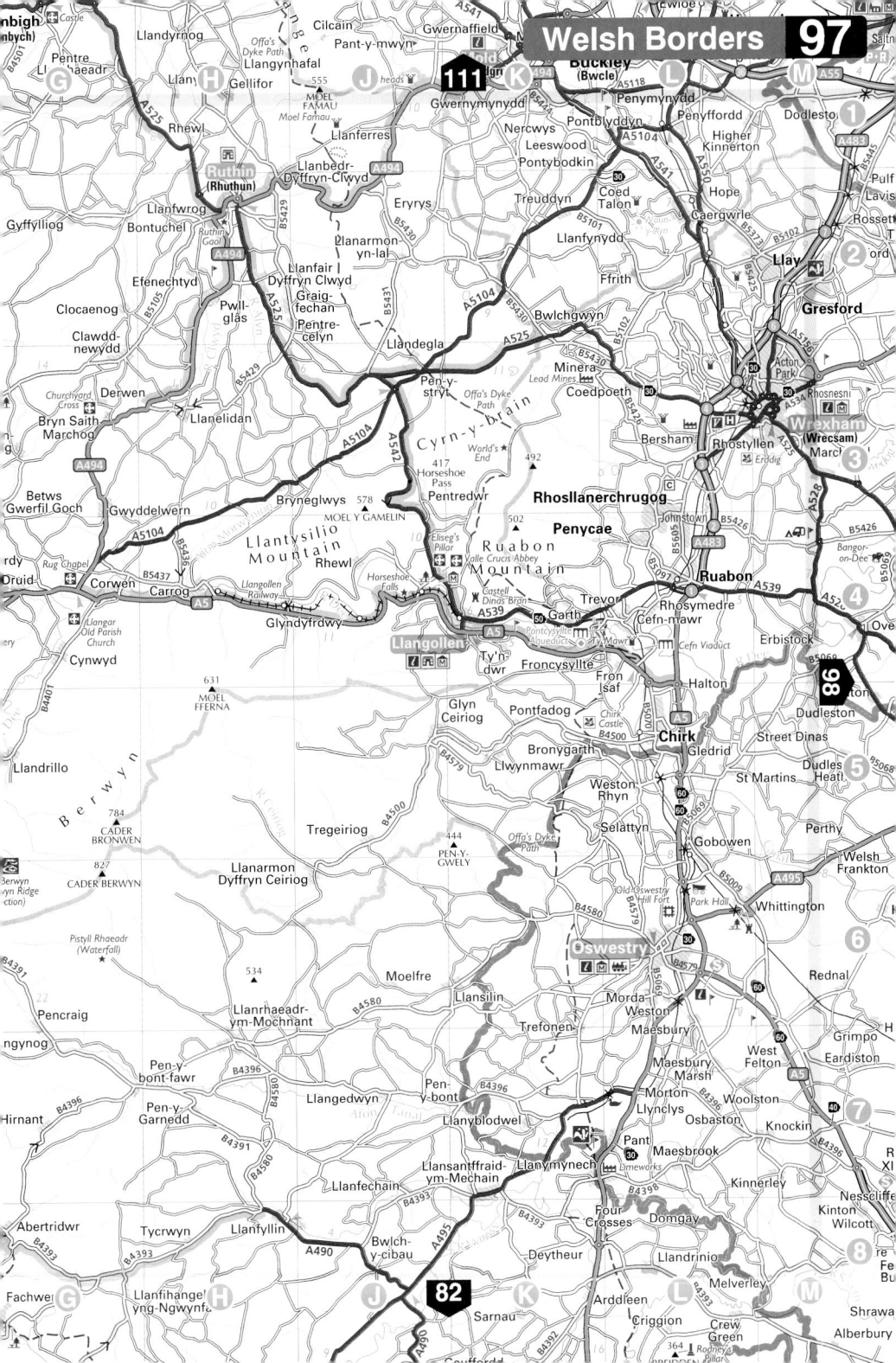

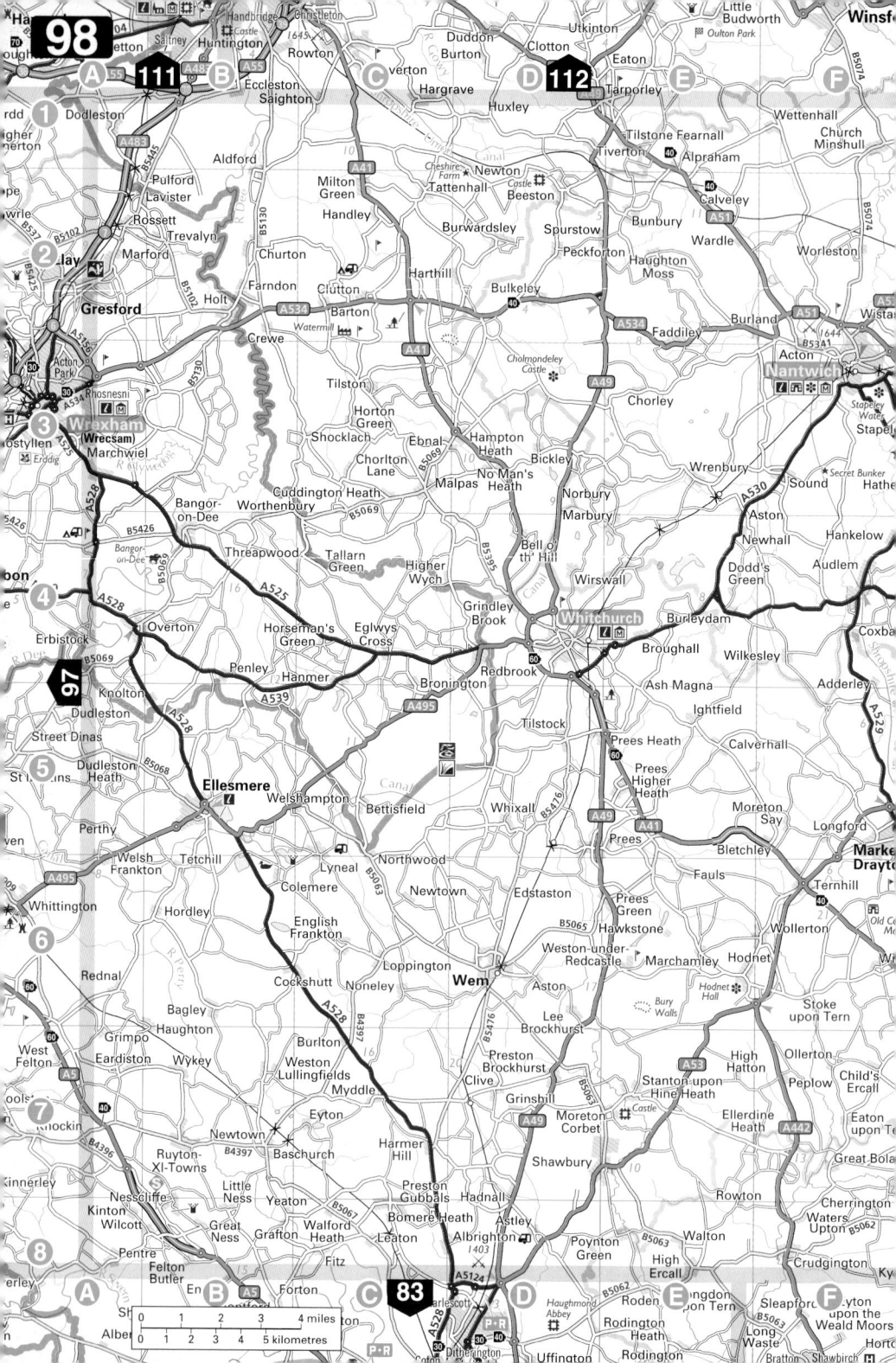

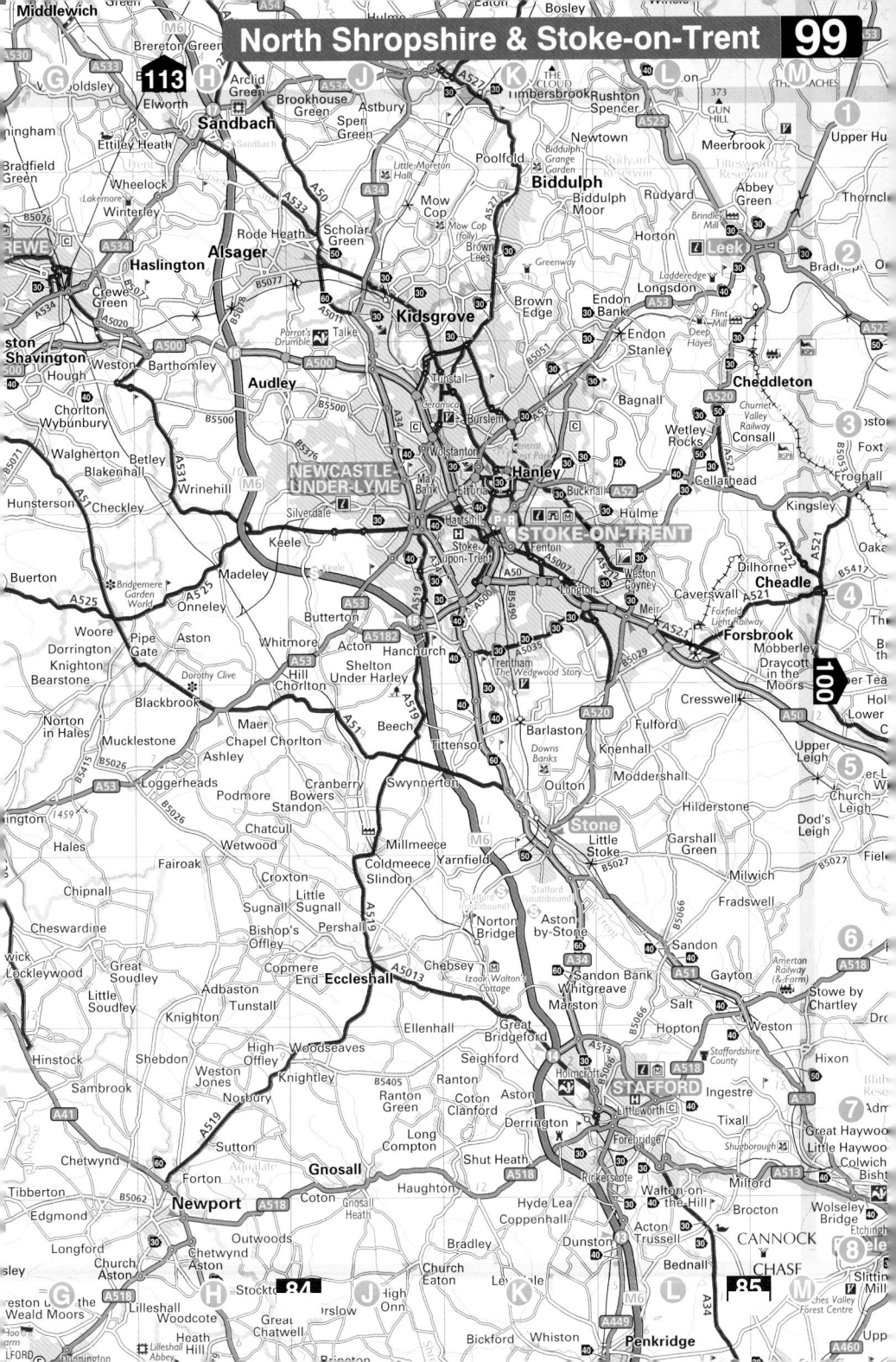

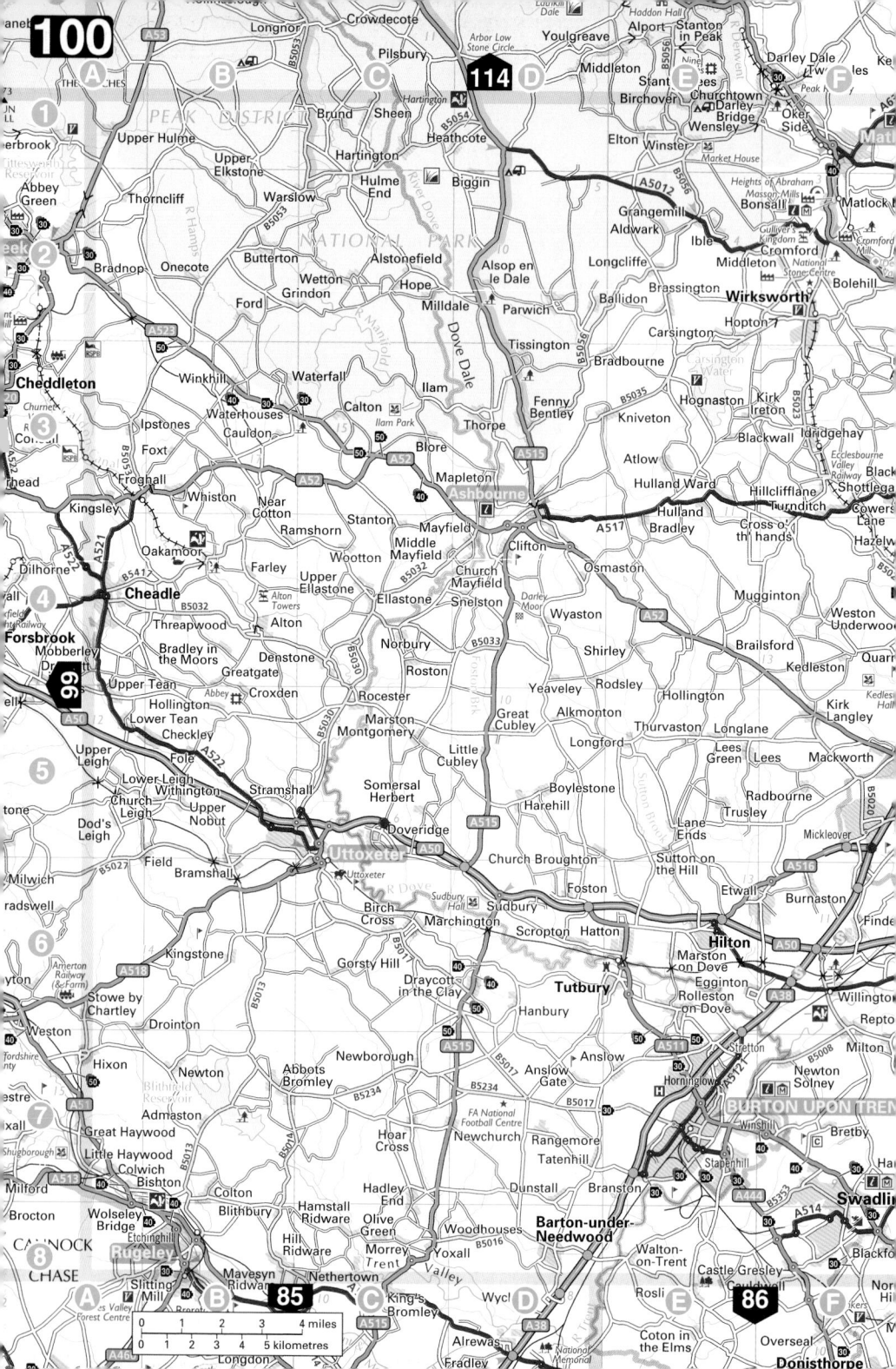

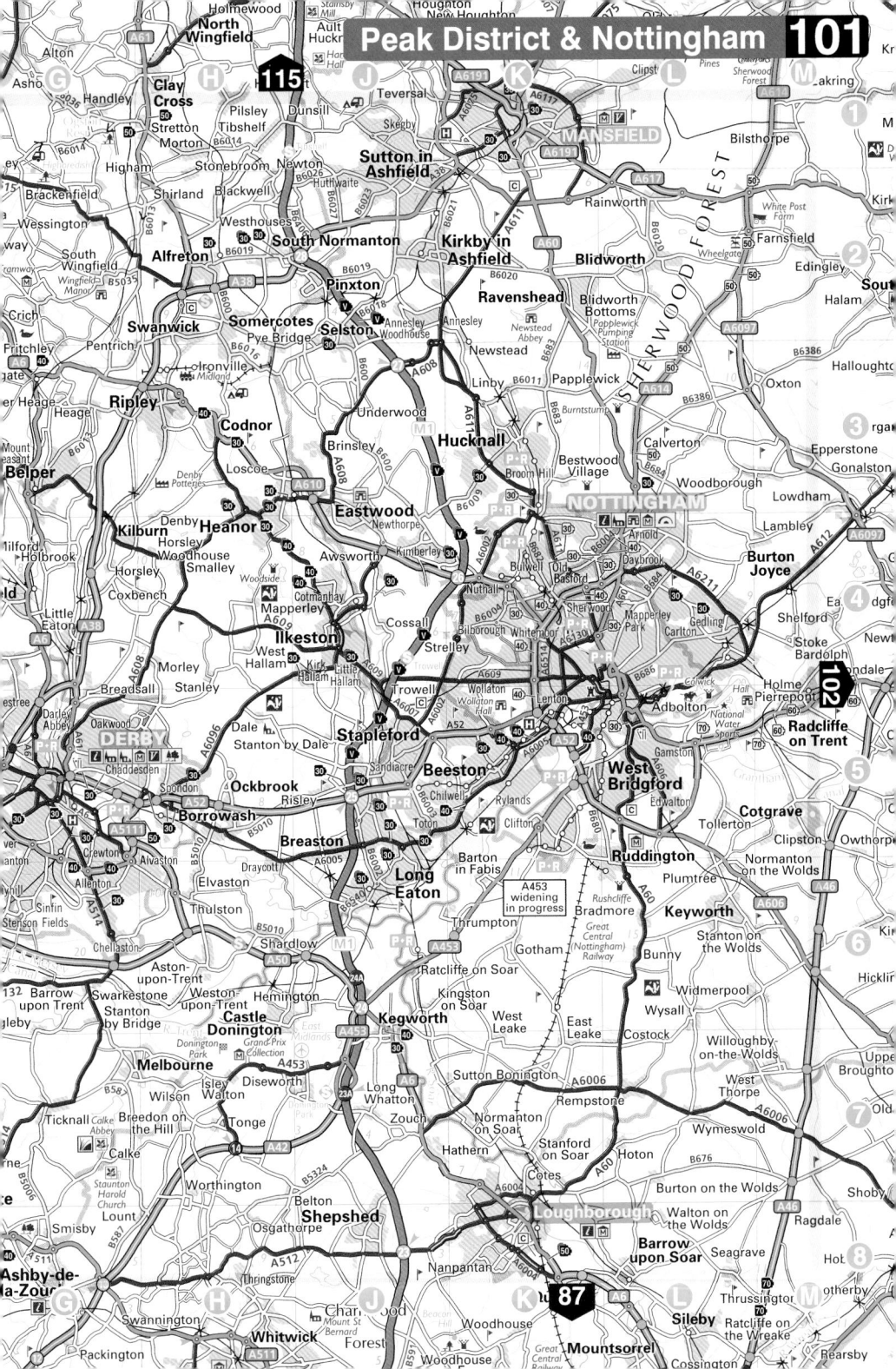

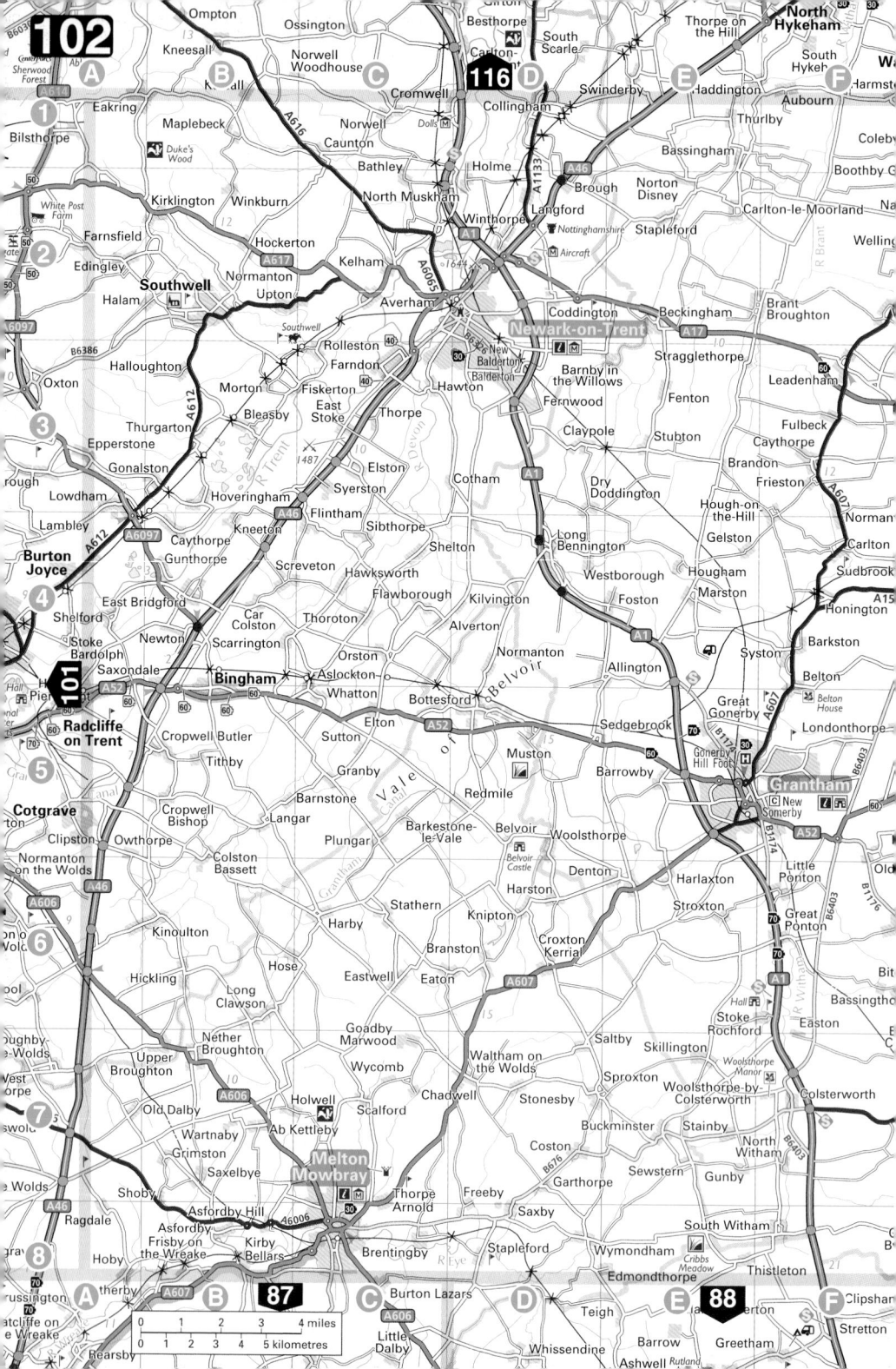

G   H   J   K   L   M

① ② ③ ④ ⑤ ⑥ ⑦ ⑧

Boston & North Norfolk **105**

North Norfolk Heritage Coast

Blakeney Poi

Brancaster Bay

Holkham Bay

Scolt Head Island

Peddars Way & Norfolk Coast Path

Holme Dunes

Holme next the Sea

Brancaster

Brancaster Staithe

Burnham Norton

Burnham Overy Staithe

Holkham

Wells-next-the-sea

Stif

Old Hunstanton

Thornham

Titchwell

Branodonum Roman Fort

Burnham Deepdale

Burnham Market

Burnham Overy

A149

Warham St Mary

106

Hunstanton

Ringstead

Burnham Thorpe

Holkham Hall

Wells & Walsingham Light Railway

Warham All Saints

Wighton

Heacham

Norfolk Lavender

Peddars Way & Norfolk Coast Path

Summerfield

Docking

North Creake

Creake Abbey

The Shrine of Our Lady

Little Walsingham

Priory Market Cros

Great Walsingham

Sedgeford

Stanhoe

South Creake

North Barsham

Hindringham

Houghton St Giles

Great Snoring

Thursford

Snettisham

Park Farm

Shernborne

Fring

Bircham Newton

Syderstone

West Barsham

East Barsham

A148

Croxt

Ingoldisthorpe

Dersingham

Great Bircham

Bircham Tofts

Wicken Green Village

Sculthorpe

Little Snoring

Kettlestone

Fakenham

Dersingham Bog

Anmer

Houghton Hall

Tattersett

Dunton Coxford

Shereford

Hempton

Tatterford

Toftrees

Colkirk

Little Ryburgh

Great Ryburgh

orpe owl rk

Volferton

Sandringham West Newton

New Houghton

West Rudham

East Rudham

East Raynham

A1067

Flitcham

Helhoughton

Castle Rising

Hillington

Harpley

West Raynham

South Raynham

Horningtoft

Gateley

Little Massingham

Weasenham St Peter

Whissonsett

Brisley

North Elmham

Congham

Roydon

A148

Grimston

Great Massingham

Wellingham

Tittleshall

Stanfield

East Bilney

Old Beetley

 on

Castle

th Wootton

A149

ywood

King's Lynn

Weasenham All Saints

Rougham

Mileham

Fairstead

Gayton

Ashwicken

Gayton Thorpe

B1145

Litcham

B1145

Gressenhall

Dereha

A47

Fair Green

East Winch

East Walton

91

Ac

Priory

e Acre

Newton

West xham

East Lexham

Bee

Longham

Gressenhall Green
Gressenhall

North Runcton

Middleton

Blackborough End

West Bilney

South

B1153

Great Dunham

G   H   J   K   L   M

1
2
3
4
5
6
7
8

Lynas

Dulas
Bay

V Seawatch Centre

Moelfre
Llanallgo

A5108
B5108

Benllech
anbedrgoch   Red Wharf
Bay   Red Wharf Bay
ddyfnan   Llanddona
Pentraeth   Llangoed
B5109   B5109   Gaol

Talwrn   A5025   Beaumaris
Castle
B5420   Llansadwrn   Beaumaris
enmynydd   Llandegfan   Courthouse
Llanfair P G   Anglesey
Column   **Menai
Bridge
(Porthaethwy)**   **Bangor**
Bryn   Britannia   Penrhyn
Celli Ddu   Bridge   Llandygai
b   Plas   A4087   Tal-y-
Newydd   bont

Puffin Island
Penmon Priory
Toll   Black Point

GREAT ORMES HEAD

Great Orme
Heritage Coast

Little Ormes
Penrh
ay

B5115

110

Llandudno
Llandrillo-
yn-Rhos
Deganwy   A470
A55   B5115
Conwy   **Llandudno
Junction**
Conwy
Castle   Llansanffraid
Glan Conwy

Dwygyfylchi
Penmaenmawr   Capelulo   A470
Llanfairfechan   Henryd
A55

Conwy
Bay

SNOWDONIA

610
TAL-Y-FAN   Rowen   B5106
Graig
Ty'n-y-Groes   Tal-y-Cafn
Eglwysbach

A4080   Llanfair P G
Y Felinheli   GreenWood   B4547   Pentir   groes
Forest Park
Bethel   Seion   Glasinfryn   Rhyd-y-
Llanddeiniolen   Tregarth   Rachub
Saron   **Bethesda**
A487   Llanrug   Rhiwlas
A4086   Deiniolen
Caeathro   Cwm-y-glo   Brynrefail
Segontium   Llanberis Lake
ant   442
ontnewydd   Llanberis
Electric Mountain

95

rwic   923
ELIDIR
FAWR
Slate   Dolbadarn
Castle
946
Y GARN
917

Abergwyngregyn
Coedydd
Aber
580
MOEL
WINION   Aber Falls
757   942
Y DROSGL   FOEL-FRAS
Afon Caseg   Afon Anafon

Llanbedr-y-Cennin
Tal-y-Bont
Dolgarrog

Vale of Conwy

NATIONAL
PARK
Llyn
Eigiau
Afon Dulyn
1062
CARNEDD
LLEWELYN   Llyn
Cowlyd
1044
CARNEDD
DAFYDD
Afon Llugwy   Llyn Ogwen

Trefriw Woollen Mills
Trefriw
Llanddoget

Llanrwst   96   Pentre-
tafarn-y-fedw
Gwydir
Uchaf Chapel
Llyn
Crafnant   Geirionydd   The Ugly House
National

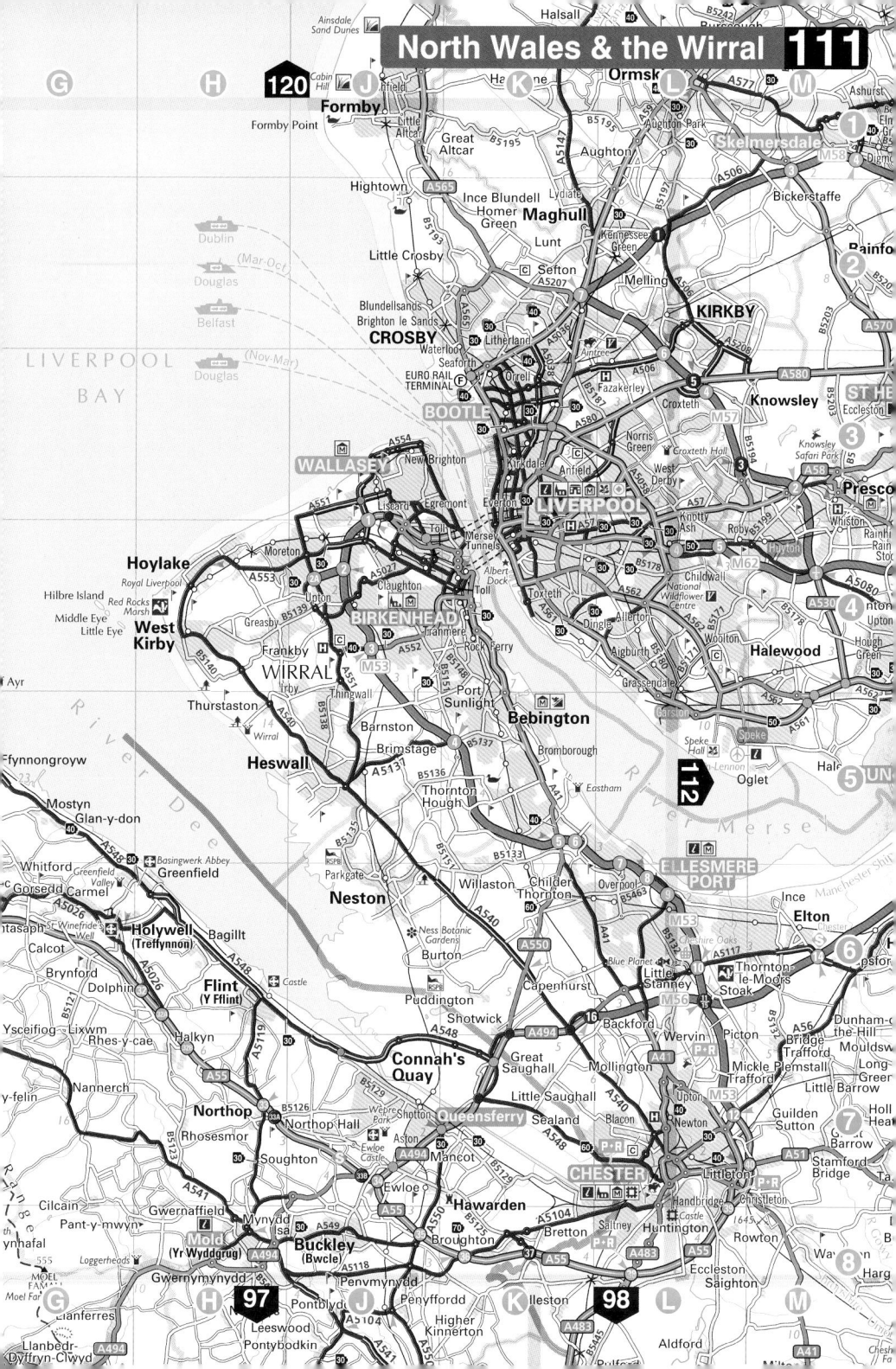

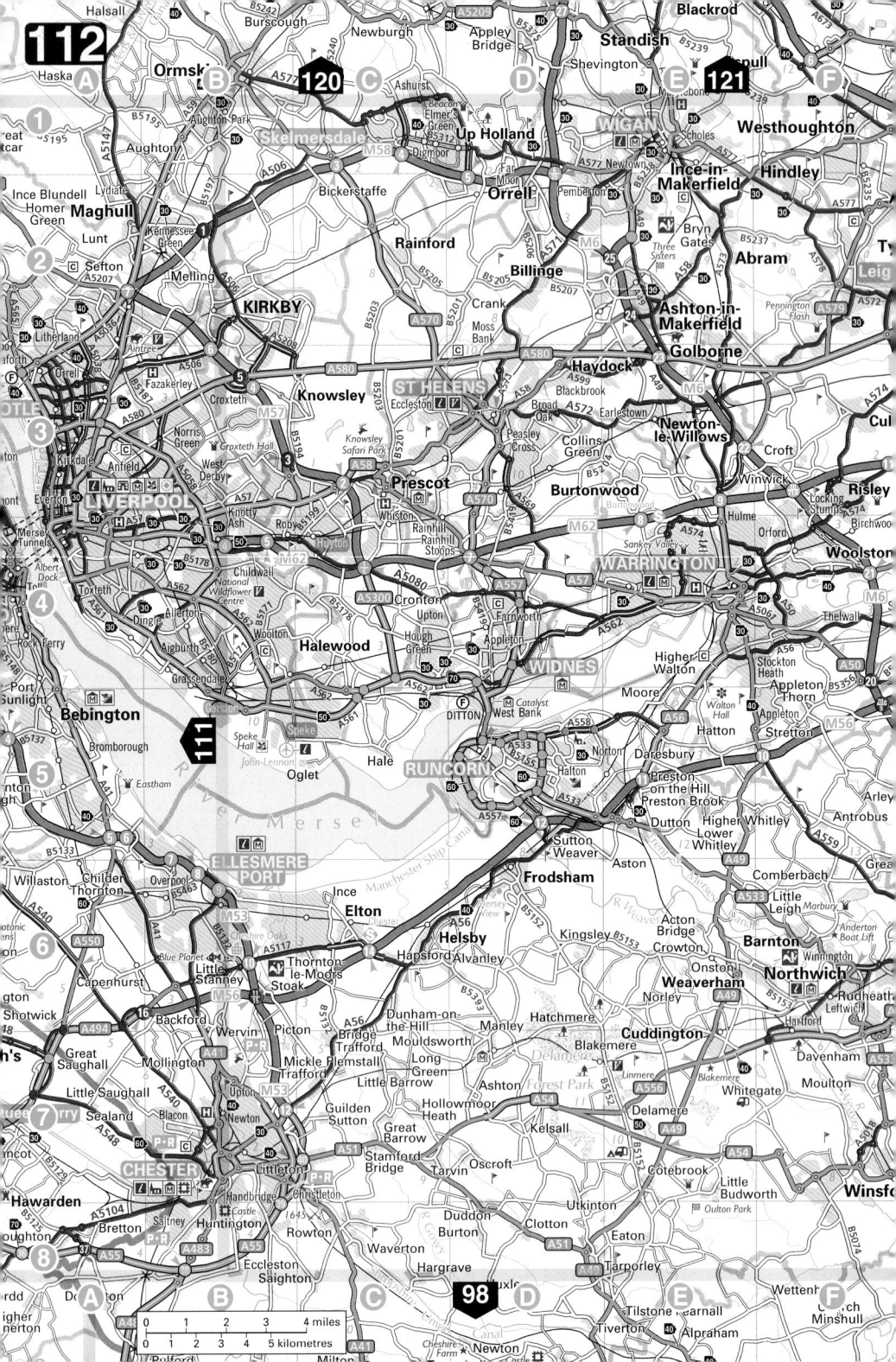

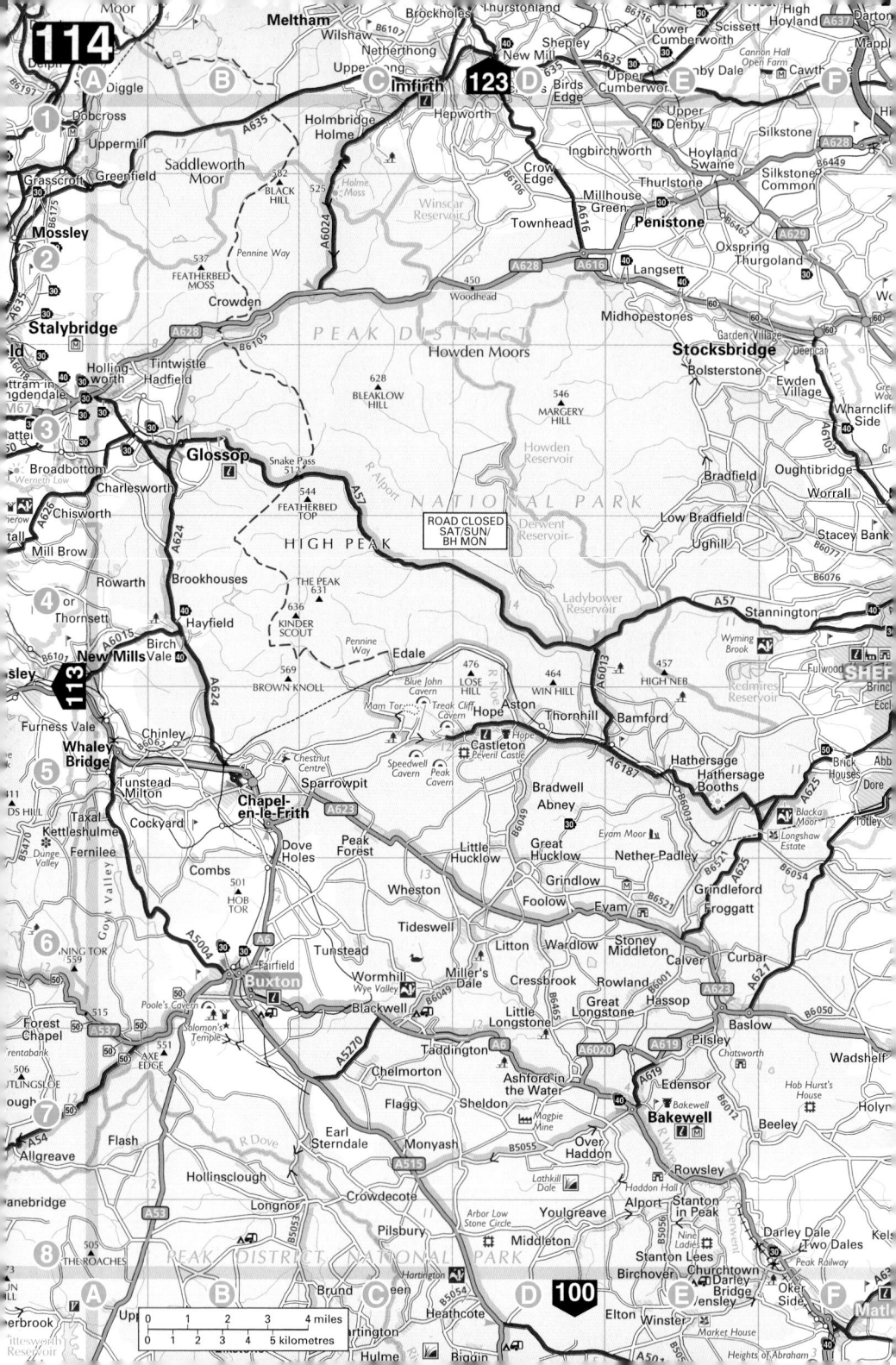

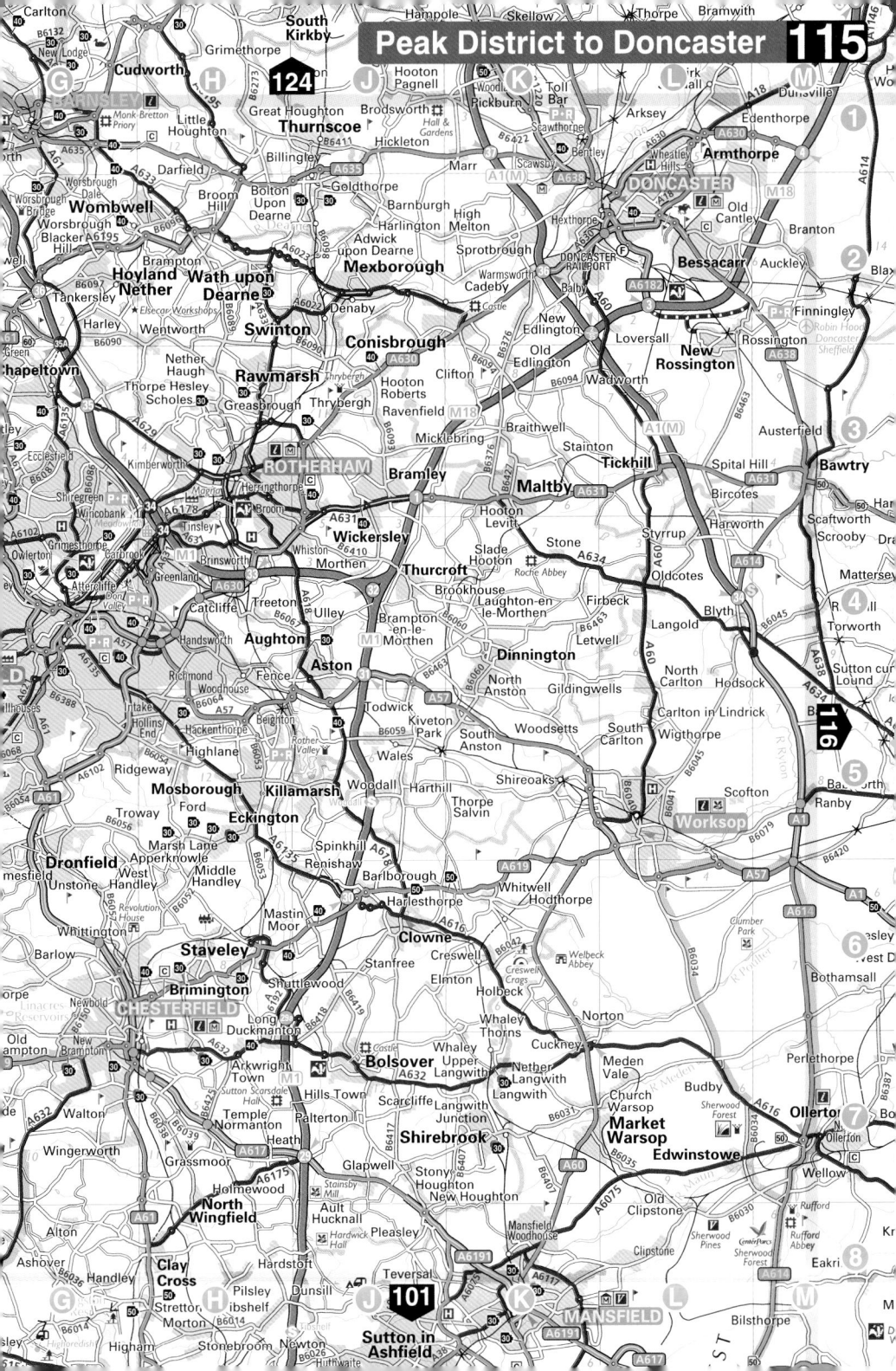

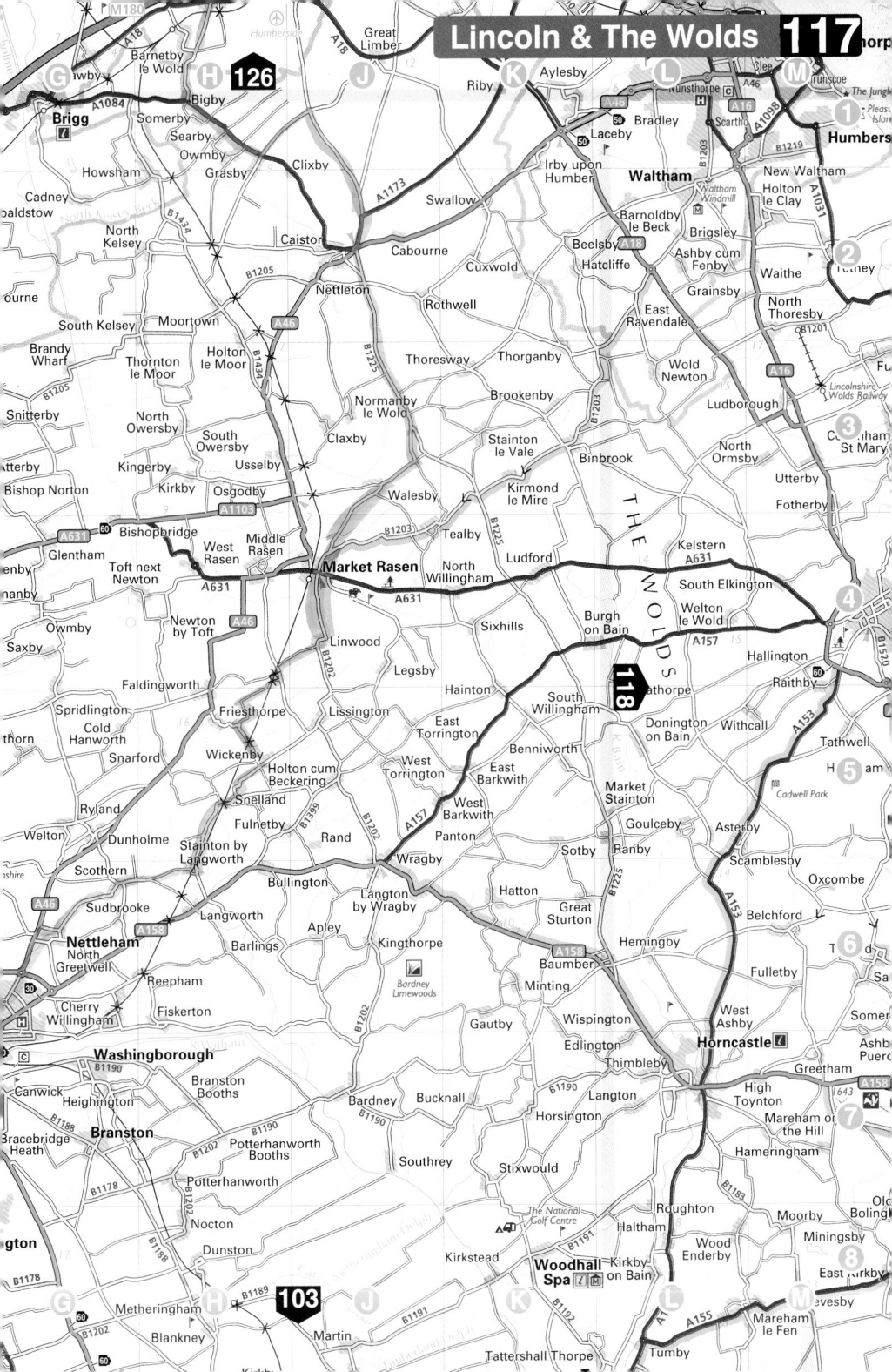

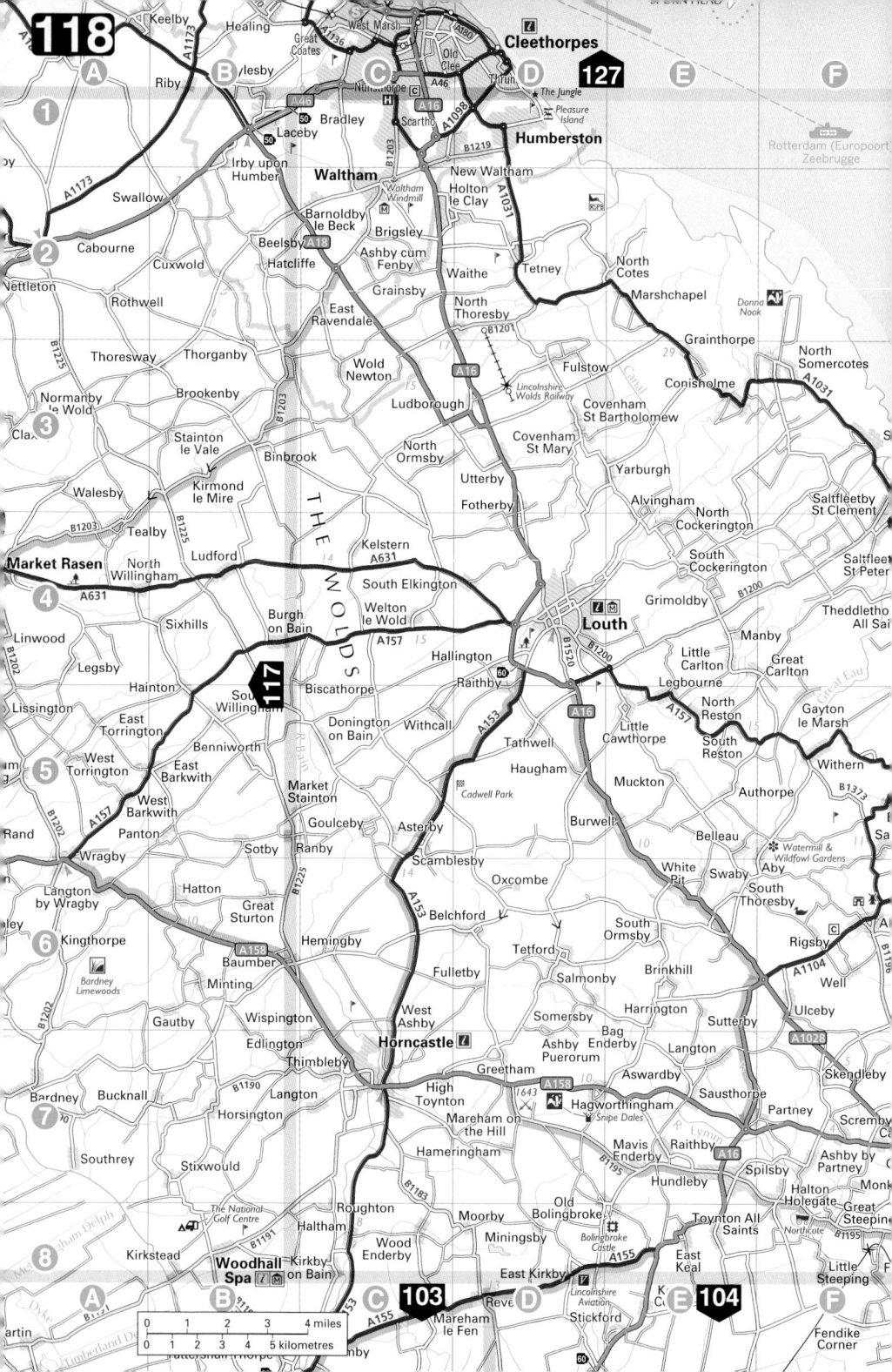

G · H · J · K · L · M

① ② ③ ④ ⑤ ⑥ ⑦ ⑧

etby
ts
Theddlethorpe
St Helen
A1031
Mablethorpe ℹ
A1104
Trusthorpe
ltby
Marsh
A52
Sutton on Sea
Sandilands
A1111
Markby
A52
Huttoft
Bilsby
Thurlby
Anderby Creek
B1449
Anderby
Farlesthorpe
Mumby
mberworth
Chapel Point
Hogsthorpe
**Chapel
St Leonards**
illoughby
Sloothby
Habertoft
Addlethorpe
☵ Fantasy Island
Welton
Marsh
Ingoldmells
A52
by
Ingoldmells
Point
Orby
Burgh le Marsh
ratoft
A158
ℹ 🏛 ✈ ⚓
by in the Marsh
Skegness

G · H · J · K · L · M

104
Croft
Thorpe St Peter

120

Ⓐ Ⓑ Ⓒ Ⓓ Ⓔ **129** Ⓕ

Glasson

Cockersand

① Cockerham

Knott End-on-Sea
Pilling
Preesall
COCKERHAM M
Winmarleigh

Fleetwood
Rossall Point
River Wyre
A588
Stalmine
Eagland Hill
② Staynall
Moss Edge
Cleveleys
Hambleton
Out Rawcliffe
Church
Thornton
Great Eccleston

A584
Warbreck
C
Little Singleton
Copp
Poulton-le-Fylde
Singleton
Elswick
Thistleton
B5269
③ North Shore
Marton
Esprick
Wharles
Ca
BLACKPOOL
H
Staining
A585
M55
South Shore
Model Village
Great Marton
Weeton
Great Plumpton
Wesham
Treales
Kirkham
④ Blackpool
Westby
Wrea Green
Newton with Scales
Clifton
A584
St Anne's
Ansdell
Kellamergh
Freckleton
Royal Lytham & St Anne's
Fairhaven
Warton
Lytham St Anne's
RSPB
Discovery Centre
A584 Lytham
River Ribble

Long
Wa
Bri
Hesketh Bank
West Lanc
Light Rail
⑤

Becconsall
Banks
Tarleton
⑥
A565
Bre
SOUTHPORT
Mere Brow
A59
New Pleasureland
P·R
Leisure Lakes
Holmeswood
Rufford
B5246
Birkdale
H
P·R
C
Windmill Animal Farm
The Royal Birkdale
Wildfowl & Wetlands Trust
Scarisbrick
Bescar
Burscough Bridge
⑦
Shirdley Hill
A570
Heaton's Bridge
B5242
Ainsdale
A565
Halsall
Burscough
Ne
Ainsdale Sand-Dunes
Barton
Haskayne
Ormskirk
A577
⑧
Cabin Hill
Freshfield
Little Altcar
Great Altcar
Aughton Park
Skelmersdale
Formby
B5
A5147
Aughton
A506
111 Ⓒ Ⓓ Ⓔ Ⓕ
Hightown A565

Ⓐ Ⓑ Ⓒ Ⓓ Ⓔ Ⓕ

0 1 2 3 4 miles
0 1 2 3 4 5 kilometres

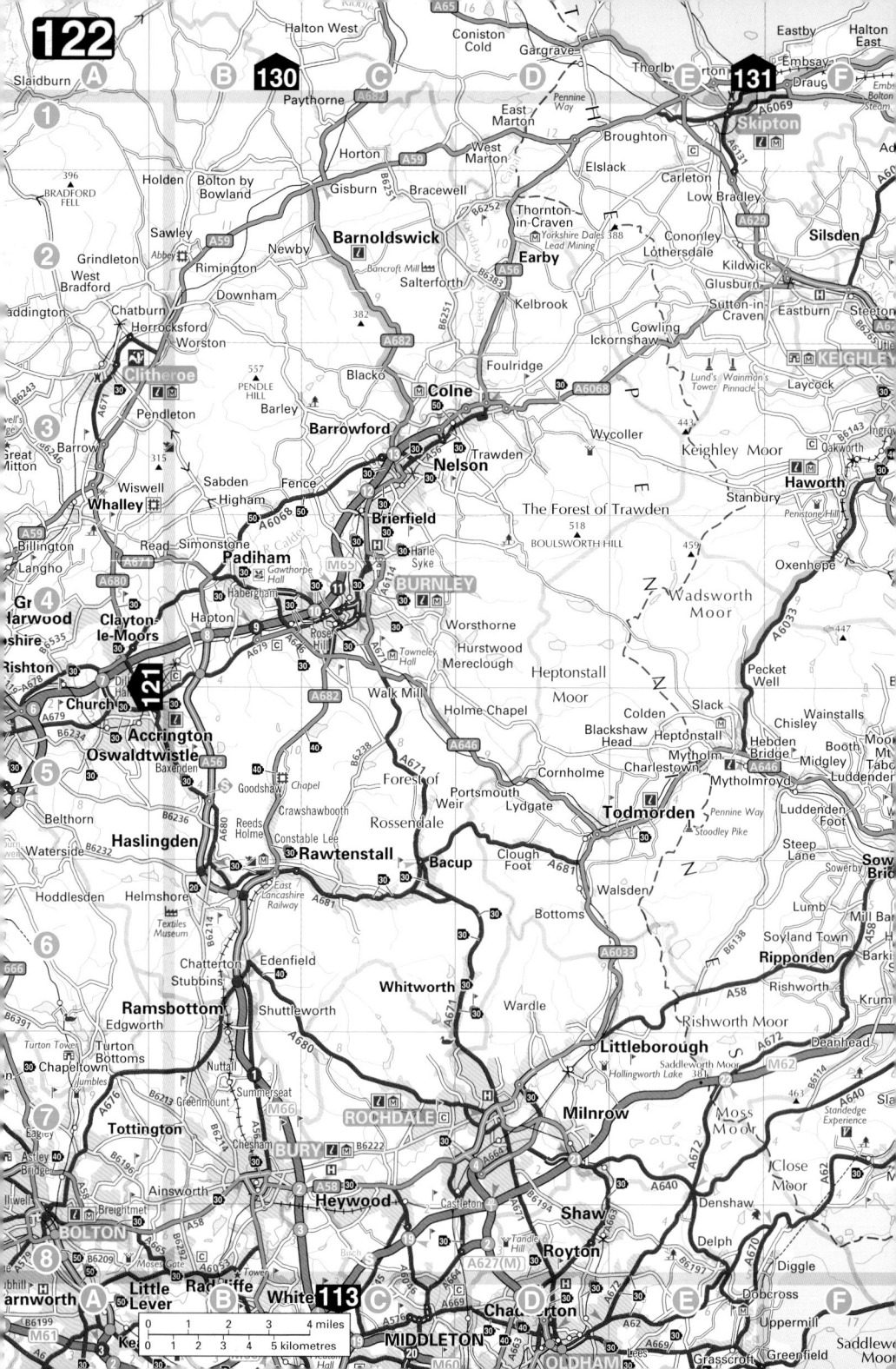

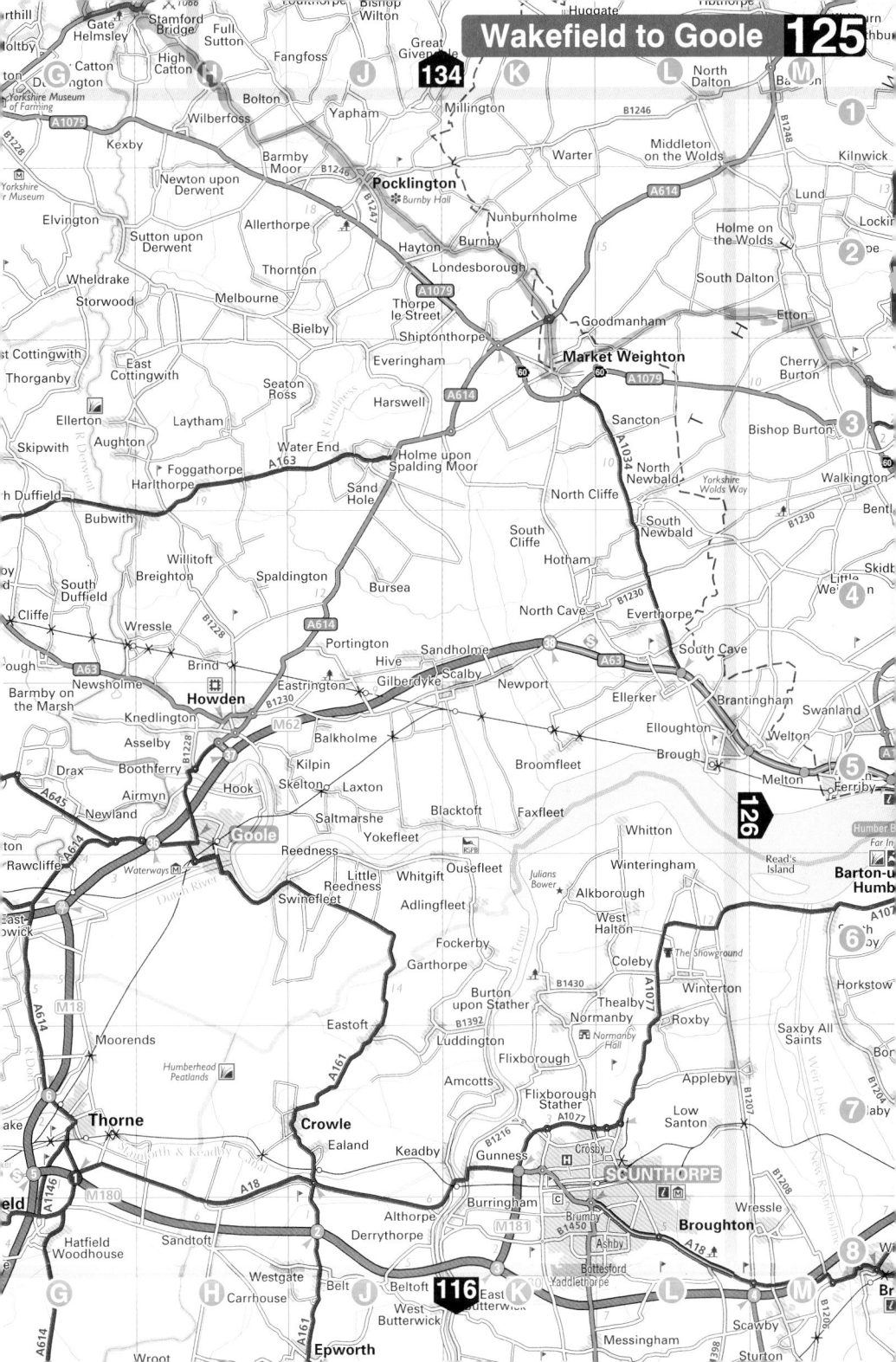

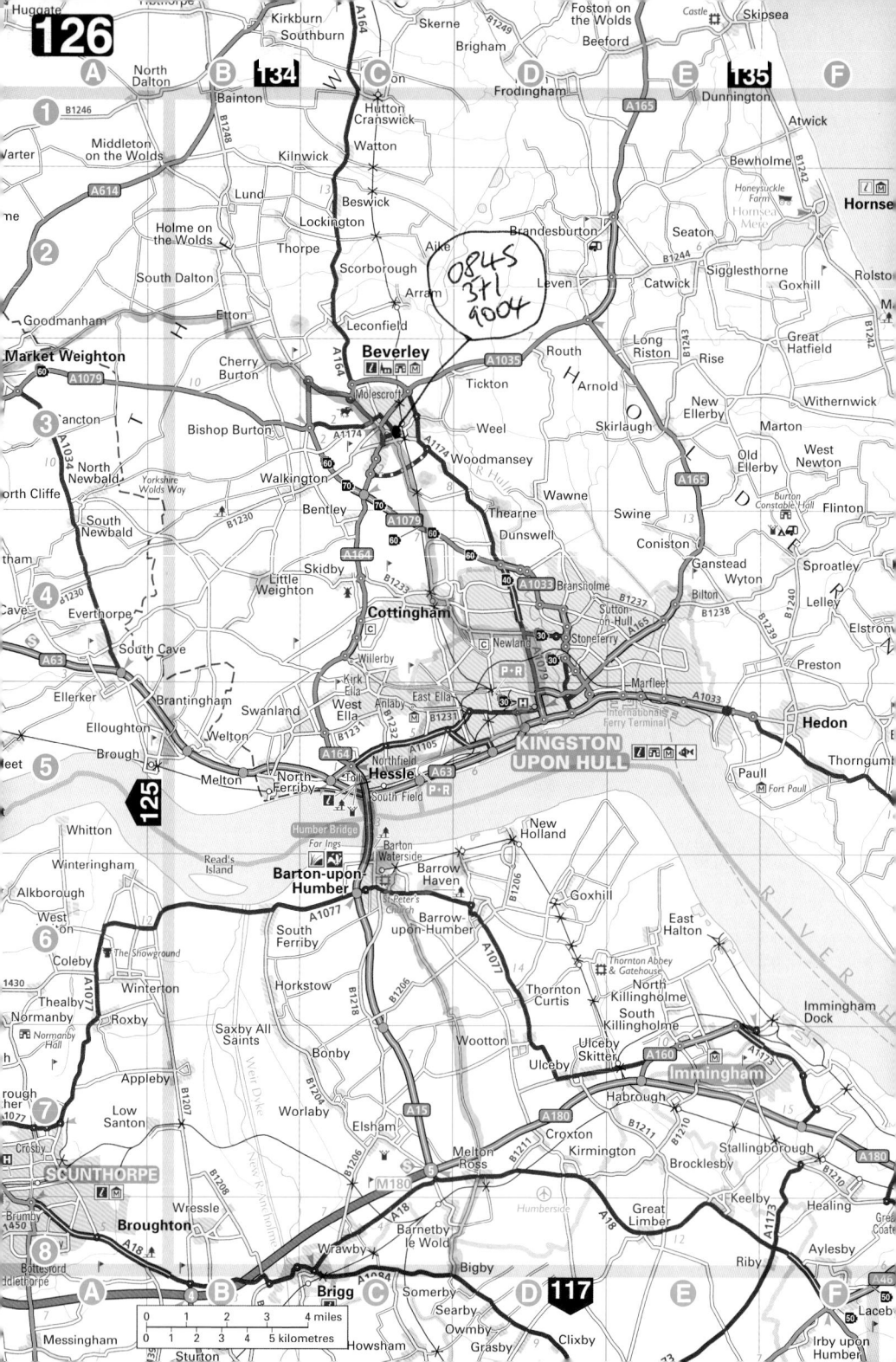

G H J K L M

1
2
3

leton Sands
len

Aldbrough

B1242

eton Hilston
Owstwick Tunstall

Burton Roos
Pidsea B1242 Rimswell
B1362 Owthorne
ck S Withernsea
Halsham B1362
eyingham S Hollym
ngham Winestead A1033 Holmpton
Patrington
Patrington Welwick
Haven Weeton Easington
Skeffling B1445
Spurn
Heritage Coast
Kilnsea

SPURN HEAD

Spurn Heritage Coast

Rotterdam (Europoort)
Zeebrugge

M
B
E
R

GRIMSBY

West Marsh
Old
Clee
Cleethorpes
Nunsthorpe C A46 Thrunscoe
The Jungle
ey A16 sure
G nd H
A1098
ham B1219
New Waltham Humberston

118 J

4
5
6
7
8

G H 118 J K L M

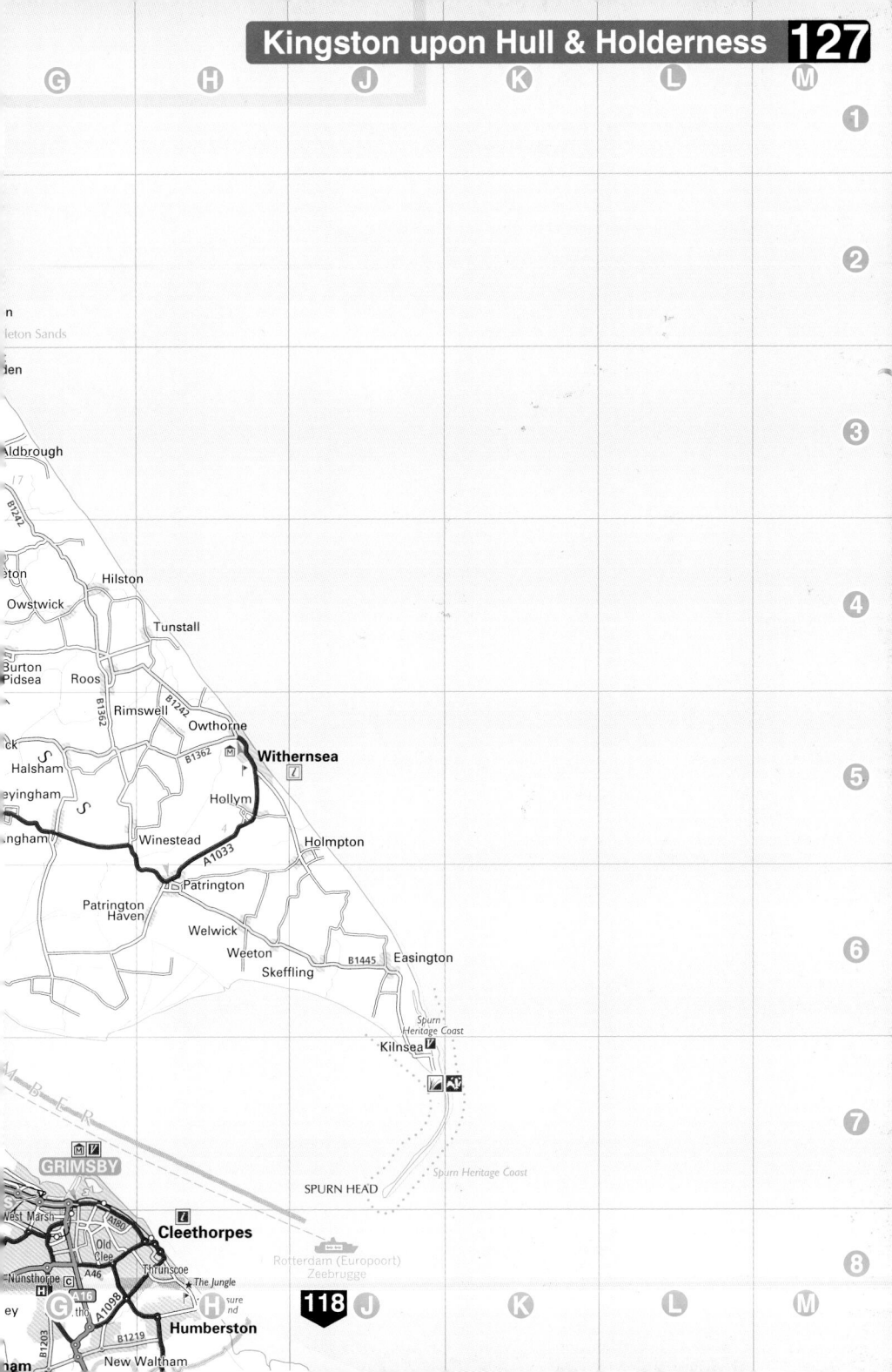

Seascale
Hallsenna Moor
Drigg Holmrook
Muncaster Mill

Green
Eskdale

652
HARTER
FELL

Fu

Seathwait
Tarn

A

B

C

D

Ravenglass and Eskdale Railway

Devoke Water

E

F

1

Ravenglass
Roman Bath House

Muncaster

A595

Hall Dunnerdale

136

River Esk

Seathwaite

137

Waberthwaite

573
WHITFELL

Ulpha

A593

LAKE DISTRICT

Broughton Mills

2

Hycemoor

Selker Bay

Bootle

NATIONAL

Swinside Stone Circle

Broughton-in-Furn

PARK

A595

Lady Hall

Foxfield

Grizebe

3

Gutterby Spa

600
BLACK COMBE

Whitbeck

The Green

A5093

The Hill

Kirkby-in-Fu
Beck Side

Whicham

Silecroft

The Hill

A595

4

Kirksanton

Soutergate

Millom

U

RSPB

Penr

Haverigg

Haverigg Point

Ireleth

Askam in Furness

Lindal in Furness
South Lakes Animal Park

Little Urswic

5

Sandscale Haws

North Walney

Dalton-in-Furness

Newton

Stain with Ac

BARROW-IN-FURNESS

Furness Abbey

Bow Bridge

Dendron

Leec

G

6

Vickerstown

A590

Barrow Island

30

A5087

Rampsi

ISLE OF WALNEY

Sheep Island

Piel Castle

Foulr

Piel Island

7

Hilpsford Point

South Walney

Piel Bar

8

A

B

C

D

E

F

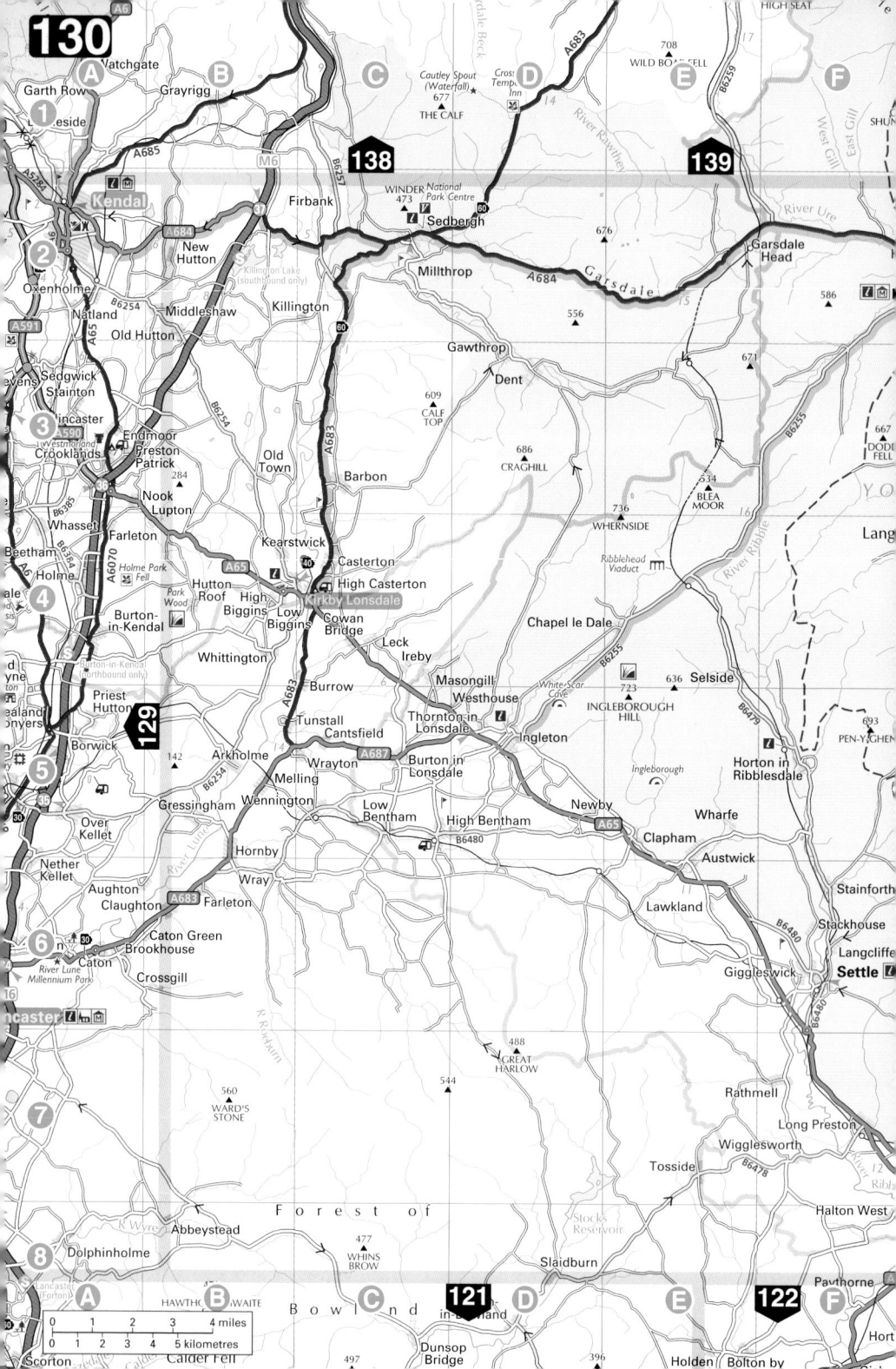

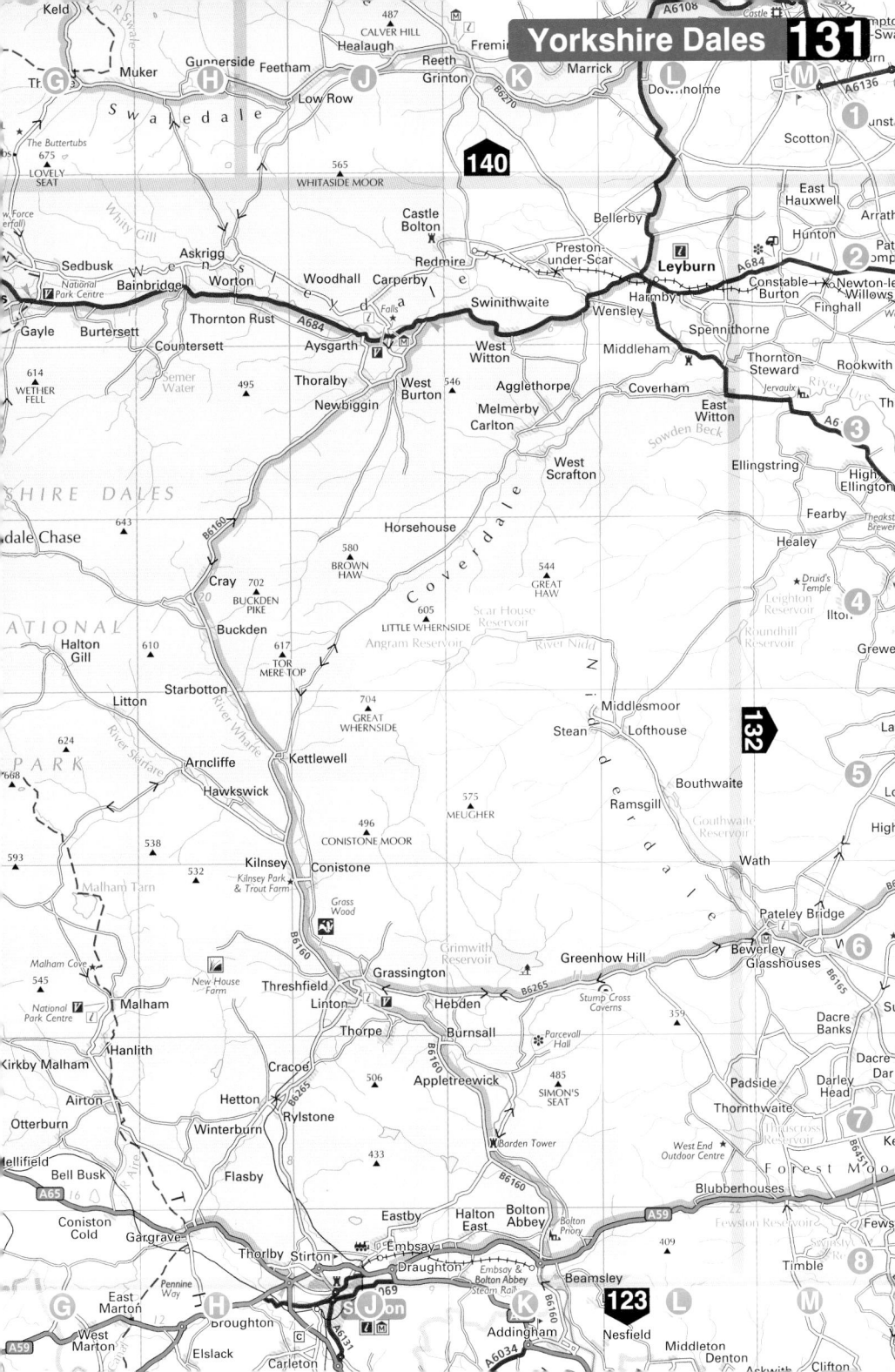

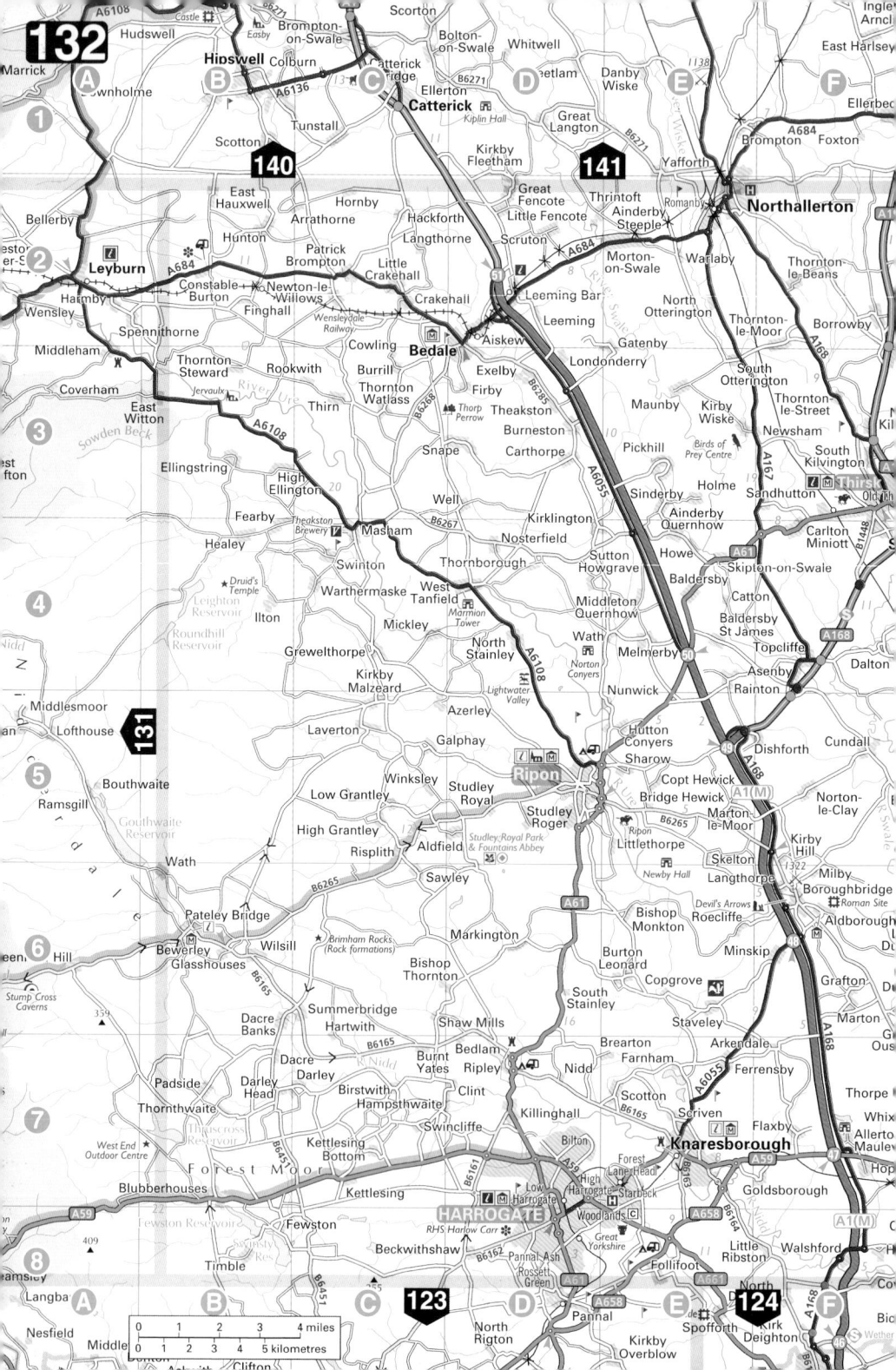

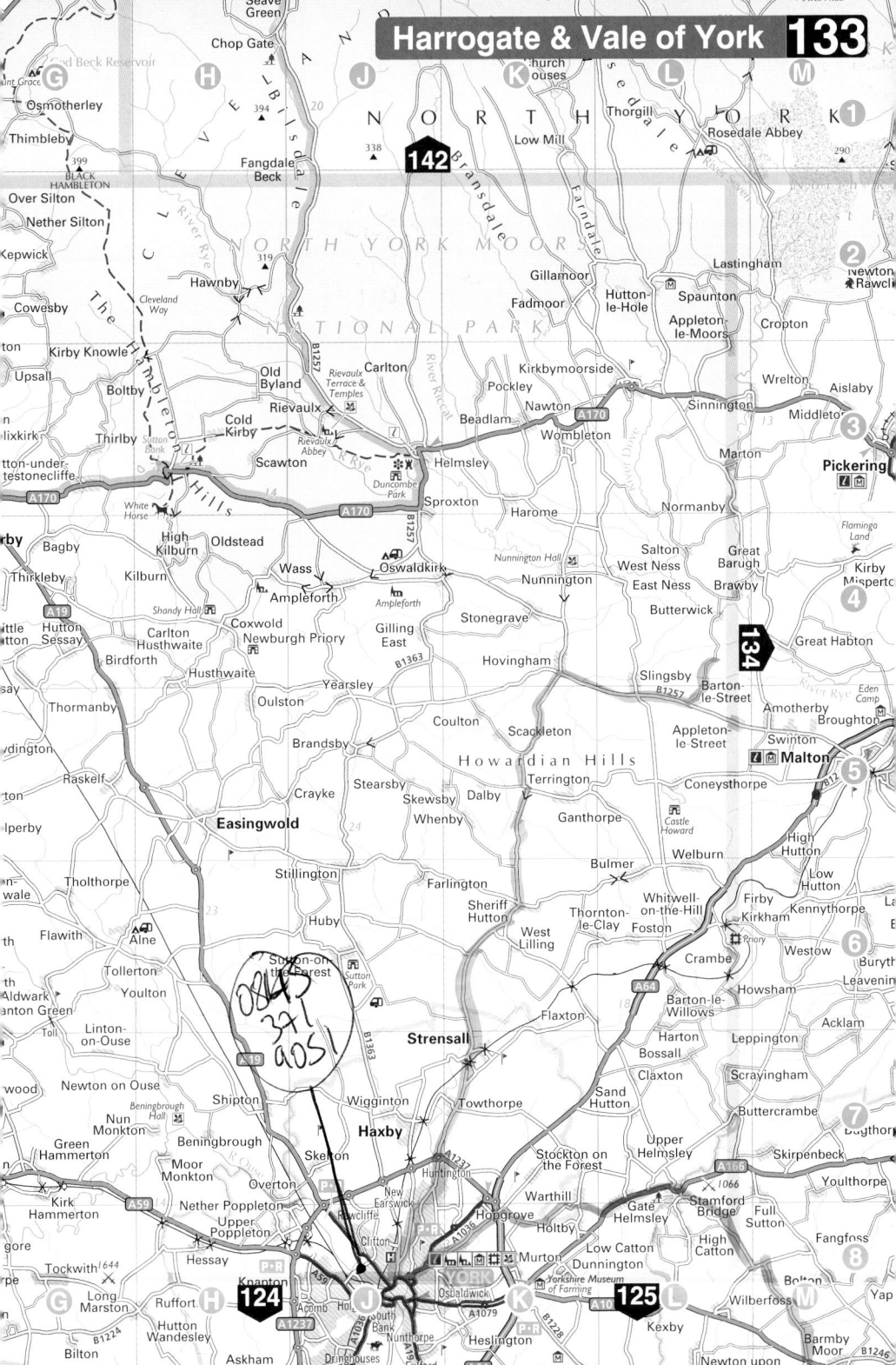

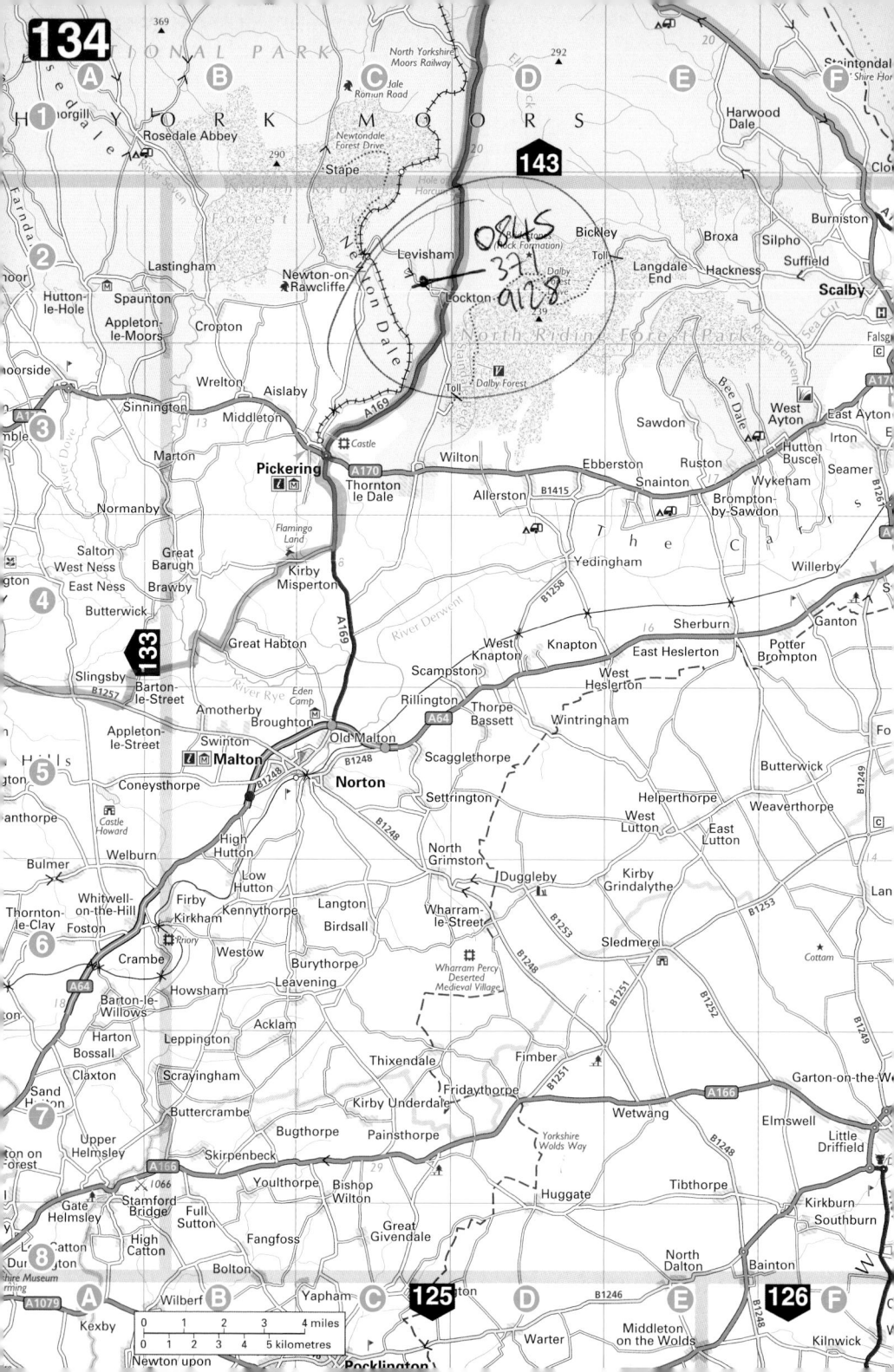

G   H   J   K   L   M

1

2

**Cloughton
Wyke**

romer Point

leveland Way

3

Scarborough
Castle
*Hatherleigh
Deep Sea Trawler*
Oliver's Mount

A165

P•R Osgodby
B1261
gates
Cayton Bay
The
Lebberston Wyke
Gristhorpe Filey Brigg
Folkton Muston A1039 Filey
Flixton A1039

4

Filey Bay

Yorkshire
ds Way
Hunmanby
Fordon Reighton
Speeton Flamborough Head
Wold B1229 Bempton Heritage Coast
Newton Cliffs Thornwick
Burton Buckton Bay
Fleming Bempton North Landing
Grindale A165 B1229 Selwicks
Thwing B1259 Bay
Lighthouse FLAMBOROUGH
B1255 HEAD
Sewerby Flamborough
B1253 ★ Bondville
Rudston ⚑ Monolith Miniature Village
Boynton Bridlington
Bessingby BRIDLINGTON
Carnaby Hilderthorpe BAY
Haisthorpe
Kilham Thornholme
Burton Agnes ⚑ Norman
Harpham Manor House
Ruston Parva A165
Lowthorpe Fraisthorpe
A614 Nafferton Gransmoor
ield Great Kelk Lissett Barmston
B1242
Wansford Gembling Ulrome
Skerne Foston on Castle ⚑ Skipsea
B1249 the Wolds
Brigham Beeford
North
Frodingham
wick A165 **126** Dunnington Atwick
Bewholme
B1242

5

6

7

8

G   H   J   K   L   M

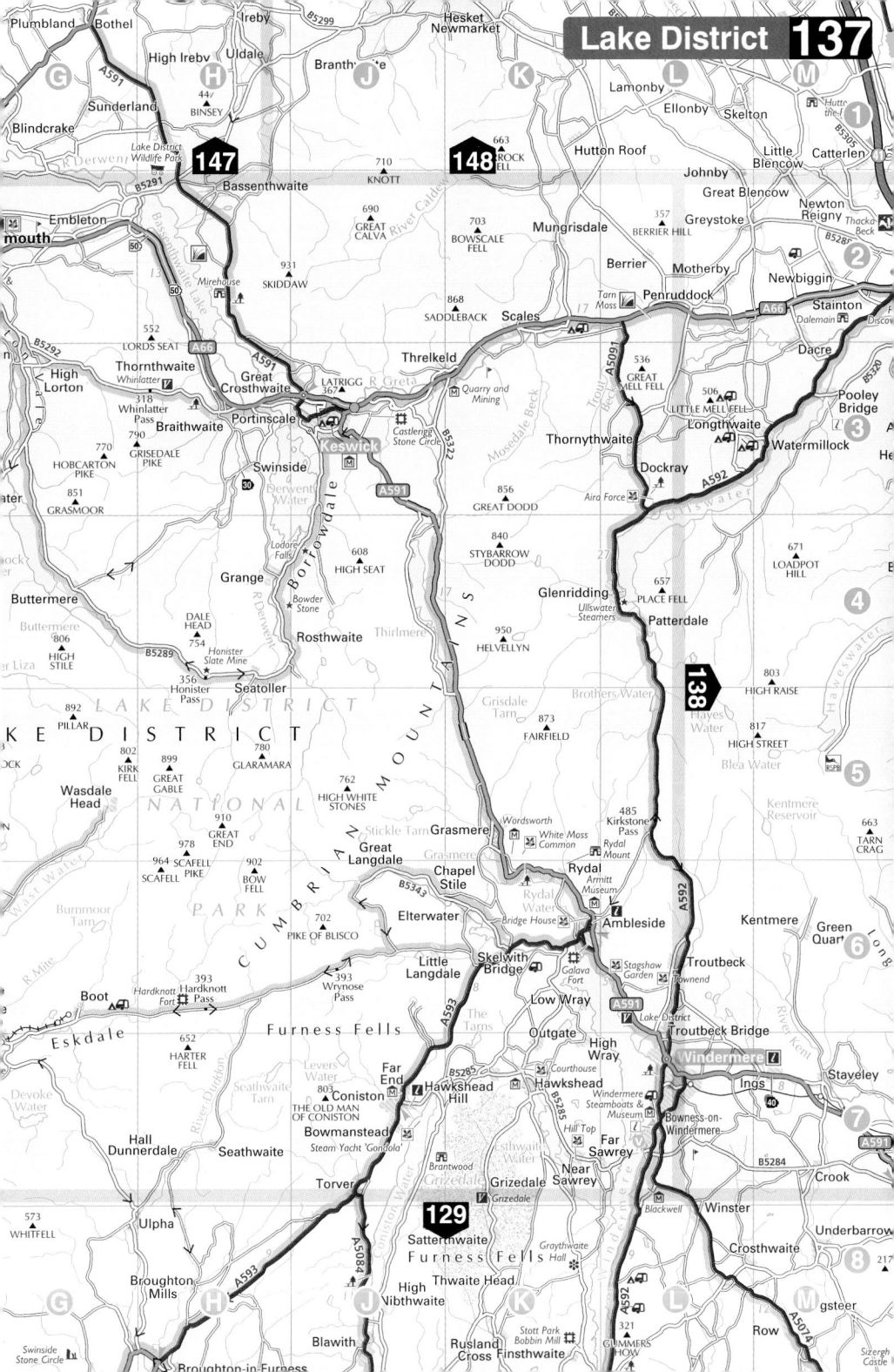

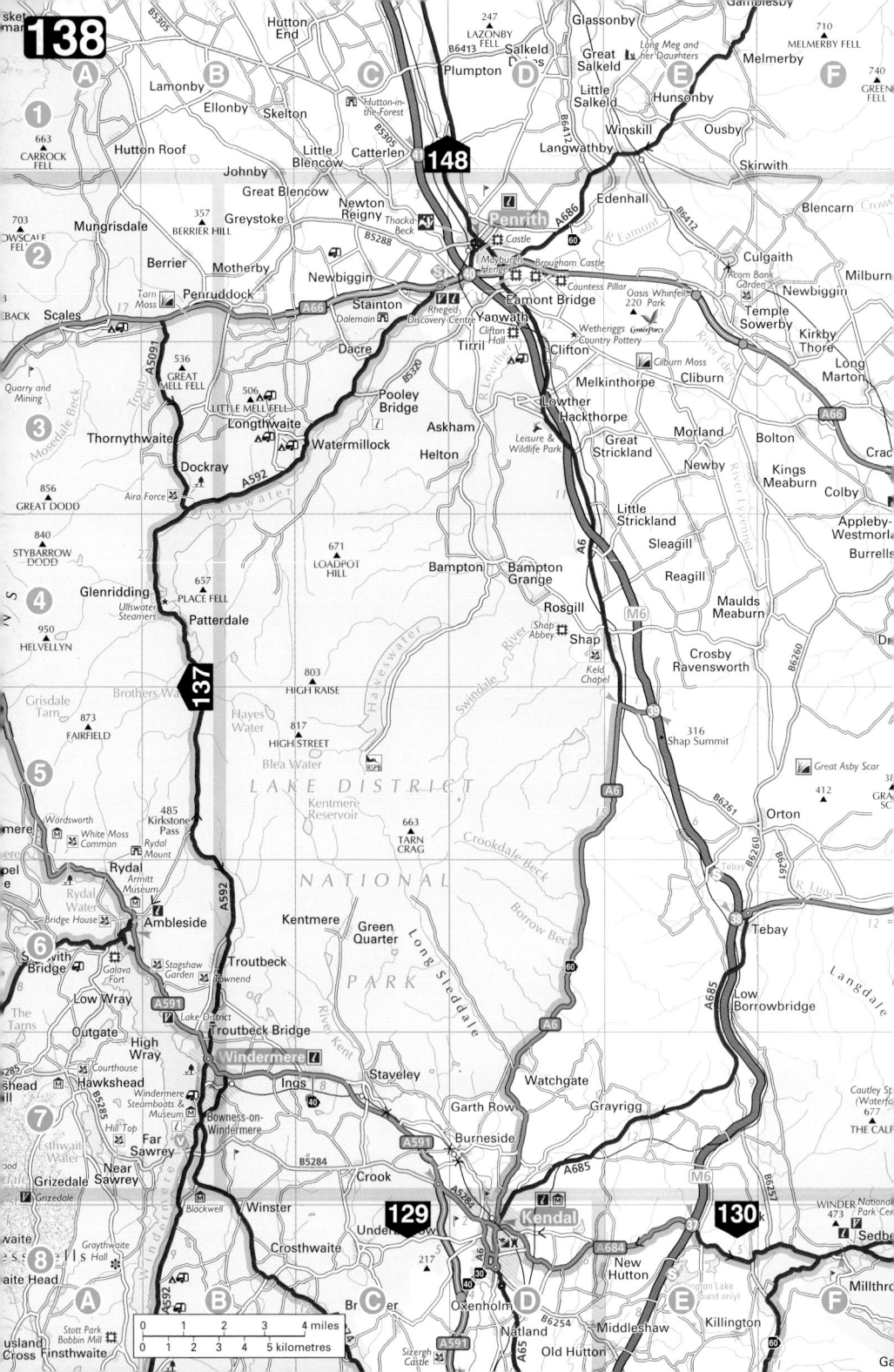

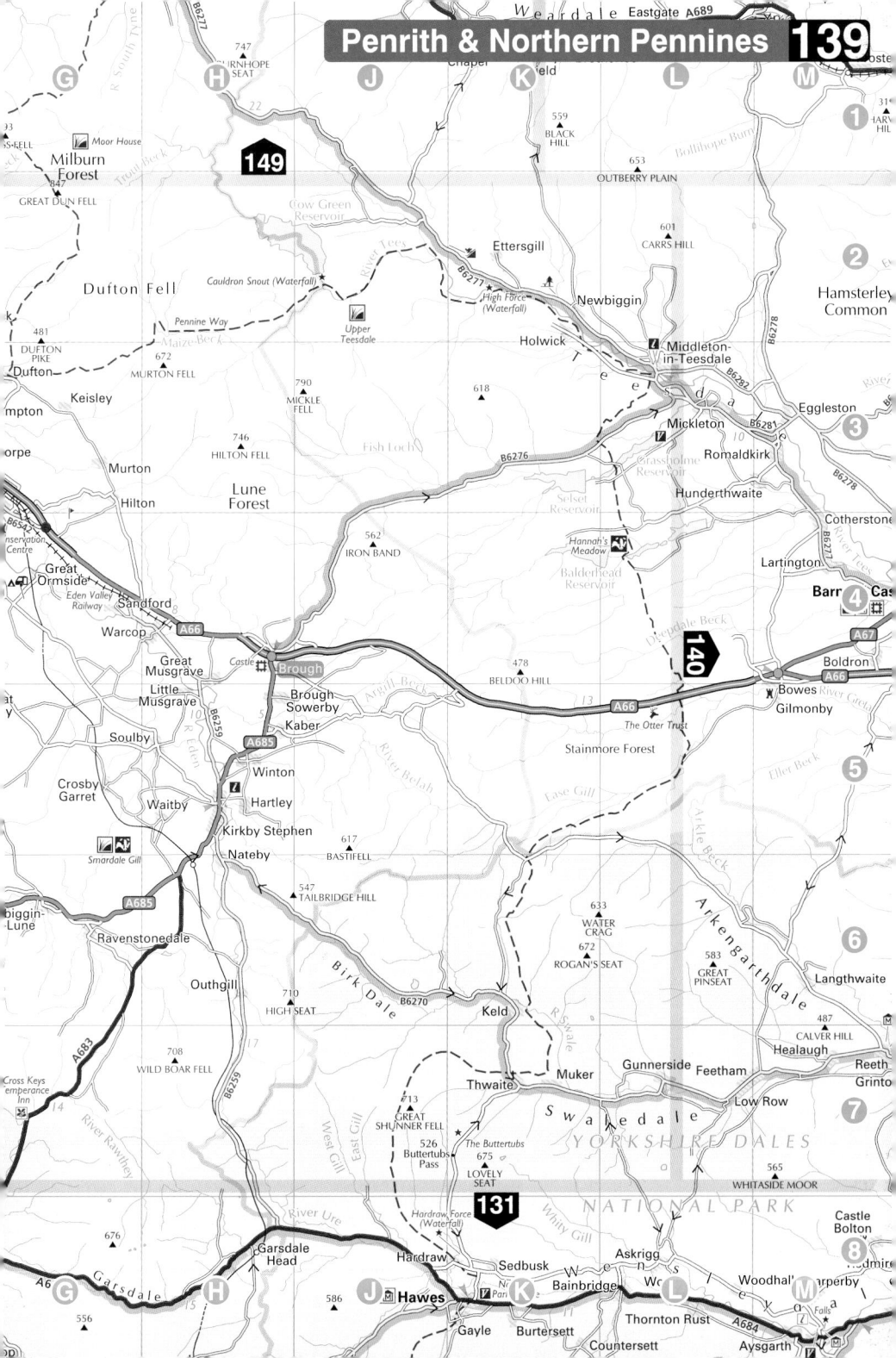

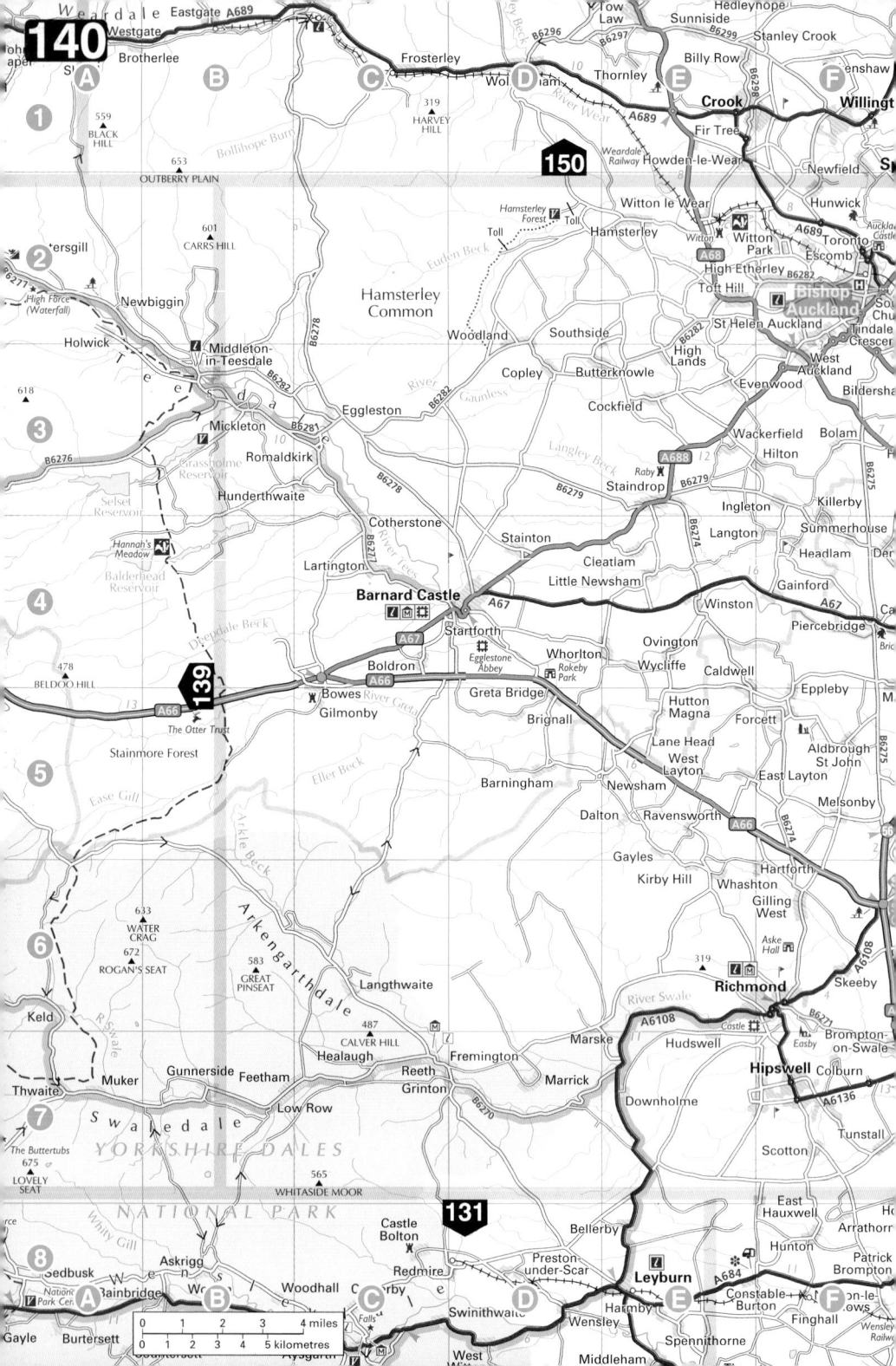

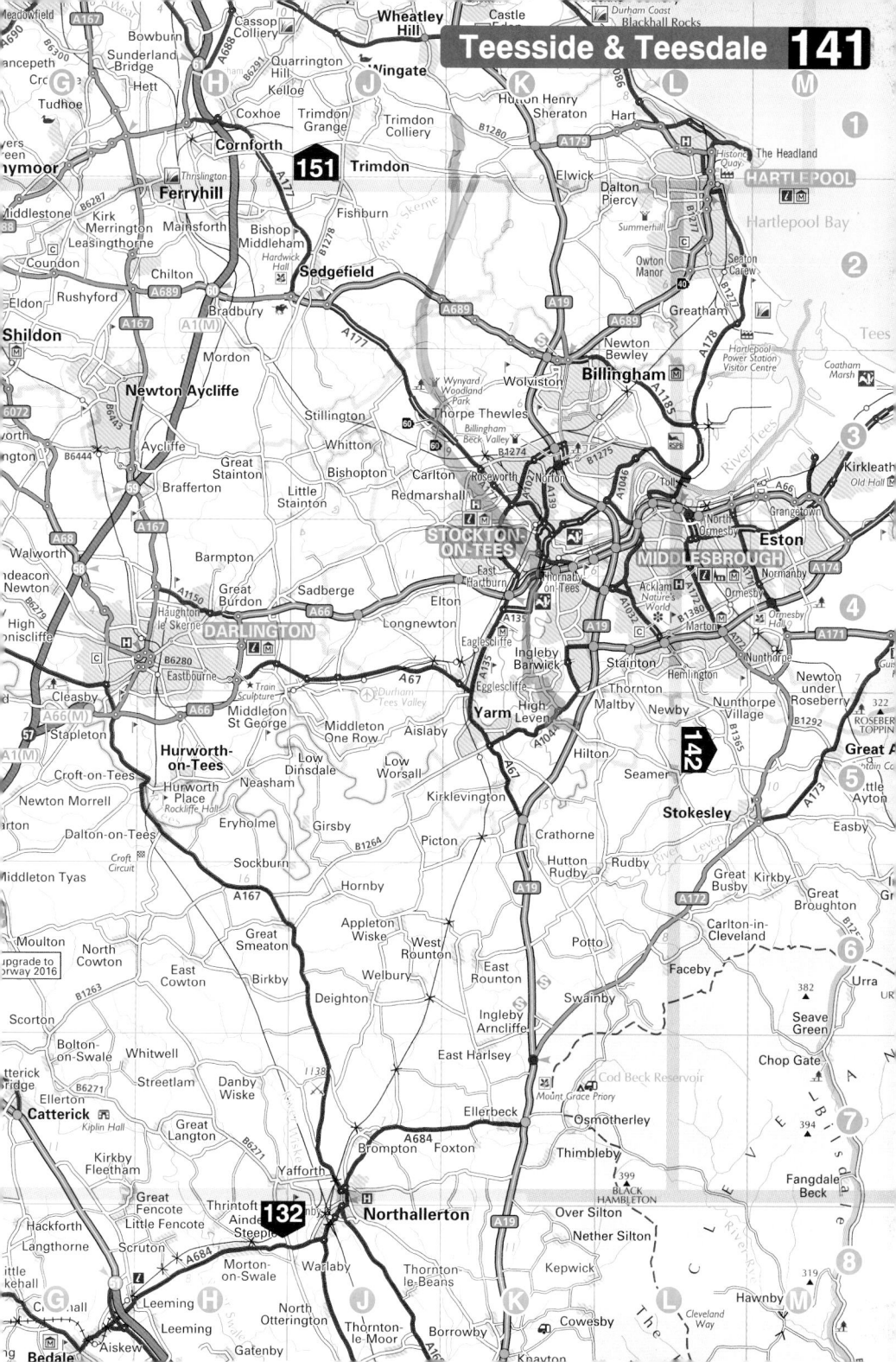

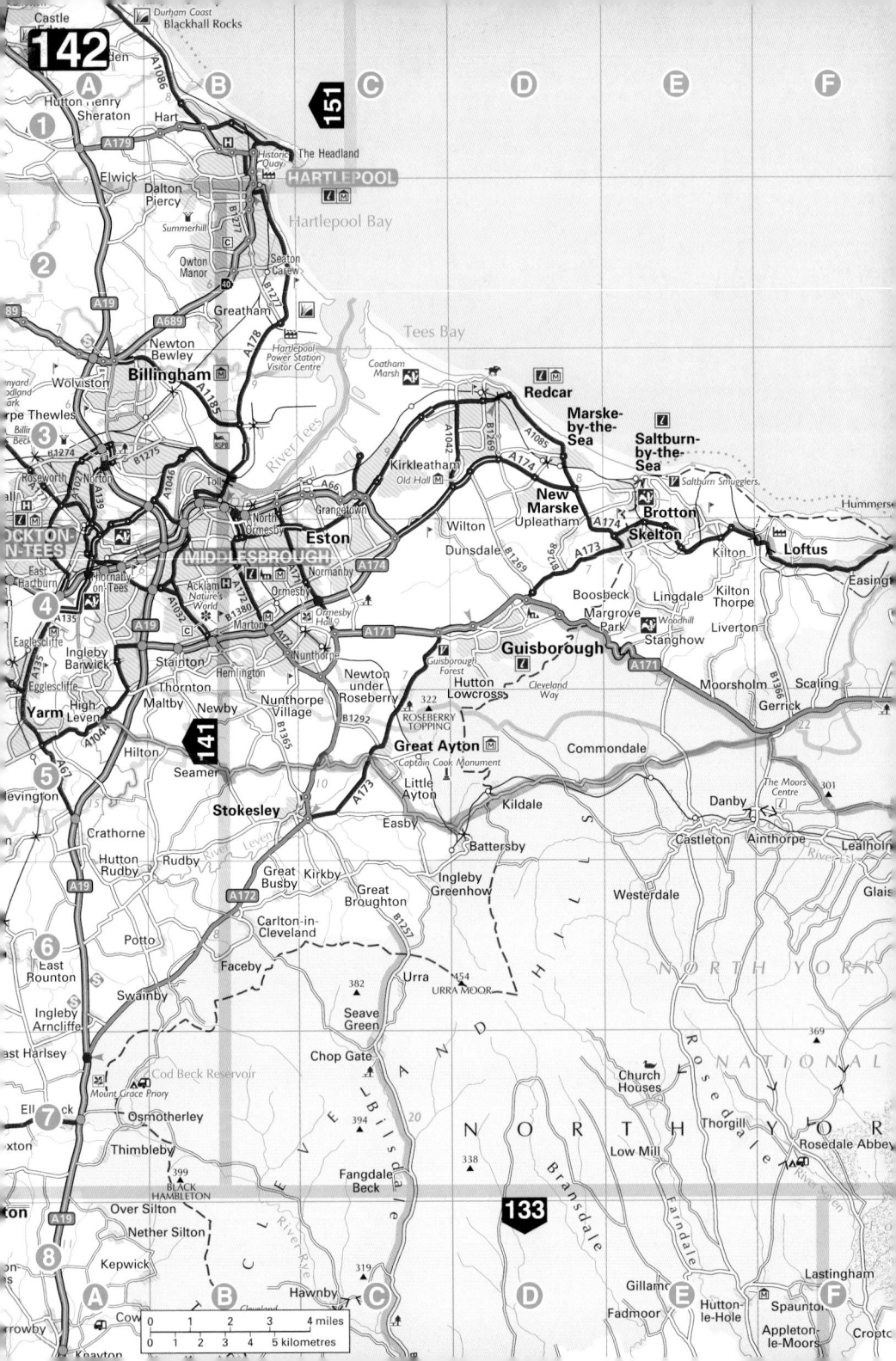

0845 371 9049

0845 371 9504.

Drumlamford
Creebank
Glen Trool
Bargrennan
Bruce's
716
LAMACHAN
HILL
675
LA
L
654
MILLF
Bruce & Wildlife Centre
ay
Loch
A712
M
325
CAIRN
EDWAR
1

Loch
Ochiltree
1027
G
H
J
K
L
440
GARLICK
HILL
Galloway Deer Range
402
ROUND
FELL
471
FELL OF FLEET
Knowe
RSPB
`153`
Pencill Burn
G A L L O W A Y
184
URRALL
FELL
Carseriggan
Challoch
Minnigaff
710
CAIRNSMORE
OF FLEET
208
AUCHENCLOY HILL
Skerrow
2
Loch
Grannoch
Loch
Fleet
Barfad
214
CULVENNAN
FELL
Newton
Stewart
Creebridge
Kirroughtree
Big Water of Fleet
335
WHITE TOP
OF CULREACH
Carstramon
Wood
Shennanton
Palnure
A714
Upper
Ruscoe
B796
367
BENGI
Craighlaw
B733
A75
Kirkcowan
15
Causeway
End
Baltersan
A75
Gem Rock
Creetown
Gatehouse
of Fleet
B7
Littleto
Wh
`146`
4
Clugston
Torhouse
Stone Circle
B733
THE
Wigtown
Bladnoch
Kirkmabreck
455
CAIRNHARROW
Cairnholy
Chambered Cairns
Carsluith
Anwoth
Cardoness
Castle
Girthon
18
Fell
Loch
MACHARS
Kirwaugh
Carsluith
Castle
Braehead
Ravenshall
Point
Mossyard
Fleet
Bay
Lennox
Plunton
Margrie
Gle
5
Culshabbin
B7005
Barrachan
Kirkinner
Orchardton
Bay
Culscadden
Islands
of Fleet
Kirkandrews
Chapel
Finian
(ruin)
B7052
Whauphill
B7004
Wigtown Bay
Borness
Ba
Elrig
Little
Airies
A746
B7052
Garlieston
Cruggleton
Bay
Ringdoo Point
6
1747
13
Mochrum
Druchtag
Motte
B7085
Sorbie
Pouton
B7004
Drumtrodden
Cup & Ring
Drummoddie
Drumtrodden
Standing Stones
Broughton
Mains
B7063
Port William
Big Balcraig
B7021
Priory
Barsalloch Fort
'Wren's Egg'
Standing Stones
Monreith
Whithorn
Story
Rispain
Camp
Whithorn
Portyerrock
Point of Leg
A747
A746
St Ninian's
Cave
Kidsdale
B7004
Isle of Whithorn
St Ninian's
Chapel
(ruin)
Cutcloy
BURROW HEAD
7

8

G
H
J
K
L
M

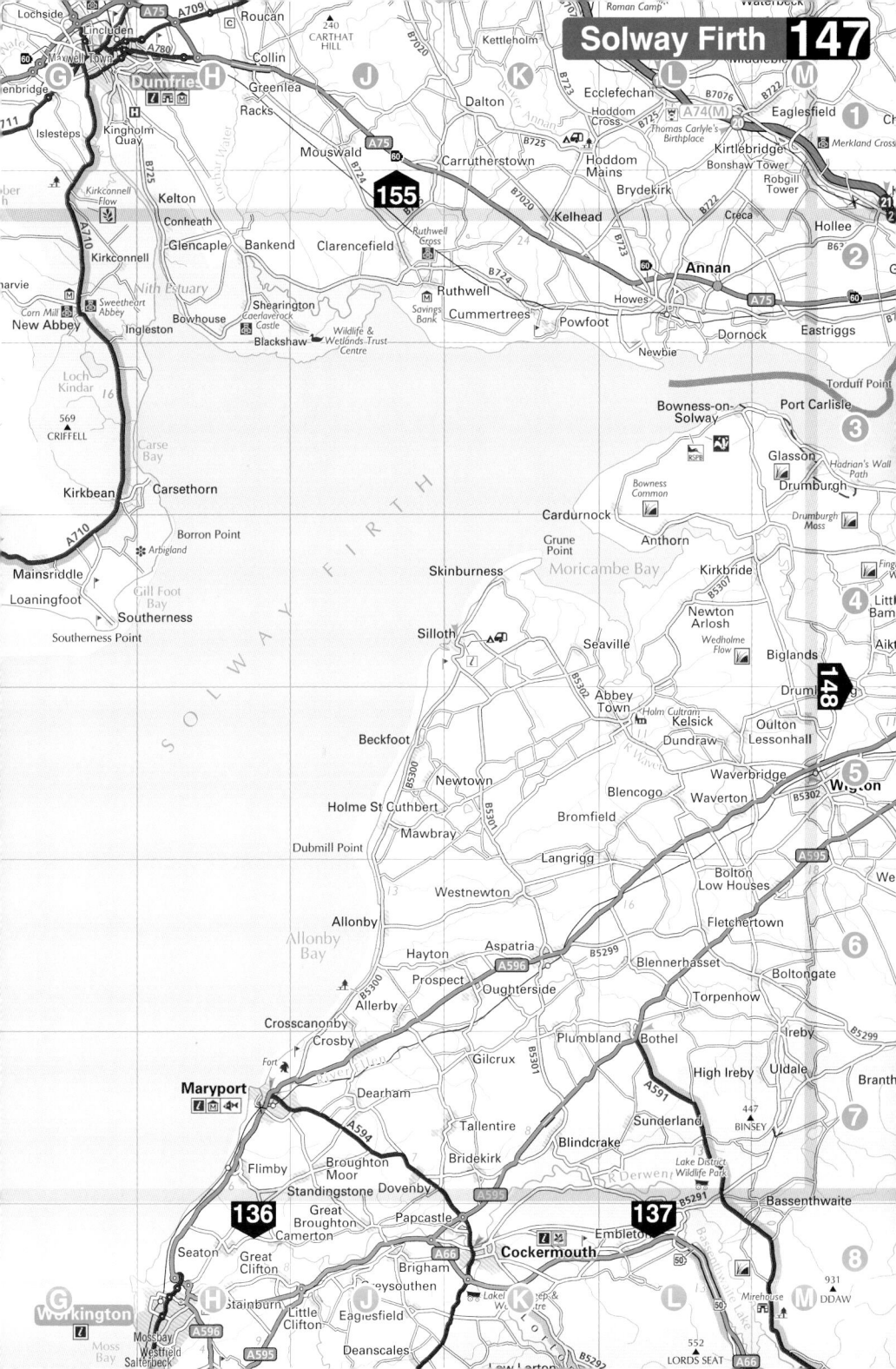

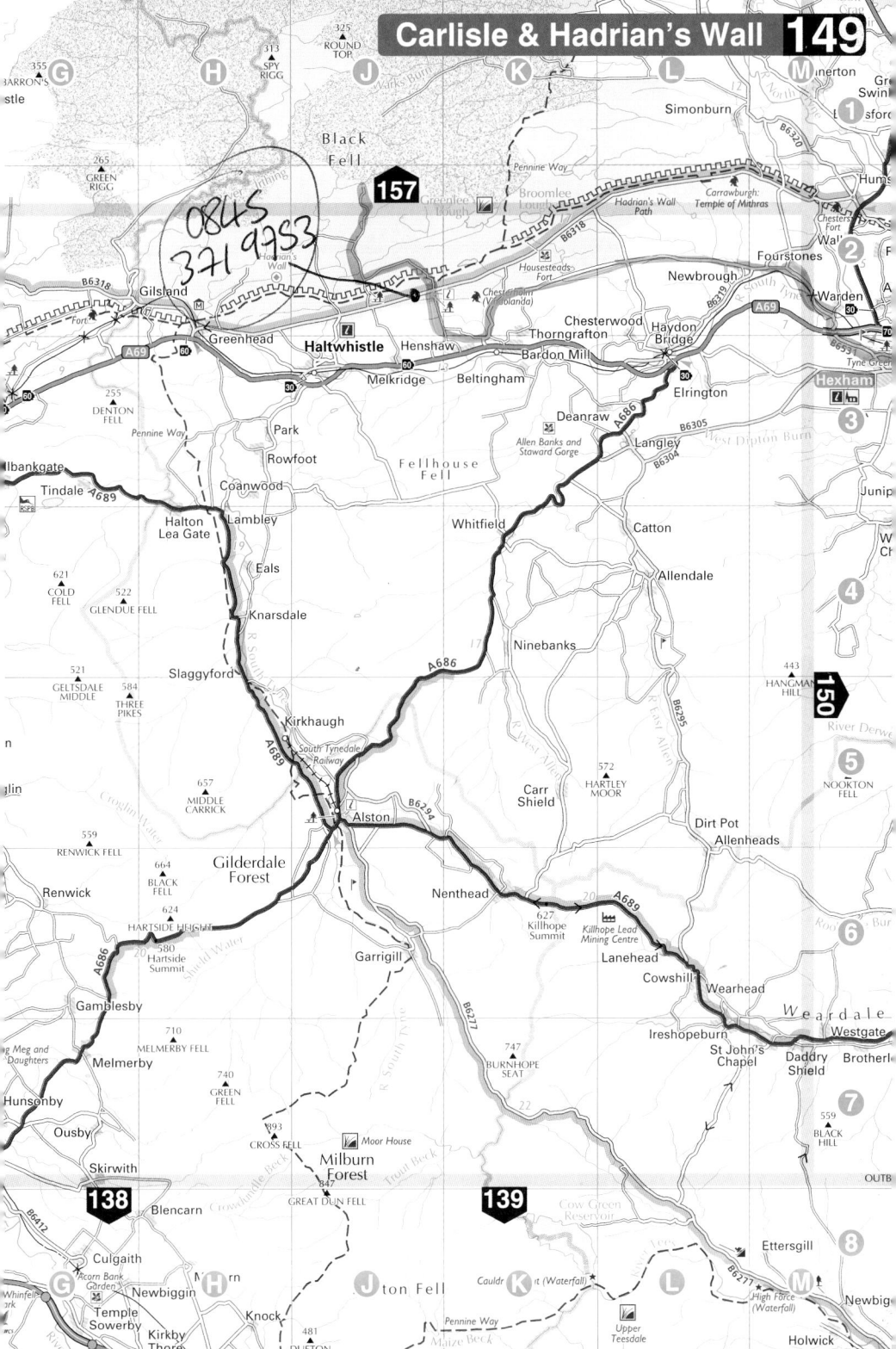

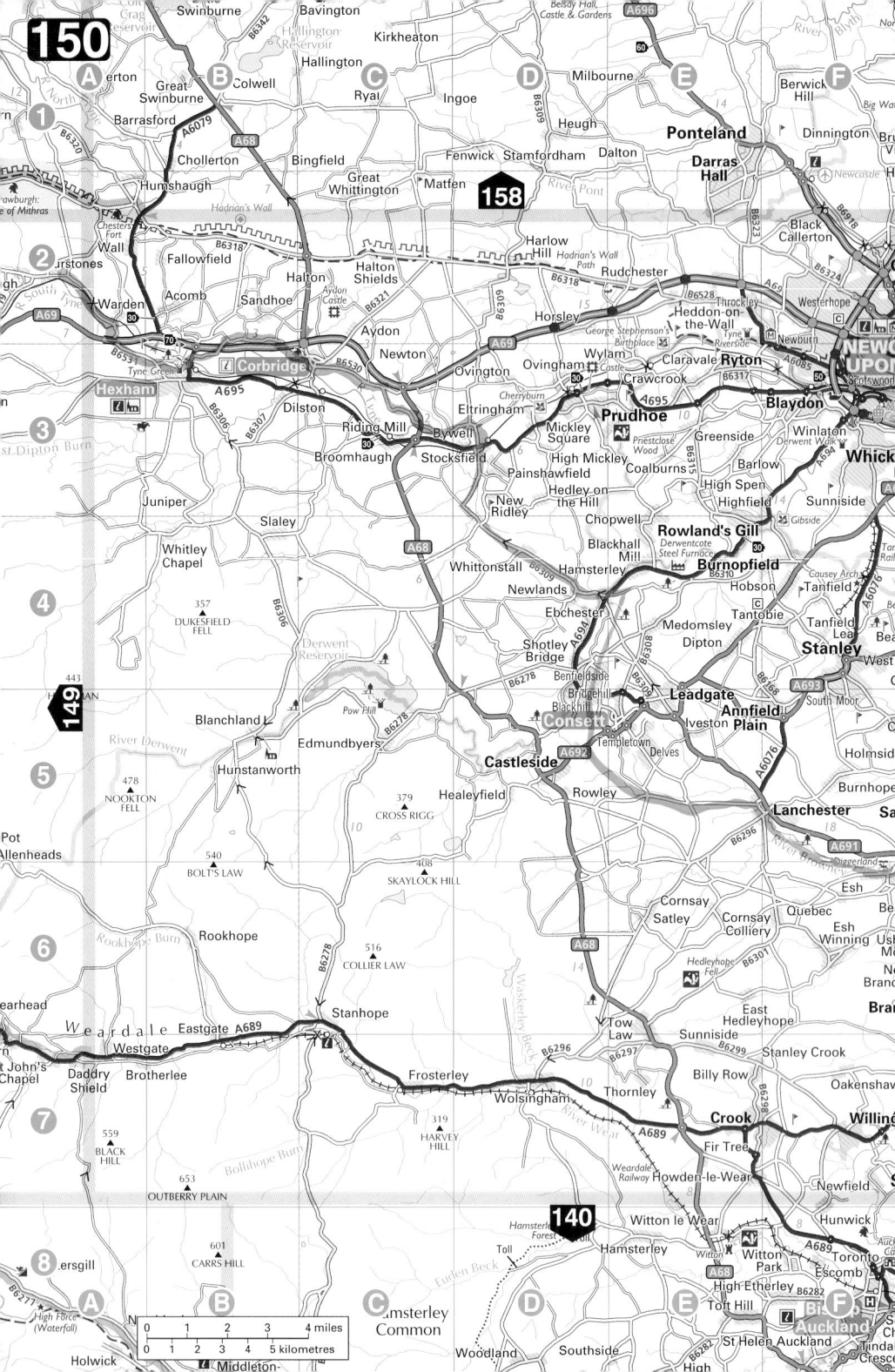

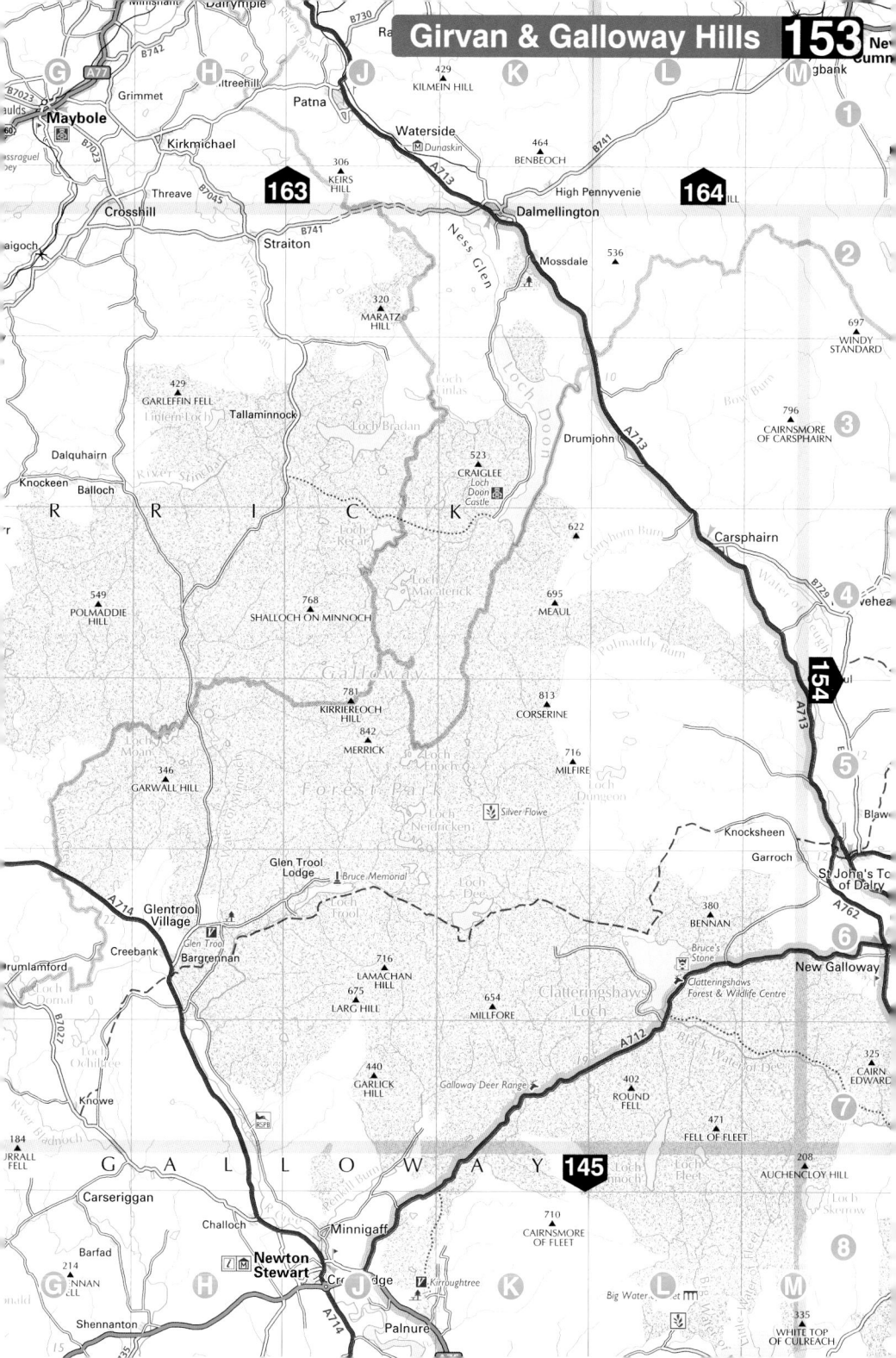

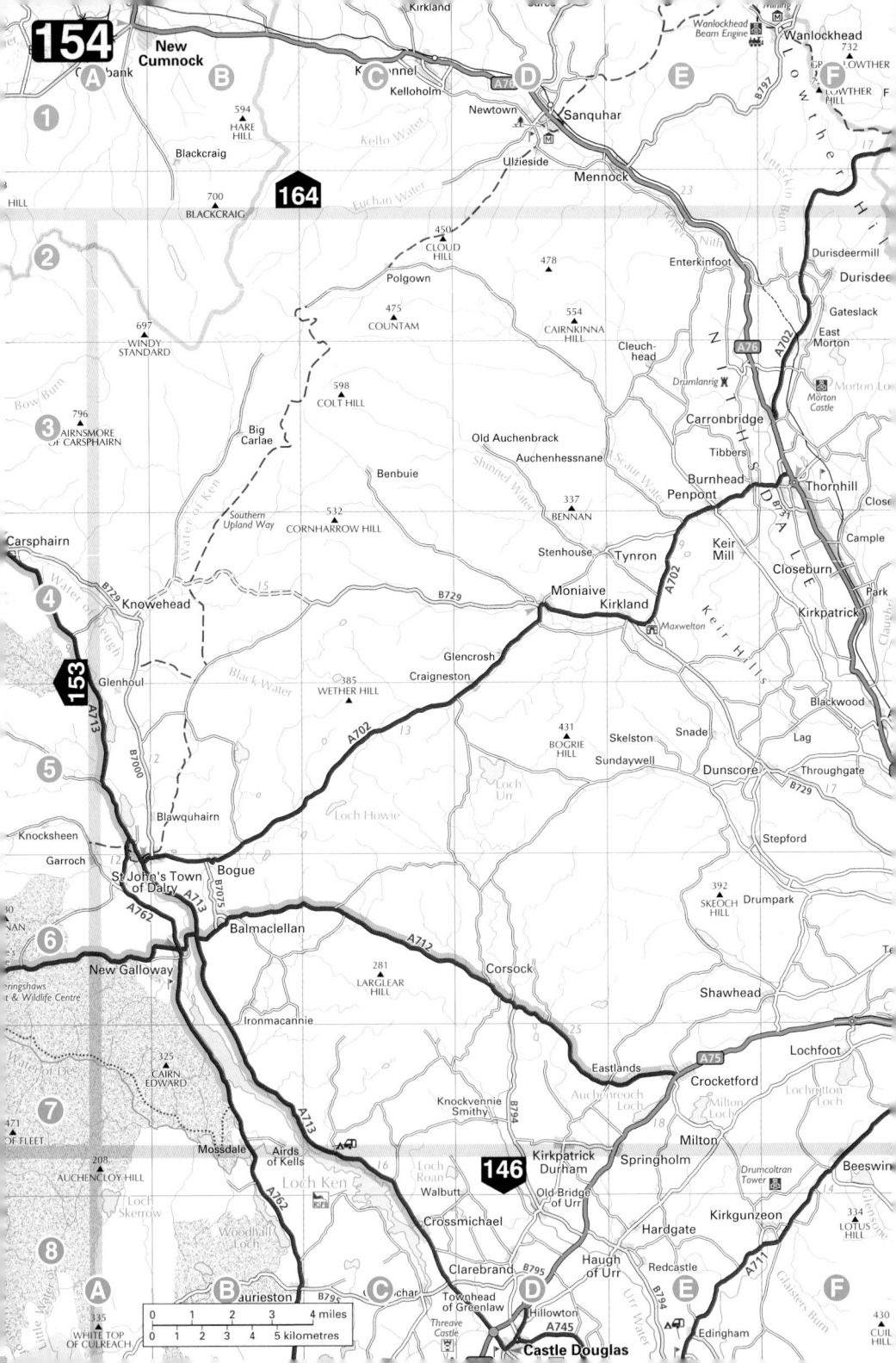

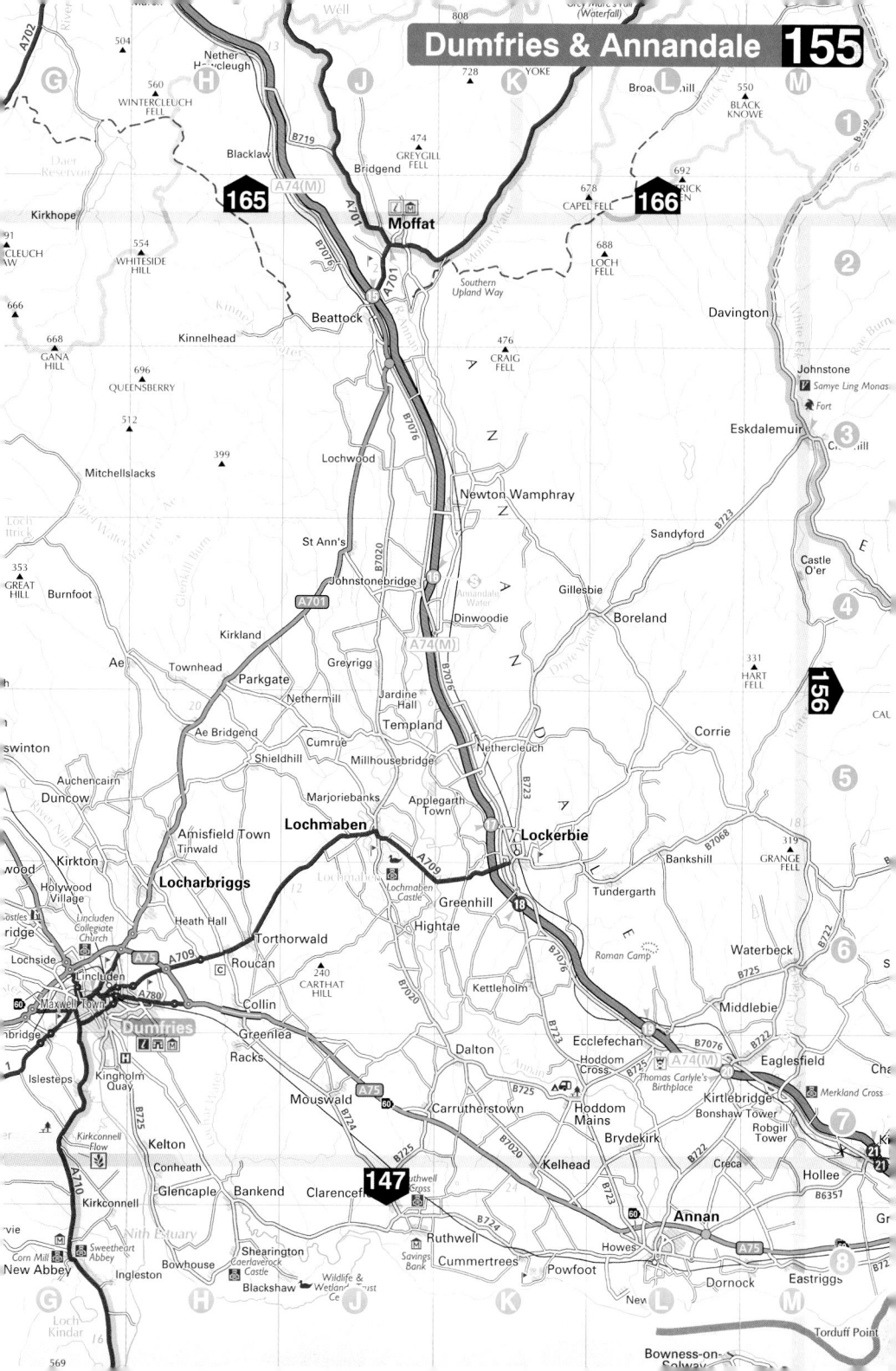

G
323
BIG
HILL
STER
Chesters
H
Abbotrule
Jedforest Deer
& Farm Park
Camptown
60
A68
Combs
J
BROWNDEAN
41
K
L
M
GUSHAT
LAW
1

River A

A6088
Letham
60
Carter
Bar
THE CHEVIOT HILLS
SHILLHOPE
LAW
500
393
WOFFEE
HEAD
Crag Bank Wood
167
417
500
HUNGRY
LAW
Alwinton
Ha

Whitelee
Moor
Ramshope
BLACK KIP
448
NORTHUMBERLAND
168
2
H

553
CARTER
FELL
Catcleugh
Reservoir
Byrness
CORBY PIKE
368
NATIONAL
THE

602
PEEL FELL
OH ME
EDGE
551
River Rede
A68
Camp
Rochester
Horsley
PARK
3

Myredykes
Kielder
Head
HINDHOPE
LAW
425
Pennine Way

513
MONKSIDE
1388
Otterburn
Elsdon
4

403
LOCH
KNOWE
Toll
Kielder
Kielder Castle
& Observatory
EARLS
SEAT
397
Otterburn Mill
A68

Kielder
Water
Black Middens
Bastle House
West
Woodburn
Fort
East
Woodburn
158

WHITE HILL
307
Gatehouse
B6320
9

Falstone
Tower
Knowe
Stannersburn
Greenhaugh
Greenhaugh
Charlton
Fort
hnsdale
5

er Forest Park
395
BOLTS
LAW
Chirdon Burn
Bellingham
Redesmouth
Birtley
6
Tho
Reservoir

519
SIGHIY
CRAG
492
BLACK KNOWE
NORTHUMBERLAND
Wark
Gunnerton
Gre
Swinb
Barrasfor

ARRON'S PIKE
355
stle
SPY
RIGG
313
ROUND
TOP
325
NATIONAL
Simonburn
B6320
7
Hums

GREEN
RIGG
265
PARK
Pennine Way
Carrawburgh:
Temple of Mithras
Chester
Fort
Wall

Black
Fell
Greenlee
Lough
Broomlee
Lough
Hadrian's Wall
Path
Fourstones
Newbrough
8

149
B6318
A69
War

B6318
Gilsland
Fort
60
reenhead
A69
60
H
Haltwh
J
Henshaw
Hadrian's
Wall
Chesterholm
(Vindolanda)
Housesteads
Fort
Chesterwood
Thorngrafton
Havdon
L
Newbrough
B6531
70
M

255
TON
60
Melkridge
60
Beltingham
30
Elrington
Tyne Green
Hexham

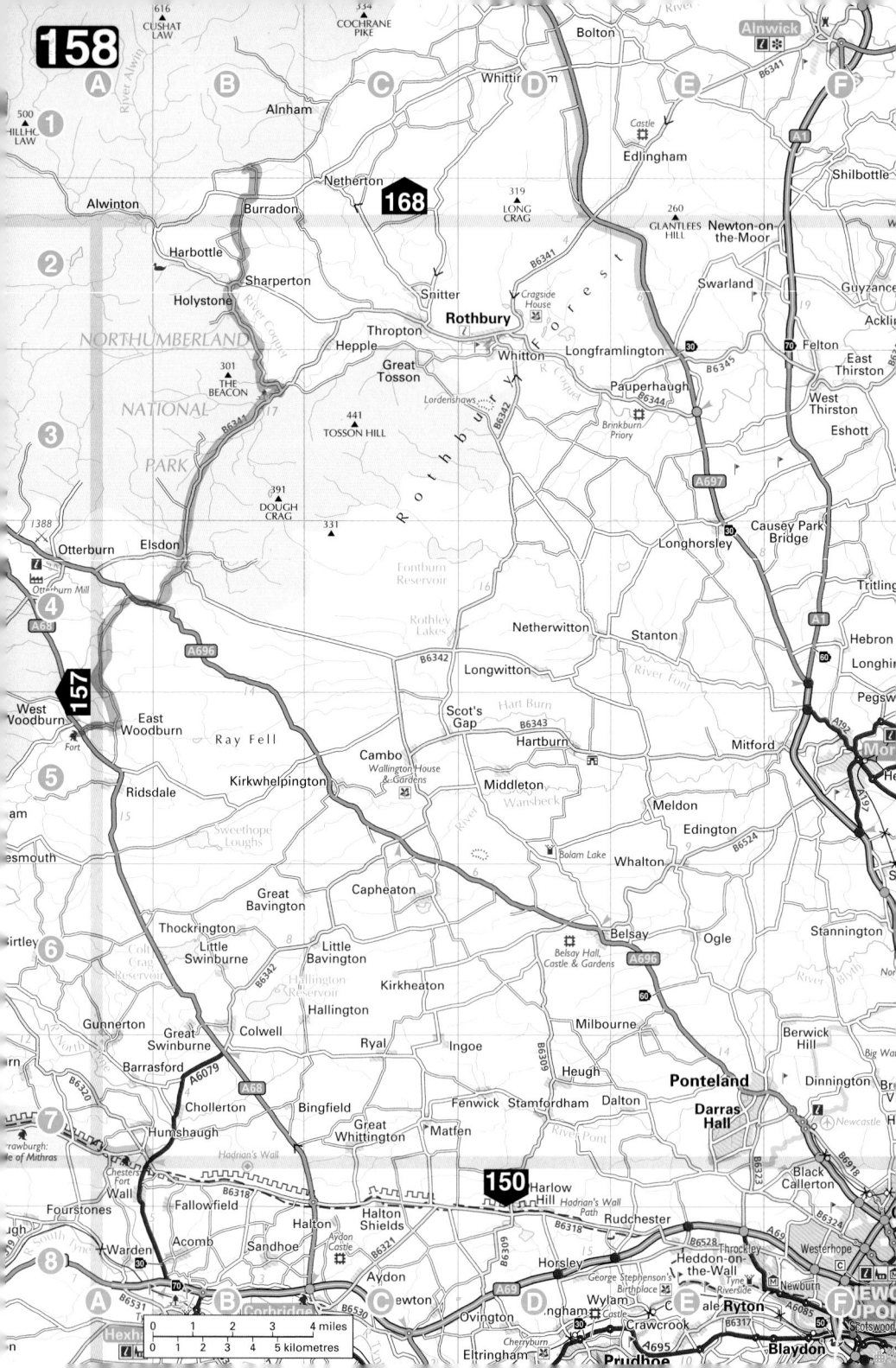

Lesbury
Seaton Point
G **H** **J** **K** **L** **M**
Alnmouth
1

Alnmouth Bay

A1068

169
Castle
toge
Warkworth
2
Amble
Coquet Island
loster Hill
High
Hauxley
Togston
Broomhill
outh
omhill
ed Row
Druridge Bay
3
Druridge Bay
swood
Widdrington
North Northumberland Heritage Coast
Widdrington
Station
Cresswell
4
Ulgham
A1068
Ellington
Lynemouth
A189
Beacon Point
Woodhorn
Ashington
A197
Newbiggin-by-the-Sea
A197
Bothal
Wansbeck Riverside
A196
Stakeford
Guide Post
5
opington
30
Bedlington
B1331
A193
B1331
Blyth
ton
B568
Cowpen
on
A189
Newsham
A192
A1061
New
Hartley
Seaton
Sluice
6
A192
A193
B1326
A190
Seaton
**Seaton
Delaval**
St Mary's Lighthouse
ramlington
50
A19
B1322
Earsdon
A192
A1148
Dudley
Wide
Open
**Whitley
Bay**
7
Killingworth
Monkseaton
Cullercoats
Forest Hall
Tynemouth
Shiremoor
A191
Rising
Sun
151
Amsterdam
(IJmuiden)
rth
Longbenton
**North
Shields**
Tynemouth Priory
& Castle
A19
Willington
Quay
**SOUTH
SHIELDS**
8
Jesmond
50
Wallsend
A187
Int. Ferry
Terminal
A183
TLE
NE
Heaton
Tyne Tunnel
Westoe
*Marsden
Bay*
40
A167
Walker
Jarrow
A194
Souter Lighthouse
G **H** **J** **K** **L** **M**
swick
Hebburn
Monkton
Felling
West
Souter Point
Cleadon
Whitburn

BEINN SHOLUM
346

Eilean
a' Chuirn

171

Rudha Mòr

Port
Ellen

Rudha na
Gainmhich

165
MAOL BUIDHE

A846

Ardbeg
Lagavulin

THE   OA

Laphroaig

I S L A Y

Lower
Killeyan

Risabus

Texa

RSPB

Kinnabus

American
Monument

Loch
Kinnabus

MULL
OF OA

Rudha nan Leacan

Kilnaughton Bay

Port Ellen, Kennacraig

Earadale

MUL
OF
KINTY

| 0 | 1 | 2 | 3 | 4 miles |
| 0 | 1 | 2 | 3 | 4 | 5 kilometres |

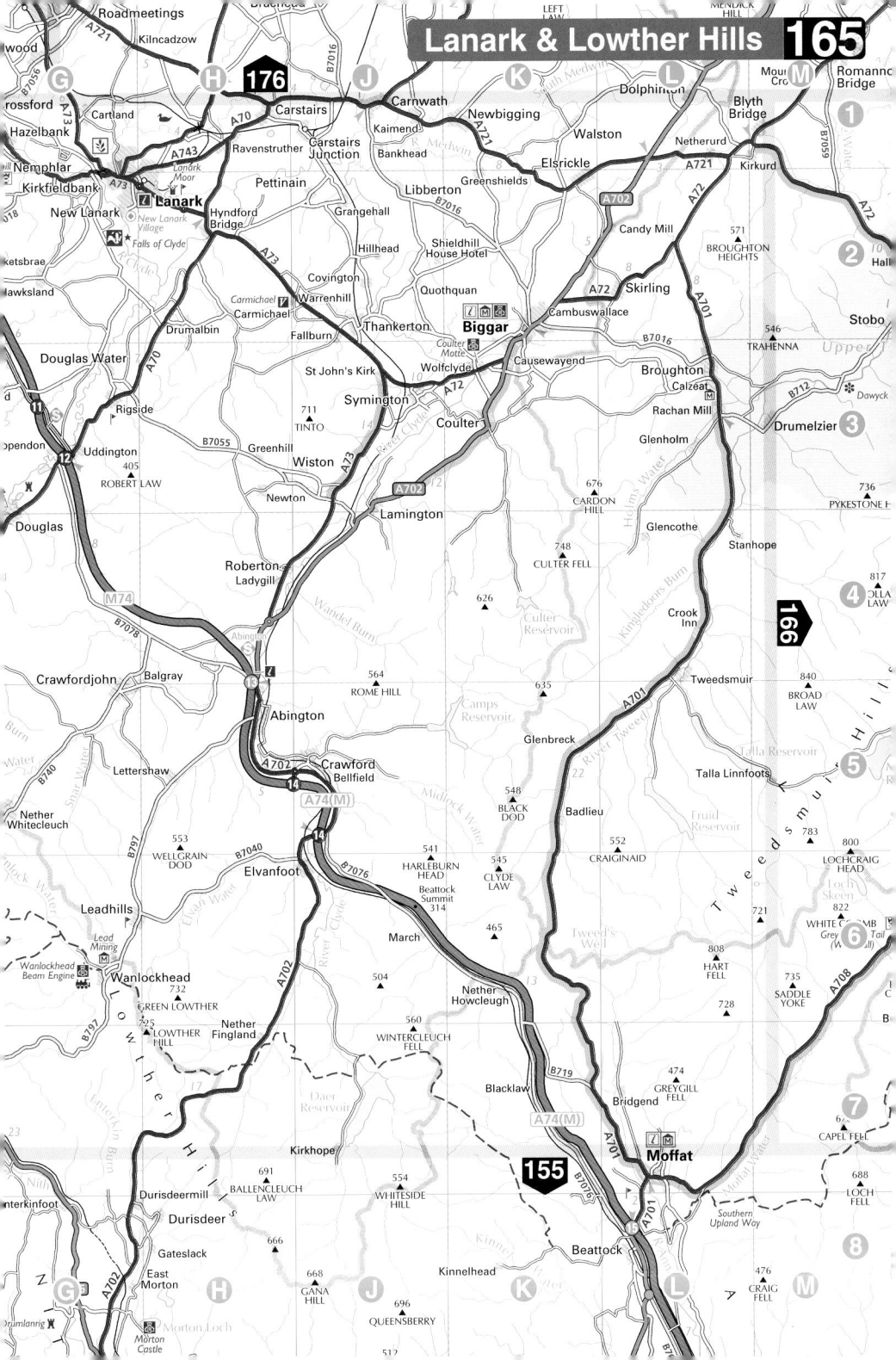

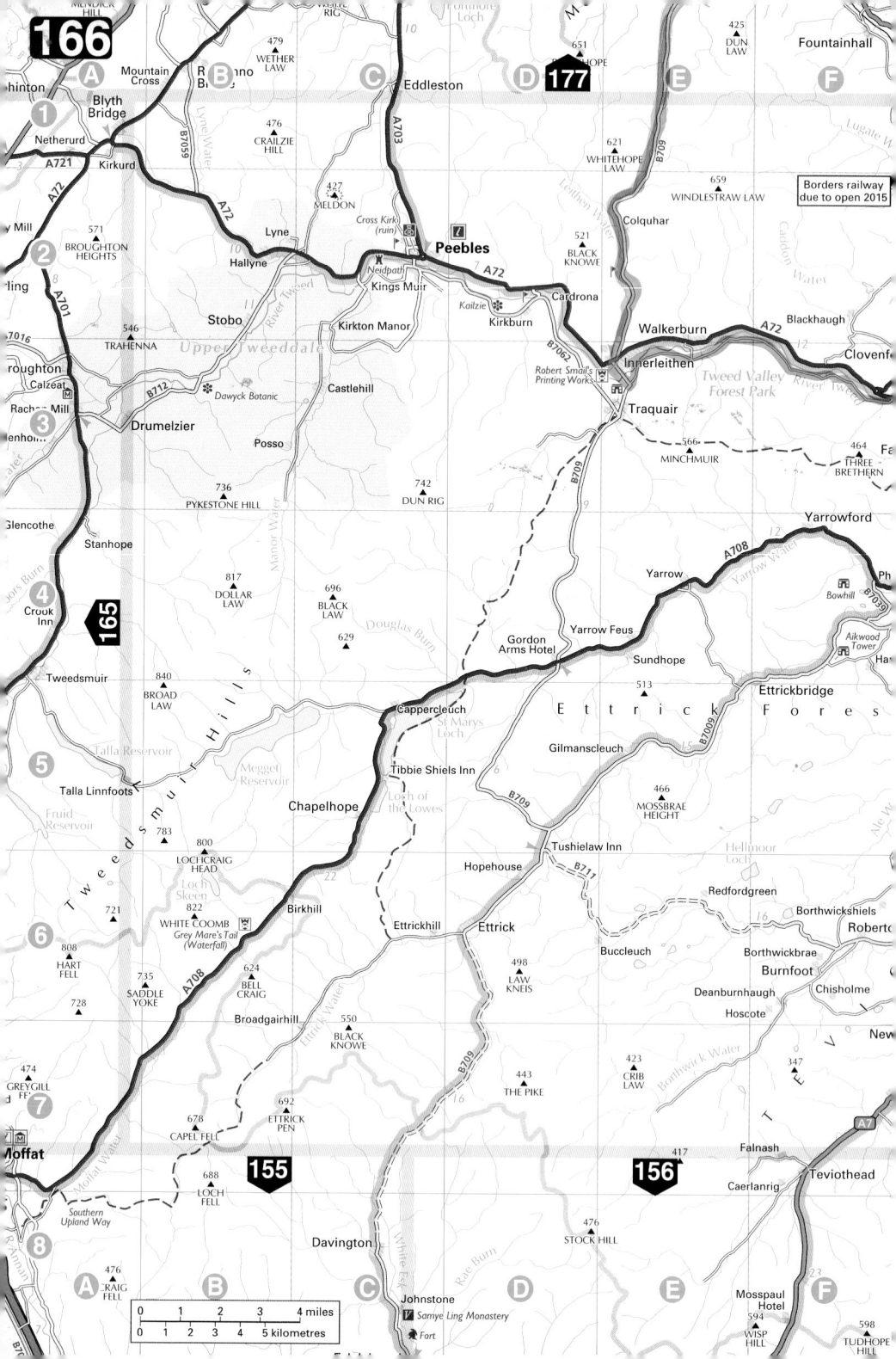

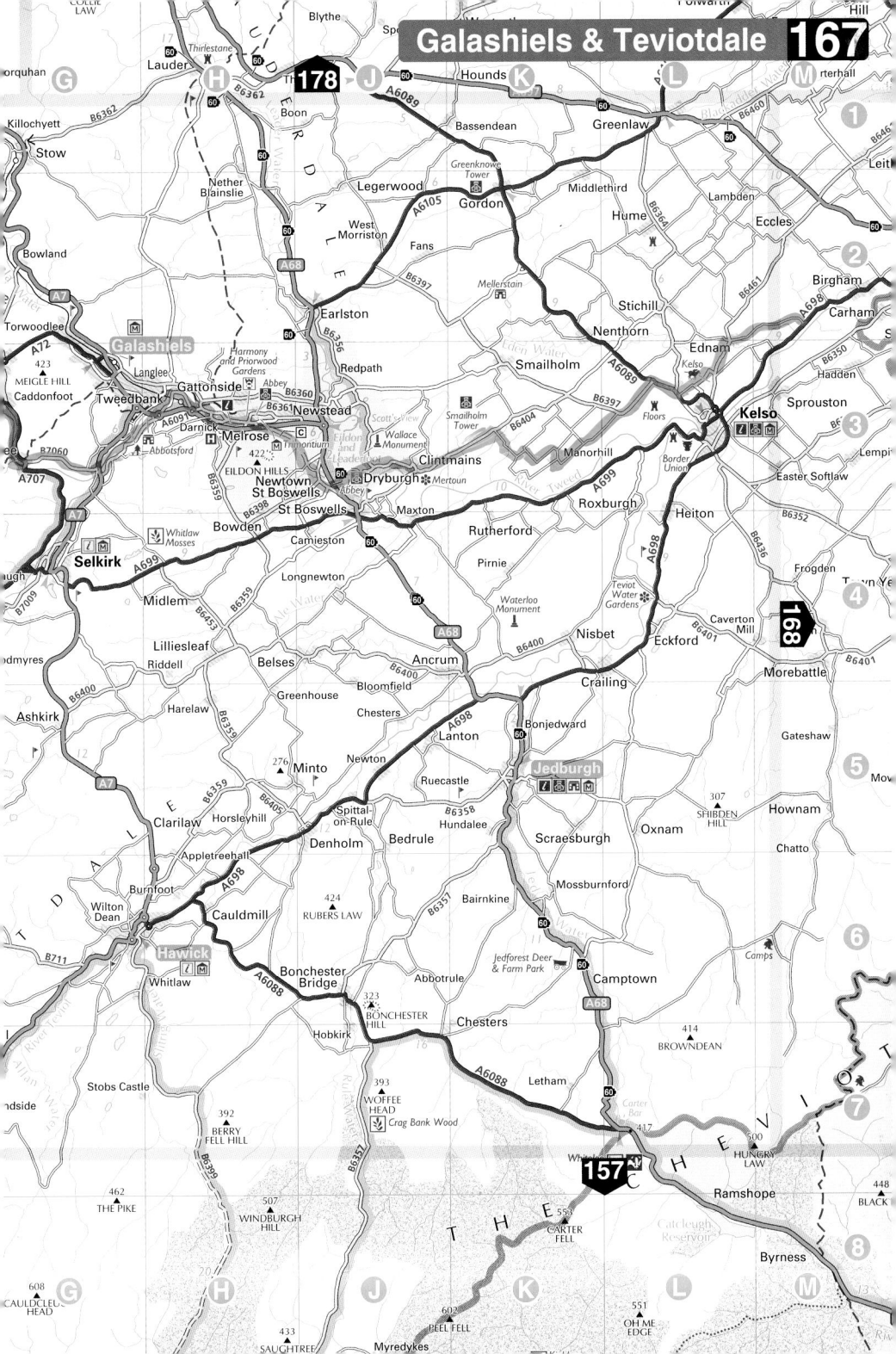

G H J K L M

1

2

3

4

5

6

7

8

CAUSEWAY
FLOODED
AT HIGH TIDE

HOLY ISLAND

eal

Holy
Island

Lindisfarne
Castle

Lindisfarne
Priory

Castle Point

Guile Point

kton

Longstone
Lighthouse

FARNE
ISLANDS

Staple
Sound

North Northumberland
Heritage Coast

Inner
Sound

Budle
Bay

Bamburgh

B1342

Belford

Bamburgh

B7340

B6349

B1341

Lucker

B6348

Warenford

Seahouses

North Sunderland

Beadnell

Swinhoe

Beadnell
Bay

Chathill

B1340

Newstead

Tughall

Ellingham

Preston

Newton-by-the-Sea

d Cattle
Park

Preston
Pele Tower

Ros
Castle

Embleton &
Newton Links

267
CATERAN
HILL

Christon
Bank

Embleton

North
Charlton

Fallodon

B5347

Embleton
Bay

ld Bewick

Dunstanburgh Castle

B6346

South
Charlton

B1339

Eglingham

Dunstan

Craster

w
ick

B6341

Rock

Stamford

Beanley

Rennington

Howick
Hall

Howick

burn

Cullernose Point

B6346

Longhoughton

Denwick

Boulmer

Bolton

River Aln

Alnwick

Séaton Point

B6341

Lesbury

ham

Alnmouth

Castle

Alnmouth
Bay

Edlingham

A1

A1068

Shilbottle

260
GLANTLEES
HILL

Newton-on-
the-Moor

Warkworth Castle
& Hermitage

Warkworth

159

B6341

Amble

Coquet Island

Swarland

Guyzance

Gloster Hill

gside
ouse

Acklington

High
Hauxley

amlington

30

70

Felton

Togston

Pauperhaugh

East
Thirston

Broomhill

B6344

Swarland

South
Broomhill

West
Thirston

B1330

Red Row

Druridge Bay

A B C D E F

1

2

3

Dubh Eilea

ISLAY

Nave Island

Ardnave
Point

Gortanta
Point

4

Ton Mhòr

Kilnave

Sanaigmore

Eilean Mòr

Loch
Gorr

Rudha Lamanais

Lecht Gruinart

RSPB

Loch Gruinart

Saligo Bay

B8018

B8017

Gleann Mòr

Gruinart

5

Loch
Gorm

Coul Point

B8018

Sunderland

A847

Kilchoman

Machir
Bay

6

Bruichladdich

Loch
Indaal

Kilchiaran Bay

R H I N N S   O F   I S L A Y

15

M

Bowmore

Port
Charlotte

River Lay

231
▲
BEINN TART A'MHILL

Dush R

A846

Lossit Bay

Nereabolls

7

Rudha na
Faing

A847

Laggan

Islay

Portnahaven

Port Wemyss

Orsay

Bay

RHINNS
POINT

8

Rudha Mòr

Kintra

A B C D E 160 F

165
▲
MAOL BU

THE O

Lower

Risabus

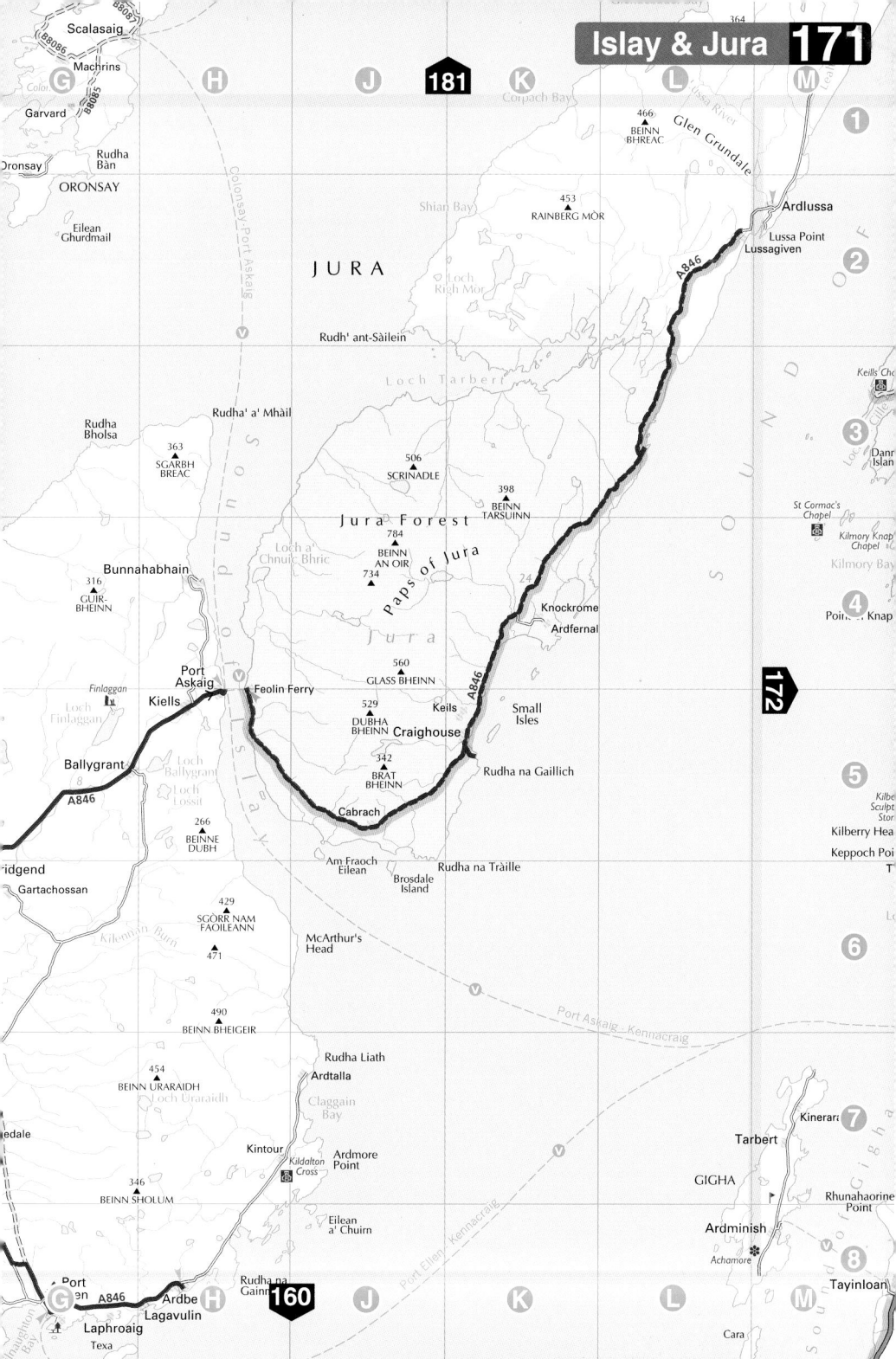

B8087

Scalasaig

Machrins

G

Garvard

Colon

Oronsay

Rudha
Bàn

ORONSAY

Eilean
Ghurdmail

H

Colonsay–Port Askaig

J

181

K

L

364

466
BEINN
BHREAC

Glen Grundale

Lussa River

SOUND

M

1

453
RAINBERG MÒR

Shian Bay

JURA

Corpach Bay

A846

Ardlussa

Lussa Point
Lussagiven

2

Rudh' ant-Sàilein

Loch
Righ Mòr

Keills' Cho

Rudha
Bholsa

Rudha 'a' Mhàil

Loch Tarbert

363
SGARBH
BREAC

506
SCRINADLE

398
BEINN
TARSUINN

St Cormac's
Chapel

Danr
Islan

3

Jura Forest

784
BEINN
AN OIR

734

Paps of Jura

24

Kilmory Knap
Chapel

Kilmory Bay

Bunnahabhain

316
GUIR-
BHEINN

Jura

Knockrome
Ardfernal

Poin , Knap

4

Port
Askaig

Finlaggan

Kiells

Loch
Finlaggan

Feolin Ferry

Loch
Ballygrant

Loch
Lossit

560
GLASS BHEINN

529
DUBHA
BHEINN

Keils

Craighouse

Small
Isles

A846

172

Kilbe
Sculpt
Stor

Kilberry Hea

Keppoch Poi
T

5

Ballygrant

A846

266
BEINNE
DUBH

342
BRAT
BHEINN

Cabrach

Rudha na Gaillich

dgend

Gartachossan

Kilennan Burn

429
SGÒRR NAM
FAOILEANN

471

Am Fraoch
Eilean

Brosdale
Island

Rudha na Tràille

6

490
BEINN BHEIGEIR

McArthur's
Head

Port Askaig – Kennacraig

454
BEINN URARAIDH

Loch Uraraidh

Rudha Liath

Ardtalla

Claggain
Bay

Kintour

Kildalton
Cross

Ardmore
Point

Tarbert

GIGHA

Kinerara

Rhunahaorine
Point

7

edale

346
BEINN SHOLUM

Eilean
a' Chuirn

Port Ellen – Kennacraig

Ardminish

Achamore

8

Port
en

A846

Ardbe
Lagavulin

Laphroaig

Texa

H

Rudha na
Gaint

160

J

K

L

Cara

Sound of Gigha

Tayinloan

M

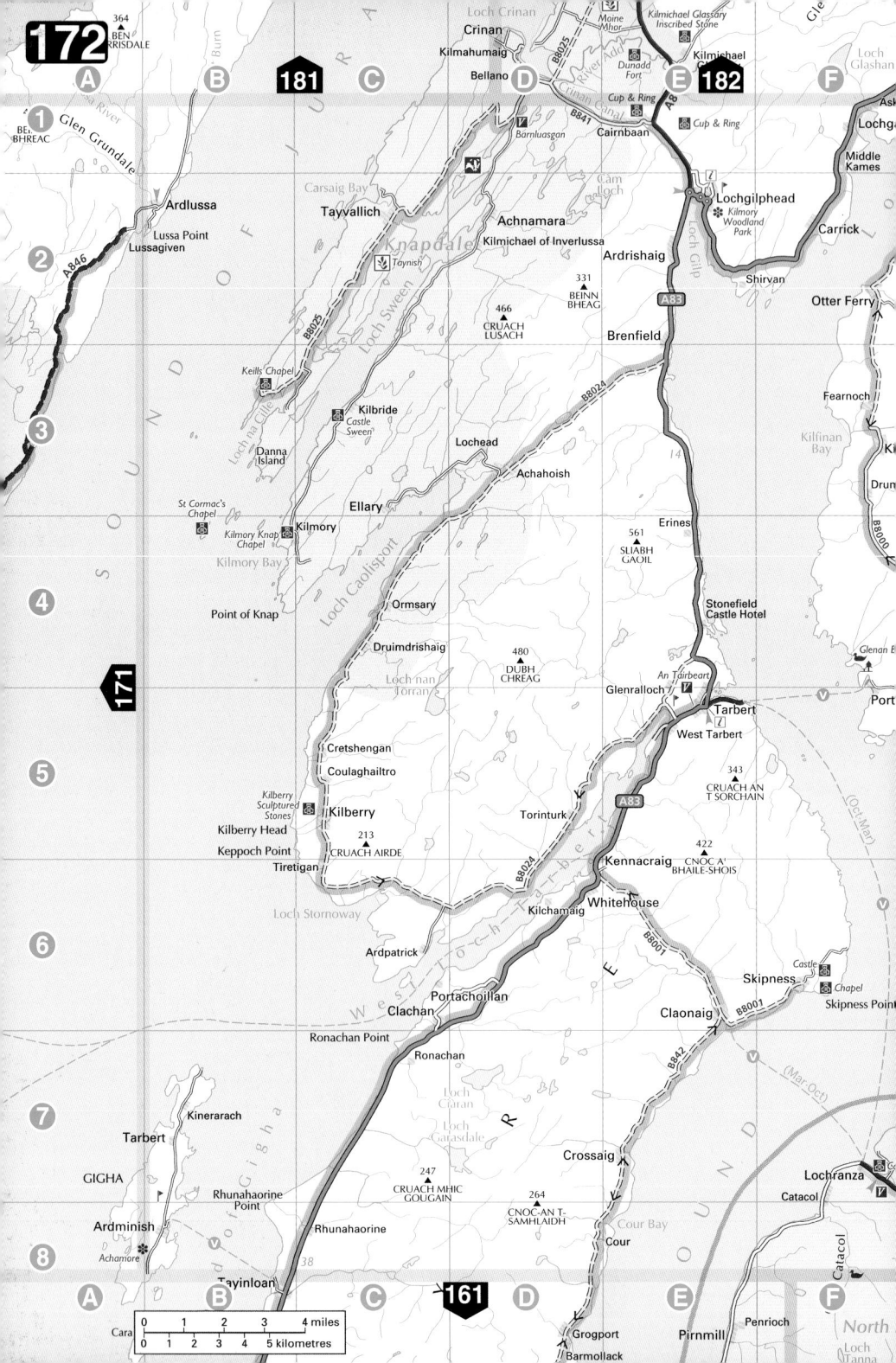

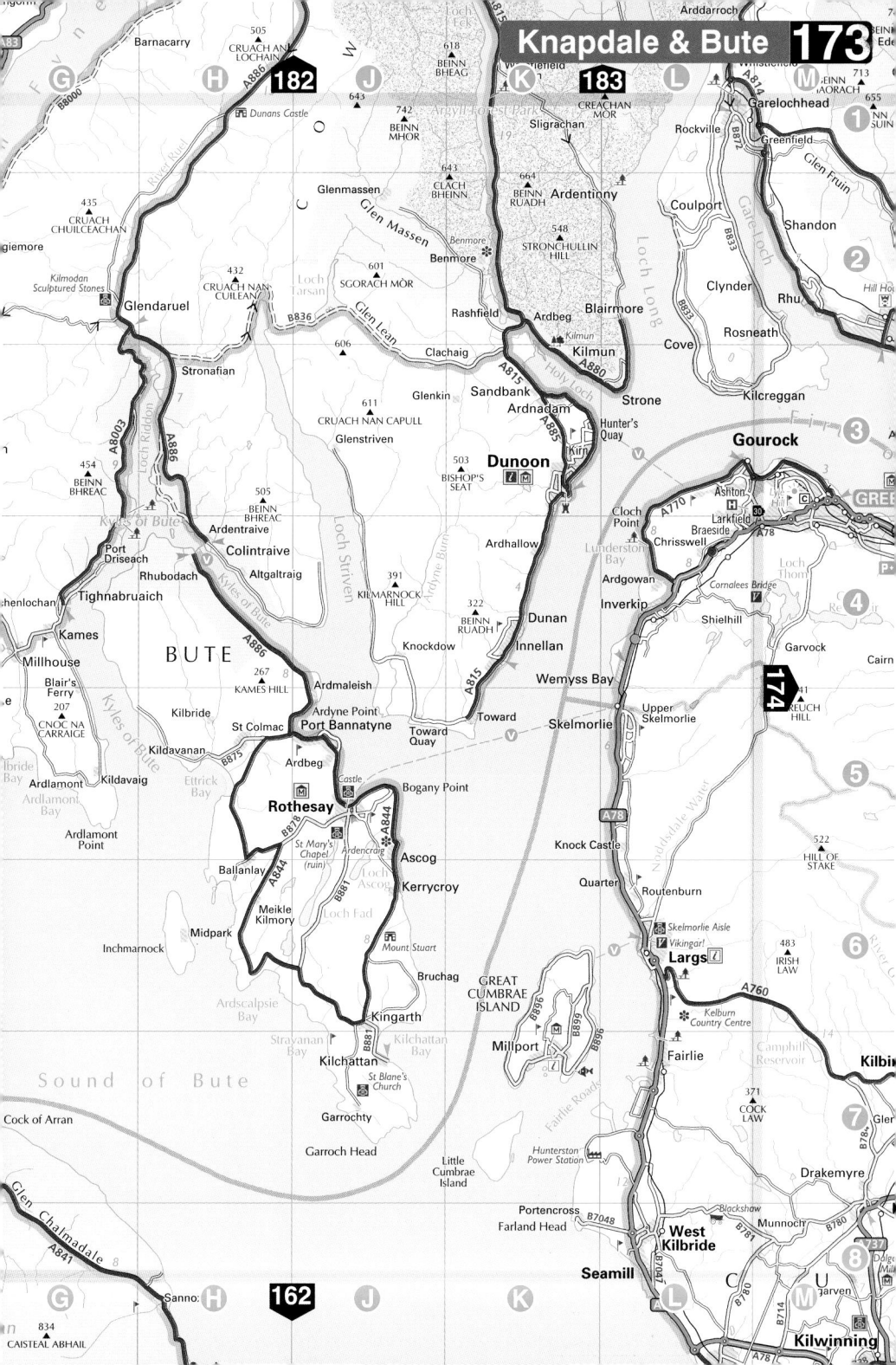

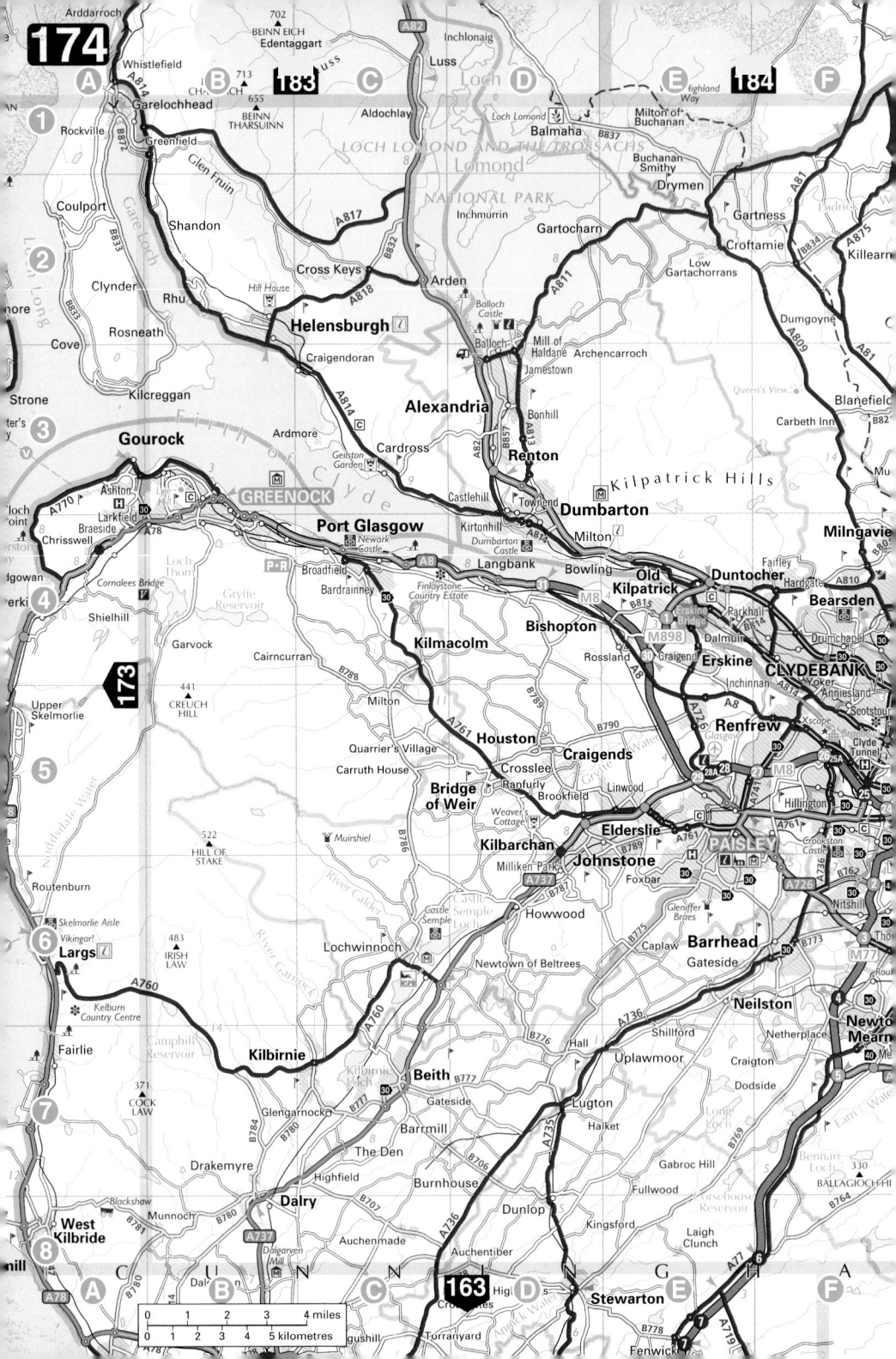

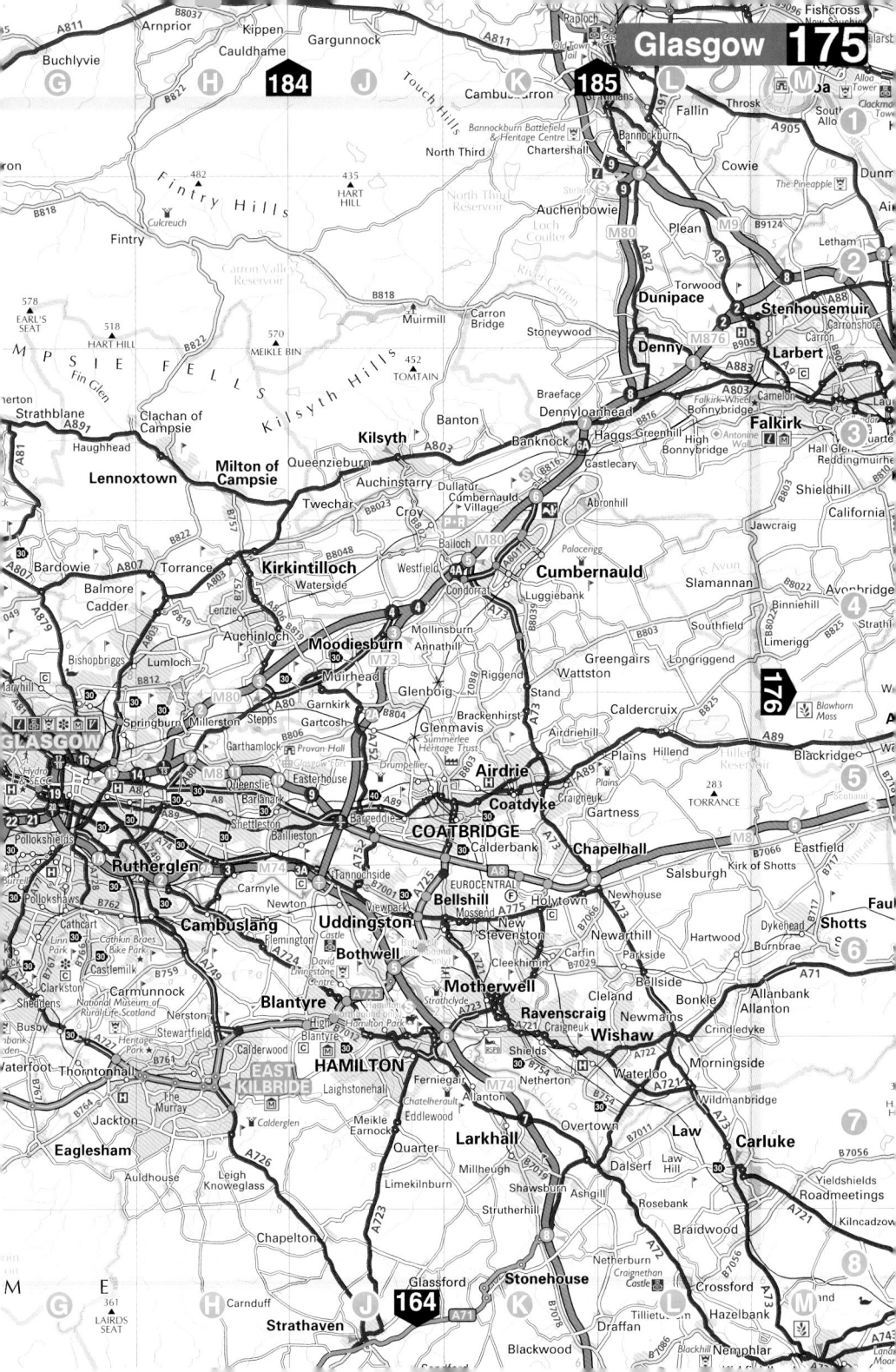

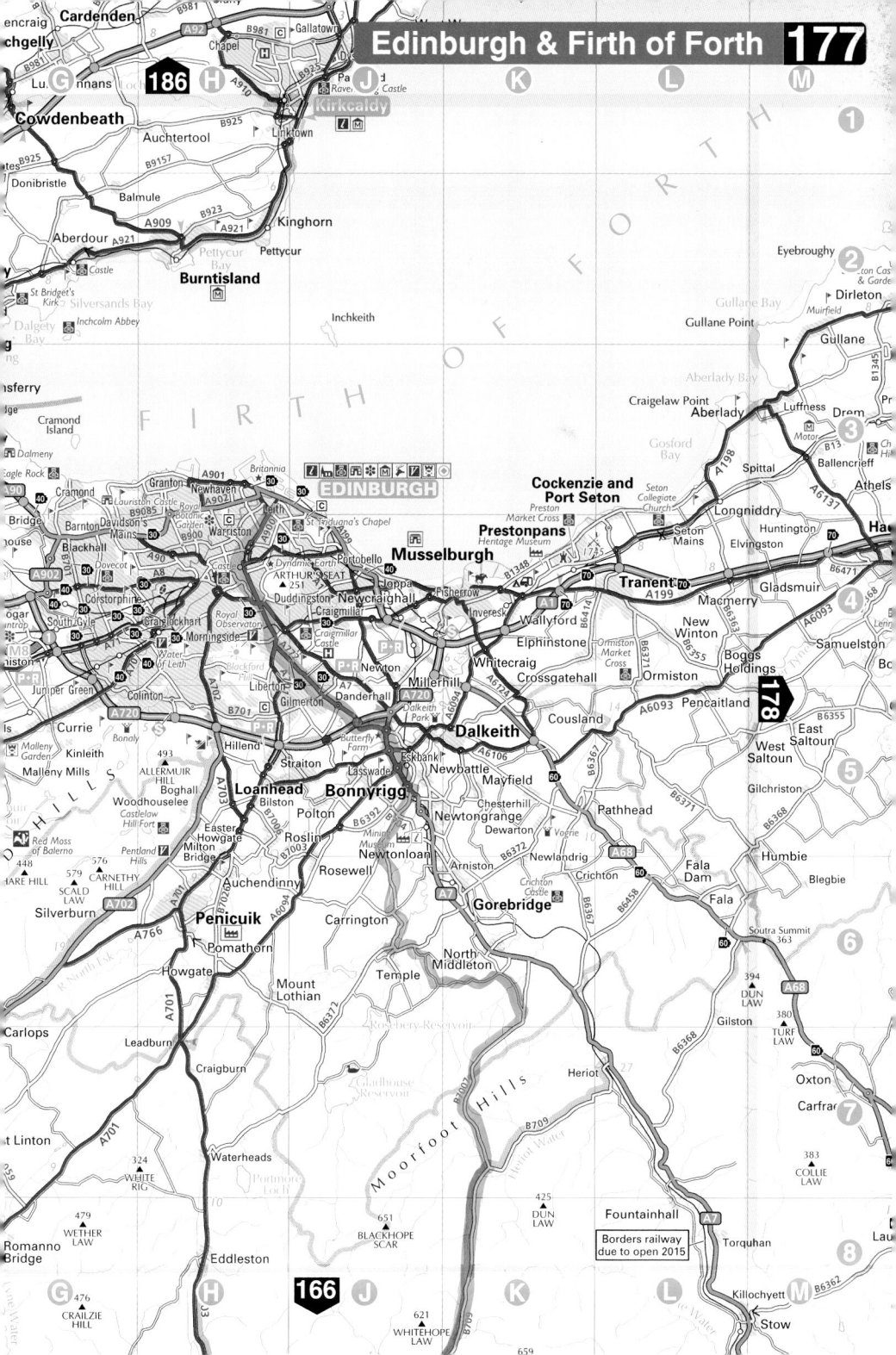

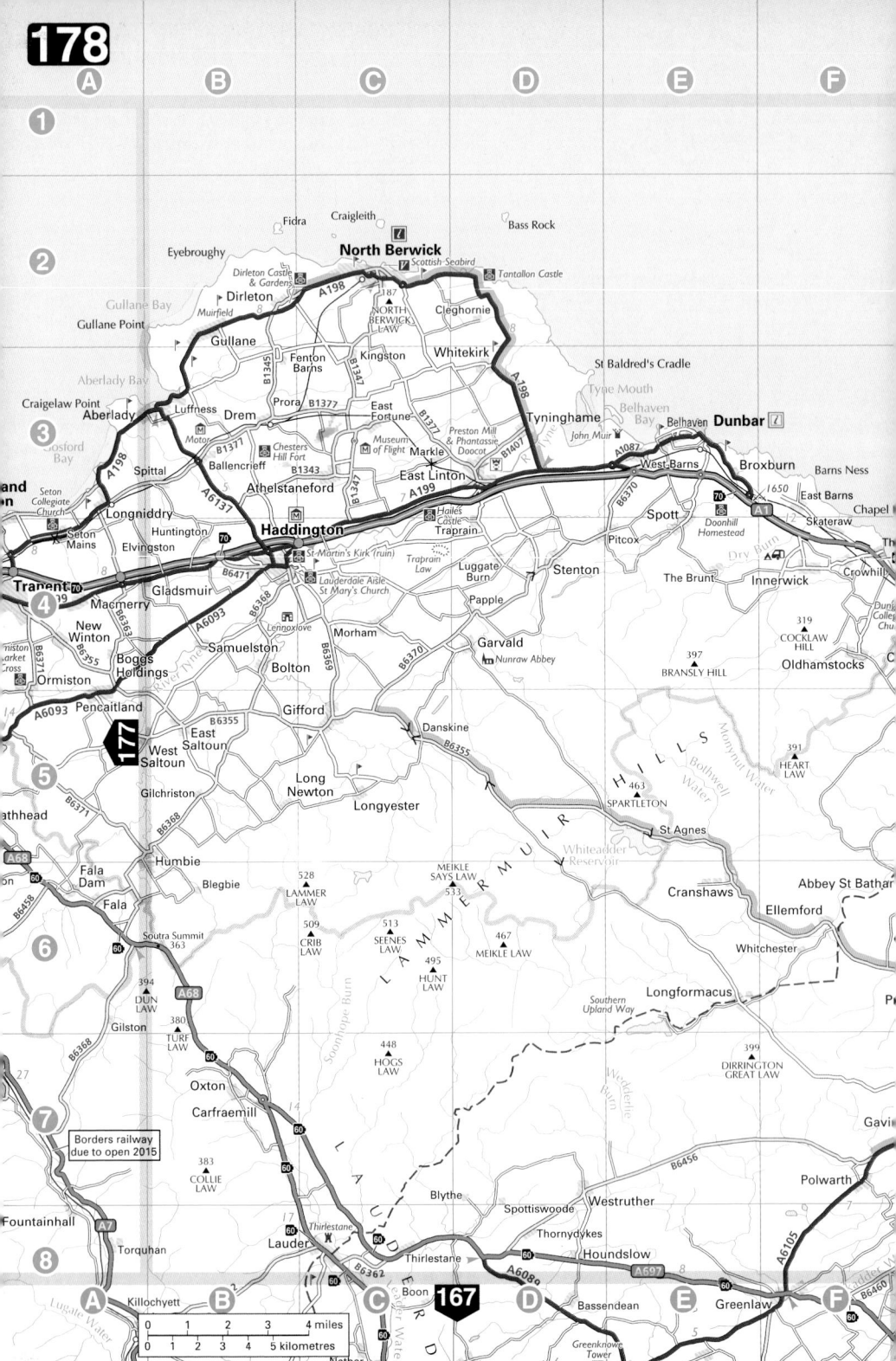

G   H   J   K   L   M

1   2   3   4   5   6   7   8

Reed Point Cove
Pease Bay
Siccar Point
Fast Castle Head
ST ABB'S HEAD
rnspath
A1107
Pease Dean
196
BROWN RIG
Coldingham Loch
St Abbs
Southern Upland Way
Grantshouse
Coldingham
Coldingham Bay
Butterdean
Houndwood
Heugh Head
Cairncross
Eyemouth
262
HORSELEY HILL
Reston
Burnmouth
uixwood
Ayton
B6438
Auchencrow
Marygold
Lamberton
Lintlaw
Preston
Cumledge
Edrom Church
Chirnside
Foulden
Marshall Meadows Bay
ehill
B6355
Chirnsidebridge
North Northumberland Heritage Coast
Edrom
Manderston
Broadhaugh
Edington
Foulden Tithe Barn
1333
Allanton
Hutton
A6105
Berwick-upon-Tweed
Castle
Duns
A6105
Paxton
Town Ramparts
Barracks
Blackadder
B6461
Tweedmouth
Whitsome
Hilton
Paxton
Spittal
Nisbet Hill
Sinclair's Hill
Huds Head
Horndean
Horncliffe
Scremerston
Murton
Swinton
Ladykirk
Castle
Norham
Thornton
A1
harterhall
Upsettlington
168
Cheswick
Simprim
Ancroft
Leitholm
Haggerston

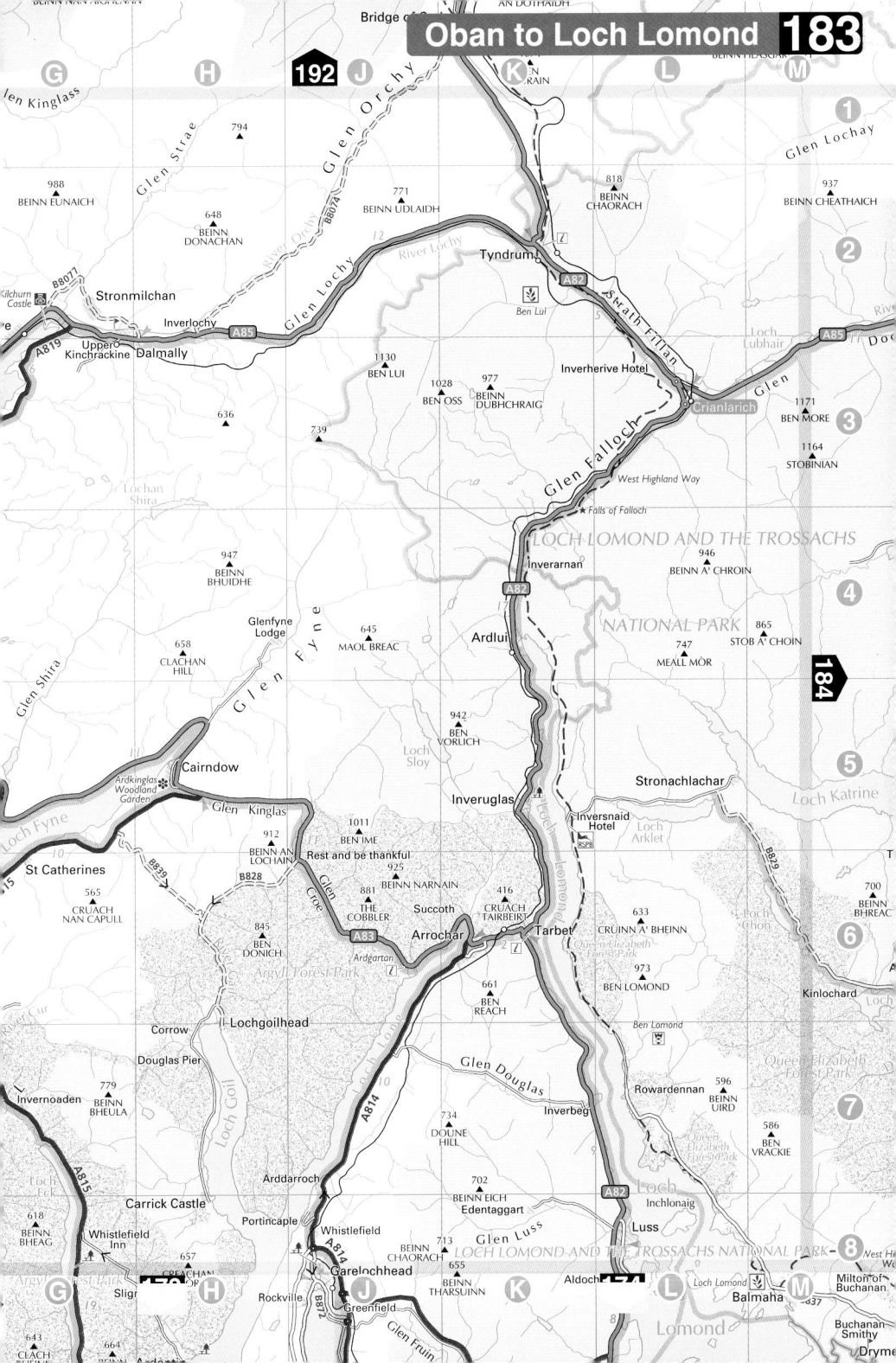

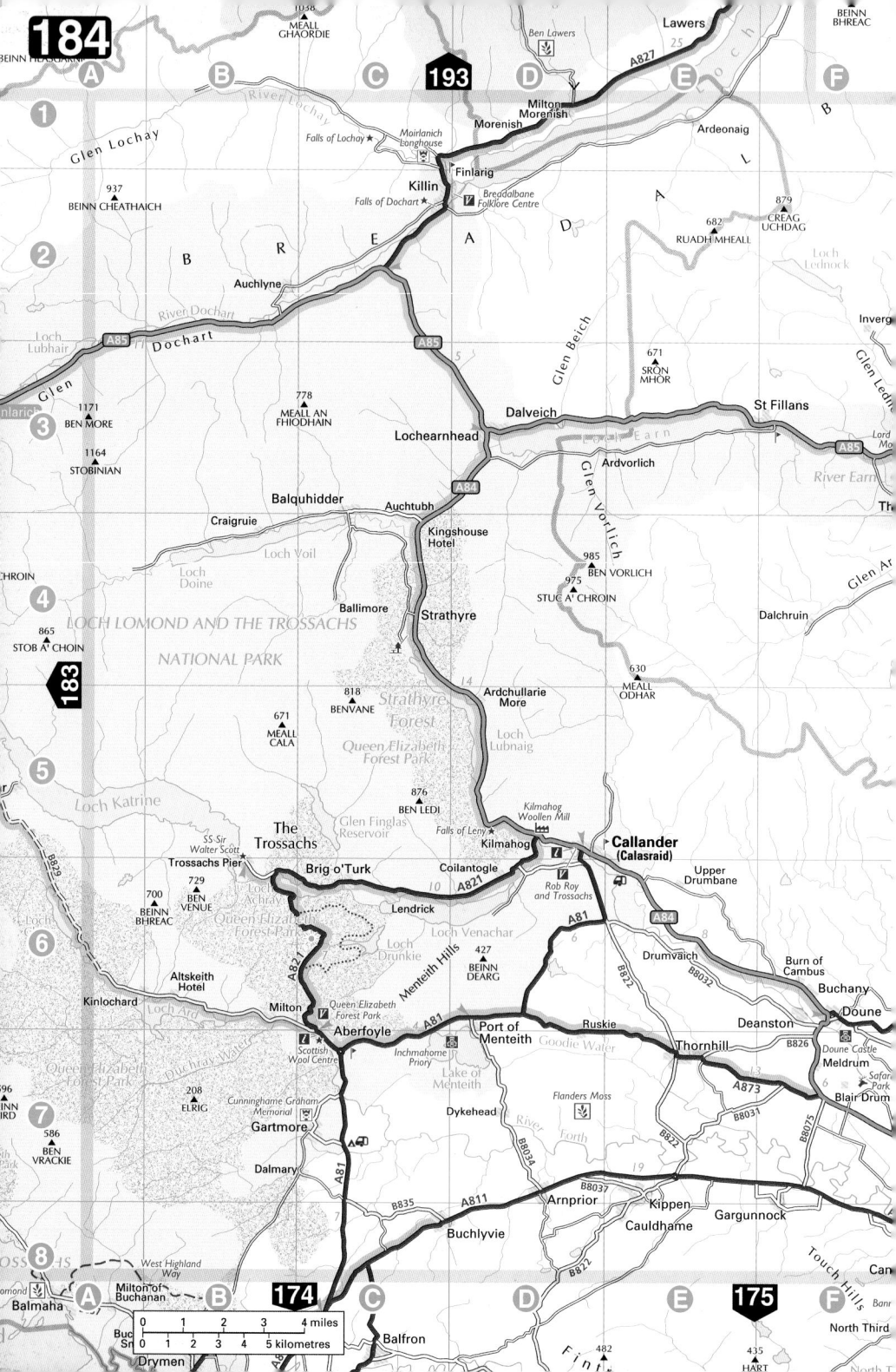

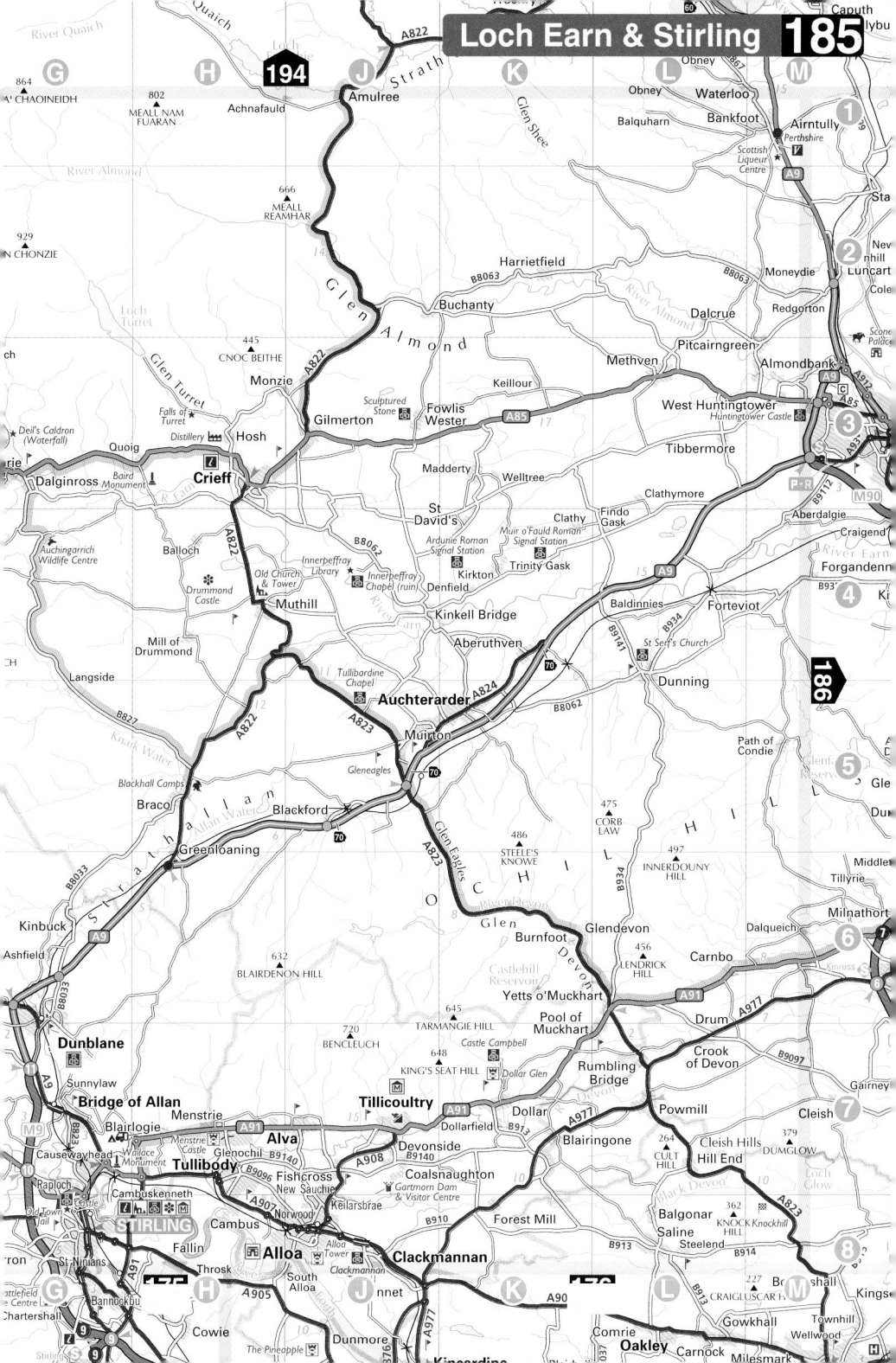

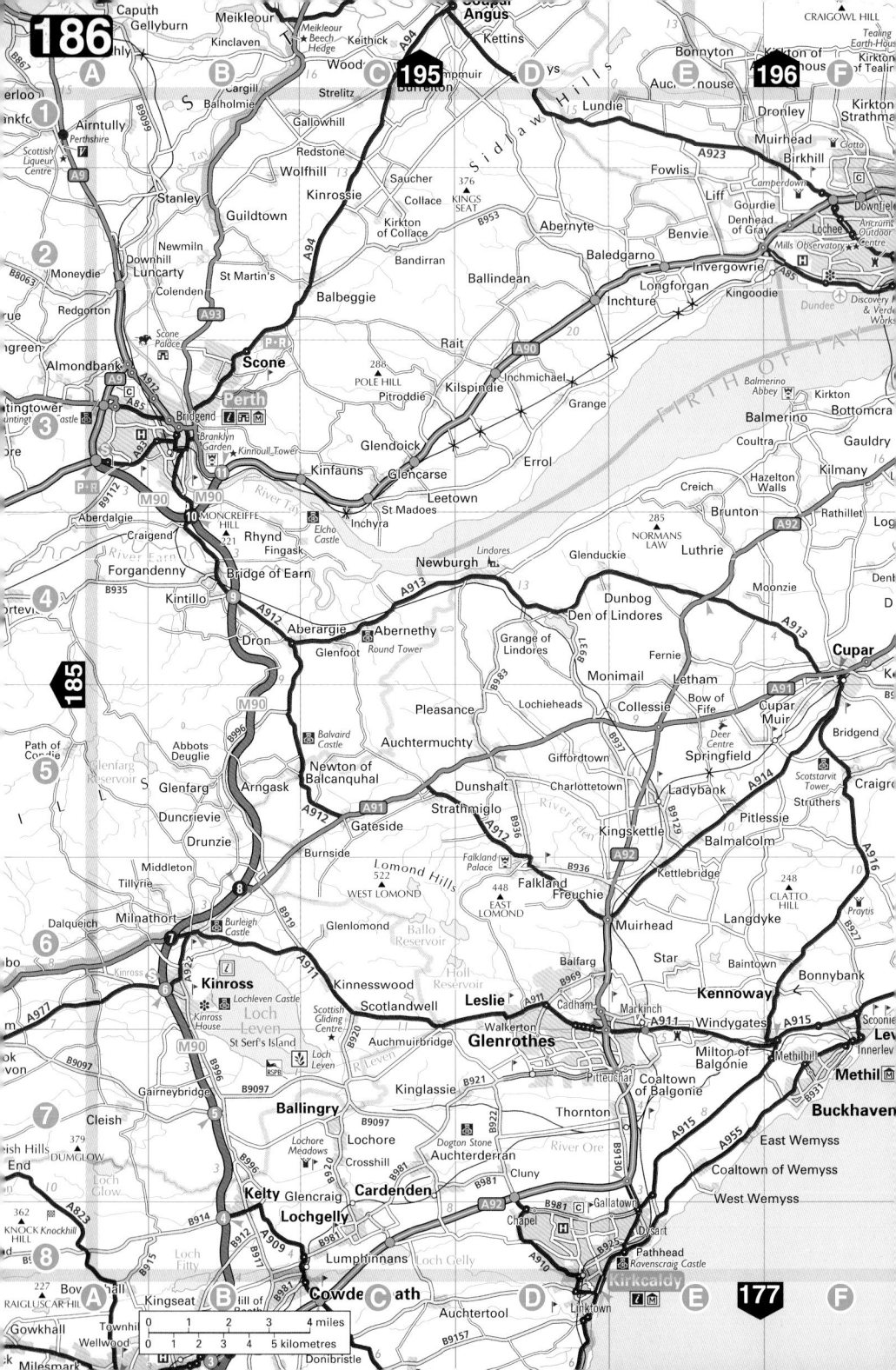

Petterden
Todhills
Crombie
Monikie
Bonnington
Arbirloy
Arbroath

CARROT HILL
Monikie
B9128

N ging
Kirkton of Monikie
A92

Wellban.
B961
196
Muirdr

Newbigging
Carlungie Earth-House
Upper Victoria
East Haven

Kellas
Ardestie Earth-House
Panbride

Murroes
B961
Barry
West Haven

Whitfield
Baldovie
B962
Carnoustie

Douglas and Angus
A92
A930
Carnoustie

A90
Barnhills
B961

Claypotts Castle
Monifieth

3959
North Carr ghtship
BUDDON NESS

DUNDEE
Broughty Ferry
Broughty Castle

A92 Tay Bridge
Tayport
Tentsmuir Point

te rn'
Newport-on-Tay
B945

A994
★ Scottish National Golf Centre
Tentsmuir Point

nit
ST ANDREWS BAY

A919
Leuchars
RAF Leuchars

Balmullo
A914

Guardbridge
St Andrews

Kincaple
A91
Castle
St Andrews

Strathkinness
Botanic Garden
Brownhills

B939
Craigtoun
A917
Boarhills

Blebocraigs
A915

Denhead
Dunino
Kingsbarns

Pitscottie
Cameron Reservoir
Balcomie Links

res
Baldinnie
B940
Kingsmuir
FIFE NESS

Peat Inn
Radernie
B940
★ Scotland's Secret Bunker
Crail

New Gilston
B941
Lathones
Lochty

Woodside
Largoward
Carnbee
Easter Pitkierie

A915
Kellie Castle
B9171
Wester Pitkierie
B9131
A917
Kilrenny

Upper Largo
Arncroach
B9171
Newton of Balcormo
Cellardyke

Colinsburgh
B942
Fisheries
Anstruther

Lower Largo
Drumeldrie
B941
B942
Kilconquhar
Pittenweem

Largo Bay
A917
St Monans

Earlsferry
Elie
Isle of May

Ⓐ   Ⓑ   Ⓒ   Ⓓ   Ⓔ   Ⓕ

❶

❷

❸

❹

Arnabo
Grishipoll
Clabhach   Loch Cliad
Hogh Bay   Ballyhaugh   Ar

❺   Bagh a Chaisteil
(Castlebay)   Totronald
         Feall   Coll   Acha
         Bay   Arileod
             Uig
       (Mar Og)   Calgary Point   Rudha
                Crossapoll   Fàsachd
           Gunna   Bay

❻   Rudha Port   Clachan   Caoles
          Bhiosd   Mor   Balephetrish   Rudha Dubh
         Haugh   Loch   Bay   B8068   Ruaig
         Bay   Bhasapoll   B8069
       Ballevullin   Cornoigmore   Kenovay   Gott
      Kilkenneth   Tiree   Bay

❼   Moss   B8068   B8065   Scarinish
     Middleton   Heylipoll
    Barrapoll   B8065   Crossapoll   TIREE
      Loch a   Hynish Bay
      Phuil   B8067   Balemartine
    Rinn   Mannel
   Thorbhais   Balephuil
        Bay   Hynish

❽

Ⓐ   Ⓑ   Ⓒ   Ⓓ   Ⓔ   Ⓕ

| 0 | 1 | 2 | 3 | 4 miles |
| 0 | 1 | 2 | 3 | 4 | 5 kilometres |

G   H   J   K   L   M

1

2

Eilean nan Each

MUCK

Port Mor

Kildonnan

393

c L tail

Ockle Point

R D

3

Sanna Point

Sanna Bay

Sanna Bay

Portuairk

Achnaha

Kilmory

Branault

Ockle

Ardnamurchan Point

Achosnich

436
MEALL NAN CON

ARDNAMU

B8007

4

Bagh a Chasteil
(Castlebay)
Loch Baghasdail
(Lochboisdale)

342
BEINN NA SEILG

Kilchoan

Ormsaigmore

Mingary

527
BEN HIANT

Ardslignish

Eilean Mòr

Rudha Mòr

Rudha Sgor-innis

Bousd   Sorisdale

B8072

COLL

Coll - Oban

Eilean Ornsay

Ardmore Point

Sorne Point

Quinish Point

Glengorm Castle

Tobermory

190

Auliston Point

Or

5

Caliach Point

292
'S AIRDE BEINN

Calve Island

Drim

6

Dervaig

Achnadrish House

Calgary

B8073

Calgary Bay

Ensay

342
CÀRN MÒR

ISLE
OF
MULL

444
SPEINNE MÒR

A848

Glen Aros

Aro

7

Treshnish Point

Rudh' a' Chaoil

Burg

Fladda

Fanmore

390
CNOC AN DÀ CHINN

Ballygown

Eas Fors (Waterfall)

333
BEINN NAN CÀRN

Glenaros House

Killiechronan

Gruline

B8035

8

Lunga

Gometra

ULVA

Oskamull

B8073

Macquarie Mausoleum

TRESHNISH ISLES

Bac Mòr or Dutchmans Cap

Bac Beag

Little Colonsay

Loch Tuath

Loch na Keal, Isle of Mull

Eorsa

Loch na Keal

591
BEINN A' GH

G   H   J   K   L   M

180

Staffa
Fingal's Cave

Inch neth
Inchkenne apel
(ruin)

Balnahard

966

70

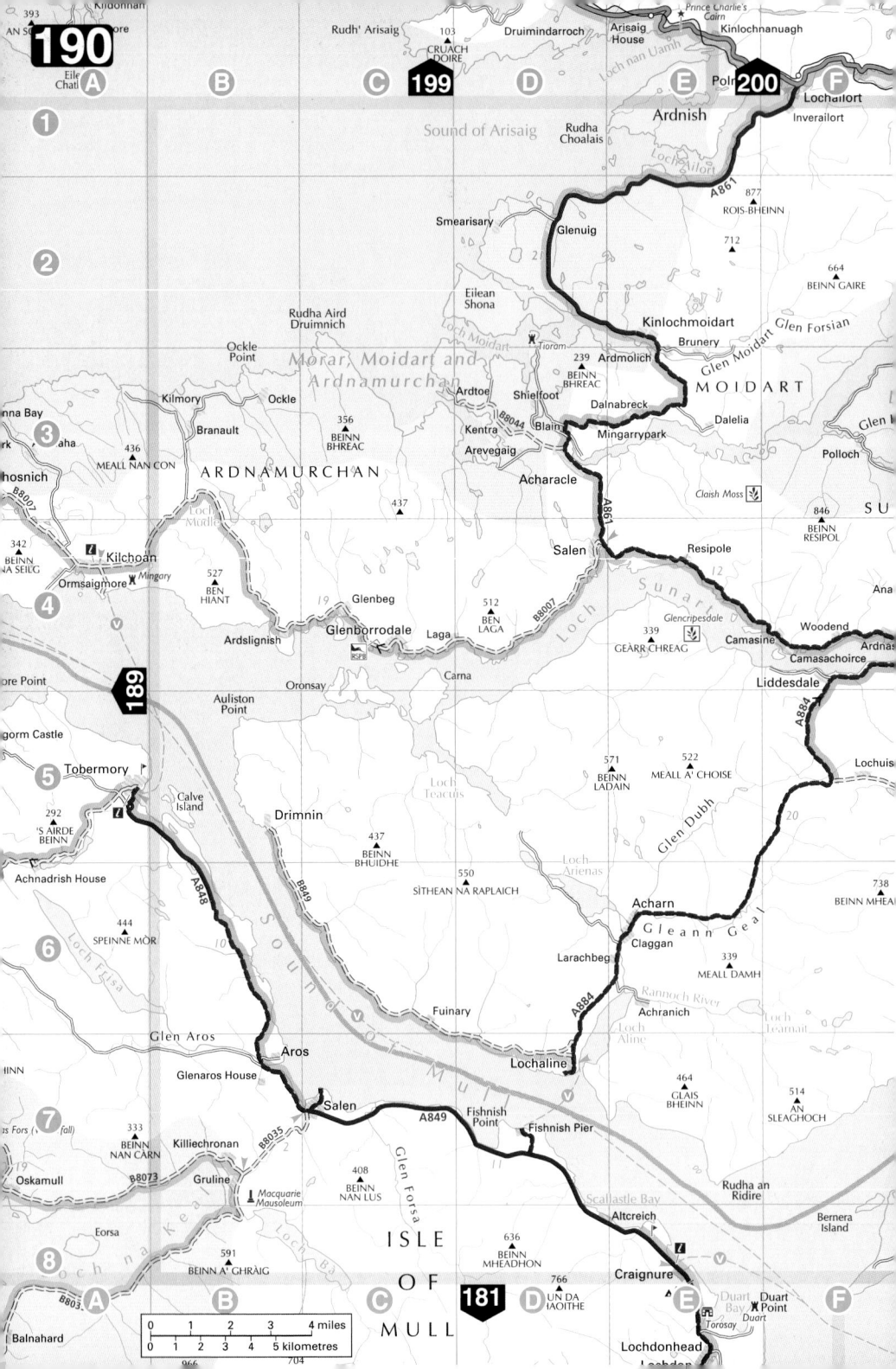

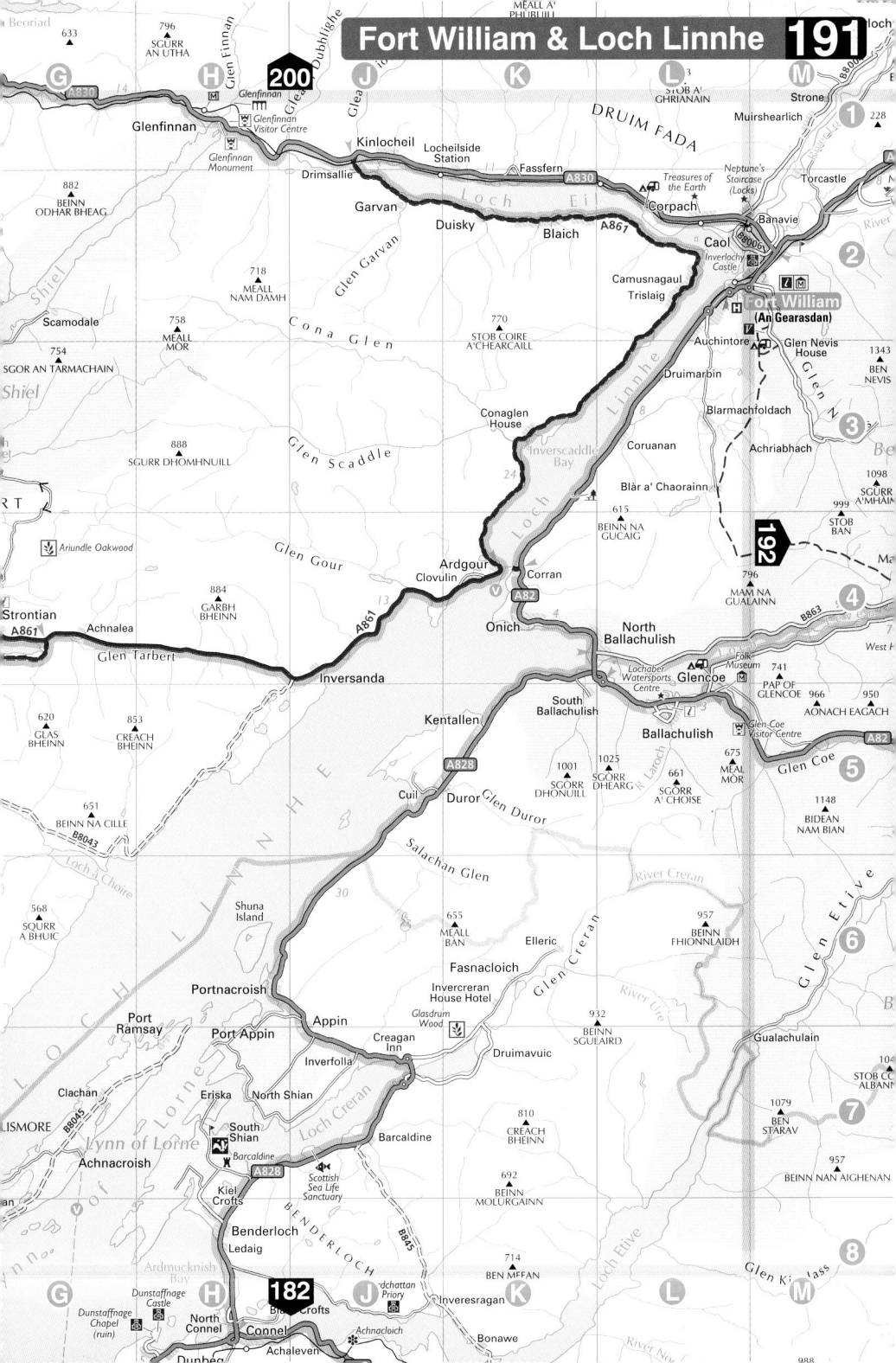

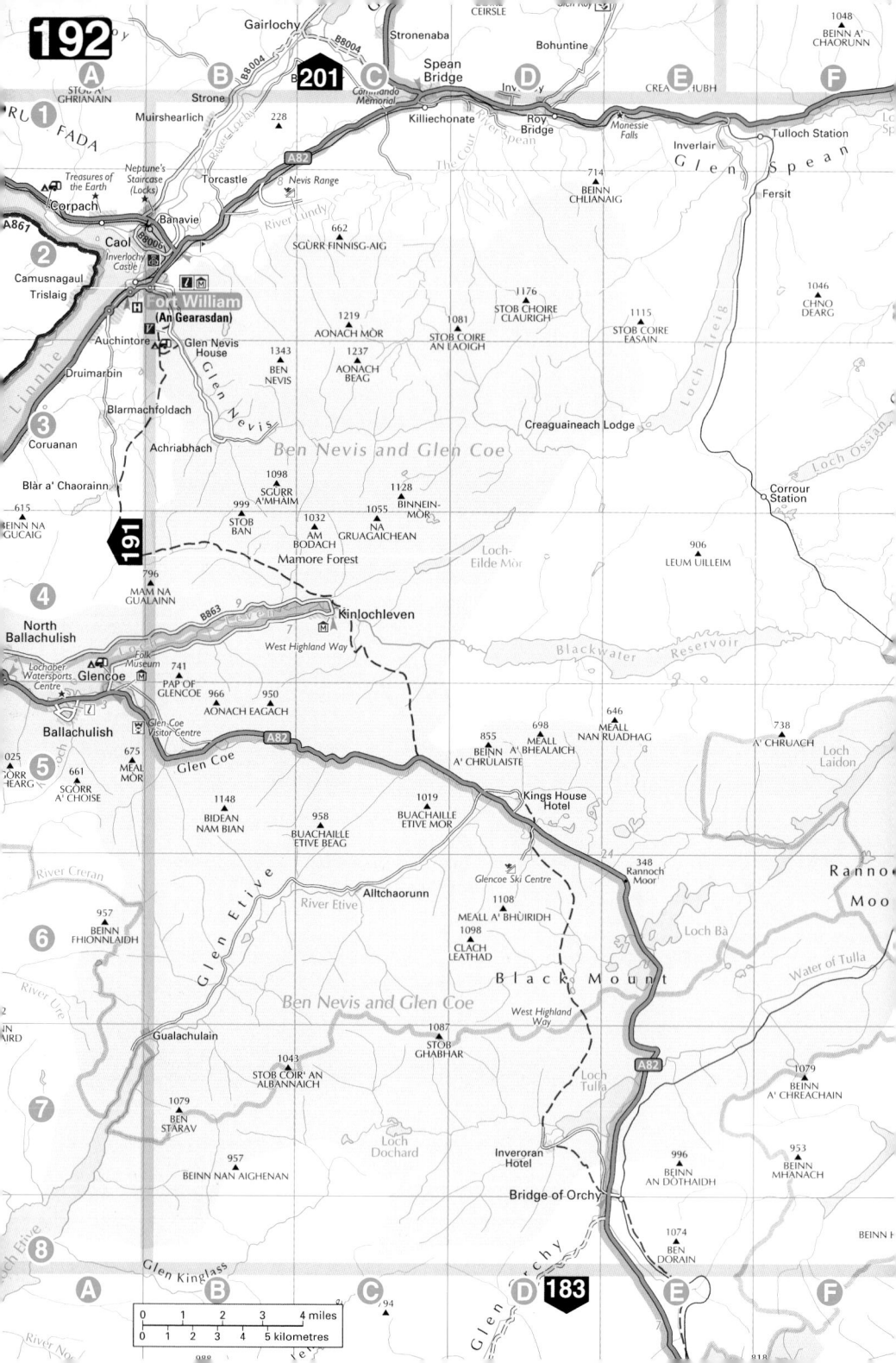

202

G Moy

H

J

K

L

M

747 BINNEIN SHUAS

1049 GEAL CHÀRN

896 MEALL CRUAIDH

769 CREAGAN MÒR

94 CÀRN NA CAIM

Loch an Dù...

1

Loch Pattack

1088 BEINN A' CHLACHAIR

1034 CÀRN DEARG

975 A' MHARCONAICH

459 Drumochter Summit

926 GLAS MHÉALL MÒR

Loch Ericht

2

ch lbin

1101 BEINN EIBHINN

1008 BEINN UDLAMAIN

991 SGAIRNEACH MHOR

Dalnaspidal

1145 BEN ALDER

Loch Garry

Glen Garry

Dalnacardoch

3

844 MEALL A' BHEALAICH

952 SGÒR GAIBHRE

626 SRON A CHLAONAIDH

841 BEINN MHOLACH

Loch Con

Loch Errochty

Trinafour

B847

4

864 BEINN PHARIAGAIN

892 BEINN A' CHUALLAICH

511 TORR DUBH

194

B846

Rannoch Station

R Ericht

Bridge of Ericht

Killichonan

16

Loch Rannoch

Kinloch Rannoch

Drumchastle

Dunalastair

R Tummel

Tummel Bridge

Dunan B846

Finnart

Inverhadden

Tempar

Dunalastair Water

Loch Eigheach

Bridge of Gaur

Carie

5

Camghouran

Tay Forest Park

1081 SCHIEHALLION

Glengoulandie Deer Park

6

Loch Rannoch and Glen Lyon

745 MEALL A' MHUIC

1042 CÀRN MAIRG

931 MEALL BUIDHE

860 CAM CHREAG

824 BEINN DEARG

1027 CÀRN GORM

Ke... urn

Loch an Daimh

Glen Lyon

River Lyon

Fortingall

Kenmore

Bridge of Balgie

Fearnan

Acharn

780 MEALL LUAIDHE

924 MEALL A' CHOIRE LEITH

1116 MEALL GARBH

1000 MEALL GREIGH

7

...ann... ...tre

Loch Lyon

908 BEINN NAN OIGHREAG

1214 BEN LAWERS

Leckbuie

713 BEINN BHREAC

1038 MEALL GHAORDIE

Lochan na Làirige

Lawers

A827

25

GARNICH

Ben Lawers

184

Milton Morenish

8

G Glen Lochay

H Glen Lochay

J Morenish Longhouse

Falls of Lochay ★

K ...renish

Finlarig

River Lochay

L Arde...g

M SRÒN A'

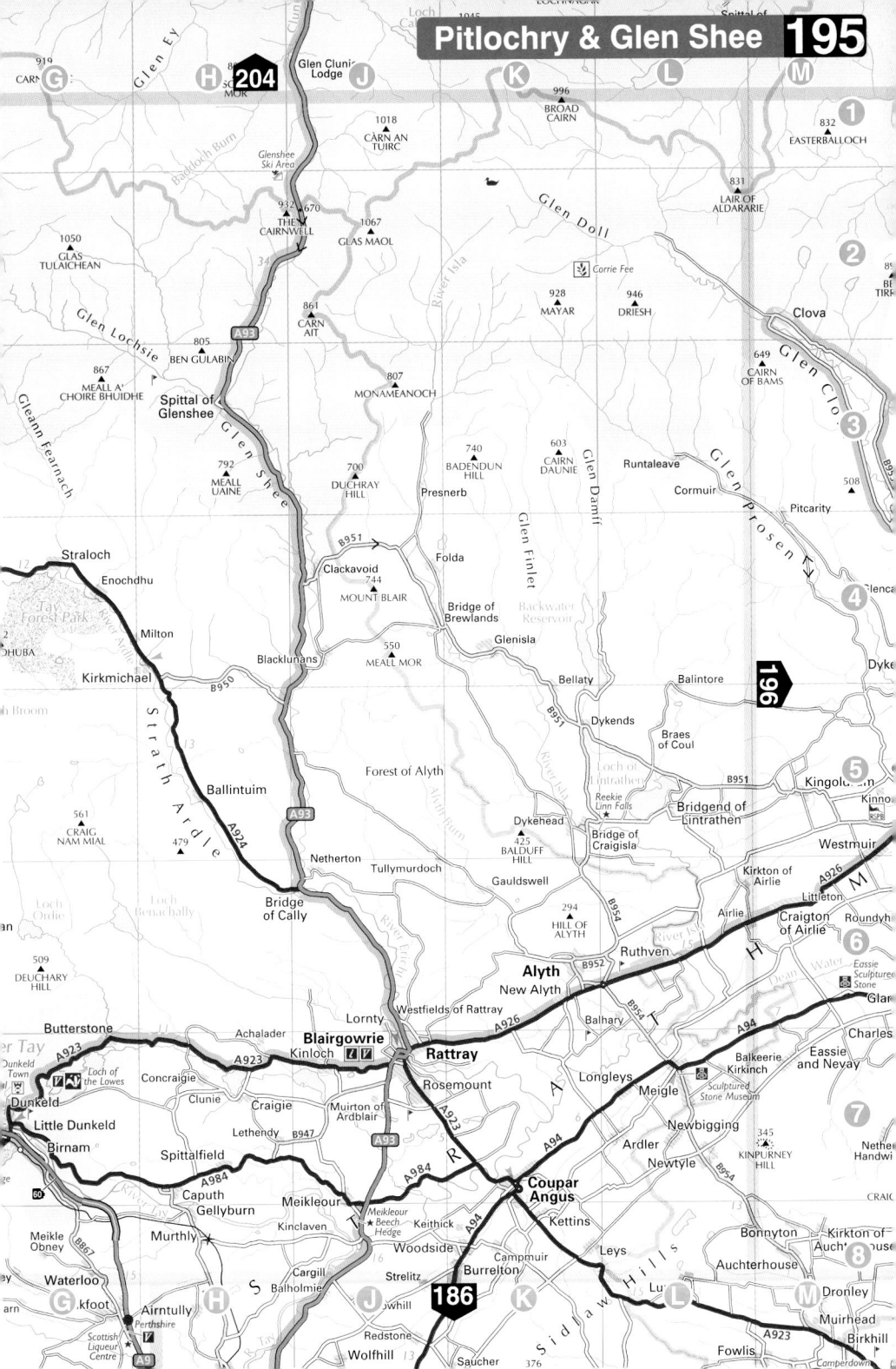

204

196

186

G · H · J · K · L · M

1
EASTERBALLOCH

2

3

4

5

6

7

8

Glen Ey
Glen Clunie Lodge
CARN

919
CARN

Glen Doll

1045

Spittal of

1018
CARN AN TUIRC

996
BROAD CAIRN

832
EASTERBALLOCH

831
LAIR OF ALDARARIE

Glenshee Ski Area

932 670
THE CAIRNWELL

1067
GLAS MAOL

Corrie Fee

928
MAYAR

946
DRIESH

Clova

649
CAIRN OF BAMS

Glen Clo

1050
GLAS TULAICHEAN

861
CARN AIT

805
BEN GULABIN

Glen Lochsie

807
MONAMEANOCH

603
CAIRN DAUNIE

Glen Damff

Runtaleave

Cormuir

Glen Prosen

Pitcarity

508

Glenca

867
MEALL A' CHOIRE BHUIDHE

Spittal of Glenshee

Gleann Fearnach

792
MEALL UAINE

700
DUCHRAY HILL

740
BADENDUN HILL

Presnerb

Glen Finlet

Glen Shee

B951

Clackavoid

Folda

744
MOUNT BLAIR

Bridge of Brewlands

Bridge of Craigisla

Glenisla

Backwater Reservoir

Bellaty

Balintore

Dyke

Straloch

Enochdhu

Milton

Kirkmichael

Blacklunans

550
MEALL MOR

Dykends

Braes of Coul

B951

Tay Forest Park

DHUBA

River Ardle

Strath Ardle

B950

Ballintuim

Forest of Alyth

Loch of Lintrathen

Reekie Linn Falls

Bridgend of Lintrathen

Kingoldrum

Kinno

Westmuir

561
CRAIG NAM MIAL

479

Milk Burn

Dykehead

425
BALDUFF HILL

Kirkton of Airlie

Littleton

Craigton of Airlie

Roundyh

509
DEUCHARY HILL

A924

Netherton

Tullymurdoch

Gauldswell

294
HILL OF ALYTH

B954

Ruthven

Airlie

B952

Alyth

New Alyth

Eassie Sculptured Stone

Butterstone

Bridge of Cally

Lornty

Achalader

Westfields of Rattray

Balhary

Longleys

Meigle

Balkeerie Kirkinch

Eassie and Nevay

Glar

Charles

Loch of the Lowes

Concraigie

Blairgowrie

Kinloch

Rattray

Rosemount

Sculptured Stone Museum

Newbigging

345
KINPURNEY HILL

Nethe Handwi

Dunkeld Town

A923

A923

Clunie

Craigie

Muirton of Ardblair

Ardler

Newtyle

CRAIG

Dunkeld

Little Dunkeld

Birnam

Spittalfield

Lethendy

B947

A93

A984

Caputh

Meikleour

Kinclaven

Coupar Angus

Kettins

Campmuir

Bonnyton

Kirkton of Auch house

Meikle Obney

B867

Gellyburn

Murthly

Meikleour Beech Hedge

Keithick

Woodside

Burrelton

Leys

Auchterhouse

Waterloo

Airntully

Perthshire

Cargill

Balholmie

Strelitz

Lu

Dronley

Muirhead

Birkhill

Scottish Liqueur Centre

kfoot

A9

ghill

Redstone

Wolfhill

Saucher

Sidlaw Hills

Fowlis

A923

Camperdown

376

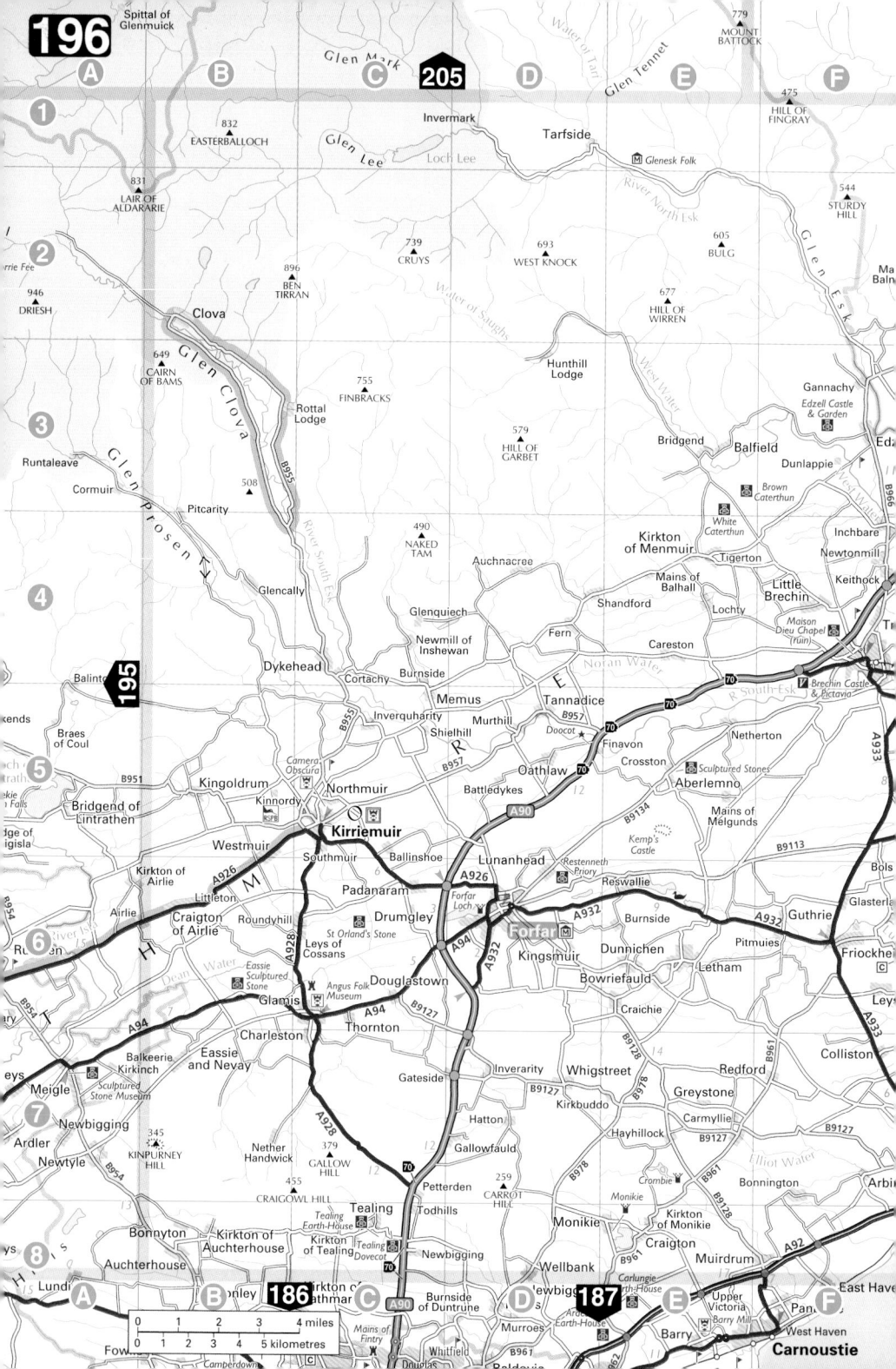

LEACHIE HILL

Goosecruives

Goyle Water

v Mill

Ta

206

G | H | J | K | L | M

1

465
GOYLE
HILL

Drumlithie

Temple
of Fiddes

Crawton

Fowlsheugh
Trelong
Bay

454
Cairn
O'Mount

Glenbervie

Mondynes

Kinneff

Catterline

Auchenblae

414
FINELLA
HILL

70

Todhead Point

2

B966

Fordoun

B967

Arbuthnott

A92

Pittarrow

Redmyre

Inverbervie

ttercairn

Mains of
Haulkerton

70

Bervie
Bay

Bogmuir

B9120

Laurencekirk

Gourdon

3

Sauchieburn

B9120

Redford

Bervie Bay

Edzell
Woods

50

B974

Dykelands

Benholm

Luthermuir

70

A937

Johnshaven

70

A90

13

River North

Marykirk

Bush

Logie Pert

70

Craigo

Lochside

St Cyrus

Milton Ness

4

Logie

Morphie

A92

Hillside

House of
Dun

Montrose Air Station

chin

Dun

Montrose

A935

Caledonian
Railway

Montrose
Basin

haughs of
Kinnaird

Barnhead

Scurdie Ness

5

Maryton

Ferryden

ell

A934

Craig

Usan

Westerton
of Rossie

Boddin Point

132
WUDDY
LAW

Braehead

Lunan

Boysack

Lunan Bay

6

Water

Inverkeilor

Red Head

13

Chapelton

Cauldcots

etham
range

A92

Marywell

7

St Vigeans

Auchmithie

Carlingheugh
Bay

The Deil's
Head

Arbroath

8

G | H | J | K | L | M

A B C D E F

208

1

2

3

4

5

6

7

8

A B C D E

189

F

Talisker
Bay

147
BEINN
BHREAC

Gr

Loch Eynort

434
AN CRUACHIN
Glenbrittle House
Bualintur

Loch Brittle

CEANN

Rudh' an Dùnain

So

C U I L

CANNA
210
CARN A' GHAILL
Garrisdale Point
A'Chill
Canna
Harbour
Sanday

Kilmory
Bay
Rudha
Shamhnan Insir

Sound of Canna

A Bhrideanach

302
MULLACH
MÓR

570
ORVAL

Kinloch

Oigh-sgeir

RÙM

Harris
Bay

810
ASKIVAL

763
SGÙRR NAN
GILLEAN

The Small Isles

Rudha nam
Meirleach

Sound o

Rudha an Fha

Eilean
nan Each

MUCK

Pe

0   1   2   3   4 miles
0 1 2 3 4 5 kilometres

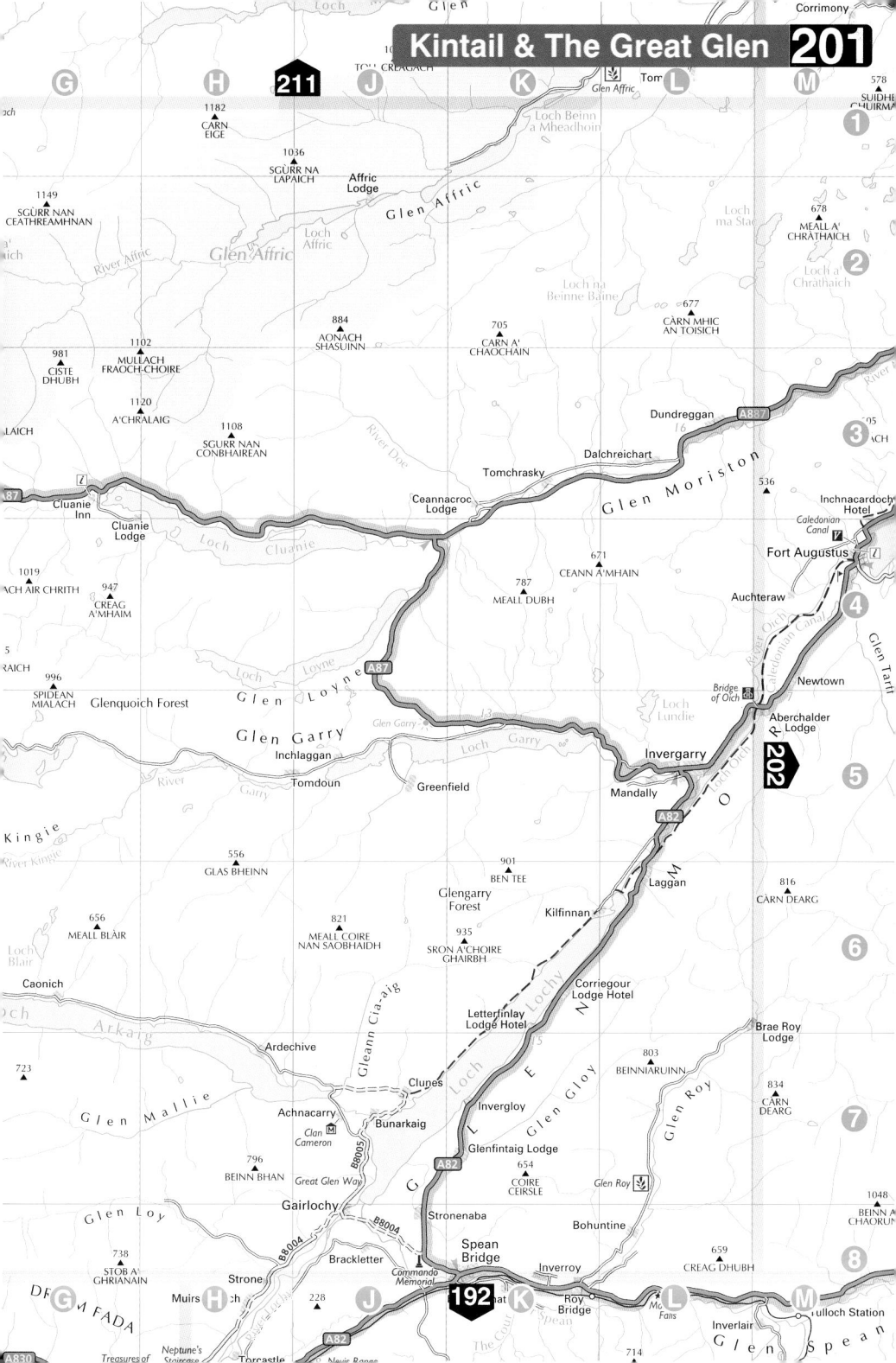

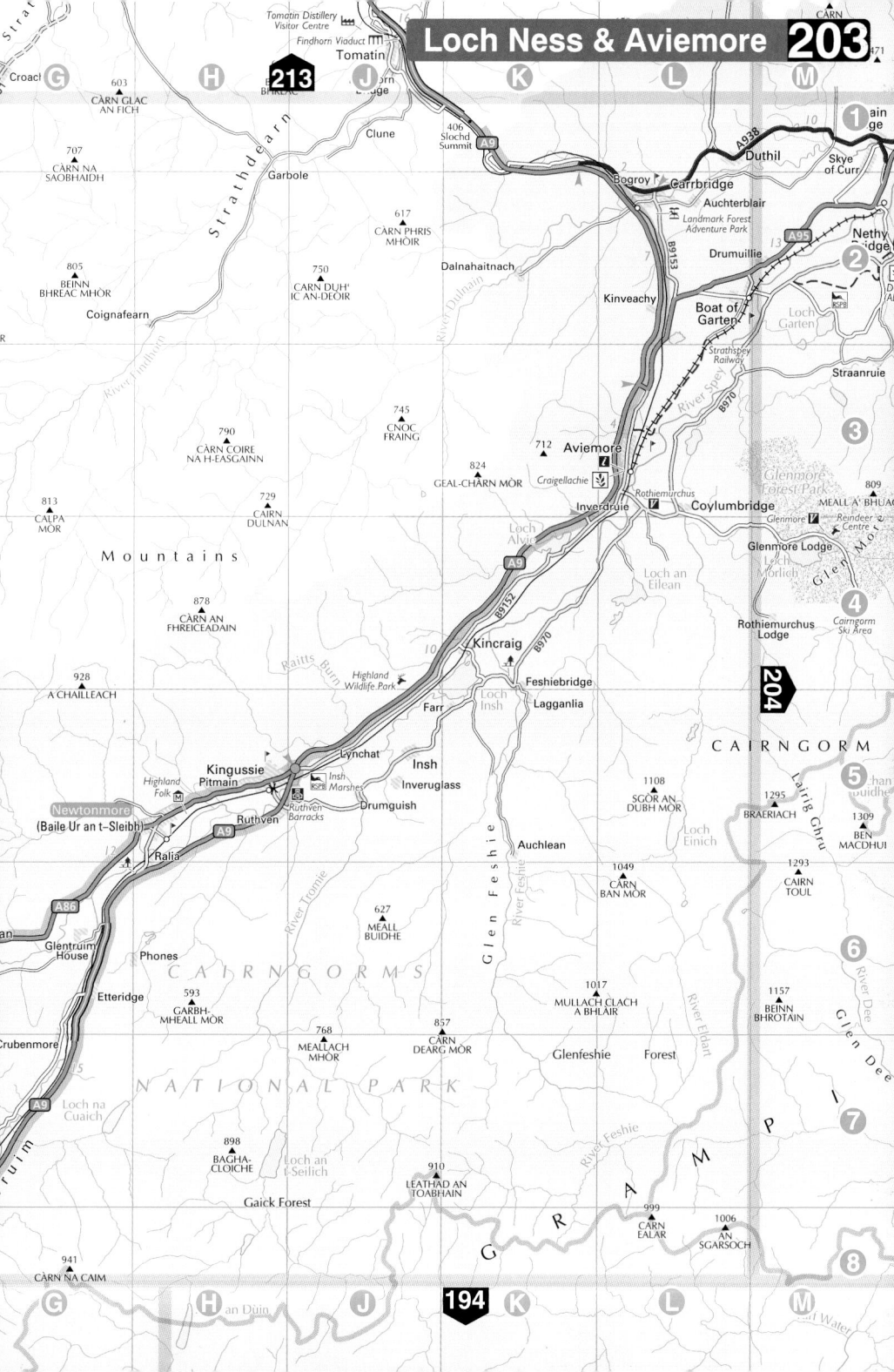

G **H** **J** **K** **L** **M**

Tomatin Distillery Visitor Centre
Findhorn Viaduct
Tomatin
213
Clune
Croac
603
CÀRN GLAC AN FICH
707
CÀRN NA SAOBHAIDH
Strathdearn
Garbole
406 Slochd Summit
Bogroy
CARN
Skye of Curr
Duthil
Carrbridge
1
Strath
Auchterblair
Landmark Forest Adventure Park
A95
Nethy Bridge
2
617 CÀRN PHRIS MHÒIR
Dalnahaitnach
B9153
Drumuillie
Boat of Garten
RSPB
De Al
805
BEINN BHREAC MHÒR
750
CARN DUH' IC AN-DEOIR
Kinveachy
Loch Garten
Coignafearn
River Dulnain
Strathspey Railway
Straanruie
790
CÀRN COIRE NA H-EASGAINN
745
CNOC FRAING
824
GEAL-CHARN MÒR
712
Aviemore
Craigellachie
River Spey
B970
3
Glenmore Forest Park
809
MEALL A' BHUAC
813
CALPA MÒR
729
CAIRN DULNAN
Inverdruie
Rothiemurchus
Coylumbridge
Glenmore
Reindeer Centre
Loch Alvie
Glenmore Lodge
A9
Loch an Eilean
Loch Morlich
Glen Mor
Mountains
878
CÀRN AN FHREICEADAIN
B9152
Rothiemurchus Lodge
Cairngorm Ski Area
4
928
A CHAILLEACH
Raitts Burn
10
Kincraig
B970
Feshiebridge
204
5
chan Buidhe
Highland Wildlife Park
Farr
Loch Insh
Laggantia
CAIRNGORM
1295
BRAERIACH
1309
BEN MACDHUI
Lynchat
Insh
Inveruglass
1108 SGÒR AN DUBH MOR
Kingussie
Insh Marshes
Highland Folk
Pitmain
Ruthven Barracks
Drumguish
Auchlean
Loch Einich
1293
CAIRN TOUL
Newtonmore
(Baile Ur an t–Sleibh)
Ruthven
A9
Glen Feshie
1049 CÀRN BAN MÒR
6
River Dee
Ralia
12
A86
627
MEALL BUIDHE
1017
MULLACH CLACH A BHLÀIR
1157
BEINN BHROTAIN
Glen Dee
Glentruim House
Phones
CAIRNGORMS
593
GARBH-MHEALL MÒR
Etteridge
768
MEALLACH MHÒR
857
CÀRN DEARG MÒR
Glenfeshie
Forest
7
Crubenmore
River Feshie
River Eidart
I
NATIONAL PARK
Loch na Cuaich
A9
898
BAGHA-CLOICHE
Loch an t-Seilich
910
LEATHAD AN TOABHAINN
River Feshie
M
P
999
CÀRN EALAR
1006
AN SGARSOCH
G
R
A
8
941
CÀRN NA CAIM
Gaick Forest
Water

G **H** an Dùin **J** **194** **K** **L** **M**

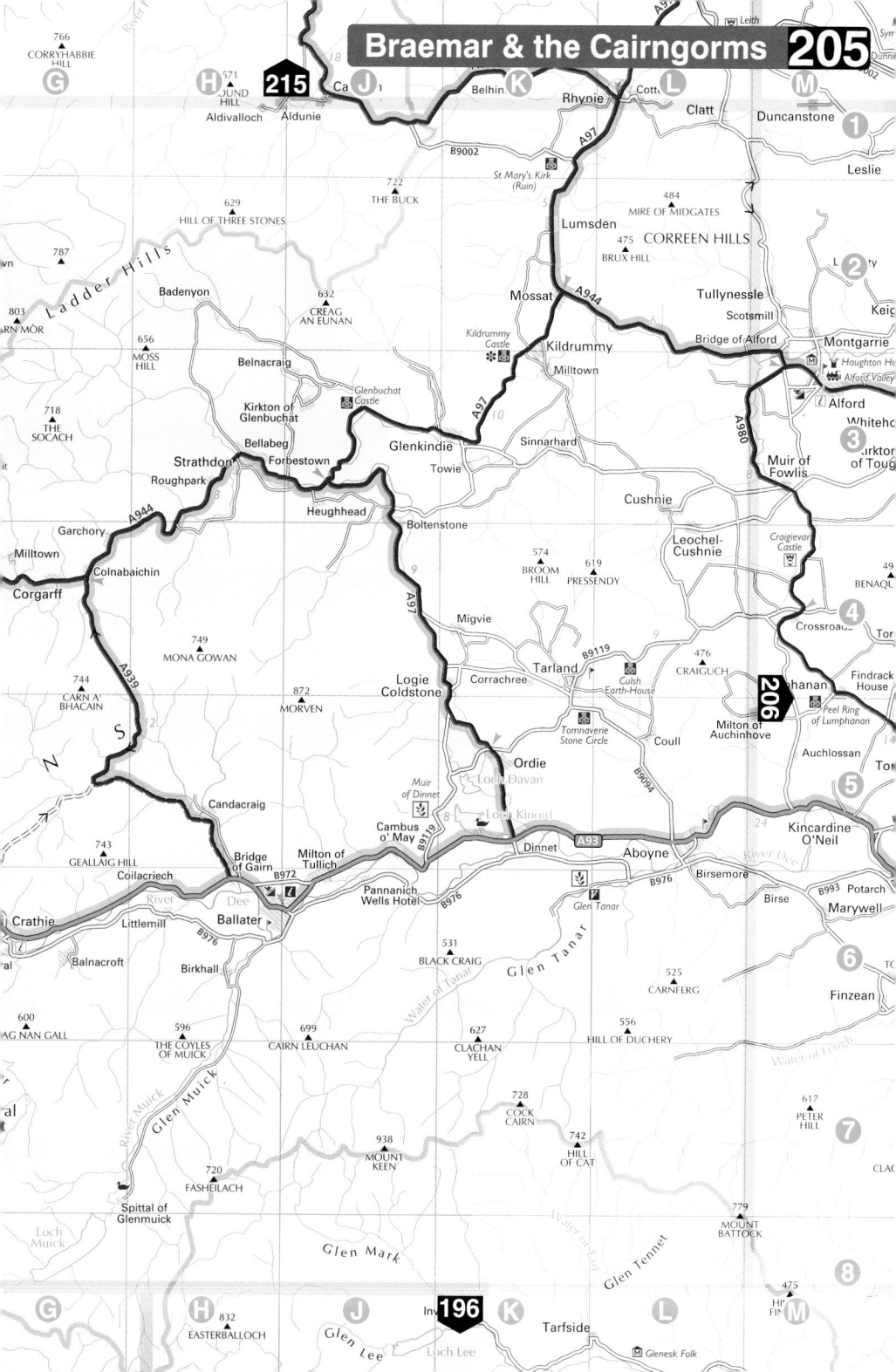

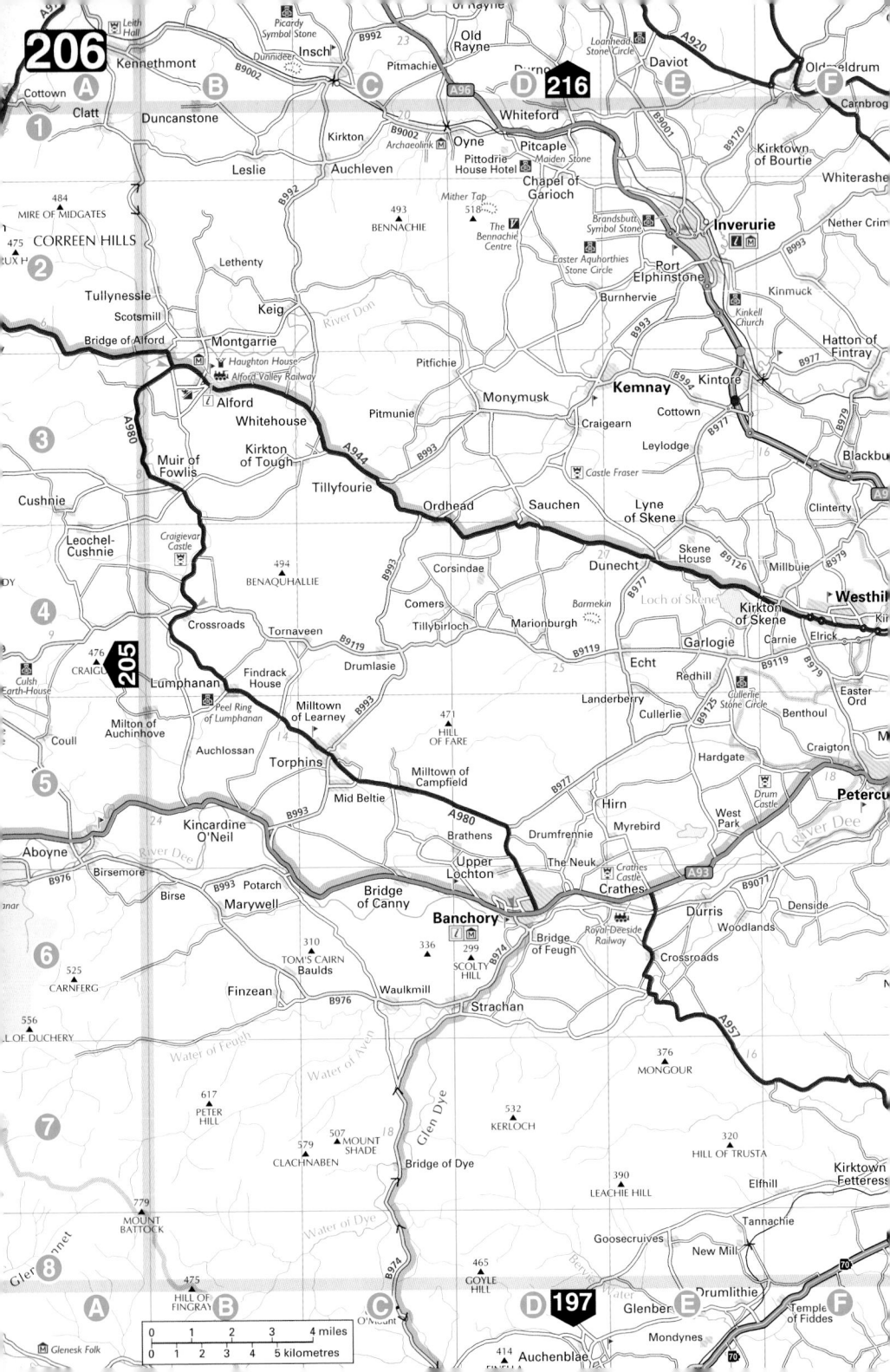

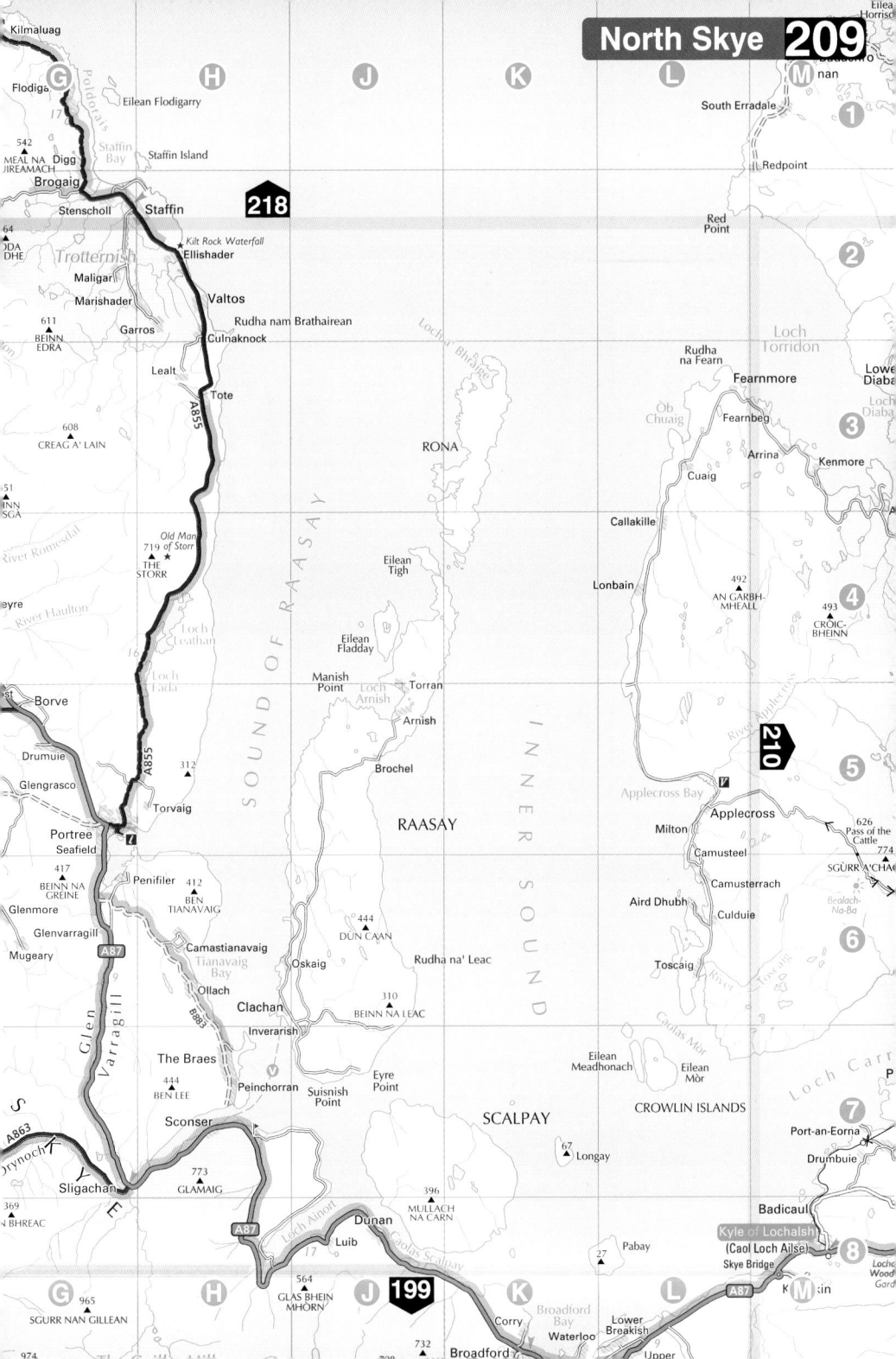

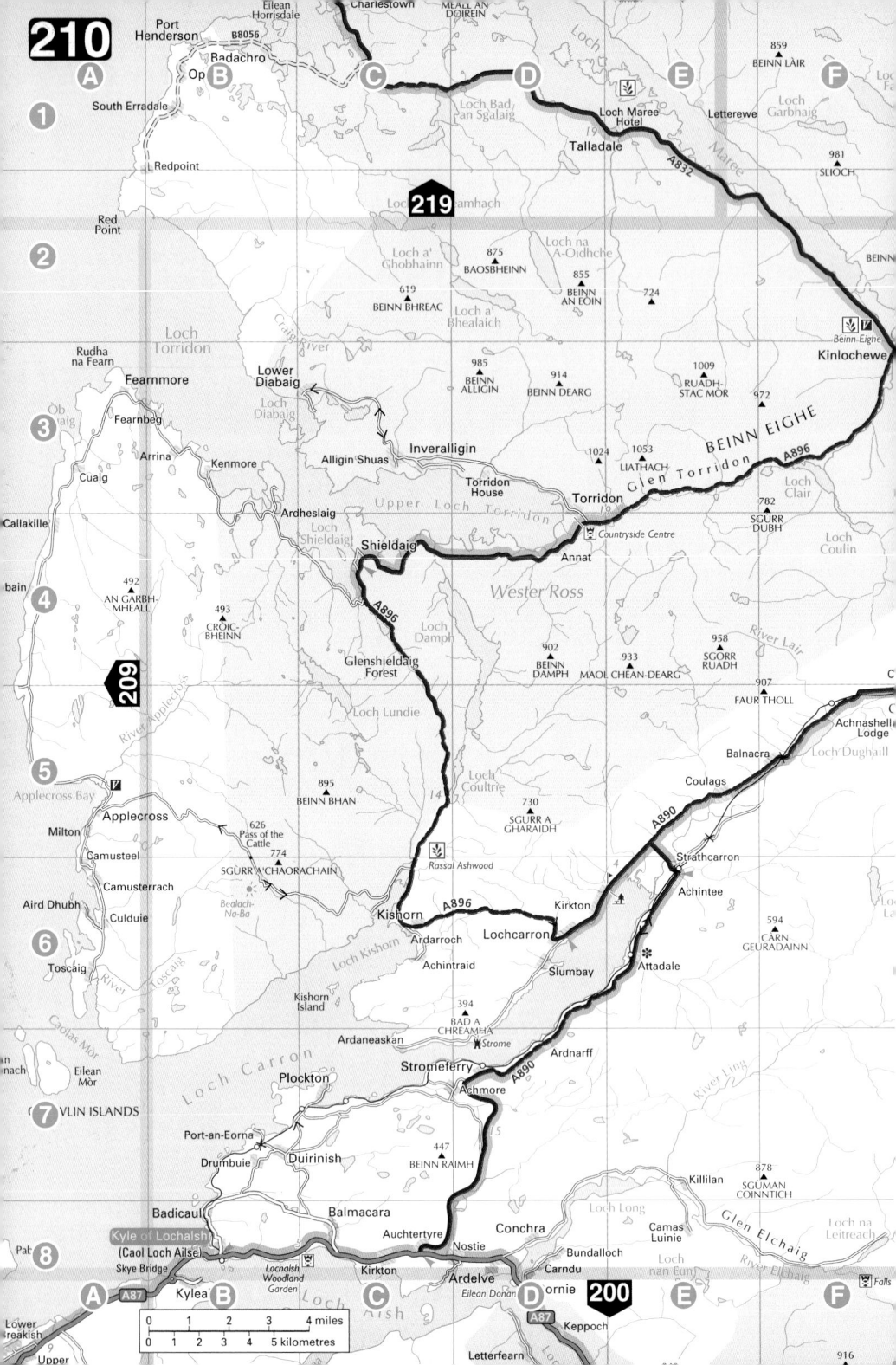

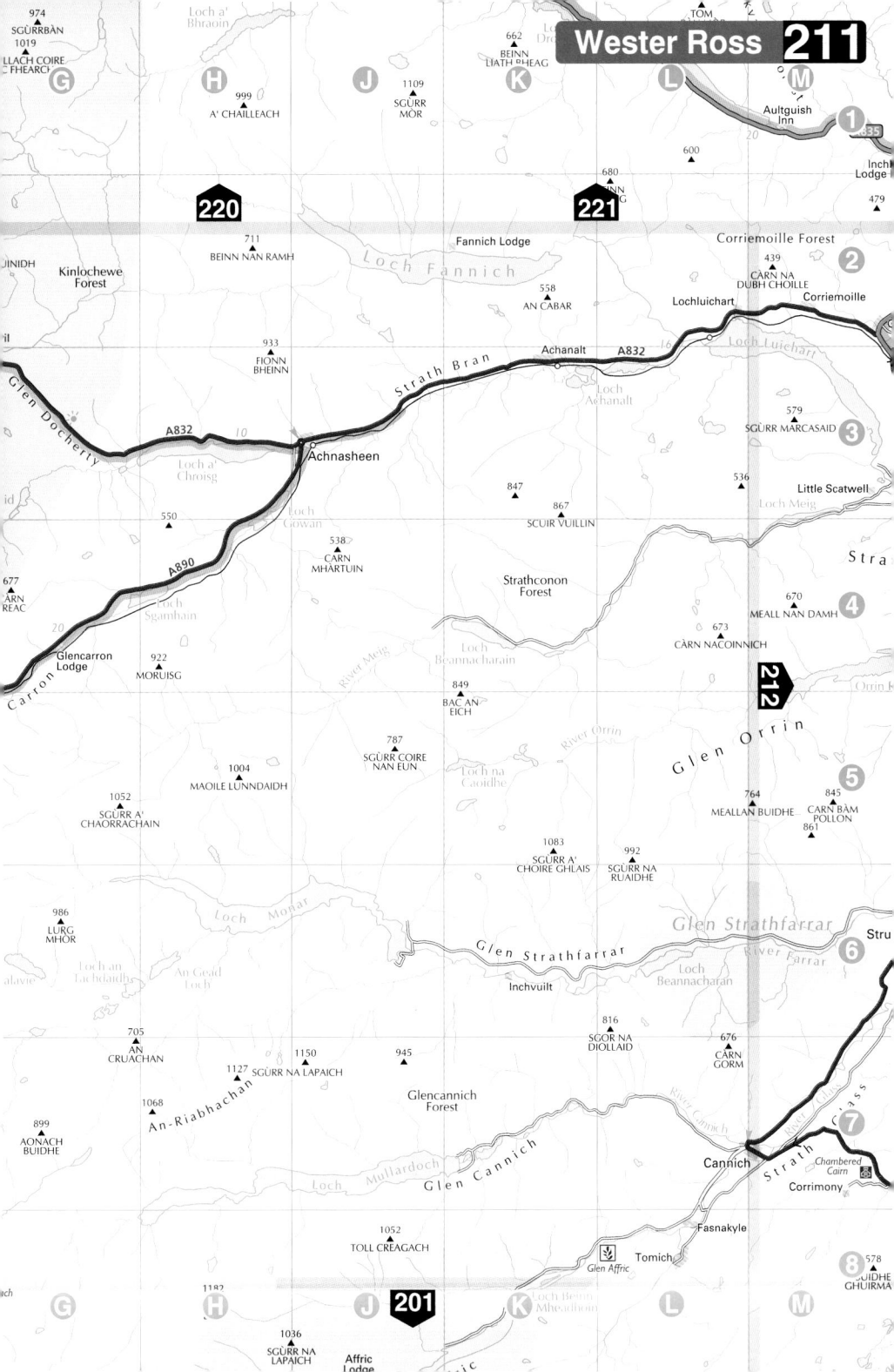

974
SGURRBAN
1019
LLACH COIRE
E FHEARCH
G

H
999
A' CHAILLEACH

J
1109
SGÙRR
MÒR

K
662
BEINN
LIATH BHEAG

TOM

L

M
Aultguish
Inn
1
A835

600

Inch
Lodge

479

680
N
G

220

221

711
BEINN NAN RAMH

Fannich Lodge

Loch Fannich

Corriemoille Forest

439
CÀRN NA
DUBH CHOILLE
2

558
AN CABAR

Lochluichart

Corriemoille

Kinlochewe
Forest

JINIDH

il

Glen Docherty

933
FIONN
BHEINN

Strath Bran

Achanalt

A832

Loch
Achanalt

Loch Luichart

579
SGÙRR MARCASAID
3

A832

10

Achnasheen

Loch a'
Chroisg

536

Little Scatwell

Loch Meig

Stra

id

550

Loch
Gowan

847

867
SCUIR VUILLIN

A890

538
CÀRN
MHÀRTUIN

Strathconon
Forest

670
MEALL NAN DAMH
4

677
ÀRN
REAC

Loch
Sgamhain

Loch
Beannacharain

673
CÀRN NACOINNICH

River Meig

Glencarron
Lodge

922
MORUISG

Carron

20

849
BAC AN
EICH

River Orrin

212

Glen Orrin

Orrin

787
SGÙRR COIRE
NAN EUN

Loch na
Caoidhe

5

1004
MAOILE LUNNDAIDH

1052
SGÙRR A'
CHAORRACHAIN

845
CÀRN BÀN
POLLON
861

764
MEALLAN BUIDHE

1083
SGÙRR A'
CHOIRE GHLAIS

992
SGÙRR NA
RUAIDHE

986
LURG
MHÒR

Loch Monar

Glen Strathfarrar

Glen Strathfarrar

River Farrar

Stru
6

Loch an
Laoigh

An Geàd
Loch

Inchvuilt

Loch
Beannacharan

alavie

705
AN
CRUACHAN

1150

816
SGOR NA
DIOLLAID

676
CÀRN
GORM

1068

1127
SGÙRR NA LAPAICH

945

An-Riabhachan

Glencannich
Forest

River Cannich

7

899
AONACH
BUIDHE

Loch Mullardoch

Glen Cannich

Cannich

Chambered
Cairn

Strath
Glass

Corrimony

1052
TOLL CREAGACH

Fasnakyle

Tomich

578
UIDHE
GHUIRMA
8

G

H

J
201

Glen Affric

Loch Beinn
Mheadhoin

K

L

M

ch

1182

1036
SGÙRR NA
LAPAICH

Affric
Lodge

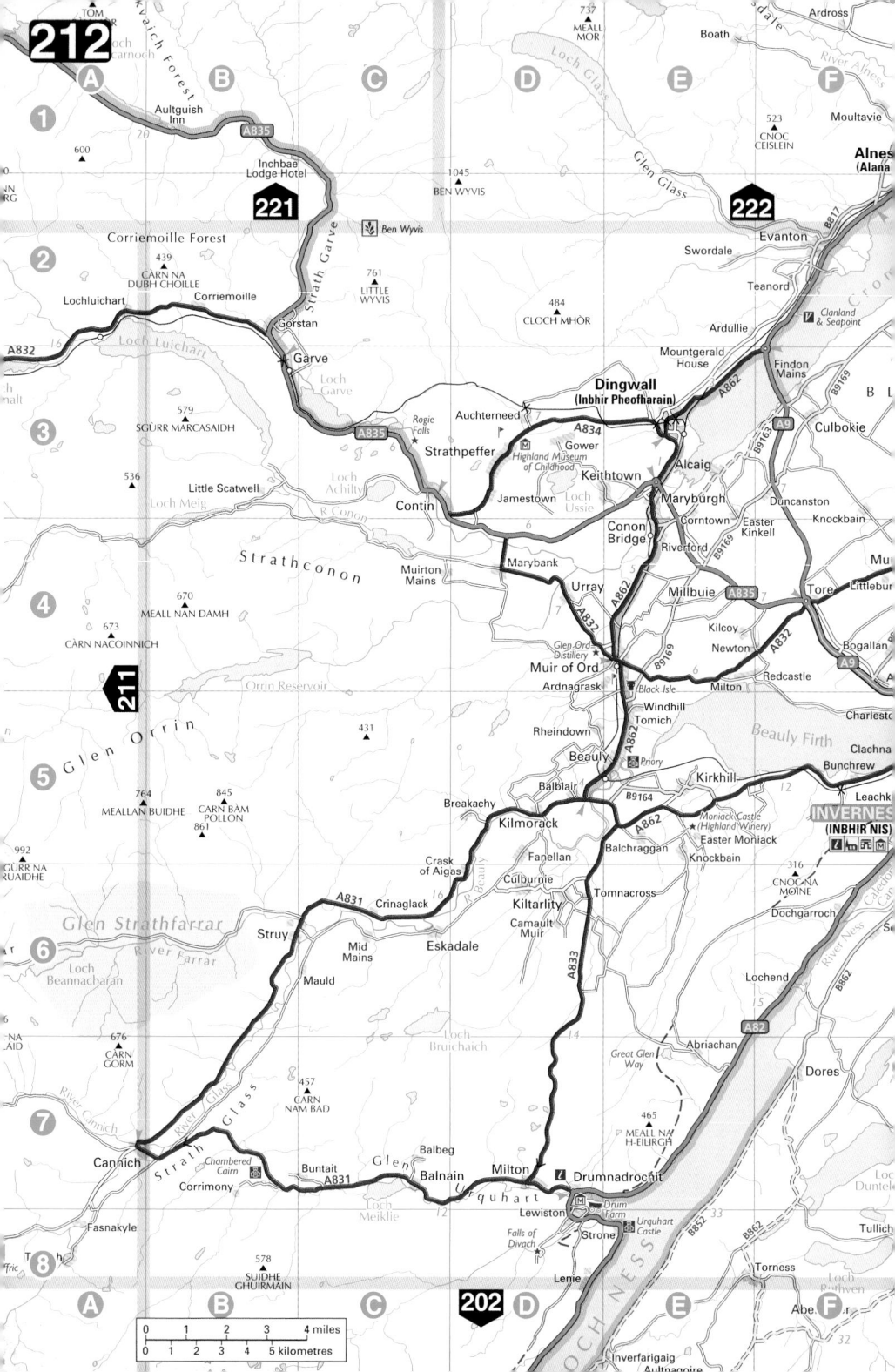

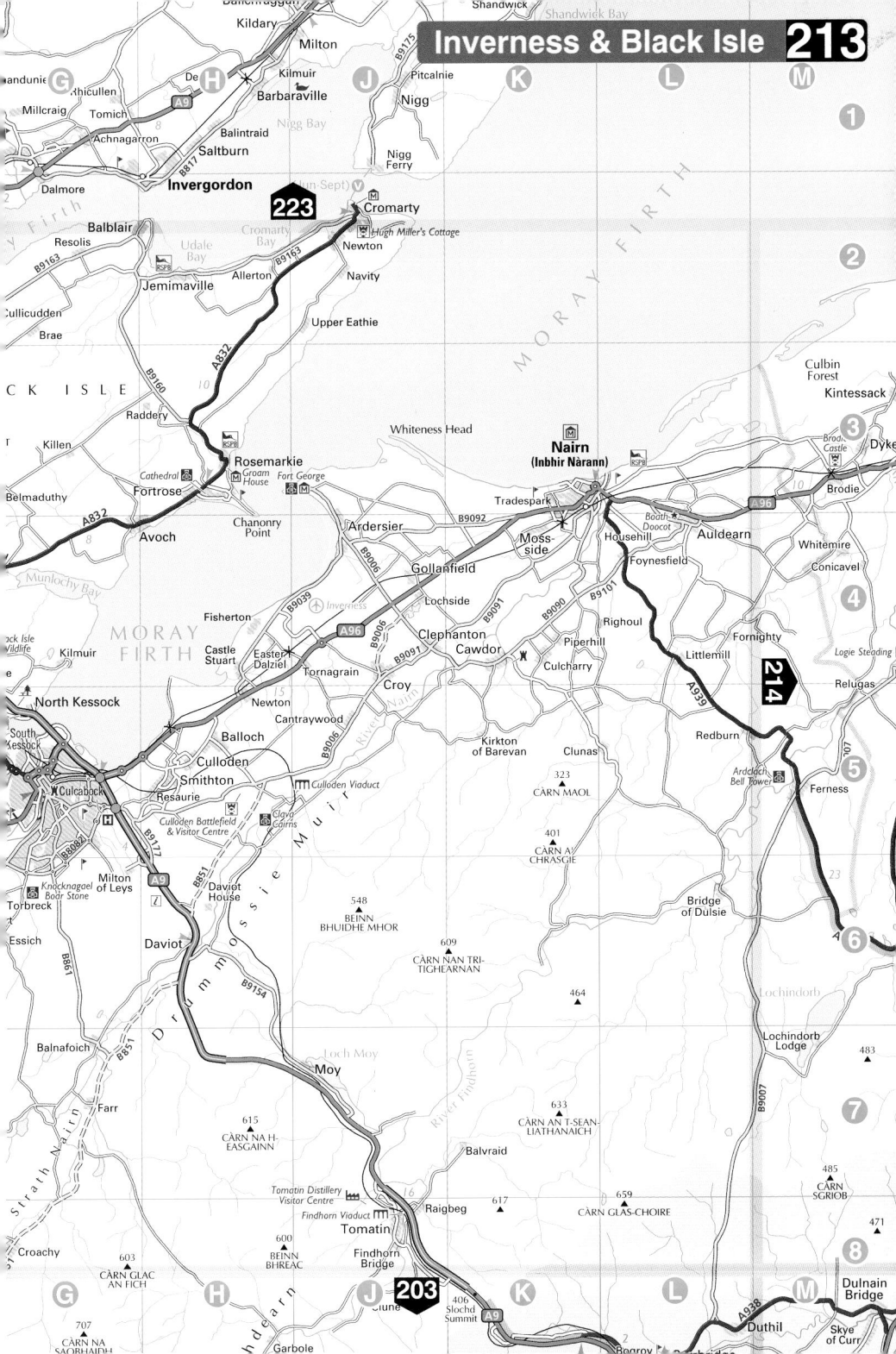

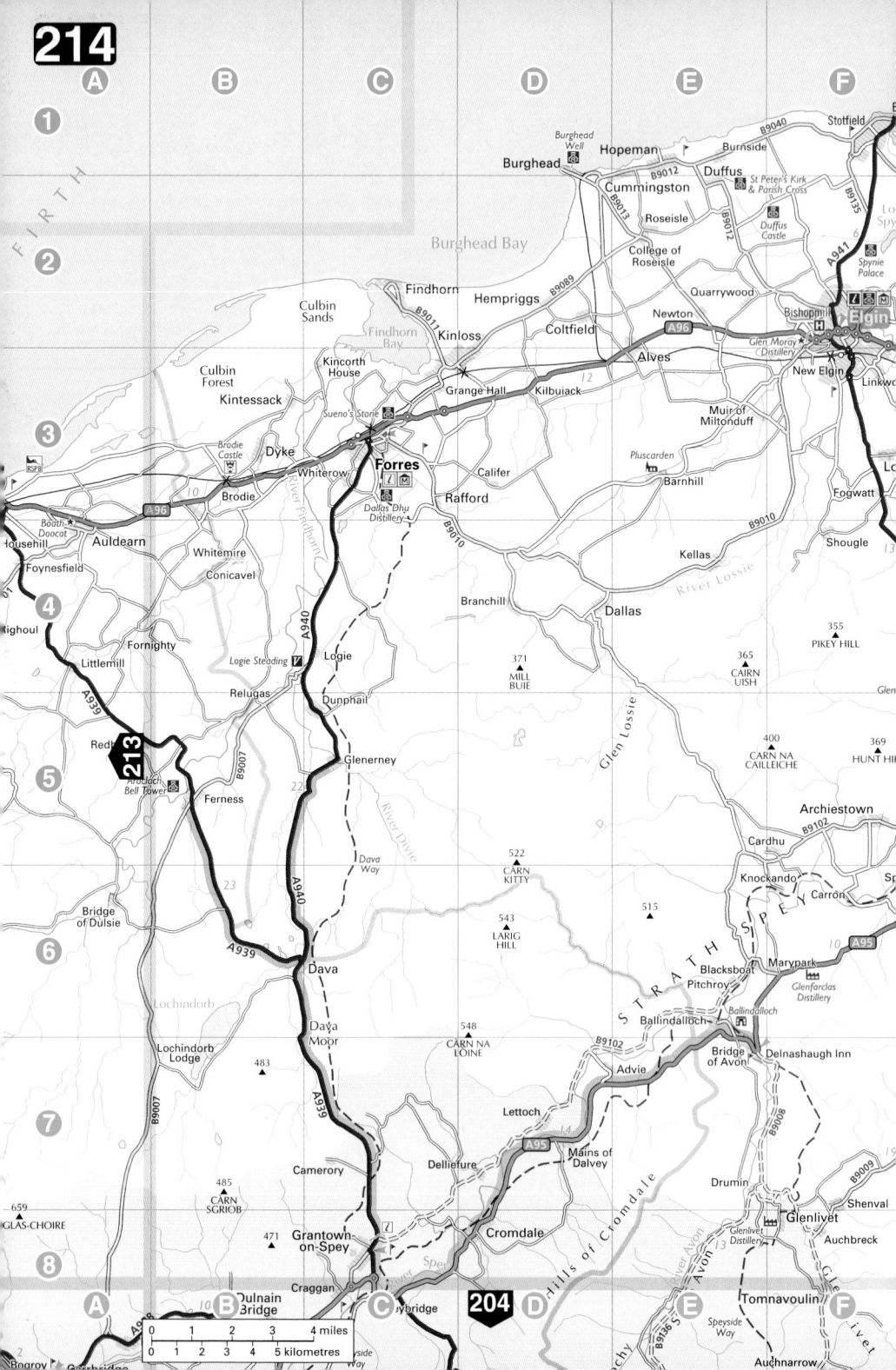

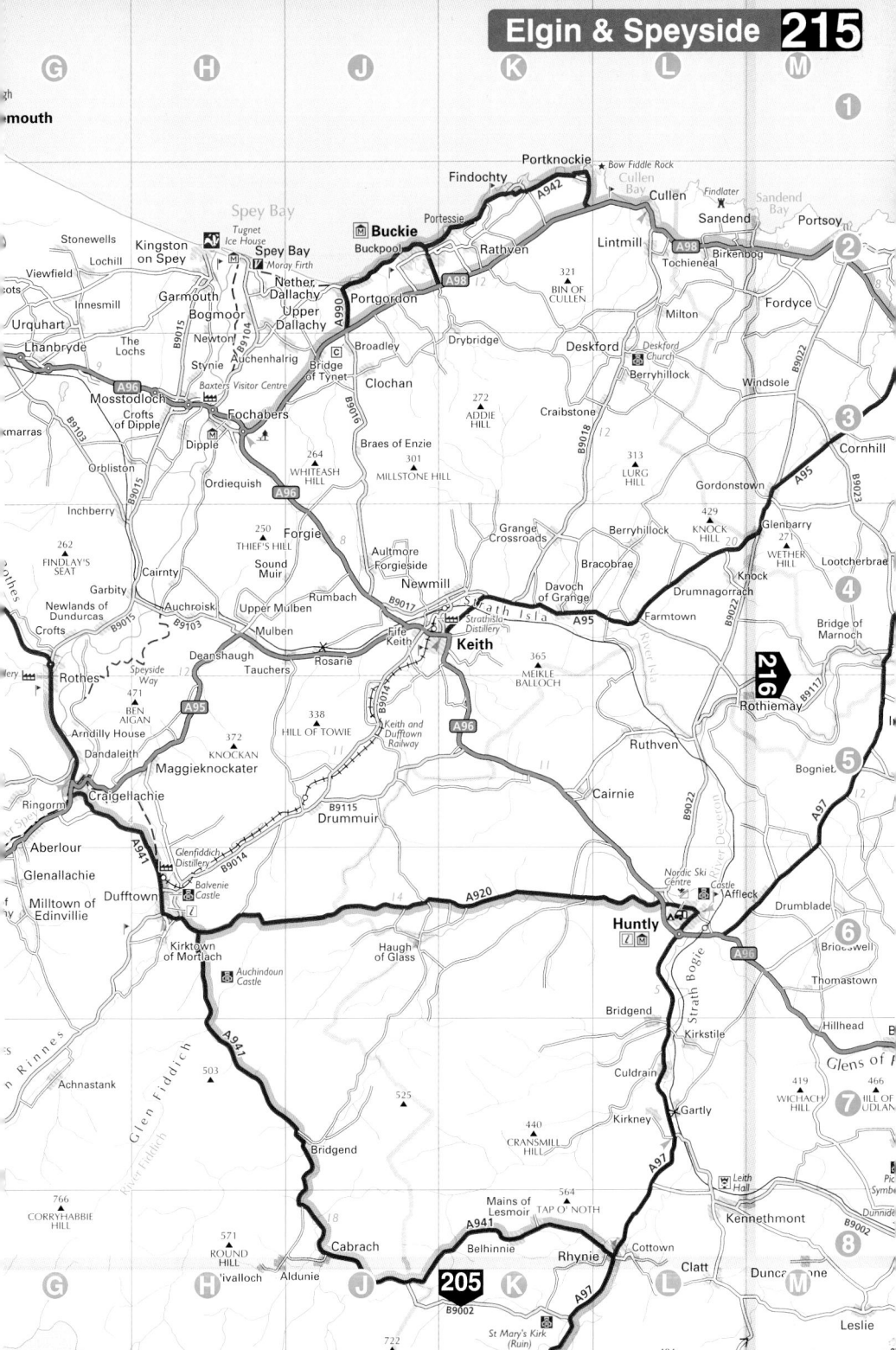

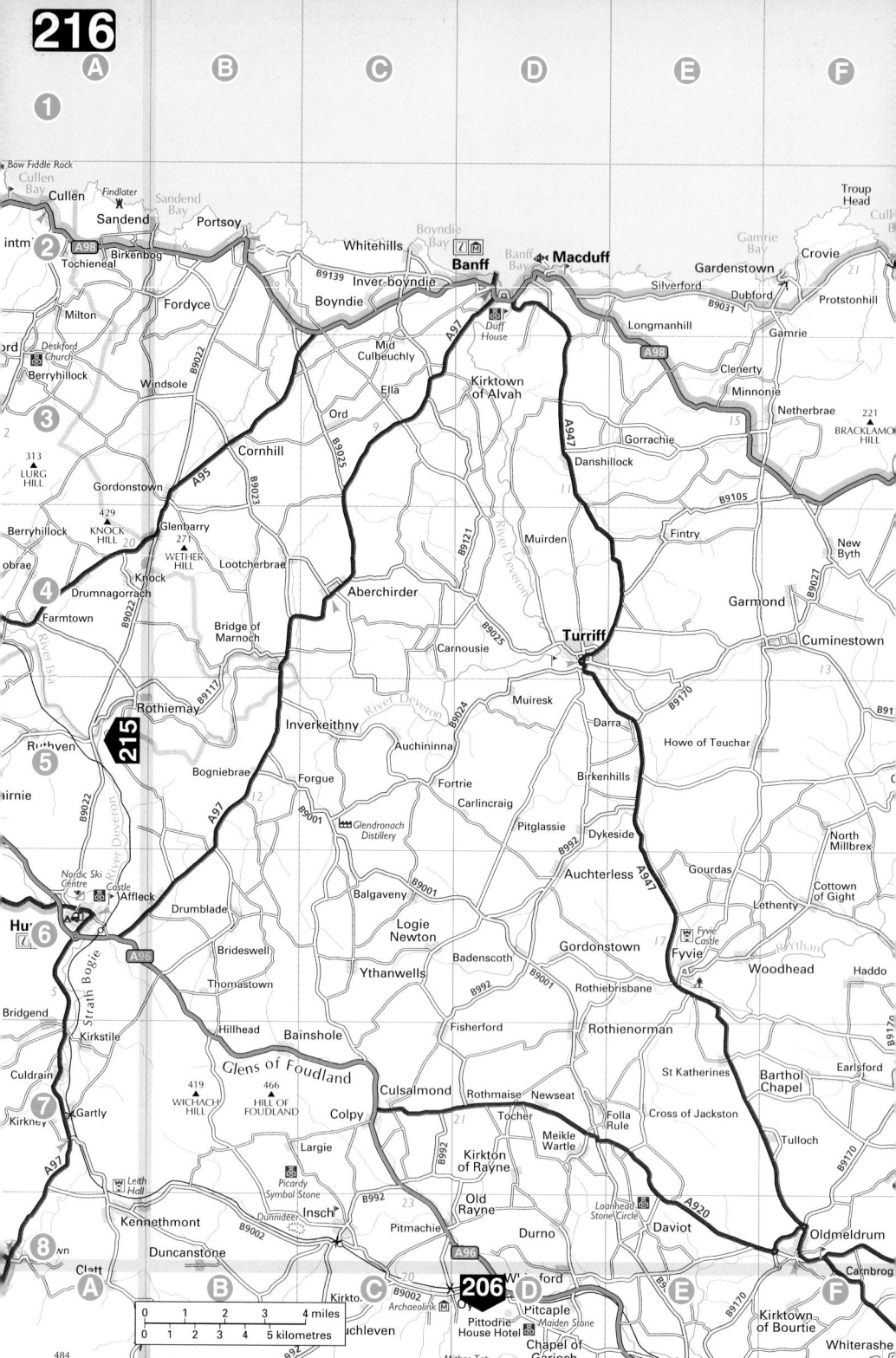

G   H   J   K   L   M

1
2
3
4
5
6
7
8

Rosehearty
Pittulie
Sandhaven
Castle Lighthouse & Museum
Kinnaird Head
Peathill
Kirktown
Fraserburgh
Craigiefold
Percyhorner
Fraserburgh Bay
Maggie's Hoosie
Cairnbulg
Inverallochy
Aberdour Bay
Coburty
Pitblae
Whitelinks Bay
New berdour
Boyndlie
Mid Ardlaw
B9031
Memsie
St Combs
B9032
A98
A381
Memsie Cairn
Rathen
New Pitsligo
Newburgh
Lonmay
Crofts of Savoch
B9093
234 WAUGHTON HILL
Strichen
Crimond
Blackhill
Rattray Head
Loch of Strathbeg
Bonnykelly
New Leeds
A952
B9093
Leys
Kirktown
St Fergus
A981
A950
Denhead
Backfolds
Rora
A90
Fetterangus
Deer Abbey
Dunshillock
Maud
B9106
Aden
Mintlaw
Longside
Inverugie
Peterhead
New Deer
B9029
Old Deer
B9029
Stuartfield
Inverquhomery
Buchanhaven
Peterhead Bay
B9028
A948
Drymuir
Blackhill of Clackriach
Bulwack
Millbreck
Nether Kinmundy
Hillhead of Cocklaw
Burnhaven
Nethermuir
Clola
Blackhill
Stirling
Buchan Ness
Boddam
Knaven
B9030
Kinnadie
Kinknockie
Lendrum Terrace
Auchnagatt
Cairnorrie
Coldwells
Ardallie
Longhaven
Brownhill
A952
Bullers of Buchan
lethlick
Inkhorn
A948
Hatton
A90
Auchiries
North Haven
Arthrath
Muirtack
Slains
Cruden Bay
Ythan
Bogbrae
Chapel Hill
Bay of Cruden
B9005
Ythanbank
Birness
Whinnyfold
The Skares
derlairs
Auchedly
Artrochie
A975
Altar Tomb of William Forbes
Kinharrachie
Ellon
P·R
Kirktown of Slains
Ythsie
Esslemont
Kirkton of Logie Buchan
Collieston
Iquhon Castle
A920
B9005
Pitmedden Garden
Pitmedden
Logierieve
Forvie
B999
Ud Gre
Housieside
B90
B9000
Newburgh
Udny Station
A90
Woodland
Pettymuk
Cultercullen
Foveran

207

G   H   J   K   L   M

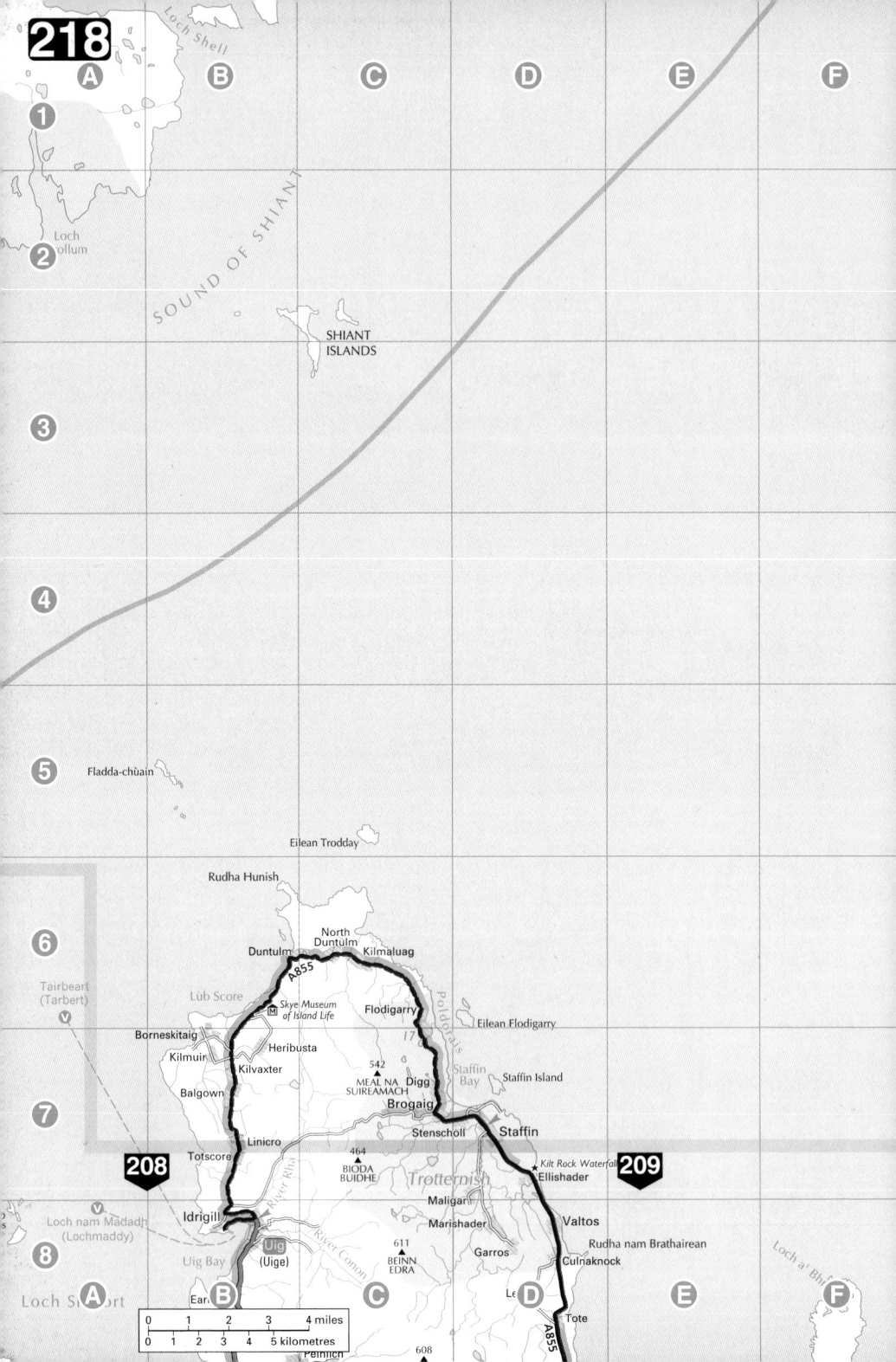

A B C D E F

1

2

Loch Shell

Loch Sollum

SOUND OF SHIANT

SHIANT
ISLANDS

3

4

5

Fladda-chùain

Eilean Trodday

Rudha Hunish

North
Duntulm
Duntulm Kilmaluag

A855

6

Tairbeart
(Tarbert)

Lùb Score

Skye Museum
of Island Life Flodigarry

Eilean Flodigarry

Borneskitaig

Kilmuir Heribusta

Kilvaxter

542
MEAL NA Digg
SUIREAMACH

Staffin
Bay Staffin Island

Balgown

Brogaig

7

Totscore Linicro

Stenscholl Staffin

208

464
BIODA
BUIDHE Trotternish

Kilt Rock Waterfall
Ellishader

209

Idrigill

River Rha

Maligar

Marishader

Valtos

Rudha nam Brathairean
Culnaknock

Loch nam Madadh
(Lochmaddy)

Uig Bay

Uig
(Uige)

River Conon

611
BEINN
EDRA

Garros

Lea

A855

8

Loch Sport

A B C D E F

Earl

Tote

0 1 2 3 4 miles
0 1 2 3 4 5 kilometres

Peinlich

608

G H J K L M

Polba

1

Badentarb Bay

Tanera Beg
Tanera Mòr

Steornabhagh (Stornoway)

Glas-leac Beag

Hor Isla

2

Priest Island

Eilean Dubh

Scorai

Greenstone Point

Rudha Beag

Cailleach Head

3

Mellon Udrigle

Stattic Point

GRUINARD ISLAND

Badluarach

Foura

Cove

Laide

Gruinard Bay

A832

Badc

Rudha Reidh

Mellon Charles

Ormiscaig

Aultbea

Little Gruinard River

Gruinard

4

296
AN CUAIDH

B8057

ISLE OF EWE

Little Gruinard River

Gruinard River

347
CREAG-MHEAL BEAG

220

Melvaig

Loch Ewe

Aultgrishin

Inverasdale

Loch Fada

293
CNOC BREAC

Naast

Inverewe Garden

13

Londubh

250
MEALL NA MEINE

681
BEINN A' CHAISGEIN BEAG

5

North Erradale

B8021

Poolewe

Wester Ross

B

Big Sand

Strath

A832

Dubh Loch

Longa Island

Smithstown

Lonemore

Auchtercairn

Heritage

Charlestown

421
MEALL AN DOIREIN

791
BEINN AIRIDH CHARR

6

Loch Gairloch

Gairloch

Eilean Horrisdale

Port Henderson

B8056

Badachro

Opinan

South Erradale

Redpoint

Loch

859
BEINN LAIR

Loch Maree Hotel

Letterewe

Loch Garbhaig

7

Talladale

A832

Maree

981
SLIOCH

Red Point

Loch Ghaineamhach

19

210

Loch Gholbhan

875
BAOSBHEINN

Loch na A'Oidhche

855
BEINN AN EOIN

724

8

Beinn E

Kinloch

619
BEINN BHREAC

Loch a' Bhealaich

914
BEINN DEARG

Rudha na Fearn

Fearnn.

Loch Torridon

Lower Diabaig

Craig River

B.
ALLIGIN

1009
RUADH-STAC MOR

972

Òb Chuaig

Fearnbeg

Loch Diabaig

N EIGHE

G H J K L M

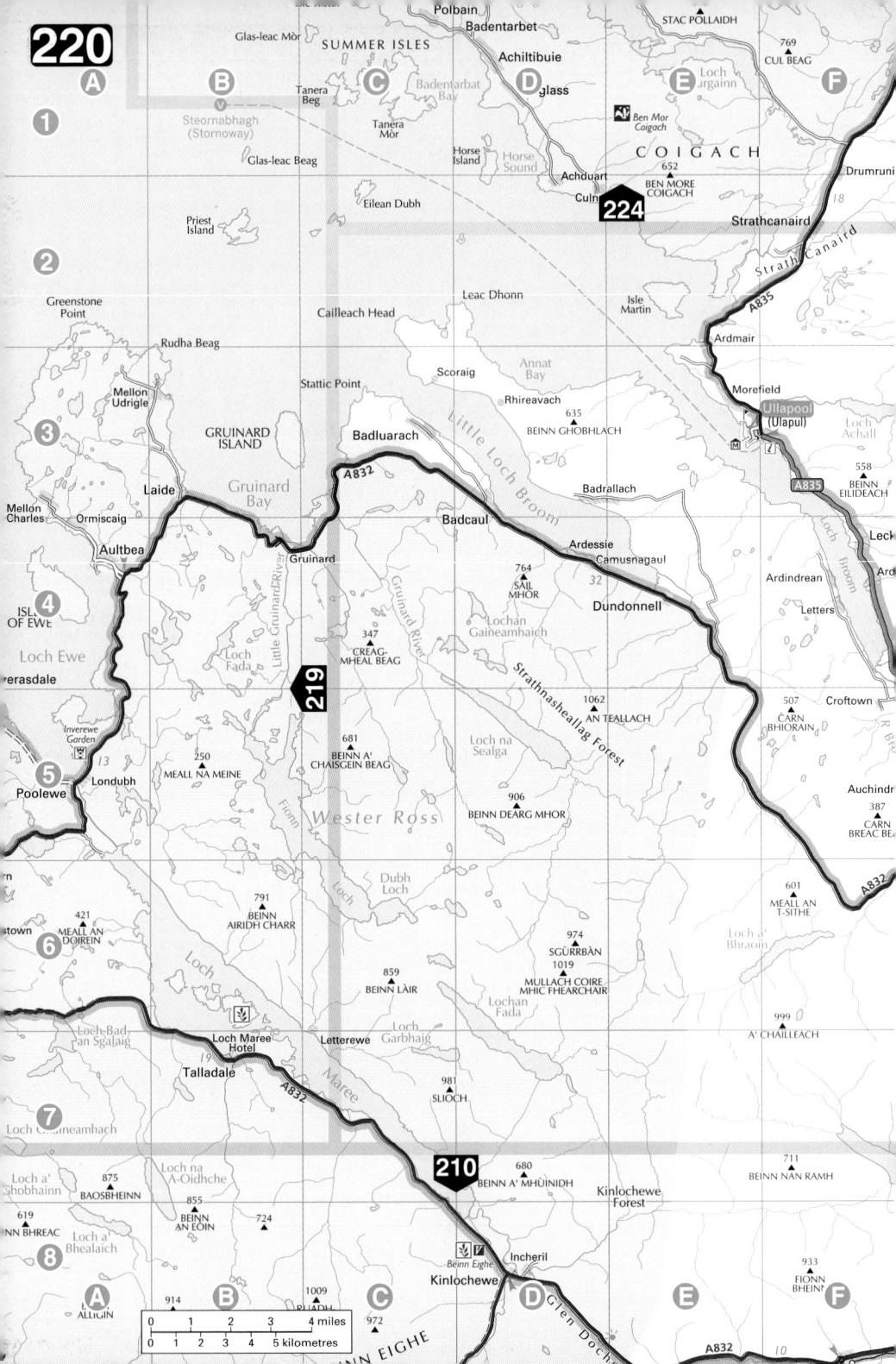

Col

G **H** **J** **K** **L** **M**

Loch
Urigill

nockan Cliff

1

Loch na
Cluise Moire

364
AN STICHD

BEINN AN

402
CNOC A' CHOIRE

A839

Cromalt Hills

307
CN
GLAS ... LLE

225

River Oykel

Rosehall
A837

27

2

Rappach

e

Glen Einig

Oykel Bridge
Hotel

Oykel Bridge
Hotel

Doune

31

Altass

Linside

Strath Oykel

408
DROMANNAN

Rappach Water

Glen Achall

412
CREAG
LOISGTE

493
BEINN
ULBHAIDH

463
BREAC BHEINN

Brealangwell
Lodge

3

Loch an
Daimh

Strath Mulzie

Giasha Burn

701
CARN A'
CHOIN DEIRG

506
MEALL
DHEIRGIDH

Croick

Strathcarron

677
MEALL NAM
BRADHAN

River Carron

642
MEALL
DUBH

ch

842
CARN
BAN

63
CARN BHREN

4

647
CARN MOR

Loch a'
Choire Mhoir

ael

Glencalvie Forest

River Laol

Gleann Beag

Crom Loch

838
CARN
CHUINNEAG

222

5

710
BEINN
THARSUINN

66
CARN CAS NAN GABHAR

Braemore

628

1081
BEINN
DEARG

E

Corrieshalloch
Gorge

Loch
Coire Lair

Loch a'
Chaorunn

of
och

618
MEALL
LEACACHAIN

771
MEALL A'
GHRIANAIN

Loch
Morie

Strathvaich Forest

Loch
Vaich

742
BEINN
NAN EUN

6

737
MEALL
MOR

662
BEINN
LIATH BHEAG

Loch
Droma

742
TOM
BAN MOR

Loch Glass

Loch
Glascarnoch

1109
SGURR
MOR

Glen Gl...

Aultguish
Inn

20

A835

1045
BEN WYVIS

7

680
BEINN
DEARG

600

Inchbae
Lodge Hotel

479

Ben Wyvis

Fannich Lodge

211

Corriemoille Forest

212

Strath Garve

h Fannich

558
AN CABAR

439
CARN NA
DUBH CHOILLE

Corriemoille

761
LITTLE
WYVIS

484
CLOCH MHOR

8

Lochluichart

Strath ran

Achanalt

A832

16

Gorstan

Garve

Loch
Garve

Loch Luichart

Dingwall
(Inbhir Pheotharai...)

M

h
Achanalt

579
SGURR MARCASAIDH

Rogie
Falls

Auchterneed

A834

A835

G **H** **J** **K** **L** **M**

G H J K L M

1
2
3
4
5
6
7
8

Strath b
River Brora
Dalreavoch
Lodge

COL-
BHEINN
Lothbeg

520
BEN
HORN
Loch
Horn

Dalchalm
Brora

378
CAGAR
FEOSAIG
Doll

227

ogart
Golspie Burn

446
BEN LUNDIE
Backies
Carn Liath
A9

383
BEN BHRAGGIE
Rhives
Dunrobin Castle

Torboll
Golspie

Cambusavie
Platform
Loch
Fleet

Badninish
Skelbo
Skelbo Street
Fourpenny
Embo

rquhar
Birichin
Astle
Embo Street
Pitgrudy

Evelix
A949
Royal Dornoch

Clashmore
A9
3
Camore
Dornoch
Historylinks

Cuthill
Tarbat Ness

ouscurrie
Ferry Point
Innis Mhor
Brucefield
Wilkhaven

Dornoch Firth
Portmahomack

Glenmorangie
Distillery
Inver

Morangie
Arboll
Rockfield
B9165

284
Tain
(Baile Dhubhthaich)
Toulvaddie
Lochslin

Loch
Eye
Rhynie
Balmuchy

Newfield
B9165
Hill of
Fearn
Hilton of Cadboll
Chapel (ruin)

Fearn
Tullich
Hilton
Balintore

Ballchraggan
B9166
Arabella
Shandwick
Shandwick Bay

Kildary
Ankerville

Milton
B9175
Pitcalnie

elny
Kilmuir
Nigg

Barbaraville
Nigg Bay

Balintraid
Nigg
Ferry

Saltburn

ergordon
(Jun-Sept)

Cromarty
Hugh Miller's Cottage
213

Cromarty
Bay
B9163
Newton
Allerton
Navity

dale
ay
ville
Upper Eathie

A832

214

Burghe

Findhorn
B9011
H

Culbin
Sands
Findhorn
Bay

Culbin
Forest
Kincorth
House

Kintessack
Sueno's Stone
Grange

MORAY FIRTH

Whiteness Head

G H J K L M

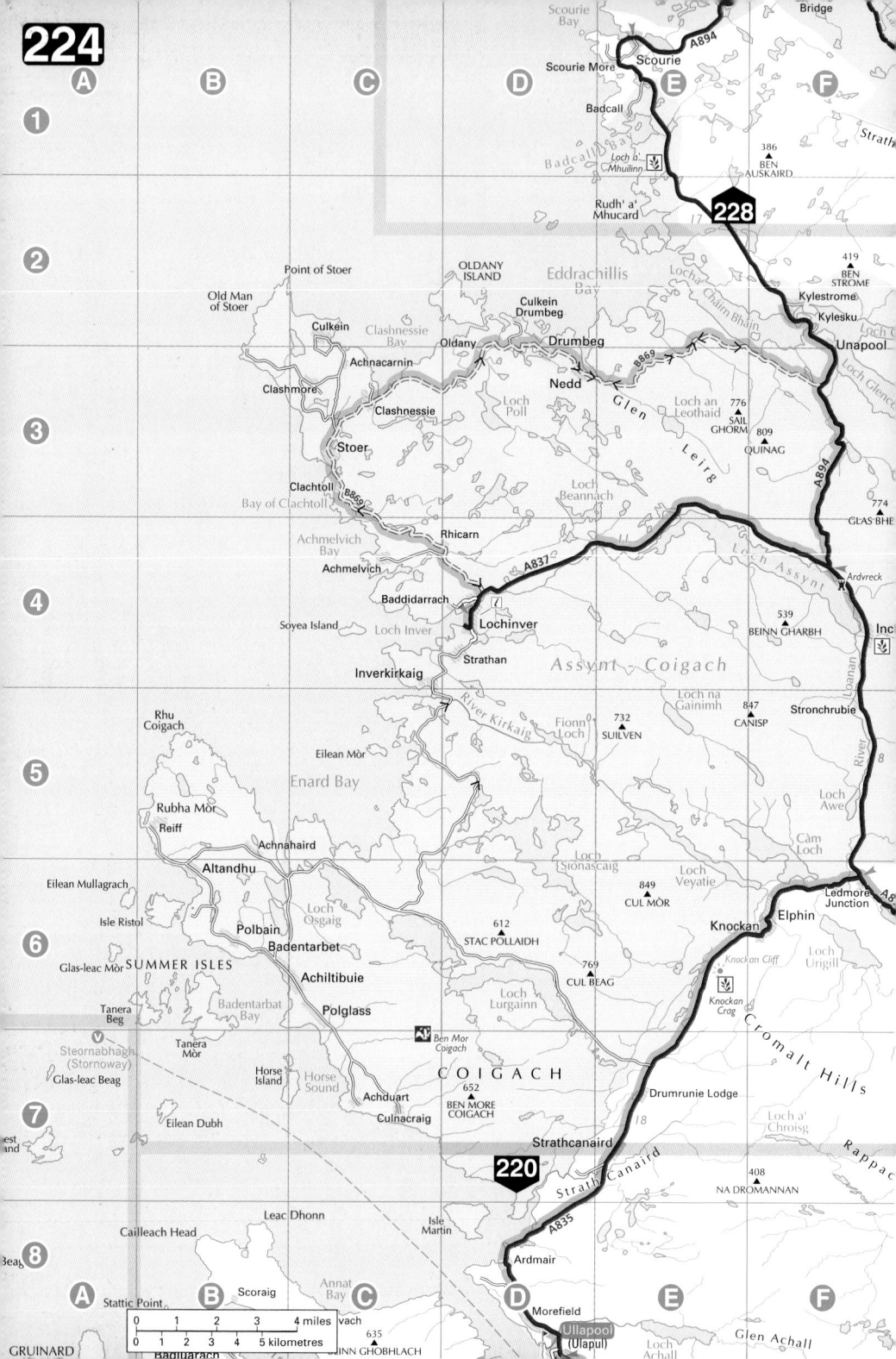

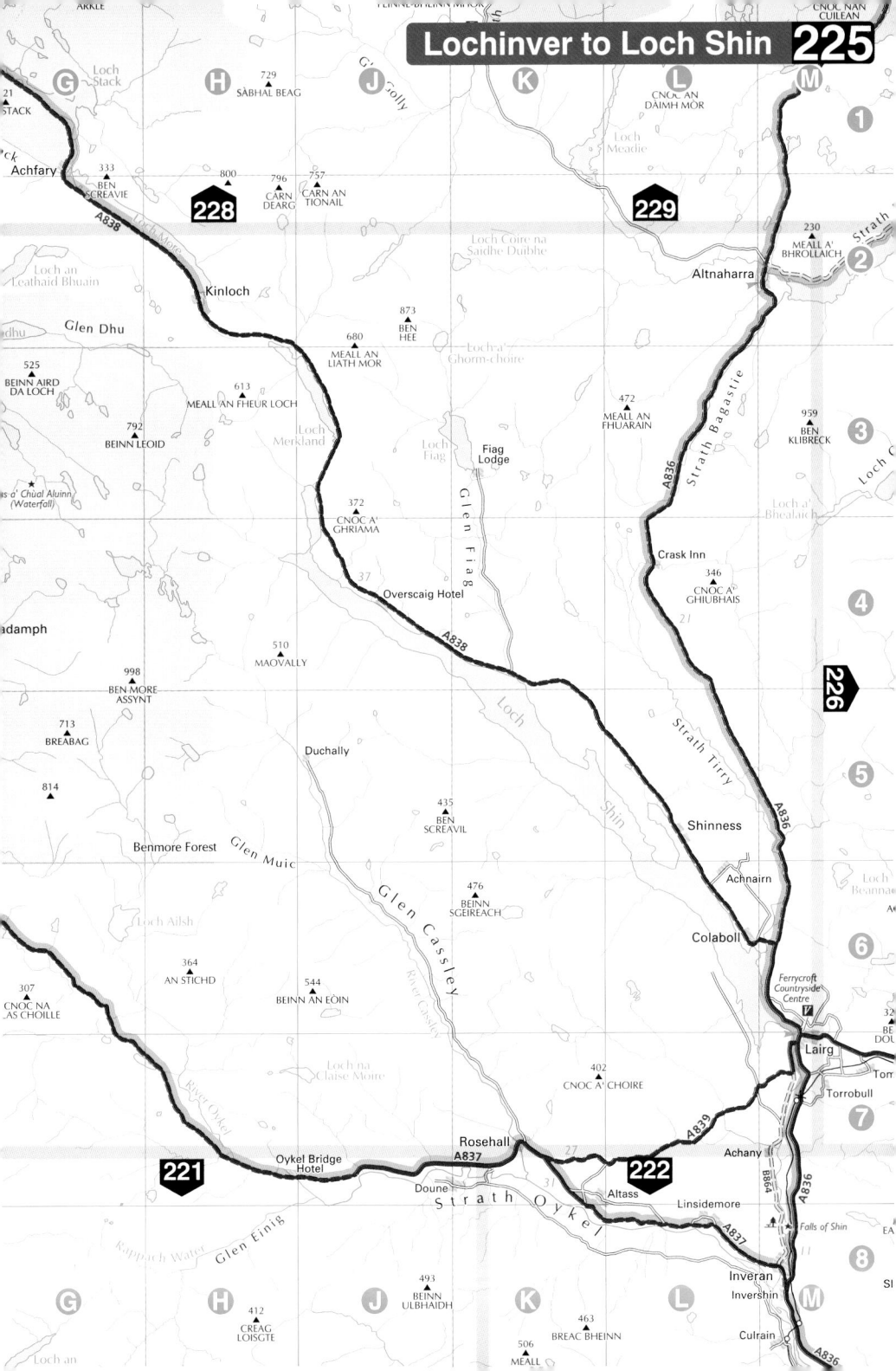

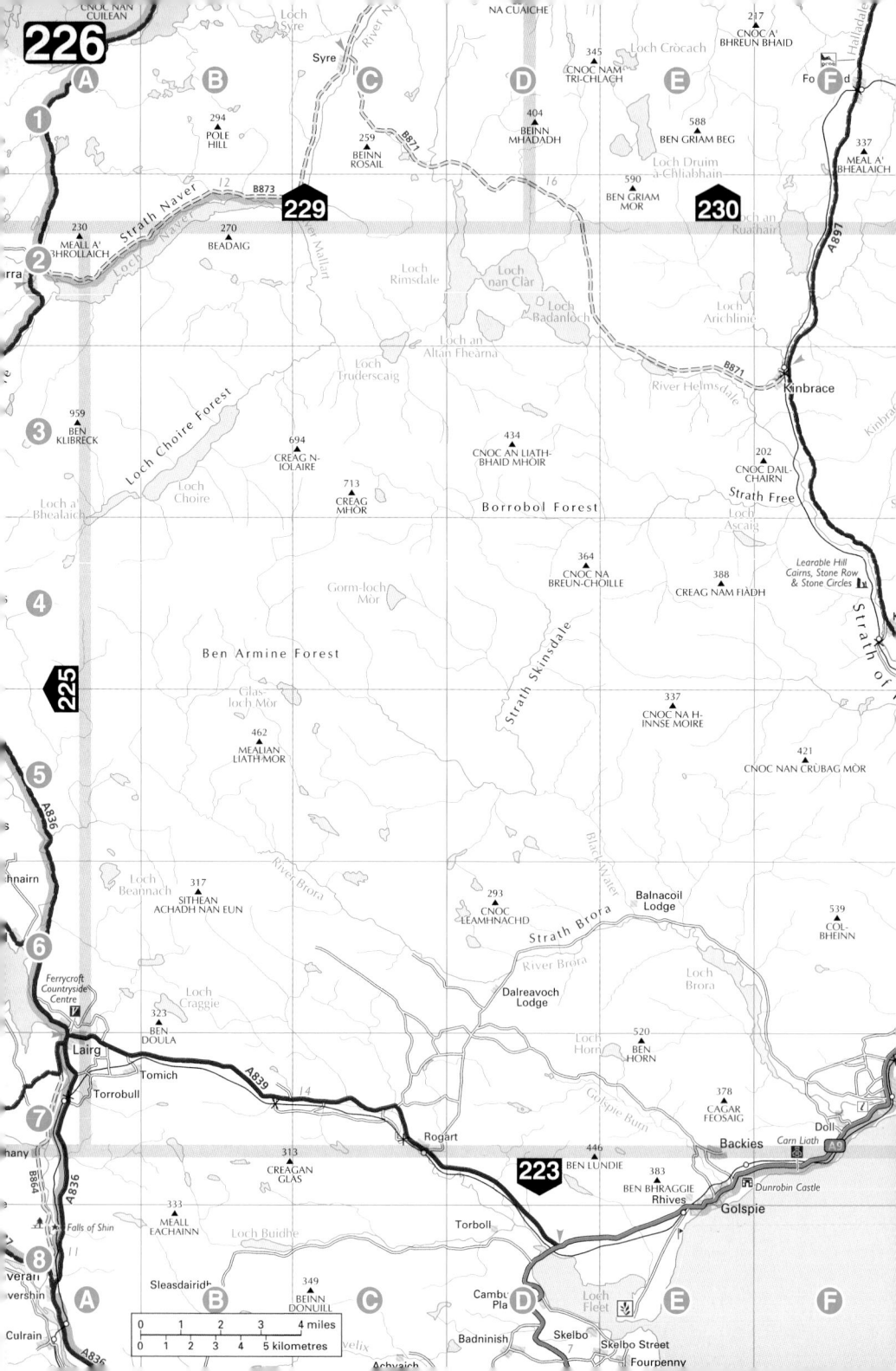

A · B · C · D · E · F

229 · 230

225 · 223

CNOC NAN CUILEAN

Loch Syre

Syre

River Naver

NA CUAICHE

CNOC A' BHREUN BHAID 217

Fo F d

294 POLE HILL

259 BEINN ROSAIL

B871

B873

Strath Naver 12

345 CNOC NAM TRI-CHLACH

Loch Cròcach

404 BEINN MHADADH

Beinn Griam Beg 588

590 BEN GRIAM MÓR

337 MEAL A' BHEALAICH

230 BEADAIG

270

Loch Druim a-Chliabhain

Loch an Ruathair

230 MEALL A' BHROLLAICH

rra

Loch Naver

River Mallart

Loch Rimsdale

Loch nan Clàr

Loch Badanloch

Loch Arichlinie

A897

959 BEN KLIBRECK

Loch Choire Forest

694 CREAG N-IOLAIRE

Loch Truderscaig

Loch an Altan Fhearna

Loch Choire

713 CREAG MHÓR

434 CNOC AN LIATH-BHAID MHÓIR

Borrobol Forest

River Helmsdale

B871

Kinbrace

Loch a' Bhealaich

202 CNOC DAIL-CHAIRN

Strath Free

Loch Ascaig

Gorm-loch Mór

364 CNOC NA BREUN-CHOILLE

388 CREAG NAM FIÀDH

Learable Hill Cairns, Stone Row & Stone Circles

Strath of

Ben Armine Forest

Glas-loch Mór

Strath Skinsdale

337 CNOC NA H-INNSE MOIRE

462 MEALLAN LIATH-MÓR

421 CNOC NAN CRÙBAG MÓR

A836

River Brora

317 SITHEAN ACHADH NAN EUN

Loch Beannach

293 CNOC LEAMHNACHD

Balnacoil Lodge

539 COL-BHEINN

hnairn

Ferrycroft Countryside Centre

Loch Craggie

River Brora

Strath Brora

Dalreavoch Lodge

Loch Brora

323 BEN DOULA

Lairg

Tomich

A839

Loch Horn

520 BEN HORN

378 CAGAR FEOSAIG

Doll

Torrobull

14

Rogart

Golspie Burn

Backies

Carn Liath

A9

446 BEN LUNDIE

223

Dunrobin Castle

hany

B864

A836

313 CREAGAN GLAS

383 BEN BHRAGGIE

Rhives

Golspie

Falls of Shin 11

333 MEALL EACHAINN

Torboll

veran

Loch Buidhe

Sleasdairidh

349 BEINN DONUILL

Cambu Pla

Loch Fleet

Badninish

Skelbo

Skelbo Street

Culrain

A836

A · B · C · D · E · F

Fourpenny

SLETILL HILL

Altnabreac Station

G

CNOC NAN GALL

Rumsdale Water

H

Dalnawillan Lodge

Strathmore

J

Loch an Thulachan

Loch Sand

K

Achavanich

L

Loch Stemster

STEMSTER HILL

Grey of C

M

226
COIRE NA BEINN

Loch Rangag

Re

1

230

348
BEN ALISKY

Glutt Lodge

287
BEN-A-CHIELT

231

Upper Lybster

2

440

432

KNOCKFIN HEIGHTS

264
CNOCAN CONACHREAG

Houstry

Smerral

Land-hallow

Forse

Swiney

Invershore

Lybster

Lybster Bay

317
CNOC LOCH MHADADH

Dunbeath Water

Latheronwheel

Janetstown

Latheron

A9

3

437
CNOC COIRE NA FEARNA

Berriedale Water

484
MAIDEN PAP

Braemore

Knockally

Laidhay Croft

Dunbeath

705
MORVEN

518
CNOC AN EIREANNAICH

626
SCARABEN

Ramscraigs

Borgue

20

Sill Burn

Langwell Forest

Newport

Langwell House

Berriedale

4

554
CREAG SCALABSDALE

401
CNOC NA MAOILE

A9

onan Lodge

Kildonan 416
BENN DUBHAIN

A897

Torrish

River Helmsdale

404
CREAG THORARAIDH

Ord of Caithness

Navidale House Hotel

5

624
BEINN DHORAIN

591
BEINN NA MEILICH

West Helmsdale

Gartymore

Portgower

Timespan

East Helmsdale

Helmsdale

onan

Glen Loth

Lothmore

Lothbeg

21

6

7

Dalchalm

rora

8

G   H   J   K   L   M

A B C D E F

1

2

CAPE WRATH

Cléit
Dhubh

Faraid
Head

371
SGRIBHIS-
BHEINN

297
CNOC A
GHIUBHAIS

300
MAOVALLY

Balnakeil
Bay

Sango
Bay

THE PARPH

Balnakeil

Durness
Sangomore

Smoo
Cave

3

457
FASHVEN

Keoldale

Smoo

Sangobeg

Sandwood
Bay

Loch Airigh
na Beinne

Loch
Meadaidh

Sandwood
Loch

485
CREAG
RIABACH

Rudh' an Fhir Leithe

468
BEINN
DEARG MHÒR

464
MEALL
NA MÒINE

331
GHLAS-
BHEINN

423
MEALL
MEADHONACH

Strath Shinary

Sheigra

4

Balchreick

Blairmore

Oldshoremore

355
AN
SOCACH

521
FARVEALL

489
MEALL
NA CRÀ

Laid

Kinlochbervie

Badcall

773
BEINN
SPIONNAIDH

Loch Clash

Achriesgill

801
CRANSTACKIE

Strath Beag

Strath Dionard

Rhiconich

520
AN LEAN-CHÀRN

5

Rudha Ruadh

Skerricha

Loch na
Claise Càrnaich

River Dionard

908
FOINAVEN

Fanagmore

Tarbet

Foindle

HANDA
ISLAND

North-west Sutherland

Loch na Tuadh

786
ARKLE

FEINNE-BH

6

Laxford
Bridge

River Laxford

A838

Scourie Bay

A894

Scourie

729
SÀBHAL BEAG

Glen Golly

Dur

Scourie More

Loch
Stack

Badcall

721
BEN STACK

Strath Stack

Achfary

333
BEN
SCREAVIE

800

796
CÀRN
DEARG

757
CARN AN
TIONAIL

7

Badcall Bay

386
BEN
AUSKAIRD

Loch a'
Mhuilinn

Rudh' a'
Mhucard

A838

Loch More

224

OLDANY
ISLAND

Eddrachillis
Bay

419
BEN
STROME

Kylestrome

225

Kinloch

Culkein
Drumbeg

Kyleskul

Loch an
Leathaid Bhuain

873
BEN
HEE

8

Drumbeg

B869

Nedd

Unapool

Loch Glendhu

Glen Dhu

680
MEALL AN
LIATH-MÒR

A B C D E F

Loch
Poll

0   1   2   3   4 miles

0 1 2 3 4 5 kilometres

525
BEINN
DA LOC

613
MEALL AN FHEUR LOCH

792

Loch
Merkland

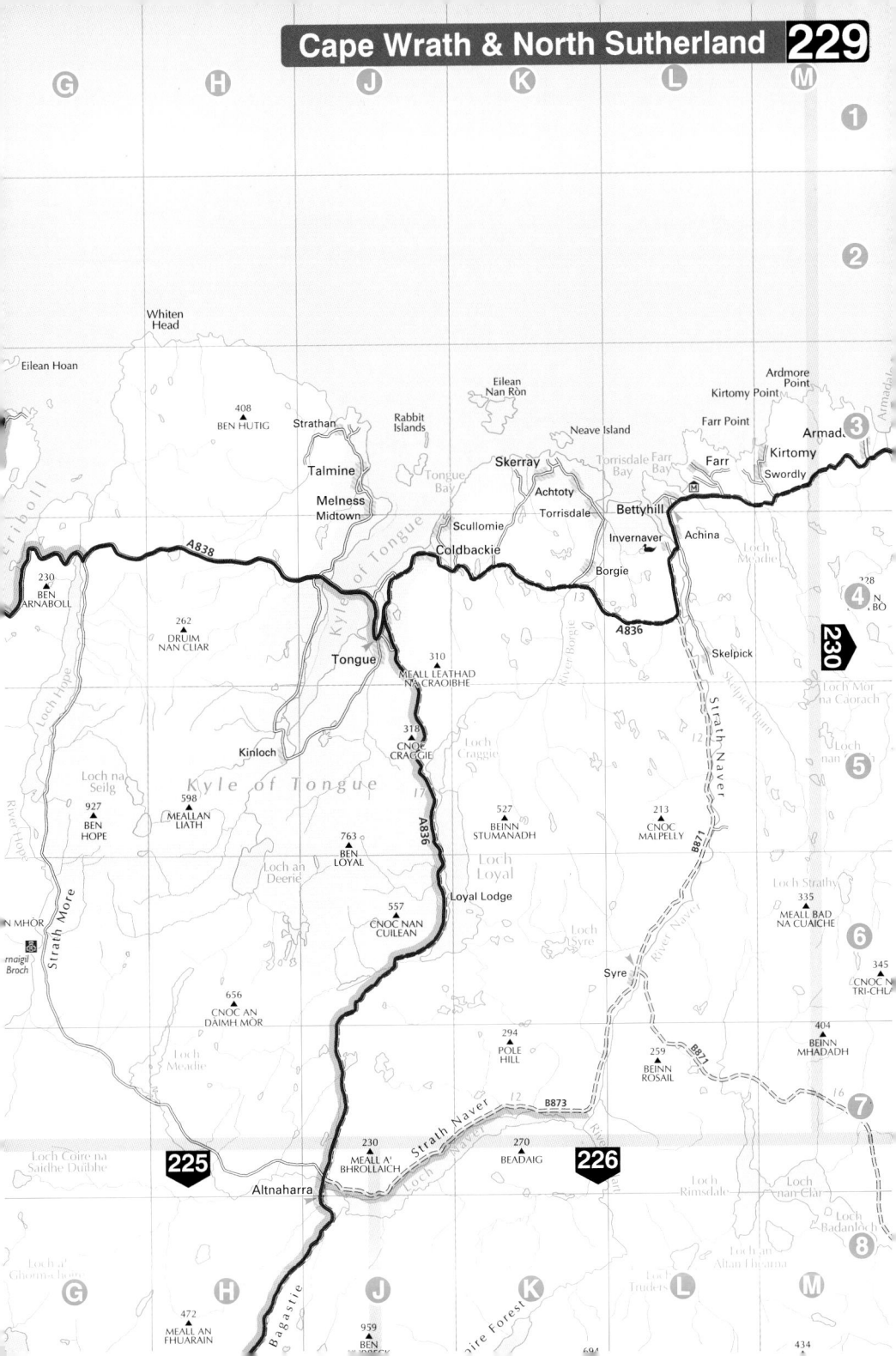

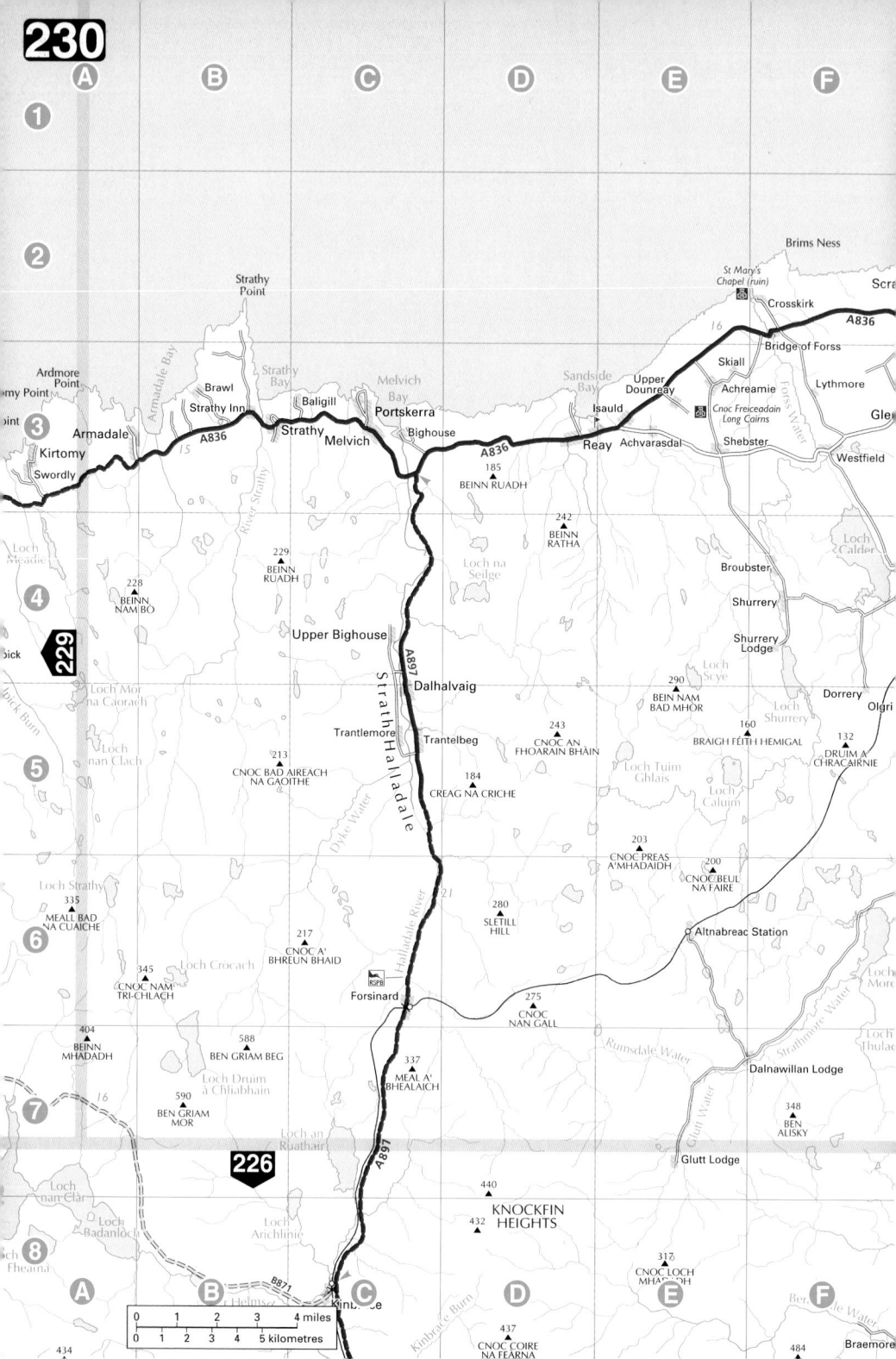

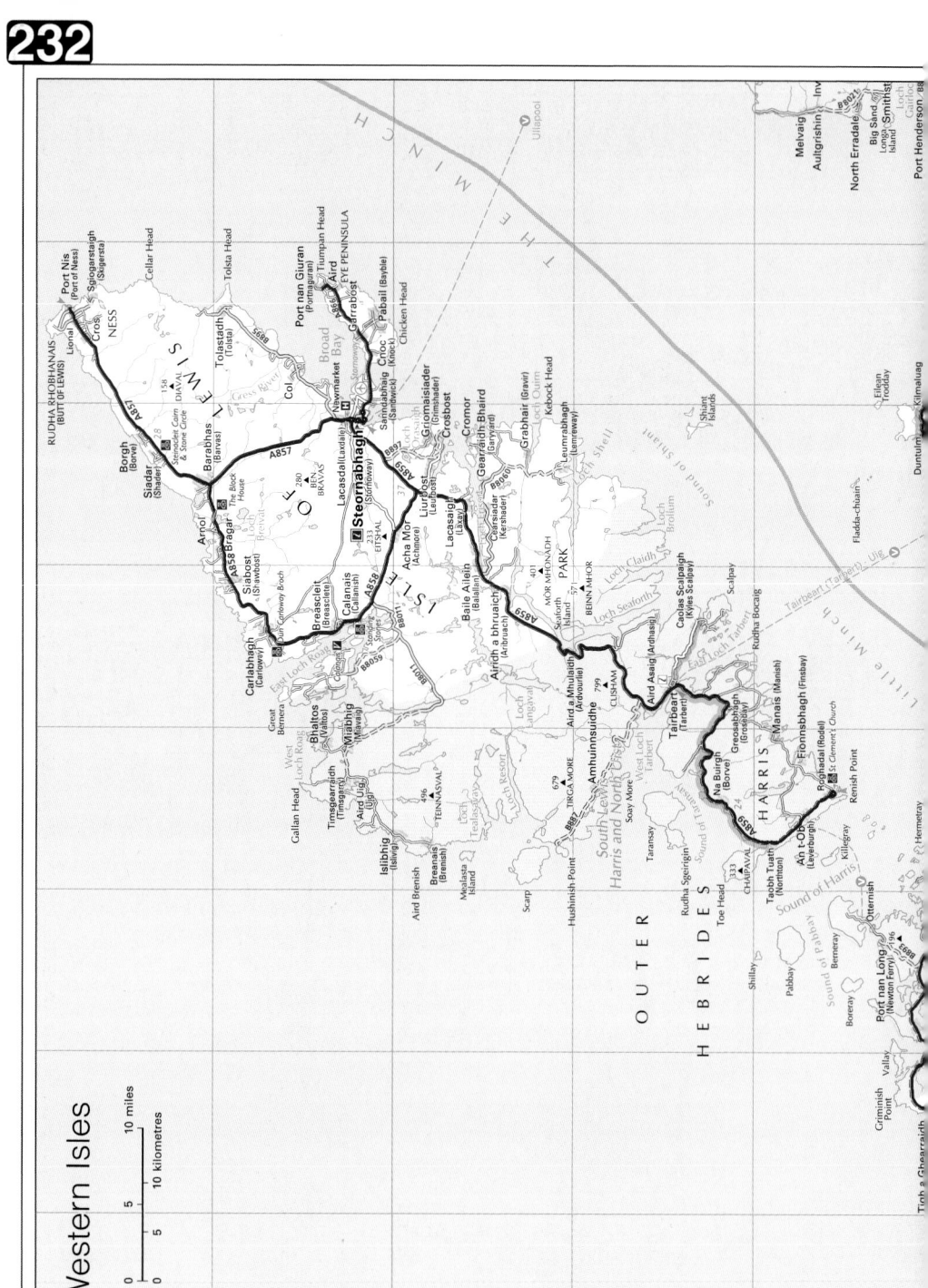

Western Isles

10 miles

10 kilometres

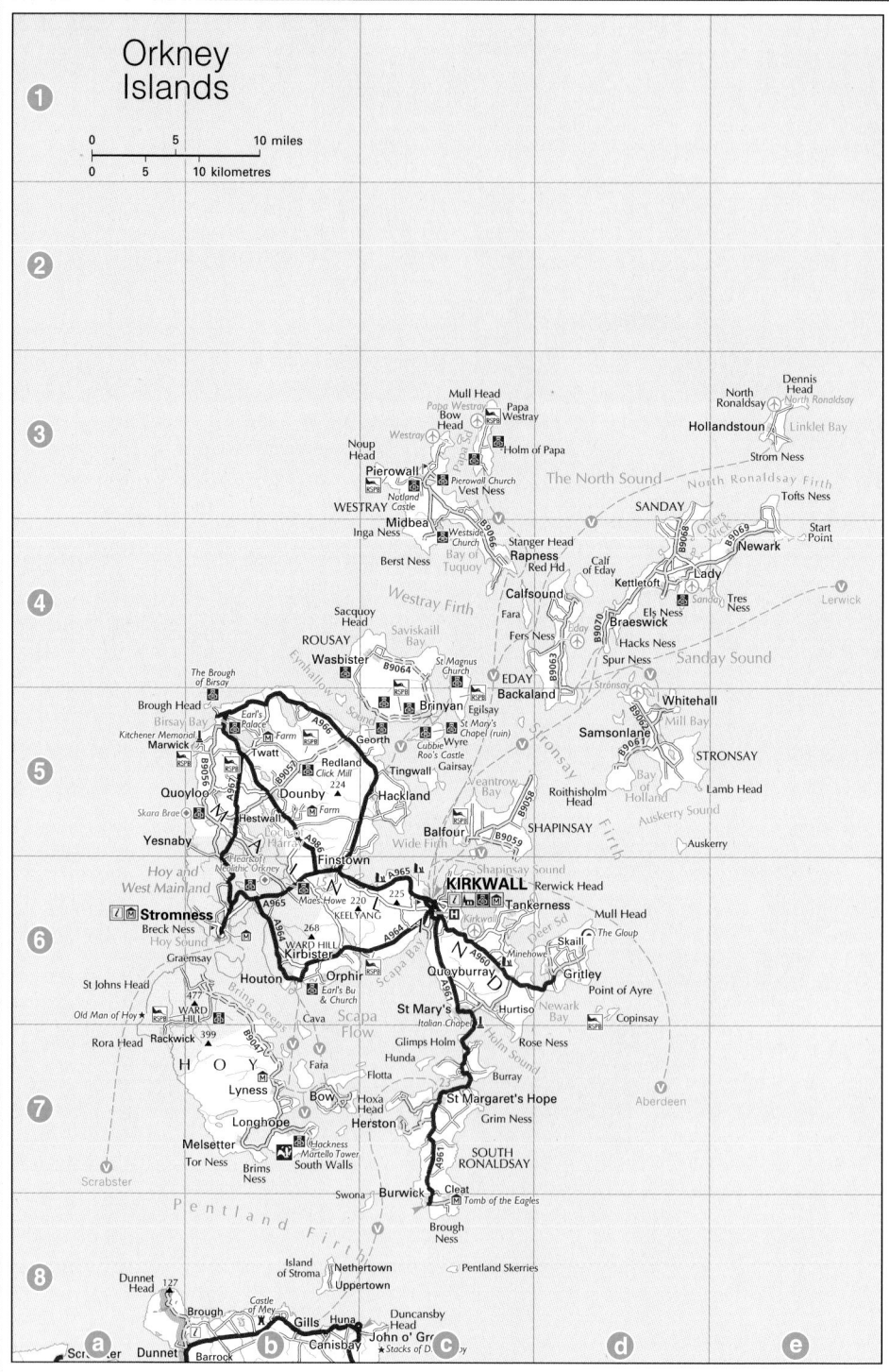

Orkney
Islands

0 5 10 miles
0 5 10 kilometres

Mull Head
Papa Westray
Bow Head
Papa Westray
Holm of Papa
Noup Head
Pierowall
Pierowall Church
Notland Castle
Vest Ness
WESTRAY Midbea
Inga Ness
Westside Church
Berst Ness
Bay of Tuquoy

Dennis Head
North Ronaldsay
North Ronaldsay
Hollandstoun
Linklet Bay
Strom Ness
The North Sound
North Ronaldsay Firth
Tofts Ness
SANDAY
Otters Wick
Start Point
Newark
B9069
Lady
Sanday
Lerwick

Stanger Head
Rapness
Red Hd.
Calf of Eday
Kettletoft
Calfsound
Els Ness
Braeswick
B9070
Fers Ness
Hacks Ness
Spur Ness
Sanday Sound
Tres Ness

Sacquoy Head
Westray Firth
ROUSAY
Wasbister
Saviskaill Bay
St Magnus Church
B9064
Fara
Egilsay
EDAY
Backaland
Stronsay
Whitehall
Mill Bay
Samsonlane
STRONSAY

The Brough of Birsay
Brough Head
Birsay Bay
Earl's Palace
Farm
Kitchener Memorial
Marwick
Twatt
A986
Redland
Click Mill
224
Quoyloo
Dounby
Hackland
Roo's Castle
St Mary's Chapel (ruin)
Wyre
Gairsay
Cubbie
Georth
Tingwall
Balfour
Brinyan
Veantrow Bay
SHAPINSAY
Roithisholm Head
Bay of Holland
Lamb Head
Bay of Holland

Skara Brae
A967
Hestwall
Farm
Yesnaby
Heart of Neolithic Orkney
Harray
A986
Finstown
A965
Maes Howe 220
KEELYANG
225
A964
Wide Firth
B9059
Auskerry Sound
Auskerry

Hoy and West Mainland
Stromness
Breck Ness
Hoy Sound
Graemsay
St Johns Head
WARD HILL
477
Old Man of Hoy
Rora Head
Rackwick
399
HOY

Houton
WARD HILL
268
Kirbister
Orphir
Earl's Bu & Church
Cava
Scapa Flow
St Mary's
Italian Chapel
Glimps Holm
Hunda
Bow
Hoxa Head
Burray

KIRKWALL
Renwick Ness
Tankerness
Mull Head
Deer Sd.
Skaill
The Gloup
Minehowe
Quoyburray
Gritley
Point of Ayre
Hurtiso
Newark Bay
Copinsay
Rose Ness
Holm Sound

Lyness
Longhope
Flotta
Melsetter
Tor Ness
Brims Ness
Hackness
Martello Tower
South Walls
Swona
Burwick
Cleat
Tomb of the Eagles

St Margaret's Hope
Grim Ness
SOUTH RONALDSAY
A961
Brough Ness

Aberdeen

Scrabster
Pentland Firth
Island of Stroma
Netherton
Uppertown
Pentland Skerries

Dunnet Head
127
Brough
Castle of Mey
Gills
Huna
Duncansby Head
John o' Gro
Stacks of D.
Dunnet
Barrock
Canisbay

a b c d e

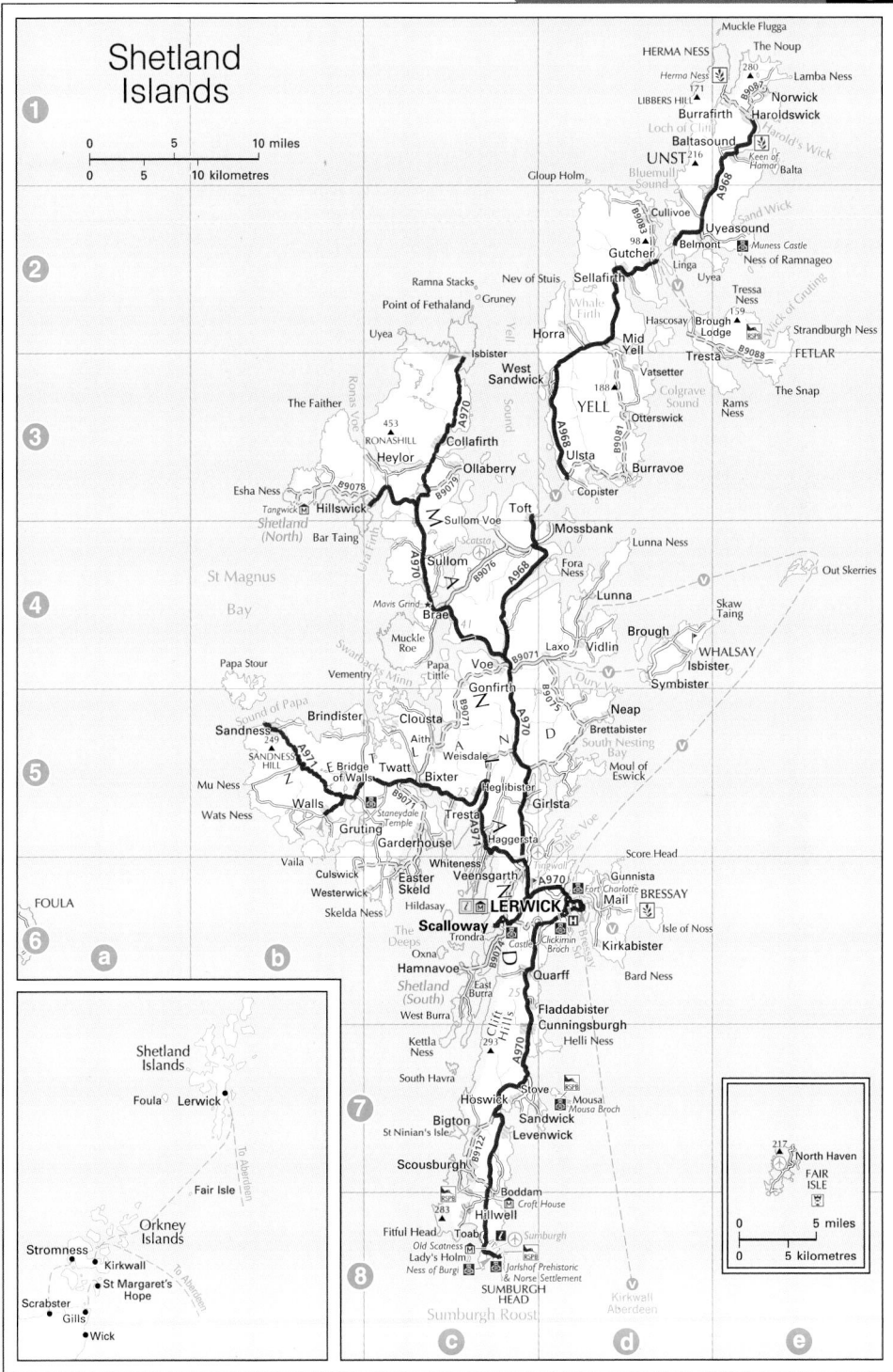

Shetland
Islands

0   5   10 miles

0   5   10 kilometres

Muckle Flugga
The Noup
HERMA NESS
Herma Ness *171* 280
LIBBERS HILL A907 Lamba Ness
Burrafirth   Norwick
Loch of Cliff   Haroldswick
Baltasound
Bluemull UNST *216* Keen of Hamar
Gloup Holm Sound   Balta
Culivoe   Uyeasound
Ramna Stacks B9083 98 Belmont Muness Castle
Point of Fethaland Gruney   Gutcher   Ness of Ramnageo
Uyea   Nev of Stuis   Linga Uyea
Isbister   Horra   Tressa
Sellafirth   Ness
West   Hascosay Brough 159
The Faither   Sandwick   Mid   Lodge   Strandburgh Ness
453   Yell   Tresta   FETLAR
RONASHILL   188 Vatsetter   A9088
Heylor   Collafirth   YELL   The Snap
Esha Ness   Ollaberry   Ulsta   Otterswick   Rams
B9078   Ness
Tangwick Hillswick   Toft   Burravoe
Shetland   Copister
(North) Bar Taing   Sullom Voe   Mossbank
Scatsta   Lunna Ness
St Magnus   Sullom   Fora   Lunna   Skaw
Ness   Taing Out Skerries
Bay   Mavis Grind   Laxo   Brough
Brae   Muckle   Vidlin   WHALSAY
Roe   Papa   Voe   Isbister
Papa Stour   Little   B9071   Symbister
Vementry   Gonfirth   Neap
Brindister   Brettabister
Sandness   Clousta   Weisdale   South Nesting   Moul of
249   Aith   Bay   Eswick
SANDNESS   E Bridge   Twatt
HILL   of Walls   Bixter   Score Head
Mu Ness   Weisdale   Girlsta
Walls   Tresta   Haggersta   Gunnista
Wats Ness   Gruting   A970   Mail   BRESSAY
Vaila   Garderhouse   Whiteness   Fort Charlotte Isle of Noss
Culswick   Veensgarth LERWICK
FOULA   Easter   Hildasay   Clickimin   Kirkabister
Westerwick   Skeld   Scalloway   Broch
Skelda Ness   Trondra Castle   Bard Ness
The   Oxna   Hamnavoe   Quarff
Deeps   East   Fladdabister
Burra   Cunningsburgh
Shetland   Helli Ness
(South)   Clift
West Burra   Hills 293
Kettla   Hoswick
Ness   Sand   Sandwick
South Havra   Bigton   Levenwick
St Ninian's Isle   Stove
Scousburgh   Mousa
Mousa Broch
Boddam
Croft House
Fitful Head   Hillwell
283   Toab
Old Scatness   Sumburgh
Lady's Holm   Jarlshof Prehistoric
Ness of Burgi   & Norse Settlement
SUMBURGH
HEAD
Sumburgh Roost

FOULA

Shetland
Islands

Foula Lerwick

Fair Isle

Orkney
Islands

Stromness
Kirkwall
St Margaret's
Scrabster   Hope
Gills
Wick

217
North Haven
FAIR
ISLE

0   5 miles

0   5 kilometres

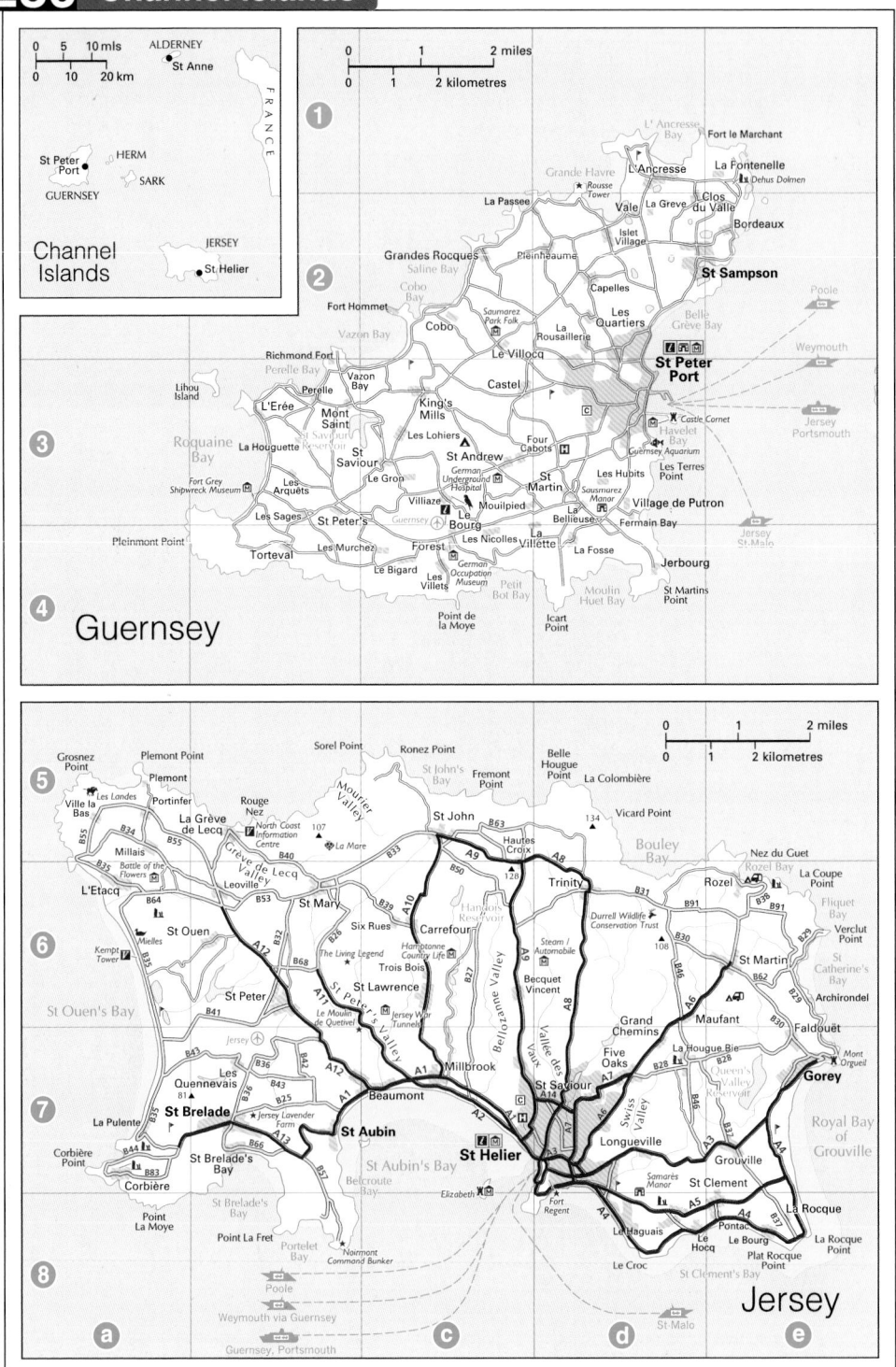

Channel Islands

0 5 10 mls
0 10 20 km

ALDERNEY
● St Anne

FRANCE

St Peter Port ● HERM

SARK

GUERNSEY

JERSEY
● St Helier

1

0 1 2 miles
0 1 2 kilometres

L'Ancresse Bay
Fort le Marchant
L'Ancresse
La Fontenelle
★ Rousse Tower
Dehus Dolmen
La Passee
Vale
La Greve
Clos du Valle
Bordeaux
Grande Havre

2

Grandes Rocques
Saline Bay
Pleinheaume
Capelles
Les Quartiers
St Sampson
Poole

Fort Hommet
Cobo Bay
Cobo
Saumarez Park Folk
La Rousaillerie
Belle Greve Bay
Weymouth

Vazon Bay
Le Villocq
St Peter Port
Richmond Fort
Perelle Bay
Perelle
Castel
Jersey Portsmouth

3

Lihou Island
L'Erée
Vazon Bay
King's Mills
Les Lohiers
Four Cabots
Castle Cornet
Guernsey Aquarium
Havelet Bay

Roquaine Bay
La Hougette
Mont Saint
St Saviour's Reservoir
St Saviour
Le Gron
St Andrew
German Underground Hospital
St Martin
Les Hubits
Les Terres Point

Fort Grey Shipwreck Museum
Les Arquêts
Les Sages
St Peter's
Villiaze
Le Bourg
Moulpied
La Bellieuse
Sausmarez Manor
Village de Putron
Fermain Bay

4

Pleinmont Point
Torteval
Les Murchez
Le Bigard
Forest
Les Nicolles
La Villette
La Fosse
Jerbourg
Guernsey
German Occupation Museum
Les Villets
Petit Bot Bay
Moulin Huet Bay
St Martins Point
Point de la Moye
Icart Point

Guernsey

5

0 1 2 miles
0 1 2 kilometres

Grosnez Point
Plemont Point
Sorel Point
Ronez Point
Belle Hougue Point
La Colombière
Plemont
St John's Bay
Fremont Point

Ville la Bas
Les Landes
Portinfer
Rouge Nez
Mourier Valley
St John
B63
Hautes Croix
A8
Vicard Point
Bouley Bay
Nez du Guet
Rozel Bay
La Coupe Point

6

La Grève de Lecq
North Coast Information Centre
107
La Mare
B40
B33
B50
A9
128
Trinity
Durrell Wildlife Conservation Trust
Rozel
B91
Fliquet Bay
Verclut Point

Millais
Battle of the Flowers
B35
Grève de Lecq Valley
Leoville
B53
St Mary
B39
Six Rues
A10
Hamptonne Reservoir
Carrefour
B27
Steam / Automobile
106
St Martin
B62
St Catherine's Bay
Archirondel

L'Etacq
B64
St Ouen
Mielles
A12
B72
B68
Trois Bois
The Living Legend
St Lawrence
Hamptonne Country Life
Becquet Vincent
A8
B46
Faldouët
B30

6

Kempt Tower
B35
St Peter
B41
Le Moulin de Quetivel
Jersey War Tunnels
Grand Chemins
Maufant
La Hougue Bie
Mont Orgueil
B29

St Ouen's Bay
Jersey
Five Oaks
B28
Gorey
B26
Queen's Valley Reservoir

7

Les Quennevais
B43
B25
A1
Millbrook
St Saviour
A14
A7
Longueville
Royal Bay of Grouville

La Pulente
St Brelade
B66
St Aubin
Beaumont
A2
St Helier
Swiss Valley
Grouville
A4

Corbière Point
B44
B83
St Brelade's Bay
B37
St Aubin's Bay
Elizabeth
Fort Regent
Samarès Manor
St Clement
La Rocque

8

Corbière
Point La Moye
St Brelade's Bay
Belcroute Bay
Point La Fret
Portelet Bay
Noirmont Command Bunker
Le Haguais
Le Croc
Le Hocq
Le Bourg
Plat Rocque Point
La Rocque Point

Poole
Weymouth via Guernsey
Guernsey, Portsmouth
St-Malo

Jersey

a   c   d   e

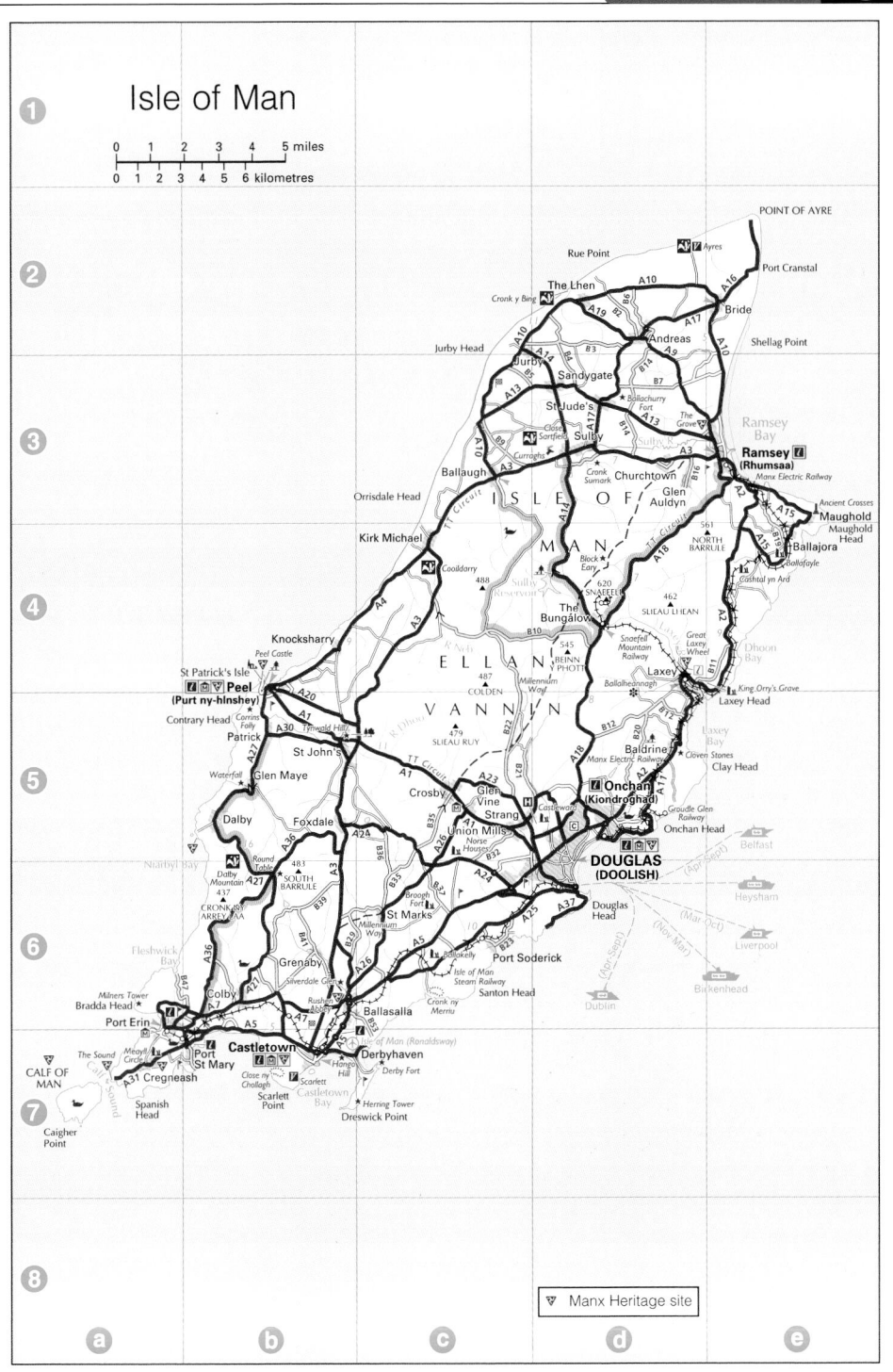

Isle of Man

0 1 2 3 4 5 miles
0 1 2 3 4 5 6 kilometres

POINT OF AYRE

Ayres
Rue Point
Port Cranstal
The Lhen
A10
Cronk y Bing
A19
A17
Bride
A16
Shellag Point
Jurby Head
A10
Andreas
A9
A10
Jurby
A4
Sandygate
B3
B7
St Jude's
A13
Ballachurry Fort
Close Sartfield
Sulby
A17
The Grove
B14
Ramsey Bay
Curraghs
Ballaugh
A10
Churchtown
Sulby
A3
Ramsey (Rhumsaa)
Manx Electric Railway
Orrisdale Head
A14
Cronk Surnark
Glen Auldyn
B16
A2
Ancient Crosses
Maughold
Kirk Michael
Block Eary
TT Circuit
A18
561 NORTH BARRULE
A15
Maughold Head
Cooildarry
488
Sulby Reservoir
620 SNAEFELL
462 SLIEAU LHEAN
Ballajora
Ballafayle
Cashtal yn Ard
Knocksharry
A4
A3
The Bungalow
B10
Snaefell Mountain Railway
Great Laxey Wheel
Dhoon Bay
Peel Castle
Corrins Folly
ELLAN
545 BEINN Y PHOTT
A3
King Orry's Grave
St Patrick's Isle
Peel (Purt ny-hInshey)
A20
487 COLDEN
Millennium Way
Ballaheannagh
Laxey
B11
Laxey Head
Contrary Head
A1
VANNIN
479 SLIEAU RUY
TT Circuit
B12
Laxey Bay
Patrick
A30
Tynwald Hill
St John's
A1
B20
Cloven Stones
Clay Head
Glen Maye
Waterfall
A23
Crosby
B35
Baldrine
Manx Electric Railway
Dalby
Foxdale
Glen Vine
Strang
Castletown
Onchan (Kiondroghad)
Groudle Glen Railway
Onchan Head
Union Mills
Norse House
A24
A5
Belfast
Nnarbyl Bay
Dalby Mountain 437
483 SOUTH BARRULE
A36
A25
DOUGLAS (DOOLISH)
Heysham
CRONK NY ARREY LAA
B39
St Marks
Brooghr Fort
Millennium Way
A25
A37
Douglas Head
Liverpool
Fleshwick Bay
A36
Grenaby
Silverdale Glen
Rushen Abbey
A5
Ballakilley
Port Soderick
Isle of Man Steam Railway
Santon Head
Birkenhead
Milners Tower
Bradda Head
Colby
A7
Ballasalla
A5
Cronk ny Merriu
Dublin
Port Erin
B47
A27
Isle of Man (Ronaldsway)
Castletown
Derbyhaven
A3
Port St Mary
Meayll Circle
A31 Cregneash
Close ny Chollagh
Hango Hill
Derby Fort
The Sound
Scarlett
Castletown Bay
CALF OF MAN
Scarlett Point
Castletown Head
Herring Tower
Spanish Head
Dreswick Point
Caigher Point

∀ Manx Heritage site

1 2 3 4 5 6 7 8
a b c d e

Restricted junctions

Motorway and Primary Route junctions which have access or exit restrictions are shown on the map pages thus:

M1 London - Leeds

Junction	Northbound	Southbound
2	Access only from A1 *(northbound)*	Exit only to A1 *(southbound)*
4	Access only from A41 *(northbound)*	Exit only to A41 *(southbound)*
6A	Access only from M25 *(no link from A405)*	Exit only to M25 *(no link from A405)*
7	Access only from A414	Exit only to A414
17	Exit only to M45	Access only from M45
19	Exit only to M6 *(northbound)*	Access only from M6
21A	Exit only, no access	Access only, no exit
23A	Access only from A42	No restriction
24A	Access only, no exit	Exit only, no access
35A	Exit only, no access	Access only, no exit
43	Access only from M621	Access only from M621
48	Exit only to A1(M) *(northbound)*	Access only from A1(M) *(southbound)*

M2 Rochester - Faversham

Junction	Westbound	Eastbound
1	No exit to A2 *(eastbound)*	No access from A2 *(westbound)*

M3 Sunbury - Southampton

Junction	Northeastbound	Southwestbound
8	Access only from A303, no exit	Exit only to A303, no access
10	Exit only, no access	Access only, no exit
14	Access from M27 only, no exit	No access to M27 *(westbound)*

M4 London - South Wales

Junction	Westbound	Eastbound
1	Access only from A4 *(westbound)*	Exit only to A4 *(eastbound)*
21	Exit only to M48	Access only from M48
23	Access only from M48	Exit only to M48
25	Exit only, no access	Access only, no exit
25A	Exit only, no access	Access only, no exit
29	Exit only to A48(M)	Access only from A48(M)
38	Exit only, no access	No restriction
39	Access only, no exit	No access or exit

M5 Birmingham - Exeter

Junction	Northeastbound	Southwestbound
10	Access only, no exit	Exit only, no access
11A	Access only from A417 *(westbound)*	Exit only to A417 *(eastbound)*
18A	Exit only to M49	Access only from M49
18	Exit only, no access	Access only, no exit
29	No restriction	Access only from A30 *(westbound)*

M6 Toll Motorway

Junction	Northwestbound	Southeastbound
T1	Access only, no exit	No access or exit
T2	No access or exit	Access only, no exit
T3	Staggered junction, follow signs - access only from A38 *(northbound)*	Staggered junction, follow signs - access only from A38 *(southbound)*
T5	Access only, no exit	Exit only to A5148 *(northbound)*, no access
T7	Exit only, no access	Access only, no exit
T8	Exit only, no access	Access only, no exit

M6 Rugby - Carlisle

Junction	Northbound	Southbound
3A	Exit only to M6 Toll	Access only from M6 Toll
4A	Access only from M42 *(southbound)*	Exit only to M42
5	Exit only, no access	Access only, no exit
10A	Exit only to M54	Access only from M54

11A	Access only from M6 Toll	Exit only to M6 Toll
with M56 (jct 20A)	No restriction	Access only from M56 *(eastbound)*
20	Access only, no exit	No restriction
24	Access only, no exit	Exit only, no access
25	Exit only, no access	Access only, no exit
29	No direct access, use adjacent slip road to jct 29A	No direct exit, use adjacent slip road from jct 29A
29A	Access only, no exit	Exit only, no access
30	Access only from M61	Exit only to M61
31A	Exit only, no access	Access only, no exit
45	Exit only, no access	Access only, no exit

M8 Edinburgh - Bishopton

Junction	Westbound	Eastbound
8	No access from M73 *(southbound)* or from A8 *(eastbound)* & A89	No exit to M73 *(northbound)* or to A8 *(westbound)* & A89
9	Access only, no exit	Exit only, no access
13	Access only from M80 *(southbound)*	Exit only to M80 *(northbound)*
14	Access only, no exit	Exit only, no access
16	Exit only to A804	Access only from A879
17	Exit only to A82	No restriction
18	Access only from A82 *(eastbound)*	Exit only to A814
19	No access from A814 *(westbound)*	Exit only to A814 *(westbound)*
20	Access only, no exit	Exit only, no access
21	Access only, no exit	Exit only to A8
22	Exit only to M77 *(southbound)*	Access only from M77 *(northbound)*
23	Exit only to B768	Access only from B768
25	No access or exit from or to A8	No access or exit from or to A8
25A	Exit only, no access	Access only, no exit
28	Exit only, no access	Access only, no exit
28A	Exit only to A737	Access only from A737

M9 Edinburgh - Dunblane

Junction	Northwestbound	Southeastbound
1A	Exit only to M9 spur	Access only from M9 spur
2	Access only, no exit	Exit only, no access
3	Exit only, no access	Access only, no exit
6	Access only, no exit	Exit only to A905
8	Exit only to M876 *(southwestbound)*	Access only from M876 *(northeastbound)*

M11 London - Cambridge

Junction	Northbound	Southbound
4	Access only from A406 *(eastbound)*	Exit only to A406
5	Access only, no exit	Exit only, no access
9	Exit only to A11	Access only from A11
13	Access only, no exit	Access only, no exit
14	Exit only, no access	Access only, no exit

M20 Swanley - Folkestone

Junction	Northwestbound	Southeastbound
2	Staggered junction; follow signs - access only	Staggered junction; follow signs - exit only
3	Exit only to M26 *(westbound)*	Access only from M26 *(eastbound)*
5	Access only from A20	For access follow signs - exit only to A20
6	No restriction	For exit follow signs
11A	Access only, no exit	Exit only, no access

M23 Hooley - Crawley

Junction	Northbound	Southbound
7	Exit only to A23 *(northbound)*	Access only from A23 *(southbound)*
10A	Access only, no exit	Exit only, no access

M25 London Orbital Motorway

Junction	Clockwise	Anticlockwise
1B	No direct access, use slip road to Jct 2. Exit only	Access only, no exit
5	No exit to M26 *(eastbound)*	No access from M26
19	Access only, no exit	Access only, no exit
21	Access only from M1 *(southbound)*. Exit only to M1 *(northbound)*	Access only from M1 *(southbound)*. Exit only to M1 *(northbound)*
31	No exit (use slip road via jct 30), access only	No access (use slip road via jct 30), exit only

M26 Sevenoaks - Wrotham

Junction	Westbound	Eastbound
with M25 (jct 5)	Exit only to clockwise M25 *(westbound)*	Access only from anticlockwise M25 *(eastbound)*
with M20 (jct 3)	Access only from M20 *(northwestbound)*	Exit only to M20 *(southeastbound)*

M27 Cadnam - Portsmouth

Junction	Westbound	Eastbound
4	Staggered junction; follow signs - access only from M3 *(southbound)*. Exit only to M3 *(northbound)*	Staggered junction; follow signs - access only from M3 *(southbound)*. Exit only to M3 *(northbound)*
10	Exit only, no access	Access only, no exit
12	Staggered junction; follow signs - exit only to M275 *(southbound)*	Staggered junction; follow signs - access only from M275 *(northbound)*

M40 London - Birmingham

Junction	Northwestbound	Southeastbound
3	Exit only, no access	Access only, no exit
7	Exit only, no access	Access only, no exit
8	Exit only to M40/A40	Access only from M40/A40
13	Exit only, no access	Access only, no exit
14	Access only, no exit	Exit only, no access
16	Access only, no exit	Exit only, no access

M42 Bromsgrove - Measham

Junction	Northeastbound	Southwestbound
1	Access only, no exit	Exit only, no access
7	Exit only to M6 *(northwestbound)*	Access only from M6 *(northwestbound)*
7A	Exit only to M6 *(southeastbound)*	No access or exit
8	Access only from M6 *(southeastbound)*	Exit only to M6 *(northwestbound)*

M45 Coventry - M1

Junction	Westbound	Eastbound
Dunchurch (unnumbered)	Access only from A45	Exit only, no access
with M1 (jct 17)	Access only from M1 *(northbound)*	Exit only to M1 *(southbound)*

M53 Mersey Tunnel - Chester

Junction	Northbound	Southbound
11	Access only from M56 *(westbound)*. Exit only to M56 *(eastbound)*	Access only from M56 *(westbound)*. Exit only to M56 *(eastbound)*

M54 Telford

Junction	Westbound	Eastbound
with M6 (jct 10A)	Access only from M6 *(northbound)*	Exit only to M6 *(southbound)*

M56 North Cheshire

Junction	Westbound	Eastbound
1	Access only from M60 (westbound)	Exit only to M60 (eastbound) & A34 (northbound)
2	Exit only, no access	Access only, no exit
3	Access only, no exit	Exit only, no access
4	Exit only, no access	Access only, no exit
7	Exit only, no access	No restriction
8	Access only, no exit	No access or exit
15	Exit only to M53	Access only from M53
16	No access or exit	No restrictions

M57 Liverpool Outer Ring Road

Junction	Northwestbound	Southeastbound
3	Access only, no exit	Exit only, no access
5	Access only from A580 (westbound)	Exit only, no access

M58 Liverpool - Wigan

Junction	Westbound	Eastbound
1	Exit only, no access	Access only, no exit

M60 Manchester Orbital

Junction	Clockwise	Anticlockwise
2	Access only, no exit	Exit only, no access
3	No access from M56	Access only from A34 (northbound)
4	Access only from A34 (northbound). Exit only to M56	Access only from M56 (eastbound). Exit only to A34 (southbound)
5	Access and exit only from and to A5103 (northbound)	Access and exit only from and to A5103 (southbound)
7	Access only from A56. slip road to jct 8. Exit only to A56	Access only from A56. No exit - use jct 8
14	Access from A580 (eastbound)	Exit only to A580 (westbound)
16	Access only, no exit	Exit only, no access
20	Exit only, no access	Access only, no exit
22	No restriction	Exit only, no access
25	Exit only, no access	No restriction
26	No restriction	Exit only, no access
27	Access only, no exit	Exit only, no access

M61 Manchester - Preston

Junction	Northwestbound	Southeastbound
3	No access or exit	Exit only, no access
with M6 (jct 30)	Exit only to M6 (northbound)	Access only from M6 (southbound)

M62 Liverpool - Kingston upon Hull

Junction	Westbound	Eastbound
23	Access only, no exit	Exit only, no access
32a	No access to A1(M) (southbound)	No restriction

M65 Preston - Colne

Junction	Northeastbound	Southwestbound
9	Exit only, no access	Access only, no exit
11	Access only, no exit	Exit only, no access

M66 Bury

Junction	Northbound	Southbound
with A56	Exit only to A56 (northbound)	Access only from A56 (southbound)
1	Exit only, no access	Access only, no exit

M67 Hyde Bypass

Junction	Westbound	Eastbound
1	Access only, no exit	Exit only, no access
2	Exit only, no access	Access only, no exit
3	Exit only, no access	No restriction

M69 Coventry - Leicester

Junction	Northbound	Southbound
2	Exit only, no access	Exit only, no access

M73 East of Glasgow

Junction	Northbound	Southbound
2	No access from or exit to A89. No access from M8 (eastbound).	No access from or exit to A89. No exit to M8 (westbound)

M74 and A74(M) Glasgow - Gretna

Junction	Northbound	Southbound
3	Exit only, no access	Access only, no exit
3a	Access only, no exit	Exit only, no access
7	Access only, no exit	Exit only, no access
9	No access or exit	Exit only, no access
10	No restrictions	Access only, no exit
11	Access only, no exit	Exit only, no access
12	Exit only, no access	Access only, no exit
18	Access only, no exit	Access only, no exit

M77 South of Glasgow

Junction	Northbound	Southbound
with M8 (jct 22)	No exit to M8 (westbound)	No access from M8 (eastbound)
4	Access only, no exit	Exit only, no access
6	Access only, no exit	Exit only, no access
7	Access only, no exit	No restriction

M80 Glasgow - Stirling

Junction	Northbound	Southbound
4a	Exit only, no access	Access only, no exit
6a	Access only, no exit	Exit only, no access
8	Exit only to M876 (northeastbound)	Access only from M876 (southwestbound)

M90 Forth Road Bridge - Perth

Junction	Northbound	Southbound
2a	Exit only to A92 (eastbound)	Access only from A92 (westbound)
7	Access only, no exit	Exit only, no access
8	Exit only, no access	Access only, no exit
10	No access from A912. No exit to A912 (southbound)	No access from A912 (northbound). No exit to A912

M180 Doncaster - Grimsby

Junction	Westbound	Eastbound
1	Access only, no exit	Exit only, no access

M606 Bradford Spur

Junction	Northbound	Southbound
2	Exit only, no access	No restriction

M621 Leeds - M1

Junction	Clockwise	Anticlockwise
2a	Access only, no exit	Exit only, no access
4	No exit or access	No restriction
5	Access only, no exit	Exit only, no access
6	Access only, no exit	Access only, no exit
with M1 (jct 43)	Exit only to M1 (southbound)	Access only from M1 (northbound)

M876 Bonnybridge - Kincardine Bridge

Junction	Northeastbound	Southwestbound
with M80 (jct 5)	Access only from M80 (northbound)	Exit only to M80 (southbound)
with M9 (jct 8)	Exit only to M9 (eastbound)	Access only from M9 (westbound)

A1(M) South Mimms - Baldock

Junction	Northbound	Southbound
2	Exit only, no access	Access only, no exit
3	No restriction	Exit only, no access
5	Access only, no exit	No access or exit

A1(M) Pontefract - Bedale

Junction	Northbound	Southbound
41	No access to M62 (eastbound)	No restriction
43	Access only from M1 (northbound)	Exit only to M1 (southbound)

A1(M) Scotch Corner - Newcastle upon Tyne

Junction	Northbound	Southbound
57	Exit only to A66(M) (eastbound)	Access only from A66(M) (westbound)
65	No access Exit only to A194(M) & A1 (northbound)	No exit Access only from A194(M) & A1 (southbound)

A3(M) Horndean - Havant

Junction	Northbound	Southbound
1	Access only from A3	Exit only to A3
4	Exit only, no access	Access only, no exit

A48(M) Cardiff Spur

Junction	Westbound	Eastbound
29	Access only from M4 (westbound)	Exit only to M4 (eastbound)
29a	Exit only to A48 (westbound)	Access only from A48 (eastbound)

A66(M) Darlington Spur

Junction	Westbound	Eastbound
with A1(M) (jct 57)	Exit only to A1(M) (southbound)	Access only from A1(M) (northbound)

A194(M) Newcastle upon Tyne

Junction	Northbound	Southbound
with A1(M) (jct 65)	Access only from A1(M) (northbound)	Exit only to A1(M) (southbound)

A12 M25 - Ipswich

Junction	Northeastbound	Southwestbound
13	Access only, no exit	No restriction
14	No access, no exit	Access only, no exit
20a	Access only, no exit	Access only, no exit
20b	Access only, no exit	Exit only, no access
21	No restriction	Access only, no exit
23	Exit only, no access	Access only, no exit
24	Access only, no exit	Exit only, no access
27	Exit only, no access	Access only, no exit
Dedham & Stratford St Mary (unnumbered)	Exit only	Access only

A14 M1 - Felixstowe

Junction	Westbound	Eastbound
with M1/M6 (jct19)	Exit only to M6 and M1 (northbound)	Access only from M6 and M1 (southbound)
4	Exit only, no access	Access only, no exit
31	Access only from A1307	Exit only to A1307
34	Access only, no exit	Exit only, no access
36	Exit only to A11, access only from A1303	Access only from A11
38	Access only from A11	Exit only to A11
39	Exit only, no access	Access only, no exit
61	Access only, no exit	Exit only, no access

A55 Holyhead - Chester

Junction	Westbound	Eastbound
8a	Access only, no exit	Access only, no exit
23a	Access only, no exit	Exit only, no access
24a	Exit only, no access	No access or exit
33a	Exit only, no access	No access or exit
33b	Access only, no exit	Access only, no exit
37	Exit only to A5104	Access only from A5104

Index to place names

This index lists places appearing in the main-map section of the atlas in alphabetical order. The reference following each name gives the atlas page number and grid reference of the square in which the place appears. The map shows counties and administrative areas, together with a list of the abbreviated name forms used in the index. The top 100 places of tourist interest are indexed in **red**, World Heritage sites in **green**, motorway service areas in **blue**, airports in blue *italic* and National Parks in green *italic*.

Scotland

Abers	**Aberdeenshire**
Ag & B	**Argyll and Bute**
Angus	**Angus**
Border	**Scottish Borders**
C Aber	**City of Aberdeen**
C Dund	**City of Dundee**
C Edin	**City of Edinburgh**
C Glas	**City of Glasgow**
Clacks	**Clackmannanshire (1)**
D & G	**Dumfries & Galloway**
E Ayrs	**East Ayrshire**
E Duns	**East Dunbartonshire (2)**
E Loth	**East Lothian**
E Rens	**East Renfrewshire (3)**
Falk	**Falkirk**
Fife	**Fife**
Highld	**Highland**
Inver	**Inverclyde (4)**
Mdloth	**Midlothian (5)**
Moray	**Moray**
N Ayrs	**North Ayrshire**
N Lans	**North Lanarkshire (6)**
Ork	**Orkney Islands**
P & K	**Perth & Kinross**
Rens	**Renfrewshire (7)**
S Ayrs	**South Ayrshire**
Shet	**Shetland Islands**
S Lans	**South Lanarkshire**
Stirlg	**Stirling**
W Duns	**West Dunbartonshire (8)**
W Isls	**Western Isles (Na h-Eileanan an Iar)**
W Loth	**West Lothian**

Wales

Blae G	**Blaenau Gwent (9)**
Brdgnd	**Bridgend (10)**
Caerph	**Caerphilly (11)**
Cardif	**Cardiff**
Carmth	**Carmarthenshire**
Cerdgn	**Ceredigion**
Conwy	**Conwy**
Denbgs	**Denbighshire**
Flints	**Flintshire**
Gwynd	**Gwynedd**
IoA	**Isle of Anglesey**
Mons	**Monmouthshire**
Myr Td	**Merthyr Tydfil (12)**
Neath	**Neath Port Talbot (13)**
Newpt	**Newport (14)**
Pembks	**Pembrokeshire**
Powys	**Powys**
Rhondd	**Rhondda Cynon Taff (15)**
Swans	**Swansea**
Torfn	**Torfaen (16)**
V Glam	**Vale of Glamorgan (17)**
Wrexhm	**Wrexham**

Channel Islands & Isle of Man

Guern	**Guernsey**
Jersey	**Jersey**
IoM	**Isle of Man**

England

BaNES	**Bath & N E Somerset (18)**
Barns	**Barnsley (19)**
Bed	**Bedford**
Birm	**Birmingham**
Bl w D	**Blackburn with Darwen (20)**
Bmouth	**Bournemouth**
Bolton	**Bolton (21)**
Bpool	**Blackpool**
Br & H	**Brighton & Hove (22)**
Br For	**Bracknell Forest (23)**
Bristl	**City of Bristol**
Bucks	**Buckinghamshire**
Bury	**Bury (24)**
C Beds	**Central Bedfordshire**
C Brad	**City of Bradford**
C Derb	**City of Derby**
C KuH	**City of Kingston upon Hull**
C Leic	**City of Leicester**
C Nott	**City of Nottingham**
C Pete	**City of Peterborough**
C Plym	**City of Plymouth**
C Port	**City of Portsmouth**
C Sotn	**City of Southampton**
C Stke	**City of Stoke-on-Trent**
C York	**City of York**
Calder	**Calderdale (25)**
Cambs	**Cambridgeshire**
Ches E	**Cheshire East**
Ches W	**Cheshire West and Chester**
Cnwll	**Cornwall**
Covtry	**Coventry**
Cumb	**Cumbria Darltn**
Derbys	**Derbyshire**
Devon	**Devon**
Donc	**Doncaster (27)**
Dorset	**Dorset**
Dudley	**Dudley (28)**
Dur	**Durham**
E R Yk	**East Riding of Yorkshire**
E Susx	**East Sussex**
Essex	**Essex**
Gatesd	**Gateshead (29)**
Gloucs	**Gloucestershire**
Gt Lon	**Greater London**
Halton	**Halton (30)**
Hants	**Hampshire**
Hartpl	**Hartlepool (31)**
Herefs	**Herefordshire**
Herts	**Hertfordshire**
IoS	**Isles of Scilly**
IoW	**Isle of Wight**
Kent	**Kent**
Kirk	**Kirklees (32)**
Knows	**Knowsley (33)**
Lancs	**Lancashire**
Leeds	**Leeds**
Leics	**Leicestershire**
Lincs	**Lincolnshire**
Lpool	**Liverpool**
Luton	**Luton**
M Keyn	**Milton Keynes**
Manch	**Manchester**
Medway	**Medway**
Middsb	**Middlesbrough**
NE Lin	**North East Lincolnshire**
N Linc	**North Lincolnshire**
N Som	**North Somerset (34)**
N Tyne	**North Tyneside (35)**
N u Ty	**Newcastle upon Tyne**
N York	**North Yorkshire**
Nhants	**Northamptonshire**
Norfk	**Norfolk**
Notts	**Nottinghamshire**
Nthumb	**Northumberland**
Oldham	**Oldham (36)**
Oxon	**Oxfordshire**
Poole	**Poole**
R & Cl	**Redcar & Cleveland**
Readg	**Reading**
Rochdl	**Rochdale (37)**
Rothm	**Rotherham (38)**
Rutlnd	**Rutland**
S Glos	**South Gloucestershire (39)**
S on T	**Stockton-on-Tees (40)**
S Tyne	**South Tyneside (41)**
Salfd	**Salford (42)**
Sandw	**Sandwell (43)**
Sefton	**Sefton (44)**
Sheff	**Sheffield**
Shrops	**Shropshire**
Slough	**Slough (45)**
Solhll	**Solihull (46)**
Somset	**Somerset**
St Hel	**St Helens (47)**
Staffs	**Staffordshire**
Sthend	**Southend-on-Sea**
Stockp	**Stockport (48)**
Suffk	**Suffolk**
Sundld	**Sunderland**
Surrey	**Surrey**
Swindn	**Swindon**
Tamesd	**Tameside (49)**
Thurr	**Thurrock (50)**
Torbay	**Torbay**
Traffd	**Trafford (51)**
W & M	**Windsor and Maidenhead (52)**
W Berk	**West Berkshire**
W Susx	**West Sussex**
Wakefd	**Wakefield (53)**
Warrtn	**Warrington (54)**
Warwks	**Warwickshire**
Wigan	**Wigan (55)**
Wilts	**Wiltshire**
Wirral	**Wirral (56)**
Wokham	**Wokingham (57)**
Wolves	**Wolverhampton (58)**
Worcs	**Worcestershire**
Wrekin	**Telford & Wrekin (59)**
Wsall	**Walsall (60)**

240

ORKNEY
ISLANDS

SHETLAND
ISLANDS

WESTERN ISLES (Na h-Eileanan an Iar)

HIGHLAND

MORAY

S C O T L A N D

Aberdeen

ABERDEENSHIRE

ANGUS

PERTH &
KINROSS

Dundee

ARGYLL
& BUTE

STIRLING

FIFE

1

8 2 FALK
4 7 6
Glasgow

Edinburgh

W
LOTH

E LOTH

E LOTH

3

5

NORTH
AYRSHIRE

S LANS

S LANS

SCOTTISH
BORDERS

E AYRS

S AYRS

DUMFRIES &
GALLOWAY

NORTHUMBERLAND

Newcastle
upon Tyne 35
29 41
Sunderland

CUMBRIA

DURHAM 31

26 40 R & CL
Middlesbrough

IoM

NORTH YORKSHIRE

Blackpool

LANCASHIRE

Bradford York

Leeds

EAST RIDING
OF YORKSHIRE

Kingston
upon Hull

20 25
21 24 37 36
55 32 53
19
44 47 42 54
33 49 27
Liverpool 54 51 38
56 30 48 Sheffield
CHES Manchester
E

N LINC

N E
LIN

IoA

CONWY

FLINTS CHES
W

DENBGS

DERBYS

NOTTS

LINCOLNSHIRE

WREXHAM

Stoke-
on-Trent

GWYNEDD

STAFFS

Derby

Nottingham

59

LEICS

RUTLAND

Peterborough

NORFOLK

SHROPSHIRE

58 60
43
78 23

Birmingham
Coventry

46

NHANTS

Leicester

CAMBS

SUFFOLK

POWYS

WORCS

WARWKS

Milton
Keynes

BED

CERDGN

HEREFS

GLOUCS

OXON

BUCKS

BEDS Luton

ESSEX

PEMBKS

CARMTH

W A L E S

MONS

9
12
16

E N G L A N D

HERTS

GREATER
LONDON

Southend-
on-Sea

13
15 11
10 14
Swansea 17 Cardiff Bristol
34
18

39

Swindon

Reading

W BERK

52 45
57 23

SURREY

50

MEDWAY

WILTSHIRE

KENT

SOMERSET

HAMPSHIRE

W SUSX

E SUSX

22

DEVON

DORSET

Southampton

Portsmouth

CORNWALL

Plymouth Torbay

Bournemouth
Poole

IoW

CHANNEL
ISLANDS

Guernsey

Jersey

IoS

A

Abbas Combe Somset 27 G6
Abberley Worcs 70 D2
Abberley Common
Worcs 70 D2
Abberton Essex 62 B4
Abberton Worcs 71 H4
Abbess Roding Essex.... 60 F5
Abbeydale Sheff............ 114 H4
Abbey Dore Herefs 54 B3
Abbey Green Staffs........ 99 L2
Abbey St Bathans
Border 178 F6
Abbeystead Lancs 130 B8
Abbey Town Cumb......... 147 L5
Abbey Village Lancs....... 121 J6
Abbey Wood Gt Lon........ 45 J4
Abbotrule Border 167 J6
Abbots Bickington
Devon 9 K3
Abbots Bromley Staffs.. 100 B7
Abbotsbury Dorset........ 14 B5
Abbots Deuglie P & K.... 186 B5
Abbotsham Devon.......... 22 F6
Abbotskerswell
Devon 7 K3
Abbots Langley Herts.... 59 H7
Abbots Leigh N Som...... 38 D5
Abbotsley Cambs 75 J3
Abbots Morton Worcs.... 71 H4
Abbots Ripton Cambs.... 89 J7
Abbot's Salford
Warwks 71 J4
Abbots Worthy Hants.... 29 J5
Abbotts Ann Hants 29 G3
Abbott Street Dorset.... 15 J3
Abdon Shrops 83 L6
Aberaeron Cerdgn 66 B3
Aberaman Rhondd 52 F7
Aberangell Gwynd......... 81 J2
Aberarder Highld 202 F1
Aberargie P & K............ 186 B4
Aberarth Cerdgn 66 B2
Aberavon Neath............. 51 L7
Abercanaid Myr Td........ 53 G7
Abercarn Caerph........... 37 K2
Abercastle Pembks 64 B7
Abercegir Powys 81 H3
Aberchalder Lodge
Highld 202 B5
Aberchirder Abers 216 C4
Abercraf Powys 52 C5
Abercregan Neath.......... 36 D2
Abercwmboi Rhondd..... 52 F7
Abercych Pembks 65 H6
Abercynon Rhondd 37 G2
Aberdalgie P & K........... 185 M4
Aberdare Rhondd 52 F7
Aberdaron Gwynd......... 94 C7
Aberdeen C Aber........... 207 H4
Aberdeen Airport
C Aber 207 G3
Aberdeen
Crematorium
C Aber 207 G4
Aberdour Fife................ 177 G2
Aberdulais Neath.......... 52 B7
Aberdyfi Gwynd............. 80 D2
Aberedw Powys 68 C5
Abereiddy Pembks........ 48 D2
Abererch Gwynd............ 95 G5
Aberfan Myr Td.............. 53 G7
Aberfeldy P & K............. 194 D6
Aberffraw IoA............... 108 D7
Aberford Leeds............. 124 C3
Aberfoyle Stirlg 184 C7
Abergavenny Mons........ 53 L5
Abergele Conwy............ 110 C6
Abergorlech Carmth...... 66 D7
Abergwesyn Powys........ 67 J4
Abergwili Carmth.......... 50 F2
Abergwynfi Neath........... 36 D2
Abergwyngregyn
Gwynd 109 J6

Abergynolwyn
Gwynd 80 F3
Aberkenfig Brdgnd......... 36 D4
Aberlady E Loth............. 178 B3
Aberlemno Angus......... 196 E5
Aberllefenni Gwynd....... 81 G2
Aberllynfi Powys........... 68 D6
Aberlour Moray 215 G5
Abermule Powys........... 82 D5
Abernant Carmth.......... 50 D2
Aber-nant Rhondd........ 52 F7
Abernethy P & K............ 186 C4
Abernyte P & K.............. 186 D2
Aberporth Cerdgn 65 J4
Abersoch Gwynd............ 94 E6
Abersychan Torfn.......... 53 K7
Aberthin V Glam............. 36 F5
Abertillery Blae G......... 53 K7
Abertridwr Caerph......... 37 H3
Abertridwr Powys.......... 97 G8
Aberuthven P & K.......... 185 K4
Aberystwyth Cerdgn...... 80 D6
Aberystwyth
Crematorium
Cerdgn 80 E6
Abingdon-on-
Thames Oxon............... 41 J2
Abinger Common
Surrey 31 J3
Abinger Hammer
Surrey 31 H2
Abington Nhants........... 73 L3
Abington S Lans............ 165 H5
Abington Pigotts
Cambs 75 K5
Abington Services
S Lans 165 H4
Abingworth W Susx....... 18 F3
Ab Kettleby Leics 102 B7
Ablington Gloucs 56 C6
Abney Derbys................ 114 D5
Aboyne Abers 205 L5
Abram Wigan 112 E2
Abriachan Highld........... 212 E7
Abridge Essex............... 45 J2
Abronhill N Lans 175 K3
Abson S Glos................. 39 G5
Abthorpe Nhants 73 J5
Aby Lincs...................... 118 F5
Acaster Malbis C York... 124 E2
Acaster Selby N York.... 124 E3
Accrington Lancs 121 L5
Accrington
Crematorium
Lancs 121 L5
Acha Ag & B.................. 188 F5
Achahoish Ag & B......... 172 D3
Achalader P & K............ 195 H7
Achaleven Ag & B......... 182 D1
Acha Mor W Isls............ 232 f3
Achanalt Highld............. 211 K3
Achandunie Highld........ 222 E6
Achany Highld............... 222 D2
Acharacle Highld........... 190 D3
Acharn Highld............... 190 E6
Acharn P & K................. 194 B7
Achavanich Highld......... 231 H6
Achduart Highld............ 224 C7
Achfary Highld.............. 228 D7
A'Chill Highld................. 198 D4
Achiltibuie Highld.......... 224 C6
Achina Highld................ 229 L4
Achinhoan Ag & B......... 161 J6
Achintee Highld............. 210 E6
Achintraid Highld.......... 210 C6
Achlyness Highld........... 228 C4
Achmelvich Highld......... 224 C4
Achmore Highld............. 210 D7
Achmore W Isls............. 232 f3
Achnacarnin Highld....... 224 C3
Achnacarry Highld......... 201 J7
Achnacloich Highld........ 199 J4
Achnaconeran Highld 202 C2
Achnacroish Ag & B...... 191 G7
Achnadrish House
Ag & B 189 L6
Achnafauld P & K.......... 185 J2

Achnagarron Highld...... 222 F7
Achnaha Highld............. 189 L3
Achnahaird Highld......... 224 B5
Achnairn Highld............ 225 L6
Achnalea Highld............ 191 G4
Achnamara Ag & B........ 172 D2
Achnasheen Highld........ 211 J3
Achnashellach Lodge
Highld 210 F5
Achnastank Moray......... 215 G2
Achosnich Highld........... 189 K3
Achranich Highld........... 190 E6
Achreamie Highld.......... 230 E3
Achriabhach Highld........ 192 B3
Achriesgill Highld.......... 228 C5
Achtoty Highld.............. 229 K3
Achurch Nhants............ 88 E6
Achvaich Highld............. 222 F3
Achvarasdal Highld........ 230 E3
Ackergill Highld............. 231 L5
Acklam Middsb............. 141 L4
Acklam N York.............. 134 B7
Ackleton Shrops........... 84 D4
Acklington Nthumb....... 159 G2
Ackton Wakefd............. 124 C6
Ackworth Moor Top
Wakefd 124 C7
Acle Norfk.................... 93 J2
Acock's Green Birm 85 K6
Acol Kent..................... 35 J2
Acomb C York............... 124 E1
Acomb Nthumb............. 150 B2
Aconbury Herefs 54 D2
Acton Ches E................ 98 F2
Acton Gt Lon 44 D4
Acton Staffs................. 99 J4
Acton Suffk.................. 77 K5
Acton Beauchamp
Herefs 70 C4
Acton Bridge Ches W.... 112 E6
Acton Burnell Shrops ... 83 K3
Acton Green Herefs 70 C4
Acton Park Wrexhm...... 97 M3
Acton Round Shrops 84 B4
Acton Scott Shrops....... 83 J5
Acton Trussell Staffs.... 99 L8
Acton Turville S Glos.... 39 J4
Adbaston Staffs............ 99 H6
Adber Dorset................ 26 E7
Adbolton Notts............. 101 L5
Adderbury Oxon............ 72 F7
Adderley Shrops........... 98 F4
Addiewell W Loth.......... 176 D5
Addingham C Brad........ 123 G1
Addington Bucks........... 58 C3
Addington Gt Lon.......... 45 G7
Addington Kent............. 33 H2
Addiscombe Gt Lon....... 45 G6
Addlestone Surrey......... 43 H7
Addlethorpe Lincs......... 119 H7
Adeyfield Herts............. 59 H6
Adfa Powys................... 82 B4
Adforton Herefs 69 H1
Adisham Kent............... 35 G4
Adlestrop Gloucs.......... 56 E3
Adlingfleet E R Yk......... 125 K6
Adlington Lancs............ 121 J7
Admaston Staffs........... 100 B7
Admaston Wrekin.......... 84 B2
Adpar Cerdgn 65 J6
Adsborough Somset...... 25 L5
Adscombe Somset......... 25 J4
Adstock Bucks.............. 58 C3
Adstone Nhants............ 73 H4
Adversane W Susx........ 31 H6
Advie Highld................. 214 D7
Adwick Le Street
Donc 124 E8
Adwick upon Dearne
Donc 115 J2
Ae D & G....................... 155 H4
Ae Bridgend D & G........ 155 H5
Afan Forest Park
Neath 36 D2
Affleck Abers 216 B6
Affpuddle Dorset.......... 14 F4

Affric Lodge Highld........ 201 J2
Afon-wen Flints............ 110 F6
Afton IoW.................... 16 D5
Agecroft
Crematorium
Salfd 113 J2
Agglethorpe N York....... 131 K3
Aigburth Lpool 111 L4
Aike E R Yk................... 126 C2
Aiketgate Cumb............ 148 E5
Aikton Cumb................. 148 B4
Ailsworth C Pete.......... 89 G4
Ainderby Quernhow
N York............................ 132 E4
Ainderby Steeple
N York............................ 132 E2
Aingers Green Essex..... 62 D4
Ainsdale Sefton............ 120 D7
Ainstable Cumb............ 148 F5
Ainsworth Bury............. 121 L8
Ainthorpe N York.......... 142 E5
Ainville W Loth............. 176 F5
Aird Ag & B.................. 181 M7
Aird D & G.................... 144 D3
Aird W Isls................... 232 g2
Aird a Mhulaidh W Isls.. 232 e3
Aird Asaig W Isls.......... 232 e4
Aird Dhubh Highld......... 209 L6
Airdeny Ag & B............. 182 E2
Aird of Kinloch
Ag & B 181 H2
Aird of Sleat Highld....... 199 J5
Airdrie N Lans.............. 175 K5
Airdriehill N Lans.......... 175 K5
Airds of Kells D & G....... 154 B7
Aird Uig W Isls.............. 232 d2
Airidh a bhruaich
W Isls 232 e3
Airieland D & G............. 146 D4
Airlie Angus................. 195 L6
Airmyn E R Yk............... 125 H5
Airntully P & K.............. 186 A1
Airor Highld.................. 199 L4
Airth Falk.................... 176 B2
Airton N York................ 131 G7
Aisby Lincs................... 103 G5
Aisby Lincs................... 116 E3
Aish Devon................... 7 G4
Aish Devon................... 7 J4
Aisholt Somset............. 25 J4
Aiskew N York............... 132 D2
Aislaby N York.............. 134 B3
Aislaby N York.............. 143 H5
Aislaby S on T.............. 141 J5
Aisthorpe Lincs............ 116 F5
Aith Shet..................... 235 c5
Akeld Nthumb............... 168 E4
Akeley Bucks................ 73 K6
Albaston Cnwll.............. 6 B2
Alberbury Shrops.......... 83 G1
Albourne W Susx.......... 19 H3
Albrighton Shrops......... 84 E3
Albrighton Shrops......... 98 C8
Alburgh Norfk............... 92 F6
Albury Herts................. 60 C3
Albury Surrey............... 31 H2
Albury Heath Surrey...... 31 H3
Alcaig Highld................ 212 E3
Alcaston Shrops........... 83 J6
Alcester Warwks.......... 71 K3
Alciston E Susx............ 20 B5
Alcombe Somset........... 24 F3
Alconbury Cambs.......... 89 H7
Alconbury Weston
Cambs 89 H7
Aldborough N York........ 132 F6
Aldborough Norfk......... 106 E5
Aldbourne Wilts............ 40 E5
Aldbrough E R Yk.......... 127 G3
Aldbrough St John
N York............................ 140 F5
Aldbury Herts............... 58 F5
Aldcliffe Lancs............. 129 K7
Aldclune P & K.............. 194 E4
Aldeburgh Suffk........... 79 K3
Aldeby Norfk................. 93 J5

Aldenham Herts 43 J2
Alderbury Wilts.............28 D6
Alderford Norfk.........106 D8
Alderholt Dorset..........28 C8
Alderley Gloucs.............39 H3
Alderley Edge Ches E ...113 J5
Aldermans Green
Covtry.......................86 D6
Aldermaston W Berk 41 L7
Alderminster Warwks 72 B5
Aldershot Hants............30 E2
Alderton Gloucs............55 M2
Alderton Nhants............73 K5
Alderton Suffk...............79 H6
Alderton Wilts...............39 J4
Aldfield N York............132 D5
Aldford Ches W..............98 B2
Aldgate Rutlnd................88 E3
Aldham Essex................61 L3
Aldham Suffk................78 C5
Aldingbourne
W Susx.....................18 C5
Aldingham Cumb.........129 G5
Aldington Kent..............34 E2
Aldington Worcs...........71 J5
Aldington Corner
Kent.........................34 E7
Aldivalloch Moray 205 H1
Aldochlay Ag & B........174 C1
Aldreth Cambs..............90 C8
Aldridge Wsall...............85 J4
Aldringham Suffk...........79 J3
Aldsworth Gloucs..........56 D6
Aldunie Moray.............215 H8
Aldwark Derbys...........100 E1
Aldwark N York...........133 G6
Aldwick W Susx............18 C6
Aldwincle Nhants...........88 E6
Aldworth W Berk...........41 K4
Alexandria W Duns.......174 D3
Aley Somset..................25 J4
Alfington Devon.............12 E3
Alfold Surrey.................31 H5
Alfold Crossways
Surrey......................31 H4
Alford Abers...............206 B3
Alford Lincs................118 F6
Alford Somset...............26 E5
Alford Crematorium
Lincs......................118 F6
Alfreton Derbys...........101 H2
Alfrick Worcs................70 D4
Alfrick Pound Worcs......70 D4
Alfriston E Susx.............20 B5
Algarkirk Lincs............103 M5
Alhampton Somset.........26 F4
Alkborough N Linc.......125 K6
Alkham Kent.................35 H6
Alkmonton Derbys.......100 D5
Allaleigh Devon...............7 J5
Allanaquoich Abers 204 D6
Allanbank N Lans........175 L6
Allanton Border...........179 H7
Allanton N Lans..........175 L6
Allanton S Lans...........175 K7
Allaston Gloucs..............54 F6
Allbrook Hants...............29 J7
All Cannings Wilts.........40 B7
Allendale Nthumb.........149 L4
Allenheads Nthumb......149 L6
Allen's Green Herts........60 D5
Allensmore Herefs.........69 J7
Allenton C Derb...........101 G6
Aller Devon...................24 B6
Aller Somset..................26 B5
Allerby Cumb..............147 J6
Allercombe Devon.........12 D4
Allerford Somset............24 D3
Allerston N York..........134 D4
Allerthorpe E R Yk.......125 J2
Allerton C Brad...........123 G4
Allerton Highld............213 H2
Allerton Lpool.............111 L4
Allerton Bywater
Leeds.....................124 C5

Allerton Mauleverer
N York....................132 F7
Allesley Covtry..............86 C7
Allestree C Derb...........101 G5
Allexton Leics................88 B4
Allgreave Ches E..........113 L7
Allhallows Medway........46 D4
Alligin Shuas Highld.....210 C3
Allington Dorset............13 L4
Allington Lincs............102 E4
Allington Wilts...............28 D4
Allington Wilts...............39 K5
Allington Wilts...............40 B7
Allithwaite Cumb.........129 J4
Alloa Clacks................185 J8
Allonby Cumb..............147 J6
Alloway S Ayrs............163 J5
Allowenshay Somset......26 B8
All Stretton Shrops........83 J4
Alltchaorunn Highld.....192 C6
Alltwalis Carmth............66 B7
Alltwen Neath................51 K5
Alltyblaca Cerdgn..........66 C5
Allweston Dorset...........26 F8
Almeley Herefs...............69 G4
Almington Staffs............99 G5
Almodbank P & K........185 M3
Almondbury Kirk...........123 H7
Almondsbury S Glos......38 E4
Alne N York.................133 G6
Alness Highld..............222 E7
Alnham Nthumb...........168 E7
Alnmouth Nthumb........169 J7
Alnwick Nthumb...........169 J6
Alperton Gt Lon.............44 D4
Alphamstone Essex 77 K7
Alpheton Suffk...............77 K4
Alphington Devon...........11 L6
Alport Derbys...............114 E8
Alpraham Ches E...........98 E1
Alresford Essex.............62 C4
Alrewas Staffs...............85 L1
Alsager Ches E..............99 H2
Alsop en le Dale
Derbys....................100 D2
Alston Cumb................149 J5
Alston Devon.................13 H2
Alstone Gloucs..............55 M2
Alstonefield Staffs.......100 C2
Alston Sutton Somset....26 B2
Alswear Devon...............23 L6
Altandhu Highld...........224 B6
Altarnun Cnwll................9 G8
Altass Highld .:............222 C2
Altcreich Ag & B..........190 D8
Altgaltraig Ag & B........173 H4
Althorne Essex...............61 L7
Althorpe N Linc............125 K8
Altnabreac Station
Highld....................230 E6
Altnaharra Highld........225 M2
Alton Derbys...............115 G8
Alton Hants...................30 B4
Alton Staffs.................100 B4
Alton Barnes Wilts.........40 C7
Alton Pancras Dorset....14 D3
Alton Priors Wilts..........40 C7
Alton Towers Staffs.....100 B4
Altrincham Traffd........113 H4
Altrincham
Crematorium
Traffd....................113 G4
Altskeith Hotel Stirlg ...184 B6
Alva Clacks................185 J7
Alvanley Ches W..........112 D6
Alvaston C Derb...........101 H5
Alvechurch Worcs..........85 J8
Alvecote Warwks...........86 B3
Alvediston Wilts.............27 L6
Alveley Shrops...............84 D6
Alverdiscott Devon........23 H6
Alverstoke Hants...........17 H3
Alverstone IoW.............17 H5
Alverthorpe Wakefd.....123 L6
Alverton Notts..............102 C4
Alves Moray................214 E3

Alvescot Oxon...............56 F6
Alveston S Glos.............38 F3
Alveston Warwks...........72 B3
Alvingham Lincs..........118 E4
Alvington Gloucs...........54 E7
Alwalton C Pete.............89 G4
Alwinton Nthumb........168 D7
Alwoodley Leeds.........123 K3
Alyth P & K.................195 K6
Ambergate Derbys......101 G3
Amberley Gloucs...........55 J7
Amberley W Susx..........18 D3
Amble Nthumb.............159 G2
Amblecote Dudley.........84 F6
Ambler Thorn C Brad...123 G5
Ambleside Cumb..........137 K6
Ambleston Pembks........49 G3
Ambrosden Oxon...........57 L4
Amcotts N Linc............125 K7
Amersham Bucks...........42 F2
Amersham Common
Bucks......................42 F2
Amersham Old Town
Bucks......................42 F2
Amersham on the
Hill Bucks................58 F7
Amerton Railway &
Farm Staffs..............99 M6
Amesbury Wilts.............28 D3
Amhuinnsuidhe W Isls .232 d4
Amington Staffs.............86 B3
Amisfield Town D & G ..155 H5
Amlwch IoA.................108 F3
Ammanford Carmth.......51 J3
Amotherby N York.......134 B5
Ampfield Hants..............29 H6
Ampleforth N York.......133 J4
Ampney Crucis
Gloucs.....................56 B7
Ampney St Mary
Gloucs.....................56 C7
Ampney St Peter
Gloucs.....................56 B7
Amport Hants................28 F3
Ampthill C Beds............74 F6
Ampton Suffk................77 J1
Amroth Pembks.............49 K6
Amulree P & K.............185 J1
Amwell Herts.................59 K5
Anaheilt Highld............191 G4
Ancaster Lincs............103 G4
Ancroft Nthumb...........168 E1
Ancrum Border............167 K4
Anderby Lincs.............119 G6
Andover Hants...............29 G3
Andoversford Gloucs.....56 A4
Andreas IoM.................237 d2
Anerley Gt Lon..............45 G6
Anfield Lpool...............111 K3
Anfield Crematorium
Lpool......................111 K3
Angarrack Cnwll..............3 G4
Angelbank Shrops..........83 L7
Angle Pembks................48 E6
Anglesey IoA...............108 E5
Anglesey Abbey
Cambs.....................76 D3
Angmering W Susx........18 E5
Angram N York...........124 D2
Ankerville Highld.........223 H6
Anlaby E R Yk.............126 C5
Anmer Norfk...............105 H6
Anmore Hants................17 J1
Annan D & G...............147 L2
Annandale Water
Services D & G........155 J4
Annat Highld...............210 D4
Annathill N Lans..........175 J4
Anna Valley Hants.........29 G3
Annbank S Ayrs...........163 K5
Anne Hathaway's
Cottage Warwks......71 L4
Annesley Notts............101 J2
Annesley
Woodhouse Notts...101 J2
Annfield Plain Dur 150 F5

Anniesland C Glas.......174 F5
Ansdell Lancs..............120 D5
Ansford Somset.............26 F5
Ansley Warwks..............86 C5
Anslow Staffs..............100 E7
Anslow Gate Staffs......100 D7
Anstey Herts..................60 C2
Anstey Leics..................87 G2
Anstruther Fife............187 J6
Ansty W Susx................19 J2
Ansty Warwks................86 E6
Ansty Wilts....................27 L6
Anthorn Cumb.............147 L4
Antingham Norfk.........106 F5
An t-Ob W Isls.............232 d5
Antonine Wall Falk 175 L3
Anton's Gowt Lincs......103 M3
Antony Cnwll...................6 B5
Antrobus Ches W.........112 F5
Anwick Lincs...............103 J3
Anwoth D & G.............145 M4
Aperfield Gt Lon............32 D2
Apethorpe Nhants.........88 E4
Apley Lincs.................117 J6
Apperknowle Derbys...115 G5
Apperley Gloucs............55 K3
Appin Ag & B..............191 J6
Appleby N Linc............126 B7
Appleby-in-
Westmorland
Cumb....................139 G3
Appleby Magna Leics ...86 C2
Appleby Parva Leics......86 C2
Applecross Highld.......209 L5
Appledore Devon...........23 G5
Appledore Devon...........25 G8
Appledore Kent............34 C8
Appleford Oxon.............41 K2
Applegarth Town
D & G.....................155 J5
Appleshaw Hants...........28 F2
Appleton Halton..........112 D4
Appleton Oxon..............57 H7
Appleton Warrtn.........112 F5
Appleton-le-Moors
N York....................133 L3
Appleton-le-Street
N York....................134 B5
Appleton Roebuck
N York....................124 E3
Appleton Thorn
Warrtn....................112 F5
Appleton Wiske
N York....................141 J6
Appletreehall Border....167 H6
Appletreewick N York ..131 K7
Appley Somset..............25 G6
Appley Bridge Lancs....121 G8
Apse Heath IoW...........17 G5
Apsley End C Beds........59 J2
Apuldram W Susx..........18 A5
Arabella Highld............223 H6
Arbirlot Angus.............196 F7
Arboll Highld...............223 J5
Arborfield Wokham.......42 C6
Arborfield Cross
Wokham..................42 C6
Arbroath Angus...........197 G7
Arbuthnott Abers.........197 K2
Archddu Carmth...........50 F5
Archdeacon Newton
Darltn.....................141 G4
Archencarroch
W Duns...................174 D3
Archiestown Moray......214 F5
Arclid Green Ches E......99 H1
Ardallie Abers..............217 J6
Ardanaiseig Hotel
Ag & B....................182 F3
Ardaneaskan Highld.....210 C7
Ardarroch Highld.........210 D6
Ardbeg Ag & B............160 D1
Ardbeg Ag & B............173 J5
Ardbeg Ag & B............173 K2
Ardcharnich Highld.....220 F4
Ardchiavaig Ag & B.....180 E4

Ardchonnel Ag & B 182 D5
Ardchullarie More
  Stirlg 184 D5
Arddarroch Ag & B.........183 J7
Arddleen Powys 82 F1
Ardechive Highld...........201 H7
Ardeer N Ayrs.................163 H2
Ardeley Herts...................60 A3
Ardelve Highld................210 D8
Arden Ag & B...................174 C2
Ardens Grafton
  Warwks 71 K4
Ardentallen Ag & B........182 B3
Ardentinny Ag & B..........173 L2
Ardentraive Ag & B.........173 H4
Ardeonaig Stirlg 184 E1
Ardersier Highld 213 J4
Ardessie Highld...............220 D4
Ardfern Ag & B...............182 A6
Ardfernal Highld.............171 H4
Ardgay Highld.................222 D4
Ardgour Highld...............191 K4
Ardgowan Inver..............173 L4
Ardhallow Ag & B............173 L4
Ardhasig W Isls...............232 e4
Ardheslaig Highld...........210 B3
Ardindrean Highld...........220 F4
Ardingly W Susx...............32 C7
Ardington Oxon................41 H3
Ardlamont Ag & B...........173 G5
Ardleigh Essex.................62 C3
Ardleigh Heath Essex......62 C2
Ardler P & K.....................195 L7
Ardley Oxon......................57 K3
Ardlui Ag & B...................183 K4
Ardlussa Ag & B...............172 B2
Ardmair Highld................220 E2
Ardmaleish Ag & B..........173 J5
Ardminish Ag & B............172 B8
Ardmolich Highld.............190 E3
Ardmore Ag & B...............174 C3
Ardmore Highld...............222 F4
Ardnadam Ag & B............173 K3
Ardnagrask Highld...........212 E4
Ardnarff Highld................210 D7
Ardnastang Highld...........190 F4
Ardpatrick Ag & B............172 C6
Ardrishaig Ag & B............172 E2
Ardross Highld.................222 E6
Ardrossan N Ayrs.............163 G2
Ardsley East Leeds..........123 K5
Ardslignish Highld...........190 B4
Ardtalla Ag & B................171 J7
Ardtoe Highld..................190 C3
Arduaine Ag & B..............182 A5
Ardullie Highld.................212 E2
Ardvasar Highld...............199 K5
Ardvorlich P & K..............184 D3
Ardvourlie W Isls.............232 e3
Ardwell D & G..................144 D5
Ardwick Manch.................113 J3
Areley Kings Worcs...........70 E1
Arevegaig Highld..............190 D3
Arford Hants.....................30 D4
Argoed Caerph...................53 J7
Argyll Forest Park
  Ag & B..........................183 J6
Aribruach W Isls...............232 e3
Aridhglas Ag & B..............180 D3
Arileod Ag & B.................188 F5
Arinagour Ag & B.............189 G5
Ariogan Ag & B................182 C3
Arisaig Highld...................199 K7
Arisaig House Highld........199 L7
Arkendale N York.............132 F7
Arkesden Essex.................76 C7
Arkholme Lancs................130 B5
Arkleton D & G.................156 C4
Arkley Gt Lon.....................44 E2
Arksey Donc....................115 L1
Arkwright Town
  Derbys 115 H7
Arle Gloucs.......................55 L4
Arlecdon Cumb................136 E4
Arlesey C Beds..................75 H7
Arleston Wrekin.................84 B2

Arley Ches E....................112 F5
Arley Warwks.....................86 C5
Arlingham Gloucs..............55 G6
Arlington Devon................23 K4
Arlington E Susx................20 B4
Armadale Highld..............199 K5
Armadale Highld..............230 A3
Armadale W Loth.............176 C5
Armathwaite Cumb..........148 E5
Arminghall Norfk...............92 F3
Armitage Staffs.................85 J1
Armley Leeds..................123 K4
Armscote Warwks..............72 B5
Armthorpe Donc..............115 L1
Arnabost Ag & B..............188 F4
Arncliffe N York...............131 H5
Arncroach Fife.................187 H6
Arndilly House Moray......215 G5
Arne Dorset......................15 H5
Arnesby Leics....................87 H5
Arngask P & K..................186 B5
Arnisdale Highld..............200 C3
Arnish Highld....................209 J5
Arniston Mdloth...............177 K6
Arnol W Isls.....................232 f1
Arnold E R Yk..................126 E3
Arnold Notts....................101 L4
Arnprior Stirlg..................184 D7
Arnside Cumb..................129 K4
Aros Ag & B.....................190 B7
Arrad Foot Cumb.............129 G4
Arram E R Yk...................126 C2
Arran N Ayrs....................162 B3
Arrathorne N York...........132 C2
Arreton IoW.......................17 G5
Arrina Highld....................210 B3
Arrington Cambs...............75 K4
Arrochar Ag & B..............183 K6
Arrow Warwks...................71 J3
Arscott Shrops..................83 J2
Artafallie Highld...............212 F4
Arthington Leeds.............123 K2
Arthingworth Nhants.........87 L7
Arthrath Abers.................217 H6
Artrochie Abers................217 J7
Arundel W Susx.................18 D4
Asby Cumb.......................136 E3
Ascog Ag & B...................173 J5
Ascot W & M......................42 F6
Ascott-under-
  Wychwood Oxon..........56 F4
Asenby N York.................132 F4
Asfordby Leics.................102 B8
Asfordby Hill Leics...........102 B8
Asgarby Lincs..................103 J4
Ash Kent............................35 H3
Ash Kent............................45 L6
Ash Somset.......................26 C7
Ash Surrey........................30 E2
Ashampstead W Berk......41 K5
Ashbocking Suffk..............78 E4
Ashbourne Derbys...........100 D3
Ashbrittle Somset.............25 G6
Ashburton Devon................7 H2
Ashbury Devon..................10 D5
Ashbury Oxon....................40 E4
Ashby N Linc....................125 L8
Ashby by Partney
  Lincs 118 F7
Ashby cum Fenby
  NE Lin 118 C2
Ashby de la Launde
  Lincs 103 H2
Ashby-de-la-Zouch
  Leics 86 D3
Ashby Folville Leics..........87 K2
Ashby Magna Leics...........87 H5
Ashby Parva Leics.............87 G5
Ashby Puerorum
  Lincs 118 D7
Ashby St Ledgers
  Nhants...........................73 H2
Ashby St Mary Norfk.........93 G3
Ashchurch Gloucs.............55 L2
Ashcombe Devon...............11 L8
Ashcombe N Som..............37 M7

Ashcott Somset.................26 C4
Ashdon Essex....................76 E6
Ashe Hants........................29 K2
Asheldham Essex..............62 A7
Ashen Essex......................77 H6
Ashendon Bucks...............58 B5
Asheridge Bucks...............58 F6
Ashfield Stirlg..................185 G6
Ashfield cum Thorpe
  Suffk.............................78 E3
Ashfield Green Suffk........92 F8
Ashford Devon....................7 G6
Ashford Devon..................23 H4
Ashford Kent.....................34 D6
Ashford Surrey..................43 H6
Ashford Bowdler
  Shrops...........................69 K1
Ashford Carbonell
  Shrops...........................69 K1
Ashford Hill Hants.............41 K7
Ashford in the Water
  Derbys.........................114 D7
Ashgill S Lans..................175 K7
Ash Green Surrey..............30 E2
Ash Green Warwks............86 D6
Ashill Devon......................12 E1
Ashill Norfk.......................91 K3
Ashill Somset....................25 L7
Ashingdon Essex...............46 E2
Ashington Nthumb...........159 G5
Ashington Somset.............26 E6
Ashington W Susx.............18 F3
Ashkirk Border................167 G5
Ashleworth Gloucs............55 J3
Ashleworth Quay
  Gloucs...........................55 J3
Ashley Cambs....................77 G3
Ashley Ches E..................113 H5
Ashley Devon....................10 F3
Ashley Gloucs....................39 L2
Ashley Hants.....................16 B4
Ashley Hants.....................29 G5
Ashley Kent.......................35 J5
Ashley Nhants....................87 L5
Ashley Staffs.....................99 H5
Ashley Wilts.......................39 J6
Ashley Green Bucks..........58 F6
Ash Magna Shrops............98 E4
Ashmansworth Hants........41 H8
Ashmansworthy
  Devon............................22 E7
Ash Mill Devon..................24 C6
Ashmore Dorset................27 K7
Ashmore Green
  W Berk...........................41 J6
Ashorne Warwks................72 C3
Ashover Derbys................115 G8
Ashow Warwks...................72 C1
Ashperton Herefs..............70 B6
Ashprington Devon.............7 J4
Ash Priors Somset.............25 J5
Ashreigney Devon.............10 F3
Ash Street Suffk................78 B5
Ashtead Surrey..................44 D8
Ash Thomas Devon...........12 C1
Ashton Ches W................112 D7
Ashton Cnwll......................3 G5
Ashton Devon....................11 K7
Ashton Herefs...................69 K2
Ashton Inver....................173 L3
Ashton Nhants...................73 L5
Ashton Nhants...................88 F5
Ashton Common
  Wilts..............................39 K8
Ashton-in-Makerfield
  Wigan..........................112 E2
Ashton Keynes Wilts.........40 B2
Ashton under Hill
  Worcs............................71 H6
Ashton-under-Lyne
  Tamesd........................113 L2
Ashurst Hants...................16 D1
Ashurst Kent.....................32 F5
Ashurst Lancs..................121 G8
Ashurst W Susx.................19 G3
Ashurstwood W Susx........32 D5

Ash Vale Surrey.................30 E2
Ashwater Devon..................9 K5
Ashwell Herts....................75 J6
Ashwell Rutlnd..................88 C2
Ashwell End Herts............75 J6
Ashwellthorpe Norfk.........92 D4
Ashwick Somset................26 F2
Ashwicken Norfk..............105 H8
Askam in Furness
  Cumb..........................128 F4
Askern Donc....................124 E7
Askerswell Dorset.............14 A4
Askett Bucks......................58 D6
Askham Cumb..................138 D3
Askham Notts...................116 C6
Askham Bryan C York......124 E2
Askham Richard
  C York..........................124 E2
Asknish Ag & B.................172 F1
Askrigg N York.................131 H2
Askwith N York.................123 H2
Aslackby Lincs.................103 H6
Aslacton Norfk...................92 D5
Aslockton Notts...............102 C4
Aspatria Cumb.................147 K6
Aspenden Herts.................60 B3
Aspley Guise C Beds.........74 D7
Aspley Heath C Beds.........74 D7
Aspull Wigan...................121 J8
Asselby E R Yk.................125 H5
Assington Suffk.................77 L6
Assington Green
  Suffk.............................77 H4
Astbury Ches E..................99 J1
Astcote Nhants.................73 J4
Asterby Lincs...................118 C5
Asterley Shrops.................83 H3
Asterton Shrops................83 H5
Asthall Oxon......................56 F5
Asthall Leigh Oxon............56 F5
Astle Highld.....................223 G3
Astley Shrops....................98 D8
Astley Warwks...................86 C5
Astley Wigan....................113 G2
Astley Worcs.....................70 D2
Astley Abbots Shrops........84 C4
Astley Bridge Bolton........121 K7
Astley Cross Worcs...........70 E1
Aston Ches E.....................98 E3
Aston Ches E....................112 E5
Aston Derbys...................114 D5
Aston Flints.....................111 J7
Aston Herts.......................59 L4
Aston Oxon........................57 G7
Aston Rothm....................115 J4
Aston Shrops.....................84 E5
Aston Shrops.....................98 D6
Aston Staffs.......................99 H4
Aston Staffs.......................99 K7
Aston Wokham..................42 C4
Aston Wrekin.....................84 B2
Aston Abbotts Bucks........58 D4
Aston Botterell
  Shrops...........................84 B6
Aston-by-Stone Staffs.......99 K6
Aston Cantlow
  Warwks.........................71 K3
Aston Clinton Bucks.........58 E5
Aston Crews Herefs..........54 F4
Aston End Herts................59 L3
Aston Fields Worcs...........71 G1
Aston Flamville Leics........86 F5
Aston Ingham Herefs........55 G4
Aston le Walls Nhants.......72 F4
Aston Magna Gloucs.........71 L7
Aston Munslow
  Shrops...........................83 K6
Aston on Clun Shrops.......83 H6
Aston Pigott Shrops..........83 G3
Aston Rogers Shrops.........83 G3
Aston Rowant Oxon..........58 B7
Aston Somerville
  Worcs............................71 J6
Aston-sub-Edge
  Gloucs...........................71 K6
Aston Tirrold Oxon............41 K3

Aston-upon-Trent
Derbys **101** H6
Aston Upthorpe Oxon.....**41** K3
Astwick C Beds.................**75** G6
Astwood M Keyn **74** D5
Astwood Worcs **71** G2
Astwood Bank Worcs **71** J3
Astwood
  Crematorium
  Worcs **70** F3
Aswarby Lincs................**103** H4
Aswardby Lincs..............**118** E7
Atcham Shrops................**83** K2
Athelhampton Dorset.....**14** E4
Athelington Suffk **78** E1
Athelney Somset............**25** M5
Athelstaneford
  E Loth.......................**178** C3
Atherington Devon..........**23** J7
Atherstone Warwks **86** C4
Atherstone on Stour
  Warwks **72** B4
Atherton Wigan.............**113** G2
Atlow Derbys **100** E3
Attadale Highld **210** E6
Atterby Lincs.................**117** G3
Attercliffe Sheff **115** G4
Atterton Leics **86** D4
Attingham Park
  Shrops........................**83** K2
Attleborough Norfk **92** C4
Attleborough Warwks **86** D5
Attlebridge Norfk **92** D1
Attleton Green Suffk.......**77** G4
Atwick E R Yk.................**126** F1
Atworth Wilts **39** J7
Aubourn Lincs................**116** F8
Auchbreck Moray............**214** F8
Auchedly Abers **217** G7
Auchenblae Abers..........**197** H1
Auchenbowie Stirlg **185** L2
Auchencairn D & G.........**146** D5
Auchencairn D & G.........**155** G5
Auchencairn N Ayrs **162** D4
Auchencrow Border **179** H6
Auchendinny Mdloth.......**177** H6
Auchengray S Lans **176** D7
Auchenhalrig Moray........**215** J3
Auchenheath S Lans........**164** F1
Auchenhessnane
  D & G **154** E3
Auchenlochan
  Ag & B **173** G4
Auchenmade N Ayrs **174** C8
Auchenmalg D & G..........**144** F4
Auchentiber N Ayrs.........**174** C8
Auchindrain Ag & B.........**182** E6
Auchindrean Highld........**221** G5
Auchininna Abers...........**216** C5
Auchinleck E Ayrs...........**164** B5
Auchinloch N Lans **175** H4
Auchinstarry N Lans........**175** J3
Auchintore Highld...........**191** L2
Auchiries Abers **217** K6
Auchlean Highld.............**203** K5
Auchlee Abers................**207** G6
Auchleven Abers **206** C1
Auchlochan S Lans **164** F3
Auchlossan Abers **206** B5
Auchlyne Stirlg **184** B2
Auchmillan E Ayrs **164** A4
Auchmithie Angus **197** G7
Auchmuirbridge Fife.......**186** C6
Auchnacree Angus **196** D4
Auchnagatt Abers...........**217** H6
Auchnarrow Moray..........**204** F2
Auchroisk Moray **215** H4
Auchterarder P & K.........**185** K5
Auchteraw Highld..........**202** B4
Auchterblair Highld........**203** L2
Auchtercairn Highld.........**219** J6
Auchterderran Fife **186** C7
Auchterhouse Angus **196** B8
Auchterless Abers..........**216** D6
Auchtermuchty Fife.....**186** D5

Auchterneed Highld **212** D3
Auchtertool Fife **177** H1
Auchtertyre Highld........**210** C8
Auchtubh Stirlg **184** C4
Auckengill Highld..........**231** L3
Auckley Donc................**115** M2
Audenshaw Tamesd **113** K3
Audlem Ches E................**98** F4
Audley Staffs..................**99** J3
Audley End Essex...........**76** D6
Audley End House &
  Gardens Essex **76** D6
Aughton E R Yk.............**125** G3
Aughton Lancs...............**111** L1
Aughton Lancs...............**129** L6
Aughton Rothm.............**115** J4
Aughton Wilts **28** E1
Aughton Park Lancs......**112** B1
Auldearn Highld **213** L4
Aulden Herefs **69** J4
Auldgirth D & G............**154** F5
Auldhouse S Lans **175** H7
Ault a' chruinn
  Highld.......................**200** E2
Aultbea Highld **219** K4
Aultgrishin Highld **219** H4
Aultguish Inn Highld......**221** J7
Ault Hucknall Derbys.....**115** J7
Aultmore Moray **215** J4
Aultnagoire Highld **202** E2
Aultnamain Inn
  Highld.......................**222** F5
Aunsby Lincs.................**103** H5
Aust S Glos......................**38** E3
Austerfield Donc............**116** A3
Austrey Warwks..............**86** C3
Austwick N York.............**130** E5
Authorpe Lincs..............**118** E5
Avebury Wilts..................**40** C6
Avebury Wilts..................**40** C6
Aveley Thurr....................**45** L4
Avening Gloucs **39** K2
Averham Notts..............**102** C2
Aveton Gifford Devon **7** G6
Aviemore Highld............**203** L3
Avington W Berk **41** G6
Avoch Highld.................**213** G4
Avon Hants......................**15** L3
Avonbridge Falk............**176** B4
Avon Dassett
  Warwks **72** E4
Avonmouth Bristl............**38** D5
Avonwick Devon **7** G4
Awbridge Hants...............**28** F6
Awkley S Glos **38** D3
Awliscombe Devon **12** E3
Awre Gloucs **55** G6
Awsworth Notts............**101** J4
Axbridge Somset............**26** B1
Axford Hants **29** L3
Axford Wilts **40** E6
Axminster Devon **13** H3
Axmouth Devon **13** G4
Aycliffe Dur..................**141** G3
Aydon Nthumb...............**150** C2
Aylburton Gloucs............**54** E7
Aylesbeare Devon **12** D4
Aylesbury Bucks.............**58** D5
Aylesby NE Lin..............**126** F8
Aylesford Kent................**33** J2
Aylesham Kent................**35** H4
Aylestone C Leic............**87** H4
Aylmerton Norfk............**106** E5
Aylsham Norfk...............**106** K6
Aylton Herefs..................**70** B6
Aylworth Gloucs.............**56** C4
Aymestrey Herefs...........**69** H2
Aynho Nhants..................**57** K2
Ayot St Lawrence
  Herts..........................**59** K5
Ayr S Ayrs......................**163** J5
Aysgarth N York.............**131** J2
Ayshford Devon **25** G7
Ayside Cumb..................**129** J3
Ayston Rutlnd..................**88** C4
Ayton Border **179** J6
Azerley N York...............**132** C5

B

Babbacombe Torbay **7** L3
Babbs Green Herts..........**60** C5
Babcary Somset **26** E5
Babraham Cambs **76** D4
Babworth Notts..............**116** B5
Backaland Ork **234** d4
Backfolds Abers **217** J4
Backford Ches W............**111** L6
Backies Highld **223** H2
Back of Keppoch
  Highld.......................**199** K7
Backwell N Som **38** C6
Baconsthorpe Norfk **106** D5
Bacton Herefs **54** A2
Bacton Norfk **107** H5
Bacton Suffk **78** C2
Bacup Lancs **122** C6
Badachro Highld **219** J6
Badbury Swindn **40** D4
Badby Nhants **73** H3
Badcall Highld **228** B7
Badcall Highld **228** C4
Badcaul Highld **220** D3
Baddeley Clinton
  Warwks **86** B8
Baddesley Ensor
  Warwks **86** C4
Baddidarrach Highld **224** D4
Baddinsgill Border **176** F7
Badenscoth Abers **216** D6
Badentarbet Highld........**224** B6
Badenyon Abers.............**205** H2
Badger Shrops **84** D4
Badgeworth Gloucs **55** K4
Badgworth Somset **26** B2
Badicaul Highld **210** B8
Badingham Suffk **79** G2
Badlesmere Kent **34** D4
Badlieu Border **165** K5
Badlipster Highld **231** J5
Badluarach Highld **220** C3
Badninish Highld **223** G3
Badrallach Highld **220** D3
Badsey Worcs **71** J5
Badshot Lea Surrey.........**30** E2
Badsworth Wakefd **124** C7
Badwell Ash Suffk **78** B2
Bagber Dorset **27** H8
Bagby N York **133** G4
Bag Enderby Lincs **118** E6
Bagendon Gloucs **56** A6
Bagh a Chaisteil
  W Isls........................**233** b9
Bagh a Tuath W Isls.......**233** b9
Bagillt Flints **111** H6
Baginton Warwks **86** D8
Baglan Neath **51** L6
Bagley Shrops **98** B6
Bagley Somset **26** C3
Bagnall Staffs **99** L3
Bagshot Surrey................**42** E7
Bagstone S Glos **39** G3
Bagworth Leics **86** F2
Bagwy Llydiart
  Herefs........................**54** C3
Baildon C Brad **123** H3
Baildon Green C Brad ...**123** H3
Baile Ailein W Isls.........**232** f3
Baile a Mhanaich
  W Isls........................**233** b6
Baile Mor Ag & B..........**180** D3
Baillieston C Glas **175** J5
Bainbridge N York.........**131** H2
Bainshole Abers **216** B7
Bainton C Pete **89** G3
Bainton E R Yk..............**126** B1
Baintown Fife **186** F6
Bairnkine Border **167** K6
Bakewell Derbys............**114** E7
Bala Gwynd **96** E5
Balallan W Isls...............**232** f3
Balbeg Highld **212** C7
Balbeggie P & K.............**186** C2

Balblair Highld **212** D5
Balblair Highld **213** G2
Balby Donc....................**115** K2
Balcary D & G **146** E5
Balchraggan Highld **212** E5
Balchreick Highld **228** B4
Balcombe W Susx............**32** B6
Balcomie Links Fife **187** K5
Baldersby N York...........**132** E4
Baldersby St James
  N York........................**132** E4
Balderstone Lancs **121** J4
Balderton Notts.............**102** D3
Baldinnie Fife **187** G5
Baldinnies P & K............**185** L4
Baldock Herts **75** J7
Baldock Services
  Herts..........................**75** J6
Baldovie C Dund............**187** G2
Baldrine IoM **237** d5
Baldslow E Susx **20** F3
Bale Norfk **106** B5
Baledgarno P & K...........**186** D2
Balemartine Ag & B **188** C7
Balerno C Edin **177** G5
Balfarg Fife **186** D6
Balfield Angus **196** E3
Balfour Ork **234** C5
Balfron Stirlg **174** F1
Balgaveny Abers **216** C6
Balgonar Fife **185** L8
Balgowan D & G **144** D6
Balgowan Highld............**202** F6
Balgown Highld **218** B7
Balgracie D & G **144** B3
Balgray S Lans................**165** H5
Balham Gt Lon **44** F5
Balhary P & K.................**195** L6
Balholmie P & K **186** B1
Baligill Highld **230** C3
Balintore Angus **195** L5
Balintore Highld **223** J6
Balintraid Highld **223** G7
Balivanich W Isls **233** b6
Balkeerie Angus **196** B7
Balkholme E R Yk **125** J5
Ballachulish Highld **191** L5
Ballajora IoM **237** e4
Ballanlay Ag & B **173** H6
Ballantrae S Ayrs **152** C5
Ballasalla IoM................**237** b6
Ballater Abers **205** J6
Ballaugh IoM **237** c3
Ballchraggan Highld **223** G6
Ballencrieff E Loth.........**178** B3
Ballevullin Ag & B **188** B6
Ballidon Derbys **100** D2
Balliekine N Ayrs............**161** L2
Balliemore Ag & B **182** F7
Balligmorrie S Ayrs.........**152** F4
Ballimore Stirlg **184** C4
Ballindalloch Moray **214** E6
Ballindean P & K **186** D2
Ballinger Common
  Bucks.........................**58** E7
Ballingham Herefs **54** E2
Ballingry Fife **186** C7
Ballinluig P & K **194** F6
Ballinshoe Angus **196** C5
Ballintuim P & K **195** H5
Balloch Highld **213** H5
Balloch N Lans **175** K4
Balloch P & K **185** H4
Balloch S Ayrs **153** G3
Balloch W Duns **174** D3
Balls Cross W Susx **31** G6
Balls Green E Susx **32** E6
Ballygown Ag & B **189** K7
Ballygrant Ag & B **171** G5
Ballyhaugh Ag & B **188** C5
Balmaclellan D & G **154** B6
Balmae D & G **146** C6
Balmaha Stirlg **174** D1
Balmalcolm Fife **186** E5
Balmangan D & G **146** B5
Balmedie Abers **207** H2

Balmerino Fife..............186 F3
Balmichael N Ayrs.......162 B3
Balmore E Duns...........175 G4
Balmuchy Highld..........223 J5
Balmule Fife..................177 G2
Balmullo Fife................187 G4
Balnacoil Lodge
  Highld........................226 E6
Balnacra Highld............210 F5
Balnacroft Abers...........205 G6
Balnafoich Highld..........213 G7
Balnaguard P & K..........194 E6
Balnahard Ag & B..........180 F1
Balnahard Ag & B..........180 F7
Balnain Highld...............212 C4
Balnakeil Highld............228 F2
Balne N York..................124 F6
Balquharn P & K............185 L1
Balquhidder Stirlg.........184 C3
Balsall Common Solhll....86 B7
Balsall Heath Birm..........85 J6
Balscote Oxon................72 E6
Balsham Cambs..............76 E4
Baltasound Shet............235 e1
Baltersan D & G.............145 J3
Baltonsborough
  Somset.........................26 D4
Balvicar Ag & B.............181 M4
Balvraid Highld...............200 C3
Balvraid Highld...............213 K7
Bamber Bridge Lancs....121 H5
Bamber's Green
  Essex...........................60 F4
Bamburgh Nthumb........169 H3
Bamburgh Castle
  Nthumb.......................169 H3
Bamford Derbys............114 E5
Bampton Cumb.............138 D4
Bampton Devon..............24 E6
Bampton Oxon.................56 F7
Bampton Grange
  Cumb..........................138 D4
Banavie Highld..............191 L2
Banbury Oxon..................72 F6
Banbury
  Crematorium
  Oxon............................72 F6
Bancffosfelen
  Carmth..........................50 F3
Banchory Abers.............206 D6
Banchory-Devenick
  Abers..........................207 G5
Bancycapel Carmth........50 E3
Bancyfelin Carmth..........50 D2
Bandirran P & K............186 C2
Banff Abers....................216 D2
Bangor Gwynd..............109 H6
Bangor Crematorium
  Gwynd.........................109 H6
Bangor-on-Dee
  Wrexhm........................98 B4
Bangors Cnwll...................9 G5
Banham Norfk.................92 C6
Bank Hants.....................16 C2
Bankend D & G.............147 H2
Bankfoot P & K..............185 M1
Bankglen E Ayrs............164 C6
Bankhead C Aber...........207 G4
Bankhead S Lans...........165 J1
Banknock Falk................175 K3
Banks Lancs..................120 E6
Bankshill D & G.............155 L5
Banningham Norfk........106 F6
Bannister Green
  Essex...........................61 H4
Bannockburn Stirlg.......175 L1
Banstead Surrey.............44 E7
Bantham Devon................6 F6
Banton N Lans...............175 K3
Banwell N Som...............38 B8
Bapchild Kent.................34 C3
Bapton Wilts....................27 M4
Barabhas W Isls...........232 f1
Barassie S Ayrs.............163 J3
Barbaraville Highld........223 G6
Barbieston S Ayrs.........163 K5

Barbon Cumb.................130 C3
Barbrook Devon..............23 L2
Barby Nhants..................73 G1
Barcaldine Ag & B.........191 J7
Barcombe E Susx...........19 L3
Barcombe Cross
  E Susx...........................19 L3
Barden Park Kent...........33 G4
Bardfield End Green
  Essex...........................61 G2
Bardfield Saling Essex....61 G3
Bardney Lincs...............117 J7
Bardon Leics...................86 F2
Bardon Mill Nthumb......149 K3
Bardowie E Duns...........175 G4
Bardrainney Inver.........174 C4
Bardsea Cumb...............129 G5
Bardsey Leeds...............124 B2
Bardsey Island Gwynd....94 B7
Bardwell Suffk.................91 L8
Bare Lancs....................129 K6
Barfad D & G.................145 G2
Barford Norfk..................92 D3
Barford Warwks..............72 C3
Barford St John Oxon....57 H2
Barford St Martin
  Wilts.............................28 B5
Barford St Michael
  Oxon............................57 H2
Barfrestone Kent............35 H5
Bargeddie N Lans..........175 J5
Bargoed Caerph.............53 J7
Bargrennan D & G.........153 H6
Barham Cambs...............89 G7
Barham Kent...................35 G5
Barham Suffk..................78 D4
Barham
  Crematorium
  Kent.............................35 G5
Bar Hill Cambs...............75 L2
Barholm Lincs.................88 F2
Barkby Leics...................87 J2
Barkby Thorpe Leics......87 J2
Barkestone-le-Vale
  Leics...........................102 C5
Barkham Wokham...........42 C6
Barking Gt Lon...............45 H3
Barking Suffk..................78 C4
Barkingside Gt Lon.........45 H3
Barking Tye Suffk...........78 C4
Barkisland Calder.........122 F6
Barkla Shop Cnwll............3 J2
Barkston Lincs..............102 F4
Barkston Ash N York....124 D4
Barkway Herts................75 L7
Barlanark C Glas...........175 H5
Barlaston Staffs..............99 K5
Barlavington W Susx......18 C3
Barlborough Derbys.......115 J6
Barlby N York................124 F4
Barlestone Leics.............86 E3
Barley Herts...................76 B6
Barley Lancs.................122 B3
Barleythorpe Rutlnd.......88 B2
Barling Essex..................46 F3
Barlings Lincs...............117 H6
Barlochan D & G...........146 E4
Barlow Derbys...............115 G6
Barlow Gatesd..............150 E3
Barlow N York...............124 F5
Barmby Moor E R Yk....125 J2
Barmby on the
  Marsh E R Yk.............125 G5
Barmollack Ag & B........161 K1
Barmouth Gwynd...........80 E1
Barmpton Darltn...........141 H4
Barmston E R Yk..........135 J7
Barnacarry Ag & B........182 E8
Barnack C Pete...............88 F3
Barnard Castle Dur.......140 D4
Barnard Gate Oxon........57 H6
Barnardiston Suffk.........77 G5
Barnbarroch D & G........146 E4
Barnburgh Donc............115 J2
Barnby Suffk...................93 K5
Barnby Dun Donc..........124 F8

Barnby in the
  Willows Notts...........102 E3
Barnby Moor Notts......116 A5
Barncorkrie D & G.......144 D7
Barnes Gt Lon................44 E5
Barnes Street Kent.........33 H4
Barnet Gt Lon.................44 E2
Barnetby le Wold
  N Linc.........................126 C8
Barney Norfk.................106 B6
Barnham Suffk................91 K7
Barnham W Susx............18 C5
Barnham Broom
  Norfk............................92 C3
Barnhead Angus...........197 G5
Barnhill C Dund.............187 H2
Barnhill Moray..............214 E3
Barnhills D & G.............152 B7
Barningham Dur...........140 D5
Barningham Suffk..........91 L7
Barnoldby le Beck
  NE Lin.........................118 C2
Barnoldswick Lancs......122 C2
Barns Green W Susx......31 J6
Barnsley Barns.............115 G1
Barnsley Gloucs.............56 B6
Barnsley
  Crematorium
  Barns...........................115 G1
Barnstaple Devon..........23 J5
Barnston Essex..............61 G4
Barnston Wirral............111 J5
Barnstone Notts...........102 B5
Barnt Green Worcs.........85 H8
Barnton C Edin..............177 G4
Barnton Ches W............112 F6
Barnwell All Saints
  Nhants..........................88 F6
Barnwell St Andrew
  Nhants..........................88 F6
Barnwood Gloucs...........55 K4
Barr S Ayrs....................153 G4
Barra W Isls..................233 b9
Barra Airport W Isls......233 b9
Barrachan D & G...........145 H5
Barraigh W Isls..............233 b9
Barrapoll Ag & B............188 B7
Barrasford Nthumb........158 A7
Barrhead E Rens............174 F6
Barrhill S Ayrs...............152 F5
Barrington Cambs...........76 B5
Barrington Somset..........26 B7
Barripper Cnwll.................3 H4
Barrmill N Ayrs.............174 C7
Barrock Highld..............231 J2
Barrow Gloucs................55 K3
Barrow Lancs................121 L3
Barrow Rutlnd.................88 C1
Barrow Somset................27 G5
Barrow Suffk...................77 H2
Barrowby Lincs.............102 E5
Barrowden Rutlnd...........88 D4
Barrowford Lancs.........122 C3
Barrow Gurney
  N Som...........................38 D6
Barrow Haven N Linc...126 D6
Barrow-in-Furness
  Cumb..........................128 E5
Barrow Island Cumb.....128 E5
Barrow-upon-
  Humber N Linc...........126 D6
Barrow upon Soar
  Leics...........................101 L8
Barrow upon Trent
  Derbys.........................101 G6
Barry Angus..................187 J1
Barry V Glam.................37 H6
Barry Island V Glam.......37 H6
Barsby Leics...................87 K2
Barsham Suffk................93 H5
Barston Solhll................86 B7
Bartestree Herefs...........69 L6
Barthol Chapel Abers...216 F7
Bartholomew Green
  Essex...........................61 H4
Barthomley Ches E........99 H3

Bartley Hants.................28 F8
Bartley Green Birm........85 H6
Bartlow Cambs...............76 E5
Barton Cambs................76 B4
Barton Ches W...............98 C2
Barton Gloucs.................56 C3
Barton Lancs.................120 E8
Barton Lancs.................121 G3
Barton N York...............141 G5
Barton Oxon....................57 K6
Barton Torbay...................7 K3
Barton Bendish Norfk.....91 G3
Barton End Gloucs.........39 J2
Barton Hartshorn
  Bucks............................57 M2
Barton in Fabis Notts....101 K6
Barton in the Beans
  Leics.............................86 E3
Barton-le-Clay C Beds....59 H2
Barton-le-Street
  N York.........................133 L5
Barton-le-Willows
  N York.........................133 L6
Barton Mills Suffk..........91 G8
Barton-on-Sea Hants.....16 B4
Barton-on-the-Heath
  Warwks.........................56 E2
Barton St David
  Somset.........................26 D5
Barton Seagrave
  Nhants..........................88 C7
Barton Stacey Hants.....29 H3
Barton Town Devon.......23 L4
Barton Turf Norfk.........107 H7
Barton-under-
  Needwood Staffs....100 D8
Barton-upon-
  Humber N Linc..........126 C6
Barton Waterside
  N Linc.........................126 C6
Barvas W Isls...............232 f1
Barway Cambs................90 D7
Barwell Leics..................86 F4
Barwick Devon...............10 E4
Barwick Somset..............26 E8
Barwick in Elmet
  Leeds..........................124 B3
Baschurch Shrops..........98 B7
Bascote Warwks.............72 E2
Bashall Eaves Lancs......121 K2
Basildon Essex................46 B3
Basildon & District
  Crematorium
  Essex...........................46 C3
Basingstoke Hants.........29 M2
Basingstoke
  Crematorium
  Hants............................29 K3
Baslow Derbys..............114 E6
Bason Bridge Somset.....25 M3
Bassaleg Newpt..............37 L3
Bassendean Border.......167 K1
Bassenthwaite Cumb....137 H2
Bassett C Sotn................29 H7
Bassingbourn Cambs......75 K5
Bassingham Lincs.........102 E1
Bassingthorpe Lincs.....102 F6
Bassus Green Herts........60 A3
Baston Lincs...................89 G2
Bastwick Norfk..............107 J8
Batchworth Herts............43 H2
Batcombe Dorset...........14 C2
Batcombe Somset...........27 G4
Batford Herts..................59 J5
Bath BaNES....................39 H7
Bathampton BaNES........39 H7
Bath, City of BaNES.......39 H7
Bathealton Somset.........25 G6
Batheaston BaNES..........39 H6
Bathford BaNES.............39 H6
Bathgate W Loth...........176 D5
Bathley Notts................102 C2
Bathpool Cnwll.................5 L2
Bathpool Somset...........25 K6
Bath Side Essex..............62 F2
Bathville W Loth...........176 C5

Bathway Somset............26 E2
Batley Kirk..................123 J5
Batsford Gloucs...........71 L7
Battersby N York........142 D5
Battersea Gt Lon.........44 F5
Battisford Tye Suffk.....78 B4
Battle E Susx..............20 F3
Battle Powys..............52 F2
Battledykes Angus....196 D5
Battlesbridge Essex....46 C2
Battleton Somset.........24 E6
Baughton Worcs..........70 F6
Baughurst Hants.........41 L7
Baulds Abers.............206 B6
Baulking Oxon............40 F3
Baumber Lincs..........117 L6
Baunton Gloucs..........56 A6
Baverstock Wilts..........28 B5
Bawburgh Norfk..........92 D2
Bawdeswell Norfk......106 C7
Bawdrip Somset..........25 M4
Bawdsey Suffk............79 H6
Bawtry Donc.............115 M3
Baxenden Lancs........122 B5
Baxterley Warwks........86 C4
Bay Devon.................208 D4
Bayble W Isls.............232 g2
Baybridge Hants..........29 K6
Baycliff Cumb............129 G5
Baydon Wilts..............40 F5
Bayford Herts..............60 A6
Bayford Somset...........27 G5
Bayhead W Isls..........233 b6
Baylham Suffk.............78 D4
Bayston Hill Shrops......83 J2
Baythorne End Essex....77 G6
Bayton Worcs.............84 C8
Bayworth Oxon............57 J7
Beachampton Bucks.....73 L6
Beachamwell Norfk......91 H3
Beachy Head E Susx....20 C6
Beacon Devon.............12 F2
Beacon End Essex........62 A3
Beacon Hill Surrey.......30 E4
Beacon's Bottom
  Bucks....................42 C2
Beaconsfield Bucks.....42 F3
Beaconsfield
  Services Bucks........42 F3
Beadlam N York.........133 K3
Beadlow C Beds..........75 G6
Beadnell Nthumb........169 J4
Beaford Devon.............10 E2
Beal N York...............124 E5
Beal Nthumb..............169 G2
Bealsmill Cnwll..............6 A1
Beaminster Dorset........13 L3
Beamish Dur.............150 F4
Beamish Museum
  Dur.....................150 F4
Beamsley N York........131 K8
Beanacre Wilts.............39 K7
Beanley Nthumb........169 H4
Beardon Devon............10 D7
Beare Green Surrey......31 K3
Bearley Warwks...........71 L3
Bearpark Dur.............151 G6
Bearsden E Duns.......174 F4
Bearsted Kent.............33 K3
Bearstone Shrops.........99 G5
Bearwood Birm...........85 H6
Bearwood Herefs.........69 H4
Bearwood Poole..........15 K3
Beattock D & G...........155 J2
Beauchamp Roding
  Essex....................60 F6
Beaufort Blae G..........53 J3
Beaulieu Hants............16 E3
Beauly Highld............212 E5
Beaumaris IoA............109 H6
Beaumaris Castle IoA.....109 J6
Beaumont Cumb........148 C3
Beaumont Essex...........62 E3
Beaumont Jersey.......236 c7
Beausale Warwks.........72 B1

Beauworth Hants..........29 L6
Beaworthy Devon.........10 C5
Beazley End Essex........61 H3
Bebington Wirral........111 K5
Beccles Suffk..............93 J5
Becconsall Lancs........120 F6
Beckbury Shrops..........84 D3
Beckenham Gt Lon......45 G6
Beckenham
  Crematorium
  Gt Lon...................45 G6
Beckermet Cumb........136 E6
Beckfoot Cumb...........147 J5
Beckford Worcs...........71 H7
Beckhampton Wilts......40 C6
Beckingham Lincs......102 E2
Beckingham Notts......116 C4
Beckington Somset.......27 J2
Beckjay Shrops............83 H7
Beckley E Susx............21 G2
Beckley Oxon..............57 K5
Beck Row Suffk............91 G7
Beck Side Cumb.........128 F3
Beckton Gt Lon............45 H4
Beckwithshaw N York..132 D8
Becontree Gt Lon.........45 J3
Bedale N York............132 D2
Bedchester Dorset........27 J7
Beddau Rhondd...........37 G4
Beddgelert Gwynd........95 K3
Beddingham E Susx.....19 L4
Beddington Gt Lon.......44 F6
Beddington Corner
  Gt Lon...................44 F6
Bedfield Suffk..............78 F2
Bedford Bed...............74 F5
Bedford
  Crematorium Bed.....75 G4
Bedhampton Hants.......17 K2
Bedingfield Suffk..........78 E2
Bedlam N York...........132 D7
Bedlington Nthumb.....159 G5
Bedlinog Myr Td..........53 H7
Bedminster Bristl.........38 E6
Bedminster Down
  Bristl....................38 E6
Bedmond Herts...........59 J7
Bednall Staffs..............99 L8
Bedrule Border...........167 J5
Bedstone Shrops..........83 G7
Bedwas Caerph...........37 J3
Bedwellty Caerph........53 J7
Bedworth Warwks........86 D6
Beeby Leics................87 J2
Beech Hants...............30 B4
Beech Staffs...............99 J5
Beech Hill W Berk........42 B7
Beechingstoke Wilts.....40 C8
Beedon W Berk...........41 J5
Beeford E R Yk..........135 H8
Beeley Derbys............114 E7
Beelsby NE Lin..........117 K2
Beenham W Berk.........41 L6
Beer Devon.................13 G5
Beer Somset...............26 B5
Beercrocombe
  Somset...................25 L7
Beer Hackett Dorset.....14 B1
Beesands Devon............7 J7
Beesby Lincs.............118 F5
Beeson Devon...............7 J7
Beeston C Beds...........75 H5
Beeston Ches W..........98 D2
Beeston Leeds...........123 K4
Beeston Norfk.............91 K1
Beeston Notts............101 K5
Beeston Regis Norfk...106 E4
Beeswing D & G.........146 F2
Beetham Cumb...........129 K4
Beetham Somset..........25 L8
Beetley Norfk.............106 A8
Begbroke Oxon............57 J5
Begelly Pembks...........49 J6
Beguildy Powys...........82 D7
Beighton Norfk............93 H2
Beighton Sheff...........115 H5

Beinn Na Faoghla
  W Isls....................233 c7
Beith N Ayrs..............174 C7
Bekesbourne Kent.......35 G4
Belaugh Norfk............107 G8
Belbroughton Worcs.....85 G7
Belchalwell Dorset........14 E1
Belchamp Otten
  Essex....................77 J6
Belchamp St Paul
  Essex....................77 H6
Belchamp Walter
  Essex....................77 J6
Belchford Lincs..........118 D6
Belford Nthumb..........169 G3
Belgrave C Leic...........87 H3
Belhaven E Loth.........178 E3
Belhelvie Abers..........207 H2
Belhinnie Abers..........215 K8
Bellabeg Abers...........205 H3
Bellanoch Ag & B........182 A8
Bellaty Angus............195 K4
Bell Busk N York.........131 G7
Belleau Lincs.............118 E5
Bell End Worcs............85 G7
Bellerby N York...........131 L2
Belle Vue Cumb..........148 C4
Belle Vue Wakefd.......123 L6
Bellfield S Lans..........164 F3
Bellfield S Lans..........165 J5
Bellingdon Bucks.........58 F6
Bellingham Nthumb.....157 L5
Belloch Ag & B............161 H2
Bellochantuy Ag & B....161 H3
Bell o' th' Hill Ches W....98 D4
Bellshill N Lans..........175 J6
Bellside N Lans..........175 L6
Bellsquarry W Loth.....176 E5
Bells Yew Green
  E Susx...................33 G6
Belluton BaNES...........38 E7
Belmaduthy Highld......213 G3
Belmont Bl w D..........121 K7
Belmont Gt Lon...........44 E7
Belmont S Ayrs..........163 J5
Belmont Shet.............235 d2
Belnacraig Abers........205 J3
Belper Derbys............101 G3
Belsay Nthumb..........158 D6
Belses Border.............167 J4
Belsford Devon..............7 H4
Belsize Herts...............59 G7
Belstead Suffk.............78 D6
Belstone Devon...........10 F6
Belthorn Lancs...........121 L5
Beltinge Kent..............47 K6
Beltingham Nthumb....149 K3
Beltoft N Linc.............116 D1
Belton Leics..............101 H7
Belton Lincs..............102 F4
Belton N Linc.............116 C1
Belton Norfk...............93 K3
Belton Rutlnd..............88 B3
Belton House Lincs.....102 F5
Belvedere Gt Lon.........45 J4
Belvoir Leics.............102 D5
Bembridge IoW............17 J5
Bemerton Wilts............28 C5
Bempton E R Yk........135 J5
Benacre Suffk.............93 K6
Benbecula W Isls........233 c7
Benbecula Airport
  W Isls....................233 c6
Benbuie D & G...........154 C3
Benderloch Ag & B.....191 H8
Benfieldside Dur.........150 D4
Bengeo Herts..............60 A5
Bengeworth Worcs.......71 J5
Benhall Green Suffk.....79 H3
Benhall Street Suffk.....79 H3
Benholm Abers..........197 K3
Beningbrough N York..133 H7
Benington Herts..........59 M4
Benington Lincs..........104 C3
Benllech IoA..............109 G5

Benmore Ag & B........173 K2
Bennan N Ayrs...........162 C5
Ben Nevis Highld........192 B3
Benniworth Lincs........117 K5
Benover Kent...............33 J4
Ben Rhydding C Brad..123 H2
Benslie N Ayrs...........163 J2
Benson Oxon...............41 L3
Benthoul C Aber.........206 F5
Bentley Donc.............115 K1
Bentley E R Yk..........126 C4
Bentley Hants.............30 C3
Bentley Suffk..............78 D6
Bentley Warwks..........86 C4
Bentley
  Crematorium
  Essex....................45 L2
Bentpath D & G..........156 B4
Bentwichen Devon.......24 B5
Bentworth Hants.........30 A4
Benvie Angus............186 E2
Benville Dorset............14 A2
Benwick Cambs...........89 L5
Beoley Worcs..............71 J1
Beoraidbeg Highld......199 L6
Bepton W Susx............18 B3
Berden Essex..............60 D3
Berea Pembks..............48 D2
Bere Alston Devon.........6 C3
Bere Ferrers Devon........6 C3
Bere Regis Dorset........14 F4
Bergh Apton Norfk.......93 G4
Berinsfield Oxon..........41 L2
Berkeley Gloucs..........55 G7
Berkhamsted Herts......59 G6
Berkley Somset...........27 J2
Berkswell Solhll...........86 B7
Bermondsey Gt Lon.....45 G4
Bernera Highld..........200 C2
Bernisdale Highld.......208 F4
Berrick Prior Oxon.......41 L2
Berrick Salome Oxon....41 L2
Berriedale Highld.......227 K4
Berrier Cumb.............137 L2
Berriew Powys............82 D4
Berrington Shrops........83 K3
Berrington Worcs.........69 L2
Berrington Green
  Worcs...................69 L2
Berrow Somset............25 L2
Berrow Green Worcs....70 D3
Berryhillock Moray.....215 L3
Berryhillock Moray.....215 L4
Berrynarbor Devon......23 J3
Berry Pomeroy
  Devon......................7 J4
Bersham Wrexhm........97 L3
Berwick E Susx............20 B5
Berwick Bassett Wilts...40 C5
Berwick Hill Nthumb...158 F6
Berwick St James
  Wilts......................28 B4
Berwick St John Wilts...27 L6
Berwick St Leonard
  Wilts......................27 L5
Berwick-upon-
  Tweed Nthumb........179 K7
Bescar Lancs.............120 E7
Besford Worcs.............71 G5
Bessacarr Donc.........115 L2
Bessingby E R Yk......135 J6
Bessingham Norfk......106 E5
Besthorpe Norfk..........92 C4
Besthorpe Notts........116 D8
Bestwood Village
  Notts....................101 K3
Beswick E R Yk..........126 C2
Betchworth Surrey......31 K2
Bethel Gwynd............109 G7
Bethel IoA.................108 E7
Bethersden Kent.........34 C6
Bethesda Gwynd........109 J7
Bethesda Pembks........49 J4
Bethlehem Carmth......51 K1
Bethnal Green Gt Lon..45 G4
Betley Staffs...............99 H3

Betsham Kent....................45 L5
Betteshanger Kent..........35 J4
Bettiscombe Dorset....13 K3
Bettisfield Wrexhm........98 C5
Bettws Newpt.................37 L3
Bettws Bledrws
  Cerdgn......................66 D4
Bettws Cedewain
  Powys........................82 C4
Bettws Evan Cerdgn......65 J5
Bettws-Newydd
  Mons.........................54 A6
Bettyhill Highld.............229 L3
Betws Brdgnd.................36 D3
Betws Gwerfil Goch
  Denbgs.....................97 G3
Betws-y-Coed Conwy...96 C2
Betws-yn-Rhos
  Conwy......................110 C6
Beulah Cerdgn..............65 J5
Beulah Powys................67 K4
Bevercotes Notts........116 B6
Beverley E R Yk............126 C3
Beverston Gloucs.........39 K2
Bewcastle Cumb..........156 F7
Bewdley Worcs..............84 D7
Bewerley N York..........132 B6
Bewholme E R Yk.........126 E1
Bexhill E Susx................20 E4
Bexley Gt Lon.................45 J5
Bexleyheath Gt Lon......45 J5
Bexwell Norfk.................90 F3
Beyton Suffk...................77 L2
Beyton Green Suffk........77 L2
Bhaltos W Isls..............232 d2
Bhatarsaigh W Isls......233b10
Bibury Gloucs.................56 C6
Bicester Oxon.................57 L4
Bickenhill Solhll.............85 L6
Bicker Lincs..................103 L5
Bickerstaffe Lancs......112 C2
Bickerton N York..........124 C1
Bickford Staffs..............84 F2
Bickington Devon............7 J2
Bickington Devon..........23 H5
Bickleigh Devon...............6 D4
Bickleigh Devon............12 B2
Bickley Ches W.............98 D3
Bickley Gt Lon................45 H6
Bickley N York..............134 E2
Bicknacre Essex............61 J7
Bicknoller Somset........25 H4
Bicknor Kent..................33 L2
Bicton Shrops................82 F6
Bicton Shrops................83 J1
Bidborough Kent...........32 F5
Biddenden Kent.............33 L5
Biddenham Bed.............74 E4
Biddestone Wilts...........39 K5
Biddisham Somset........26 B2
Biddlesden Bucks..........73 J6
Biddulph Staffs..............99 K2
Biddulph Moor Staffs....99 K2
Bideford Devon..............23 G6
Bidford-on-Avon
  Warwks....................71 K4
Bielby E R Yk................125 J2
Bieldside C Aber..........207 G5
Bierley IoW.....................17 G6
Bierton Bucks.................58 D5
Big Balcraig D & G.......145 H6
Bigbury Devon..................6 F6
Bigbury-on-Sea
  Devon...........................6 F6
Bigby Lincs....................117 H1
Big Carlae D & G..........154 B3
Biggar S Lans...............165 K2
Biggin Derbys...............100 D2
Biggin Hill Gt Lon..........32 D2
Biggin Hill Airport
  Gt Lon........................45 H7
Biggleswade C Beds......75 H5
Bigholms D & G............156 B6
Bighouse Highld...........230 C3
Bighton Hants...............29 L4
Biglands Cumb.............148 A4

Bignor W Susx................18 D3
Bigrigg Cumb................136 D5
Big Sand Highld............219 H5
Bigton Shet..................235 c7
Bilborough C Nott........101 K4
Bilbrook Somset...........25 G3
Bilbrough N York..........124 E2
Bilbster Highld..............231 K5
Bildershaw Dur............140 F3
Bildeston Suffk...............78 B5
Billericay Essex.............46 B2
Billesdon Leics.............87 K3
Billesley Warwks...........71 K3
Billingborough Lincs....103 J5
Billinge St Hel..............112 D2
Billingford Norfk............92 E7
Billingford Norfk..........106 B7
Billingham S on T........141 K3
Billinghay Lincs............103 J2
Billingley Barns...........115 H1
Billingshurst W Susx.....31 H6
Billingsley Shrops.........84 C6
Billington C Beds...........58 F4
Billington Lancs...........121 L4
Billockby Norfk...............93 J2
Billy Row Dur...............150 E7
Bilsborrow Lancs..........121 G3
Bilsby Lincs...................119 G6
Bilsham W Susx.............18 D5
Bilsington Kent..............34 D7
Bilsthorpe Notts..........101 M1
Bilston Mdloth.............177 H5
Bilston Wolves...............85 G4
Bilstone Leics................86 D3
Bilton E R Yk.................126 E4
Bilton N York................124 D1
Bilton N York................132 D7
Bilton Warwks................86 F8
Binbrook Lincs..............117 K3
Bincombe Dorset...........14 D5
Binegar Somset.............26 E2
Binfield Br For................42 D6
Binfield Heath Oxon......42 C5
Bingfield Nthumb.........158 B7
Bingham Notts.............102 B4
Bingley C Brad.............123 G3
Binham Norfk...............106 B5
Binley Covtry.................86 E7
Binley Hants..................29 H2
Binley Woods Warwks....86 E7
Binnegar Dorset.............15 G5
Binniehill Falk..............176 B4
Binscombe Surrey.........30 F3
Binstead IoW.................17 H4
Binsted Hants................30 C3
Binsted W Susx.............18 D4
Binton Warwks..............71 K4
Bintree Norfk...............106 B7
Birch Essex....................61 M4
Bircham Newton
  Norfk.......................105 J5
Bircham Tofts Norfk.....105 J6
Birchanger Essex..........60 E4
Birchanger Green
  Services Essex.........60 E4
Birch Cross Staffs........100 C6
Bircher Herefs................69 J2
Birch Green Essex.........61 M4
Birchgrove Cardif..........37 J4
Birchgrove Swans.........51 K5
Birchgrove W Susx........32 D7
Birchington Kent...........35 J2
Birchley Heath
  Warwks....................86 C5
Birchover Derbys.........100 E1
Birch Services Rochdl..122 C8
Birch Vale Derbys........114 A4
Birch Wood Somset......25 K8
Birchwood Warrtn........112 F4
Bircotes Notts..............115 M3
Birdbrook Essex............77 G6
Birdforth N York...........133 G4
Birdham W Susx............17 M3
Birdingbury Warwks......72 E2
Birdlip Gloucs................55 L5

Birdsall N York.............134 C6
Birds Edge Kirk............123 J8
Birds Green Essex.........60 F6
Birdsgreen Shrops........84 D6
Birdsmoorgate
  Dorset.......................13 K3
Birdwell Barns.............115 G2
Birgham Border...........168 B2
Birichin Highld.............223 G3
Birkby N York...............141 H6
Birkdale Sefton...........120 D7
Birkenbog Abers.........215 L2
Birkenhead Wirral........111 K4
Birkenhills Abers.........216 E5
Birkenshaw Kirk..........123 J5
Birkhall Abers..............205 H6
Birkhill Angus..............186 F1
Birkhill D & G...............166 B6
Birkin N York................124 E5
Birley Herefs..................69 J4
Birley Carr Sheff..........115 G3
Birling Kent....................46 B7
Birlingham Worcs..........71 G5
Birmingham Birm..........85 J6
Birmingham Airport
  Solhll........................85 L6
Birnam P & K................195 G7
Birness Abers...............217 J7
Birse Abers...................206 B6
Birsemore Abers..........205 L5
Birstall Kirk...................123 J5
Birstall Leics..................87 H2
Birstwith N York...........132 C7
Birtley Gatesd..............151 G4
Birtley Herefs.................69 G2
Birtley Nthumb.............157 L6
Birtley Crematorium
  Gatesd.....................151 G4
Birts Street Worcs........70 D7
Bisbrooke Rutlnd..........88 C4
Biscathorpe Lincs........118 C5
Bisham W & M................42 D4
Bishampton Worcs........71 H4
Bish Mill Devon.............24 B6
Bishop Auckland Dur...140 F2
Bishopbridge Lincs......117 G4
Bishopbriggs E Duns...175 G4
Bishop Burton E R Yk...126 B3
Bishop Middleham
  Dur..........................141 H2
Bishopmill Moray.........214 F2
Bishop Monkton
  N York......................132 E6
Bishop Norton Lincs....117 G3
Bishopsbourne Kent.....35 G4
Bishops Cannings
  Wilts.........................40 B7
Bishop's Castle
  Shrops......................83 G5
Bishop's Caundle
  Dorset.......................27 G8
Bishop's Cleeve
  Gloucs......................55 L3
Bishop's Frome
  Herefs.......................70 B5
Bishop's Green Essex...61 G4
Bishops Hull Somset.....25 J6
Bishop's Itchington
  Warwks....................72 E3
Bishops Lydeard
  Somset.....................25 J5
Bishop's Norton
  Gloucs......................55 J3
Bishop's Nympton
  Devon.......................24 B6
Bishop's Offley Staffs...99 H6
Bishop's Stortford
  Herts........................60 D4
Bishop's Sutton
  Hants........................29 L5
Bishop's Tachbrook
  Warwks....................72 C3
Bishop's Tawton
  Devon.......................23 J5
Bishopsteignton
  Devon.........................7 K2

Bishopstoke Hants.........29 J7
Bishopston Swans.........51 H7
Bishopstone Bucks........58 D6
Bishopstone E Susx......19 M5
Bishopstone Herefs.......69 H5
Bishopstone Kent...........47 K6
Bishopstone Swindn......40 E4
Bishopstone Wilts.........28 B6
Bishopstrow Wilts..........27 L3
Bishop Sutton BaNES....38 E7
Bishop's Waltham
  Hants........................29 K7
Bishopswood Somset....25 K8
Bishop's Wood Staffs....84 E2
Bishopsworth Bristl......38 E6
Bishop Thornton
  N York......................132 D6
Bishopthorpe C York....124 F2
Bishopton Darltn.........141 J3
Bishopton Rens............174 E4
Bishop Wilton E R Yk....134 C7
Bishton Newpt...............38 B3
Bishton Staffs..............100 A7
Bisley Gloucs.................55 K6
Bisley Surrey..................42 F8
Bissoe Cnwll....................3 K3
Bisterne Hants...............15 L3
Bitchfield Lincs.............103 G6
Bittadon Devon..............23 J3
Bittaford Devon................6 F4
Bitterley Shrops.............83 L7
Bitterne C Sotn..............29 J8
Bitteswell Leics..............87 G6
Bitton S Glos.................39 G6
Bix Oxon........................42 B4
Bixter Shet...................235 c5
Blaby Leics.....................87 H4
Blackadder Border........179 H7
Blackawton Devon...........7 J5
Blackborough Devon......12 E1
Blackborough End
  Norfk.........................90 F1
Black Bourton Oxon.......56 F6
Blackboys E Susx...........20 B2
Blackbrook Derbys.......101 G3
Blackbrook St Hel........112 D3
Blackbrook Staffs...........99 H5
Blackburn Abers...........206 F3
Blackburn Bl w D..........121 K5
Blackburn W Loth.........176 D5
Blackburn with
  Darwen Services
  Bl w D......................121 K5
Black Callerton N u Ty..150 F2
Blackcraig E Ayrs.........164 C7
Black Crofts Ag & B......182 D1
Blackdog Abers.............207 H3
Black Dog Devon............11 J3
Blackdown Dorset.........13 K2
Blacker Hill Barns.........115 G2
Blackfen Gt Lon.............45 J5
Blackfield Hants.............16 E3
Blackford P & K............185 J5
Blackford Somset..........26 B2
Blackford Somset..........26 F6
Blackfordby Leics.........101 G8
Blackhall C Edin...........177 G4
Blackhall Colliery Dur...151 K6
Blackhall Mill Gatesd...150 E4
Blackhaugh Border.......166 F2
Blackheath Gt Lon.........45 G5
Blackheath Sandw.........85 H6
Blackheath Suffk...........93 J8
Blackheath Surrey.........31 G3
Blackhill Abers.............217 K3
Blackhill Abers.............217 K5
Blackhill Dur.................150 D5
Blackhill of
  Clackriach Abers.....217 H5
Blackhorse Devon.........12 C4
Blacklaw D & G.............165 K7
Blackley Manch............113 J2
Blackley
  Crematorium
  Manch......................113 J2
Blacklunans P & K........195 J4

Blackmarstone
Herefs.............................69 K6
Blackmill Brdgnd.............36 E3
Blackmoor Hants..............30 C5
Blackmoor N Som.............38 C7
Blackmoorfoot Kirk.........123 G7
Blackmore Essex..............60 F7
Blackmore End Essex......61 H2
Blackness Falk................176 E3
Blacknest Hants..............30 D3
Black Notley Essex..........61 J4
Blacko Lancs.................122 C3
Black Pill Swans..............51 J7
Blackpool Bpool............120 D4
Blackpool Devon..............7 K6
Blackpool Airport
Lancs.............................120 D4
Blackridge W Loth.........176 B5
Blackrod Bolton.............121 J7
Blacksboat Moray...........214 E6
Blackshaw D & G.............147 J2
Blackshaw Head
Calder.........................122 E5
Blackstone W Susx.........19 H3
Black Street Suffk...........93 K6
Blackthorn Oxon.............57 L4
Blackthorpe Suffk............77 K2
Blacktoft E R Yk.............125 J5
Blacktop C Aber............207 G4
Black Torrington
Devon.............................10 C4
Blackwall Derbys............100 E3
Blackwater Cnwll..............3 J3
Blackwater Hants.............42 D7
Blackwater IoW................17 G5
Blackwater Somset.........25 K7
Blackwaterfoot
N Ayrs..........................162 A4
Blackwell Cumb..............148 D4
Blackwell Derbys............101 H2
Blackwell Derbys............114 C6
Blackwell Warwks............72 B5
Blackwell Worcs..............71 H1
Blackwood Caerph...........37 J2
Blackwood D & G............154 F5
Blackwood S Lans...........164 F1
Blacon Ches W................111 L2
Bladnoch D & G..............145 J4
Bladon Oxon....................57 J5
Blaenannerch Cerdgn......65 H5
Blaenau Ffestiniog
Gwynd............................96 A4
Blaenavon Torfn...............53 K6
Blaenavon Big Pit
Torfn.............................53 K6
Blaenffos Pembks............65 H6
Blaengarw Brdgnd............36 D2
Blaengwrach Neath..........52 D6
Blaengwynfi Neath...........36 D2
Blaenpennal Cerdgn.........66 E2
Blaenplwyf Cerdgn...........80 D7
Blaenporth Cerdgn...........65 J5
Blaenrhondda
Rhondd...........................52 E7
Blaenwaun Carmth............50 B1
Blaen-y-Coed Carmth.......50 D2
Blaen-y-cwm Rhondd........52 E7
Blagdon N Som................38 D8
Blagdon Somset...............25 K7
Blagdon Torbay..................7 K4
Blagdon Hill Somset........25 K7
Blaich Highld..................191 K2
Blain Highld....................190 D3
Blaina Blae G....................53 J6
Blair Atholl P & K...........194 D4
Blair Drummond
Stirlg............................184 F7
Blairgowrie P & K...........195 J7
Blairhall Fife..................176 D2
Blairingone P & K...........185 K7
Blairlogie Stirlg.............185 H7
Blairmore Ag & B............173 L2
Blairmore Highld............173 G4
Blair's Ferry Ag & B........173 G4
Blaisdon Gloucs..............55 G5
Blakebrook Worcs............84 E7

Blakedown Worcs.............84 F7
Blake End Essex..............61 H4
Blakemere Ches W...........112 D7
Blakemere Herefs.............69 G6
Blakenall Heath Wsall.......85 H3
Blakeney Gloucs..............54 F6
Blakeney Norfk...............106 B4
Blakenhall Ches E............99 G3
Blakenhall Wolves............85 G4
Blakesley Nhants..............73 J4
Blanchland Nthumb.........150 B5
Blandford Forum
Dorset...........................15 G2
Blandford St Mary
Dorset...........................15 G2
Blanefield Stirlg.............174 F3
Blankney Lincs................103 H1
Blantyre S Lans...............175 J6
Blar a' Chaorainn
Highld...........................191 L3
Blargie Highld................202 F6
Blarmachfoldach
Highld...........................191 L3
Blaston Leics...................88 B4
Blatherwycke Nhants........88 B4
Blawith Cumb..................129 G2
Blawquhairn D & G..........154 B5
Blaxhall Suffk..................79 H3
Blaxton Donc..................116 A2
Blaydon Gatesd...............150 F3
Bleadney Somset...............26 C3
Bleadon N Som.................25 M1
Blean Kent........................34 F3
Bleasby Notts.................102 B3
Blebocraigs Fife.............187 G4
Bleddfa Powys...................68 E2
Bledington Gloucs............56 E4
Bledlow Bucks..................58 C7
Bledlow Ridge Bucks........42 D2
Blegbie E Loth................178 B6
Blencarn Cumb................138 F2
Blencogo Cumb...............147 L5
Blendworth Hants.............30 B8
Blenheim Palace
Oxon..............................57 H5
Blennerhasset Cumb.......147 L6
Bletchingdon Oxon...........57 J4
Bletchingley Surrey..........32 B3
Bletchley M Keyn.............58 D2
Bletchley Shrops...............98 F5
Bletherston Pembks.........49 H4
Bletsoe Bed......................74 E3
Blewbury Oxon.................41 K4
Blickling Norfk................106 E6
Blidworth Notts..............101 L2
Blidworth Bottoms
Notts...........................101 L2
Blindcrake Cumb.............147 K7
Blindley Heath Surrey......32 C4
Blisland Cnwll....................5 H2
Blissford Hants.................28 D8
Bliss Gate Worcs..............84 D8
Blisworth Nhants..............73 K4
Blithbury Staffs..............100 B8
Blockley Gloucs................71 L7
Blofield Norfk...................93 G2
Blofield Heath Norfk.........93 G2
Blo Norton Norfk..............92 B7
Bloomfield Border...........167 J4
Blore Staffs.....................100 C3
Bloxham Oxon...................72 E7
Bloxholm Lincs...............103 H2
Bloxwich Wsall..................85 H3
Bloxworth Dorset..............15 G4
Blubberhouses
N York...........................132 B7
Blue Anchor Somset.........24 F3
Blue Bell Hill Kent............46 C7
Blue John Cavern
Derbys.........................114 C5
Blundellsands Sefton......111 J2
Blundeston Suffk..............93 L4
Blunham Bed....................75 H4
Blunsdon St Andrew
Swindn...........................40 C3
Bluntington Worcs............84 F8

Bluntisham Cambs............89 L8
Blyborough Lincs...........116 F3
Blyford Suffk....................93 J7
Blymhill Staffs..................84 E2
Blyth Notts.....................115 L4
Blyth Nthumb.................159 H5
Blyth Bridge Border........165 M1
Blythburgh Suffk...............93 J7
Blyth Crematorium
Nthumb.........................159 H5
Blythe Border.................178 D7
Blyton Lincs...................116 D3
Boarhills Fife..................187 J5
Boarhunt Hants.................17 H2
Boarstall Bucks................57 L5
Boath Highld...................222 D6
Boat of Garten Highld......203 L2
Bobbing Kent....................46 E6
Bobbington Staffs.............84 E5
Bocking Essex...................61 J4
Bocking
Churchstreet
Essex.............................61 J3
Boddam Abers................217 L6
Boddam Shet...................235 c7
Boddington Gloucs...........55 K3
Bodedern IoA.................108 D5
Bodelwyddan
Denbgs.........................110 D6
Bodenham Herefs.............69 K4
Bodenham Wilts...............28 D6
Bodenham Moor
Herefs............................69 K4
Bodewryd IoA.................108 E4
Bodfari Denbgs...............110 F7
Bodffordd IoA.................108 F6
Bodfuan Gwynd.................94 F5
Bodham Norfk.................106 D4
Bodiam E Susx..................33 K7
Bodiam Castle E Susx.......33 K7
Bodicote Oxon..................72 F6
Bodinnick Cnwll..................5 H5
Bodle Street Green
E Susx............................20 D3
Bodmin Cnwll.....................5 G3
Bodmin Moor Cnwll............5 J1
Bodsham Kent...................34 E5
Bodwen Cnwll.....................5 G4
Bogallan Highld...............212 F4
Bogbrae Abers.................217 J7
Bogend S Ayrs................163 K3
Boggs Holdings
E Loth...........................177 L4
Boghall Mdloth................177 H5
Boghall W Loth...............176 D5
Boghead S Lans...............164 F2
Bogmoor Moray...............215 H2
Bogmuir Abers.................197 G3
Bogniebrae Abers............216 B3
Bognor Regis
W Susx............................18 C6
Bogroy Highld.................203 L2
Bogue D & G....................154 B6
Bohortha Cnwll...................3 L5
Bohuntine Highld............201 L8
Bolam Dur......................140 F3
Bolberry Devon...................7 G7
Boldmere Birm..................85 K5
Boldre Hants.....................16 C3
Boldron Dur.....................140 C4
Bole Notts.......................116 C4
Bolehill Derbys................100 F2
Bolham Devon...................24 E7
Bolham Water Devon.........25 J8
Bolingey Cnwll....................3 K1
Bollington Ches E...........113 L6
Bolney W Susx...................31 L6
Bolnhurst Bed...................74 F3
Bolshan Angus................197 G6
Bolsover Derbys...............115 J7
Bolsterstone Sheff..........114 F3
Boltby N York..................133 G3
Boltenstone Abers...........205 J3
Bolton Bolton...................121 L8
Bolton Cumb....................138 F3
Bolton E Loth..................178 B4

Bolton E R Yk..................125 J1
Bolton Nthumb................169 G6
Bolton Abbey N York........131 K8
Bolton by Bowland
Lancs............................122 B3
Boltonfellend Cumb.........148 E2
Boltongate Cumb............147 M6
Bolton le Sands Lancs......129 K6
Bolton Low Houses
Cumb............................147 M6
Bolton-on-Swale
N York...........................141 G7
Bolton Percy N York.........124 E3
Bolton Upon Dearne
Barns...........................115 J2
Bolventor Cnwll..................5 J1
Bomere Heath Shrops........98 C8
Bonar Bridge Highld........222 E3
Bonawe Ag & B................182 E2
Bonby N Linc...................126 C7
Boncath Pembks................65 H6
Bonchester Bridge
Border...........................167 J6
Bondleigh Devon...............10 F4
Bonds Lancs....................121 G2
Bo'ness Falk....................176 D3
Boney Hay Staffs...............85 J2
Bonhill W Duns................174 D3
Boningale Shrops..............84 E3
Bonjedward Border..........167 K5
Bonkle N Lans..................175 L6
Bonnington Angus...........196 F7
Bonnington Kent................34 E7
Bonnybank Fife................186 F6
Bonnybridge Falk............175 L3
Bonnykelly Abers............217 G4
Bonnyrigg Mdloth............177 J5
Bonnyton Angus..............196 B8
Bonsall Derbys................100 F2
Bonshaw Tower
D & G...........................155 M7
Bont-Dolgadfan
Powys.............................81 J4
Bont-goch or Elerch
Cerdgn...........................80 F6
Bontnewydd Cerdgn..........66 E2
Bontnewydd Gwynd...........95 H1
Bontuchel Denbgs.............97 G2
Bonvilston V Glam.............37 G5
Boode Devon.....................23 H4
Booker Bucks.....................42 D3
Boon Border....................167 J1
Boosbeck R & Cl..............142 E4
Boose's Green Essex........61 K2
Boot Cumb......................137 G6
Booth Calder...................122 F5
Boothby Graffoe
Lincs............................103 G2
Boothby Pagnell
Lincs............................102 F6
Boothferry E R Yk............125 H5
Boothstown Salfd............113 G2
Bootle Cumb...................128 D2
Bootle Sefton.................111 K3
Boraston Shrops................70 B1
Bordeaux Guern...............236 e2
Borden Kent.....................34 B3
Border Forest Park.........157 G5
Borders
Crematorium
Border...........................167 H3
Boreham Essex..................61 J6
Boreham Wilts...................27 K3
Boreham Street
E Susx............................20 D4
Borehamwood Herts.........44 D2
Boreland D & G................155 L4
Boreraig Highld...............208 C4
Borgh W Isls....................232 f1
Borgh W Isls....................233 b9
Borgie Highld..................229 K4
Borgue D & G...................146 B5
Borgue Highld..................227 K4
Borley Essex.....................77 J6
Borneskitaig Highld........218 B7
Borness D & G.................146 A5

Boroughbridge
N York 132 F6
Borough Green Kent 33 G2
Borrowash Derbys 101 H5
Borrowby N York 132 F2
Borrowstoun Falk 176 D3
Borstal Medway 46 B6
Borth Cerdgn 80 E5
Borthwickbrae
Border 166 F6
Borthwickshiels
Border 166 F6
Borth-y-Gest Gwynd 95 K5
Borve Highld 209 G5
Borve W Isls 232 d4
Borve W Isls 232 f1
Borve W Isls 233 b9
Borwick Lancs 129 L5
Bosbury Herefs 70 C5
Boscastle Cnwll 8 E6
Boscombe Bmouth 15 L4
Boscombe Wilts 28 D4
Bosham W Susx 17 L2
Bosherston Pembks 49 G8
Bosley Ches E 113 K7
Bossall N York 133 L7
Bossiney Cnwll 8 E6
Bossingham Kent 34 F5
Bossington Somset 24 D2
Bostock Green
Ches W 112 F7
Boston Lincs 104 B4
Boston Crematorium
Lincs 104 A4
Boston Spa Leeds 124 C2
Boswinger Cnwll 4 F7
Botallack Cnwll 2 C5
Botany Bay Gt Lon 59 M7
Botesdale Suffk 92 C7
Bothal Nthumb 159 G5
Bothamsall Notts 116 A6
Bothel Cumb 147 L6
Bothenhampton
Dorset 13 L4
Bothwell S Lans 175 J6
Bothwell Services
S Lans 175 J6
Botley Bucks 59 G7
Botley Hants 29 K8
Botley Oxon 57 J6
Botolph Claydon
Bucks 58 B3
Botolphs W Susx 19 G4
Bottesford Leics 102 D5
Bottesford N Linc 116 E1
Bottisham Cambs 76 D3
Bottomcraig Fife 186 F3
Bottoms Calder 122 D6
Botusfleming Cnwll 6 B4
Botwnnog Gwynd 94 E6
Bough Beech Kent 32 E4
Boughrood Powys 68 C6
Boughton Nhants 73 L2
Boughton Norfk 91 G3
Boughton Notts 116 B7
Boughton Aluph Kent 34 D5
Boughton Green
Kent 33 K3
Boughton
Monchelsea Kent 33 K3
Boughton Street
Kent 34 E3
Bouldon Shrops 83 K6
Boulmer Nthumb 169 K6
Boultham Lincs 116 F7
Bourn Cambs 75 K3
Bourne Lincs 103 H7
Bournebridge Essex 45 J2
Bournebrook Birm 85 J6
Bourne End Bucks 42 E3
Bourne End C Beds 74 D5
Bourne End Herts 59 G6
Bournemouth
Bmouth 15 K4
Bournemouth
Airport Dorset 15 L3

Bournemouth
Crematorium
Bmouth 15 L4
Bournes Green
Sthend 46 E3
Bournheath Worcs 85 G8
Bournmoor Dur 151 H5
Bournville Birm 85 J7
Bourton Dorset 27 H5
Bourton Oxon 40 E3
Bourton Shrops 83 L4
Bourton Wilts 40 B7
Bourton on
Dunsmore Warwks 72 E1
Bourton-on-the-Hill
Gloucs 56 D2
Bourton-on-the-
Water Gloucs 56 D4
Bousd Ag & B 189 G4
Bouth Cumb 129 H3
Bouthwaite N York 131 L5
Boveridge Dorset 28 B7
Bovey Tracey Devon 7 J1
Bovingdon Herts 59 G7
Bow Devon 11 G4
Bow Gt Lon 45 G4
Bow Ork 234 b7
Bow Brickhill M Keyn 74 C7
Bowbridge Gloucs 55 J6
Bowburn Dur 151 H7
Bowcombe IoW 16 F5
Bowd Devon 12 E4
Bowden Border 167 H4
Bowden Hill Wilts 39 L6
Bowdon Traffd 113 H4
Bower Highld 231 J3
Bowerchalke Wilts 28 A6
Bowermadden Highld 231 J3
Bowers Staffs 99 J5
Bowers Gifford Essex 46 C3
Bowershall Fife 176 F1
Bower's Row Leeds 124 B5
Bowes Dur 140 C4
Bowgreave Lancs 121 G2
Bowhouse D & G 147 H2
Bowland Border 167 G2
Bowley Herefs 69 K4
Bowlhead Green
Surrey 30 E4
Bowling C Brad 123 H4
Bowling W Duns 174 E4
Bowmanstead Cumb 137 J7
Bowmore Ag & B 170 F6
Bowness-on-Solway
Cumb 147 L3
Bowness-on-
Windermere
Cumb 137 L7
Bow of Fife Fife 186 E5
Bowriefauld Angus 196 E6
Bowsden Nthumb 168 E2
Bow Street Cerdgn 80 E6
Box Gloucs 55 K7
Box Wilts 39 J6
Boxford Suffk 77 L6
Boxford W Berk 41 H6
Boxgrove W Susx 18 B4
Boxley Kent 33 K2
Boxmoor Herts 59 H6
Boxted Essex 62 B2
Boxted Essex 62 B2
Boxted Suffk 77 J4
Boxted Cross Essex 62 B2
Boxworth Cambs 75 L2
Boyden Gate Kent 47 L6
Boylestone Derbys 100 D5
Boyndie Abers 216 C2
Boyndlie Abers 217 G2
Boynton E R Yk 135 H4
Boysack Angus 197 G6
Boyton Cnwll 9 J6
Boyton Suffk 79 H5
Boyton Wilts 27 L4
Boyton Cross Essex 61 G6
Boyton End Suffk 77 G5
Bozeat Nhants 74 C3

Brabourne Kent 34 E6
Brabourne Lees Kent 34 E6
Brabstermire Highld 231 K2
Bracadale Highld 208 E6
Braceborough Lincs 88 F2
Bracebridge Heath
Lincs 117 G7
Bracebridge Low
Fields Lincs 116 F7
Braceby Lincs 103 G5
Bracewell Lancs 122 C2
Brackenfield Derbys 101 G2
Brackenhirst N Lans 175 K5
Bracklesham W Susx 17 L3
Brackletter Highld 201 J8
Brackley Nhants 73 H6
Bracknell Br For 42 E6
Braco P & K 185 H5
Bracobrae Moray 215 L4
Bracon Ash Norfk 92 E4
Bracora Highld 199 L6
Bracorina Highld 199 L6
Bradbourne Derbys 100 D3
Bradbury Dur 141 H2
Bradden Nhants 73 J5
Bradenham Bucks 42 D2
Bradenstoke Wilts 39 M4
Bradfield Devon 12 D1
Bradfield Essex 62 D2
Bradfield Norfk 106 F5
Bradfield Sheff 114 F3
Bradfield W Berk 41 L6
Bradfield Combust
Suffk 77 K3
Bradfield Green
Ches E 99 G2
Bradfield Heath Essex ... 62 D3
Bradfield St Clare
Suffk 77 K3
Bradfield St George
Suffk 77 K3
Bradford C Brad 123 H4
Bradford Devon 9 L4
Bradford Abbas
Dorset 26 E8
Bradford Leigh Wilts 39 J7
Bradford-on-Avon
Wilts 39 J7
Bradford-on-Tone
Somset 25 J6
Bradford Peverell
Dorset 14 C4
Bradiford Devon 23 J5
Brading IoW 17 H5
Bradley Derbys 100 E4
Bradley Hants 29 M3
Bradley NE Lin 118 C1
Bradley Staffs 99 K8
Bradley Wolves 85 G4
Bradley Worcs 71 H3
Bradley Green Worcs 71 H3
Bradley in the Moors
Staffs 100 B4
Bradley Stoke S Glos 38 E4
Bradmore Notts 101 L6
Bradninch Devon 12 C2
Bradnop Staffs 100 A2
Bradpole Dorset 13 L4
Bradshaw Calder 123 G4
Bradstone Devon 9 K8
Bradwall Green
Ches E 113 H8
Bradwell Derbys 114 D5
Bradwell Essex 61 J4
Bradwell M Keyn 74 B6
Bradwell Norfk 93 K3
Bradwell
Crematorium
Staffs 99 J3
Bradwell-on-Sea
Essex 62 B6
Bradwell Waterside
Essex 62 B6
Bradworthy Devon 9 J3
Brae Highld 213 G2
Brae Shet 235 c4

Braeface Falk 175 K3
Braehead Angus 197 H5
Braehead D & G 145 J4
Braehead S Lans 176 C7
Braemar Abers 204 E6
Braemore Highld 221 G5
Braemore Highld 227 J3
Brae Roy Lodge
Highld 201 L6
Braeside Inver 173 L4
Braes of Coul Angus 195 L5
Braes of Enzie Moray ... 215 J3
Braeswick Ork 234 d4
Braevallich Ag & B 182 D6
Brafferton Darltn 141 H3
Brafferton N York 132 F5
Brafield-on-the-
Green Nhants 74 B3
Bragar W Isls 232 f2
Bragbury End Herts 59 L4
Braidwood S Lans 175 L8
Brailsford Derbys 100 E4
Braintree Essex 61 J4
Braiseworth Suffk 78 D1
Braishfield Hants 29 G6
Braithwaite Cumb 137 H3
Braithwell Donc 115 K3
Bramber W Susx 19 G4
Bramcote Warwks 86 E5
Bramcote
Crematorium
Notts 101 J5
Bramdean Hants 29 L5
Bramerton Norfk 93 G3
Bramfield Herts 59 M5
Bramfield Suffk 93 H8
Bramford Suffk 78 D5
Bramhall Stockp 113 K5
Bramham Leeds 124 C2
Bramhope Leeds 123 K2
Bramley Hants 41 M8
Bramley Leeds 123 K4
Bramley Rothm 115 J3
Bramley Surrey 31 G3
Bramley Corner
Hants 41 M8
Bramling Kent 35 G4
Brampford Speke
Devon 11 L5
Brampton Cambs 75 J1
Brampton Cumb 138 F3
Brampton Cumb 148 F3
Brampton Lincs 116 D5
Brampton Norfk 106 F7
Brampton Rothm 115 H2
Brampton Suffk 93 J6
Brampton Abbotts
Herefs 54 E3
Brampton Ash
Nhants 87 L6
Brampton Bryan
Herefs 83 G8
Brampton-en-le-
Morthen Rothm 115 J4
Bramshall Staffs 100 B6
Bramshaw Hants 28 F7
Bramshott Hants 30 D5
Bramwell Somset 26 B5
Branault Highld 190 B3
Brancaster Norfk 105 J4
Brancaster Staithe
Norfk 105 J4
Brancepeth Dur 150 F7
Branchill Moray 214 D4
Branderburgh Moray ... 214 F1
Brandesburton E R Yk .. 126 E2
Brandeston Suffk 78 F3
Brandiston Norfk 106 D7
Brandon Dur 151 G7
Brandon Lincs 102 E3
Brandon Suffk 91 H6
Brandon Warwks 86 E7
Brandon Parva Norfk 92 C2
Brandsby N York 133 J5
Brandy Wharf Lincs 117 G3
Bran End Essex 61 G3

Branksome Poole 15 K4
Branksome Park
  Poole 15 K4
Bransbury Hants 29 H3
Bransby Lincs 116 E5
Branscombe Devon 12 F5
Bransford Worcs 70 E4
Bransgore Hants 16 A3
Bransholme C KuH 126 D4
Bransley Shrops 84 B7
Branston Leics 102 D6
Branston Lincs 117 G2
Branston Staffs 100 E7
Branston Booths
  Lincs 117 H7
Branstone IoW 17 G5
Brant Broughton
  Lincs 102 E2
Brantham Suffk 78 D7
Branthwaite Cumb. 136 E3
Branthwaite Cumb. 148 B7
Brantingham E R Yk 125 L5
Branton Donc 115 M2
Branton Nthumb. 168 F6
Branton Green
  N York 132 F6
Branxton Nthumb 168 D2
Brassington Derbys 100 E2
Brasted Kent 32 E3
Brasted Chart Kent 32 E3
Brathens Abers. 206 D5
Bratoft Lincs 119 G8
Brattleby Lincs 116 F5
Bratton Wilts 27 K2
Bratton Wrekin 84 B2
Bratton Clovelly
  Devon 10 C6
Bratton Fleming
  Devon 23 K4
Bratton Seymour
  Somset 26 F5
Braughing Herts. 60 C3
Braunston Nhants. 73 G2
Braunston Rutlnd 88 B3
Braunstone Leics 87 G3
Braunton Devon 23 H4
Brawby N York 134 B4
Brawl Highld 230 B3
Bray W & M. 42 E4
Braybrooke Nhants 87 L6
Brayford Devon 23 L4
Bray Shop Cnwll 5 M2
Brayton N York 124 F4
Braywick W & M. 42 E4
Breachwood Green
  Herts. 59 J4
Breadsall Derbys 101 G5
Breadstone Gloucs. 55 G7
Breage Cnwll. 3 G5
Breakachy Highld. 212 D5
Breakspear
  Crematorium
  Gt Lon 43 H3
Brealangwell Lodge
  Highld 222 C3
Bream Gloucs. 54 E6
Breamore Hants 28 D7
Brean Somset 25 L1
Breanais W Isls 232 d3
Brearton N York 132 E7
Breascleit W Isls 232 e2
Breasclete W Isls 232 e2
Breaston Derbys. 101 J5
Brechfa Carmth. 66 C7
Brechin Angus 196 F4
Breckles Norfk 91 L5
Brecon Powys 53 G3
Brecon Beacons
  National Park 52 F3
Bredbury Stockp 113 L3
Brede E Susx 21 G3
Bredenbury Herefs 69 L3
Bredfield Suffk 78 F4
Bredgar Kent 34 B3
Bredhurst Kent. 46 D7
Bredon Worcs 71 G6

Bredon's Hardwick
  Worcs 71 G7
Bredon's Norton
  Worcs 71 G6
Bredwardine Herefs 69 G5
Breedon on the Hill
  Leics 101 H7
Breich W Loth 176 C6
Breightmet Bolton........ 121 L8
Breighton E R Yk 125 G4
Breinton Herefs. 69 J6
Bremhill Wilts. 39 L5
Brenchley Kent. 33 H5
Brendon Devon 24 B2
Brenfield Ag & B. 172 E2
Brenish W Isls 232 d3
Brent Eleigh Suffk. 77 L5
Brentford Gt Lon. 44 D5
Brentingby Leics 102 C8
Brent Knoll Somset. 25 M2
Brent Mill Devon............. 7 G4
Brent Pelham Herts. 60 C2
Brentwood Essex 45 L2
Brenzett Kent. 21 K1
Brenzett Green Kent 34 D8
Brereton Staffs. 85 J1
Brereton Green
  Ches E 113 H8
Bressay Shet. 235 d6
Bressingham Norfk 92 C7
Bretby Derbys 100 F7
Bretby Crematorium
  Derbys 100 F7
Bretford Warwks 86 E7
Bretforton Worcs. 71 K5
Bretherton Lancs 121 G6
Brettabister Shet. 235 d5
Brettenham Norfk 91 L6
Brettenham Suffk. 77 L4
Bretton Flints. 111 K8
Brewood Staffs. 84 F2
Briantspuddle Dorset..... 14 F4
Brickendon Herts. 60 A6
Bricket Wood Herts 59 J7
Brick Houses Sheff. 114 F5
Brickhampton
  Worcs 71 H6
Bride IoM 237 e2
Bridekirk Cumb. 147 K7
Bridestowe Devon 10 D6
Brideswell Abers 216 B6
Bridford Devon 11 J7
Bridge Kent 35 G4
Bridgehampton
  Somset 26 E6
Bridge Hewick
  N York 132 E5
Bridgehill Dur 150 D5
Bridgemary Hants.......... 17 H2
Bridgend Abers 215 L7
Bridgend Ag & B. 161 K2
Bridgend Ag & B. 171 G6
Bridgend Angus 196 E3
Bridgend Brdgnd 36 E4
Bridgend D & G. 165 L7
Bridgend Devon. 6 E6
Bridgend Fife. 186 F5
Bridgend Moray............ 215 J7
Bridgend P & K. 186 B3
Bridgend W Loth 176 E3
Bridgend of
  Lintrathen Angus... 195 L5
Bridge of Alford
  Abers 206 B2
Bridge of Allan Stirlg... 185 G7
Bridge of Avon Moray. 204 E2
Bridge of Avon Moray.. 214 E7
Bridge of Balgie
  P & K. 193 J6
Bridge of Brewlands
  Angus 195 J4
Bridge of Brown
  Highld 204 D2
Bridge of Cally P & K ... 195 J6
Bridge of Canny
  Abers 206 C6

Bridge of Craigisla
  Angus 195 K5
Bridge of Dee D & G.... 146 C3
Bridge of Don C Aber.. 207 H4
Bridge of Dulsie
  Highld 213 L6
Bridge of Dye Abers 206 C7
Bridge of Earn P & K. .. 186 B4
Bridge of Ericht P & K.. 193 H5
Bridge of Feugh
  Abers 206 D6
Bridge of Forss
  Highld 230 F2
Bridge of Gairn Abers.. 205 H6
Bridge of Gaur P & K ... 193 H5
Bridge of Marnoch
  Abers 216 B4
Bridge of Orchy
  Ag & B 192 F2
Bridge of Tilt P & K 194 D4
Bridge of Tynet
  Moray 215 J3
Bridge of Walls Shet.... 235 b5
Bridge of Weir Rens 174 D5
Bridgerule Devon............. 9 H4
Bridge Sollers Herefs.. 69 H6
Bridge Street Suffk. 77 K5
Bridgetown Somset 24 E5
Bridge Trafford
  Ches W 112 C7
Bridgham Norfk 91 L6
Bridgnorth Shrops. 84 C5
Bridgwater Somset 25 L4
Bridgwater Services
  Somset 25 L4
Bridlington E R Yk........ 135 J6
Bridport Dorset 13 L4
Bridstow Herefs. 54 E3
Brierfield Lancs. 122 C3
Brierley Barns 124 C7
Brierley Gloucs. 54 F5
Brierley Hill Dudley 85 G6
Brigg N Linc. 117 G1
Briggate Norfk 107 G6
Briggswath N York 143 H5
Brigham Cumb. 136 F2
Brigham E R Yk. 135 G8
Brighouse Calder. 123 H6
Brighstone IoW 16 E5
Brighthampton Oxon...... 57 G7
Brightley Devon 10 E5
Brightling E Susx 20 D2
Brightlingsea Essex 62 C5
Brighton Br & H. 19 J3
Brighton le Sands
  Sefton 111 J2
Brightons Falk 176 C3
Brightwalton W Berk...... 41 H5
Brightwell Suffk. 78 F5
Brightwell Baldwin
  Oxon 41 M2
Brightwell-cum-
  Sotwell Oxon 41 L3
Brightwell Upperton
  Oxon 42 A2
Brignall Dur. 140 D5
Brig o'Turk Stirlg 184 C6
Brigsley NE Lin. 118 C2
Brigsteer Cumb. 129 K2
Brigstock Nhants 88 D6
Brill Bucks 58 A5
Brill Cnwll........................ 3 J5
Brilley Herefs 68 F5
Brimfield Herefs. 69 K2
Brimfield Cross
  Herefs. 69 K2
Brimington Derbys 115 H6
Brimley Devon 7 J1
Brimpsfield Gloucs. 55 L5
Brimpton W Berk. 41 K7
Brimscombe Gloucs. 55 K7
Brimstage Wirral 111 J5
Brincliffe Sheff 115 F4
Brind E R Yk. 125 H4
Brindister Shet. 235 c5
Brindle Lancs 121 J5

Brineton Staffs 84 E2
Bringhurst Leics 88 B5
Bringsty Common
  Herefs. 70 C4
Brington Cambs 88 F7
Briningham Norfk 106 C5
Brinkhill Lincs. 118 E6
Brinkley Cambs 76 F4
Brinklow Warwks 86 E7
Brinkworth Wilts. 40 A4
Brinscall Lancs 121 J6
Brinsley Notts 101 J3
Brinsworth Rothm......... 115 H4
Brinton Norfk 106 C5
Brinyan Ork 234 c5
Brisley Norfk 105 M7
Brislington Bristl 38 F6
Brissenden Green
  Kent 34 C6
Bristol Bristl. 38 E5
Bristol Airport N Som.... 38 D7
Bristol Zoo Gardens
  Bristl 38 E5
Briston Norfk 106 C6
Britford Wilts 28 D5
Brithdir Caerph. 53 J7
Brithdir Gwynd 96 B8
British Legion Village
  Kent 33 J2
Briton Ferry Neath 51 L6
Britwell Salome Oxon... 42 A2
Brixham Torbay 7 L5
Brixton Devon 6 E5
Brixton Gt Lon 44 F5
Brixton Deverill Wilts 27 K4
Brixworth Nhants 73 L1
Brize Norton Oxon.......... 56 F6
Brize Norton Airport
  Oxon. 56 F6
Broad Alley Worcs......... 70 F2
Broad Blunsdon
  Swindn 40 D3
Broadbottom Tamesd.. 113 M3
Broadbridge W Susx..... 17 M2
Broadbridge Heath
  W Susx 31 J5
Broad Campden
  Gloucs. 71 L6
Broad Carr Calder....... 123 G6
Broad Chalke Wilts. 28 B6
Broadclyst Devon 12 C3
Broadfield Inver 174 C4
Broadford Highld 199 K2
Broadford Bridge
  W Susx 31 H6
Broadgairhill Border.... 166 C7
Broad Green Worcs........ 70 D4
Broadhaugh Border 117 H7
Broad Haven Pembks.... 48 E5
Broadheath Traffd...... 113 H4
Broadhembury
  Devon 12 E2
Broadhempston
  Devon 7 J3
Broad Hinton Wilts 40 C5
Broadland Row
  E Susx 21 G2
Broad Layings Hants...... 41 H7
Broadley Moray 215 J3
Broad Marston Worcs.... 71 K5
Broadmayne Dorset 14 D5
Broadmoor Pembks 49 J6
Broadoak Dorset. 13 K3
Broad Oak E Susx 20 C2
Broad Oak E Susx 21 G2
Broad Oak Herefs. 54 C4
Broad Oak Kent 35 G3
Broad Oak St Hel. 112 D3
Broad's Green Essex 61 H5
Broadstairs Kent. 35 K2
Broadstone Poole 15 J4
Broadstone Shrops. 83 K5
Broad Street E Susx 21 H3
Broad Street Kent. 33 L2
Broad Town Wilts 40 C5
Broadwas Worcs........... 70 D4

Broadwater Herts 59 L4
Broadwater W Susx 18 F5
Broadwaters Worcs 84 E7
Broadway Pembks 48 E5
Broadway Somset 25 L7
Broadway Worcs 71 K6
Broadwell Gloucs 54 E5
Broadwell Gloucs 56 D3
Broadwell Oxon 56 E6
Broadwell Warwks 72 F2
Broadwindsor Dorset 13 K2
Broadwood Kelly
   Devon 10 F4
Broadwoodwidger
   Devon 9 K6
Brochel Highld 209 J5
Brochroy Ag & B 182 E2
Brockamin Worcs 70 D4
Brockbridge Hants 29 L7
Brockdish Norfk 92 E7
Brockenhurst Hants 16 C3
Brocketsbrae S Lans ... 164 F2
Brockford Street
   Suffk 78 D2
Brockhall Nhants 73 J2
Brockham Surrey 31 K2
Brockhampton
   Gloucs 56 B4
Brockhampton Hants 17 K2
Brockhampton
   Herefs 54 E2
Brockholes Kirk 123 H7
Brocklesby Lincs 126 E7
Brockley N Som 38 C6
Brockley Suffk 77 J1
Brockley Green Suffk 77 G5
Brockley Green Suffk 77 J4
Brockton Shrops 83 G3
Brockton Shrops 83 G6
Brockton Shrops 83 L5
Brockweir Gloucs 54 D7
Brockworth Gloucs 55 K5
Brocton Staffs 99 L8
Brodick N Ayrs 162 C3
Brodie Moray 214 B3
Brodsworth Donc 115 J1
Brogaig Highld 218 C7
Brokenborough Wilts 39 K3
Broken Cross Ches E ... 113 K6
Brokerswood Wilts 27 J2
Bromborough Wirral ... 111 K5
Brome Suffk 92 D7
Brome Street Suffk 92 D7
Bromeswell Suffk 79 G4
Bromfield Cumb 147 L5
Bromfield Shrops 83 J7
Bromham Bed 74 E4
Bromham Wilts 39 L7
Bromley Gt Lon 45 H6
Bromley Shrops 84 D4
Brompton Medway 46 C6
Brompton N York 141 J7
Brompton-by-
   Sawdon N York 134 E3
Brompton-on-Swale
   N York 140 F7
Brompton Ralph
   Somset 25 G5
Brompton Regis
   Somset 24 E5
Bromsberrow Gloucs 70 D7
Bromsberrow Heath
   Gloucs 55 G2
Bromsgrove Worcs 71 G1
Bromyard Herefs 70 B4
Bronant Cerdgn 66 E2
Brongest Cerdgn 65 K5
Bronington Wrexhm 98 C4
Bronllys Powys 68 D7
Bronwydd Carmth 50 E2
Bronygarth Shrops 97 K5
Bron-y-Nant
   Crematorium
   Conwy 110 A5
Brook Hants 28 F8
Brook IoW 16 E5

Brook Kent 34 E6
Brook Surrey 30 F4
Brooke Norfk 93 G4
Brooke Rutlnd 88 B3
Brookenby Lincs 117 K3
Brookfield Rens 174 D5
Brookhampton
   Somset 26 F5
Brook Hill Hants 28 F8
Brookhouse Lancs 129 L6
Brookhouse Rothm ... 115 K4
Brookhouse Green
   Ches E 99 J1
Brookhouses Derbys ... 114 B4
Brookland Kent 21 K1
Brooklands Traffd 113 H4
Brookmans Park
   Herts 59 L7
Brook Street Essex 45 L2
Brook Street Kent 34 C7
Brookthorpe Gloucs 55 J5
Brookwood Surrey 42 F8
Broom C Beds 75 H6
Broom Rothm 115 H3
Broom Warwks 71 K4
Broome Norfk 93 H5
Broome Shrops 83 H7
Broome Worcs 84 F7
Broomedge Warrtn ... 113 G4
Broomfield Essex 61 H5
Broomfield Kent 33 L3
Broomfield Kent 47 K6
Broomfield Somset 25 K5
Broomfleet E R Yk 125 K5
Broomhaugh
   Nthumb 150 C3
Broom Hill Barns 115 H2
Broom Hill Notts 101 K3
Broomhill Nthumb 159 G3
Broompark Dur 151 G6
Brora Highld 226 F7
Broseley Shrops 84 C3
Brotherlee Dur 150 A7
Brotherton N York ... 124 D5
Brotton R & Cl 142 E4
Broubster Highld 230 F4
Brough Cumb 139 H4
Brough E R Yk 125 L5
Brough Highld 231 J2
Brough Notts 102 D2
Brough Shet 235 d4
Broughall Shrops 98 E4
Brough Lodge Shet ... 235 d2
Brough Sowerby
   Cumb 139 H5
Broughton Border 165 L3
Broughton Cambs 89 K7
Broughton Flints 111 K8
Broughton Hants 28 F5
Broughton Lancs 121 G4
Broughton M Keyn 74 C6
Broughton N Linc 126 B8
Broughton N York ... 122 D1
Broughton N York ... 134 B5
Broughton Nhants 88 B7
Broughton Oxon 72 E6
Broughton Salfd 113 J2
Broughton V Glam 36 E6
Broughton Astley
   Leics 87 G5
Broughton Gifford
   Wilts 39 K7
Broughton Green
   Worcs 71 G3
Broughton Hackett
   Worcs 71 G4
Broughton-in-
   Furness Cumb 128 F3
Broughton Mains
   D & G 145 J6
Broughton Mills
   Cumb 128 F2
Broughton Moor
   Cumb 147 J7
Broughton Poggs
   Oxon 56 E7

Broughty Ferry
   C Dund 187 H2
Brown Candover
   Hants 29 L4
Brown Edge Staffs 99 K2
Brownhill Abers 217 G6
Brownhills Fife 187 H4
Brownhills Wsall 85 J3
Browninghill Green
   Hants 41 L7
Brown Lees Staffs 99 K2
Brownsea Island
   Dorset 15 J5
Browns Hill Gloucs 55 K7
Brownston Devon 7 G5
Broxa N York 134 E2
Broxbourne Herts 60 B6
Broxburn E Loth 178 E3
Broxburn W Loth 176 K4
Broxted Essex 60 F3
Bruan Highld 231 K7
Bruar P & K 194 C3
Brucefield Highld 223 K4
Bruchag Ag & B 173 J6
Bruichladdich Ag & B. 170 E6
Bruisyard Suffk 79 G2
Bruisyard Street
   Suffk 79 G2
Brumby N Linc 125 K8
Brund Staffs 100 C1
Brundall Norfk 93 G2
Brundish Suffk 78 F1
Brundish Street Suffk .. 78 F1
Brunery Highld 190 E3
Brunswick Village
   N u Ty 159 G7
Brunthwaite C Brad... 122 F2
Bruntingthorpe Leics ... 87 H5
Brunton Fife 186 E3
Brunton Wilts 28 E1
Brushford Devon 11 G4
Brushford Somset 24 E6
Bruton Somset 27 G4
Bryan's Green Worcs ... 70 F2
Bryanston Dorset 15 G2
Brydekirk D & G 155 L7
Bryher IoS 2 a1
Brympton Somset 26 D7
Bryn Carmth 51 G5
Bryn Neath 36 C3
Brynamman Carmth 51 K3
Brynberian Pembks 64 F7
Bryncir Gwynd 95 H4
Bryn-coch Neath 51 L5
Bryncroes Gwynd 94 D6
Bryncrug Gwynd 80 E3
Bryneglwys Denbgs 97 H3
Brynford Flints 111 G6
Bryn Gates Wigan 112 E2
Bryngwran IoA 108 D6
Bryngwyn Mons 54 B6
Bryngwyn Powys 68 D5
Bryn-Henllan Pembks... 64 E6
Brynhoffnant Cerdgn ... 65 K4
Brynmawr Blae G 53 J5
Bryn-mawr Gwynd 94 D5
Brynmenyn Brdgnd..... 36 D4
Brynmill Swans 51 J6
Brynna Rhondd 36 F4
Brynrefail Gwynd 109 H8
Brynsadler Rhondd..... 37 G4
Bryn Saith Marchog
   Denbgs 97 G3
Brynsiencyn IoA 108 F7
Brynteg IoA 109 G5
Bryn-y-Maen Conwy .. 110 B6
Bualintur Highld 198 F2
Bubbenhall Warwks 86 D8
Bubwith E R Yk 125 H4
Buccleuch Border 166 E6
Buchanan Smithy
   Stirlg 174 E1
Buchanhaven Abers ... 217 L5
Buchanty P & K 185 J2
Buchany Stirlg 184 F6
Buchlyvie Stirlg 184 C8

Buckabank Cumb 148 C5
Buckden Cambs 75 H2
Buckden N York 131 H4
Buckenham Norfk 93 H3
Buckerell Devon 12 E3
Buckfast Devon 7 H3
Buckfastleigh Devon 7 H3
Buckhaven Fife 186 F7
Buckholt Mons 54 D5
Buckhorn Weston
   Dorset 27 H6
Buckhurst Hill Essex ... 45 H2
Buckie Moray 215 J2
Buckingham Bucks 73 K7
Buckland Bucks 58 E5
Buckland Devon 7 G6
Buckland Gloucs 71 J7
Buckland Herts 75 L7
Buckland Kent 35 J6
Buckland Oxon 41 G2
Buckland Surrey 31 K2
Buckland Brewer
   Devon 22 F7
Buckland Common
   Bucks 58 F6
Buckland Dinham
   Somset 27 H2
Buckland Filleigh
   Devon 10 C3
Buckland in the
   Moor Devon 7 G2
Buckland
   Monachorum
   Devon 6 D3
Buckland Newton
   Dorset 14 D2
Buckland Ripers
   Dorset 14 C6
Buckland St Mary
   Somset 25 L8
Buckland-Tout-
   Saints Devon 7 H6
Bucklebury W Berk 41 K6
Bucklers Hard Hants ... 16 E3
Bucklesham Suffk 78 F6
Buckley Flints 111 J8
Bucklow Hill Ches E.. 113 G5
Buckminster Leics 102 E7
Bucknall C Stke 99 K3
Bucknall Lincs 117 K7
Bucknell Oxon 57 K3
Bucknell Shrops 83 G8
Buckpool Moray 215 J2
Bucksburn C Aber ... 207 G4
Buck's Cross Devon 22 E6
Bucks Green W Susx ... 31 H5
Buckshaw Village
   Lancs 121 H6
Bucks Horn Oak
   Hants 30 D3
Buck's Mills Devon 22 E6
Buckton E R Yk 135 J5
Buckton Nthumb 169 G2
Buckworth Cambs 89 G7
Budby Notts 115 L7
Bude Cnwll 9 G4
Budge's Shop Cnwll 5 M4
Budleigh Salterton
   Devon 12 D6
Budock Water Cnwll 3 K5
Buerton Ches E 99 G4
Bugbrooke Nhants 73 J3
Bugle Cnwll 4 F4
Bugley Dorset 27 H6
Bugthorpe E R Yk 134 B7
Buildwas Shrops 84 B3
Builth Wells Powys 68 B4
Bulbridge Wilts 28 C5
Bulford Wilts 28 D3
Bulkeley Ches E 98 D2
Bulkington Warwks 86 E6
Bulkington Wilts 39 L8
Bulkworthy Devon 9 K3
Bullbrook Br For 42 E6
Bullington Hants 29 J3
Bullington Lincs 117 H6

Bulmer Essex 77 J6
Bulmer N York 133 L6
Bulmer Tye Essex 77 J6
Bulphan Thurr 45 M3
Bulwark Abers 217 H5
Bulwick Nhants 88 D5
Bumble's Green Essex 60 C6
Bunacaimb Highld 199 K7
Bunarkaig Highld 201 J7
Bunbury Ches E 98 E2
Bunchrew Highld 212 F5
Bundalloch Highld 210 D8
Bunessan Ag & B 180 E3
Bungay Suffk 93 G5
Bunnahabhain
  Ag & B 171 H4
Bunny Notts 101 L6
Buntait Highld 212 C7
Buntingford Herts 60 B3
Bunwell Norfk 92 D5
Burbage Leics 86 F5
Burbage Wilts 40 E7
Burchett's Green
  W & M 42 D4
Burcombe Wilts 28 B5
Burcott Bucks 58 E4
Bures Essex 77 K7
Burford Oxon 56 E5
Burford Shrops 69 L2
Burg Ag & B 189 J7
Burgates Hants 30 C5
Burgess Hill W Susx 19 J2
Burgh Suffk 78 F4
Burgh by Sands
  Cumb 148 B3
Burgh Castle Norfk 93 K3
Burghclere Hants 41 J7
Burghead Moray 214 D1
Burghfield W Berk 42 A6
Burghfield Common
  W Berk 42 A6
Burgh Heath Surrey 44 E7
Burghill Herefs 69 J5
Burgh Island Devon 6 F6
Burgh le Marsh Lincs 119 G7
Burgh next Aylsham
  Norfk 106 F7
Burgh on Bain Lincs 117 L4
Burgh St Margaret
  Norfk 93 J2
Burgh St Peter Norfk 93 K5
Burghwallis Donc 124 E7
Burham Kent 46 B7
Buriton Hants 30 C7
Burland Ches E 98 E2
Burlawn Cnwll 4 F2
Burleigh Gloucs 55 K7
Burlescombe Devon 25 G7
Burleston Dorset 14 E4
Burley Hants 16 B2
Burley Rutlnd 88 C2
Burleydam Ches E 98 E4
Burley Gate Herefs 69 L5
Burley in Wharfedale
  C Brad 123 H2
Burley Street Hants 16 B2
Burley Wood Head
  C Brad 123 H2
Burlton Shrops 98 C7
Burmarsh Kent 34 E7
Burmington Warwks 72 C6
Burn N York 124 F5
Burnage Manch 113 K3
Burnaston Derbys 100 F6
Burnbrae N Lans 176 B6
Burnby E R Yk 125 K2
Burneside Cumb 138 D7
Burneston N York 132 D3
Burnett BaNES 38 F7
Burnfoot Border 166 F6
Burnfoot Border 167 H6
Burnfoot D & G 155 G4
Burnfoot D & G 156 C3
Burnfoot D & G 156 C4
Burnfoot P & K 185 K6

Burnham Bucks 42 F4
Burnham Deepdale
  Norfk 105 J4
Burnham Market
  Norfk 105 K4
Burnham Norton
  Norfk 105 K4
Burnham-on-Crouch
  Essex 46 F2
Burnham-on-Sea
  Somset 25 L2
Burnham Overy
  Norfk 105 K4
Burnham Overy
  Staithe Norfk 105 K4
Burnham Thorpe
  Norfk 105 K4
Burnhaven Abers 217 L5
Burnhead D & G 154 E3
Burnhervie Abers 206 D2
Burnhill Green Staffs 84 E4
Burnhope Dur 150 F5
Burnhouse N Ayrs 174 D7
Burniston N York 134 F2
Burnley Lancs 122 C4
Burnley
  Crematorium
  Lancs 122 B4
Burnmouth Border 179 K6
Burn of Cambus
  Stirlg 184 F6
Burnopfield Dur 150 F4
Burnsall N York 131 J7
Burnside Angus 196 C4
Burnside Angus 196 E6
Burnside Fife 186 B5
Burnside Moray 214 E1
Burnside W Loth 176 E3
Burnside of
  Duntrune Angus 187 G1
Burntisland Fife 177 H2
Burntwood Staffs 85 J2
Burntwood Green
  Staffs 85 J2
Burnt Yates N York 132 C7
Burnworthy Somset 25 J7
Burpham Surrey 31 G2
Burpham W Susx 18 E4
Burradon Nthumb 168 E7
Burrafirth Shet 235 e1
Burravoe Shet 235 d3
Burrells Cumb 138 F4
Burrelton P & K 195 K8
Burridge Devon 13 H2
Burridge Hants 17 G1
Burrill N York 132 C3
Burringham N Linc 125 K8
Burrington Devon 10 F2
Burrington Herefs 69 J1
Burrington N Som 38 C8
Burrough Green
  Cambs 76 F4
Burrough on the Hill
  Leics 87 L2
Burrow Lancs 130 C4
Burrow Somset 24 E3
Burrow Bridge
  Somset 26 A5
Burrowhill Surrey 42 F7
Burry Green Swans 50 F7
Burry Port Carmth 50 F5
Burscough Lancs 120 F7
Burscough Bridge
  Lancs 120 F7
Bursea E R Yk 125 J4
Bursledon Hants 16 F1
Burslem C Stke 99 K3
Burstall Suffk 78 D5
Burstock Dorset 13 K2
Burston Norfk 92 D6
Burstow Surrey 32 B5
Burstwick E R Yk 126 F5
Burtersett N York 131 G2
Burtholme Cumb 148 F3
Burthorpe Green
  Suffk 77 H2

Burtoft Lincs 103 L5
Burton Ches W 111 K6
Burton Ches W 112 D8
Burton Dorset 15 M4
Burton Lincs 116 F6
Burton Pembks 49 G6
Burton Somset 25 J3
Burton Wilts 39 J4
Burton Agnes E R Yk 135 H6
Burton Bradstock
  Dorset 13 L4
Burton Coggles Lincs 103 G7
Burton End Essex 60 E4
Burton Fleming
  E R Yk 135 G5
Burton Hastings
  Warwks 86 E5
Burton-in-Kendal
  Cumb 129 L4
Burton-in-Kendal
  Services Cumb 129 L4
Burton in Lonsdale
  N York 130 C5
Burton Joyce Notts 101 M4
Burton Latimer
  Nhants 88 C8
Burton Lazars Leics 87 L1
Burton Leonard
  N York 132 E6
Burton on the Wolds
  Leics 101 L7
Burton Overy Leics 87 J4
Burton Pedwardine
  Lincs 103 J4
Burton Pidsea E R Yk 127 G4
Burton Salmon
  N York 124 D5
Burton's Green Essex 61 K3
Burton upon Stather
  N Linc 125 K6
Burton upon Trent
  Staffs 100 E7
Burton Waters Lincs 116 F6
Burtonwood Warrtn 112 E3
Burtonwood
  Services Warrtn 112 E4
Burwardsley Ches W 98 D2
Burwarton Shrops 84 B6
Burwash E Susx 33 H7
Burwash Common
  E Susx 20 D2
Burwash Weald
  E Susx 20 D2
Burwell Cambs 76 E2
Burwell Lincs 118 E5
Burwen IoA 108 E3
Burwick Ork 234 c8
Bury Bury 122 B7
Bury Cambs 89 K6
Bury Somset 24 E6
Bury W Susx 18 D3
Bury Green Herts 60 D4
Bury St Edmunds
  Suffk 77 J2
Burythorpe N York 134 C6
Busby E Rens 175 G6
Buscot Oxon 40 E2
Bush Abers 197 J4
Bush Bank Herefs 69 J4
Bushbury Wolves 85 G3
Bushbury
  Crematorium
  Wolves 85 G3
Bushey Herts 43 J2
Bushey Heath Herts 43 J2
Bush Hill Park Gt Lon 45 G2
Bushley Worcs 70 F7
Bushmoor Shrops 83 J6
Bushton Wilts 40 B5
Bussage Gloucs 55 K7
Bussex Somset 26 A4
Butcombe N Som 38 D7
Bute Ag & B 173 H4
Butleigh Somset 26 D5
Butleigh Wootton
  Somset 26 D4

Butlers Marston
  Warwks 72 D4
Butley Suffk 79 H4
Buttercrambe
  N York 133 L7
Butterdean Border 179 G5
Butterknowle Dur 140 E3
Butterleigh Devon 12 C2
Buttermere Cumb 137 G4
Buttershaw C Brad 123 H5
Butterstone P & K 195 G7
Butterton Staffs 99 J4
Butterton Staffs 100 B2
Butterwick Lincs 104 C4
Butterwick N York 133 L4
Butterwick N York 134 F5
Buttington Powys 82 E2
Buttonoak Shrops 84 D7
Buxhall Suffk 78 B3
Buxted E Susx 20 A2
Buxton Derbys 114 B6
Buxton Norfk 106 F7
Buxton Heath Norfk 106 E7
Bwlch Powys 53 J4
Bwlchgwyn Wrexhm 97 K2
Bwlchllan Cerdgn 66 D3
Bwlchtocyn Gwynd 94 E7
Bwlch-y-cibau Powys 97 J8
Bwlch-y-ffridd Powys 82 B4
Bwlch-y-groes
  Pembks 65 H7
Bwlch-y-sarnau
  Powys 82 B8
Byers Green Dur 150 F7
Byfield Nhants 73 G4
Byfleet Surrey 43 H7
Byford Herefs 69 H6
Byker N u Ty 151 G3
Bylchau Conwy 110 D8
Byley Ches W 113 G7
Byrness Nthumb 157 K2
Bystock Devon 12 D5
Bythorn Cambs 88 F7
Byton Herefs 69 G2
Bywell Nthumb 150 D3
Byworth W Susx 31 G7

C

Cabourne Lincs 117 J2
Cabrach Ag & B 171 J5
Cabrach Moray 215 J8
Cabus Lancs 121 G2
Cadbury Devon 11 L4
Cadbury World Birm 85 J7
Cadder E Duns 175 G4
Caddington C Beds 59 H4
Caddonfoot Border 167 G3
Cadeby Donc 115 K2
Cadeby Leics 86 E3
Cadeleigh Devon 11 L4
Cade Street E Susx 20 C2
Cadgwith Cnwll 3 J7
Cadham Fife 186 D6
Cadishead Salfd 113 G3
Cadle Swans 51 J6
Cadley Lancs 121 G4
Cadley Wilts 28 E2
Cadley Wilts 40 E6
Cadmore End Bucks 42 C3
Cadnam Hants 28 F8
Cadney N Linc 117 G2
Cadoxton V Glam 37 H6
Cadoxton Juxta-
  Neath Neath 51 L5
Caeathro Gwynd 95 J1
Caenby Lincs 117 G4
Caeo Carmth 66 F6
Caerau Brdgnd 36 D2
Caerau Cardif 37 H5
Caer Farchell Pembks 48 D3
Caergeiliog IoA 108 D5
Caergwrle Flints 97 L2
Caerlanrig Border 156 D2
Caerleon Newpt 37 M3

Caernarfon Gwynd......108 F8
Caernarfon Castle
   Gwynd......108 F8
Caerphilly Caerph.......37 J3
Caersws Powys......82 B5
Caerwedros Cerdgn......65 L4
Caerwent Mons......38 C3
Caerwys Flints......110 F6
Cairinis W Isls......233 c6
Cairnbaan Ag & B......172 E1
Cairnbulg Abers......217 J2
Cairncross Border......179 J5
Cairncurran Inver......174 C4
Cairndow Ag & B......183 H5
Cairneyhill Fife......176 E2
Cairngarroch D & G......144 C5
Cairngorms
   National Park......204 C5
Cairnie Abers......215 K5
Cairnorrie Abers......217 G6
Cairnryan D & G......144 C2
Cairnty Moray......215 H4
Caister-on-Sea Norfk......93 L2
Caistor Lincs......117 J2
Caistor St Edmund
   Norfk......92 F3
Calanais W Isls......232 e2
Calbourne IoW......16 E5
Calcot Flints......111 G6
Calcot Gloucs......56 C6
Calcot Row W Berk......42 A6
Calcots Moray......215 G2
Caldbeck Cumb......148 B6
Caldecote Cambs......75 L3
Caldecote Cambs......89 G5
Caldecote Highfields
   Cambs......75 L3
Caldecott Nhants......74 E2
Caldecott Oxon......41 J2
Caldecott Rutlnd......88 C5
Calderbank N Lans......175 K5
Calder Bridge Cumb......136 E6
Caldercruix N Lans......175 L5
Calder Grove Wakefd......123 L6
Caldermill S Lans......164 D2
Calder Vale Lancs......121 G2
Calderwood S Lans......175 H7
Caldey Island Pembks......49 K7
Caldicot Mons......38 C3
Caldmore Wsall......85 H4
Caldwell N York......140 E5
Calf of Man IoM......237 a7
Calfsound Ork......234 d4
Calgary Ag & B......189 J6
Califer Moray......214 D3
California Falk......176 B3
California Norfk......93 K1
Calke Derbys......101 G7
Calke Abbey Derbys......101 G7
Callakille Highld......209 L4
Callander Stirlg......184 D5
Callanish W Isls......232 e2
Callestick Cnwll......3 K2
Calligarry Highld......199 K5
Callington Cnwll......6 A3
Callow Herefs......69 J7
Callow End Worcs......70 E4
Callow Hill Wilts......40 B4
Calmore Hants......29 G7
Calmsden Gloucs......56 B6
Calne Wilts......39 M6
Calshot Hants......16 F3
Calstock Cnwll......6 C3
Calstone Wellington
   Wilts......40 B6
Calthorpe Norfk......106 E6
Calthorpe Street
   Norfk......107 J7
Calthwaite Cumb......148 E6
Calton Staffs......100 C3
Calveley Ches E......98 E2
Calver Derbys......114 E6
Calverhall Shrops......98 E5
Calverleigh Devon......11 L3
Calverton M Keyn......73 L6
Calverton Notts......101 L3

Calvine P & K......194 C3
Calzeat Border......165 L3
Cam Gloucs......55 H7
Camasachoirce
   Highld......190 F4
Camasine Highld......190 F4
Camas Luinie Highld......210 E8
Camastianavaig
   Highld......209 H6
Camault Muir Highld......212 D6
Camber E Susx......21 J2
Camberley Surrey......42 E7
Camberwell Gt Lon......44 F5
Camblesforth N York......124 F5
Cambo Nthumb......158 C5
Camborne Cnwll......3 H4
Camborne and
   Redruth Mining
   District Cnwll......3 H4
Cambourne Cambs......75 K3
Cambridge Cambs......76 C3
Cambridge Gloucs......55 H7
Cambridge Airport
   Cambs......76 C3
Cambridge City
   Crematorium
   Cambs......76 B3
Cambrose Cnwll......3 H3
Cambus Clacks......185 H8
Cambusavie
   Platform Highld......223 G3
Cambusbarron Stirlg......185 G8
Cambuskenneth
   Stirlg......185 G8
Cambuslang S Lans......175 H6
Cambus o' May Abers......205 J5
Cambuswallace
   S Lans......165 K2
Camden Town Gt Lon......44 F4
Cameley BaNES......38 E8
Camelford Cnwll......8 E7
Camelon Falk......176 B3
Camerory Highld......214 C7
Camerton BaNES......39 G8
Camerton Cumb......136 E2
Camghouran P & K......193 J5
Camieston Border......167 J4
Cammachmore Abers......207 G6
Cammeringham Lincs......116 F5
Camore Highld......223 G4
Campbeltown Ag & B......161 J5
Campbeltown Airport
   Ag & B......161 H5
Cample D & G......154 F4
Campmuir P & K......195 K8
Camps W Loth......176 E5
Campsall Donc......124 E7
Campsea Ash Suffk......79 G4
Campton C Beds......75 G6
Camptown Border......167 K6
Camrose Pembks......48 F4
Camserney P & K......194 C6
Camusnagaul Highld......191 L2
Camusnagaul Highld......220 D4
Camusteel Highld......209 L6
Camusterrach Highld......209 L6
Canada Hants......28 F7
Candacraig Abers......205 H5
Candlesby Lincs......118 F7
Candy Mill Border......165 L2
Cane End Oxon......42 B4
Canewdon Essex......46 E2
Canford Cliffs Poole......15 K5
Canford
   Crematorium
   Bristl......38 E5
Canford Heath Poole......15 J4
Canisbay Highld......231 L2
Canley Covtry......86 C7
Canley Crematorium
   Covtry......86 C7
Cann Dorset......27 K7
Canna Highld......198 C4
Cannich Highld......211 L7
Cannington Somset......25 K4
Canning Town Gt Lon......45 H4

Cannock Staffs......85 H2
Cannock Chase Staffs......99 M8
Cannon Bridge Herefs......69 H6
Canonbie D & G......156 C6
Canon Frome Herefs......70 B5
Canon Pyon Herefs......69 J5
Canons Ashby Nhants......73 H4
Canonstown Cnwll......2 F4
Canterbury Kent......34 F3
Canterbury
   Cathedral Kent......34 F3
Cantley Norfk......93 H3
Canton Cardif......37 J5
Cantraywood Highld......213 J5
Cantsfield Lancs......130 C5
Canvey Island Essex......46 D4
Canwick Lincs......117 G7
Canworthy Water
   Cnwll......9 G6
Caol Highld......191 L2
Caolas Scalpaigh
   W Isls......232 e4
Caoles Ag & B......188 D6
Caonich Highld......201 G6
Capel Kent......33 H4
Capel Surrey......31 K4
Capel Bangor Cerdgn......80 E7
Capel Coch IoA......108 F5
Capel Curig Conwy......96 A2
Capel Dewi Carmth......50 F2
Capel Dewi Cerdgn......66 B6
Capel-Dewi Cerdgn......80 E6
Capel Garmon Conwy......96 C2
Capel Hendre Carmth......51 H4
Capel Iwan Carmth......65 J7
Capel le Ferne Kent......35 H6
Capel Parc IoA......108 F4
Capel St Andrew
   Suffk......79 H5
Capel St Mary Suffk......78 C6
Capel Seion Cerdgn......80 E7
Capelulo Conwy......109 L6
Capenhurst Ches W......111 K6
Capheaton Nthumb......158 C6
Caplaw E Rens......174 E6
Cappercleuch Border......166 C5
Capton Devon......7 J5
Caputh P & K......195 H7
Caradon Mining
   District Cnwll......5 K2
Carbeth Inn Stirlg......174 F3
Carbis Bay Cnwll......2 F4
Carbost Highld......208 F5
Carbost Highld......208 F7
Carbrook Sheff......115 G4
Carbrooke Norfk......91 L3
Car Colston Notts......102 B4
Carcroft Donc......124 E8
Cardenden Fife......186 C7
Cardhu Moray......214 F5
Cardiff Cardif......37 J5
Cardiff Airport V Glam......37 G6
Cardiff Gate Services
   Cardif......37 K4
Cardiff West Services
   Cardif......37 H4
Cardigan Cerdgn......65 G5
Cardington Bed......74 F5
Cardington Shrops......83 K4
Cardinham Cnwll......5 H3
Cardrain D & G......144 D8
Cardrona Border......166 D2
Cardross Ag & B......174 C3
Cardross
   Crematorium
   Ag & B......174 C3
Cardryne D & G......144 D7
Cardurnock Cumb......147 L3
Careby Lincs......88 E1
Careston Angus......196 E4
Carew Pembks......49 H6
Carew Cheriton
   Pembks......49 H6
Carew Newton
   Pembks......49 H6
Carey Herefs......54 E2

Carfin N Lans......175 K6
Carfraemill Border......178 B7
Cargate Green Norfk......93 H2
Cargenbridge D & G......155 G6
Cargill P & K......195 J8
Cargo Cumb......148 C3
Cargreen Cnwll......6 C4
Carham Nthumb......168 B2
Carhampton Somset......24 F3
Carharrack Cnwll......3 J3
Carie P & K......193 K5
Carinish W Isls......233 c6
Carisbrooke IoW......16 F5
Cark Cumb......129 H4
Carkeel Cnwll......6 B4
Carlabhagh W Isls......232 e2
Carlbury Darltn......140 F4
Carlby Lincs......88 F2
Carleen Cnwll......3 G5
Carleton N York......122 E1
Carleton
   Crematorium
   Bpool......120 D3
Carleton Forehoe
   Norfk......92 C3
Carleton Rode Norfk......92 D5
Carleton St Peter
   Norfk......93 H3
Carlincraig Abers......216 D5
Carlingcott BaNES......39 G8
Carlisle Cumb......148 D4
Carlisle Airport Cumb......148 E3
Carlisle Crematorium
   Cumb......148 C4
Carlops Border......177 G6
Carloway W Isls......232 e2
Carlton Barns......124 B7
Carlton Bed......74 D4
Carlton Cambs......76 F4
Carlton Leeds......123 L5
Carlton Leics......86 E3
Carlton N York......124 F5
Carlton N York......131 K3
Carlton N York......133 J3
Carlton Notts......101 L4
Carlton S on T......141 J3
Carlton Suffk......79 H2
Carlton Colville Suffk......93 K5
Carlton Curlieu Leics......87 K4
Carlton Green Cambs......76 F4
Carlton Husthwaite
   N York......133 G4
Carlton-in-Cleveland
   N York......142 B6
Carlton in Lindrick
   Notts......115 L5
Carlton-le-Moorland
   Lincs......102 E2
Carlton Miniott
   N York......132 F4
Carlton-on-Trent
   Notts......116 D8
Carlton Scroop Lincs......102 F4
Carluke S Lans......175 L7
Carmacoup S Lans......164 F4
Carmarthen Carmth......50 E2
Carmel Carmth......51 H3
Carmel Flints......111 G6
Carmel Gwynd......95 H2
Carmichael S Lans......165 H2
Carmountside
   Crematorium
   C Stke......99 K3
Carmunnock C Glas......175 G6
Carmyle C Glas......175 H6
Carmyllie Angus......196 E7
Carnaby E R Yk......135 H6
Carnbee Fife......187 J2
Carnbo P & K......185 L6
Carn Brea Cnwll......3 H3
Carnbrogie Abers......216 F8
Carndu Highld......210 D8
Carnduff S Lans......164 D1
Carnell E Ayrs......163 L3
Carnforth Lancs......129 K5
Carn-gorm Highld......200 E2

Carnhell Green Cnwll 3 G4
Carnie Abers 206 F4
Carnkie Cnwll 3 H4
Carnkie Cnwll 3 J4
Carno Powys 81 K4
Carnock Fife 176 E1
Carnon Downs Cnwll 4 C7
Carnousie Abers 216 C4
Carnoustie Angus 187 J1
Carnwath S Lans 165 J1
Carol Green Solhll 86 C7
Carperby N York 131 J2
Carradale Ag & B 161 K2
Carrbridge Highld 203 L2
Carrefour Jersey 236 c6
Carreglefn IoA 108 E4
Carr Gate Wakefd 123 L5
Carrhouse N Linc 116 C1
Carrick Ag & B 172 F2
Carrick Castle Ag & B... 183 H8
Carriden Falk 176 D3
Carrington Mdloth 177 J6
Carrington Traffd 113 H3
Carrog Denbgs 97 H4
Carron Falk 176 B2
Carron Moray 214 F6
Carronbridge D & G 154 F3
Carron Bridge Stirlg 175 K2
Carronshore Falk 176 B2
Carr Shield Nthumb 149 K5
Carrutherstown
   D & G 155 J7
Carruth House Inver 174 C5
Carrville Dur 151 H6
Carsaig Ag & B 181 H3
Carseriggan D & G 145 G2
Carsethorn D & G 147 H3
Carshalton Gt Lon 44 F6
Carsington Derbys 100 E2
Carskey Ag & B 161 H7
Carsluith D & G 145 K4
Carsphairn D & G 153 L4
Carstairs S Lans 165 H1
Carstairs Junction
   S Lans 165 J1
Carterton Oxon 56 F6
Carthew Cnwll 4 F5
Carthorpe N York 132 D3
Cartland S Lans 165 G1
Cartmel Cumb 129 H4
Carway Carmth 50 F4
Cashe's Green Gloucs 55 J6
Cassington Oxon 57 J5
Cassop Colliery Dur 151 J7
Castel Guern 236 c3
Casterton Cumb 130 C4
Castle Acre Norfk 91 J1
Castle Ashby Nhants 74 C3
Castlebay W Isls 233 b9
Castle Bolton N York 131 J2
Castle Bromwich
   Solhll 85 K5
Castle Bytham Lincs 103 G8
Castlebythe Pembks 49 H2
Castle Caereinion
   Powys 82 D3
Castle Camps Cambs 76 F6
Castle Carrock Cumb ... 148 F4
Castlecary Falk 175 K3
Castle Cary Somset 26 F5
Castle Combe Wilts 39 J5
Castle Donington
   Leics 101 H6
Castle Douglas D & G... 146 D3
Castle Eaton Swindn 40 C2
Castle Eden Dur 151 K7
Castleford Wakefd 124 C5
Castle Frome Herefs 70 C5
Castle Gresley Derbys .. 100 F8
Castle Hedingham
   Essex 77 H7
Castlehill Border 166 C3
Castlehill Highld 231 H2
Castle Hill Suffk 78 D5
Castlehill W Duns 174 D3
Castle Howard N York . 133 L5

Castle Kennedy D & G.. 144 D3
Castle Lachlan Ag & B.. 182 K2
Castlemartin Pembks 48 F7
Castlemilk C Glas 175 G6
Castlemorton Worcs 70 E6
Castlemorton
   Common Worcs 70 E6
Castle O'er D & G 156 A4
Castle Pulverbatch
   Shrops 83 H3
Castle Rising Norfk 105 G7
Castleside Dur 150 D5
Castle Stuart Highld 213 H4
Castlethorpe M Keyn 74 B5
Castleton Border 156 E4
Castleton Derbys 114 D5
Castleton N York 142 E5
Castleton Newpt 37 K4
Castleton Rochdl 122 D7
Castletown Highld 231 H3
Castletown IoM 237 b7
Castletown Sundld 151 J4
Castley N York 123 K2
Caston Norfk 91 L4
Castor C Pete 89 G4
Catacol N Ayrs 172 F7
Catcliffe Rothm 115 H4
Catcomb Wilts 40 A5
Catcott Somset 26 B4
Catcott Burtle
   Somset 26 B3
Caterham Surrey 32 C3
Catfield Norfk 107 H7
Catford Gt Lon 45 G5
Catforth Lancs 121 G4
Cathcart C Glas 175 G6
Cathedine Powys 53 H3
Catherington Hants 30 B8
Catherston
   Leweston Dorset 13 J4
Catisfield Hants 17 G2
Catlodge Highld 202 F6
Catmere End Essex 76 C6
Catmore W Berk 41 J4
Caton Lancs 129 L6
Caton Green Lancs 129 L6
Catrine E Ayrs 164 B4
Catsfield E Susx 20 E3
Catsgore Somset 26 D6
Catshill Worcs 85 G8
Cattadale Ag & B 161 H7
Cattal N York 133 G8
Cattawade Suffk 62 D2
Catterall Lancs 121 G3
Catterick N York 141 G7
Catterick Bridge
   N York 141 G7
Catterlen Cumb 148 E7
Catterline Abers 197 L2
Catterton N York 124 D2
Catteshall Surrey 31 G3
Catthorpe Leics 87 G7
Cattistock Dorset 14 B3
Catton N York 132 E4
Catton Nthumb 149 L4
Catwick E R Yk 126 E2
Catworth Cambs 88 F8
Caudle Green Gloucs 55 L6
Caulcott Oxon 57 K3
Cauldcots Angus 197 G6
Cauldhame Stirlg 184 E8
Cauldmill Border 167 H6
Cauldon Staffs 100 B3
Cauldwell Derbys 86 B1
Caulkerbush D & G 147 G4
Caulside D & G 156 D6
Caundle Marsh
   Dorset 27 G8
Caunton Notts 102 C1
Causeway End D & G... 145 J3
Causeway End Essex 61 G4
Causewayend S Lans ... 165 K3
Causewayhead Stirlg .. 185 G7
Causeyend Abers 207 H2
Causey Park Bridge
   Nthumb 158 F3

Cavendish Suffk 77 J5
Cavenham Suffk 77 H1
Caversfield Oxon 57 L3
Caversham Readg 42 B5
Caverswall Staffs 99 L4
Caverton Mill Border ... 167 M4
Cawdor Highld 213 K4
Cawood N York 124 E3
Cawsand Cnwll 6 C5
Cawston Norfk 106 D7
Cawthorne Barns 123 K8
Caxton Cambs 75 K3
Caynham Shrops 83 K8
Caythorpe Lincs 102 F3
Caythorpe Notts 102 B4
Cayton N York 135 G3
Ceann a Bhaigh W Isls .. 233 b6
Ceannacroc Lodge
   Highld 201 K3
Cearsiadar W Isls 232 f3
Cefn Newpt 37 L3
Cefn-brith Conwy 96 E3
Cefn-bryn-brain
   Carmth 51 L3
Cefn Cribwr Brdgnd 36 D4
Cefneithin Carmth 51 G3
Cefngorwydd Powys 67 J5
Cefn-mawr Wrexhm 97 L4
Cefn-y-pant Carmth 49 K3
Cellardyke Fife 187 J6
Cellarhead Staffs 99 L3
Cemaes IoA 108 E3
Cemmaes Powys 81 H3
Cemmaes Road
   Powys 81 H3
Cenarth Cerdgn 65 J6
Ceres Fife 186 F5
Cerne Abbas Dorset 14 C3
Cerney Wick Gloucs 40 B2
Cerrigydrudion
   Conwy 96 E3
Ceunant Gwynd 95 J1
Chaceley Gloucs 55 J2
Chacewater Cnwll 3 K3
Chackmore Bucks 73 K7
Chacombe Nhants 72 F5
Chadbury Worcs 71 H5
Chadderton Oldham 113 K1
Chaddesden C Derb 101 G5
Chaddesley Corbett
   Worcs 84 F8
Chaddlehanger
   Devon 6 C1
Chaddleworth W Berk ... 41 H5
Chadlington Oxon 57 G4
Chadshunt Warwks 72 D4
Chadwell Leics 102 C7
Chadwell Heath
   Gt Lon 45 J3
Chadwell St Mary
   Thurr 45 M4
Chadwick Worcs 70 E2
Chadwick End Solhll 86 B8
Chaffcombe Somset 13 J1
Chagford Devon 11 G7
Chailey E Susx 19 K2
Chainhurst Kent 33 J4
Chaldon Surrey 32 B3
Chale IoW 16 F6
Chale Green IoW 16 F6
Chalfont Common
   Bucks 43 G3
Chalfont St Giles
   Bucks 43 G2
Chalfont St Peter
   Bucks 43 G3
Chalford Gloucs 55 K7
Chalford Wilts 27 K2
Chalgrove Oxon 41 M2
Chalk Kent 46 A5
Chalkwell Kent 34 B2
Challacombe Devon 23 L3
Challoch D & G 145 H2
Challock Kent 34 D5
Chalton C Beds 59 G3
Chalton Hants 30 B7

Chalvey Slough 42 F4
Chalvington E Susx 20 B4
Chandler's Cross
   Herts 43 H2
Chandler's Ford
   Hants 29 H7
Chanterlands
   Crematorium
   C KuH 126 D4
Chantry Somset 27 G3
Chantry Suffk 78 D5
Chapel Fife 186 D8
Chapel Allerton Leeds .. 123 L3
Chapel Allerton
   Somset 26 B2
Chapel Amble Cnwll 4 F2
Chapel Brampton
   Nhants 73 K2
Chapel Chorlton
   Staffs 99 J5
Chapelend Way Essex ... 77 G6
Chapel-en-le-Frith
   Derbys 114 B5
Chapel Green Warwks ... 72 F3
Chapel Haddlesey
   N York 124 E5
Chapelhall N Lans 175 K5
Chapel Hill Abers 217 K7
Chapel Hill Lincs 103 K2
Chapel Hill Mons 54 D7
Chapel Hill N York 123 L2
Chapelhope Border 166 C5
Chapelknowe D & G 156 B7
Chapel Lawn Shrops 82 F7
Chapel le Dale N York . 130 E4
Chapel Leigh Somset 25 H5
Chapel of Garioch
   Abers 206 D1
Chapel Rossan D & G .. 144 D6
Chapel Row W Berk 41 L6
Chapel St Leonards
   Lincs 119 H6
Chapel Stile Cumb 137 K6
Chapelton Angus 197 G6
Chapelton Devon 23 J6
Chapelton S Lans 175 J8
Chapeltown Bl w D 121 L7
Chapeltown Moray 204 F2
Chapeltown Sheff 115 G3
Chapmanslade Wilts 27 J2
Chapmans Well
   Devon 9 J6
Chapmore End Herts 60 B5
Chappel Essex 61 L3
Chard Somset 13 H2
Chard Junction
   Somset 13 J2
Chardleigh Green
   Somset 13 H1
Chardstock Devon 13 H2
Charfield S Glos 39 G3
Charing Kent 34 C5
Charing
   Crematorium
   Kent 34 C5
Charingworth Gloucs 71 L6
Charlbury Oxon 57 G4
Charlcombe BaNES 39 H6
Charlcutt Wilts 39 M5
Charlecote Warwks 72 C3
Charlemont Sandw 85 H5
Charles Devon 23 L5
Charleston Angus 196 C7
Charlestown C Aber 207 H5
Charlestown C Brad 123 H3
Charlestown Calder 122 E5
Charlestown Cnwll 5 G5
Charlestown Cnwll 5 G2
Charlestown Fife 176 E2
Charlestown Highld 213 G5
Charlestown Highld 219 J6
Charlestown Salfd 113 J2
Charles Tye Suffk 78 B4
Charlesworth Derbys .. 114 A3
Charlottetown Fife 186 E5

Charlton Gt Lon 45 H4
Charlton Nhants 73 G7
Charlton Nthumb 157 K5
Charlton Oxon 41 H3
Charlton Somset 25 L6
Charlton Somset 27 G2
Charlton W Susx 18 B3
Charlton Wilts 27 K6
Charlton Wilts 39 L3
Charlton Worcs 71 H5
Charlton Wrekin 83 L2
Charlton Abbots
   Gloucs 56 B3
Charlton Adam
   Somset 26 D5
Charlton All Saints
   Wilts 28 D6
Charlton Down
   Dorset 14 D4
Charlton Horethorne
   Somset 26 F6
Charlton Kings Gloucs ... 55 L4
Charlton Mackrell
   Somset 26 D5
Charlton Marshall
   Dorset 15 G2
Charlton Musgrove
   Somset 27 G5
Charlton-on-Otmoor
   Oxon 57 K5
Charlton on the Hill
   Dorset 15 G2
Charlton St Peter
   Wilts 28 C1
Charlwood Hants 30 A5
Charlwood Surrey 31 L3
Charminster Dorset 14 D4
Charmouth Dorset............ 13 J4
Charndon Bucks 58 A3
Charney Bassett
   Oxon 41 G2
Charnock Richard
   Lancs 121 H7
Charnock Richard
   Crematorium
   Lancs 121 H6
Charnock Richard
   Services Lancs 121 H7
Charsfield Suffk................ 78 F3
Charter Alley Hants.......... 41 L8
Charterhall Border 179 G8
Charterhouse Somset 26 D1
Chartershall Stirlg 175 K1
Chartham Kent................. 34 E4
Chartham Hatch Kent 34 E4
Chartridge Bucks 58 F7
Chart Sutton Kent............ 33 K4
Charvil Wokham 42 C5
Charwelton Nhants 73 G4
Chase Terrace Staffs........ 85 J2
Chasetown Staffs............. 85 J2
Chastleton Oxon 56 E3
Chasty Devon 9 J4
Chatburn Lancs 121 L2
Chatcull Staffs.................. 99 H5
Chatham Medway 46 C6
Chatham Green Essex 61 H5
Chathill Nthumb............. 169 J4
Chatsworth House
   Derbys 114 E7
Chattenden Medway 46 C5
Chatteris Cambs............... 90 B6
Chatterton Lancs 122 B6
Chattisham Suffk.............. 78 C6
Chatto Border................. 168 B5
Chatton Nthumb............. 168 F4
Chawleigh Devon 11 G3
Chawton Hants................. 30 B4
Cheadle Staffs................. 100 A4
Cheadle Stockp............... 113 K4
Cheadle Hulme
   Stockp 113 K4
Cheam Gt Lon 44 E7
Chearsley Bucks 58 B6
Chebsey Staffs.................. 99 J6
Checkendon Oxon 42 A4

Checkley Ches E 99 G4
Checkley Staffs............... 100 B5
Chedburgh Suffk.............. 77 H3
Cheddar Somset............... 26 C2
Cheddington Bucks 58 F4
Cheddleton Staffs............. 99 L3
Cheddon Fitzpaine
   Somset 25 K6
Chedgrave Norfk 93 H4
Chedington Dorset........... 13 L2
Chediston Suffk................ 93 H7
Chedworth Gloucs 56 B5
Chedzoy Somset 25 M4
Cheetham Hill Manch 113 J2
Cheldon Devon 11 H3
Chelford Ches E 113 J6
Chellaston C Derb 101 G6
Chellington Bed 74 D4
Chelmarsh Shrops............ 84 C5
Chelmondiston Suffk 78 E6
Chelmorton Derbys 114 C7
Chelmsford Essex 61 H6
Chelmsford
   Crematorium
   Essex 61 H6
Chelmsley Wood
   Solhll 85 L6
Chelsea Gt Lon 44 F4
Chelsfield Gt Lon 45 J7
Chelsworth Suffk 77 L5
Cheltenham Gloucs.......... 55 L4
Cheltenham
   Crematorium
   Gloucs 55 L4
Chelveston Nhants 74 E1
Chelvey N Som 38 C6
Chelwood BaNES.............. 38 F7
Chelwood Gate
   E Susx 32 D6
Cheney Longville
   Shrops 83 H6
Chenies Bucks.................. 43 G2
Chepstow Mons 38 D2
Cherhill Wilts 40 B6
Cherington Gloucs 55 K7
Cherington Warwks 72 C6
Cheriton Hants 29 L5
Cheriton Kent 35 G7
Cheriton Swans 50 F6
Cheriton Bishop
   Devon 11 H6
Cheriton Fitzpaine
   Devon 11 K4
Cheriton or
   Stackpole Elidor
   Pembks 49 G7
Cherrington Wrekin 98 F8
Cherry Burton E R Yk 126 B3
Cherry Hinton Cambs....... 76 C3
Cherry Orchard
   Worcs 70 F4
Cherry Willingham
   Lincs 117 G6
Chertsey Surrey 43 H6
Cherwell Valley
   Services Oxon 57 K3
Cheselbourne Dorset 14 E3
Chesham Bucks 58 F7
Chesham Bury 122 B7
Chesham Bois Bucks........ 58 F7
Cheshire Farm Ice
   Cream Ches W 98 D2
Cheshunt Herts 60 B7
Chesil Beach Dorset......... 14 B6
Cheslyn Hay Staffs........... 85 H3
Chessetts Wood
   Warwks 85 L8
Chessington Gt Lon 44 D7
Chessington World
   of Adventures
   Gt Lon 44 D7
Chester Ches W 112 B7
Chesterblade Somset 26 F3
Chester
   Crematorium
   Ches W 111 L7

Chesterfield Derbys 115 G7
Chesterfield
   Crematorium
   Derbys 115 H6
Chesterhill Mdloth 177 K5
Chester-le-Street Dur... 151 G5
Chester Moor Dur.......... 151 G5
Chesters Border 167 J5
Chesters Border 167 K7
Chester Services
   Ches W 112 C6
Chesterton Cambs 76 C3
Chesterton Cambs 89 G4
Chesterton Gloucs 56 A7
Chesterton Oxon 57 K4
Chesterton Shrops........... 84 D4
Chesterton Green
   Warwks 72 D3
Chesterwood
   Nthumb 149 L2
Chester Zoo Ches W....... 112 B7
Chestfield Kent................ 47 J6
Cheston Devon 7 G4
Cheswardine Shrops 99 G6
Cheswick Nthumb 168 F1
Chetnole Dorset 14 B2
Chettisham Cambs 90 D6
Chettle Dorset 27 L8
Chetton Shrops 84 B5
Chetwynd Wrekin 99 G7
Chetwynd Aston
   Wrekin 99 H8
Cheveley Cambs............... 76 F3
Chevening Kent................ 32 E2
Chevington Suffk 77 H3
Cheviot Hills 168 A7
Chevithorne Devon 24 F7
Chew Magna BaNES........ 38 E7
Chew Stoke BaNES.......... 38 E7
Chewton Keynsham
   BaNES 38 F6
Chewton Mendip
   Somset 26 E2
Chicheley M Keyn............. 74 C5
Chichester W Susx........... 18 B5
Chichester
   Crematorium
   W Susx 18 B4
Chickerell Dorset.............. 14 C6
Chicklade Wilts 27 K4
Chidden Hants.................. 30 A7
Chiddingfold Surrey 30 D4
Chiddingly E Susx............ 20 B3
Chiddingstone Kent 32 E4
Chiddingstone
   Causeway Kent 32 F4
Chideock Dorset............... 13 K4
Chidham W Susx............... 17 L2
Chidswell Kirk 123 K6
Chieveley W Berk 41 J5
Chignall St James
   Essex 61 G6
Chignall Smealy Essex..... 61 G5
Chigwell Essex 45 H2
Chigwell Row Essex......... 45 J2
Chilbolton Hants 29 H4
Chilcomb Hants 29 J5
Chilcombe Dorset 13 M4
Chilcompton Somset........ 26 F2
Chilcote Leics 86 C2
Childer Thornton
   Ches W 111 K6
Child Okeford
   Dorset 27 J8
Childrey Oxon 41 G3
Child's Ercall Shrops 98 F7
Childswickham
   Worcs 71 J6
Childwall Lpool 112 B4
Chilfrome Dorset.............. 14 B3
Chilgrove W Susx.............. 18 A3
Chilham Kent 34 E4
Chillaton Devon................ 10 C8
Chillenden Kent................ 35 H4
Chillerton IoW 16 F5
Chillesford Suffk.............. 79 H4

Chillington Devon 7 J7
Chillington Somset 13 K1
Chilmark Wilts 27 L5
Chilmington Green
   Kent 34 C6
Chilson Oxon 56 F4
Chilsworthy Cnwll.............. 6 B2
Chilsworthy Devon 9 J4
Chiltern Hills 42 C2
Chilterns
   Crematorium
   Bucks 43 F2
Chilthorne Domer
   Somset 26 D7
Chilton Bucks 58 B5
Chilton Dur..................... 141 H2
Chilton Oxon 41 J4
Chilton Candover
   Hants 29 L4
Chilton Cantelo
   Somset 26 E6
Chilton Foliat Wilts 40 F6
Chilton Polden
   Somset 26 B4
Chilton Street Suffk......... 77 H5
Chilton Trinity
   Somset 25 L4
Chilwell Notts 101 K5
Chilworth Hants 29 H7
Chilworth Surrey 31 G3
Chimney Oxon 57 G7
Chineham Hants............... 30 A1
Chingford Gt Lon............. 45 G2
Chinley Derbys 114 B5
Chinnor Oxon................... 58 C7
Chipnall Shrops................ 99 G6
Chippenham Cambs 76 F1
Chippenham Wilts............ 39 L5
Chipperfield Herts 59 H7
Chipping Herts................. 60 B2
Chipping Lancs 121 J2
Chipping Campden
   Gloucs 71 L6
Chipping Norton
   Oxon 56 F3
Chipping Ongar Essex 60 E7
Chipping Sodbury
   S Glos 39 G4
Chipping Warden
   Nhants 72 F5
Chipstable Somset 25 G6
Chipstead Kent................. 32 E3
Chipstead Surrey.............. 32 B2
Chirbury Shrops 82 F4
Chirk Wrexhm 97 L5
Chirnside Border 179 H6
Chirnsidebridge
   Border 179 H7
Chirton Wilts 40 B8
Chisbury Wilts 40 F6
Chiselborough
   Somset 26 C8
Chiseldon Swindn 40 D4
Chiselhampton Oxon 57 L7
Chisholme Border 166 F6
Chislehurst Gt Lon........... 45 H6
Chislet Kent 47 L6
Chisley Calder 122 F5
Chiswell Green Herts 59 J6
Chiswick Gt Lon 44 E4
Chisworth Derbys 113 M3
Chithurst W Susx.............. 30 D6
Chittering Cambs 76 C1
Chitterne Wilts................. 27 M3
Chittlehamholt
   Devon 23 K7
Chittlehampton
   Devon 23 K6
Chittoe Wilts 39 L6
Chivelstone Devon.............. 7 H7
Chivenor Devon 23 H4
Chlenry D & G 144 D3
Chobham Surrey 42 F7
Cholderton Wilts 28 E3
Cholesbury Bucks 58 F6
Chollerton Nthumb 158 B7

Cholsey Oxon...................41 L3
Cholstrey Herefs 69 J3
Chop Gate N York 142 C7
Choppington
Nthumb...................159 G5
Chopwell Gatesd...........150 E4
Chorley Ches E................98 E3
Chorley Lancs................121 H6
Chorley Shrops................84 C6
Chorleywood Herts 43 H2
Chorleywood West
Herts.........................43 G2
Chorlton Ches E..............99 G3
Chorlton-cum-Hardy
Manch....................113 J3
Chorlton Lane Ches W....98 C3
Choulton Shrops.............83 H5
Chrishall Essex................76 C6
Chriswell Inver..............173 L4
Christchurch Cambs........90 C4
Christchurch Dorset 15 M4
Christchurch Newpt 37 M3
Christian Malford
Wilts.........................39 L5
Christleton Ches W 112 C7
Christon N Som...............38 B8
Christon Bank
Nthumb...................169 J5
Christow Devon...............11 J7
Chudleigh Devon............11 K8
Chudleigh Knighton
Devon..........................7 J1
Chulmleigh Devon 11 L3
Church Lancs................121 L5
Churcham Gloucs.............55 H4
Church Aston Wrekin......99 H8
Church Brampton
Nhants......................73 K2
Church Broughton
Derbys....................100 D5
Church Cove Cnwll...........3 J8
Church Crookham
Hants........................30 D2
Churchdown Gloucs........55 K4
Church Eaton Staffs........99 J8
Church End C Beds..........59 G4
Church End C Beds..........75 H6
Churchend Essex.............47 G2
Church End Essex............61 H3
Church End Gt Lon...........44 E3
Church Enstone Oxon......57 G3
Church Fenton
N York......................124 D3
Churchfield Sandw..........85 H5
Church Green Devon 12 F3
Church Hanborough
Oxon..........................57 H5
Church Houses
N York......................142 E7
Churchill Devon...............13 H3
Churchill N Som..............38 C7
Churchill Oxon.................56 F3
Churchill Worcs...............71 G4
Churchill Worcs...............84 F7
Churchinford Somset.......25 K8
Church Knowle
Dorset........................15 H6
Church Langton Leics......87 K5
Church Lawford
Warwks......................86 F7
Church Leigh Staffs........100 A5
Church Lench Worcs........71 H4
Church Mayfield
Staffs........................100 D4
Church Minshull
Ches E........................98 E1
Church Norton
W Susx........................18 B6
Churchover Warwks........87 G7
Church Preen Shrops.......83 K4
Church Pulverbatch
Shrops........................83 H3
Churchstanton
Somset.......................25 J8
Churchstoke Powys.........82 F5
Churchstow Devon............7 G6

Church Stowe Nhants 73 J3
Church Street Kent.........46 B5
Church Stretton
Shrops........................83 J5
Churchtown Cnwll............5 H1
Churchtown Derbys.......114 E8
Churchtown IoM...........237 d3
Churchtown Lancs.........121 G2
Church Village
Rhondd......................37 G3
Church Warsop Notts....115 K7
Churston Ferrers
Torbay.........................7 K5
Churt Surrey...................30 D4
Churton Ches W..............98 B2
Churwell Leeds..............123 K5
Chwilog Gwynd...............95 G5
Chyandour Cnwll...............2 E5
Cilcain Flints................111 G7
Cilcennin Cerdgn............66 C3
Cilfrew Neath..................52 B7
Cilfynydd Rhondd............37 G3
Cilgerran Pembks............65 H6
Cilmaengwyn Neath........51 L4
Cilmery Powys.................67 L4
Cilsan Carmth.................51 H2
Ciltalgarth Gwynd............96 D4
Cilycwm Carmth..............67 G6
Cimla Neath...................36 B2
Cinderford Gloucs...........54 F5
Cippenham Slough..........42 F4
Cirencester Gloucs..........56 A7
City Gt Lon.....................45 G4
City Airport Gt Lon...........45 H4
City of London
Crematorium
Gt Lon......................45 H3
Clabhach Ag & B............188 F5
Clachaig Ag & B 173 J3
Clachan Ag & B..............172 C6
Clachan Ag & B..............182 A4
Clachan Ag & B..............191 G7
Clachan Highld..............209 H6
Clachan-a-Luib W Isls....233 c6
Clachan Mor Ag & B......188 C6
Clachan na Luib W Isls...233 c6
Clachan of Campsie
E Duns.....................175 G3
Clachan-Seil Ag & B......181 M4
Clachnaharry Highld......213 G5
Clachtoll Highld.............224 C3
Clackavoid P & K...........195 J4
Clacket Lane
Services Surrey.........32 D3
Clackmannan Clacks......185 J8
Clackmarras Moray......214 F3
Clacton-on-Sea Essex.....62 E5
Cladich Ag & B 182 F3
Cladswell Worcs..............71 J3
Claggan Highld..............190 E6
Claigan Highld...............208 C4
Clanfield Hants................30 B7
Clanfield Oxon.................56 F7
Clanville Hants................28 F2
Clanville Somset..............26 F5
Claonaig Ag & B............172 E6
Clapgate Herts................60 C3
Clapham Bed...................74 F4
Clapham Gt Lon..............44 F5
Clapham N York.............130 E5
Clapham W Susx.............18 F4
Clapton Somset...............13 K2
Clapton Somset...............26 F2
Clapton-in-Gordano
N Som........................38 C5
Clapton-on-the-Hill
Gloucs.......................56 D4
Claravale Gatesd...........150 E3
Clarbeston Pembks.........49 H3
Clarbeston Road
Pembks.....................49 H4
Clarborough Notts 116 B5
Clare Suffk......................77 H5
Clarebrand D & G..........146 D2
Clarencefield D & G.......147 J2
Clarilaw Border..............167 H4

Clarkston E Rens 175 G6
Clashmore Highld..........223 G4
Clashmore Highld..........224 C3
Clashnessie Highld........224 C3
Clashnoir Moray............204 F2
Clathy P & K..................185 K4
Clathymore P & K..........185 L3
Clatt Abers....................205 L1
Clatter Powys..................81 L5
Clatworthy Somset..........25 G5
Claughton Lancs............121 G3
Claughton Lancs............130 B6
Claughton Wirral...........111 J4
Claverdon Warwks 71 L2
Claverham N Som............38 C6
Clavering Essex...............60 D2
Claverley Shrops.............84 E5
Claverton BaNES............39 H7
Clawdd-coch V Glam.......37 G5
Clawdd-newydd
Denbgs......................97 G3
Clawton Devon..................9 J5
Claxby Lincs...................117 J3
Claxton N York...............133 L7
Claxton Norfk..................93 H3
Claybrooke Magna
Leics..........................86 F5
Clay Coton Nhants..........87 H7
Clay Cross Derbys..........115 H8
Claydon Oxon..................72 F4
Claydon Suffk..................78 D5
Claygate D & G..............156 D6
Claygate Kent..................33 J4
Claygate Surrey...............44 D7
Clayhall Gt Lon................45 H3
Clayhanger Devon...........24 F6
Clayhidon Devon..............25 J7
Clayhill E Susx................21 G2
Clayock Highld...............231 H4
Claypits Gloucs................55 H6
Claypole Lincs................102 D3
Clayton C Brad...............123 G4
Clayton Donc..................124 C8
Clayton W Susx................19 J3
Clayton-le-Moors
Lancs.......................121 L4
Clayton-le-Woods
Lancs.......................121 H6
Clayton West Kirk..........123 K7
Clayworth Notts.............116 B4
Cleadale Highld.............199 G2
Cleadon S Tyne..............151 J3
Clearbrook Devon.............6 D3
Clearwell Gloucs..............54 E6
Cleasby N York...............141 G5
Cleat Ork......................234 c8
Cleatlam Dur.................140 E4
Cleator Cumb.................136 D4
Cleator Moor Cumb.......136 E4
Cleckheaton Kirk...........123 J5
Cleehill Shrops................83 L7
Cleekhimin N Lans.........175 K6
Clee St Margaret
Shrops........................83 L6
Cleethorpes NE Lin........127 H8
Cleeton St Mary
Shrops........................84 B7
Cleeve N Som..................38 C7
Cleeve Oxon....................41 L4
Cleeve Hill Gloucs...........55 M3
Cleeve Prior Worcs..........71 J5
Cleghornie E Loth..........178 D2
Clehonger Herefs............69 J6
Cleish P & K..................186 A7
Cleland N Lans...............175 L6
Clenamacrie Ag & B.......182 C2
Clenchwarton Norfk.......104 F7
Clenerty Abers...............216 E3
Clent Worcs....................85 G7
Cleobury Mortimer
Shrops........................84 C7
Cleobury North
Shrops........................84 B6
Cleongart Ag & B...........161 H3
Clephanton Highld.........213 J4
Clerkhill D & G...............156 A3

Cleuch-head D & G........154 E3
Clevancy Wilts..................40 B5
Clevedon N Som..............38 B6
Cleveleys Lancs..............120 D2
Cleverton Wilts................39 L4
Clewer Somset.................26 C2
Cley next the Sea
Norfk.......................106 C4
Cliburn Cumb.................138 E3
Cliddesden Hants............29 M2
Cliffe Medway..................46 C5
Cliffe N York..................125 G4
Cliff End E Susx...............21 H3
Cliffe Woods Medway......46 C5
Clifford Herefs.................68 E5
Clifford Leeds................124 C2
Clifford Chambers
Warwks......................71 L4
Clifford's Mesne
Gloucs........................55 G4
Clifton Bristl....................38 E5
Clifton C Beds.................75 H6
Clifton C Nott.................101 K5
Clifton C York................133 J8
Clifton Calder................123 H6
Clifton Cumb.................138 D2
Clifton Derbys................100 D4
Clifton Devon..................23 J3
Clifton Donc..................115 K3
Clifton Lancs..................120 F4
Clifton N York................123 J2
Clifton Oxon....................57 J2
Clifton Worcs..................70 F5
Clifton Campville
Staffs.........................86 B2
Clifton Hampden
Oxon..........................41 K2
Clifton Reynes
M Keyn......................74 C4
Clifton upon
Dunsmore Warwks...87 G7
Clifton upon Teme
Worcs........................70 C3
Cliftonville Kent..............35 K1
Climping W Susx.............18 D5
Clink Somset...................27 H2
Clint N York..................132 D7
Clinterty C Aber.............206 F3
Clint Green Norfk............92 B2
Clintmains Border..........167 J3
Clippesby Norfk...............93 J2
Clipsham Rutlnd..............88 D1
Clipston Nhants...............87 K7
Clipston Notts................101 M5
Clipstone C Beds.............58 F3
Clipstone Notts..............115 L8
Clitheroe Lancs..............121 L3
Clive Shrops....................98 D7
Cliveden Bucks...............42 E4
Clixby Lincs...................117 J2
Cloatley Wilts..................39 M3
Clocaenog Denbgs...........97 G2
Clochan Moray...............215 J3
Clodock Herefs................53 L3
Clola Abers....................217 J5
Clophill C Beds................74 F6
Clopton Nhants...............88 F7
Clopton Suffk..................78 F4
Clopton Corner Suffk......78 F4
Clos du Valle Guern........236 d2
Closeburn D & G............154 F4
Closeburnmill D & G.......154 F3
Closworth Somset...........14 B1
Clothall Herts..................59 L2
Clotton Ches W...............112 D8
Clough Foot Calder........122 D5
Clough Head Calder........123 G6
Cloughton N York...........143 K7
Clousta Shet..................235 C5
Clova Angus..................196 B2
Clovelly Devon................22 E6
Clovenfords Border........167 G3
Clovulin Highld..............191 K4
Clowne Derbys...............115 J6
Clows Top Worcs.............70 C1
Cluanie Inn Highld.........201 G3

Cluanie Lodge Highld ... 201 G3
Clugston D & G 145 H4
Clun Shrops 82 F7
Clunas Highld 213 K5
Clunbury Shrops 83 G7
Clunderwen Carmth 49 J4
Clune Highld 203 J1
Clunes Highld 201 J7
Clungunford Shrops 83 H7
Clunie P & K 195 H7
Clunton Shrops 83 G7
Cluny Fife 186 D7
Clutton BaNES 38 F8
Clutton Ches W 98 C2
Clutton Hill BaNES 38 F8
Clydach Mons 53 K5
Clydach Swans 51 K5
Clydach Vale Rhondd 36 F2
Clydebank
  Crematorium
  W Duns 174 E4
Clyffe Pypard Wilts 40 B5
Clynder Ag & B 174 A2
Clyne Neath 52 C7
Clynnog-fawr Gwynd 95 G3
Clyro Powys 68 E5
Clyst Honiton Devon 12 C4
Clyst Hydon Devon 12 D3
Clyst St George
  Devon 12 C5
Clyst St Lawrence
  Devon 12 D3
Clyst St Mary Devon 12 C4
Cnoc W Isls 232 g2
Cnwch Coch Cerdgn 80 F8
Coad's Green Cnwll 5 L1
Coalburn S Lans 164 F3
Coalburns Gatesd 150 E3
Coaley Gloucs 55 H7
Coalhill Essex 61 J7
Coalpit Heath S Glos 38 F4
Coalport Wrekin 84 C3
Coalsnaughton
  Clacks 185 J7
Coaltown of
  Balgonie Fife 186 E7
Coaltown of Wemyss
  Fife 186 E7
Coalville Leics 86 E2
Coanwood Nthumb 149 H3
Coat Somset 26 C7
Coatbridge N Lans 175 J5
Coatdyke N Lans 175 K5
Coate Swindn 40 D4
Coate Wilts 40 B7
Coates Cambs 89 K4
Coates Gloucs 55 L7
Coates Lincs 116 E5
Coates W Susx 18 D3
Cobbaton Devon 23 K6
Coberley Gloucs 55 L5
Cobham Kent 46 A6
Cobham Surrey 43 J7
Cobham Services
  Surrey 43 J8
Cobnash Herefs 69 J3
Cobo Guern 236 c2
Coburby Abers 217 H2
Cockayne Hatley
  C Beds 75 J5
Cock Bridge Abers 205 G4
Cockburnspath
  Border 179 G4
Cock Clarks Essex 61 K7
Cockenzie and Port
  Seton E Loth 177 L4
Cockerham Lancs 120 F1
Cockermouth Cumb 136 F2
Cockernhoe Herts 59 J4
Cockett Swans 51 J6
Cockfield Dur 140 E3
Cockfield Suffk 77 K4
Cockfosters Gt Lon 44 F2
Cock Green Essex 61 H4
Cocking W Susx 18 B3

Cocking Causeway
  W Susx 18 B2
Cockington Torbay 7 K3
Cocklake Somset 26 C2
Cockley Cley Norfk 91 H3
Cock Marling E Susx 21 H2
Cockpole Green
  Wokham 42 D4
Cockshutt Shrops 98 B6
Cockthorpe Norfk 106 B4
Cockwood Devon 12 C6
Cockyard Derbys 114 B5
Coddenham Suffk 78 D4
Coddington Herefs 70 C6
Coddington Notts 102 D2
Codford St Mary Wilts 27 L4
Codford St Peter
  Wilts 27 L4
Codicote Herts 59 K4
Codmore Hill W Susx 31 H7
Codnor Derbys 101 H3
Codrington S Glos 39 G5
Codsall Staffs 84 F3
Codsall Wood Staffs 84 F3
Coedpoeth Wrexhm 97 L3
Coed Talon Flints 97 L2
Coed-y-paen Mons 53 K7
Coffinswell Devon 7 K3
Cofton Devon 12 C6
Cofton Hackett
  Worcs 85 H7
Cogan V Glam 37 J6
Cogenhoe Nhants 74 B3
Coggeshall Essex 61 K4
Coignafearn Highld 203 H2
Coilacriech Abers 205 H6
Coilantogle Stirlg 184 D6
Coillore Highld 208 E6
Coity Brdgnd 36 E4
Col W Isls 232 g2
Colaboll Highld 225 L6
Colan Cnwll 4 D4
Colaton Raleigh
  Devon 12 D5
Colbost Highld 208 C5
Colburn N York 140 F7
Colby Cumb 138 F3
Colby IoM 237 b6
Colchester Essex 62 B3
Colchester
  Crematorium
  Essex 62 B4
Colchester Zoo Essex 62 A4
Cold Ash W Berk 41 K6
Cold Ashby Nhants 87 J7
Cold Ashton S Glos 39 H6
Cold Aston Gloucs 56 C4
Coldbackie Highld 229 J4
Cold Brayfield M Keyn 74 D4
Coldean Br & H 19 J4
Coldeast Devon 7 J2
Colden Calder 122 E5
Colden Common
  Hants 29 J6
Cold Hanworth Lincs 117 G5
Coldharbour Surrey 31 J3
Cold Higham Nhants 73 J4
Coldingham Border 179 J5
Cold Kirby N York 133 H3
Coldmeece Staffs 99 J6
Cold Norton Essex 61 K7
Cold Overton Leics 88 B2
Coldred Kent 35 H5
Coldridge Devon 11 G4
Coldstream Border 168 C2
Coldwaltham W Susx 18 D3
Coldwells Herefs 69 H7
Coldwells Abers 217 H6
Cole Somset 26 F5
Colebatch Shrops 83 G6
Colebrook Devon 12 C2
Colebrooke Devon 11 H5
Coleby Lincs 102 F1
Coleby N Linc 125 L6
Coleford Devon 11 H5
Coleford Gloucs 54 E6

Coleford Somset 27 G2
Colegate End Norfk 92 E6
Colehill Dorset 15 J3
Coleman's Hatch
  E Susx 32 D6
Colemere Shrops 98 B6
Colemore Hants 30 B5
Colenden P & K 186 B2
Colerne Wilts 39 J6
Colesbourne Gloucs 56 A5
Coleshill Bucks 42 F2
Coleshill Oxon 40 E2
Coleshill Warwks 85 L5
Coley BaNES 26 E1
Colgate W Susx 31 L5
Colinsburgh Fife 187 H6
Colinton C Edin 177 H5
Colintraive Ag & B 173 H4
Colkirk Norfk 105 L7
Coll Ag & B 189 G5
Collace P & K 186 C2
Collafirth Shet 235 c3
Coll Airport Ag & B 188 F5
Collaton Devon 7 G7
Collaton St Mary
  Torbay 7 K4
College of Roseisle
  Moray 214 E2
College Town Br For 42 D7
Collessie Fife 186 E5
Collier Row Gt Lon 45 J2
Collier's End Herts 60 B4
Collier Street Kent 33 J4
Colliston Abers 217 K6
Collin D & G 155 H6
Collingbourne Ducis
  Wilts 28 E2
Collingbourne
  Kingston Wilts 28 E1
Collingham Leeds 124 B2
Collingham Notts 102 D1
Collington Herefs 70 B3
Collingtree Nhants 73 L4
Collins Green Warrtn 112 E3
Colliston Angus 196 F7
Colliton Devon 12 E2
Collyweston Nhants 88 E3
Colmonell S Ayrs 152 D5
Colmworth Bed 75 G3
Colnabaichin Abers 205 G4
Colnbrook Slough 43 G5
Colne Cambs 89 L7
Colne Lancs 122 D3
Colne Engaine Essex 61 K3
Colney Norfk 92 E3
Colney Heath Herts 59 K6
Coln Rogers Gloucs 56 B6
Coln St Aldwyns
  Gloucs 56 C6
Coln St Dennis Gloucs 56 B5
Colonsay Ag & B 180 E7
Colonsay Airport
  Ag & B 180 E8
Colpy Abers 216 C7
Colquhar Border 166 E2
Colsterworth Lincs 102 F7
Colston Bassett Notts 102 B5
Coltfield Moray 214 D2
Coltishall Norfk 106 F8
Colton Cumb 129 G3
Colton Leeds 124 B4
Colton N York 124 D2
Colton Norfk 92 D2
Colton Staffs 100 B7
Colt's Hill Kent 33 H4
Colvend D & G 146 F4
Colwall Herefs 70 D6
Colwell Nthumb 158 B6
Colwich Staffs 100 A7
Colwinston V Glam 36 E5
Colworth W Susx 18 C5
Colwyn Bay Conwy 110 B5
Colyford Devon 13 G4
Colyton Devon 13 G4
Combe Oxon 57 H5
Combe W Berk 41 G7

Combe Down BaNES 39 H7
Combe Fishacre
  Devon 7 J3
Combe Florey Somset 25 J5
Combe Hay BaNES 39 G7
Combeinteignhead
  Devon 7 K2
Combe Martin Devon 23 J3
Combe Raleigh
  Devon 12 F3
Comberbach Ches W 112 F6
Comberford Staffs 85 L3
Comberton Cambs 75 L4
Comberton Herefs 69 K2
Combe St Nicholas
  Somset 13 H1
Combrook Warwks 72 C4
Combs Derbys 114 B6
Combs Suffk 78 C3
Combs Ford Suffk 78 C3
Combwich Somset 25 K4
Comers Abers 206 D4
Comhampton Worcs 70 E2
Commins Coch Powys 81 J3
Commondale N York 142 E5
Common End Cumb 136 D3
Common Moor Cnwll 5 K2
Compstall Stockp 113 L4
Compstonend D & G 146 B4
Compton Devon 7 K3
Compton Hants 29 J6
Compton Staffs 84 E6
Compton Surrey 30 F3
Compton W Berk 41 K4
Compton W Susx 30 C7
Compton Wilts 28 C2
Compton Abbas
  Dorset 27 K7
Compton Abdale
  Gloucs 56 B5
Compton Bassett
  Wilts 40 B6
Compton
  Beauchamp Oxon 40 F3
Compton Bishop
  Somset 26 B1
Compton
  Chamberlayne
  Wilts 28 B5
Compton Dando
  BaNES 38 F7
Compton Dundon
  Somset 26 C5
Compton Durville
  Somset 26 B7
Compton Greenfield
  S Glos 38 E4
Compton Martin
  BaNES 38 D8
Compton
  Pauncefoot
  Somset 26 F6
Compton Valence
  Dorset 14 B4
Comrie Fife 176 D1
Comrie P & K 185 G3
Conaglen House
  Highld 191 K3
Conchra Highld 210 D8
Concraigie P & K 195 H7
Conderton Worcs 71 G6
Condicote Gloucs 56 D3
Condorrat N Lans 175 K4
Condover Shrops 83 J3
Coney Hill Gloucs 55 J4
Coneyhurst Common
  W Susx 31 J6
Coneysthorpe N York 133 L5
Coney Weston Suffk 91 L7
Congerstone Leics 86 D3
Congham Norfk 105 H7
Congleton Ches E 113 J8
Congresbury N Som 38 C7
Conheath D & G 147 H2
Conicavel Moray 214 B4
Coningsby Lincs 103 L2

Conington Cambs 75 K2
Conington Cambs 89 H6
Conisbrough Donc....115 K2
Conisholme Lincs 118 E3
Coniston Cumb 137 J7
Coniston E R Yk 126 E4
Coniston Cold N York..131 G8
Conistone N York 131 J6
Connah's Quay Flints...111 J7
Connel Ag & B..............182 C1
Connel Park E Ayrs......164 C6
Connor Downs Cnwll......3 G4
Conon Bridge Highld ...212 E4
Cononley N York..........122 E2
Consall Staffs 99 M3
Consett Dur 150 E5
Constable Burton
  N York 132 B2
Constable Lee Lancs ..122 B5
Constantine Cnwll............3 J5
Constantine Bay
  Cnwll............................4 D2
Contin Highld...............212 C3
Conwy Conwy..............109 L6
Conwy Castle Conwy ...109 L6
Conyer's Green Suffk...77 K2
Cooden E Susx 20 E4
Cookbury Devon..............9 K4
Cookham W & M............42 E4
Cookham Dean
  W & M........................42 E4
Cookham Rise W & M 42 E4
Cookhill Worcs................71 J3
Cookley Suffk 93 H7
Cookley Worcs 84 E7
Cookley Green Oxon....42 B3
Cookney Abers 207 G6
Cook's Green Essex......62 E4
Cooks Green Suffk 77 L4
Cooksmill Green
  Essex 61 G6
Coolham W Susx............31 J6
Cooling Medway............46 C5
Coombe Cnwll..................4 E5
Coombe Devon 7 L2
Coombe Devon 12 E4
Coombe Gloucs 39 H2
Coombe Hants 30 A7
Coombe Abbey
  Warwks 86 E7
Coombe Bissett Wilts ..28 C6
Coombe Cellars
  Devon 7 K2
Coombe Hill Gloucs 55 K3
Coombe Keynes
  Dorset 14 F5
Coombe Pafford
  Torbay..........................7 L3
Coombes W Susx 19 G4
Coombes-Moor
  Herefs..........................69 G2
Coopersale Common
  Essex 60 D7
Copdock Suffk 78 D6
Copford Green Essex....61 L4
Copgrove N York..........132 E6
Copister Shet...............235 d3
Cople Bed 75 G5
Copley Dur 140 D3
Copmanthorpe
  C York 124 E2
Copmere End Staffs 99 J6
Copp Lancs 120 F3
Coppenhall Staffs 99 K8
Copperhouse Cnwll........2 F4
Coppingford Cambs 89 G8
Copplestone Devon......11 H4
Coppull Lancs 121 H7
Copsale W Susx............31 K6
Copster Green Lancs ..121 K4
Copston Magna
  Warwks 86 F5
Cop Street Kent............35 J3
Copt Hewick N York....132 E5
Copthorne W Susx 32 B5
Copt Oak Leics 86 F2

Copythorne Hants 28 F8
Corbets Tey Gt Lon......45 K3
Corbiere Jersey...........236 a7
Corbridge Nthumb 150 C3
Corby Nhants 88 C5
Corby Glen Lincs 103 G7
Cordon N Ayrs.............162 D4
Coreley Shrops 84 B8
Corfe Somset................25 K7
Corfe Castle Dorset....15 H6
Corfe Mullen Dorset....15 J3
Corfton Shrops 83 J6
Corgarff Abers 205 G4
Corhampton Hants........29 L7
Corley Warwks 86 C6
Corley Services
  Warwks 86 C6
Cormuir Angus............195 L3
Cornard Tye Suffk 77 K6
Cornforth Dur 151 H7
Cornhill Abers 216 B3
Cornhill-on-Tweed
  Nthumb 168 C2
Cornholme Calder 122 D5
Cornoigmore Ag & B ..188 C6
Cornsay Dur 150 E6
Cornsay Colliery Dur ..150 F6
Corntown Highld.........212 E3
Corntown V Glam..........36 E5
Cornwell Oxon..............56 F3
Cornwood Devon............6 E4
Cornworthy Devon..........7 J5
Corpach Highld...........191 L2
Corpusty Norfk...........106 D6
Corrachree Abers 205 K4
Corran Highld..............191 K4
Corran Highld..............200 C4
Corrie D & G................155 L5
Corrie N Ayrs 162 C2
Corriecravie N Ayrs....162 B5
Corriegills N Ayrs.......162 D3
Corriegour Lodge
  Hotel Highld 201 K6
Corriemoille Highld....212 B2
Corrimony Highld........212 B7
Corringham Lincs........116 E4
Corringham Thurr........46 B4
Corris Gwynd................81 G2
Corris Uchaf Gwynd 81 G2
Corrow Ag & B.............183 H7
Corry Highld................199 K1
Corscombe Devon........10 F5
Corscombe Dorset......13 M2
Corse Gloucs.................55 H3
Corse Lawn Gloucs.......55 J2
Corsham Wilts...............39 K6
Corsindae Abers 206 D4
Corsley Wilts 27 J3
Corsley Heath Wilts 27 J3
Corsock D & G.............154 D6
Corston BaNES.............39 G7
Corston Wilts 39 L4
Corstorphine C Edin ..177 G4
Cortachy Angus..........196 C4
Corton Suffk.................93 L4
Corton Wilts 27 L4
Corton Denham
  Somset 26 F6
Coruanan Highld.........191 L3
Corwen Denbgs............97 G4
Coryton Devon 10 C7
Coryton Thurr...............46 C4
Cosby Leics 87 G4
Coseley Dudley 85 G5
Cosgrove Nhants..........73 L6
Cosham C Port..............17 J2
Cosheston Pembks 49 G6
Coshieville P & K........194 C6
Cossall Notts..............101 J4
Cossington Leics 87 H2
Cossington Somset......26 A4
Costessey Norfk 92 E2
Costock Notts.............101 L7
Coston Leics 102 D7
Coston Norfk 92 C3
Cote Oxon....................57 G7

Cotebrook Ches W......112 E7
Cotehill Cumb.............148 E5
Cotes Leics................101 K7
Cotesbach Leics...........87 G6
Cotford St Luke
  Somset 25 J6
Cotgrave Notts..........101 M5
Cothal Abers 207 G3
Cotham Notts..............102 C3
Cotherstone Dur........140 C4
Cothill Oxon.................57 J7
Cotleigh Devon 13 G3
Cotmanhay Derbys.....101 J4
Coton Cambs 76 B3
Coton Nhants 73 J1
Coton Staffs 99 J7
Coton Clanford Staffs...99 K7
Coton Hill Shrops.........83 J2
Coton in the Elms
  Derbys 86 B1
Cotswolds 55 M6
Cotswold Wildlife
  Park & Gardens
  Oxon 56 E6
Cott Devon 7 H4
Cottam Lancs 121 G4
Cottam Notts..............116 D5
Cottenham Cambs........76 C2
Cottered Herts.............60 A3
Cotterstock Nhants.....88 F5
Cottesbrooke Nhants...87 K8
Cottesmore Rutlnd......88 C2
Cottingham E R Yk 126 C4
Cottingham Nhants......88 B5
Cottingley C Brad.......123 G3
Cottingley Hall
  Crematorium
  Leeds 123 K4
Cottisford Oxon............57 L2
Cotton Suffk.................78 C2
Cottown Abers 206 E3
Cottown Abers 215 L8
Cottown of Gight
  Abers 216 F6
Cotts Devon 6 C3
Coughton Warwks 71 J3
Coulaghailtro Ag & B...172 C5
Coulags Highld...........210 E5
Coull Abers 205 L5
Coulport Ag & B..........173 L2
Coulsdon Gt Lon..........32 B2
Coulston Wilts..............27 L2
Coulter S Lans.............165 K3
Coulton N York...........133 K5
Coultra Fife................186 F3
Cound Shrops 83 L3
Coundon Dur...............141 G2
Countersett N York.....131 H2
Countess Wear
  Devon 12 B4
Countesthorpe Leics....87 H4
Countisbury Devon.......24 B2
Coupar Angus P & K...195 K7
Coupland Nthumb.......168 D3
Cour Ag & B................172 D8
Courteachan Highld ...199 L6
Courteenhall Nhants....73 L4
Court Henry Carmth 51 H2
Courtsend Essex..........47 G2
Courtway Somset.........25 J5
Cousland Mdloth........177 K5
Cousley Wood E Susx ...33 H6
Cove Ag & B................173 L2
Cove Border 179 G4
Cove Devon 24 E7
Cove Hants...................30 E1
Cove Highld................219 J3
Cove Bay C Aber.........207 H5
Covehithe Suffk............93 L6
Coven Staffs.................85 G3
Coveney Cambs 90 C6
Covenham St
  Bartholomew
  Lincs 118 D3
Covenham St Mary
  Lincs 118 D3

Coventry Covtry...........86 D7
Coventry Airport
  Warwks 86 D8
Coverack Cnwll 3 K7
Coverack Bridges
  Cnwll............................3 H5
Coverham N York 131 L3
Covington Cambs 74 F1
Covington S Lans........165 J2
Cowan Bridge Lancs ..130 C4
Cowbeech E Susx 20 C3
Cowbit Lincs...............103 L8
Cowbridge V Glam 36 F5
Cowden Kent................32 E5
Cowdenbeath Fife.......177 G1
Cowers Lane Derbys...100 F3
Cowes IoW 16 F3
Cowesby N York 133 G2
Cowfold W Susx...........31 K6
Cowhill S Glos..............38 E3
Cowie Stirlg.................175 L1
Cowley Devon...............11 K5
Cowley Gloucs 55 L5
Cowley Gt Lon..............43 H4
Cowley Oxon.................57 K7
Cowling Lancs.............121 H6
Cowling N York 122 E2
Cowling N York 132 C3
Cowlinge Suffk 77 G4
Cowpen Nthumb 159 H5
Cowplain Hants............17 K1
Cowshill Dur 149 L6
Cowslip Green N Som...38 C7
Cowthorne N York 132 F8
Coxbank Ches E............98 F4
Coxbench Derbys.......101 G4
Coxford Cnwll 8 F5
Coxford Norfk 105 K6
Coxheath Kent.............33 J3
Coxhoe Dur 151 H7
Coxley Somset 26 D3
Coxley Wick Somset 26 D3
Coxtie Green Essex......45 K2
Coxwold N York 133 H4
Coychurch Brdgnd......36 E4
Coychurch
  Crematorium
  Brdgnd 36 E4
Coylton S Ayrs............163 K5
Coylumbridge Highld ...203 L3
Coytrahen Brdgnd........36 D4
Crabbs Cross Worcs 71 J2
Crabtree W Susx 31 K6
Crackenthorpe Cumb...138 F3
Crackington Haven
  Cnwll............................8 F5
Crackleybank Shrops...84 D2
Cracoe N York.............131 J7
Craddock Devon...........25 G8
Cradley Dudley 85 G6
Cradley Herefs.............70 D5
Cradley Heath Sandw...85 G6
Cradoc Powys 52 F2
Crafthole Cnwll 6 B5
Craggan Highld...........204 C1
Craghead Dur 150 F5
Cragside House &
  Garden Nthumb 158 D2
Crai Powys 52 D3
Craibstone Moray.......215 L3
Craichie Angus............196 E6
Craig Angus................197 H5
Craig Highld...............211 G4
Craigbank E Ayrs........164 C6
Craigburn Border 177 H7
Craigcleuch D & G......156 C5
Craigdam Abers..........216 F7
Craigdhu Ag & B.........182 B6
Craigearn Abers 206 D3
Craigellachie Moray...215 G5
Craigend P & K............186 B4
Craigend Rens 174 E4
Craigendoran Ag & B...174 C3
Craigends Rens 174 D5
Craighlaw D & G.........145 G3
Craighouse Ag & B.....171 K5

Craigie P & K 195 H7
Craigie S Ayrs 163 K3
Craigiefold Abers 217 H2
Craigley D & G 146 D4
Craig Llangiwg Neath....51 K4
Craiglockhart C Edin 177 H4
Craigmillar C Edin 177 J4
Craigneston D & G 154 D5
Craigneuk N Lans 175 K5
Craigneuk N Lans 175 K6
Craignure Ag & B...........190 E8
Craigo Angus 197 H4
Craigrothie Fife 186 F5
Craigruie Stirlg 184 B4
Craigton Angus 196 E8
Craigton C Aber 206 F5
Craigton E Rens 174 F7
Craigton
  Crematorium
  C Glas 174 F5
Craigton of Airlie
  Angus 196 B6
Crail Fife 187 K5
Crailing Border 167 L4
Craiselound N Linc 116 C2
Crakehall N York 132 C2
Crambe N York 133 L6
Cramlington Nthumb 159 G6
Cramond C Edin 177 G3
Cramond Bridge
  C Edin 177 G4
Cranage Ches E 113 H7
Cranberry Staffs 99 J5
Cranborne Dorset 28 B8
Cranbourne Br For..........42 F5
Cranbrook Kent..............33 K6
Cranfield C Beds 74 D6
Cranford Gt Lon..............43 J5
Cranford St Andrew
  Nhants 88 D7
Cranford St John
  Nhants 88 D7
Cranham Gloucs 55 K5
Crank St Hel. 112 D2
Cranleigh Surrey 31 H4
Cranmore Somset 26 F3
Cranoe Leics 87 L4
Cransford Suffk 79 G2
Cranshaws Border 178 E6
Crantock Cnwll 4 C4
Cranwell Lincs 103 G3
Cranwich Norfk 91 H4
Cranworth Norfk 92 B3
Craobh Haven Ag & B...182 A6
Crarae Ag & B. 182 E7
Crask Inn Highld 225 L4
Crask of Aigas Highld ...212 D6
Craster Nthumb 169 K5
Cratfield Suffk 93 G7
Crathes Abers 206 E6
Crathie Abers 205 G6
Crathie Highld. 202 E6
Crathorne N York 141 K5
Craven Arms Shrops 83 H6
Crawcrook Gatesd 150 E3
Crawford S Lans 165 J5
Crawfordjohn S Lans 165 G5
Crawley Hants 29 H4
Crawley Oxon 57 G5
Crawley W Susx 31 L4
Crawley Down
  W Susx 32 C5
Crawshawbooth
  Lancs 122 B5
Crawton Abers 197 L1
Cray N York 131 H4
Crayford Gt Lon..............45 K5
Crayke N York 133 H5
Crays Hill Essex 46 B2
Creacombe Devon 24 C7
Creagan Inn Ag & B......191 J7
Creag Ghoraidh W Isls ..233 c7
Creagorry W Isls 233 c7
Creaguaineach
  Lodge Highld. 192 E3
Creaton Nhants 73 K1

Creca D & G 155 M7
Credenhill Herefs 69 J5
Crediton Devon 11 J3
Creebank D & G 153 H6
Creebridge D & G 145 J2
Creech Heathfield
  Somset 25 L6
Creech St Michael
  Somset 25 L6
Creed Cnwll 4 E6
Creekmouth Gt Lon 45 J4
Creeting St Mary
  Suffk 78 D3
Creeton Lincs 103 G8
Creetown D & G 145 K3
Cregneash IoM 237 a7
Creich Fife 186 E3
Creigiau Cardif 37 G4
Cremyll Cnwll 6 C5
Cressage Shrops 83 L3
Cressbrook Derbys 114 D6
Cresselly Pembks 49 H6
Cressex Bucks 42 D3
Cressing Essex 61 J4
Cresswell Nthumb 159 H4
Cresswell Pembks 49 H6
Cresswell Staffs 99 L5
Creswell Derbys 115 K6
Cretingham Suffk 78 F3
Cretshengan Ag & B 172 C5
Crewe Ches E 99 G2
Crewe Ches W 98 B2
Crewe Crematorium
  Ches E 99 G2
Crewe Green Ches E 99 G2
Crew Green Powys 83 G1
Crewkerne Somset 13 K1
Crewton C Derb.............101 G5
Crianlarich Stirlg...........183 L3
Cribyn Cerdgn 66 C4
Criccieth Gwynd 95 J5
Crich Derbys 101 G2
Crichton Mdloth 177 K6
Crick Nhants 87 H8
Crickadarn Powys 68 C6
Cricket St Thomas
  Somset 13 J2
Crickhowell Powys 53 K4
Cricklade Wilts 40 C2
Cricklewood Gt Lon 44 E3
Crieff P & K 185 H5
Criggion Powys 82 F1
Crigglestone Wakefd 123 L7
Crimond Abers 217 K3
Crimplesham Norfk 90 F3
Crimscote Warwks 72 B5
Crinaglack Highld 212 C6
Crinan Ag & B. 182 A8
Crindledyke N Lans 175 L6
Cringleford Norfk 92 E3
Crinow Pembks 49 J5
Croachy Highld 213 G8
Crockenhill Kent.............45 J6
Crocker End Oxon 42 B3
Crockernwell Devon 11 H6
Crockerton Wilts 27 K3
Crocketford D & G 154 E7
Crockham Hill Kent.........32 D3
Croeserw Neath 36 D2
Croes-goch Pembks 48 D2
Croes-lan Cerdgn 65 L5
Croesor Gwynd 95 L4
Croesyceiliog Carmth....50 E3
Croesyceiliog Torfn 37 L2
Croft Leics 87 G4
Croft Lincs 104 E1
Croft Warrtn 112 F3
Croftamie Stirlg 174 E2
Crofton Wakefd 124 B6
Croft-on-Tees N York 141 H5
Croftown Highld 220 F5
Crofts Moray 215 G4
Crofts of Dipple
  Moray 215 H3
Crofts of Savoch
  Abers 217 K3

Crofty Swans 51 G6
Croggan Ag & B.............181 L3
Croglin Cumb. 148 F5
Croick Highld. 222 B3
Cromarty Highld. 223 H7
Crombie Fife 176 E2
Cromdale Highld 214 D8
Cromer Herts 59 M3
Cromer Norfk 106 F4
Cromford Derbys 100 F2
Cromhall S Glos. 39 G3
Cromor W Isls. 232 f3
Cromwell Notts. 102 D1
Cronberry E Ayrs 164 C5
Crondall Hants 30 C2
Cronton Knows. 112 C4
Crook Cumb. 138 C7
Crook Dur. 150 E7
Crookedholm E Ayrs 163 L3
Crookham Nthumb. 168 D2
Crookham W Berk 41 K7
Crookham Village
  Hants 30 C2
Crook Inn Border 165 L4
Crooklands Cumb. 129 L3
Crook of Devon P & K ...185 L7
Cropredy Oxon 72 F5
Cropston Leics 87 G2
Cropthorne Worcs 71 H5
Cropton N York 134 B2
Cropwell Bishop
  Notts. 102 B5
Cropwell Butler Notts....102 B5
Cros W Isls. 232 g1
Crosbost W Isls. 232 f3
Crosby Cumb. 147 J7
Crosby IoM 237 c5
Crosby N Linc. 125 K7
Crosby Sefton 111 J2
Crosby Garret Cumb 139 G5
Crosby Ravensworth
  Cumb. 138 F4
Croscombe Somset. 26 E3
Cross Somset 26 B1
Crossaig Ag & B. 172 E7
Crossapol Ag & B. 188 C2
Cross Ash Mons 54 B4
Cross-at-Hand Kent. 33 K4
Crosscanonby Cumb. 147 J6
Crossdale Street
  Norfk 106 F5
Cross Flatts C Brad........123 G3
Crossford Fife. 176 E2
Crossford S Lans 175 L8
Crossgatehall E Loth 177 K5
Crossgates E Ayrs. 163 J1
Crossgates Fife. 176 F1
Cross Gates Leeds 124 B4
Crossgates N York 134 F3
Crossgill Lancs 129 L6
Cross Green Leeds........123 L4
Cross Green Suffk 77 K4
Cross Green Suffk 78 B4
Cross Hands Carmth......51 H3
Crosshands E Ayrs 163 L4
Crosshill Fife. 186 C7
Crosshill S Ayrs. 163 J7
Crosshouse E Ayrs. 163 K2
Cross Houses Shrops 83 K3
Cross in Hand E Susx 20 B2
Cross Inn Cerdgn 65 L3
Cross Keys Ag & B. 174 C2
Crosskeys Caerph. 37 K3
Crosskirk Highld. 230 F2
Cross Lane IoW. 17 G4
Cross Lane Head
  Shrops. 84 C4
Crosslee Rens 174 D5
Crossmichael D & G 146 C2
Cross of Jackston
  Abers. 216 D7
Cross o' th' hands
  Derbys. 100 F4
Crossroads Abers. 206 B4
Crossroads Abers. 206 E6
Cross Street Suffk 92 E7

Crosston Angus 196 E5
Cross Town Ches E........113 H5
Crossway Green
  Worcs 70 E2
Crossways Dorset 14 E5
Crosswell Pembks 64 F6
Crosthwaite Cumb 129 J2
Croston Lancs 121 G6
Crostwick Norfk 92 F1
Crostwight Norfk 92 F1
Crouch End Gt Lon 44 F3
Crouchestown Wilts 28 B6
Crouch Hill Dorset 14 D1
Croughton Nhants 73 G7
Crovie Abers. 216 F2
Crowan Cnwll. 3 H4
Crowborough E Susx. 32 F6
Crowcombe Somset 25 H4
Crowdecote Derbys. 114 C7
Crowden Derbys. 114 B2
Crow Edge Barns. 114 D2
Crowell Oxon 58 C7
Crowfield Suffk 78 D3
Crowhill E Loth 178 F4
Crow Hill Herefs. 54 F3
Crowhurst E Susx. 20 F3
Crowhurst Surrey. 32 D4
Crowland Lincs 89 J2
Crowland Suffk 78 B1
Crowlas Cnwll. 2 F5
Crowle N Linc. 125 J7
Crowle Worcs. 71 G4
Crowle Green Worcs. 71 G3
Crowmarsh Gifford
  Oxon 41 L3
Crown Corner Suffk........78 F1
Crownhill C Plym. 6 C4
Crownhill
  Crematorium
  M Keyn. 74 B6
Crownthorpe Norfk. 92 C3
Crowntown Cnwll. 3 H5
Crows-an-Wra Cnwll. 2 D5
Crowthorne Wokham. 42 D7
Crowton Ches W. 112 E6
Croxdale Dur. 151 G7
Croxden Staffs 100 B5
Croxley Green Herts. 43 H2
Croxteth Lpool 111 L3
Croxton Cambs 75 J3
Croxton N Linc. 126 D7
Croxton Norfk 91 K6
Croxton Norfk 106 B6
Croxton Staffs. 99 H6
Croxton Kerrial Leics....102 D6
Croy Highld. 213 J4
Croy N Lans 175 J3
Croyde Devon 23 G4
Croydon Cambs 75 K5
Croydon Gt Lon 44 F6
Croydon
  Crematorium
  Gt Lon. 44 F6
Crubenmore Highld. 203 G7
Cruckmeole Shrops 83 H2
Cruckton Shrops 83 H2
Cruden Bay Abers 217 K6
Crudgington Wrekin 98 F8
Crudwell Wilts. 39 L2
Crumlin Caerph. 37 K2
Crumplehorn Cnwll. 5 K5
Crumpsall Manch 113 J2
Crundale Kent. 34 E5
Crunwear Pembks 49 K5
Crux Easton Hants 29 H1
Crwbin Carmth 50 F3
Cryers Hill Bucks. 42 E2
Crymych Pembks 65 G4
Crynant Neath 52 C6
Crystal Palace Gt Lon.....45 G5
Cuaig Highld. 209 L3
Cuan Ag & B. 181 L4
Cubbington Warwks 72 D2
Cubert Cnwll. 4 C4
Cublington Bucks. 58 D4
Cublington Herefs. 69 H6
Cuckfield W Susx. 32 B7

Cucklington Somset 27 H6
Cuckney Notts 115 K7
Cuddesdon Oxon 57 L7
Cuddington Bucks 58 C5
Cuddington Ches W 112 E7
Cuddington Heath
Ches W 98 C3
Cudham Gt Lon 32 D2
Cudliptown Devon 10 D8
Cudnell Bmouth 15 K3
Cudworth Barns 124 B8
Cudworth Somset 13 J1
Cuffley Herts 59 M7
Cuil Highld 191 J5
Culbokie Highld 212 F3
Culburnie Highld 212 D6
Culcabock Highld 213 G5
Culcharry Highld 213 K4
Culcheth Wartn 112 F3
Culdrain Abers 215 L7
Culduie Highld 209 L6
Culford Suffk 77 J1
Culgaith Cumb 138 E2
Culham Oxon 41 J2
Culkein Highld 224 C2
Culkein Drumbeg
Highld 224 D2
Culkerton Gloucs 39 L2
Cullen Moray 215 L2
Cullercoats N Tyne 159 J2
Cullerlie Abers 206 E5
Cullicudden Highld 213 G2
Cullingworth C Brad 123 G3
Cuillin Hills Highld 199 G2
Cullipool Ag & B 181 L5
Cullivoe Shet 235 d2
Culloden Highld 213 H5
Cullompton Devon 12 C2
Cullompton Services
Devon 12 D2
Culm Davy Devon 25 H7
Culmington Shrops 83 J6
Culmstock Devon 25 H8
Culnacraig Highld 224 C7
Culnaightrie D & G 146 D5
Culnaknock Highld 209 H2
Culrain Highld 222 D3
Culross Fife 176 D2
Culroy S Ayrs 163 H6
Culsalmond Abers 216 C7
Culscadden D & G 145 K5
Culshabbin D & G 145 G5
Culswick Shet 235 b6
Cultercullen Abers 207 H1
Cults C Aber 207 G5
Culverstone Green
Kent 45 M7
Culverthorpe Lincs 103 G4
Culworth Nhants 73 G5
Culzean Castle &
Country Park
S Ayrs 163 G7
Cumbernauld N Lans 175 K4
Cumbernauld Village
N Lans 175 K3
Cumberworth Lincs 119 G6
Cuminestown Abers 216 F4
Cumledge Border 179 G6
Cummersdale Cumb 148 D4
Cummertrees D & G 147 K2
Cummingston Moray 214 E1
Cumnock E Ayrs 164 B5
Cumnor Oxon 57 J7
Cumrew Cumb 148 F5
Cumrue D & G 155 J5
Cumwhinton Cumb 148 D4
Cumwhitton Cumb 148 E4
Cundall N York 132 F5
Cunninghamhead
N Ayrs 163 J2
Cunningsburgh Shet ... 235 c7
Cupar Fife 186 F4
Cupar Muir Fife 186 F5
Curbar Derbys 114 E6
Curbridge Hants 17 G1
Curbridge Oxon 57 J7

Curdridge Hants 29 K8
Curdworth Warwks 85 L5
Curland Somset 25 L7
Curridge W Berk 41 J6
Currie C Edin 177 G5
Curry Mallet Somset 25 L6
Curry Rivel Somset 26 B6
Curtisden Green Kent 33 J5
Curtisknowle Devon 7 H5
Cury Cnwll 3 H6
Cushnie Abers 205 L3
Cutcloy D & G 145 J7
Cutcombe Somset 24 E4
Cuthill Highld 223 G4
Cutnall Green Worcs 70 F2
Cutsdean Gloucs 56 C3
Cutthorpe Derbys 115 G6
Cuxham Oxon 42 A2
Cuxton Medway 46 B6
Cuxwold Lincs 117 K2
Cwm Denbgs 110 E6
Cwmafan Neath 36 B3
Cwmaman Rhondd 52 F7
Cwmbach Carmth 50 B1
Cwmbach Powys 68 D6
Cwmbach Rhondd 52 F7
Cwmbach Llechrhyd
Powys 68 B4
Cwmbran Torfn 37 L2
Cwmcarn Caerph 37 K2
Cwmcarvan Mons 54 C6
Cwm-cou Cerdgn 65 J6
Cwm Crawnon Powys 53 H4
Cwmdare Rhondd 52 F7
Cwmdu Powys 53 J4
Cwmdu Swans 51 J6
Cwmduad Carmth 65 L7
Cwmfelin Brdgnd 36 D3
Cwmfelin Myr Td 53 H7
Cwmfelin Boeth
Carmth 49 K4
Cwmfelinfach Caerph ... 37 J3
Cwmffrwd Carmth 50 E3
Cwmgiedd Powys 52 C5
Cwmgorse Carmth 51 K4
Cwmgwili Carmth 51 H4
Cwmhiraeth Carmth 65 K6
Cwm Llinau Powys 81 J2
Cwmllynfell Neath 51 L3
Cwmmawr Carmth 51 G3
Cwmparc Rhondd 36 E2
Cwmpengraig
Carmth 65 K6
Cwmtillery Blae G 53 K6
Cwm-twrch Isaf
Powys 52 B6
Cwm-twrch Uchaf
Powys 51 L4
Cwm-y-glo Gwynd 109 H8
Cwmystwyth Cerdgn 81 H8
Cwrt-newydd Cerdgn ... 66 C5
Cyfarthfa Castle
Museum Myr Td 53 G6
Cylibebyll Neath 51 L5
Cymer Neath 36 D2
Cymmer Rhondd 36 F3
Cynghordy Carmth 67 H6
Cynonville Neath 36 C2
Cynwyd Denbgs 97 G4
Cynwyl Elfed Carmth 65 L8

Daccombe Devon 7 K3
Dacre Cumb 138 C2
Dacre N York 132 B7
Dacre Banks N York 132 B6
Daddry Shield Dur 149 M7
Dadford Bucks 73 J6
Dadlington Leics 86 E4
Dagenham Gt Lon 45 J3
Daglingworth Gloucs 55 M6
Dagnall Bucks 59 G5
Dailly S Ayrs 152 F2
Dairsie Fife 187 G4

Dalabrog W Isls 233 b8
Dalavich Ag & B 182 D5
Dalbeattie D & G 146 E3
Dalby IoM 237 b5
Dalby N York 133 K5
Dalcapon P & K 194 F5
Dalchalm Highld 226 F7
Dalchreichart Highld ... 201 L3
Dalchruin P & K 184 F4
Dalcrue P & K 185 L2
Dalditch Devon 12 D5
Daldowie
Crematorium
C Glas 175 J6
Dale Derbys 101 H5
Dale Pembks 48 D6
Dalelia Highld 190 E3
Dalgarven N Ayrs 163 H1
Dalgety Bay Fife 177 G2
Dalgig E Ayrs 164 B6
Dalginross P & K 185 G3
Dalguise P & K 194 F6
Dalhalvaig Highld 230 C5
Dalham Suffk 77 G3
Daliburgh W Isls 233 b8
Dalkeith Mdloth 177 K5
Dallas Moray 214 D4
Dallinghoo Suffk 78 F4
Dallington E Susx 20 D2
Dallington Nhants 73 K3
Dalmally Ag & B 183 H3
Dalmary Stirlg 184 C7
Dalmellington E Ayrs ... 153 K2
Dalmeny C Edin 176 F3
Dalmore Highld 222 F7
Dalmuir W Duns 174 E4
Dalnabreck Highld 190 E3
Dalnacardoch P & K 194 B3
Dalnahaitnach Highld .. 203 K2
Dalnaspidal P & K 193 K2
Dalnawillan Lodge
Highld 230 F7
Daloist P & K 194 C5
Dalqueich P & K 186 A6
Dalquhairn S Ayrs 153 G3
Dalreavoch Lodge
Highld 226 D6
Dalry N Ayrs 174 B7
Dalrymple E Ayrs 163 J6
Dalserf S Lans 175 L7
Dalsmeran Ag & B 161 G6
Dalston Cumb 148 C5
Dalston Gt Lon 45 G3
Dalswinton D & G 155 G5
Dalton D & G 155 K7
Dalton N York 132 F4
Dalton N York 140 E5
Dalton Nthumb 158 E7
Dalton-in-Furness
Cumb 128 F5
Dalton-le-Dale Dur 151 K5
Dalton-on-Tees
N York 141 H5
Dalton Piercy Hartpl ... 141 L2
Dalveich Stirlg 184 D3
Dalwhinnie Highld 202 F7
Dalwood Devon 13 G3
Damerham Hants 28 C7
Damgate Norfk 93 J2
Danbury Essex 61 J6
Danby N York 142 F5
Danby Wiske N York 141 H7
Dandaleith Moray 215 G5
Danderhall Mdloth 177 J4
Danebridge Ches E 113 L7
Dane End Herts 60 B4
Danehill E Susx 32 D7
Dane Hills C Leic 87 H3
Dane Street Kent 34 E4
Danshillock Abers 216 D3
Danskine E Loth 178 C5
Darenth Kent 45 K5
Daresbury Halton 112 E5
Darfield Barns 115 H1
Dargate Kent 34 E3
Darite Cnwll 5 K3

Darlaston Wsall 85 H4
Darlaston Green Wsall .. 85 H4
Darley N York 132 C7
Darley Abbey C Derb ... 101 G5
Darley Bridge Derbys .. 100 E1
Darley Dale Derbys 114 F8
Darley Green Solhll 85 L8
Darleyhall Herts 59 J4
Darley Head N York 132 B7
Darlingscott Warwks 72 B6
Darlington Darltn 141 H4
Darlington
Crematorium
Darltn 141 G4
Darlton Notts 116 C6
Darnick Border 167 H3
Darowen Powys 81 H3
Darra Abers 216 E5
Darracott Devon 9 G2
Darracott Devon 23 G4
Darras Hall Nthumb 158 E7
Darrington Wakefd 124 D6
Darsham Suffk 79 J1
Darshill Somset 26 E3
Dartford Kent 45 K5
Dartington Devon 7 H4
Dartmoor
National Park
Devon 11 G8
Dartmouth Devon 7 K5
Darton Barns 123 L7
Darvel E Ayrs 164 B2
Darwen Bl w D 121 K6
Datchet W & M 43 G5
Datchworth Herts 59 L4
Daubhill Bolton 121 K8
Daugh of Kinnermony
Moray 214 F6
Dauntsey Wilts 39 M4
Dava Highld 214 C6
Davenham Ches W 112 F7
Daventry Nhants 73 H3
Davidson's Mains
C Edin 177 G3
Davidstow Cnwll 8 F7
Davington D & G 155 M2
Davington Hill Kent 34 D3
Daviot Abers 216 E8
Daviot Highld 213 H6
Daviot House Highld ... 213 H6
Davoch of Grange
Moray 215 K4
Dawesgreen Surrey 31 K3
Dawley Wrekin 84 C2
Dawlish Devon 12 C6
Dawlish Warren
Devon 12 C6
Daybrook Notts 101 L4
Daylesford Gloucs 56 E3
Deal Kent 35 K4
Dean Cumb 136 E3
Dean Devon 7 H3
Dean Devon 23 L2
Dean Hants 29 K7
Dean Oxon 57 G4
Dean Somset 26 F3
Dean Bottom Kent 45 L6
Deanburnhaugh
Border 166 F6
Deancombe Devon 7 G3
Dean Court Oxon 57 J6
Deane Bolton 121 K8
Deane Hants 29 K2
Deanhead Kirk 122 F7
Deanland Dorset 27 M7
Dean Prior Devon 7 H3
Deanraw Nthumb 149 L3
Deans W Loth 176 D5
Deanscales Cumb 136 F2
Deanshanger Nhants 73 L6
Deanshaugh Moray 215 H4
Deanston Stirlg 184 F6
Dearham Cumb 147 J7
Debach Suffk 78 F4
Debden Essex 45 H2
Debden Essex 60 E2

Debenham Suffk 78 E2
Deblin's Green Worcs 70 G5
Dechmont W Loth 176 E4
Dechmont Road
　W Loth 176 D4
Deddington Oxon 57 J2
Dedham Essex 62 C2
Dedworth W & M 42 F5
Deene Nhants 88 D5
Deenethorpe Nhants......88 D5
Deepcar Sheff 114 F3
Deeping Gate C Pete 89 G2
Deeping St James
　Lincs 89 H2
Deeping St Nicholas
　Lincs 89 J1
Deerhurst Gloucs 55 K3
Defford Worcs 71 G5
Defynnog Powys 52 E3
Deganwy Conwy 109 L5
Degnish Ag & B. 182 A5
Deighton C York 124 F2
Deighton N York 141 J6
Deiniolen Gwynd 109 H8
Delabole Cnwll..................8 E7
Delamere Ches W.........112 E7
Delfrigs Abers 207 H2
Delliefure Highld..........214 D7
Dell Quay W Susx 18 A5
Delnabo Moray 204 E3
Delnashaugh Inn
　Moray 214 E7
Delny Highld.................223 G6
Delph Oldham 122 E8
Delves Dur. 150 E5
Dembleby Lincs 103 H5
Denaby Donc 115 J2
Denbigh Denbgs 110 E7
Denbrae Fife 186 F4
Denbury Devon 7 J3
Denby Derbys 101 H4
Denby Dale Kirk 123 J8
Denchworth Oxon 41 G3
Dendron Cumb. 128 F5
Denfield P & K. 185 K4
Denford Nhants..............88 E7
Dengie Essex 62 B7
Denham Bucks. 43 H3
Denham Suffk 77 H3
Denham Suffk 92 E8
Denham Green Bucks....43 H3
Denhead Abers 217 J4
Denhead Fife 187 G5
Denhead of Gray
　C Dund 186 F2
Denholm Border 167 J3
Denholme C Brad. 123 G4
Denmead Hants..............30 A8
Denmore C Aber. 207 H3
Dennington Suffk 79 G2
Denny Falk 175 L2
Dennyloanhead Falk 175 L3
Den of Lindores Fife 186 D4
Denshaw Oldham 122 E7
Denside Abers 206 F6
Densole Kent 35 G6
Denston Suffk 77 H4
Denstone Staffs. 100 C4
Denstroude Kent 34 E3
Dent Cumb. 130 D3
Denton Cambs. 89 G6
Denton Darltn 140 F4
Denton E Susx 19 L5
Denton Kent 35 G5
Denton Lincs 102 E6
Denton N York 123 H2
Denton Nhants 74 B3
Denton Norfk 93 G5
Denton Tamesd 113 L3
Denver Norfk 90 E3
Denwick Nthumb. 169 J6
Deopham Norfk 92 C4
Deopham Green
　Norfk 92 C4
Depden Suffk 77 H3
Deptford Gt Lon 45 G4

Deptford Wilts 28 A4
Derby C Derb 101 G5
Derby Devon 23 J5
Derbyhaven IoM 237 b7
Derculich P & K. 194 D5
Dereham Norfk 92 B2
Deri Caerph 53 H7
Derringstone Kent 35 G5
Derrington Staffs 99 K7
Derry Hill Wilts 39 L6
Derrythorpe N Linc. 125 J8
Dersingham Norfk 105 H6
Dervaig Ag & B. 189 K6
Derwen Denbgs 97 G3
Derwenlas Powys 80 F4
Derwent Valley Mills
　Derbys 100 F2
Derwent Water
　Cumb. 137 J3
Desborough Nhants 88 B6
Desford Leics 86 F3
Deskford Moray. 215 L3
Detling Kent 33 K2
Devauden Mons 54 C7
Devil's Bridge Cerdgn...81 G7
Devizes Wilts 40 A7
Devonport C Plym 6 C5
Devonside Clacks 185 J7
Devoran Cnwll 4 C7
Devoran & Perran
　Cnwll 3 K4
Dewarton Mdloth 177 K5
Dewlish Dorset 14 E3
Dewsbury Kirk 123 K6
Dewsbury Moor
　Crematorium Kirk 123 J6
Deytheur Powys 97 K8
Dial Post W Susx 18 F2
Dibden Hants 16 E2
Dibden Purlieu Hants....16 E2
Dickleburgh Norfk 92 E6
Didbrook Gloucs 56 B2
Didcot Oxon 41 K3
Diddington Cambs. 75 H2
Diddlebury Shrops 83 K6
Didling W Susx 18 A3
Didmarton Gloucs 39 J3
Didsbury Manch 113 J3
Digby Lincs 103 H2
Digg Highld 218 C7
Diggle Oldham 122 F8
Digmoor Lancs 112 C1
Dihewyd Cerdgn 66 C4
Dilham Norfk 107 G7
Dilhorne Staffs 99 L4
Dill Hall Lancs 121 L4
Dillington Cambs. 75 G2
Dilston Nthumb. 150 B3
Dilton Wilts 27 K2
Dilton Marsh Wilts 27 K2
Dilwyn Herefs 69 H4
Dinas Gwynd 94 E5
Dinas Pembks 64 E6
Dinas-Mawddwy
　Gwynd 81 J1
Dinas Powys V Glam 37 J6
Dinder Somset 26 E3
Dinedor Herefs 69 K6
Dingestow Mons 54 C6
Dingle Lpool 111 K4
Dingley Nhants 87 L6
Dingwall Highld 212 E3
Dinnet Abers 205 K5
Dinnington N u Ty. 158 F7
Dinnington Rothm..........115 K4
Dinnington Somset. 26 B8
Dinorwic Gwynd 95 K1
Dinton Bucks. 58 C5
Dinton Wilts 28 A5
Dinwoodie D & G. 155 K4
Dinworthy Devon 9 J2
Dipford Somset 25 J6
Dippen Ag & B. 161 K2
Dippen N Ayrs 162 D5
Dippertown Devon 10 C7
Dipple Moray 215 H3

Dipple S Ayrs 152 E2
Diptford Devon 7 G4
Dipton Dur 150 E4
Dirleton E Loth 178 B2
Dirt Pot Nthumb 149 L5
Diseworth Leics.............101 J7
Dishforth N York 132 F5
Disley Ches E. 113 L5
Diss Norfk 92 D7
Distington Cumb. 136 D3
Distington Hall
　Crematorium
　Cumb. 136 E3
Ditchampton Wilts.........28 C5
Ditcheat Somset. 26 F4
Ditchingham Norfk..........93 G5
Ditchling E Susx. 19 J3
Ditherington Shrops.......83 K2
Ditteridge Wilts 39 J6
Dittisham Devon 7 K5
Ditton Kent 33 J2
Ditton Green Cambs. 76 F3
Ditton Priors Shrops.......83 L5
Dixton Mons 54 D5
Dobcross Oldham..........113 M1
Dobwalls Cnwll 5 K3
Doccombe Devon 11 H7
Dochgarroch Highld......212 F6
Docking Norfk 105 J5
Docklow Herefs 69 L3
Dockray Cumb. 137 L3
Doddinghurst Essex 60 F7
Doddington Cambs. 90 B5
Doddington Kent 34 C4
Doddington Lincs 116 E7
Doddington Nthumb. 168 E3
Doddington Shrops 84 B7
Doddiscombsleigh
　Devon. 11 K7
Dodd's Green Ches E. 98 E4
Dodford Nhants 73 H3
Dodford Worcs 85 G8
Dodington S Glos 39 H4
Dodington Somset. 25 J4
Dodleston Ches W. 98 A1
Dodside E Rens. 174 F7
Dod's Leigh Staffs 100 A5
Dodworth Barns.............114 F1
Dogdyke Lincs 103 K2
Dogmersfield Hants 30 C2
Dolanog Powys................82 B2
Dolbenmaen Gwynd 95 J4
Dolfach Powys 81 K3
Dolfor Powys 82 C6
Dolgarrog Conwy 109 L7
Dolgellau Gwynd 96 B8
Doll Highld 226 F7
Dollar Clacks 185 K7
Dollarfield Clacks 185 K7
Dolphin Flints 111 H6
Dolphinholme Lancs.....129 L8
Dolphinton S Lans. 176 F8
Dolton Devon. 10 E3
Dolwen Conwy 110 B6
Dolwyddelan Conwy 96 B3
Domgay Powys 97 L8
Doncaster Donc 115 L2
Doncaster North
　Services Donc. 125 G7
Donhead St Andrew
　Wilts 27 K6
Donhead St Mary
　Wilts 27 K6
Donibristle Fife 177 G2
Doniford Somset. 25 G3
Donington Lincs 103 K5
Donington on Bain
　Lincs 118 C5
Donington Park
　Services Leics. 101 J7
Donisthorpe Leics. 86 C2
Donnington Gloucs. 56 D3
Donnington Shrops 83 L2
Donnington W Berk 41 J6
Donnington W Susx 18 B5
Donnington Wrekin 84 C2

Donnington Wood
　Wrekin 84 C2
Donyatt Somset 25 M8
Doonfoot S Ayrs 163 H5
Dorback Lodge
　Highld 204 D3
Dorchester Dorset 14 D4
Dorchester Oxon. 41 L2
Dordon Warwks 86 C4
Dore Sheff 114 F5
Dores Highld 212 F7
Dorking Surrey 31 K2
Dormans Land Surrey. 32 D5
Dormington Herefs 69 L6
Dormston Worcs 71 H3
Dorney Bucks. 42 F5
Dornie Highld 200 D1
Dornoch Highld 223 H4
Dornock D & G. 147 M2
Dorrery Highld 230 F5
Dorridge Solhll 85 L8
Dorrington Lincs 103 H2
Dorrington Shrops 83 J3
Dorrington Shrops 99 G4
Dorsington Warwks 71 K4
Dorstone Herefs 69 G6
Dorton Bucks. 58 B5
Douglas IoM 237 d6
Douglas S Lans 165 G4
Douglas and Angus
　C Dund 187 G2
Douglas Borough
　Crematorium IoM 237 d5
Douglas Pier Ag & B. 183 H7
Douglastown Angus......196 C6
Douglas Water S Lans...165 G3
Douglas West S Lans 164 F3
Doulting Somset 26 F3
Dounby Ork. 234 b5
Doune Highld 221 L2
Doune Stirlg 184 F6
Dounepark S Ayrs. 152 E3
Dounie Highld 222 D4
Dousland Devon................6 D3
Dove Holes Derbys 114 B6
Dovenby Cumb. 147 J7
Dover Kent 35 J6
Dover Castle Kent 35 J6
Dovercourt Essex. 62 F2
Doverdale Worcs 70 F2
Doveridge Derbys 100 C5
Doversgreen Surrey. 31 L2
Dowally P & K. 194 F6
Dowdeswell Gloucs. 55 M4
Dowlais Myr Td................53 G6
Dowland Devon. 10 E3
Dowlish Wake
　Somset. 26 A8
Down Ampney Gloucs....40 C2
Downderry Cnwll. 5 L5
Downe Gt Lon 45 H7
Downend Gloucs. 39 J2
Downend S Glos 38 F5
Downfield C Dund 186 F2
Downgate Cnwll. 6 A2
Downham Essex. 45 H5
Downham Gt Lon 45 H5
Downham Lancs. 122 B2
Downham Market
　Norfk 90 E3
Down Hatherley
　Gloucs. 55 K4
Downhead Somset 26 E6
Downhead Somset...........27 G3
Downhill P & K. 186 A2
Downholme N York 140 E7
Downies Abers 207 H6
Downley Bucks. 42 D2
Down St Mary Devon 11 H4
Downs Crematorium
　Br & H. 19 J4
Downside Surrey 43 J8
Down Thomas Devon. 6 D6
Downton Wilts 28 D6
Dowsby Lincs 103 J6
Doynton S Glos 39 G5

Draethen Caerph............37 K3
Draffan S Lans...............164 F1
Drakeholes Notts........116 B4
Drakemyre N Ayrs......174 B7
Drakes Broughton
Worcs.........................71 G5
Draughton N York........131 M8
Draughton Nhants........87 L7
Drax N York..................125 G5
Draycote Warwks..........72 F1
Draycott Derbys...........101 H6
Draycott Gloucs............71 L7
Draycott Somset...........26 C2
Draycott in the Clay
Staffs......................100 D6
Draycott in the
Moors Staffs............99 M4
Drayton C Port..............17 J2
Drayton Leics................88 B5
Drayton Norfk...............92 E2
Drayton Oxon................41 J2
Drayton Oxon................72 E6
Drayton Somset............26 B6
Drayton Worcs..............85 G7
Drayton Bassett
Staffs.........................85 L4
Drayton Beauchamp
Bucks........................58 E5
Drayton Manor Park
Staffs.........................85 L4
Drayton Parslow
Bucks........................58 D3
Drayton St Leonard
Oxon.........................41 L2
Dreen Hill Pembks.........48 F5
Drefach Carmth.............51 G3
Drefach Carmth.............65 K6
Drefach Cerdgn.............66 C5
Dreghorn N Ayrs..........163 J2
Drellingore Kent............35 H6
Drem E Loth................178 B3
Drewsteignton
Devon........................11 H6
Driffield E R Yk............134 F7
Driffield Gloucs.............56 B7
Drift Cnwll......................2 D5
Drigg Cumb.................136 E7
Drighlington Leeds.......123 J5
Drimnin Highld.............190 B5
Drimpton Dorset...........13 K2
Drimsallie Highld..........191 J1
Dringhouses C York.....124 E2
Drinkstone Suffk............77 L3
Drinkstone Green
Suffk.........................77 L3
Drointon Staffs............100 A6
Droitwich Worcs............70 F2
Dron P & K..................186 B4
Dronfield Derbys..........115 G5
Drongan E Ayrs...........163 K5
Dronley Angus.............186 E1
Droop Dorset................14 E2
Droxford Hants..............29 L7
Droylsden Tamesd........113 K2
Druid Denbgs................97 G4
Druidston Pembks..........48 E4
Druimarbin Highld........191 L3
Druimavuic Ag & B.......191 K7
Druimdrishaig Ag & B...172 C4
Druimindarroch
Highld......................199 L7
Drum Ag & B................172 F3
Drum P & K..................185 L7
Drumalbin S Lans.........165 H2
Drumbeg Highld...........224 D3
Drumblade Abers.........216 B6
Drumbreddon D & G.....144 C6
Drumbuie Highld..........210 B7
Drumburgh Cumb.........148 A3
Drumburn D & G..........146 F4
Drumchapel C Glas......174 F4
Drumchastle P & K.......193 L5
Drumclog S Lans..........164 C2
Drumeldrie Fife............187 G6
Drumelzier Border........165 M3
Drumfearn Highld........199 L3

Drumfrennie Abers.......206 D5
Drumgley Angus...........196 C6
Drumguish Highld.........203 J5
Drumin Moray...............214 E7
Drumjohn D & G...........153 L3
Drumlamford S Ayrs.....153 G6
Drumlasie Abers...........206 C4
Drumleaning Cumb.......148 A5
Drumlemble Ag & B......161 H5
Drumlithie Abers...........197 J1
Drummoddie D & G.......145 H6
Drummore D & G..........144 D7
Drummuir Moray...........215 J5
Drumnadrochit
Highld......................212 D7
Drumnaglaur D & G......144 D7
Drumnagorrach
Moray......................215 L4
Drumpark D & G...........154 F6
Drumrunie Lodge
Highld......................224 E7
Drumshang S Ayrs.......163 G6
Drumuie Highld............209 G5
Drumuillie Highld..........204 B2
Drumvaich Stirlg..........184 E6
Drunzie P & K..............186 B5
Drybeck Cumb..............138 F4
Drybridge Moray..........215 K2
Drybridge N Ayrs.........163 J3
Drybrook Gloucs............54 F4
Dryburgh Border..........167 J3
Dry Doddington
Lincs.......................102 D3
Dry Drayton Cambs........75 L3
Drymen Stirlg...............174 E2
Drymuir Abers..............217 G5
Drynoch Highld............208 F7
Dubford Abers..............216 F2
Duchally Highld............225 J5
Ducklington Oxon..........57 G6
Duddenhoe End
Essex........................76 C7
Duddingston C Edin.....177 J4
Duddington Nhants........88 E4
Duddlestone Somset......25 K7
Duddo Nthumb............168 D2
Duddon Ches W...........112 D8
Dudleston Shrops..........97 M5
Dudleston Heath
Shrops......................98 A5
Dudley Dudley...............85 G5
Dudley N Tyne.............159 G7
Dudley Port Sandw........85 G5
Dudsbury Dorset...........15 K3
Duffield Derbys............101 G4
Duffryn Neath...............36 C2
Dufftown Moray............215 H6
Duffus Moray...............214 E2
Dufton Cumb................139 G3
Duggleby N York..........134 D6
Duirinish Highld...........210 B7
Duisdalemore Highld....199 L3
Duisky Highld...............191 K2
Duke Street Suffk..........78 C6
Dukinfield Tamesd........113 L2
Dukinfield
Crematorium
Tamesd....................113 L2
Dulcote Somset.............26 E3
Dulford Devon...............12 D2
Dull P & K...................194 C6
Dullatur N Lans............175 K3
Dullingham Cambs.........76 F3
Dulnain Bridge Highld...204 B1
Duloe Bed.....................75 H3
Duloe Cnwll....................5 K4
Dulverton Somset..........24 E5
Dulwich Gt Lon..............45 G5
Dumbarton W Duns......174 D4
Dumbleton Gloucs.........71 H7
Dumfries D & G............155 G6
Dumgoyne Stirlg..........174 F2
Dummer Hants...............29 L3
Dumpton Kent...............35 K2
Dun Angus..................197 G4
Dunalastair P & K.........193 L5

Dunan Ag & B..............173 K4
Dunan Highld...............209 J8
Dunan P & K................193 G5
Dunaverty Ag & B.........161 H7
Dunball Somset.............25 L3
Dunbar E Loth..............178 E3
Dunbeath Highld..........227 L3
Dunbeg Ag & B............182 C2
Dunblane Stirlg............185 G6
Dunbog Fife.................186 E4
Duncanston Highld.......212 F3
Duncanstone Abers......216 B8
Dunchideock Devon.......11 K7
Dunchurch Warwks........72 F1
Duncow D & G..............155 G5
Duncrievie P & K..........186 B5
Duncton W Susx............18 C3
Dundee C Dund............186 F2
Dundee Airport
C Dund....................186 F2
Dundee
Crematorium
C Dund....................186 F2
Dundon Somset.............26 C5
Dundonald S Ayrs........163 J3
Dundonnell Highld........220 E4
Dundraw Cumb.............147 L5
Dundreggan Highld.......201 L3
Dundrennan D & G........146 D5
Dundry N Som................38 E6
Dunecht Abers..............206 E4
Dunfermline Fife............176 F2
Dunfermline
Crematorium Fife....176 F2
Dunfield Gloucs............40 C2
Dungavel S Lans..........164 D3
Dungeness Kent............21 L3
Dunham Notts..............116 D6
Dunham-on-the-Hill
Ches W.....................112 C6
Dunhampton Worcs.......70 F2
Dunham Town
Traffd......................113 H4
Dunham
Woodhouses
Traffd......................113 G4
Dunholme Lincs............117 G5
Dunino Fife.................187 J3
Dunipace Falk.............175 L2
Dunkeld P & K..............195 G7
Dunkerton BaNES..........39 G8
Dunkeswell Devon........12 E2
Dunkeswick N York......123 L2
Dunkirk Kent.................34 E3
Dunkirk S Glos..............39 H4
Dunk's Green Kent.........33 G3
Dunlappie Angus..........196 F3
Dunley Worcs................70 E2
Dunlop E Ayrs..............174 D8
Dunmaglass Highld......202 F2
Dunmore Falk...............176 B1
Dunnet Highld..............231 J2
Dunnichen Angus.........196 E6
Dunning P & K..............185 L4
Dunnington C York.......133 K8
Dunnington E R Yk.......126 E1
Dunnington Warwks.......71 J4
Dunoon Ag & B............173 K3
Dunphail Moray............214 C5
Dunragit D & G............144 B4
Duns Border................179 G7
Dunsby Lincs...............103 J6
Dunscore D & G............154 F5
Dunscroft Donc............124 F8
Dunsdale R & Cl...........142 D4
Dunsden Green Oxon......42 C5
Dunsdon Devon..............9 J3
Dunsfold Surrey............31 G4
Dunsford Devon............11 J6
Dunshalt Fife...............186 D5
Dunshillock Abers.........217 J5
Dunsill Notts................101 J1
Dunsley N York............143 H5
Dunsley Staffs...............84 F6
Dunsmore Bucks...........58 E6
Dunsop Bridge Lancs....121 K1

Dunstable C Beds..........59 G4
Dunstall Staffs.............100 D7
Dunstan Nthumb..........169 K5
Dunster Somset.............24 F3
Duns Tew Oxon.............57 J3
Dunston Gatesd............151 G3
Dunston Lincs..............117 H8
Dunston Norfk...............92 F3
Dunston Staffs...............99 L8
Dunstone Devon..............6 E5
Dunstone Devon..............7 G2
Dunsville Donc.............124 F8
Dunswell E R Yk...........126 D4
Dunsyre S Lans............176 E8
Dunterton Devon............6 B1
Duntisbourne
Abbots Gloucs............55 L6
Duntisbourne Rouse
Gloucs......................55 M6
Duntish Dorset..............14 D2
Duntocher W Duns.......174 E4
Dunton Bucks................58 D3
Dunton C Beds..............75 J5
Dunton Norfk...............105 L6
Dunton Bassett Leics.....87 G5
Dunton Green Kent........32 F2
Duntulm Highld............218 C6
Dunure S Ayrs..............163 G6
Dunvant Swans.............51 H6
Dunvegan Highld..........208 D5
Dunwich Suffk...............79 K1
Durgan Cnwll..................3 K5
Durham Dur.................151 G6
Durham Cathedral
Dur.........................151 G6
Durham
Crematorium Dur...151 G6
Durham Services Dur...151 H7
Durham Tees Valley
Airport S on T..........141 J5
Durisdeer D & G...........154 F2
Durisdeermill D & G.....154 F2
Durleigh Somset............25 L4
Durley Hants.................29 K7
Durley Wilts..................40 E7
Durley Street Hants.......29 K7
Durlock Kent.................35 H3
Durlock Kent.................35 J2
Durness Highld............228 F3
Durno Abers................216 D8
Duror Highld................191 K5
Durran Ag & B.............182 D5
Durrington W Susx........18 F5
Durrington Wilts............28 D3
Durris Abers................206 E6
Dursley Gloucs..............39 H2
Dursley Cross Gloucs.....55 G4
Durston Somset.............25 L5
Durweston Dorset..........15 G2
Duston Nhants...............73 K3
Duthil Highld...............203 L1
Dutton Ches W.............112 E5
Duxford Cambs..............76 C5
Duxford Oxon................57 G7
Duxford IWM Cambs......76 C5
Dwygyfylchi Conwy.......109 L6
Dwyran IoA.................108 F7
Dyce C Aber.................207 G3
Dyffryn Ardudwy
Gwynd.......................95 K7
Dyffryn Cellwen
Neath........................52 D6
Dyke Lincs..................103 J7
Dyke Moray.................214 B3
Dykehead Angus..........195 K5
Dykehead Angus..........196 C4
Dykehead N Lans.........176 B6
Dykehead Stirlg...........184 D7
Dykelands Abers..........197 H3
Dykends Angus............195 K5
Dykeside Abers............216 D5
Dymchurch Kent............34 E8
Dymock Gloucs.............55 G2
Dyrham S Glos...............39 H5
Dysart Fife..................186 F8
Dyserth Denbgs............110 E5

E

Eagland Hill Lancs 120 F2
Eagle Lincs 116 E7
Eaglescliffe S on T 141 K4
Eaglesfield Cumb........ 136 F2
Eaglesfield D & G........ 155 M7
Eaglesham E Rens........ 175 G7
Eagley Bolton 121 L7
Eakring Notts 102 A1
Ealand N Linc 125 J7
Ealing Gt Lon................ 44 D4
Eals Nthumb.............. 149 H4
Eamont Bridge Cumb.. 138 D2
Earby Lancs 122 D2
Eardington Shrops........ 84 C5
Eardisland Herefs........ 69 H3
Eardisley Herefs.......... 68 F5
Eardiston Shrops.......... 98 A7
Eardiston Worcs.......... 70 C2
Earith Cambs............... 89 L8
Earlestown St Hel 112 E3
Earley Wokham............ 42 C6
Earlham Norfk............. 92 E2
Earlham
   Crematorium
   Norfk..................... 92 E2
Earlish Highld............ 208 F3
Earls Barton Nhants .. 74 C2
Earls Colne Essex........ 61 K3
Earls Common Worcs .. 71 G3
Earl's Croome Worcs .. 70 F6
Earlsdon Covtry.......... 86 D7
Earlsferry Fife............ 187 H7
Earlsfield Gt Lon 44 E5
Earlsford Abers 216 F7
Earlsheaton Kirk........ 123 K6
Earl Shilton Leics........ 86 F4
Earl Soham Suffk........ 78 F2
Earl Sterndale Derbys.. 114 C7
Earlston Border.......... 167 J2
Earlston E Ayrs........... 163 K3
Earlswood Surrey........ 32 B4
Earlswood Warwks...... 85 K8
Earnley W Susx............ 17 M3
Earsdon N Tyne.......... 159 H7
Earsham Norfk............ 93 G5
Eartham W Susx.......... 18 C4
Easby N York 142 C5
Easdale Ag & B........... 181 L4
Easebourne W Susx...... 30 E6
Easenhall Warwks........ 86 F7
Eashing Surrey............ 30 F3
Easington Bucks.......... 58 B6
Easington Dur............ 151 K6
Easington E R Yk........ 127 J6
Easington R & Cl........ 142 F4
Easington Colliery
   Dur........................ 151 K6
Easington Lane
   Sundld................... 151 J5
Easingwold N York...... 133 H5
Eassie and Nevay
   Angus.................... 196 B7
East Aberthaw
   V Glam.................... 37 G6
East Allington Devon......7 H6
East Anstey Devon...... 24 D6
East Ashey IoW........... 17 H5
East Ashling W Susx...... 17 M2
East Ayton N York...... 134 F3
East Barkwith Lincs.... 117 K5
East Barming Kent...... 33 J3
East Barnby N York.... 143 G5
East Barnet Gt Lon...... 44 F2
East Barns E Loth...... 178 F3
East Barsham Norfk.... 105 L5
East Beckham Norfk.. 106 E4
East Bedfont Gt Lon.... 43 H5
East Bergholt Suffk...... 78 C7
East Bilney Norfk...... 106 A8
East Blatchington
   E Susx..................... 20 A5
East Boldon S Tyne.... 151 J3
East Boldre Hants........ 16 D3

Eastbourne Darltn 141 H4
Eastbourne E Susx........ 20 C5
Eastbourne
   Crematorium
   E Susx..................... 20 D5
East Bradenham
   Norfk..................... 91 L2
East Brent Somset 25 M2
Eastbridge Suffk.......... 79 J2
East Bridgford Notts.... 102 B4
East Buckland Devon.. 23 L5
East Budleigh Devon.... 12 D5
Eastburn C Brad........ 122 F2
Eastbury Herts............ 43 J2
Eastbury W Berk.......... 41 G5
East Butterwick
   N Linc................... 116 D1
Eastby N York............ 131 J8
East Calder W Loth.... 176 E5
East Carleton Norfk...... 92 E3
East Carlton Leeds...... 123 J2
East Carlton Nhants.... 88 B5
East Chaldon
   (Chaldon Herring)
   Dorset................... 14 E5
East Challow Oxon...... 41 G3
East Charleton Devon....7 H7
East Chelborough
   Dorset................... 14 A2
East Chiltington
   E Susx..................... 19 K3
East Chinnock
   Somset................... 26 C8
East Chisenbury Wilts .. 28 C2
Eastchurch Kent.......... 47 G5
East Clandon Surrey.... 31 H2
East Claydon Bucks.... 58 C3
East Coker Somset...... 26 D8
Eastcombe Gloucs...... 55 K6
East Compton
   Somset................... 26 E3
East Cornworthy
   Devon......................7 J5
Eastcote Gt Lon.......... 43 J3
Eastcote Nhants........ 73 K4
Eastcote Solhll........... 85 L7
Eastcott Wilts............. 28 A1
East Cottingwith
   E R Yk................... 125 G3
Eastcourt Wilts............ 40 E7
East Cowes IoW.......... 16 F4
East Cowick E R Yk...... 125 G6
East Cowton N York.... 141 H6
East Cranmore
   Somset................... 27 G3
East Dean E Susx........ 20 B6
East Dean Gloucs........ 54 F4
East Dean Hants.......... 28 F6
East Dean W Susx........ 18 B3
East Devon
   Crematorium
   Devon................... 12 D4
East Drayton Notts...... 116 C6
East Dulwich Gt Lon.... 45 G5
East Dundry N Som...... 38 E7
East Ella C KuH.......... 126 C5
Eastend Essex............ 46 F2
East End Hants............ 16 D3
East End Hants............ 41 H7
East End Kent.............. 33 L6
East End Oxon............. 57 H5
East End Somset........ 26 F3
Easter Balmoral
   Abers..................... 205 G6
Easter Compton
   S Glos.................... 38 E4
Easter Dalziel Highld .. 213 H4
Eastergate W Susx...... 18 C5
Easterhouse C Glas.... 175 J5
Easter Howgate
   Mdloth................... 177 H5
Easter Kinkell Highld .. 212 E4
Easter Moniack
   Highld................... 212 E5
Eastern Green Covtry.. 86 C7
Easter Ord Abers........ 206 F4

Easter Pitkierie Fife...... 187 J6
Easter Skeld Shet...... 235 c6
Easter Softlaw
   Border................... 168 A3
Easterton Wilts............ 28 A1
East Everleigh Wilts...... 28 D2
East Farleigh Kent........ 33 J3
East Farndon Nhants.... 87 K6
East Ferry Lincs.......... 116 D2
Eastfield N Lans........ 176 B5
Eastfield N York........ 135 G3
East Fortune E Loth.... 178 C3
East Garston W Berk.... 41 G5
Eastgate Dur.............. 150 B7
Eastgate Norfk.......... 106 D7
East Goscote Leics...... 87 J2
East Grafton Wilts........ 40 E7
East Grimstead Wilts.... 28 E5
East Grinstead
   W Susx................... 32 D5
East Guldeford E Susx.. 21 J2
East Haddon Nhants.... 73 J2
East Hagbourne
   Oxon..................... 41 K3
East Halton N Linc...... 126 E6
East Ham Gt Lon........ 45 H4
Easthampstead Park
   Crematorium
   Br For................... 42 D6
Easthampton Herefs.... 69 H2
East Hanney Oxon...... 41 H2
East Hanningfield
   Essex..................... 61 J7
East Hardwick
   Wakefd................... 124 C6
East Harling Norfk...... 92 B6
East Harlsey N York.... 141 K7
East Harnham Wilts...... 28 C5
East Harptree BaNES.... 26 E1
East Hartburn S on T.. 141 K4
East Harting W Susx...... 30 D7
East Hatch Wilts.......... 27 L5
East Hatley Cambs...... 75 K4
East Hauxwell N York.. 132 B2
East Haven Angus...... 187 J1
East Heckington
   Lincs..................... 103 K4
East Hedleyhope Dur.. 150 E6
East Helmsdale
   Highld................... 227 H5
East Hendred Oxon...... 41 J3
East Heslerton N York.. 134 E4
East Hoathly E Susx...... 20 B3
East Holme Dorset...... 15 G5
Easthope Shrops........ 83 L4
Easthorpe Essex........ 61 L4
East Horrington
   Somset................... 26 E3
East Horsley Surrey...... 31 H2
East Howe Bmouth...... 15 K4
East Huntspill Somset .. 25 M3
East Ilsley W Berk........ 41 J4
Eastington Devon........ 11 H3
Eastington Gloucs...... 55 H6
Eastington Gloucs...... 56 C5
East Keal Lincs.......... 118 E8
East Kennett Wilts...... 40 C6
East Keswick Leeds.... 124 B2
East Kilbride S Lans.... 175 H7
East Kirkby Lincs........ 118 D8
East Knighton Dorset.. 14 F5
East Knoyle Wilts........ 27 K5
East Lambrook
   Somset................... 26 B7
East Lancashire
   Crematorium
   Bury...................... 122 B8
Eastlands D & G........ 154 E7
East Langdon Kent...... 35 J5
East Langton Leics...... 87 K5
East Lavant W Susx...... 18 B4
East Lavington
   W Susx................... 18 C3
East Layton N York...... 140 E5
Eastleach Martin
   Gloucs................... 56 D6

Eastleach Turville
   Gloucs................... 56 D6
East Leake Notts........ 101 K7
Eastleigh Devon.......... 23 H5
Eastleigh Hants.......... 29 J7
East Lexham Norfk...... 105 K8
Eastling Kent.............. 34 C4
East Linton E Loth...... 178 D3
East Lockinge Oxon...... 41 H3
East London
   Crematorium
   Gt Lon................... 45 H4
East Lound N Linc...... 116 C2
East Lulworth Dorset.... 15 G6
East Lutton N York.... 134 E5
East Lydford Somset.... 26 E5
East Malling Kent........ 33 J2
East Marden W Susx...... 30 D8
East Markham Notts.... 116 C6
East Martin Hants........ 28 B7
East Marton N York.... 122 D1
East Meon Hants........ 30 B6
East Mersea Essex...... 62 C5
East Midlands Airport
   Leics..................... 101 J7
East Molesey Surrey...... 43 J6
East Morden Dorset...... 15 G4
East Morton C Brad.... 123 G3
East Morton D & G...... 154 F3
East Ness N York........ 133 L4
Eastney C Port............ 17 J3
Eastnor Herefs............ 70 D6
East Norton Leics...... 87 L4
Eastoft N Linc............ 125 J7
East Ogwell Devon........7 J2
Easton Cambs............ 75 G1
Easton Devon............ 11 G6
Easton Dorset............ 14 D7
Easton Hants............. 29 K5
Easton Lincs............. 102 F6
Easton Norfk............. 92 D2
Easton Somset........... 26 D3
Easton Suffk............. 79 G3
Easton Wilts.............. 39 K6
Easton Grey Wilts........ 39 K3
Easton-in-Gordano
   N Som..................... 38 D5
Easton Maudit
   Nhants................... 74 C3
Easton-on-the-Hill
   Nhants................... 88 E3
Easton Royal Wilts...... 40 D7
East Orchard Dorset.... 27 J7
East Peckham Kent...... 33 H4
East Pennar Pembks.... 49 G6
East Pennard Somset.... 26 E4
East Perry Cambs........ 75 G2
East Portlemouth
   Devon......................7 H7
East Prawle Devon........7 H8
East Preston W Susx...... 18 E5
East Putford Devon......9 K2
East Quantoxhead
   Somset................... 25 H3
East Rainton Sundld.... 151 H5
East Ravendale
   NE Lin................... 118 C2
East Raynham Norfk.... 105 L7
Eastrea Cambs............ 89 K4
East Riding
   Crematorium
   E R Yk................... 134 F5
Eastriggs D & G........ 147 M2
East Rigton Leeds...... 124 B2
Eastrington E R Yk...... 125 J4
Eastrop Swindn.......... 40 D2
East Rounton N York.. 141 K6
East Rudham Norfk.... 105 K6
East Runton Norfk.... 106 E4
East Ruston Norfk...... 107 H6
Eastry Kent............... 35 J4
East Saltoun E Loth.... 178 B5
East Sheen Gt Lon...... 44 E5
East Shefford W Berk.... 41 H5
East Stockwith Lincs.. 116 C3
East Stoke Dorset........ 15 G5

East Stoke Notts 102 C3
East Stour Dorset 27 J6
East Stourmouth
　Kent 35 H3
East Stowford Devon 23 K6
East Stratton Hants 29 K4
East Studdal Kent 35 J5
East Taphouse Cnwll 5 J3
East-the-Water
　Devon 23 G6
East Thirston
　Nthumb 158 F3
East Tilbury Thurr 46 B5
East Tisted Hants 30 B5
East Torrington Lincs .. 117 J5
East Tuddenham
　Norfk 92 C2
East Tytherley Hants 28 F5
East Tytherton Wilts 39 L5
East Village Devon 11 J4
Eastville Bristl 38 E5
Eastville Lincs 104 C2
East Walton Norfk 91 G1
East Week Devon 10 F6
Eastwell Leics 102 C6
East Wellow Hants 28 F7
East Wemyss Fife 186 E7
East Whitburn W Loth .. 176 C5
Eastwick Herts 60 C5
East Wickham Gt Lon 45 J5
East Williamston
　Pembks 49 J6
East Winch Norfk 91 G1
East Winterslow Wilts .. 28 E5
East Wittering W Susx .. 17 L3
East Witton N York 131 L3
Eastwood Notts 101 J3
Eastwood Sthend 46 D3
East Woodburn
　Nthumb 158 A5
East Woodhay Hants 41 H7
East Worldham Hants 30 C4
East Wretham Norfk 91 K5
East Youlstone Devon 9 H2
Eathorpe Warwks 72 E2
Eaton Ches E 113 K7
Eaton Ches W 112 E8
Eaton Leics 102 D6
Eaton Norfk 92 E3
Eaton Notts 116 B6
Eaton Oxon 57 H7
Eaton Shrops 83 K5
Eaton Bray C Beds 58 F4
Eaton Constantine
　Shrops 83 L3
Eaton Green C Beds 58 F4
Eaton Hastings Oxon 56 E7
Eaton Mascott
　Shrops 83 K3
Eaton Socon Cambs 75 H3
Eaton upon Tern
　Shrops 98 F7
Ebberston N York 134 D3
Ebbesborne Wake
　Wilts 27 M6
Ebbw Vale Blae G 53 J6
Ebchester Dur 150 D4
Ebford Devon 12 C5
Ebley Gloucs 55 J6
Ebnal Ches W 98 C3
Ebrington Gloucs 71 L6
Ecchinswell Hants 41 J8
Ecclaw Border 178 F5
Ecclefechan D & G 155 L7
Eccles Border 168 A2
Eccles Kent 46 B7
Eccles Salfd 113 H2
Ecclesall Sheff 114 F5
Eccles Crematorium
　Salfd 113 H3
Ecclesfield Sheff 115 G3
Eccleshall Staffs 99 J6
Eccleshill C Brad 123 H4
Ecclesmachan W Loth .. 176 E4
Eccles Road Norfk 92 B5
Eccleston Ches W 112 B8

Eccleston Lancs 121 G6
Eccleston St Hel 112 C3
Echt Abers 206 E4
Eckford Border 167 L4
Eckington Derbys 115 H5
Eckington Worcs 71 G6
Ecton Nhants 74 B2
Edale Derbys 114 C4
Eday Ork 234 d4
Eday Airport Ork 234 d4
Edburton W Susx 19 H4
Edderton Highld 222 F4
Eddleston Border 177 H8
Eddlewood S Lans 175 J7
Edenbridge Kent 32 D4
Edenfield Lancs 122 B6
Edenhall Cumb 138 E2
Edenham Lincs 103 H7
Eden Park Gt Lon 45 G6
Eden Project Cnwll 5 G5
Edensor Derbys 114 E7
Edentaggart Ag & B 183 K8
Edenthorpe Donc 115 L1
Edern Gwynd 94 E5
Edgbaston Birm 85 J6
Edgcott Bucks 58 B4
Edgcott Somset 24 D4
Edge Gloucs 55 J6
Edgefield Norfk 106 C5
Edgefield Green
　Norfk 106 D5
Edgerton Kirk 123 H6
Edgeworth Gloucs 55 L6
Edgmond Wrekin 99 G8
Edgton Shrops 83 H6
Edgware Gt Lon 44 D2
Edgworth Bl w D 121 L6
Edinbane Highld 208 E4
Edinburgh C Edin 177 H4
Edinburgh Airport
　C Edin 176 F4
Edinburgh Castle
　C Edin 177 H4
Edinburgh Old & New
　Town C Edin 177 H4
Edinburgh Royal
　Botanic Gardens
　C Edin 177 H4
Edinburgh Zoo C Edin .. 177 G4
Edingale Staffs 86 B2
Edingham D & G 146 E3
Edingley Notts 102 A2
Edingthorpe Norfk 107 G6
Edingthorpe Green
　Norfk 107 G6
Edington Border 179 J7
Edington Nthumb 158 E5
Edington Somset 26 B4
Edington Wilts 27 L2
Edington Burtle
　Somset 26 B3
Edingworth Somset 26 A2
Edithmead Somset 25 L2
Edith Weston Rutlnd .. 88 D3
Edlesborough Bucks 58 F4
Edlingham Nthumb 169 G7
Edlington Lincs 118 C7
Edmondsham Dorset .. 15 K1
Edmondsley Dur 151 G5
Edmondthorpe Leics .. 102 E8
Edmonton Gt Lon 45 G2
Edmundbyers Dur 150 C5
Ednam Border 167 L2
Edradynate P & K 194 D6
Edrom Border 179 H7
Edstaston Shrops 98 D6
Edstone Warwks 71 L3
Edwalton Notts 101 L5
Edwinstowe Notts 115 L7
Edworth C Beds 75 J6
Edwyn Ralph Herefs 70 B3
Edzell Angus 196 F3
Edzell Woods Abers 196 F3
Efail-fach Neath 36 B2
Efail Isaf Rhondd 37 G4
Efailnewydd Gwynd 94 F5

Efailwen Carmth 49 K3
Efenechtyd Denbgs 97 H2
Effgill D & G 156 B4
Effingham Surrey 31 J2
Efford Crematorium
　C Plym 6 D4
Egerton Bolton 121 K7
Egerton Kent 34 B5
Eggborough N York 124 E5
Eggbuckland C Plym 6 D4
Eggesford Devon 11 G3
Eggington C Beds 58 F3
Egginton Derbys 100 E6
Egglescliffe S on T 141 K4
Eggleston Dur 140 C3
Egham Surrey 43 G6
Egleton Rutlnd 88 C3
Eglingham Nthumb 169 G5
Egloshayle Cnwll 4 F3
Egloskerry Cnwll 9 H7
Eglwysbach Conwy 109 M7
Eglwys Cross Wrexhm .. 98 C4
Eglwyswrw Pembks 65 G6
Egmanton Notts 116 B7
Egremont Cumb 136 D5
Egremont Wirral 111 K3
Egton N York 143 G6
Egton Bridge N York ... 143 G6
Egypt Bucks 42 F3
Eigg Highld 199 G7
Eight Ash Green
　Essex 61 M3
Eilanreach Highld 200 C2
Eilean Donan Castle
　Highld 200 D1
Elan Valley Powys 67 J2
Elan Village Powys 67 K2
Elberton S Glos 38 E3
Elburton C Plym 6 D5
Elcombe Swindn 40 C4
Eldersfield Worcs 55 H2
Elderslie Rens 174 E5
Eldon Dur 141 G2
Elfhill Abers 206 F7
Elford Staffs 85 L2
Elgin Moray 214 F2
Elgol Highld 199 H3
Elham Kent 35 G6
Elie Fife 187 H7
Elim IoA 108 D4
Eling Hants 29 G8
Elkesley Notts 116 B6
Elkstone Gloucs 55 L5
Ella Abers 216 C3
Ellacombe Torbay 7 L3
Elland Calder 123 G6
Ellary Ag & B 172 C3
Ellastone Staffs 100 C4
Ellel Lancs 129 K7
Ellemford Border 178 F6
Ellenabeich Ag & B 181 L4
Ellenhall Staffs 99 J7
Ellen's Green Surrey 31 H4
Ellerbeck N York 141 K7
Ellerby N York 143 G4
Ellerdine Heath
　Wrekin 98 F7
Elleric Ag & B 191 K6
Ellerker E R Yk 125 L5
Ellerton E R Yk 125 G3
Ellerton N York 141 G7
Ellesborough Bucks 58 D6
Ellesmere Shrops 98 B5
Ellesmere Port
　Ches W 111 L6
Ellingham Norfk 93 H5
Ellingham Nthumb 169 H4
Ellingstring N York 132 B3
Ellington Cambs 75 H1
Ellington Nthumb 159 G4
Elliots Green Somset 27 J3
Ellisfield Hants 29 M3
Ellishader Highld 209 H2
Ellistown Leics 86 E2
Ellon Abers 217 H1
Ellonby Cumb 148 D7

Elloughton E R Yk 126 B5
Ellwood Gloucs 54 E6
Elm Cambs 90 C3
Elmbridge Worcs 70 F2
Elmdon Essex 76 C6
Elmdon Solhll 85 L6
Elmers End Gt Lon 45 G6
Elmer's Green Lancs .. 112 D1
Elmesthorpe Leics 86 F4
Elmhurst Staffs 85 K2
Elmley Castle Worcs 71 H6
Elmley Lovett Worcs 70 F1
Elmore Gloucs 55 H5
Elmore Back Gloucs 55 H5
Elm Park Gt Lon 45 K3
Elmsett Suffk 78 C5
Elmstead Market
　Essex 62 C3
Elmsted Kent 34 F5
Elmstone Kent 35 H3
Elmstone Hardwicke
　Gloucs 55 K3
Elmswell E R Yk 134 F7
Elmswell Suffk 78 B2
Elmton Derbys 115 J6
Elphin Highld 224 F6
Elphinstone E Loth 177 K4
Elrick Abers 206 F4
Elrig D & G 145 G5
Elrington Nthumb 149 L3
Elsdon Nthumb 158 B4
Elsenham Essex 60 E3
Elsfield Oxon 57 K6
Elsham N Linc 126 C7
Elsing Norfk 92 C1
Elslack N York 122 D2
Elson Hants 17 H3
Elsrickle S Lans 165 K2
Elstead Surrey 30 E3
Elsted W Susx 30 D7
Elsthorpe Lincs 103 H7
Elston Notts 102 C3
Elstow Bed 74 F5
Elstree Herts 44 D2
Elstronwick E R Yk 126 F4
Elswick Lancs 120 F3
Elswick N u Ty 151 G3
Elsworth Cambs 75 K2
Elterwater Cumb 137 K6
Eltham Gt Lon 45 H5
Eltham Crematorium
　Gt Lon 45 J5
Eltisley Cambs 75 J3
Elton Cambs 88 F5
Elton Ches W 112 C6
Elton Derbys 100 E1
Elton Herefs 69 J1
Elton Notts 102 C5
Elton S on T 141 J4
Eltringham Nthumb ... 150 D3
Elvanfoot S Lans 165 J6
Elvaston Derbys 101 H6
Elveden Suffk 91 J7
Elvetham Heath
　Hants 30 D1
Elvingston E Loth 178 A4
Elvington C York 125 G2
Elvington Kent 35 H5
Elwick Hartpl 141 K2
Elworth Ches E 99 H1
Elworthy Somset 25 G4
Ely Cambs 90 D7
Ely Cardif 37 H5
Emberton M Keyn 74 C5
Embleton Cumb 137 G2
Embleton Nthumb 169 J5
Embo Highld 223 H3
Emborough Somset 26 E2
Embo Street Highld ... 223 H3
Embsay N York 131 J8
Emery Down Hants 16 C2
Emley Kirk 123 K7
Emmington Oxon 58 C7
Emneth Norfk 90 C3
Emneth Hungate
　Norfk 90 D3

Empingham Rutlnd 88 D2
Empshott Hants 30 C5
Emstrey
   Crematorium
   Shrops 83 K2
Emsworth Hants 17 K2
Enborne W Berk 41 H7
Enborne Row W Berk 41 H7
Enderby Leics 87 G4
Endmoor Cumb 129 L3
Endon Staffs 99 L2
Endon Bank Staffs 99 L2
Enfield Gt Lon 60 B7
Enfield Crematorium
   Gt Lon 60 B7
Enfield Lock Gt Lon 60 B7
Enfield Wash Gt Lon 60 B7
Enford Wilts 28 C2
Engine Common
   S Glos 39 G4
Englefield W Berk 41 L6
Englefield Green
   Surrey 43 G6
English Bicknor
   Gloucs 54 E5
Englishcombe BaNES ...39 G7
English Frankton
   Shrops 98 C6
Enham-Alamein
   Hants 29 G2
Enmore Somset 25 K4
Enmore Green Dorset ...27 J6
Ennerdale Bridge
   Cumb 136 E4
Enochdhu P & K 195 G4
Ensay Ag & B 189 J6
Ensbury Bmouth 15 K3
Ensdon Shrops 83 H1
Enstone Oxon 57 G3
Enterkinfoot D & G 154 E2
Enville Staffs 84 E6
Eolaigearraidh W Isls ...233 b9
Epney Gloucs 55 H5
Epperstone Notts 101 M3
Epping Essex 60 D7
Epping Green Essex 60 C6
Epping Upland Essex 60 C6
Eppleby N York 140 F5
Epsom Surrey 44 E7
Epwell Oxon 72 D6
Epworth N Linc 116 C2
Erbistock Wrexhm 97 M4
Erdington Birm 85 K5
Eridge Green E Susx 32 F6
Erines Ag & B 172 E4
Eriska Ag & B 191 H7
Eriskay W Isls 233 c9
Eriswell Suffk 91 G7
Erith Gt Lon 45 K4
Erlestoke Wilts 27 L2
Ermington Devon 6 F5
Erpingham Norfk 106 E6
Errogie Highld 202 E2
Errol P & K 186 D3
Erskine Rens 174 E4
Ervie D & G 144 B2
Erwarton Suffk 78 F7
Erwood Powys 68 C6
Eryholme N York 141 H5
Eryrys Denbgs 97 J2
Escomb Dur 140 F2
Escrick N York 124 F2
Esgairgeiliog Powys 81 G3
Esh Dur 150 F6
Esher Surrey 43 J7
Eshott Nthumb 158 F3
Esh Winning Dur 150 F6
Eskadale Highld 212 C6
Eskbank Mdloth 177 J5
Eskdale Green Cumb ...137 G6
Eskdalemuir D & G 156 A3
Esprick Lancs 120 E3
Essendine Rutlnd 88 D2
Essendon Herts 59 L6
Essich Highld 213 G6
Essington Staffs 85 G3

Esslemont Abers 217 H7
Eston R & Cl 142 C4
Etal Nthumb 168 D2
Etchilhampton Wilts......40 B7
Etchingham E Susx 33 J7
Etchinghill Kent.............34 F6
Etchinghill Staffs 100 B8
Eton W & M 42 F5
Eton Wick W & M 42 F5
Etruria C Stke.................99 K3
Etteridge Highld 203 G6
Ettersgill Dur 139 K2
Ettiley Heath Ches E......99 G1
Ettingshall Wolves 85 G4
Ettington Warwks 72 C5
Etton C Pete 89 G3
Etton E R Yk 126 B2
Ettrick Border 166 D6
Ettrickbridge Border 166 F4
Ettrickhill Border 166 C6
Etwall Derbys 100 F6
Euston Suffk 91 K7
Euxton Lancs 121 H6
Evanton Highld 212 F2
Evedon Lincs 103 H3
Evelix Highld 223 G4
Evenjobb Powys 68 F3
Evenley Nhants 73 H7
Evenlode Gloucs 56 E3
Evenwood Dur 140 E3
Evercreech Somset 26 F4
Everingham E R Yk 125 J3
Everleigh Wilts 28 D2
Eversholt C Beds 59 G2
Evershot Dorset 14 B2
Eversley Hants 42 C7
Eversley Cross Hants 42 C7
Everthorpe E R Yk 125 L4
Everton C Beds 75 H4
Everton Hants 16 C4
Everton Lpool 111 K3
Everton Notts 116 B4
Evertown D & G 156 C6
Evesbatch Herefs 70 C5
Evesham Worcs 71 J5
Evington C Leic 87 J3
Ewden Village Sheff 114 F3
Ewell Surrey 44 E7
Ewell Minnis Kent 35 H6
Ewelme Oxon 41 M3
Ewen Gloucs 40 A2
Ewenny V Glam 36 D5
Ewerby Lincs 103 J3
Ewhurst Surrey 31 H3
Ewhurst Green E Susx ...20 F2
Ewhurst Green Surrey....31 H4
Ewloe Flints 111 J7
Eworthy Devon 10 C6
Ewshot Hants 30 D2
Ewyas Harold Herefs....54 B3
Exbourne Devon 10 E4
Exbridge Somset 24 E6
Exbury Hants 16 E3
Exelby N York 132 D3
Exeter Devon 11 L6
Exeter Airport Devon 12 C4
Exeter & Devon
   Crematorium
   Devon 12 B4
Exeter Services
   Devon 12 C4
Exford Somset 24 D4
Exfordsgreen Shrops 83 J3
Exhall Warwks 71 K4
Exhall Warwks 86 D6
Exlade Street Oxon 42 A4
Exminster Devon 12 B5
Exmoor
   National Park 24 D4
Exmouth Devon 12 C6
Exning Suffk 76 E2
Exton Devon 12 C5
Exton Hants 29 L1
Exton Rutlnd 88 D2
Exton Somset 24 E5
Exwick Devon 11 K6

Eyam Derbys 114 E6
Eydon Nhants 73 G4
Eye C Pete 89 J3
Eye Herefs 69 J2
Eye Suffk 92 D8
Eyemouth Border 179 K5
Eyeworth C Beds 75 J5
Eyhorne Street Kent 33 L5
Eyke Suffk 79 G4
Eynesbury Cambs 75 H3
Eynsford Kent 45 K6
Eynsham Oxon 57 H6
Eype Dorset 13 L4
Eyre Highld 208 F4
Eythorne Kent 35 H5
Eyton Herefs 69 J3
Eyton Shrops 98 C7
Eyton on Severn
   Shrops 83 L3
Eyton upon the
   Weald Moors
   Wrekin 84 B1

F

Faccombe Hants 41 H8
Faceby N York 141 L6
Fachwen Powys 82 B1
Faddiley Ches E 98 E3
Fadmoor N York 133 K2
Faerdre Swans 51 K5
Faifley W Duns 174 F4
Failand N Som 38 D6
Failford S Ayrs 163 L4
Failsworth Oldham 113 K2
Fairbourne Gwynd 80 E2
Fairburn N York 124 D5
Fairfield Derbys 114 B6
Fairfield Worcs 85 G7
Fairford Gloucs 56 D7
Fairgirth D & G 146 F4
Fair Green Norfk 90 F1
Fairhaven Lancs 120 D5
Fair Isle Shet 235 e7
Fairlands Surrey 30 F2
Fairlie N Ayrs 173 L7
Fairlight E Susx 21 G4
Fairmile Devon 12 E3
Fairmile Surrey 43 J7
Fairnilee Border 167 G3
Fair Oak Hants 29 J7
Fairoak Staffs 99 H6
Fair Oak Green Hants 42 A7
Fairseat Kent 45 L7
Fairstead Essex 61 J5
Fairstead Norfk 105 G8
Fairwarp E Susx 32 E7
Fairwater Cardif 37 H5
Fairy Cross Devon 22 F6
Fakenham Norfk 105 L6
Fakenham Magna
   Suffk 91 K7
Fala Mdloth 177 L6
Fala Dam Mdloth 177 L6
Faldingworth Lincs.......117 H5
Faldouet Jersey 236 e7
Falfield S Glos 39 G2
Falkenham Suffk 79 G6
Falkirk Falk 176 B3
Falkirk Crematorium
   Falk 176 B3
Falkirk Wheel Falk 176 A3
Falkland Fife 186 D6
Fallburn S Lans 165 J2
Fallin Stirlg 185 H8
Fallodon Nthumb 169 J5
Fallowfield Manch 113 J3
Fallowfield Nthumb 150 B2
Falls of Blarghour
   Ag & B 182 E5
Falmer E Susx 19 K4
Falmouth Cnwll 3 K5
Falnash Border 156 D2
Falsgrave N York 134 F2
Falstone Nthumb 157 J5

Fanagmore Highld 228 B5
Fancott C Beds 59 G3
Fanellan Highld 212 D5
Fangdale Beck N York ..142 C7
Fangfoss E R Yk 134 B8
Fanmore Ag & B 189 K7
Fannich Lodge Highld ...211 K2
Fans Border 167 J2
Far Bletchley M Keyn 74 C7
Farcet Cambs 89 H5
Far Cotton Nhants 73 L3
Fareham Hants 17 H2
Far End Cumb 137 J7
Farewell Staffs 85 J2
Faringdon Oxon 40 F2
Farington Lancs 121 H5
Farlam Cumb 148 F3
Farleigh N Som 38 D6
Farleigh Surrey 32 C2
Farleigh Hungerford
   Somset 39 J8
Farleigh Wallop
   Hants 29 L3
Farlesthorpe Lincs 119 G6
Farleton Cumb 129 L4
Farleton Lancs 130 B6
Farley Staffs 100 B4
Farley Wilts 28 E5
Farley Green Surrey 31 H3
Farley Hill Wokham 42 C7
Farleys End Gloucs 55 H5
Farlington C Port 17 J2
Farlington N York 133 J6
Farlow Shrops 84 B7
Farmborough BaNES......38 F7
Farmcote Gloucs 56 B3
Farmers Carmth 66 E5
Farmington Gloucs 56 C5
Farmoor Oxon 57 J6
Far Moor Wigan 112 D2
Farmtown Moray 215 L4
Farnborough Gt Lon 45 H7
Farnborough Hants 30 E2
Farnborough W Berk 41 H4
Farnborough Warwks.....72 E5
Farnborough Park
   Hants 30 E1
Farnborough Street
   Hants 30 E1
Farncombe Surrey 31 G3
Farndish Bed 74 D2
Farndon Ches W 98 B2
Farndon Notts 102 C3
Farne Islands
   Nthumb 169 K2
Farnell Angus...............197 G5
Farnham Dorset 27 L7
Farnham Essex 60 D3
Farnham N York 132 E7
Farnham Suffk 79 H3
Farnham Surrey 30 D3
Farnham Common
   Bucks 42 F4
Farnham Royal Bucks ...42 F4
Farningham Kent 45 K6
Farnley Leeds 123 K4
Farnley N York 123 J2
Farnley Tyas Kirk 123 H7
Farnsfield Notts 101 M2
Farnworth Bolton 113 G1
Farnworth Halton 112 D4
Far Oakridge Gloucs 55 L7
Farr Highld 203 K5
Farr Highld 213 G7
Farr Highld 229 L3
Farraline Highld 202 E2
Farringdon Devon 12 C4
Farrington Gurney
   BaNES 26 F1
Far Sawrey Cumb 137 K7
Farthinghoe Nhants 73 G6
Farthingstone
   Nhants 73 H4
Fartown Kirk 123 H6
Fartown Leeds 123 J4
Fasnacloich Ag & B 191 K6

Fasnakyle Highld............211 L8
Fassfern Highld.............191 K2
Fatfield Sundld...............151 H4
Fauldhouse W Loth........176 C6
Faulkbourne Essex..........61 J3
Faulkland Somset...........27 H1
Fauls Shrops...................98 E6
Faversham Kent...............34 D3
Fawdington N York.........132 F5
Fawdon N u Ty...............151 G2
Fawkham Green Kent.......45 L6
Fawler Oxon....................57 G4
Fawley Bucks..................42 C3
Fawley W Berk.................41 H4
Fawley Hants...................16 F2
Faxfleet E R Yk..............125 K5
Faygate W Susx...............31 K5
Fazakerley Lpool............111 K3
Fearby N York................132 B4
Fearn Highld..................223 H6
Fearnan P & K................194 B7
Fearnbeg Highld.............210 B3
Fearnmore Highld...........209 L3
Fearnoch Ag & B............172 F3
Featherstone Staffs..........85 G3
Featherstone Wakefd....124 C6
Feckenham Worcs............71 H3
Feering Essex...................61 L4
Feetham N York.............140 C7
Felbridge Surrey..............32 C5
Felbrigg Norfk................106 E5
Felcourt Surrey................32 C5
Felindre Carmth...............51 G2
Felindre Carmth...............65 K6
Felindre Powys................82 D7
Felindre Swans................51 J5
Felindre Farchog
  Pembks......................64 F6
Felingwm Isaf
  Carmth......................51 G2
Felingwm Uchaf
  Carmth......................51 G1
Felixkirk N York............133 G3
Felixstowe Suffk..............79 G7
Felling Gatesd...............151 G3
Felmersham Bed.............74 E3
Felmingham Norfk.........106 F6
Felpham W Susx..............18 C5
Felsham Suffk..................77 L3
Felsted Essex...................61 G4
Feltham Gt Lon...............43 J5
Felthamhill Surrey...........43 H6
Felthorpe Norfk.............106 E8
Felton Herefs..................69 L5
Felton N Som..................38 D7
Felton Nthumb...............158 F3
Felton Butler Shrops........98 B8
Feltwell Norfk..................91 G5
Fence Lancs...................122 C3
Fence Rothm..................115 H4
Fencott Oxon...................57 L5
Fendike Corner Lincs.....104 D1
Fen Ditton Cambs...........76 C3
Fen Drayton Cambs.........75 L2
Feniscowles Bl w D........121 J5
Feniton Devon.................12 E3
Fenland
  Crematorium
  Cambs........................90 B5
Fenn Green Shrops..........84 D6
Fenn Street Medway.........46 D5
Fenny Bentley Derbys....100 D3
Fenny Bridges Devon.......12 E3
Fenny Compton
  Warwks......................72 E4
Fenny Drayton Leics........86 D4
Fenstanton Cambs...........75 K2
Fen Street Norfk..............92 B4
Fenton C Stke.................99 K4
Fenton Cambs..................89 K7
Fenton Cumb..................148 E4
Fenton Lincs..................102 E3
Fenton Lincs..................116 D6
Fenton Notts..................116 C5
Fenton Nthumb..............168 E3

Fenton Barns E Loth.....178 B3
Fenwick Donc.................124 F7
Fenwick E Ayrs..............163 L2
Fenwick Nthumb............158 D7
Fenwick Nthumb............169 G2
Feock Cnwll........................4 C7
Feolin Ferry Ag & B.......171 H4
Fergushill N Ayrs...........163 J2
Feriniquarrie Highld......208 B4
Fern Angus....................196 D4
Ferndale Rhondd.............36 F2
Ferndown Dorset.............15 K3
Ferness Highld...............214 B5
Fernham Oxon..................40 F3
Fernhill Heath Worcs.......70 F3
Fernhurst W Susx............30 E5
Fernie Fife....................186 E4
Ferniegair S Lans...........175 K7
Fernilea Highld..............208 F7
Fernilee Derbys.............114 A5
Fernwood Notts..............102 D3
Ferrensby N York...........132 E7
Ferrindonald Highld.....199 K4
Ferring W Susx................18 F5
Ferrybridge Services
  Wakefd.....................124 D6
Ferryden Angus.............197 H5
Ferryhill Dur..................141 H2
Ferry Point Highld.........223 G4
Ferryside Carmth............50 D4
Ferrytown Highld...........223 G4
Fersfield Norfk................92 C6
Fersit Highld..................192 F2
Feshiebridge Highld.......203 K4
Fetcham Surrey................31 J1
Fetlar Shet....................235 e2
Fetterangus Abers..........217 J4
Fettercairn Abers...........197 J2
Fewston N York..............132 B8
Ffairfach Carmth.............51 J2
Ffair Rhos Cerdgn...........67 G2
Ffestiniog Gwynd............96 A4
Ffestiniog Railway
  Gwynd........................95 L4
Fforest Carmth................51 H5
Fforest Fach Swans.........51 J6
Ffostrasol Cerdgn...........65 L5
Ffrith Flints....................97 L2
Ffynnongroyw Flints.....111 G5
Fiag Lodge Highld..........225 K3
Ficklesholme Surrey........32 C2
Fiddington Somset...........25 K4
Fiddleford Dorset............27 J8
Fiddlers Green Cnwll.........4 C5
Field Staffs....................100 A5
Field Dalling Norfk.......106 B5
Field Head Leics.............86 F2
Fifehead Magdalen
  Dorset.......................27 H6
Fifehead Neville
  Dorset.......................14 E1
Fifehead St Quintin
  Dorset.......................14 E1
Fife Keith Moray............215 J4
Fifield Oxon....................56 F4
Fifield W & M.................42 E5
Figheldean Wilts.............28 D3
Filby Norfk......................93 K2
Filey N York...................135 H4
Filgrave M Keyn..............74 C5
Filkins Oxon...................56 E6
Filleigh Devon.................23 K5
Fillingham Lincs............116 F4
Fillongley Warwks...........86 C6
Filton S Glos...................38 E5
Fimber E R Yk................134 D7
Finavon Angus...............196 D5
Fincham Norfk................91 G3
Finchampstead
  Wokham......................42 D7
Fincharn Ag & B............182 C6
Finchdean Hants.............30 C8
Finchingfield Essex.........61 G2
Finchley Gt Lon..............44 F2
Findern Derbys..............100 F6
Findhorn Moray.............214 C2

Findhorn Bridge
  Highld.......................213 J8
Findochty Moray............215 K2
Findo Gask P & K...........185 L4
Findon Abers.................207 H6
Findon W Susx................18 F4
Findon Mains Highld.....212 F3
Findrack House Abers....206 B4
Finedon Nhants...............74 D1
Fingask P & K................186 C4
Fingest Bucks..................42 C3
Finghall N York.............132 B2
Fingland D & G..............164 E6
Finglesham Kent.............35 J4
Fingringhoe Essex...........62 B4
Finlarig Stirlg................184 C1
Finmere Oxon..................57 M2
Finnart P & K................193 H5
Finningham Suffk............78 C1
Finningley Donc............116 A2
Finsbay W Isls...............232 d5
Finstall Worcs..................71 H1
Finsthwaite Cumb..........129 H2
Finstock Oxon..................57 G5
Finstown Ork.................234 b6
Fintry Abers...................216 E4
Fintry Stirlg...................175 H2
Finzean Abers................206 B6
Fionnphort Ag & B........180 D3
Fionnsbhagh W Isls......232 d5
Firbank Cumb................130 C2
Firbeck Rothm...............115 K4
Firby N York..................132 D3
Firby N York..................134 B6
Firle E Susx.....................19 M4
Firsby Lincs...................118 F8
Fir Tree Dur..................150 E7
Fishbourne IoW...............17 G4
Fishbourne W Susx..........18 A5
Fishburn Dur.................141 J2
Fishcross Clacks.............185 J7
Fisherford Abers............216 C7
Fisherrow E Loth...........177 K4
Fisher's Pond Hants.........29 J7
Fisherton Highld............213 H4
Fisherton S Ayrs............163 H6
Fisherton de la Mere
  Wilts.........................27 M4
Fishguard Pembks...........64 D6
Fishlake Donc................125 G7
Fishnish Pier Ag & B.....190 D7
Fishponds Bristl..............38 F5
Fishtoft Lincs................104 B4
Fishtoft Drove Lincs.....104 A3
Fiskavaig Highld...........208 E7
Fiskerton Lincs...............117 H6
Fiskerton Notts..............102 C3
Fittleton Wilts..................28 D2
Fittleworth W Susx..........18 D2
Fitz Shrops......................98 C8
Fitzhead Somset..............25 H5
Fitzwilliam Wakefd........124 C7
Five Ash Down E Susx....19 M2
Five Ashes E Susx............32 F7
Fivehead Somset.............26 A6
Fivelanes Cnwll.................9 G8
Five Oak Green Kent........33 H4
Five Oaks Jersey............236 d7
Five Oaks W Susx............31 H5
Five Roads Carmth..........50 F4
Flackwell Heath
  Bucks.........................42 E3
Fladbury Worcs...............71 H5
Fladdabister Shet...........235 c6
Flagg Derbys.................114 C7
Flamborough E R Yk.....135 K5
Flamborough Head
  E R Yk.......................135 K5
Flamingo Land
  Theme Park
  N York......................134 B4
Flamstead Herts..............59 H5
Flansham W Susx............18 C5
Flanshaw Wakefd...........123 L6
Flasby N York................131 H7
Flash Staffs...................114 A7

Flashader Highld............208 E4
Flaunden Herts................59 G7
Flawborough Notts.........102 C4
Flawith N York...............133 G6
Flax Bourton N Som........38 D6
Flaxby N York................132 F7
Flaxley Gloucs..................55 G5
Flaxpool Somset..............25 H4
Flaxton N York...............133 K6
Fleckney Leics.................87 J5
Flecknoe Warwks............73 G2
Fledborough Notts.........116 D6
Fleet Dorset.....................14 C6
Fleet Hants......................30 D2
Fleet Lincs....................104 C7
Fleet Hargate Lincs........104 C7
Fleet Services Hants.........30 D1
Fleetwood Lancs............120 D2
Flemingston V Glam........36 F6
Flemington S Lans.........175 H6
Flempton Suffk................77 J1
Fletchertown Cumb........147 L6
Fletching E Susx..............19 L2
Flexbury Cnwll..................9 G4
Flexford Surrey................30 F2
Flimby Cumb..................147 H7
Flimwell E Susx...............33 J6
Flint Flints....................111 H6
Flintham Notts...............102 C4
Flinton E R Yk................126 F4
Flitcham Norfk...............105 H6
Flitton C Beds..................74 F7
Flitwick C Beds................74 F7
Flixborough N Linc........125 K7
Flixborough Stather
  N Linc.......................125 K7
Flixton N York...............135 G4
Flixton Suffk....................93 G6
Flixton Traffd................113 H3
Flockton Kirk.................123 J7
Flockton Green Kirk......123 K7
Flodigarry Highld..........218 C6
Flookburgh Cumb..........129 H4
Flordon Norfk..................92 E4
Flore Nhants...................73 J3
Flowton Suffk..................78 C5
Flushing Cnwll...................3 L4
Fluxton Devon.................12 E4
Flyford Flavell Worcs......71 H4
Fobbing Thurr.................46 B4
Fochabers Moray...........215 H3
Fochriw Caerph...............53 H6
Fockerby N Linc............125 K6
Foddington Somset.........26 E5
Foel Powys......................81 L2
Foggathorpe E R Yk......125 H3
Fogo Border...................179 G8
Fogwatt Moray...............214 F3
Foindle Highld...............228 B5
Folda Angus...................195 J4
Fole Staffs....................100 B5
Foleshill Covtry................86 D6
Folke Dorset....................26 F8
Folkestone Kent..............35 H7
Folkingham Lincs...........103 H5
Folkington E Susx............20 B5
Folksworth Cambs...........89 G5
Folkton N York...............135 G4
Folla Rule Abers............216 D7
Follifoot N York.............132 E8
Folly Gate Devon............10 E5
Fonthill Bishop Wilts......27 L5
Fonthill Gifford Wilts......27 L5
Fontmell Magna
  Dorset.......................27 K7
Fontmell Parva
  Dorset.......................27 J8
Fontwell W Susx..............18 C4
Foolow Derbys...............114 D6
Forbestown Abers..........205 H3
Forcett N York................140 F5
Ford Ag & B..................182 C6
Ford Bucks......................58 C6
Ford Derbys...................115 H5
Ford Devon......................22 F6
Ford Gloucs.....................56 C3

Ford Nthumb.................168 E2
Ford Somset....................25 H5
Ford Staffs....................100 B2
Ford W Susx....................18 D5
Ford Wilts........................39 J5
Fordcombe Kent..........32 F5
Fordell Fife................177 G2
Forden Powys.............82 E4
Ford End Essex............61 G5
Forder Green Devon........7 H3
Fordham Cambs..........76 F1
Fordham Essex.............61 L3
Fordham Norfk...........90 E4
Fordingbridge Hants...28 D8
Fordon E R Yk............135 G4
Fordoun Abers..........197 J2
Fordstreet Essex.........61 L3
Ford Street Somset....25 J7
Fordwich Kent.............35 G3
Fordyce Abers...........216 B2
Forebridge Staffs..........99 L7
Forest Guern..............236 c4
Forest Chapel Ches E..113 L6
Forest Gate Gt Lon.......45 H3
Forest Green Surrey......31 J3
Forest Hall N Tyne.....151 G2
Forest Hill Gt Lon........45 G5
Forest Hill Oxon..........57 L6
Forest Lane Head
  N York.....................132 E7
Forest Mill Clacks.....185 K8
Forest of Dean
  Gloucs.......................54 F5
Forest Park
  Crematorium
  Gt Lon.........................45 J2
Forest Row E Susx......32 D6
Forestside W Susx.......30 C8
Forfar Angus..............196 D6
Forgandenny P & K....186 A4
Forge Hammer Torfn...37 L2
Forgie Moray..............215 J4
Forgieside Moray......215 J4
Forgue Abers.............216 B5
Formby Sefton............111 J1
Forncett End Norfk......92 D5
Forncett St Mary
  Norfk...........................92 E5
Forncett St Peter
  Norfk...........................92 E5
Fornham All Saints
  Suffk...........................77 J2
Fornham St Martin
  Suffk...........................77 J2
Fornighty Highld.......213 L4
Forres Moray..............214 C3
Forsbrook Staffs...........99 L4
Forse Highld...............227 M2
Forsinard Highld........230 C6
Fort Augustus Highld..202 B4
Forteviot P & K..........185 L4
Forth S Lans...............176 C7
Forthampton Gloucs....55 K2
Fortingall P & K..........194 B6
Forton Hants................29 H3
Forton Lancs..............121 G1
Forton Shrops...............83 H1
Forton Somset.............13 J2
Forton Staffs................99 H7
Fortrie Abers.............216 C5
Fortrose Highld..........213 H3
Fortuneswell Dorset....14 D7
Fort William Highld....191 L2
Forty Hill Gt Lon.........60 B7
Fosbury Wilts..............40 F8
Foscot Oxon................56 E4
Fosdyke Lincs...........104 A5
Foss P & K.................194 C5
Fossebridge Gloucs.....56 B5
Foster Street Essex......60 D6
Foston Derbys...........100 D6
Foston Leics...............87 H4
Foston Lincs..............102 E4
Foston N York...........133 L6
Foston on the Wolds
  E R Yk......................135 H7

Fotherby Lincs...........118 D3
Fotheringhay Nhants...88 F5
Foula Shet.................235 a6
Foulden Border.........179 J7
Foulden Norfk............91 H4
Foul End Warwks........86 B4
Foulness Island Essex....47 G2
Foulon Vale
  Crematorium
  Guern........................236 d3
Foulridge Lancs.........122 D3
Foulsham Norfk.........106 B7
Fountainhall Border...177 L8
Four Ashes Suffk.........78 B1
Four Crosses Powys.....97 K8
Four Elms Kent............32 E4
Four Forks Somset......25 K4
Four Gotes Cambs.......90 C1
Four Lanes Cnwll...........3 J4
Four Marks Hants.........30 A4
Four Mile Bridge IoA..108 C5
Four Oaks Solhll..........86 B7
Fourpenny Highld.....223 H3
Four Roads Carmth......50 F4
Fourstones Nthumb...149 M2
Four Throws Kent........33 K7
Fovant Wilts................28 A5
Foveran Abers...........207 H2
Fowey Cnwll..................5 H5
Fowlhall Kent...............33 J4
Fowlis Angus.............186 E2
Fowlis Wester P & K....185 J3
Fowlmere Cambs........76 B5
Fownhope Herefs........69 L7
Foxbar Rens..............174 E6
Foxcote Somset..........27 G1
Foxdale IoM...............237 b5
Foxearth Essex............77 J5
Foxfield Cumb............128 F3
Foxhole Cnwll...............4 F5
Foxholes N York........134 F5
Foxley Norfk..............106 C7
Foxt Staffs.................100 B3
Foxton Cambs.............76 B5
Foxton Leics...............87 K5
Foxton N York...........141 K7
Foxwood Shrops.........84 B7
Foy Herefs..................54 E3
Foyers Highld...........202 D2
Foynesfield Highld....213 L4
Fraddon Cnwll..............4 E4
Fradley Staffs..............85 L2
Fradswell Staffs...........99 M6
Fraisthorpe E R Yk.....135 J2
Framfield E Susx.........20 A2
Framingham Earl
  Norfk...........................92 F3
Framingham Pigot
  Norfk...........................92 F3
Framlingham Suffk......79 G2
Frampton Dorset.........14 C4
Frampton Lincs..........104 B5
Frampton Cotterell
  S Glos..........................38 F4
Frampton Mansell
  Gloucs.......................55 L7
Frampton-on-Severn
  Gloucs.......................55 H6
Framsden Suffk...........78 E3
Framwellgate Moor
  Dur...........................151 G6
Franche Worcs............84 E7
Frankby Wirral...........111 H4
Frankley Worcs............85 H7
Frankley Services
  Worcs..........................85 H7
Frankton Warwks........72 E1
Frant E Susx................33 G6
Fraserburgh Abers....217 J2
Frating Essex...............62 C4
Frating Green Essex....62 C4
Fratton C Port..............17 J3
Freathy Cnwll................6 B5
Freckenham Suffk........76 F1
Freckleton Lancs.......120 F5
Freeby Leics..............102 D7

Freefolk Hants.............29 J2
Freeland Oxon.............57 H5
Freethorpe Norfk........93 J3
Freethorpe Common
  Norfk...........................93 J3
Freiston Lincs............104 B4
Fremington Devon......23 H5
Fremington N York.....140 D7
Frenchay S Glos..........38 F5
Frenich P & K.............194 C5
Frensham Surrey.........30 D3
Freshfield Sefton.......120 C8
Freshford Wilts...........39 H7
Freshwater IoW...........16 D5
Fressingfield Suffk.......92 F7
Freston Suffk...............78 E6
Freswick Highld.........231 L3
Fretherne Gloucs.........55 G6
Frettenham Norfk......106 F8
Freuchie Fife..............186 E6
Freystrop Pembks........49 G5
Friar Park Sandw.........85 H4
Friday Bridge Cambs...90 C3
Friday Street Suffk......79 H3
Fridaythorpe E R Yk...134 D7
Friern Barnet Gt Lon....44 F2
Friesthorpe Lincs......117 H5
Frieston Lincs............102 F3
Frieth Bucks................42 D3
Frilford Oxon...............41 H2
Frilsham W Berk..........41 K5
Frimley Surrey.............42 E8
Frindsbury Medway.....46 C6
Fring Norfk.................105 H5
Fringford Oxon............57 L3
Frinsted Kent...............34 B4
Frinton-on-Sea Essex....62 F4
Friockheim Angus......196 F6
Frisby on the
  Wreake Leics...........102 B8
Friskney Lincs............104 D2
Friston E Susx.............20 B6
Friston Suffk................79 J3
Fritchley Derbys........101 G3
Fritham Hants...............28 E8
Frithelstock Devon......23 G7
Frithelstock Stone
  Devon........................23 G7
Frithville Lincs...........104 A3
Frittenden Kent...........33 K5
Frittiscombe Devon........7 J6
Fritton Norfk................92 F5
Fritton Norfk................93 K4
Fritwell Oxon...............57 K3
Frizinghall C Brad.....123 H4
Frizington Cumb........136 E4
Frocester Gloucs.........55 H7
Frodesley Shrops........83 K3
Frodsham Ches W......112 D6
Frogden Border.........168 B4
Frog End Cambs..........76 B5
Froggatt Derbys........114 E6
Froghall Staffs...........100 A3
Frogmore Devon...........7 H7
Frognall Lincs.............89 H2
Frog Pool Worcs...........70 E2
Frogwell Cnwll...............6 A3
Frolesworth Leics........87 G5
Frome Somset..............27 H2
Frome St Quintin
  Dorset........................14 B2
Fromes Hill Herefs......70 C5
Froncysyllte Denbgs....97 K4
Fron-goch Gwynd........96 D5
Fron Isaf Wrexhm........97 L4
Frosterley Dur...........150 C7
Froxfield Wilts............40 F6
Froxfield Green Hants...30 B6
Fryern Hill Hants.........29 H7
Fryerning Essex...........61 G2
Fuinary Highld...........190 C6
Fulbeck Lincs............102 F3
Fulbourn Cambs..........76 D4
Fulbrook Oxon............56 E5
Fulflood Hants.............29 J5
Fulford C York...........124 F2

Fulford Somset.............25 K5
Fulford Staffs...............99 L5
Fulham Gt Lon.............44 E5
Fulking W Susx............19 H4
Fullarton N Ayrs.........163 H2
Fuller Street Essex......61 H5
Fullerton Hants...........29 G4
Fulletby Lincs............118 D6
Fullready Warwks........72 C5
Full Sutton E R Yk......134 B7
Fullwood E Ayrs........174 E7
Fulmer Bucks...............43 G4
Fulmodeston Norfk....106 B6
Fulnetby Lincs............117 H5
Fulney Lincs................103 L7
Fulstow Lincs.............118 D3
Fulwell Sundld...........151 J3
Fulwood Lancs...........121 H4
Fulwood Sheff............114 F4
Fundenhall Norfk........92 D4
Funtington W Susx......17 L2
Funtullich P & K.........184 F3
Furley Devon................13 H2
Furnace Ag & B..........182 E7
Furnace Carmth...........51 G5
Furness Vale Derbys...114 A5
Furneux Pelham
  Herts...........................60 C3
Furzley Hants...............28 F7
Fyfield Essex................60 F6
Fyfield Hants................28 F3
Fyfield Oxon.................57 H7
Fyfield Wilts.................40 C6
Fyfield Wilts.................40 D7
Fylingthorpe N York...143 J6
Fyning W Susx.............30 D6
Fyvie Abers................216 E6

G

Gabroc Hill E Ayrs.....174 E7
Gaddesby Leics...........87 K2
Gaddesden Row
  Herts...........................59 H5
Gadgirth S Ayrs.........163 K6
Gaer-llwyd Mons.........38 C2
Gaerwen IoA.............108 F7
Gailes N Ayrs.............163 H3
Gailey Staffs................85 G2
Gainford Dur.............140 F4
Gainsborough Lincs...116 D4
Gainsford End Essex....77 G7
Gairloch Highld.........219 J6
Gairlochy Highld.......201 J8
Gairneybridge P & K...186 B7
Gaitsgill Cumb...........148 C5
Galashiels Border......167 G3
Galgate Lancs............129 K7
Galhampton Somset....26 F5
Gallanachbeg Ag & B..182 B2
Gallanachmore
  Ag & B......................182 B3
Gallatown Fife............186 E8
Galleywood Essex.......61 H7
Gallovie Highld.........202 E7
Galloway Forest
  Park.......................153 J5
Gallowfauld Angus.....196 D7
Gallowhill P & K.........186 B1
Galltair Highld...........200 C2
Galmpton Devon...........7 G7
Galmpton Torbay..........7 K5
Galphay N York.........132 C5
Galston E Ayrs...........163 L3
Gamblesby Cumb.......149 G6
Gamlingay Cambs........75 J4
Gamlingay Great
  Heath Cambs............75 J4
Gamrie Abers.............216 F2
Gamston Notts...........101 L5
Gamston Notts...........116 B6
Ganavan Bay Ag & B..182 B2
Ganllwyd Gwynd.........96 B7
Gannachy Angus........196 F3
Ganstead E R Yk.......126 E4

Ganthorpe N York 133 L5
Ganton N York 134 F4
Garbity Moray 215 H4
Garboldisham Norfk....92 B7
Garbole Highld..............203 H1
Garchory Abers 205 G4
Gardeners Green
  Wokham 42 D6
Gardenstown Abers 216 F2
Garden Village Sheff....114 E2
Garderhouse Shet........235 c5
Gare Hill Somset 27 H4
Garelochhead Ag & B...173 L1
Garford Oxon..............41 H2
Garforth Leeds 124 B4
Gargrave N York 131 H8
Gargunnock Stirlg......184 F8
Garlic Street Norfk........92 E6
Garlieston D & G 145 K5
Garlinge Kent..............35 J2
Garlinge Green Kent....34 F4
Garlogie Abers 206 E4
Garmond Abers 216 F4
Garmouth Moray........215 H2
Garmston Shrops 83 L3
Garn-Dolbenmaen
  Gwynd 95 J4
Garnkirk N Lans 175 J5
Garrabost W Isls 232 g2
Garrallan E Ayrs 164 B5
Garras Cnwll 3 J6
Garreg Gwynd 95 K4
Garrigill Cumb 149 J6
Garroch D & G............153 M6
Garrochtrie Ag & B.....144 D7
Garrochty Ag & B........173 J7
Garros Highld..............209 H2
Garsdale Head Cumb..130 E2
Garsdon Wilts 39 L3
Garshall Green Staffs ...99 L5
Garsington Oxon..........57 L7
Garstang Lancs 121 G2
Garston Herts 59 J7
Garston Lpool 112 B5
Gartachossan Ag & B...171 G6
Gartcosh N Lans........175 J5
Garth Powys..............67 K5
Garth Wrexhm 97 K4
Garthamlock C Glas 175 H5
Garthmyl Powys..........82 E4
Garth Penrhyncoch
  Cerdgn 80 E6
Garth Row Cumb 138 D7
Gartly Abers 215 L7
Gartmore Stirlg..........184 C7
Gartness N Lans 175 K5
Gartness Stirlg..........174 F2
Gartocharn W Duns 174 D2
Garton-on-the-Wolds
  E R Yk........................134 F7
Gartymore Highld 227 H5
Garvald E Loth 178 D4
Garvan Highld............191 J2
Garvard Ag & B..........171 G1
Garve Highld..............212 B3
Garvellachs Ag & B......181 K5
Garvestone Norfk........92 B3
Garvock Inver 174 B4
Garway Herefs 54 C4
Garyvard W Isls 232 f3
Gasper Wilts 27 H5
Gastard Wilts..............39 K6
Gasthorpe Norfk..........91 L7
Gaston Green Essex......60 D5
Gatcombe IoW..............16 F5
Gate Burton Lincs........116 D5
Gateforth N York........124 E5
Gate Helmsley N York...133 L4
Gatehouse Nthumb......157 K4
Gatehouse of Fleet
  D & G 145 M4
Gateley Norfk 106 A7
Gatenby N York 132 E3

Gateshaw Border........168 B5
Gateshead Gatesd......151 G3
Gateside Angus 196 D7
Gateside E Rens........174 E6
Gateside Fife..............186 C5
Gateside N Ayrs 174 C7
Gateslack D & G 154 F2
Gatley Stockp............113 J4
Gattonside Border......167 H3
Gatwick Airport
  W Susx *32 B5*
Gaulby Leics 87 K4
Gauldry Fife..............186 F3
Gauldswell P & K........195 K6
Gautby Lincs 117 K6
Gavinton Border 179 G7
Gawcott Bucks 58 B2
Gawsworth Ches E......113 K7
Gawthrop Cumb..........130 D3
Gawthwaite Cumb......129 G3
Gaydon Warwks 72 D4
Gayhurst M Keyn..........74 B5
Gayle N York 131 G2
Gayles N York 140 E5
Gayton Nhants............73 K4
Gayton Norfk............105 H8
Gayton Staffs 99 M6
Gayton le Marsh Lincs..118 F5
Gayton Thorpe Norfk...105 H8
Gaywood Norfk..........105 G7
Gazeley Suffk..............77 G2
Gearraidh Bhaird
  W Isls........................232 f3
Geary Highld 208 D3
Gedding Suffk..............77 L3
Geddington Nhants......88 C6
Gedling Notts............101 L4
Gedney Lincs 104 C7
Gedney Broadgate
  Lincs..........................104 C7
Gedney Drove End
  Lincs..........................104 D6
Gedney Dyke Lincs......104 C7
Gedney Hill Lincs..........89 L2
Geeston Rutlnd............88 E3
Geldeston Norfk..........93 H5
Gellifor Denbgs..........110 F8
Gelligaer Caerph..........37 H2
Gellilydan Gwynd..........95 M4
Gellinudd Neath 51 K5
Gellyburn P & K..........195 H8
Gellywen Carmth..........50 C2
Gelston D & G 146 D3
Gelston Lincs............102 E4
Gembling E R Yk........135 H7
Gentleshaw Staffs........85 J2
Georgefield D & G 156 B4
George Green Bucks......43 G4
Georgeham Devon........23 G4
Georgemas Junction
  Station Highld..........231 H4
George Nympton
  Devon 23 L6
Georth Ork 234 b5
Germansweek Devon....10 C6
Gerrans Cnwll 4 D8
Gerrards Cross Bucks....43 G3
Gerrick R & Cl 142 E5
Gestingthorpe Essex....77 J6
Geuffordd Powys..........82 E2
Gidea Park Gt Lon........45 K3
Giffnock E Rens..........175 G6
Gifford E Loth 178 C5
Giffordtown Fife..........186 E5
Giggleswick N York......130 F6
Gigha Ag & B 171 L7
Gilberdyke E R Yk........125 K5
Gilchriston E Loth........178 B5
Gilcrux Cumb 147 K7
Gildersome Leeds......123 K5
Gildingwells Rothm....115 K4
Gilesgate Moor Dur....151 H6
Gileston V Glam 36 F6
Gilfach Caerph............53 J7
Gilfach Goch Brdgnd 36 F3
Gilfachrheda Cerdgn....65 L3

Gilgarran Cumb..........136 E3
Gillamoor N York........133 K2
Gillen Highld 208 D3
Gillesbie D & G 155 K4
Gilling East N York......133 J4
Gillingham Dorset........27 J6
Gillingham Medway......46 C6
Gillingham Norfk..........93 J5
Gilling West N York......140 F6
Gillock Highld............231 J4
Gills Highld 231 K2
Gilmanscleuch Border..166 E5
Gilmerton C Edin........177 J5
Gilmerton P & K 185 J3
Gilmonby Dur............140 C5
Gilmorton Leics............87 H6
Gilroes Crematorium
  C Leic 87 H3
Gilsland Nthumb........149 G2
Gilston Border............177 L6
Gilston Herts 60 D5
Gilwern Mons..............53 K5
Gimingham Norfk........107 G5
Gipping Suffk..............78 C2
Gipsey Bridge Lincs....103 M3
Girdle Toll N Ayrs......163 J2
Girlsta Shet 235 c5
Girsby N York 141 J5
Girthon D & G 146 A4
Girton Cambs..............76 B3
Girton Notts 116 D7
Girvan S Ayrs 152 E3
Gisburn Lancs............122 C2
Gisleham Suffk............93 K5
Gislingham Suffk..........78 C1
Gissing Norfk..............92 D6
Gittisham Devon..........12 E3
Gladestry Powys..........68 E4
Gladsmuir E Loth........177 M4
Glais Swans 51 K5
Glaisdale N York 143 G6
Glamis Angus 196 C6
Glanaman Carmth........51 J3
Glandford Norfk..........106 C4
Glandwr Pembks..........49 K2
Glandyfi Cerdgn..........80 F4
Glanllynfi Brdgnd 36 D3
Glan-rhyd Powys..........52 B6
Glanton Nthumb........169 G6
Glanvilles Wootton
  Dorset 14 D2
Glan-y-don Flints........111 G5
Glapthorn Nhants........88 E5
Glapwell Derbys..........115 J7
Glasbury Powys............68 D6
Glascwm Powys............68 D4
Glasfryn Conwy............96 E3
Glasgow C Glas 175 G5
Glasgow Airport Rens....*174 E5*
Glasgow Science
  Centre C Glas 175 G5
Glasinfryn Gwynd........109 H7
Glasnacardoch Bay
  Highld 199 L6
Glasnakille Highld......199 H3
Glassford S Lans 175 J8
Glasshouse Gloucs......55 G4
Glasshouses N York....132 B6
Glasson Cumb............148 A3
Glasson Lancs............129 K7
Glassonby Cumb 149 G7
Glasterlaw Angus........196 F6
Glaston Rutlnd............88 C4
Glastonbury Somset....26 D4
Glatton Cambs............89 H6
Glazebrook Warrtn......113 G3
Glazebury Warrtn........112 F3
Glazeley Shrops............84 C5
Gleaston Cumb..........128 F5
Glebe Highld 202 D2
Gledhow Leeds..........123 L3
Gledpark D & G 146 B5
Gledrid Shrops............97 L5
Glemsford Suffk............77 J5
Glenallachie Moray......215 G6
Glenancross Highld......199 K6

Glenaros House
  Ag & B 190 B7
Glen Auldyn IoM........237 d3
Glenbarr Ag & B..........161 H3
Glenbarry Abers 216 B4
Glenbeg Highld 190 C4
Glenbervie Abers........197 J1
Glenboig N Lans 175 J5
Glenborrodale Highld..190 C4
Glenbranter Ag & B.....183 G7
Glenbreck Border........165 K5
Glenbrittle House
  Highld 198 F2
Glenbuck E Ayrs 164 E4
Glencally Angus 196 B4
Glencaple D & G 147 H2
Glencarron Lodge
  Highld 211 G4
Glencarse P & K 186 C3
Glen Clunie Lodge
  Abers 204 E8
Glencoe Highld 191 L5
Glencothe Border........165 L4
Glencraig Fife............186 C7
Glencrosh D & G 154 D4
Glendale Highld..........208 B4
Glendaruel Ag & B......173 G2
Glendevon P & K........185 K6
Glendoe Lodge Highld..202 C4
Glendoick P & K 186 C3
Glenduckie Fife..........186 D4
Glenegedale Ag & B....170 F7
Glenelg Highld 200 C2
Glenerney Moray 214 C5
Glenfarg P & K 186 B5
Glenfield Leics..............87 G3
Glenfinnan Highld......191 H1
Glenfintaig Lodge
  Highld 201 K7
Glenfoot P & K 186 C4
Glenfyne Lodge
  Ag & B 183 H4
Glengarnock N Ayrs....174 C7
Glengolly Highld........231 G3
Glengorm Castle
  Ag & B 189 K5
Glengrasco Highld......209 G5
Glenholm Border........165 L3
Glenhoul D & G 154 A5
Glenisla Angus............195 K4
Glenkin Ag & B 173 K3
Glenkindie Abers 205 K3
Glenlivet Moray 214 F8
Glenlochar D & G 146 C3
Glenlomond P & K......186 C6
Glenluce D & G 144 E4
Glenmassen Ag & B.....173 J2
Glenmavis N Lans 175 K5
Glen Maye IoM............237 b6
Glenmore Highld 209 G6
Glenmore Lodge
  Highld 204 B4
Glen Nevis House
  Highld 192 B3
Glenochil Clacks........185 H7
Glen Parva Leics..........87 H4
Glenquiech Angus........196 C4
Glenralloch Ag & B......172 E5
Glenridding Cumb......137 L4
Glenrothes Fife..........186 D7
Glenshero Lodge
  Highld 202 E6
Glenstriven Ag & B......173 J3
Glentham Lincs..........117 G4
Glen Trool Lodge
  D & G 153 J6
Glentrool Village
  D & G 153 H6
Glentruim House
  Highld 203 G6
Glentworth Lincs........116 F4
Glenuig Highld..........190 D2
Glenvarragill Highld....209 G6
Glen Vine IoM............237 c5
Glenwhilly D & G 152 E7
Glespin S Lans 164 F4

Glewstone Herefs 54 E4
Glinton C Pete............... 89 H3
Glooston Leics 87 L4
Glossop Derbys 114 B3
Gloster Hill Nthumb....159 G2
Gloucester Gloucs 55 J4
Gloucester
   Crematorium
      Gloucs.................... 55 J5
Gloucestershire
   Airport Gloucs.......... 55 K4
Glusburn N York 122 F2
Glutt Lodge Highld......227 H2
Glympton Oxon............ 57 H4
Glynarthen Cerdgn...... 65 K5
Glyn Ceiriog Wrexhm... 97 J5
Glyncorrwg Neath 52 D7
Glynde E Susx............... 19 L4
Glyndyfrdwy Denbgs... 97 J4
Glynneath Neath.......... 52 D6
Glynn Valley
   Crematorium
      Cnwll........................ 5 H3
Glyntaff
   Crematorium
      Rhondd.................... 37 H3
Glyntawe Powys.......... 52 D5
Glyntawg Carmth.......... 65 K6
Gnosall Staffs 99 J7
Gnosall Heath Staffs 99 J7
Goadby Leics 87 L4
Goadby Marwood
      Leics....................102 C7
Goatacre Wilts............. 40 A5
Goathill Dorset............. 26 F7
Goathland N York 143 H6
Goathurst Somset........ 25 K5
Gobowen Shrops.......... 97 L5
Godalming Surrey 30 F3
Goddard's Green
      Kent........................ 33 L6
Godmanchester
      Cambs.................... 75 J1
Godmanstone Dorset.... 14 C3
Godmersham Kent........ 34 E5
Godney Somset............ 26 C3
Godolphin Cross
      Cnwll........................ 3 G5
Godre'r-graig Neath 51 L4
Godshill IoW................. 17 G6
Godstone Surrey.......... 32 C3
Goetre Mons 53 L6
Goff's Oak Herts.......... 60 B7
Gofilon Mons 53 K5
Gogar C Edin 177 G4
Goginan Cerdgn.......... 80 F7
Golan Gwynd............... 95 J4
Golant Cnwll................. 5 H5
Golberdon Cnwll........... 5 M2
Golborne Wigan..........112 E3
Golcar Kirk..................123 G7
Goldcliff Newpt............ 38 A4
Golden Green Kent...... 33 H4
Golden Pot Hants........ 30 B3
Golders Green Gt Lon... 44 E3
Golders Green
   Crematorium
      Gt Lon.................... 44 E3
Goldhanger Essex........ 61 L6
Goldington Bed............ 74 F4
Goldsborough N York..132 F7
Goldsborough N York..143 H4
Goldsithney Cnwll........ 2 F5
Goldsworth Park
      Surrey.................... 43 G8
Goldthorpe Barns........115 J2
Goldworthy Devon........ 22 F6
Gollanfield Highld........213 J4
Golspie Highld............223 H2
Gomeldon Wilts........... 28 D4
Gomshall Surrey........... 31 H2
Gonalston Notts..........102 B3
Gonerby Hill Foot
      Lincs......................102 E5
Gonfirth Shet..............235 c4
Good Easter Essex........ 60 F5

Gooderstone Norfk...... 91 H3
Goodleigh Devon........ 23 J5
Goodmanham E R Yk..125 K2
Goodmayes Gt Lon...... 45 J3
Goodnestone Kent...... 34 D3
Goodnestone Kent...... 35 H4
Goodrich Herefs 54 E4
Goodrich Castle
      Herefs 54 E4
Goodrington Torbay...... 7 K4
Goodshaw Lancs........122 B5
Goodwick Pembks........ 64 C6
Goodworth Clatford
      Hants...................... 29 G3
Goole E R Yk...............125 H5
Goom's Hill Worcs...... 71 H4
Goonbell Cnwll.............. 3 J2
Goonhavern Cnwll........ 3 K1
Goonvrea Cnwll............ 3 J2
Goosecruives Abers....206 E8
Gooseford Devon......... 11 G6
Goose Green Essex...... 62 D3
Goose Green S Glos...... 38 F5
Gooseham Cnwll............ 9 G2
Goosey Oxon................ 41 G3
Goosnargh Lancs........121 H3
Goostrey Ches E..........113 H7
Gordano Services
      N Som...................... 38 D5
Gordon Border............167 K2
Gordon Arms Hotel
      Border....................166 D4
Gordonstown Abers....216 D4
Gordonstown Abers....216 D6
Gorebridge Mdloth......177 K6
Gorefield Cambs.......... 90 B2
Gores Wilts.................. 40 C8
Gorey Jersey................236 e7
Goring Oxon................ 41 L4
Goring-by-Sea W Susx..18 F5
Gorleston on Sea
      Norfk...................... 93 L3
Gornal Wood
   Crematorium
      Dudley.................... 85 G5
Gorrachie Abers..........216 E3
Gorran Churchtown
      Cnwll........................ 4 F7
Gorran Haven Cnwll...... 4 F7
Gorsedd Flints............111 G6
Gorse Hill Swindn........ 40 D3
Gorseinon Swans........ 51 H5
Gorsgoch Cerdgn........ 66 C4
Gorslas Carmth............ 51 H3
Gorsley Gloucs............ 55 G3
Gorsley Common
      Herefs...................... 54 F3
Gorstan Highld............212 B2
Gorsty Hill Staffs........100 C6
Gorten Ag & B............181 L2
Gorthleck Highld........202 E2
Gorton Manch..............113 K3
Gosbeck Suffk.............. 78 D4
Gosberton Lincs..........103 L6
Gosfield Essex.............. 61 J3
Gosforth Cumb............136 E6
Gosforth N u Ty..........151 G2
Gospel End Staffs........ 84 F5
Gosport Hants.............. 17 H3
Gossington Gloucs...... 55 H7
Gotham Notts..............101 K6
Gotherington Gloucs.... 55 L3
Gotton Somset............ 25 K5
Goudhurst Kent............ 33 J5
Goulceby Lincs............118 C5
Gourdas Abers............216 E6
Gourdie C Dund..........186 F2
Gourdon Abers............197 K3
Gourock Inver............173 L3
Govan C Glas..............174 F5
Goveton Devon............. 7 H6
Gowdall E R Yk............124 F6
Gower Highld..............212 D3
Gower Swans............... 51 G7
Gowerton Swans.......... 51 H6
Gowkhall Fife..............176 E1

Goxhill E R Yk..............126 F2
Goxhill N Linc..............126 D6
Grabhair W Isls............232 f3
Graffham W Susx.......... 18 C3
Grafham Cambs............ 75 H2
Grafham Surrey............ 31 G3
Grafton N York............132 F6
Grafton Oxon................ 56 F7
Grafton Shrops............ 98 B8
Grafton Worcs.............. 71 H6
Grafton Flyford
      Worcs...................... 71 G4
Grafton Regis Nhants.... 73 L5
Grafton Underwood
      Nhants.................... 88 D7
Grafty Green Kent........ 34 B5
Graig Conwy................109 M6
Graig-fechan
      Denbgs.................... 97 J2
Grain Medway.............. 46 E5
Grainsby Lincs............118 C2
Grainthorpe Lincs........118 E3
Grampound Cnwll.......... 4 E6
Grampound Road
      Cnwll........................ 4 E5
Gramsdal W Isls..........233 c6
Gramsdale W Isls..........233 c6
Granborough Bucks...... 58 C3
Granby Notts................102 C5
Grandborough
      Warwks.................... 72 F2
Grand Chemins
      Jersey....................236 d7
Grandes Rocques
      Guern......................236 c2
Grandtully P & K..........194 E5
Grange Cumb..............137 H4
Grange Medway............ 46 D6
Grange P & K..............186 D3
Grange Crossroads
      Moray.....................215 K4
Grange Hall Moray......214 C3
Grangehall S Lans........165 J2
Grange Hill Essex........ 45 H2
Grangemill Derbys......100 E2
Grange Moor Kirk........123 J7
Grangemouth Falk......176 C3
Grange of Lindores
      Fife........................186 D4
Grange-over-Sands
      Cumb.....................129 J4
Grangepans Falk..........176 D3
Grangetown R & Cl......142 C3
Grangetown Sundld....151 K4
Grange Villa Dur..........151 K4
Gransmoor E R Yk......135 H7
Granston Pembks........ 64 C7
Grantchester Cambs.... 76 B4
Grantham Lincs............102 E5
Grantham
   Crematorium
      Lincs......................102 F5
Granton C Edin............177 H3
Grantown-on-Spey
      Highld....................214 C8
Grantshouse Border....179 G5
Grasby Lincs................117 H1
Grasmere Cumb..........137 K5
Grasscroft Oldham......113 L1
Grassendale Lpool......111 L4
Grassington N York......131 J6
Grassmoor Derbys......115 H7
Grassthorpe Notts......116 C7
Grateley Hants............ 28 F3
Graveley Cambs.......... 75 J2
Graveley Herts............ 59 L3
Graveney Kent.............. 34 E3
Gravesend Kent............ 46 A5
Gravir W Isls................232 f3
Grayingham Lincs........116 F3
Grayrigg Cumb............138 E7
Grays Thurr.................. 45 L4
Grayshott Hants.......... 30 E4
Grayswood Surrey...... 30 E4
Greasbrough Rothm....115 H3
Greasby Wirral............111 H4

Great Abington
      Cambs.................... 76 D5
Great Addington
      Nhants.................... 88 D7
Great Alne Warwks...... 71 K3
Great Altcar Lancs......111 K1
Great Amwell Herts...... 60 B5
Great Asby Cumb........138 F5
Great Ashfield Suffk.... 78 B2
Great Ayton N York......142 C5
Great Baddow Essex.... 61 H6
Great Badminton
      S Glos...................... 39 J4
Great Bardfield Essex.... 61 G2
Great Barford Bed........ 75 G4
Great Barr Sandw........ 85 J4
Great Barrington
      Gloucs.................... 56 E5
Great Barrow Ches W..112 C7
Great Barton Suffk...... 77 K2
Great Barugh N York..134 B4
Great Bavington
      Nthumb..................158 C6
Great Bealings Suffk.... 78 F5
Great Bedwyn Wilts...... 40 F7
Great Bentley Essex...... 62 D4
Great Billing Nhants...... 74 B3
Great Bircham Norfk...105 J6
Great Blakenham
      Suffk...................... 78 D4
Great Blencow Cumb..138 C2
Great Bolas Wrekin...... 98 F7
Great Bookham
      Surrey.................... 31 J1
Great Bourton Oxon.... 72 F5
Great Bowden Leics...... 87 L5
Great Bradley Suffk...... 76 F4
Great Braxted Essex...... 61 K5
Great Bricett Suffk...... 78 C4
Great Brickhill Bucks.... 58 E3
Great Bridgeford
      Staffs...................... 99 K6
Great Brington
      Nhants.................... 73 J2
Great Bromley Essex.... 62 C3
Great Broughton
      Cumb.....................136 E2
Great Broughton
      N York....................142 C6
Great Budworth
      Ches W....................112 F6
Great Burdon Darltn....141 H4
Great Burstead Essex.... 46 B2
Great Busby N York......142 B6
Great Carlton Lincs......118 E4
Great Casterton
      Rutlnd.................... 88 E2
Great Chalfield Wilts.... 39 K7
Great Chart Kent.......... 34 C6
Great Chatwell Staffs.... 84 E1
Great Chesterford
      Essex...................... 76 D6
Great Cheverell Wilts.... 27 M1
Great Chishill Cambs.... 76 B6
Great Clacton Essex.... 62 E5
Great Clifton Cumb......136 E2
Great Coates NE Lin....126 F8
Great Comberton
      Worcs...................... 71 G6
Great Corby Cumb......148 E4
Great Cornard Suffk...... 77 K6
Great Cowden E R Yk..126 F3
Great Coxwell Oxon...... 40 F2
Great Cransley
      Nhants.................... 88 B7
Great Cressingham
      Norfk...................... 91 J3
Great Crosthwaite
      Cumb.....................137 J3
Great Cubley Derbys..100 D5
Great Cumbrae
      Island N Ayrs..........173 K6
Great Dalby Leics........ 87 L2
Great Doddington
      Nhants.................... 74 C2
Great Dunham Norfk...91 K1

Great Dunmow Essex..... 61 G4
Great Durnford Wilts..... 28 C4
Great Easton Essex...... 60 F3
Great Easton Leics..... 88 B5
Great Eccleston Lancs.. 120 F3
Great Ellingham
　Norfk 92 B4
Great Elm Somset 27 H2
Great Everdon
　Nhants 73 H3
Great Eversden
　Cambs 75 L4
Great Fencote N York .. 132 D2
Great Finborough
　Suffk 78 B3
Greatford Lincs......... 88 F2
Great Fransham
　Norfk 91 K2
Great Gaddesden
　Herts 59 G5
Greatgate Staffs 100 B4
Great Gidding Cambs .. 89 G6
Great Givendale
　E R Yk 134 C8
Great Glemham Suffk ... 79 H3
Great Glen Leics....... 87 J4
Great Gonerby Lincs ... 102 E5
Great Gransden
　Cambs 75 J4
Great Green Cambs...... 75 K5
Great Green Suffk 77 K4
Great Habton N York .. 134 B4
Great Hale Lincs....... 103 J4
Great Hallingbury
　Essex 60 E4
Greatham Hants 30 C5
Greatham Hartpl 141 L2
Greatham W Susx 18 E3
Great Hampden
　Bucks 58 D7
Great Harrowden
　Nhants 74 C1
Great Harwood Lancs.. 121 L4
Great Haseley Oxon..... 57 M7
Great Hatfield E R Yk.. 126 F3
Great Haywood
　Staffs 99 M7
Great Heck N York 124 E6
Great Henny Essex...... 77 K6
Great Hinton Wilts 39 K8
Great Hockham Norfk... 91 L5
Great Holland Essex 62 E4
Great Hollands Br For.. 42 E6
Great Horkesley
　Essex 62 B2
Great Hormead Herts.... 60 C3
Great Horton C Brad ... 123 H4
Great Horwood Bucks.. 58 C2
Great Houghton
　Barns 115 H1
Great Houghton
　Nhants 73 L3
Great Hucklow
　Derbys 114 D6
Great Kelk E R Yk....... 135 H7
Great Kimble Bucks 58 D6
Great Kingshill Bucks.. 42 E2
Great Langdale Cumb.. 137 J6
Great Langton N York.. 141 H7
Great Leighs Essex...... 61 H4
Great Limber Lincs 126 E8
Great Linford M Keyn ... 74 C6
Great Livermere Suffk... 77 K1
Great Longstone
　Derbys 114 D6
Great Lumley Dur 151 H5
Great Malvern Worcs... 70 D5
Great Maplestead
　Essex 77 J7
Great Marton Bpool ... 120 D4
Great Massingham
　Norfk 105 J7
Great Milton Oxon 57 L7
Great Missenden
　Bucks 58 E7
Great Mitton Lancs 121 K3

Great Mongeham
　Kent 35 K4
Great Moulton Norfk.... 92 E5
Great Musgrave
　Cumb 139 H4
Great Ness Shrops...... 98 B8
Great Notley Essex...... 61 H4
Great Oak Mons........ 54 B6
Great Oakley Essex...... 62 E3
Great Oakley Nhants ... 88 C6
Great Offley Herts....... 59 J3
Great Ormside Cumb .. 139 G4
Great Orton Cumb 148 B4
Great Ouseburn
　N York 133 G6
Great Oxendon
　Nhants 87 K6
Great Oxney Green
　Essex 61 G6
Great Paxton Cambs ... 75 H2
Great Plumpton
　Lancs 120 E4
Great Plumstead
　Norfk 93 G2
Great Ponton Lincs 102 F6
Great Preston Leeds.... 124 B5
Great Raveley Cambs... 89 J7
Great Rissington
　Gloucs 56 D5
Great Rollright Oxon.... 56 F2
Great Ryburgh Norfk ... 106 A6
Great Ryton Shrops 83 J3
Great Saling Essex...... 61 H3
Great Salkeld Cumb... 148 F7
Great Sampford
　Essex 76 F7
Great Saughall
　Ches W 111 K7
Great Shefford
　W Berk 41 G5
Great Shelford Cambs... 76 C4
Great Smeaton
　N York 141 H6
Great Snoring Norfk.... 105 M5
Great Somerford
　Wilts 39 L4
Great Soudley Shrops... 99 G6
Great Stainton Darltn .. 141 H3
Great Stambridge
　Essex 46 E2
Great Staughton
　Cambs 75 G2
Great Steeping Lincs ... 118 F8
Great Stoke S Glos...... 38 F4
Greatstone-on-Sea
　Kent 21 L2
Great Strickland
　Cumb 138 D3
Great Stukeley
　Cambs 89 J8
Great Sturton Lincs..... 117 K6
Great Swinburne
　Nthumb 158 B6
Great Tew Oxon........ 57 H3
Great Tey Essex...... 61 L3
Great Thurlow Suffk.... 76 F4
Great Torrington
　Devon 23 H7
Great Tosson Nthumb.. 158 C3
Great Totham Essex..... 61 K5
Great Totham Essex..... 61 L5
Great Urswick Cumb... 129 G5
Great Wakering Essex.. 46 F3
Great Waldingfield
　Suffk 77 K5
Great Walsingham
　Norfk 105 M5
Great Waltham Essex.... 61 H5
Great Warley Essex 45 L2
Great Washbourne
　Gloucs 71 H7
Great Weeke Devon..... 11 G7
Great Weldon Nhants... 88 D5
Great Wenham Suffk... 78 C6
Great Whittington
　Nthumb 158 C7

Great Wigborough
　Essex 62 A5
Great Wilbraham
　Cambs 76 D3
Great Wishford Wilts ... 28 B4
Great Witcombe
　Gloucs 55 K5
Great Witley Worcs...... 70 D2
Great Wolford
　Warwks 72 B7
Greatworth Nhants 73 G6
Great Wratting Suffk.... 77 G5
Great Wymondley
　Herts 59 K3
Great Wyrley Staffs..... 85 H3
Great Yarmouth
　Norfk 93 L3
Great Yarmouth
　Crematorium
　　Norfk 93 K3
Great Yeldham Essex.... 77 H6
Greenburn W Loth 176 C6
Green End Herts......... 60 B2
Green End Herts......... 60 B4
Greenfield Ag & B..... 173 M1
Greenfield C Beds...... 74 F7
Greenfield Flints......... 111 H6
Greenfield Highld...... 201 J5
Greenfield Oldham..... 113 M2
Greenford Gt Lon 43 J4
Greengairs N Lans...... 175 K4
Greengates C Brad..... 123 J3
Greenham Somset 25 G7
Green Hammerton
　N York 133 G7
Greenhaugh Nthumb... 157 K5
Greenhead Nthumb..... 149 H3
Green Heath Staffs..... 85 H2
Greenhill D & G 155 J6
Greenhill Falk......... 175 L3
Greenhill Kent 47 K6
Greenhill S Lans....... 165 H3
Greenhithe Kent....... 45 L5
Greenholm E Ayrs..... 164 B3
Greenhouse Border ... 167 H5
Greenhow Hill N York... 131 L6
Greenland Highld...... 231 J3
Greenland Sheff....... 115 H4
Greenlaw Border 167 L1
Greenlea D & G 155 H6
Greenloaning P & K ... 185 H6
Greenmount Bury...... 122 B7
Greenock Inver....... 174 B3
Greenock
　Crematorium
　　Inver 174 B3
Greenodd Cumb....... 129 G3
Green Ore Somset..... 26 E2
Green Quarter Cumb... 138 C6
Greenshields S Lans... 165 K2
Greenside Gatesd..... 150 E3
Greenside Kirk....... 123 H7
Greens Norton
　Nhants 73 J4
Greenstead Green
　Essex 61 K3
Green Street Herts..... 59 K7
Green Street Herts..... 60 D4
Green Street Green
　Kent 45 L6
Green Tye Herts....... 60 C4
Greenway Somset..... 25 L6
Greenwich Gt Lon 45 G4
Greenwich Maritime
　Gt Lon 45 H4
Greet Gloucs....... 56 B3
Greete Shrops....... 69 L1
Greetham Lincs 118 D7
Greetham Rutlnd...... 88 D2
Greetland Calder..... 123 G6
Greinton Somset 26 B4
Grenaby IoM 237 b6
Grendon Nhants...... 74 C3
Grendon Warwks..... 86 C4
Grendon Underwood
　Bucks 58 B5

Grenoside Sheff........... 115 G3
Grenoside
　Crematorium
　　Sheff 114 F3
Greosabhagh W Isls.... 232 e4
Gresford Wrexhm....... 97 M2
Gresham Norfk......... 106 E5
Greshornish House
　Hotel Highld............ 208 E4
Gressenhall Norfk....... 91 L1
Gressenhall Green
　Norfk 91 L1
Gressingham Lancs..... 130 B5
Greta Bridge Dur....... 140 D5
Gretna D & G........ 148 B2
Gretna Green D & G... 148 B2
Gretna Services D & G.. 148 B2
Gretton Gloucs.......... 56 A2
Gretton Nhants........ 88 C5
Gretton Shrops....... 83 K4
Grewelthorpe N York.. 132 C4
Greyrigg D & G....... 155 J4
Greys Green Oxon...... 42 B4
Greysouthen Cumb.... 136 E2
Greystoke Cumb....... 138 B2
Greystone Angus..... 196 E7
Greywell Hants...... 30 B2
Griff Warwks....... 86 D5
Griffithstown Torfn..... 53 L7
Grimeford Village
　Lancs 121 J7
Grimesthorpe Sheff.... 115 G4
Grimethorpe Barns..... 124 C8
Grimley Worcs....... 70 E3
Grimmet S Ayrs....... 163 H7
Grimoldby Lincs....... 118 E4
Grimpo Shrops....... 98 A7
Grimsargh Lancs...... 121 H4
Grimsby NE Lin........ 127 G7
Grimsby
　Crematorium
　　NE Lin 118 C1
Grimscote Nhants..... 73 J4
Grimscott Cnwll....... 9 H4
Grimshader W Isls..... 232 f3
Grimsthorpe Lincs..... 103 H7
Grimston Leics....... 102 B7
Grimston Norfk....... 105 H7
Grimstone Dorset..... 14 C4
Grimstone End Suffk... 77 L2
Grindale E R Yk....... 135 H5
Grindleford Derbys..... 114 E6
Grindleton Lancs...... 121 L2
Grindley Brook
　Shrops 98 D4
Grindlow Derbys....... 114 D6
Grindon Staffs....... 100 B2
Gringley on the Hill
　Notts 116 C4
Grinsdale Cumb...... 148 C4
Grinshill Shrops....... 98 D7
Grinton N York....... 140 D7
Griomaisiader W Isls.. 232 f3
Griomsaigh W Isls..... 233 c6
Grishipoll Ag & B..... 188 F4
Gristhorpe N York..... 135 H3
Griston Norfk....... 91 L4
Gritley Ork....... 234 d6
Grittenham Wilts...... 40 B4
Grittleton Wilts....... 39 K4
Grizebeck Cumb...... 128 F3
Grizedale Cumb....... 137 K7
Groby Leics....... 87 G3
Groes Conwy....... 110 D8
Groes-faen Rhondd..... 37 G4
Groeslon Gwynd...... 95 H2
Groes-Wen Caerph..... 37 H3
Grogarry W Isls....... 233 b7
Grogport Ag & B..... 161 K1
Groigearraidh W Isls.. 233 b7
Gronant Flints....... 110 F5
Groombridge E Susx... 32 F5
Grosebay W Isls....... 232 e4
Grosmont Mons....... 54 B3
Grosmont N York..... 143 H6
Groton Suffk....... 77 L6

Grouville Jersey 236 e7
Grove Notts..................116 C5
Grove Oxon 41 H3
Grove Green Kent 33 K3
Grove Park Gt Lon.......45 H5
Grovesend Swans.........51 H5
Gruinard Highld 219 L4
Gruinart Ag & B..........170 F5
Grula Highld 208 F8
Grundisburgh Suffk....78 F4
Gruting Shet 235 c5
Gualachulain Highld ..192 B7
Guardbridge Fife 187 G4
Guarlford Worcs...........70 E5
Guay P & K....................194 F6
Guernsey Guern 236 c3
Guernsey Airport
  Guern 236 c3
Guestling Green
  E Susx 21 G3
Guestling Thorn
  E Susx 21 G3
Guestwick Norfk 106 C6
Guide Post Nthumb....159 G5
Guilden Morden
  Cambs 75 K5
Guilden Sutton
  Ches W 112 C7
Guildford Surrey..........31 G2
Guildford
  Crematorium
  Surrey 31 G3
Guildtown P & K..........186 B2
Guilsborough Nhants...87 J8
Guilsfield Powys...........82 E2
Guiltreehill S Ayrs 163 J7
Guineaford Devon 23 J4
Guisborough R & Cl ..142 D4
Guiseley Leeds 123 J3
Guist Norfk 106 B7
Guiting Power Gloucs...56 C3
Gulberwick Shet 235 d6
Gullane E Loth............178 B2
Gulval Cnwll 2 E5
Gulworthy Devon............6 C2
Gumfreston Pembks 49 J7
Gumley Leics 87 K5
Gunby Lincs................102 E7
Gunby Lincs................118 F7
Gundleton Hants 29 L5
Gun Hill E Susx 20 C3
Gunn Devon 23 K5
Gunnerside N York 139 L7
Gunnerton Nthumb....158 A7
Gunness N Linc 125 K7
Gunnislake Cnwll............6 C2
Gunnista Shet 235 d6
Gunthorpe N Linc......116 D3
Gunthorpe Norfk 106 B5
Gunthorpe Notts........102 B4
Gunwalloe Cnwll.............3 H6
Gurnard IoW 16 F4
Gurney Slade Somset ..26 F2
Gurnos Powys 52 B6
Gussage All Saints
  Dorset 15 J1
Gussage St Andrew
  Dorset 27 L8
Gussage St Michael
  Dorset 15 J1
Guston Kent 35 J5
Gutcher Shet 235 d2
Guthrie Angus............196 F6
Guyhirn Cambs 90 B3
Guyzance Nthumb......158 F2
Gwaenysgor Flints......110 F5
Gwalchmai IoA 108 E6
Gwaun-Cae-Gurwen
  Carmth 51 K3
Gweek Cnwll 3 J6
Gwenddwr Powys.........68 B6
Gwennap Cnwll 3 J4
Gwennap Mining
  District Cnwll 3 K3
Gwent Crematorium
  Mons 37 L2

Gwernaffield Flints......111 H7
Gwernesney Mons........54 B7
Gwernogle Carmth........66 C7
Gwernymynydd
  Flints 111 H8
Gwespyr Flints 110 F5
Gwinear Cnwll 3 G4
Gwithian Cnwll 3 G3
Gwyddelwern
  Denbgs 97 G3
Gwyddgrug Carmth......66 B7
Gwytherin Conwy 96 D1

H

Habberley Shrops 83 H3
Habberley Worcs...........84 E7
Habergham Lancs........122 B4
Habertoft Lincs 119 G7
Habrough NE Lin 126 E7
Hacconby Lincs...........103 J7
Haceby Lincs 103 G5
Hacheston Suffk...........79 G3
Hackbridge Gt Lon.......44 F6
Hackenthorpe Sheff...115 H5
Hackford Norfk 92 C3
Hackforth N York 132 C2
Hackland Ork 234 c5
Hackleton Nhants 74 B4
Hacklinge Kent.............35 J4
Hackness N York 134 F2
Hackney Gt Lon............45 G3
Hackthorn Lincs 117 G5
Hackthorpe Cumb......138 D3
Hadden Border 168 B3
Haddenham Bucks........58 C6
Haddenham Cambs......90 C7
Haddington E Loth......178 B4
Haddington Lincs........116 E8
Haddiscoe Norfk...........93 J4
Haddo Abers 216 F6
Haddon Cambs..............89 G5
Hadfield Derbys..........114 A3
Hadham Ford Herts......60 C4
Hadleigh Essex 46 D3
Hadleigh Suffk..............78 B6
Hadley Worcs.................70 F2
Hadley Wrekin 84 C2
Hadley End Staffs......100 C7
Hadley Wood Gt Lon....44 E1
Hadlow Kent 33 H3
Hadlow Down E Susx ..20 B2
Hadnall Shrops 98 D7
Hadrian's Wall 150 B2
Hadstock Essex 76 D5
Hadzor Worcs.................71 G3
Haggersta Shet 235 c5
Haggerston Nthumb...168 F2
Haggs Falk....................175 L3
Hagley Herefs 69 L6
Hagley Worcs.................85 G7
Hagworthingham
  Lincs 118 D7
Haile Cumb 136 E5
Hailey Oxon...................57 G5
Hailsham E Susx 20 C4
Hail Weston Cambs......75 H3
Hainault Gt Lon............45 J2
Hainford Norfk 106 F8
Hainton Lincs 117 K5
Haisthorpe E R Yk......135 H6
Hakin Pembks 48 F6
Halam Notts................102 B2
Halbeath Fife..............176 F1
Halberton Devon...........24 F8
Halcro Highld 231 J4
Hale Cumb 129 K4
Hale Halton 112 C5
Hale Hants 28 D7
Hale Surrey 30 D2
Hale Traffd 113 H4
Halebarns Traffd 113 H4
Hales Norfk 93 H4
Hales Staffs...................99 G5
Halesowen Dudley 85 G6

Hales Place Kent 34 F3
Hale Street Kent...........33 H4
Halesworth Suffk..........93 H7
Halewood Knows........112 C4
Halford Shrops 7 J2
Halford Warwks 72 C5
Halfpenny Green
  Staffs 84 E5
Halfway House
  Shrops 83 G2
Halfway Houses Kent....46 F5
Halifax Calder 123 G5
Halket E Ayrs 174 D7
Halkirk Highld 231 G4
Halkyn Flints 111 H7
Hall E Rens..................174 D7
Halland E Susx 20 A3
Hallaton Leics 87 L4
Hallatrow BaNES 38 F8
Hallbankgate Cumb ..149 G3
Hall Dunnerdale
  Cumb 137 H7
Hallen S Glos................38 D4
Hallgarth Dur..............151 H6
Hall Glen Falk 176 B3
Hall Green Birm 85 K7
Hallin Highld 208 D3
Halling Medway 46 B7
Hallington Lincs..........118 D4
Hallington Nthumb.....158 C6
Halliwell Bolton 121 K7
Halloughton Notts......102 B3
Hallow Worcs.................70 E3
Hall's Green Herts 59 L3
Hallyne Border 166 B2
Halmore Gloucs 55 G7
Halnaker W Susx...........18 B4
Halsall Lancs...............120 E7
Halse Nhants 73 H6
Halse Somset 25 H5
Halsetown Cnwll.............2 E4
Halsham E R Yk..........127 G5
Halstead Essex...............61 K2
Halstead Kent 45 J7
Halstead Leics 87 L3
Halstock Dorset 14 A2
Haltemprice
  Crematorium
  E R Yk 126 C4
Haltham Lincs 118 C8
Halton Bucks.................58 E6
Halton Halton..............112 D5
Halton Lancs 129 K6
Halton Leeds 123 L4
Halton Nthumb...........150 C2
Halton Wrexhm 97 L4
Halton East N York 131 K8
Halton Gill N York 131 G4
Halton Holegate Lincs.118 F7
Halton Lea Gate
  Nthumb 149 H4
Halton Shields
  Nthumb 150 C2
Halton West N York ...130 F8
Haltwhistle Nthumb...149 J3
Halvergate Norfk..........93 J3
Halwell Devon.................7 H5
Halwill Devon................10 C5
Halwill Junction
  Devon 10 C5
Ham Devon 13 G3
Ham Gloucs 55 G7
Ham Gt Lon...................44 D5
Ham Kent 35 J4
Ham Somset 25 L6
Ham Wilts 41 G7
Hambleden Bucks 42 C3
Hambledon Hants 29 M7
Hamble-le-Rice Hants..16 F2
Hambleton Lancs 120 E3
Hambleton N York 124 E4
Hambridge Somset 26 B6
Hambrook W Susx........17 L2
Hameringham Lincs 118 D7
Hamerton Cambs..........89 G7

Ham Green Worcs 71 H2
Hamilton S Lans...........175 J7
Hamilton Services
  S Lans 175 J6
Hamlet Dorset 14 B2
Hammersmith Gt Lon...44 E4
Hammerwich Staffs......85 J3
Hammoon Dorset 27 J8
Hamnavoe Shet 235 c6
Hampden Park E Susx...20 C5
Hampnett Gloucs 56 C5
Hampole Donc..............124 D7
Hampreston Dorset 15 K3
Hampstead Gt Lon........44 E3
Hampstead Norreys
  W Berk 41 K5
Hampsthwaite N York..132 C7
Hampton C Pete............89 H5
Hampton Gt Lon...........43 J6
Hampton Kent 47 K6
Hampton Shrops 84 D6
Hampton Swindn 40 D3
Hampton Worcs.............71 H5
Hampton Bishop
  Herefs 69 L6
Hampton Court
  Palace Gt Lon..............44 D6
Hampton Heath
  Ches W 98 D3
Hampton in Arden
  Solhll 86 B7
Hampton Lovett
  Worcs 70 F2
Hampton Lucy
  Warwks 72 B3
Hampton Magna
  Warwks 72 C2
Hampton Poyle Oxon....57 J5
Hampton Wick Gt Lon...44 D6
Hamptworth Wilts 28 E7
Hamsey E Susx..............19 L3
Hamstall Ridware
  Staffs 100 C8
Hamstead Marshall
  W Berk 41 H7
Hamsterley Dur...........140 E2
Hamsterley Dur...........150 E4
Hamstreet Kent............34 D7
Ham Street Somset......26 D4
Hamworthy Poole 15 J4
Hanbury Staffs............100 D6
Hanbury Worcs.............71 G2
Hanchurch Staffs 99 J4
Handa Island Highld ..228 A6
Hand and Pen Devon...12 D4
Handbridge Ches W....112 B7
Handcross W Susx.......31 L5
Handforth Ches E 113 J5
Handley Ches W 98 C2
Handley Derbys...........101 G1
Handsworth Birm 85 J5
Handsworth Sheff.......115 H4
Hanging Heaton Kirk..123 K6
Hanging Houghton
  Nhants 87 L8
Hanging Langford
  Wilts 28 B4
Hangleton Br & H.........19 H4
Hanham S Glos..............38 F6
Hankelow Ches E 98 F4
Hankerton Wilts 39 L3
Hanley C Stke...............99 K3
Hanley Castle Worcs....70 E6
Hanley Child Worcs......70 B2
Hanley Swan Worcs......70 E6
Hanley William Worcs...70 C2
Hanlith N York 131 G7
Hanmer Wrexhm 98 C4
Hannaford Devon 23 J5
Hannington Hants 29 K1
Hannington Nhants......74 B1
Hannington Swindn 40 D2
Hannington Wick
  Swindn 40 D2
Hanslope M Keyn.........74 B5
Hanthorpe Lincs..........103 H7

Hanwell Gt Lon 44 D4
Hanwell Oxon 72 E5
Hanwood Shrops 83 J2
Hanworth Gt Lon 43 J6
Hanworth Norfk............ 106 E5
Happendon S Lans 165 G3
Happisburgh Norfk..... 107 H6
Happisburgh
    Common Norfk 107 H6
Hapsford Ches W 112 C6
Hapton Lancs 122 B4
Hapton Norfk.................. 92 E4
Harberton Devon 7 H4
Harbertonford Devon 7 H5
Harbledown Kent 34 F3
Harborne Birm 85 H6
Harborough Magna
    Warwks 86 F7
Harbottle Nthumb...... 158 B2
Harbourneford
    Devon 7 G4
Harbury Warwks 72 D3
Harby Leics 102 C6
Harby Notts 116 E7
Harcombe Devon 11 K8
Harcombe Devon 12 F4
Harcombe Bottom
    Devon 13 J4
Harden C Brad 123 G3
Harden Wsall 85 H4
Hardenhuish Wilts 39 K5
Hardgate Abers 206 E5
Hardgate W Duns 174 F4
Hardham W Susx 18 E3
Hardingham Norfk........ 92 C3
Hardingstone Nhants.... 73 L3
Hardington Somset 27 H2
Hardington
    Mandeville
    Somset 13 M1
Hardington Marsh
    Somset 13 M1
Hardington Moor
    Somset 26 D8
Hardisworthy Devon.... 22 C7
Hardley Hants 16 E2
Hardley Street Norfk.... 93 H4
Hardraw N York............ 131 G2
Hardstoft Derbys 115 H8
Hardway Hants 17 H3
Hardway Somset............ 27 G5
Hardwick Bucks 58 D4
Hardwick Cambs............ 75 L3
Hardwick Nhants 74 B1
Hardwick Norfk.............. 92 F5
Hardwick Oxon................ 57 G6
Hardwick Oxon................ 57 L3
Hardwicke Gloucs 55 H5
Hardwicke Gloucs 55 K3
Hardwick Hall Dur 141 H2
Hardy's Green Essex 61 M4
Hare Croft C Brad 123 G4
Harefield Gt Lon 43 H3
Hare Green Essex 62 D3
Hare Hatch Wokham...... 42 D5
Harehill Derbys 100 D5
Harehills Leeds 123 L4
Harelaw Border 167 H5
Harelaw D & G 156 D6
Harescombe Gloucs...... 55 J6
Haresfield Gloucs 55 J6
Harestock Hants 29 J5
Hare Street Essex.......... 60 C6
Hare Street Herts 60 C3
Harewood Leeds 123 L2
Harewood End
    Herefs 54 D3
Harford Devon.................. 6 F4
Hargrave Ches W 98 C1
Hargrave Nhants 74 F1
Hargrave Suffk 77 H3
Harkstead Suffk 78 E7
Harlaston Staffs............ 86 B2
Harlaxton Lincs 102 E6
Harlech Gwynd 95 K6

Harlech Castle Gwynd 95 K6
Harlescott Shrops 83 K1
Harlesden Gt Lon............ 44 E4
Harlesthorpe Derbys .. 115 J6
Harleston Devon 7 J6
Harleston Norfk.............. 92 F6
Harleston Suffk 78 B3
Harlestone Nhants........ 73 K2
Harle Syke Lancs 122 C4
Harley Rothm 115 G2
Harley Shrops 83 L3
Harlington C Beds.......... 59 G2
Harlington Donc 115 J2
Harlington Gt Lon 43 H5
Harlosh Highld 208 D6
Harlow Essex 60 D6
Harlow Carr RHS
    N York......................... 132 D8
Harlow Hill Nthumb.... 150 D2
Harlthorpe E R Yk........ 125 H3
Harlton Cambs................ 76 B4
Harlyn Cnwll...................... 4 D2
Harman's Cross
    Dorset 15 J6
Harmby N York 131 L2
Harmer Green Herts...... 59 L5
Harmer Hill Shrops........ 98 C7
Harmston Lincs 116 F8
Harnage Shrops.............. 83 L3
Harnhill Gloucs.............. 56 B7
Harold Hill Gt Lon 45 K2
Haroldston West
    Pembks 48 E4
Haroldswick Shet........ 235 e1
Harold Wood Gt Lon 45 K3
Harome N York 133 K3
Harpenden Herts 59 J5
Harpford Devon.............. 12 E4
Harpham E R Yk............ 135 H7
Harpley Norfk 105 J7
Harpley Worcs 70 C3
Harpole Nhants 73 K3
Harpsdale Highld........ 231 G4
Harpswell Lincs 116 F4
Harpurhey Manch........ 113 K2
Harraby Cumb.............. 148 D4
Harracott Devon 23 J6
Harrapool Highld........ 199 K2
Harrietfield P & K........ 185 K2
Harrietsham Kent.......... 33 L3
Harringay Gt Lon............ 44 F3
Harrington Cumb........ 136 D3
Harrington Lincs 118 E6
Harrington Nhants........ 87 L7
Harringworth Nhants.... 88 D4
Harris W Isls................ 232 d4
Harrogate N York 132 D8
Harrogate
    Crematorium
    N York......................... 132 E8
Harrold Bed 74 D3
Harrow Gt Lon 44 D3
Harrowbarrow Cnwll 6 B2
Harrow Green Suffk........ 77 J4
Harrow on the Hill
    Gt Lon 44 D3
Harrow Weald Gt Lon.... 44 D2
Harston Cambs................ 76 B4
Harston Leics 102 D6
Harswell E R Yk............ 125 J3
Hart Hartpl.................... 151 L7
Hartburn Nthumb........ 158 D5
Hartest Suffk 77 J4
Hartfield E Susx 32 E6
Hartford Cambs.............. 89 J8
Hartford Ches W 112 F6
Hartfordbridge Hants .. 42 C8
Hartford End Essex........ 61 G4
Harthill N York 140 F6
Harthill Ches W 98 D7
Harthill N Lans 176 B5
Harthill Rothm.............. 115 J5
Hartington Derbys 100 C1
Hartland Devon 22 D6
Hartland Quay Devon.. 22 C6

Hartlebury Worcs.......... 70 E1
Hartlepool Hartpl 151 L7
Hartlepool
    Crematorium
    Hartpl 142 B2
Hartley Cumb 139 H5
Hartley Kent.................... 33 K6
Hartley Kent.................... 45 L6
Hartley Wespall
    Hants 42 B8
Hartley Wintney
    Hants 30 C1
Hartlip Kent.................... 46 D7
Harton N York 133 L6
Harton S Tyne 151 J2
Hartpury Gloucs 55 J3
Hartshead Kirk............ 123 J6
Hartshead Moor
    Services Calder 123 H5
Hartshill C Stke 99 K4
Hartshill Warwks 86 D5
Hartshorne Derbys 100 F7
Hartwell Nhants 73 L4
Hartwith N York 132 C6
Hartwood N Lans 175 L6
Hartwoodmyres
    Border 166 F4
Harvel Kent.................... 46 A7
Harvington Worcs.......... 71 J5
Harvington Worcs.......... 84 F8
Harwell Notts 116 B3
Harwell Oxon.................. 41 J3
Harwich Essex 62 F2
Harwood Dale N York .. 143 K7
Harwood Park
    Crematorium
    Herts............................ 59 L4
Harworth Notts............ 115 L3
Hasbury Dudley 85 G6
Hascombe Surrey.......... 31 G4
Haselbech Nhants........ 87 K7
Haselbury Plucknett
    Somset 13 L1
Haseley Warwks 72 B2
Haselor Warwks 71 K3
Hasfield Gloucs 55 J3
Haskayne Lancs 120 E8
Hasketon Suffk 78 F4
Haslemere Surrey.......... 30 E5
Haslingden Lancs 122 B6
Haslingfield Cambs...... 76 B4
Haslington Ches E.......... 99 G2
Hassingham Norfk........ 93 H3
Hassocks W Susx 19 J3
Hassop Derbys 114 E6
Haster Highld 231 K5
Hastingleigh Kent.......... 34 E5
Hastings E Susx 21 G4
Hastings Borough
    Crematorium
    E Susx 21 G3
Hastingwood Essex...... 60 D6
Hastoe Herts.................. 58 F6
Haswell Dur 151 J6
Haswell Plough Dur 151 J6
Hatch Beauchamp
    Somset 25 L7
Hatch End Gt Lon 43 J3
Hatchmere Ches W 112 D6
Hatcliffe NE Lin............ 117 K2
Hatfield Donc 125 G8
Hatfield Herefs 69 L3
Hatfield Herts 59 L6
Hatfield Broad Oak
    Essex 60 E5
Hatfield Heath Essex.... 60 E5
Hatfield Peverel
    Essex 61 J5
Hatfield Woodhouse
    Donc.......................... 125 G8
Hatford Oxon.................. 41 G2
Hatherden Hants............ 29 G2
Hatherleigh Devon 10 D4
Hathern Leics 101 J7
Hatherop Gloucs 56 D6
Hathersage Derbys 114 E5

Hathersage Booths
    Derbys 114 E5
Hatherton Ches E.......... 99 G3
Hatherton Staffs............ 85 G2
Hatley St George
    Cambs 75 K4
Hatt Cnwll 6 B4
Hattersley Tamesd...... 113 M3
Hatton Abers 217 K6
Hatton Angus 196 D7
Hatton Derbys 100 E6
Hatton Gt Lon 43 J5
Hatton Lincs 117 K6
Hatton Shrops 83 J5
Hatton Warrtn 112 E5
Hatton Warwks 72 B2
Hatton of Fintray
    Abers 206 F3
Haugh E Ayrs................ 163 L4
Haugham Lincs 118 D5
Haughhead E Duns...... 175 G3
Haughley Suffk................ 78 B3
Haughley Green Suffk.... 78 B2
Haugh of Glass Moray .. 215 J6
Haugh of Urr D & G...... 146 E2
Haughs of Kinnaird
    Angus 197 G5
Haughton Shrops.......... 98 B6
Haughton Staffs............ 99 K7
Haughton le Skerne
    Darltn 141 H4
Haughton Moss
    Ches E 98 E2
Haultwick Herts 60 B4
Haunton Staffs 86 B2
Hauxton Cambs.............. 76 B4
Havant Hants 17 K2
Havant Crematorium
    Hants............................ 17 K2
Havenstreet IoW 17 G4
Havercroft Wakefd 124 B7
Haverfordwest
    Pembks 48 F4
Haverhill Suffk 76 F5
Haverigg Cumb............ 128 E4
Havering-atte-
    Bower Gt Lon............ 45 K2
Haversham M Keyn........ 74 B6
Haverthwaite Cumb .. 129 H3
Havyat N Som.................. 38 C7
Hawarden Flints.......... 111 J7
Hawbush Green
    Essex 61 J4
Hawen Cerdgn.............. 65 K5
Hawes N York 131 G2
Hawe's Green Norfk...... 92 F4
Hawford Worcs 70 E3
Hawick Border 167 G6
Hawkchurch Devon...... 13 J3
Hawkedon Suffk 77 H4
Hawkeridge Wilts.......... 27 K2
Hawkesbury S Glos 39 H3
Hawkesbury Upton
    S Glos 39 H3
Hawkhurst Kent............ 33 K6
Hawkinge Kent.............. 35 G6
Hawkinge
    Crematorium
    Kent.............................. 35 G6
Hawkley Hants 30 C5
Hawkridge Somset 24 D5
Hawkshead Cumb 137 K7
Hawkshead Hill
    Cumb 137 K7
Hawksland S Lans 165 G2
Hawkstone Shrops........ 98 E6
Hawkswick N York 131 H5
Hawksworth Leeds...... 123 H3
Hawksworth Notts...... 102 C4
Hawkwell Essex.............. 46 E2
Hawley Hants 42 E8
Hawling Gloucs 56 B4
Hawnby N York 133 H2
Haworth C Brad.............. 122 F3
Hawstead Suffk 77 J3
Hawthorn Dur 151 K5

Hawthorn Hill Lincs 103 K2
Hawton Notts................102 C3
Haxby C York................133 J7
Haxey N Linc 116 C2
Haycombe
  Crematorium
  BaNES 39 G7
Haydock St Hel............112 E3
Haydon Bridge
  Nthumb 149 L3
Haydon Wick
  Swindn 40 C3
Hayes Gt Lon................43 J4
Hayes Gt Lon................45 H6
Hayes End Gt Lon........43 H4
Hayfield Ag & B............182 F3
Hayfield Derbys............114 B4
Hayhillock Angus........196 E7
Hayle Cnwll....................2 F4
Hayle Port Cnwll..............2 F4
Hayley Green Dudley....85 G6
Hayling Island Hants......17 K3
Hayne Devon................11 H7
Haynes (Church End)
  C Beds 74 F6
Haynes (Northwood
  End) C Beds 75 G6
Haynes (Silver End)
  C Beds 75 G6
Haynes (West End)
  C Beds 74 F6
Hay-on-Wye Powys........68 G6
Hayscastle Pembks........48 F3
Hayscastle Cross
  Pembks......................48 F3
Hay Street Herts............60 C3
Hayton Cumb................147 K6
Hayton Cumb................148 E4
Hayton E R Yk................125 J2
Hayton Notts................116 B5
Haytor Vale Devon..........7 H1
Haytown Devon..............9 K3
Haywards Heath
  W Susx 19 J2
Haywood Donc............124 E7
Hazelbank S Lans........165 G1
Hazelbury Bryan
  Dorset 14 E2
Hazeleigh Essex............61 K7
Hazel Grove Stockp......113 L4
Hazelton Walls Fife......186 E6
Hazelwood Derbys........101 G4
Hazlemere Bucks..........42 E2
Hazlerigg N u Ty............159 G7
Hazleton Gloucs............56 B4
Heacham Norfk............105 G5
Headbourne Worthy
  Hants 29 J5
Headcorn Kent..............33 L4
Headingley Leeds........123 K4
Headington Oxon..........57 K6
Headlam Dur................140 F4
Headlesscross N Lans..176 B6
Headless Cross
  Worcs........................71 J2
Headley Hants................30 D4
Headley Hants................41 K7
Headley Surrey 31 K1
Headley Down Hants....30 D4
Headon Notts................116 C6
Heads Nook Cumb........148 E4
Heage Derbys................101 D2
Healaugh N York..........124 D2
Healaugh N York..........140 C7
Heald Green Stockp......113 J4
Heale Somset................25 K7
Heale Somset................26 B6
Healey N York..............132 B4
Healeyfield Dur............150 D5
Healing NE Lin..............126 F7
Heamoor Cnwll..............2 E5
Heanor Derbys..............101 H3
Heanton
  Punchardon
  Devon........................23 H4
Heapham Lincs............116 E4

Heart of England
  Crematorium
  Warwks......................86 E5
Heart of Scotland
  Services N Lans *176 B5*
Heasley Mill Devon........24 B5
Heast Highld................199 K2
Heath Derbys................115 J7
Heath Wakefd..............123 L6
Heath and Reach
  C Beds 58 F3
Heathcote Derbys........100 D1
Heather Leics................86 E2
Heathfield E Susx..........20 C2
Heathfield Somset........25 J6
Heath Green Worcs........71 J1
Heath Hall D & G..........155 H6
Heath Hayes &
  Wimblebury Staffs..85 H2
Heath Hill Shrops..........84 D2
Heathrow Airport
  Gt Lon *43 H5*
Heathton Shrops............84 E5
Heath Town Wolves......85 G4
Heatley Warrtn............113 G4
Heaton C Brad..............123 H4
Heaton N u Ty..............151 G2
Heaton Staffs..............113 L8
Heaton's Bridge
  Lancs........................120 E7
Heaverham Kent............33 G2
Heavitree Devon............12 B4
Hebburn S Tyne............151 H3
Hebden N York..............131 J6
Hebden Bridge Calder..122 E5
Hebing End Herts..........60 A4
Hebron Carmth..............49 K3
Hebron Nthumb............158 F4
Heckfield Hants............42 B7
Heckfield Green Suffk....92 E7
Heckfordbridge
  Essex........................61 M4
Heckington Lincs..........103 J4
Heckmondwike Kirk....123 J5
Heddington Wilts..........39 M6
Heddon-on-the-Wall
  Nthumb 150 E2
Hedenham Norfk............93 G5
Hedge End Hants..........29 J8
Hedgerley Bucks..........42 F3
Hedging Somset............25 L5
Hedley on the Hill
  Nthumb 150 D3
Hednesford Staffs..........85 H2
Hedon E R Yk................126 F5
Hedsor Bucks................42 E3
Heglibister Shet............235 c5
Heighington Darltn......141 G3
Heighington Lincs........117 G7
Heightington Worcs........70 D1
Heiton Border..............167 L4
Hele Devon....................12 C2
Hele Devon....................23 H3
Helensburgh Ag & B....174 B2
Helenton S Ayrs............163 K3
Helford Cnwll..................3 K6
Helford Passage
  Cnwll..........................3 K6
Helhoughton Norfk......105 K7
Helions Bumpstead
  Essex........................76 F6
Helland Cnwll..................5 G2
Hellescott Cnwll..............5 L3
Hellesdon Norfk............92 E2
Hellidon Nhants............73 G3
Hellifield N York..........131 G7
Hellingly E Susx............20 C4
Helmdon Nhants............73 H5
Helme Kirk....................123 G7
Helmingham Suffk........78 E3
Helmsdale Highld........227 H5
Helmshore Lancs..........122 B6
Helmsley N York..........133 J3
Helperby N York..........133 G5
Helperthorpe N York....134 E5
Helpringham Lincs........103 J4

Helpston C Pete............89 G3
Helsby Ches W..............112 C6
Helston Cnwll..................3 H5
Helstone Cnwll................8 E8
Helton Cumb................138 D3
Hemel Hempstead
  Herts..........................59 H6
Hemerdon Devon............6 E4
Hemingbrough
  N York......................125 G4
Hemingby Lincs............118 C6
Hemingford Abbots
  Cambs........................75 K1
Hemingford Grey
  Cambs........................75 K1
Hemingstone Suffk........78 D4
Hemington Leics..........101 J6
Hemington Nhants........88 F6
Hemington Somset........27 G2
Hemley Suffk................79 G6
Hemlington Middsb......142 B4
Hempnall Norfk............92 F5
Hempnall Green
  Norfk........................92 F5
Hempriggs Moray........214 D2
Hempstead Essex..........76 F6
Hempstead Norfk........106 D5
Hempstead Norfk........107 J6
Hempton Norfk............105 L6
Hempton Oxon..............57 H2
Hemsby Norfk..............107 K8
Hemswell Lincs............116 F4
Hemswell Cliff Lincs....116 F4
Hemsworth Wakefd......124 C7
Hemyock Devon............25 H8
Henbury Bristl..............38 E5
Hendon Gt Lon..............44 E3
Hendon Sundld............151 K4
Hendon
  Crematorium
  Gt Lon........................44 E2
Hendy Carmth..............51 H5
Henfield W Susx............19 G3
Hengoed Caerph............37 J2
Hengoed Powys............68 E4
Hengrave Suffk............77 J2
Henham Essex..............60 E3
Heniarth Powys............82 C2
Henlade Somset............25 L6
Henley Dorset................14 D2
Henley Somset..............26 B5
Henley Suffk................78 E4
Henley W Susx..............30 E6
Henley-in-Arden
  Warwks......................71 L2
Henley-on-Thames
  Oxon..........................42 C4
Henley's Down E Susx..20 E3
Henllan Cerdgn............65 K6
Henllan Denbgs............110 E7
Henllys Torfn................37 K3
Henlow C Beds..............75 H5
Hennock Devon..............11 J8
Henny Street Essex........77 K6
Henryd Conwy..............109 L6
Henry's Moat (Castell
  Hendre) Pembks......49 H3
Hensall N York..............124 F5
Henshaw Nthumb........149 K3
Hensingham Cumb......136 D4
Henstead Suffk..............93 K6
Hensting Hants..............29 J6
Henstridge Somset........27 G7
Henstridge Ash
  Somset......................27 G7
Henton Oxon................58 C7
Henton Somset..............26 C3
Henwick Worcs..............70 E4
Henwood Cnwll..............5 L2
Heol-y-Cyw Brdgnd......36 E4
Hepple Nthumb............158 C2
Hepscott Nthumb........158 F5
Heptonstall Calder......122 E5
Hepworth Kirk............114 D1
Hepworth Suffk............92 B8
Herbrandston
  Pembks......................48 E6

Hereford Herefs............69 K6
Hereford
  Crematorium
  Herefs........................69 J6
Hereson Kent................35 K2
Heribusta Highld..........218 B7
Heriot Border................177 L7
Hermiston C Edin........177 G4
Hermitage Border........156 E3
Hermitage Dorset..........14 C2
Hermitage W Berk..........41 J5
Hermon Carmth............65 K7
Hermon Pembks............49 L2
Herne Kent....................47 K6
Herne Bay Kent............47 K6
Herne Hill Gt Lon..........44 F5
Herne Pound Kent........33 H3
Hernhill Kent..................34 E3
Herodsfoot Cnwll............5 K4
Heronsford S Ayrs........152 D5
Herriard Hants................30 A3
Herringfleet Suffk..........93 K4
Herringswell Suffk........77 G1
Herringthorpe Rothm..115 J3
Herrington Sundld........151 J4
Hersden Kent................35 G3
Hersham Surrey............43 J7
Herstmonceux E Susx....20 D3
Herston Ork..................234 c7
Hertford Herts................60 B5
Hertford Heath Herts....60 B5
Hertingfordbury
  Herts..........................60 A5
Hesketh Bank Lancs....120 F5
Hesketh Lane Lancs....121 J3
Hesket Newmarket
  Cumb........................148 C7
Hesleden Dur................151 K7
Heslington C York........124 F1
Hessay C York..............133 H8
Hessenford Cnwll............5 L4
Hessett Suffk................77 L3
Hessle E R Yk................126 C5
Hessle Wakefd..............124 C6
Hest Bank Lancs..........129 K6
Heston Gt Lon..............43 J5
Heston Services
  Gt Lon........................*43 J5*
Hestwall Ork................234 b5
Heswall Wirral..............111 J5
Hethe Oxon....................57 L3
Hethersett Norfk............92 D3
Hethersgill Cumb..........148 E2
Hett Dur........................151 G7
Hetton N York..............131 H7
Hetton-le-Hole
  Sundld......................151 J5
Heugh Nthumb............158 D7
Heughhead Abers........205 J3
Heugh Head Border......179 H6
Heveningham Suffk........93 G8
Hever Kent....................32 E4
Heversham Cumb..........129 K3
Hevingham Norfk........106 E7
Hewas Water Cnwll........4 F6
Hewelsfield Gloucs........54 E7
Hewish Somset..............13 K2
Hewood Dorset..............13 J2
Hexham Nthumb..........150 B3
Hextable Kent................45 K6
Hexthorpe Donc............115 K2
Hexton Herts..................59 J2
Hexworthy Cnwll............9 K8
Hexworthy Devon............6 F2
Heybridge Essex............61 G7
Heybridge Essex............61 K6
Heybrook Bay Devon......6 D6
Heydon Cambs..............76 B6
Heydon Norfk..............106 D6
Heydour Lincs..............103 G5
Heylipoll Ag & B............188 C2
Heylor Shet..................235 c3
Heysham Lancs..............129 J7
Heyshott W Susx............18 B3
Heytesbury Wilts..........27 L3
Heythrop Oxon..............57 G3

Heywood Rochdl.............122 C7
Heywood Wilts.............27 K2
Hibaldstow N Linc.........116 F2
Hickleton Donc...........115 J1
Hickling Norfk...........107 J7
Hickling Notts..........102 B6
Hickling Green Norfk....107 J7
Hickstead W Susx..........31 L7
Hidcote Bartrim
  Gloucs....................71 L6
Hidcote Boyce Gloucs....71 L6
High Ackworth
  Wakefd...................124 C6
Higham Barns.............114 F1
Higham Derbys............101 H2
Higham Kent...............33 G4
Higham Kent...............46 B5
Higham Lancs.............122 B3
Higham Suffk..............77 H2
Higham Suffk..............78 B7
Higham Ferrers
  Nhants....................74 D2
Higham Gobion
  C Beds....................59 J2
Higham Hill Gt Lon........45 G3
Higham on the Hill
  Leics.....................86 E4
Highampton Devon..........10 C4
Highams Park Gt Lon.......45 H2
High Ardwell D & G.......144 C6
High Auldgirth D & G....154 F5
High Bankhill Cumb.......148 F6
High Beach Essex..........60 C7
High Bentham N York......130 C5
High Bickington
  Devon.....................23 J7
High Biggins Cumb........130 B4
High Blantyre S Lans....175 J6
High Bonnybridge
  Falk......................175 L3
High Bray Devon...........23 L5
Highbridge Somset.........25 L3
Highbrook W Susx..........32 C7
High Brooms Kent..........33 G5
Highburton Kent..........123 J7
Highbury Gt Lon...........44 F3
Highbury Somset...........27 G2
High Casterton Cumb.....130 C4
High Catton E R Yk......133 L8
Highclere Hants...........41 H8
Highcliffe Dorset.........16 B4
High Coniscliffe
  Darltn...................141 G4
High Crosby Cumb.........148 E3
High Cross E Ayrs........163 K1
High Cross Hants..........30 B5
High Cross Herts..........60 B4
High Cross Warwks.........71 L2
High Drummore
  D & G....................144 D7
High Easter Essex.........60 F5
High Ellington N York...132 B3
Higher Ansty Dorset......14 E2
Higher Bartle Lancs.....121 G4
Higher
  Bockhampton
    Dorset.................14 D4
Higher Brixham
  Torbay.....................7 L5
High Ercall Wrekin.......98 E8
Higher Chillington
  Somset....................13 K1
Higher Folds Wigan......113 G2
Higher Gabwell
  Devon......................7 L3
Higher Heysham
  Lancs....................129 J7
Higher Irlam Salfd......113 G3
Higher Kinnerton
  Flints....................97 L1
Higher Muddiford
  Devon.....................23 J4
Higher Penwortham
  Lancs....................121 G5
Higher Prestacott
  Devon......................9 K5

Higher Town Cnwll..........4 C6
Higher Town Cnwll..........4 F4
Higher Town IoS............2 b1
Higher Walton Lancs.....121 H5
Higher Walton Warrtn...112 E4
Higher Wambrook
  Somset....................13 H2
Higher Waterston
  Dorset....................14 D4
Higher Wheelton
  Lancs....................121 J6
Higher Whitley
  Ches W...................112 F5
Higher Wincham
  Ches W...................113 G6
Higher Wraxhall
  Dorset....................14 B3
Higher Wych Ches W........98 C4
High Etherley Dur.......140 F2
Highfield Gatesd........150 E3
Highfield N Ayrs........174 C7
High Garrett Essex........61 J3
Highgate Gt Lon...........44 F3
High Grantley N York....132 C5
High Green Norfk..........92 D3
High Green Norfk..........92 E5
High Green Sheff........115 G3
High Halden Kent..........34 B7
High Halstow
  Medway....................46 C5
High Ham Somset...........26 B5
High Harrogate
  N York...................132 D7
High Hatton Shrops........98 E7
High Hauxley
  Nthumb...................159 G2
High Hawsker N York.....143 J5
High Hesket Cumb........148 E6
High Hoyland Barns......123 K8
High Hurstwood
  E Susx....................32 E7
High Hutton N York......134 B5
High Ireby Cumb.........147 M7
High Kilburn N York.....133 H4
High Lands Dur..........140 E3
Highlane Derbys.........115 H5
High Lane Stockp........113 L4
High Lanes Cnwll...........3 G4
Highleadon Gloucs.........55 H4
High Legh Ches E........113 G5
Highleigh W Susx..........18 A6
High Leven S on T.......141 K5
Highley Shrops............84 D6
High Littleton BaNES......38 F8
High Lorton Cumb........137 G3
High Marnham Notts.....116 D7
High Melton Donc........115 K2
High Mickley Nthumb....150 D3
Highmoor Oxon.............42 B4
Highmoor Cross Oxon.....42 B4
Highnam Gloucs............55 H4
High Newport Sundld....151 J4
High Newton Cumb........129 J3
High Nibthwaite
  Cumb.....................129 G2
High Offley Staffs........99 H7
High Ongar Essex..........60 E7
High Onn Staffs...........84 E1
High Park Corner
  Essex.....................62 C4
High Pennyvenie
  E Ayrs...................163 L7
High Roding Essex.........60 F4
High Salvington
  W Susx....................18 F4
High Spen Gatesd........150 E3
Highsted Kent.............34 B3
High Street Cnwll..........4 F5
Highstreet Kent...........34 E3
Highstreet Green
  Surrey....................31 G4
Hightae D & G...........155 J6
Hightown Sefton.........111 J2
Hightown Green
  Suffk.....................77 L4
High Toynton Lincs......118 C7

High Valleyfield Fife...176 D2
Highweek Devon.............7 J2
Highwood Hill Gt Lon.....44 E2
Highworth Swindn..........40 D2
High Wray Cumb..........137 K7
High Wych Herts...........60 D5
High Wycombe Bucks......42 E2
Hilborough Norfk..........91 J4
Hilcott Wilts.............40 C8
Hildenborough Kent.......32 F4
Hilden Park Kent..........33 G4
Hildersham Cambs..........76 D5
Hilderstone Staffs........99 L5
Hilderthorpe E R Yk.....135 J6
Hilgay Norfk..............90 E4
Hill S Glos...............38 F2
Hill Warwks...............72 F2
Hillam N York............124 D5
Hill Brow Hants...........30 C6
Hillbutts Dorset..........15 J3
Hill Chorlton Staffs......99 H5
Hillcliffane Derbys......100 F3
Hill Common Somset........25 H6
Hilldyke Lincs...........104 B3
Hillend Fife............176 F2
Hill End Fife...........185 L7
Hill End Gloucs...........70 F6
Hillend Mdloth..........177 H5
Hillend N Lans..........175 L5
Hillesden Bucks...........58 B3
Hillesley Gloucs..........39 H3
Hillfarrance Somset.......25 J6
Hill Green Kent...........46 B7
Hill Head Hants...........17 G2
Hillhead S Lans.........165 J2
Hillhead of Cocklaw
  Abers....................217 K5
Hilliclay Highld........231 H3
Hillington C Glas.......174 F5
Hillington Norfk.........105 H7
Hillmorton Warwks.........87 G8
Hill of Beath Fife......176 F1
Hill of Fearn Highld....223 H5
Hillowton D & G.........146 D3
Hill Ridware Staffs.....100 B8
Hillside Abers..........207 H5
Hillside Angus..........197 H4
Hill Side Kirk..........123 H6
Hills Town Derbys.......115 J7
Hillstreet Hants..........29 G7
Hillswick Shet..........235 c3
Hill Top Wakefd.........123 L7
Hillwell Shet...........235 c8
Hilmarton Wilts...........40 A5
Hilperton Wilts...........39 K8
Hilsea C Port.............17 J2
Hilston E R Yk..........127 G4
Hilton Border...........179 H7
Hilton Cambs..............75 K2
Hilton Cumb.............139 G3
Hilton Derbys...........100 E6
Hilton Dorset.............14 E2
Hilton Dur..............140 F3
Hilton Highld...........223 J6
Hilton S on T...........141 K5
Hilton Shrops............84 D4
Hilton Park Services
  Staffs....................85 G3
Himbleton Worcs...........71 G3
Himley Staffs.............84 F5
Hincaster Cumb..........129 L3
Hinchley Wood
  Surrey....................44 D6
Hinckley Leics............86 E5
Hinderclay Suffk..........92 B7
Hinderwell N York.......143 G4
Hindhead Surrey...........30 E4
Hindley Wigan...........112 F1
Hindlip Worcs.............70 F3
Hindolveston Norfk......106 C6
Hindon Wilts..............27 K5
Hindringham Norfk.......106 B5
Hingham Norfk............92 B3
Hinstock Shrops...........99 G7

Hintlesham Suffk..........78 C5
Hinton Herefs.............69 G6
Hinton S Glos.............39 G5
Hinton Shrops.............83 H2
Hinton Ampner Hants.....29 L6
Hinton Blewett
  BaNES.....................26 E1
Hinton Charterhouse
  BaNES.....................39 H8
Hinton-in-the-
  Hedges Nhants............73 H6
Hinton Martell Dorset....15 J2
Hinton on the Green
  Worcs.....................71 H6
Hinton Parva Swindn......40 E4
Hinton St George
  Somset....................26 B8
Hinton St Mary
  Dorset....................27 H7
Hinton Waldrist Oxon.....57 G7
Hints Staffs..............85 L3
Hinwick Bed..............74 D3
Hinxhill Kent.............34 D6
Hinxton Cambs.............76 C5
Hinxworth Herts..........75 J6
Hipperholme Calder.....123 H5
Hipswell N York.........140 F7
Hirn Abers..............206 D5
Hirnant Powys.............97 G7
Hirst Nthumb............159 G5
Hirst Courtney N York..124 F7
Hirwaun Rhondd............52 E6
Hiscott Devon.............23 J6
Histon Cambs..............76 B2
Hitcham Suffk.............78 B4
Hitcham Causeway
  Suffk.....................78 B4
Hitcham Street Suffk.....78 B4
Hitchin Herts.............59 K3
Hither Green Gt Lon......45 H5
Hittisleigh Devon.........11 H5
Hive E R Yk.............125 J4
Hixon Staffs............100 A7
Hoaden Kent...............35 H3
Hoar Cross Staffs........100 C7
Hoarwithy Herefs..........54 D3
Hoath Kent...............47 K7
Hobarris Shrops...........82 F7
Hobkirk Border..........167 J7
Hobson Dur..............150 F4
Hoby Leics..............102 A8
Hockering Norfk...........92 C2
Hockerton Notts.........102 B2
Hockley Essex.............46 D2
Hockley Heath Solhll.....85 L8
Hockliffe C Beds..........58 F3
Hockwold cum
  Wilton....................91 G6
Hockworthy Devon.........25 G7
Hoddesdon Herts..........60 B6
Hoddlesden Bl w D.......121 L6
Hoddom Cross D & G......155 L7
Hoddom Mains D & G.....155 K7
Hodgeston Pembks.........49 H7
Hodnet Shrops............98 E6
Hodsock Notts...........115 L4
Hodsoll Street Kent......45 M7
Hodson Swindn............40 D4
Hodthorpe Derbys........115 K6
Hoe Norfk................92 B1
Hogben's Hill Kent.......34 D4
Hoggeston Bucks...........58 D3
Hoggrill's End Warwks....86 B5
Hoghton Lancs...........121 J5
Hognaston Derbys........100 E3
Hogsthorpe Lincs........119 H6
Holbeach Lincs..........104 B7
Holbeach Bank Lincs.....104 B6
Holbeach Clough
  Lincs....................104 B6
Holbeach Drove Lincs....89 K2
Holbeach Hurn Lincs....104 C6
Holbeach St Johns
  Lincs....................104 B8
Holbeach St Mark's
  Lincs....................104 B6

Holbeach
St Matthew Lincs 104 C6
Holbeck Notts.................. 115 K6
Holberrow Green
Worcs 71 K3
Holbeton Devon 6 F5
Holborn Gt Lon................ 44 F4
Holbrook Derbys 101 G4
Holbrook Suffk 78 E6
Holbrooks Covtry.......... 86 D6
Holbury Hants................ 16 E2
Holcombe Devon 12 B7
Holcombe Somset.......... 26 F2
Holcombe Rogus
Devon 25 G7
Holcot Nhants................ 73 L1
Holden Lancs................ 122 B1
Holdenby Nhants............ 73 K2
Holder's Green Essex.... 61 G3
Holdgate Shrops 83 L5
Holdingham Lincs........ 103 H3
Holditch Dorset............ 13 J2
Holemoor Devon 10 B4
Holford Somset 25 J3
Holgate C York.............. 124 E1
Holker Cumb................ 129 H4
Holkham Norfk............ 105 L4
Hollacombe Devon 9 K4
Holland Fen Lincs........ 103 L3
Holland-on-Sea Essex.... 62 E5
Hollandstoun Ork........ 234 e3
Hollee D & G 148 A2
Hollesley Suffk.............. 79 H5
Hollicombe Torbay 7 K4
Hollingbourne Kent...... 33 L3
Hollingbury Br & H........ 19 J4
Hollingdon Bucks.......... 58 E3
Hollington Derbys........ 100 E5
Hollington Staffs.......... 100 B5
Hollingworth Tamesd...114 A3
Hollinsclough Staffs......114 B7
Hollins End Sheff.......... 115 G5
Hollins Green Warrtn .. 113 G4
Hollinswood Wrekin 84 C2
Hollinwood
Crematorium
Oldham.......................... 113 K2
Hollocombe Devon........ 10 F3
Holloway Derbys.......... 100 F2
Holloway Gt Lon............ 44 F3
Hollowell Nhants............ 73 K1
Hollowmoor Heath
Ches W.......................... 112 C7
Hollows D & G 156 C6
Hollybush Caerph.......... 53 J7
Hollybush E Ayrs.......... 163 K6
Hollybush Herefs.......... 70 D6
Hollym E R Yk.............. 127 H5
Holmbridge Kirk..........114 C1
Holmbury St Mary
Surrey.............................. 31 J3
Holmbush Cnwll 5 G5
Holmcroft Staffs............ 99 K7
Holme Cambs................ 89 H6
Holme Cumb................ 129 L4
Holme Kirk..................114 C1
Holme N York.............. 132 E3
Holme Notts.................. 102 D2
Holme Chapel Lancs .. 122 C5
Holme Hale Norfk.......... 91 K3
Holme Lacy Herefs........ 69 K6
Holme Marsh Herefs...... 69 G4
Holme next the Sea
Norfk.............................. 105 H4
Holme on the Wolds
E R Yk............................ 126 B2
Holme Pierrepont
Notts 101 L5
Holmer Herefs................ 69 K6
Holmer Green Bucks...... 42 E2
Holme St Cuthbert
Cumb.............................. 147 J5
Holmes Chapel
Ches E............................ 113 H7
Holmesfield Derbys........114 F6
Holmeswood Lancs 120 F6

Holmethorpe Surrey........ 32 B3
Holme upon
Spalding Moor
E R Yk............................ 125 J3
Holmewood Derbys......115 H7
Holmfirth Kirk.............. 123 H8
Holmhead E Ayrs.......... 164 B5
Holmpton E R Yk.......... 127 J5
Holmrook Cumb.......... 136 E7
Holmsford Bridge
Crematorium
N Ayrs............................ 163 J2
Holmside Dur.............. 150 F5
Holne Devon 7 G3
Holnicote Somset.......... 24 E3
Holsworthy Devon.......... 9 J4
Holsworthy Beacon
Devon 9 K3
Holt Dorset.................... 15 J2
Holt Norfk.................... 106 C5
Holt Wilts...................... 39 K7
Holt Worcs.................... 70 E3
Holt Wrexham................ 98 B2
Holtby C York.............. 133 K8
Holt End Worcs.............. 71 J1
Holt Heath Worcs.......... 70 E2
Holton Oxon.................. 57 L6
Holton Somset.............. 27 G6
Holton Suffk.................. 93 J7
Holton cum
Beckering Lincs............ 117 J5
Holton le Clay Lincs 118 C2
Holton le Moor Lincs 117 H3
Holton St Mary Suffk.... 78 C6
Holwell Dorset.............. 14 D1
Holwell Herts................ 59 K2
Holwell Leics................ 102 B7
Holwell Oxon................ 56 E6
Holwick Dur.................. 139 K2
Holybourne Hants.......... 30 B4
Holyhead IoA.............. 108 C5
Holy Island IoA.......... 108 C5
Holy Island Nthumb...... 169 H2
Holymoorside Derbys....115 G3
Holyport W & M.............. 42 E5
Holystone Nthumb........ 158 B2
Holytown N Lans.......... 175 K6
Holytown
Crematorium
N Lans.......................... 175 K6
Holywell C Beds............ 59 G5
Holywell Cambs............ 75 L1
Holywell Cnwll................ 4 B4
Holywell Dorset............ 14 B2
Holywell Flints.............. 111 G6
Holywell Green
Calder............................ 123 G6
Holywell Lake Somset.... 25 H7
Holywell Row Suffk 91 G7
Holywood D & G.......... 155 G6
Holywood Village
D & G.............................. 155 G6
Homer Shrops................ 84 B3
Homer Green Sefton 111 K2
Homersfield Suffk.......... 93 G6
Homington Wilts............ 28 C6
Honeybourne Worcs...... 71 K5
Honeychurch Devon 10 F4
Honeystreet Wilts.......... 40 C7
Honey Tye Suffk............ 77 L7
Honiley Warwks.............. 86 B8
Honing Norfk................ 107 G6
Honingham Norfk.......... 92 D2
Honington Lincs............ 102 F4
Honington Suffk............ 91 K8
Honington Warwks........ 72 C6
Honiton Devon.............. 12 F3
Honley Kirk.................. 123 H7
Honor Oak
Crematorium
Gt Lon.............................. 45 G5
Hooe C Plym.................... 6 D5
Hooe E Susx.................. 20 E4
Hoo Green Ches E........ 113 G5
Hoohill Bpool................ 120 D3
Hook E R Yk.................. 125 H5

Hook Gt Lon.................. 44 D7
Hook Hants.................... 30 B1
Hook Pembks.................. 49 G5
Hook Wilts...................... 40 B4
Hooke Dorset................ 14 A3
Hook Green Kent............ 33 H6
Hook Green Kent............ 45 L6
Hook Norton Oxon........ 57 G2
Hookway Devon.............. 11 K5
Hooley Surrey................ 32 B3
Hoo St Werburgh
Medway.......................... 46 C5
Hooton Levitt Rothm...115 K3
Hooton Pagnell Donc... 124 D8
Hooton Roberts
Rothm............................ 115 J3
Hope Derbys................ 114 D5
Hope Devon...................... 7 G7
Hope Flints.................... 97 L2
Hope Staffs.................. 100 C2
Hope Bagot Shrops........ 83 L8
Hope Bowdler Shrops 83 J5
Hopehouse Border........ 166 D6
Hopeman Moray............ 214 E1
Hope Mansell Herefs 54 F4
Hopesay Shrops............ 83 H6
Hope under Dinmore
Herefs............................ 69 K4
Hopgrove C York.......... 133 K8
Hopperton N York........ 132 F7
Hopstone Shrops............ 84 D5
Hopton Derbys.............. 100 E2
Hopton Staffs................ 99 L7
Hopton Suffk................ 92 B7
Hopton Cangeford
Shrops............................ 83 K7
Hopton Castle Shrops.... 83 G7
Hoptonheath Shrops...... 83 H7
Hopton on Sea Norfk.... 93 L4
Hopton Wafers
Shrops............................ 84 B7
Hopwas Staffs................ 85 L3
Hopwood Worcs............ 85 J7
Hopwood Park
Services Worcs............ 85 J8
Horam E Susx................ 20 C3
Horbling Lincs.............. 103 J5
Horbury Wakefd............ 123 K6
Horden Dur.................. 151 K6
Hordle Hants.................. 16 C4
Hordley Shrops.............. 98 B6
Horfield Bristl................ 38 E5
Horham Suffk................ 92 E8
Horkesley Heath
Essex.............................. 62 B3
Horkstow N Linc............ 126 B6
Horley Oxon.................. 72 E5
Horley Surrey................ 32 B5
Hornblotton Green
Somset............................ 26 E5
Hornby Lancs................ 130 B5
Hornby N York.............. 132 C2
Hornby N York.............. 141 J6
Horncastle Lincs.......... 118 C7
Hornchurch Gt Lon........ 45 K3
Horncliffe Nthumb........ 179 J7
Horndean Border.......... 179 J8
Horndean Hants............ 30 B8
Horndon Devon.............. 10 D8
Horndon on the Hill
Thurr.............................. 46 A4
Horne Surrey................ 32 C4
Horner Somset.............. 24 D3
Horning Norfk.............. 107 H8
Horninghold Leics.......... 88 B4
Horninglow Staffs........ 100 E7
Horningsea Cambs........ 76 C3
Horningsham Wilts........ 27 J3
Horningtoft Norfk........ 105 M7
Horns Cross Devon 22 F6
Hornsea E R Yk............ 126 F2
Hornsey Gt Lon............ 44 F3
Hornton Oxon................ 72 E5
Horra Shet.................... 235 d2
Horringer Suffk 77 J3

Horrocksford Lancs...... 121 L2
Horsebridge Devon 6 B2
Horsebridge E Susx...... 20 C4
Horsebridge Hants........ 29 G5
Horsehay Wrekin.......... 84 C3
Horseheath Cambs........ 76 E5
Horsehouse N York...... 131 K4
Horsell Surrey................ 43 G8
Horseman's Green
Wrexhm.......................... 98 C4
Horsey Norfk................ 107 K7
Horsey Somset.............. 25 L4
Horsford Norfk.............. 92 E1
Horsforth Leeds............ 123 J3
Horsham W Susx............ 31 K5
Horsham Worcs.............. 70 D3
Horsham St Faith
Norfk.............................. 92 E1
Horsington Lincs.......... 117 K7
Horsington Somset........ 27 G6
Horsley Derbys.............. 101 G4
Horsley Gloucs.............. 39 J2
Horsley Nthumb............ 150 D2
Horsley Nthumb............ 157 L3
Horsleycross Street
Essex.............................. 62 D3
Horsleyhill Border........ 167 H5
Horsley Woodhouse
Derbys............................ 101 H4
Horsmonden Kent.......... 33 J5
Horspath Oxon.............. 57 L6
Horstead Norfk............ 106 F8
Horsted Keynes
W Susx............................ 32 C7
Horton Bucks................ 58 F4
Horton Dorset................ 15 J2
Horton Lancs................ 122 C1
Horton Nhants.............. 74 B4
Horton S Glos................ 39 H4
Horton Somset.............. 25 L7
Horton Staffs................ 99 L2
Horton Swans................ 50 F7
Horton W & M................ 43 G5
Horton Wilts.................. 40 B7
Horton Wrekin.............. 84 C1
Horton-cum-Studley
Oxon................................ 57 L5
Horton Green
Ches W............................ 98 C3
Horton in
Ribblesdale
N York............................ 130 F5
Horton Kirby Kent.......... 45 K6
Horwich Bolton............ 121 J7
Horwood Devon............ 23 H6
Hoscote Border............ 166 F6
Hose Leics.................... 102 B6
Hosh P & K.................... 185 H3
Hoswick Shet................ 235 C7
Hotham E R Yk.............. 125 L4
Hothfield Kent................ 34 C5
Hoton Leics.................. 101 L7
Hough Ches E................ 99 G3
Hougham Lincs.............. 102 E4
Hough Green Halton...... 112 C4
Hough-on-the-Hill
Lincs.............................. 102 F3
Houghton Cambs............ 75 K1
Houghton Hants............ 29 G5
Houghton Pembks.......... 49 G6
Houghton W Susx.......... 18 D4
Houghton Conquest
C Beds............................ 74 F6
Houghton Green
E Susx............................ 21 H2
Houghton-le-Spring
Sundld............................ 151 H5
Houghton on the Hill
Leics.............................. 87 J3
Houghton Regis
C Beds............................ 59 G4
Houghton St Giles
Norfk.............................. 105 L5
Hound Green Hants........ 42 B8
Houndslow Border 178 D8
Houndwood Border...... 179 H5

Hounslow Gt Lon......**43** J5
Househill Highld..........**213** L4
Houses Hill Kirk...........**123** J6
Housieside Abers.........**207** G1
Houston Rens..............**174** D5
Houstry Highld............**227** K2
Hove Br & H...................**19** J5
Hoveringham Notts...**102** B3
Hoveton Norfk............**107** G8
Hovingham N York....**133** K4
How Caple Herefs.......**54** E3
Howden E R Yk..........**125** H5
Howden-le-Wear Dur...**150** E7
Howe Highld...............**231** K3
Howe N York...............**132** E4
Howe Norfk....................**92** F4
Howe Bridge
  Crematorium
  Wigan..................**112** F2
Howe Green Essex.......**61** J7
Howegreen Essex........**61** K7
Howell Lincs................**103** J4
Howe of Teuchar
  Abers.................**216** E5
Howes D & G..............**147** L2
Howe Street Essex......**61** H5
Howe Street Essex......**77** G7
Howey Powys................**68** B3
Howgate Cumb..........**136** D3
Howgate Mdloth........**177** H6
Howick Nthumb..........**169** K5
Howlett End Essex.......**76** E7
Howley Somset............**13** H1
How Mill Cumb...........**148** E4
Howmore W Isls.........**233** b7
Hownam Border.........**168** B5
Howsham N Linc........**117** H2
Howsham N York........**133** L6
Howtel Nthumb..........**168** D3
Howwood Rens...........**174** D6
Hoxne Suffk..................**92** E7
Hoy Ork......................**234** b7
Hoylake Wirral...........**111** H4
Hoyland Nether
  Barns..................**115** G2
Hoyland Swaine
  Barns..................**114** E1
Hubberston Pembks...**48** E6
Huby N York................**123** K2
Huby N York................**133** J6
Hucclecote Gloucs......**55** K4
Hucking Kent................**33** L2
Hucknall Notts............**101** K3
Huddersfield Kirk......**123** H7
Huddersfield
  Crematorium Kirk...**123** H6
Huddington Worcs......**71** G3
Hudswell N York.........**140** E7
Huggate E R Yk..........**134** D7
Hughenden Valley
  Bucks...................**42** E2
Hughley Shrops...........**83** L4
Hugh Town IoS...............**2** b2
Huish Devon................**10** D3
Huish Wilts....................**40** C7
Huish Champflower
  Somset..................**25** G5
Huish Episcopi
  Somset..................**26** B6
Hulcott Bucks...............**58** D5
Hulham Devon.............**12** C5
Hulland Derbys..........**100** E3
Hulland Ward Derbys...**100** E3
Hullavington Wilts......**39** K4
Hullbridge Essex..........**46** D2
Hull, Kingston upon
  C KuH..................**126** D5
Hulme Manch...............**113** J4
Hulme Staffs.................**99** L4
Hulme Warrtn.............**112** E4
Hulme End Staffs.......**100** C2
Hulme Walfield
  Ches E.................**113** J7
Hulverstone IoW..........**16** E5
Hulver Street Suffk......**93** K6

Humberside Airport
  N Linc........................126 D7
Humberston NE Lin....**118** D1
Humberstone C Leic...**87** J3
Humbie E Loth...........**178** B5
Humbleton E R Yk.....**126** F4
Humby Lincs...............**103** G6
Hume Border..............**167** L2
Humshaugh Nthumb...**158** A7
Huna Highld...............**231** L2
Huncote Leics..............**87** G4
Hundalee Border.......**167** K5
Hunderthwaite Dur....**140** C3
Hundleby Lincs..........**118** E7
Hundleton Pembks.......**49** G7
Hundon Suffk................**77** G5
Hundred House
  Powys....................**68** C4
Hungarton Leics..........**87** K3
Hungerford Somset......**25** G4
Hungerford W Berk.....**41** G6
Hungerford
  Newtown W Berk....**41** G6
Hungerstone Herefs......**69** J7
Hunmanby N York......**135** H4
Hunningham Warwks...**72** D2
Hunsbury Hill Nhants...**73** K3
Hunsdon Herts.............**60** C5
Hunsingore N York....**132** F8
Hunslet Leeds............**123** L4
Hunsonby Cumb........**149** G7
Hunstanton Norfk......**105** G4
Hunstanworth Dur....**150** B5
Hunsterson Ches E.......**99** G4
Hunston Suffk...............**77** L2
Hunston W Susx..........**18** B5
Hunstrete BaNES.........**38** F7
Hunsworth Kirk..........**123** J5
Hunter's Quay Ag & B...**173** K3
Huntham Somset........**25** M6
Hunthill Lodge Angus...**196** D3
Huntingdon Cambs....**89** J8
Huntingfield Suffk.......**93** G8
Huntington C York....**133** J7
Huntington Ches W....**112** B8
Huntington E Loth.....**178** B4
Huntington Herefs......**68** E4
Huntington Staffs.......**85** H2
Huntley Gloucs............**55** G4
Huntly Abers..............**215** L6
Hunton Kent................**33** J4
Hunton N York...........**132** B2
Huntscott Somset........**24** E3
Huntsham Devon........**24** F7
Huntshaw Devon........**23** H6
Huntspill Somset..........**25** L3
Huntstile Somset.........**25** K5
Huntworth Somset.......**25** L4
Hunwick Dur..............**140** F2
Hunworth Norfk.........**106** C5
Hurdcott Wilts.............**28** D5
Hurdsfield Ches E......**113** L6
Hurley W & M.............**42** D4
Hurley Warrtn...............**86** B4
Hurley Common
  Warwks.................**86** B4
Hurlford E Ayrs.........**163** L3
Hurn Dorset..................**15** L3
Hursley Hants...............**29** H6
Hurst Wokham............**42** C5
Hurstbourne Priors
  Hants.....................**29** H3
Hurstbourne Tarrant
  Hants.....................**29** G2
Hurst Green E Susx.....**33** J7
Hurst Green Essex........**62** C5
Hurst Green Lancs.....**121** K3
Hurst Green Surrey......**32** D3
Hurstpierpoint
  W Susx..................**19** J3
Hurstwood Lancs.......**122** C4
Hurtiso Ork.................**234** c6
Hurworth-on-Tees
  Darltn..................**141** H5
Hurworth Place
  Darltn..................**141** H5

Husbands Bosworth
  Leics......................**87** J6
Husborne Crawley
  C Beds....................**74** D7
Husthwaite N York....**133** H4
Hutcliffe Wood
  Crematorium
  Sheff....................**115** G5
Huthwaite Notts.......**101** J2
Huttoft Lincs.............**119** G6
Hutton Border...........**179** J7
Hutton E R Yk...........**134** F8
Hutton Essex................**45** M2
Hutton Lancs.............**121** G5
Hutton N Som.............**37** M8
Hutton Buscel N York...**134** F3
Hutton Conyers
  N York.................**132** E5
Hutton Cranswick
  E R Yk..................**126** C1
Hutton End Cumb.....**148** D7
Hutton Henry Dur....**151** K7
Hutton-le-Hole
  N York.................**133** L2
Hutton Lowcross
  R & Cl.................**142** D4
Hutton Magna Dur....**140** E5
Hutton Roof Cumb....**130** B4
Hutton Roof Cumb....**148** C7
Hutton Rudby N York...**141** K6
Hutton Sessay N York...**133** G4
Hutton Wandesley
  N York.................**124** D1
Huxham Devon............**12** B3
Huxley Ches W.............**98** D1
Huyton Knows...........**112** C4
Hycemoor Cumb........**128** D2
Hyde Tamesd..............**113** L3
Hyde Heath Bucks.......**58** F7
Hyde Lea Staffs...........**99** K8
Hylands House &
  Park Essex.............**61** G7
Hyndford Bridge
  S Lans..................**165** H2
Hynish Ag & B...........**188** C8
Hyssington Powys......**82** F5
Hythe Essex..................**62** B3
Hythe Hants.................**16** E2
Hythe Kent...................**34** F7
Hythe End W & M.......**43** G6

I

Ibberton Dorset............**14** E2
Ible Derbys.................**100** E3
Ibsley Hants.................**15** L1
Ibstock Leics................**86** E2
Ibstone Bucks...............**42** C2
Ibthorpe Hants............**29** G2
Iburndale N York.......**143** H5
Ibworth Hants..............**29** K1
Ichrachan Ag & B......**182** E2
Ickburgh Norfk............**91** J4
Ickenham Gt Lon........**43** H3
Ickford Bucks...............**57** M6
Ickham Kent.................**35** G3
Ickleford Herts.............**59** K2
Icklesham E Susx.........**21** H3
Ickleton Cambs............**76** C5
Icklingham Suffk..........**91** H8
Ickornshaw N York....**122** E2
Ickwell Green C Beds...**75** G5
Icomb Gloucs...............**56** E4
Idbury Oxon.................**56** E4
Iddesleigh Devon.........**10** E3
Ide Devon.....................**11** K6
Ideford Devon................**7** K1
Ide Hill Kent................**32** E3
Iden E Susx...................**21** H2
Iden Green Kent...........**33** J5
Iden Green Kent...........**33** K6
Idle C Brad.................**123** H3
Idless Cnwll....................**4** C6
Idlicote Warwks...........**72** C5
Idmiston Wilts.............**28** D4

Idole Carmth.................**50** E3
Idridgehay Derbys......**100** F3
Idrigill Highld.............**208** F2
Idstone Oxon...............**40** E4
Iffley Oxon....................**57** K7
Ifield W Susx.................**31** L4
Ifold W Susx.................**31** G5
Iford Bmouth................**15** L4
Iford E Susx...................**19** L4
Ifton Mons....................**38** C3
Ightfield Shrops............**98** D5
Ightham Kent................**33** G2
Ilam Staffs..................**100** C3
Ilchester Somset...........**26** D6
Ilderton Nthumb........**168** F5
Ilford Gt Lon................**45** H3
Ilford Somset................**26** A7
Ilfracombe Devon........**23** H2
Ilkeston Derbys...........**101** J4
Ilketshall St Andrew
  Suffk......................**93** H6
Ilketshall St
  Margaret Suffk......**93** H6
Ilkley C Brad.............**123** G2
Illand Cnwll....................**5** L1
Illey Dudley.................**85** H7
Illogan Cnwll..................**3** H3
Illston on the Hill
  Leics......................**87** K4
Ilmer Bucks..................**58** C6
Ilmington Warwks......**72** B5
Ilminster Somset..........**26** A8
Ilsington Devon..............**7** H2
Ilston Swans.................**51** H7
Ilton N York...............**132** B4
Ilton Somset.................**25** M7
Imachar N Ayrs..........**161** L2
Immingham NE Lin....**126** F7
Immingham Dock
  NE Lin.................**126** F7
Impington Cambs........**76** C2
Ince Ches W...............**112** C6
Ince Blundell Sefton...**111** K2
Ince-in-Makerfield
  Wigan..................**112** E1
Inchbae Lodge Hotel
  Highld..................**221** K7
Inchbare Angus..........**196** F4
Inchberry Moray.........**215** G4
Incheril Highld...........**211** G3
Inchinnan Rens..........**174** E5
Inchlaggan Highld.....**201** J5
Inchmichael P & K....**186** D3
Inchnacardoch Hotel
  Highld..................**202** B3
Inchnadamph Highld...**224** F4
Inchture P & K...........**186** D2
Inchvuilt Highld.........**211** K6
Inchyra P & K............**186** C4
Indian Queens Cnwll......**4** E4
Ingatestone Essex.......**61** G7
Ingbirchworth Barns...**114** E1
Ingestre Staffs..............**99** L7
Ingham Lincs..............**116** F5
Ingham Norfk.............**107** H7
Ingham Suffk................**77** J1
Ingham Corner Norfk...**107** H6
Ingleby Derbys...........**101** G6
Ingleby Arncliffe
  N York.................**141** K6
Ingleby Barwick
  S on T..................**141** K4
Ingleby Greenhow
  N York.................**142** C6
Ingleigh Green Devon...**10** E4
Inglesbatch BaNES......**39** G7
Inglesham Swindn.......**56** D7
Ingleston D & G.........**147** G2
Ingleton Dur..............**140** F3
Ingleton N York.........**130** D5
Inglewhite Lancs.......**121** H3
Ingoe Nthumb...........**158** C7
Ingol Lancs...............**121** G4
Ingoldisthorpe Norfk...**105** G6
Ingoldmells Lincs......**119** H7
Ingoldsby Lincs..........**103** G6

Ingram Nthumb 168 F6
Ingrave Essex 45 M2
Ingrow C Brad 122 F3
Ings Cumb 138 C7
Ingst S Glos 38 E3
Ingthorpe Rutlnd 88 E2
Ingworth Norfk 106 E6
Inkberrow Worcs 71 H3
Inkhorn Abers 217 H6
Inkpen W Berk 41 G7
Inkstack Highld 231 J2
Innellan Ag & B 173 K4
Innerleithen Border ...166 E3
Innerleven Fife 186 F7
Innermessan D & G ...144 C3
Innerwick E Loth 178 F4
Innesmill Moray 215 G2
Insch Abers 216 C8
Insh Highld 203 J5
Inskip Lancs 120 F3
Instow Devon 23 G5
Intake Sheff 115 H5
Inver Abers 204 F6
Inver Highld 223 J5
Inver P & K 194 F7
Inverailort Highld 190 F1
Inveralligin Highld 210 C3
Inverallochy Abers 217 K2
Inveran Highld 222 D2
Inveraray Ag & B 182 F5
Inverarish Highld 209 J7
Inverarity Angus 196 D7
Inverarnan Stirlg 183 K4
Inverasdale Highld 219 J4
Inverbeg Ag & B 183 K7
Inverbervie Abers 197 K2
Inver-boyndie Abers ...216 C2
Invercreran House
   Hotel Ag & B 191 K6
Inverdruie Highld 203 L3
Inveresk E Loth 177 K4
Inveresragan Ag & B ...182 E1
Inverey Abers 204 D7
Inverfarigaig Highld ...202 D2
Inverfolla Ag & B 191 J7
Invergarry Highld 201 L5
Invergeldie P & K 184 F2
Invergloy Highld 201 K7
Invergordon Highld 222 F7
Invergowrie P & K 186 F2
Inverguseran Highld ...200 B4
Inverhadden P & K 193 L5
Inverherive Hotel
   Stirlg 183 L3
Inverie Highld 200 B5
Inverinan Ag & B 182 E4
Inverinate Highld 200 E2
Inverkeilor Angus 197 G6
Inverkeithing Fife 176 F2
Inverkeithny Abers 216 C5
Inverkip Inver 173 L4
Inverkirkaig Highld 224 C4
Inverlael Highld 220 F4
Inverlair Highld 192 E1
Inverliever Lodge
   Ag & B 182 C6
Inverlochy Ag & B 183 H2
Invermark Angus 196 D1
Invermoriston Highld ...202 C3
Invernaver Highld 229 L4
Inverness Highld 213 G5
Inverness Airport
   Highld 213 J4
Inverness
   Crematorium
   Highld 212 F5
Invernoaden Ag & B ...183 G7
Inveroran Hotel
   Ag & B 192 D7
Inverquharity Angus 196 C5
Inverquhomery
   Abers 217 J5
Inverroy Highld 201 K8
Inversanda Highld 191 J4
Invershiel Highld 200 E2
Invershin Highld 222 D3

Invershore Highld 231 J8
Inversnaid Hotel
   Stirlg 183 K5
Inverugie Abers 217 L5
Inveruglas Ag & B 183 K5
Inveruglass Highld 203 J5
Inverurie Abers 206 E2
Inwardleigh Devon 10 E5
Inworth Essex 61 L4
Iochdar W Isls 233 b7
Iona Ag & B 180 D3
Iping W Susx 30 D6
Ipplepen Devon 7 J3
Ipsden Oxon 41 M4
Ipstones Staffs 100 A3
Ipswich Suffk 78 E5
Ipswich
   Crematorium
   Suffk 78 E5
Irby Wirral 111 J5
Irby in the Marsh
   Lincs 118 F8
Irby upon Humber
   NE Lin 117 K1
Irchester Nhants 74 D2
Ireby Cumb 147 M7
Ireby Lancs 130 C4
Ireleth Cumb 128 F4
Ireshopeburn Dur 149 L7
Irlam Salfd 113 G3
Irnham Lincs 103 G7
Iron Acton S Glos 39 G4
Ironbridge Wrekin 84 C3
Ironbridge Gorge
   Wrekin 84 C3
Ironmacannie D & G ...154 B6
Ironville Derbys 101 H3
Irstead Norfk 107 H7
Irthington Cumb 148 E3
Irthlingborough
   Nhants 74 D1
Irton N York 134 F3
Irvine N Ayrs 163 H2
Isauld Highld 230 E3
Isbister Shet 235 c2
Isbister Shet 235 d4
Isfield E Susx 19 L3
Isham Nhants 88 C8
Islington Hants 30 C3
Islay Ag & B 171 G4
Islay Airport Ag & B ...*170 F7*
Isle Abbotts Somset 26 A7
Isle Brewers Somset 26 A7
Isleham Cambs 90 F8
Isle of Dogs Gt Lon 45 G4
Isle of Grain Medway 46 E5
Isle of Lewis W Isls 232 f2
Isle of Man IoM 237 c4
Isle of Man
   Ronaldsway
   Airport IoM *237 b7*
Isle of Mull Ag & B 181 J1
Isle of Purbeck
   Dorset 15 J5
Isle of Sheppey Kent 46 F6
Isle of Skye Highld 208 F6
Isle of Thanet Kent 35 J2
Isle of Walney Cumb ...128 E6
Isle of Whithorn
   D & G 145 K7
Isle of Wight IoW 17 G5
Isle of Wight
   Crematorium IoW......17 G4
Isleornsay Highld 199 L3
Isles of Scilly St
   Mary's Airport IoS *2 b1*
Islesteps D & G 155 G7
Isleworth Gt Lon 44 D5
Isley Walton Leics 101 H7
Islibhig W Isls 232 d3
Islington Gt Lon 44 F3
Islington
   Crematorium
   Gt Lon 44 F2
Islip Nhants 88 E7
Islip Oxon 57 K5

Islivig W Isls 232 d3
Isombridge Wrekin 83 L2
Itchen Abbas Hants 29 K5
Itchen Stoke Hants 29 K5
Itchingfield W Susx 31 J5
Itteringham Norfk 106 D6
Itton Mons 38 C2
Itton Common Mons 38 C2
Ivegill Cumb 148 D6
Iver Bucks 43 G4
Iver Heath Bucks 43 G4
Iveston Dur 150 E5
Ivinghoe Bucks 58 F5
Ivinghoe Aston Bucks ...58 F4
Ivington Herefs 69 J3
Ivybridge Devon 6 F5
Ivychurch Kent 21 K1
Ivy Hatch Kent 33 G3
Iwade Kent 46 E6
Iwerne Courtney or
   Shroton Dorset 27 K8
Iwerne Minster
   Dorset 27 K8
Ixworth Suffk 77 L1
Ixworth Thorpe Suffk ...91 K8

J

Jack-in-the-Green
   Devon 12 C4
Jackton S Lans 175 G7
Jacobstow Cnwll 9 G5
Jacobstowe Devon 10 E4
Jameston Pembks 49 H7
Jamestown Highld 212 D3
Jamestown W Duns 174 D3
Janetstown Highld 227 L3
Janets-town Highld 231 L5
Jardine Hall D & G 155 J5
Jarrow S Tyne 151 H3
Jasper's Green Essex ...61 H3
Jawcraig Falk 175 L4
Jaywick Essex 62 F5
Jedburgh Border 167 K5
Jeffreyston Pembks 49 J6
Jemimaville Highld 213 H2
Jerbourg Guern 236 d4
Jersey Jersey 236 c6
Jersey Airport Jersey ...*236 b7*
Jersey Crematorium
   Jersey 236 c7
Jesmond N u Ty 151 G2
Jevington E Susx 20 B5
Jockey End Herts 59 H5
Johnby Cumb 148 D7
John Lennon Airport
   Lpool 112 B5
John o' Groats Highld ...231 L2
Johnshaven Abers 197 J3
Johnston Pembks 48 F5
Johnstone D & G 155 M3
Johnstone Rens 174 D5
Johnstonebridge
   D & G 155 J4
Johnstown Carmth 50 E2
Johnstown Wrexhm 97 L4
Joppa C Edin 177 J4
Joppa Cerdgn 66 D2
Joppa S Ayrs 163 K5
Jordanston Pembks 64 C7
Joyden's Wood Kent 45 K5
Juniper Nthumb 150 B3
Juniper Green C Edin ...177 G5
Jura Ag & B 171 J2
Jurassic Coast *13 H4*
Jurby IoM 237 C2

K

Kaber Cumb 139 H5
Kaimend S Lans 165 J1
Kames Ag & B 173 G4
Kames E Ayrs 164 D4
Kea Cnwll 4 C7

Keadby N Linc 125 K7
Keal Cotes Lincs 104 B1
Kearsley Bolton 113 H1
Kearsney Kent 35 H6
Kearstwick Cumb 130 B4
Kedington Suffk 77 G5
Kedleston Derbys 100 F4
Keelby Lincs 126 E8
Keele Staffs 99 J4
Keele Services Staffs *99 J4*
Keelham C Brad 123 G4
Keeston Pembks 48 F4
Keevil Wilts 39 L8
Kegworth Leics 101 J7
Kehelland Cnwll 3 G3
Keig Abers 206 B2
Keighley C Brad 122 F3
Keighley
   Crematorium
   C Brad 122 F3
Keilarsbrae Clacks 185 J8
Keillour P & K 185 K3
Keiloch Abers 204 E6
Keils Ag & B 171 K5
Keinton Mandeville
   Somset 26 D5
Keir Mill D & G 154 E4
Keisley Cumb 139 G3
Keiss Highld 231 L4
Keith Moray 215 J4
Keithick P & K 195 K8
Keithock Angus 196 F4
Keithtown Highld 212 E3
Kelbrook Lancs 122 D2
Kelby Lincs 103 G4
Keld N York 139 K6
Kelfield N York 124 F3
Kelham Notts 102 C2
Kelhead D & G 147 K2
Kellamergh Lancs 120 E5
Kellas Angus 187 G1
Kellas Moray 214 E4
Kellaton Devon 7 J7
Kelling Norfk 106 C4
Kellington N York 124 E5
Kelloe Dur 151 J4
Kelloholm D & G 164 E6
Kelly Devon 9 K8
Kelmarsh Nhants 87 K7
Kelmscott Oxon 56 E7
Kelsale Suffk 79 H2
Kelsall Ches W 112 D7
Kelshall Herts 75 K7
Kelsick Cumb 147 L5
Kelso Border 167 L3
Kelstedge Derbys 115 G8
Kelstern Lincs 118 C4
Kelston BaNES 39 G6
Keltneyburn P & K 194 B6
Kelton D & G 155 H7
Kelty Fife 186 B8
Kelvedon Essex 61 K4
Kelvedon Hatch
   Essex 60 F7
Kelynack Cnwll 2 C5
Kemback Fife 187 G4
Kemberton Shrops 84 D3
Kemble Gloucs 39 M2
Kemerton Worcs 71 G6
Kemeys Commander
   Mons 53 M6
Kemnay Abers 206 E3
Kempley Gloucs 54 F3
Kempley Green
   Gloucs 55 G3
Kempsey Worcs 70 F5
Kempsford Gloucs 40 D2
Kempshott Hants 29 L2
Kempston Bed 74 F5
Kempton Shrops 83 G6
Kemp Town Br & H...... 19 J5
Kemsing Kent 32 F2
Kenardington Kent 34 C7
Kenchester Herefs 69 J6
Kencot Oxon 56 E6
Kendal Cumb 129 L2

Kenfig Brdgnd 36 C4
Kenilworth Warwks....72 C1
Kenley Gt Lon..............32 B2
Kenley Shrops................83 L4
Kenmore Highld 210 B3
Kenmore P & K 194 B7
Kenn Devon..................11 L7
Kenn N Som 38 B6
Kennacraig Ag & B....172 D5
Kennall Vale Cnwll............3 J4
Kennerleigh Devon.....11 J4
Kennessee Green
  Sefton 111 L2
Kennet Clacks 176 C1
Kennethmont Abers...215 L8
Kennett Cambs.............77 G2
Kennford Devon...........11 L7
Kenninghall Norfk 92 C6
Kennington Kent 34 D5
Kennington Oxon 57 K7
Kennoway Fife............186 F6
Kennyhill Suffk 90 F7
Kennythorpe
  N York 134 C6
Kenovay Ag & B........188 C6
Kensaleyre Highld....208 F4
Kensington Gt Lon....44 E4
Kensington Palace
  Gt Lon....................44 E4
Kensworth Common
  C Beds 59 G4
Kentallen Highld.......191 K5
Kent and Sussex
  Crematorium
  Kent.........................33 G5
Kentchurch Herefs....54 B3
Kentford Suffk...........77 G2
Kent International
  Airport Kent.........35 J2
Kentisbeare Devon....12 D2
Kentisbury Devon......23 K3
Kentish Town Gt Lon.44 F3
Kentmere Cumb.........138 C6
Kenton Devon.............12 B5
Kenton Gt Lon............44 D3
Kenton N u Ty............150 F2
Kenton Suffk..............78 E2
Kentra Highld............190 D3
Kent's Green Gloucs..55 H4
Kent's Oak Hants........28 F6
Kenwyn Cnwll..............4 C6
Keoldale Highld.........228 F3
Keppoch Highld.........200 D1
Kepwick N York.........133 G2
Keresley Covtry..........86 D6
Kerrera Ag & B..........182 B2
Kerris Cnwll..................2 D5
Kerry Powys................82 D5
Kerrycroy Ag & B......173 J6
Kersall Notts 116 B8
Kersbrook Devon........12 D5
Kersey Suffk................78 B5
Kershader W Isls.......232 F3
Kerswell Devon...........12 D2
Kerswell Green Worcs..70 F5
Kesgrave Suffk.............78 F5
Kessingland Suffk......93 L6
Kestle Cnwll...................4 F6
Kestle Mill Cnwll..........4 D4
Keston Gt Lon..............45 H7
Keswick Cumb.............137 J3
Keswick Norfk..............92 E3
Kettering Nhants..........88 C7
Kettering
  Crematorium
  Nhants........................88 C7
Ketteringham Norfk....92 E3
Kettins P & K...............195 K8
Kettlebaston Suffk......77 L4
Kettlebridge Fife........186 E6
Kettlebrook Staffs.......86 B3
Kettleburgh Suffk........78 F3
Kettleholm D & G.......155 K6
Kettleshulme Ches E..113 M5
Kettlesing N York........132 C7

Kettlesing Bottom
  N York 132 C7
Kettlestone Norfk......106 A6
Kettlethorpe Lincs.....116 D6
Kettletoft Ork.............234 d4
Kettlewell N York......131 H5
Ketton Rutlnd...............88 E3
Kew Gt Lon...................44 D5
Kew Royal Botanic
  Gardens Gt Lon.....44 D5
Kewstoke N Som.........37 M7
Kexby C York..............125 G1
Kexby Lincs.................116 E4
Key Green Ches E.......113 K8
Keyham Leics...............87 J3
Keyhaven Hants...........16 C4
Keyingham E R Yk......127 G5
Keymer W Susx............19 J3
Keynsham BaNES........38 F6
Keysoe Bed..................74 F3
Keysoe Row Bed.........74 F3
Keyston Cambs............88 F7
Keyworth Notts...........101 L6
Kibblesworth Gatesd..151 G4
Kibworth
  Beauchamp Leics......87 K5
Kibworth Harcourt
  Leics..........................87 K5
Kidbrooke Gt Lon........45 H5
Kidderminster Worcs..84 E7
Kidlington Oxon...........57 J5
Kidmore End Oxon......42 B5
Kidsdale D & G 145 J7
Kidsgrove Staffs...........99 J2
Kidwelly Carmth..........50 E4
Kiel Crofts Ag & B......191 H8
Kielder Nthumb...........157 G4
Kiells Ag & B..............171 H5
Kilbarchan Rens..........174 D5
Kilbeg Highld.............199 K4
Kilberry Ag & B..........172 C5
Kilbirnie N Ayrs..........174 C7
Kilbride Ag & B..........172 C3
Kilbride Ag & B..........173 H5
Kilbuiack Moray..........214 D3
Kilburn Derbys............101 G4
Kilburn Gt Lon............44 E4
Kilburn N York...........133 H4
Kilby Leics....................87 J4
Kilchamaig Ag & B....172 D6
Kilchattan Ag & B......173 J7
Kilchattan Ag & B......180 E7
Kilcheran Ag & B......191 G8
Kilchoan Highld..........189 L4
Kilchoman Ag & B......170 D5
Kilchrenan Ag & B......182 E3
Kilconquhar Fife.........187 H6
Kilcot Gloucs................55 G3
Kilcoy Highld..............212 E4
Kilcreggan Ag & B......173 L3
Kildale N York............142 D5
Kildalloig Ag & B.......161 J5
Kildary Highld............223 G6
Kildavanan Ag & B.....173 H5
Kildonan Highld..........227 G4
Kildonan N Ayrs.........162 D5
Kildonan Lodge
  Highld......................226 F4
Kildonnan Highld.......199 G7
Kildrochet House
  D & G.......................144 C4
Kildrummy Abers........205 K2
Kildwick N York.........122 F2
Kilfinan Ag & B..........172 F3
Kilfinnan Highld.........201 K6
Kilgetty Pembks..........49 J6
Kilgrammie S Ayrs......152 F2
Kilgwrrwg Common
  Mons.........................38 C2
Kilham E R Yk.............135 G6
Kilkenneth Ag & B.....188 B7
Kilkenzie Ag & B........161 H4
Kilkerran Ag & B........161 J5
Kilkhampton Cnwll......9 H3
Killamarsh Derbys......115 J6

Killay Swans.................51 H6
Killearn Stirlg 174 F2
Killen Highld...............213 G3
Killerby Darltn...........140 F3
Killerton Devon...........12 C3
Killichonan P & K......193 J5
Killiechonate Highld.....192 D1
Killiechronan Ag & B..190 B7
Killiecrankie P & K....194 E4
Killilan Highld............210 E7
Killimster Highld........231 K4
Killin Stirlg.................184 C2
Killinghall N York.......132 D7
Killington Cumb.........130 C2
Killington Lake
  Services Cumb 130 B2
Killingworth N Tyne...159 G7
Killochyett Border......167 G1
Kilmacolm Inver.........174 C4
Kilmahog Stirlg...........184 D5
Kilmahumaig Ag & B..182 A8
Kilmaluag Highld.......218 C6
Kilmany Fife...............186 F3
Kilmarnock E Ayrs......163 K2
Kilmartin Ag & B........182 B7
Kilmaurs E Ayrs..........163 K2
Kilmelford Ag & B......182 B5
Kilmersdon Somset......27 G2
Kilmeston Hants...........29 L6
Kilmichael Ag & B......161 H5
Kilmichael Glassary
  Ag & B.....................182 B8
Kilmichael of
  Inverlussa Ag & B..172 D2
Kilmington Devon.......13 H3
Kilmington Wilts..........27 H4
Kilmington Common
  Wilts.........................27 H4
Kilmington Street
  Wilts.........................27 H4
Kilmorack Highld.......212 D5
Kilmore Ag & B..........182 C3
Kilmore Highld...........199 K4
Kilmory Ag & B..........172 C4
Kilmory Highld...........190 B3
Kilmory N Ayrs...........162 B5
Kilmuir Highld............208 D5
Kilmuir Highld............213 G4
Kilmuir Highld............218 B7
Kilmuir Highld............223 G6
Kilmun Ag & B...........173 K3
Kilnave Ag & B...........170 F4
Kilncadzow S Lans......176 B8
Kilndown Kent............33 J6
Kilninver Ag & B........182 B3
Kilnsea E R Yk.............127 J7
Kilnsey N York...........131 H6
Kilnwick E R Yk..........126 C1
Kiloran Ag & B...........180 E7
Kilpatrick N Ayrs........162 A4
Kilpeck Herefs.............54 C3
Kilpin E R Yk...............125 J5
Kilrenny Fife...............187 J6
Kilsby Nhants...............73 H1
Kilspindie P & K.........186 C3
Kilstay D & G...............144 D7
Kilsyth N Lans.............175 J3
Kiltarlity Highld.........212 D6
Kilton R & Cl..............142 E4
Kilton Thorpe R & Cl..142 E4
Kilvaxter Highld.........218 B7
Kilve Somset...............25 H3
Kilvington Notts..........102 D4
Kilwinning N Ayrs......163 H2
Kimberley Norfk..........92 C3
Kimberley Notts..........101 J4
Kimberworth Rothm...115 H3
Kimblesworth Dur......151 G5
Kimbolton Cambs........75 G2
Kimbolton Herefs........69 K3
Kimcote Leics...............87 H6
Kimmeridge Dorset......15 H6
Kimpton Hants..............28 F3
Kimpton Herts...............59 K4
Kinbrace Highld..........226 F3
Kinbuck Stirlg.............185 G6

Kincaple Fife...............187 G4
Kincardine Fife............176 C2
Kincardine Highld.......222 E4
Kincardine O'Neil
  Abers........................206 B5
Kinclaven P & K.........195 J8
Kincorth C Aber...........207 H5
Kincorth House
  Moray......................214 C3
Kincraig Highld..........203 K4
Kincraigie P & K.........194 E4
Kindallachan P & K....194 F6
Kinerarach Ag & B......172 B7
Kineton Gloucs............56 C3
Kineton Warwks...........72 D4
Kinfauns P & K...........186 C3
Kingarth Ag & B.........173 J6
Kingcausie Abers.........207 G5
Kingcoed Mons............54 B6
Kingerby Lincs............117 H3
Kingham Oxon.............56 E3
Kingholm Quay
  D & G.......................155 G7
Kinghorn Fife..............177 H2
Kinglassie Fife............186 D7
Kingoldrum Angus......196 B5
Kingoodie P & K.........186 E2
Kingsand Cnwll.............6 C5
Kingsbarns Fife...........187 K5
Kingsbridge Devon.......7 H6
Kingsbridge Somset....24 F4
King's Bromley Staffs..85 K1
Kingsburgh Highld.....208 F4
Kingsbury Gt Lon........44 D3
Kingsbury Warwks......86 B4
Kingsbury Episcopi
  Somset......................26 B7
King's Caple Herefs....54 E3
Kingsclere Hants..........41 K8
King's Cliffe Nhants....88 E4
Kingscote Gloucs.........39 J2
Kingscott Devon...........23 H7
King's Coughton
  Warwks.....................71 J3
Kingscross N Ayrs.......162 D4
Kingsdon Somset.........26 D6
Kingsdown Kent..........35 K5
Kingsdown Swindn......40 D3
Kingsdown Wilts..........39 J6
Kingsdown
  Crematorium
  Swindn.....................40 D3
Kingseat Fife...............176 F1
Kingsey Bucks..............58 C6
Kingsfold W Susx.........31 K4
Kingsford C Aber..........206 F4
Kingsford E Ayrs..........174 E8
Kingsgate Kent............35 K1
Kingshall Street Suffk..77 K3
King's Heath Birm........85 J7
Kings Hill Kent............33 H3
King's Hill Wsall..........85 H4
Kings House Hotel
  Highld......................192 D5
Kingshouse Hotel
  Stirlg........................184 C4
Kingskerswell Devon....7 K3
Kingskettle Fife...........186 E5
Kingsland Herefs..........69 J3
Kingsland IoA..............108 C5
Kings Langley Herts....59 H7
Kingsley Ches W..........112 C6
Kingsley Hants.............30 C4
Kingsley Staffs............100 A3
Kingsley Green
  W Susx......................30 E5
Kingsley Park Nhants..73 L3
King's Lynn Norfk........104 F8
Kings Meaburn Cumb..138 E3
King's Mills Guern.......236 C3
Kingsmuir Angus.........196 D6
Kingsmuir Fife............187 J5
Kingsnorth Kent..........34 D6
King's Norton Birm......85 J7
King's Norton Leics....87 K4

Kings Nympton
Devon.............................23 L7
King's Pyon Herefs 69 J4
Kings Ripton Cambs 89 J7
King's Somborne
Hants...........................29 G5
King's Stag Dorset 14 D1
King's Stanley Gloucs 55 J7
King's Sutton Nhants 72 F7
Kingstanding Birm 85 J4
Kingsteignton Devon......7 K2
Kingsthorne Herefs 54 D2
Kingsthorpe Nhants 73 L2
Kingston Cambs 75 L4
Kingston Cnwll..................6 A2
Kingston Devon.................6 F6
Kingston Dorset...............14 E1
Kingston Dorset...............15 H6
Kingston E Loth...............178 C3
Kingston IoW 16 F6
Kingston Kent...................35 G4
Kingston Bagpuize
Oxon...........................57 H7
Kingston Blount
Oxon...........................58 C7
Kingston Deverill
Wilts............................27 J4
Kingstone Herefs 69 H7
Kingstone Somset............26 B8
Kingstone Staffs.............100 B6
Kingston Lacy House
& Gardens Dorset 15 J3
Kingston Lisle Oxon........40 F3
Kingston near Lewes
E Susx 19 K4
Kingston on Soar
Notts..........................101 J6
Kingston on Spey
Moray.........................215 H2
Kingston Russell
Dorset 14 B4
Kingston St Mary
Somset.........................25 K5
Kingston Seymour
N Som 38 B6
Kingston upon Hull
C KuH.........................126 D5
Kingston upon
Thames Gt Lon............44 D6
Kingston upon
Thames
Crematorium
Gt Lon........................44 D6
King's Walden Herts......59 K4
Kingswear Devon..............7 K5
Kingswells C Aber 207 G4
Kings Weston Bristl........38 D5
Kingswinford Dudley.....84 F5
Kingswood Bucks 58 B4
Kingswood Gloucs 39 H3
Kingswood S Glos 38 F5
Kingswood Somset...........25 H4
Kingswood Surrey 31 L1
Kingswood Warwks 71 L1
Kingswood Common
Staffs...........................84 E3
Kings Worthy Hants........29 J5
Kingthorpe Lincs...........117 J6
Kington Herefs 68 F3
Kington S Glos 38 F3
Kington Worcs..................71 H4
Kington Langley Wilts...39 L5
Kington Magna
Dorset 27 H6
Kington St Michael
Wilts............................39 K5
Kingussie Highld..........203 H5
Kingweston Somset.........26 D5
Kinharrachie Abers.......217 H7
Kinharvie D & G.............147 G2
Kinkell Bridge P & K....185 J4
Kinknockie Abers..........217 J6
Kinleith C Edin.............177 G5
Kinlet Shrops...................84 C7
Kinloch Highld..............198 F5
Kinloch Highld..............225 H2

Kinloch Highld..............229 H5
Kinloch P & K................195 J7
Kinlochard Stirlg...........184 B6
Kinlochbervie Highld.....228 C4
Kinlocheil Highld...........191 J1
Kinlochewe Highld.........210 F3
Kinloch Hourn Highld....200 E4
Kinlochlaggan Highld....202 E7
Kinlochleven Highld......192 C4
Kinlochmoidart
Highld.........................190 E2
Kinlochnanuagh
Highld.........................200 B8
Kinloch Rannoch
P & K..........................193 L5
Kinloss Moray...............214 C3
Kinmel Bay Conwy.........110 D5
Kinmuck Abers..............206 F2
Kinmundy Abers............207 G2
Kinnabus Ag & B............160 B2
Kinnadie Abers..............217 H5
Kinnaird P & K...............194 F5
Kinneff Abers.................197 K2
Kinnelhead D & G...........155 H2
Kinnell Angus................196 F6
Kinnerley Shrops.............97 M7
Kinnersley Herefs...........69 G5
Kinnersley Worcs............70 F5
Kinnerton Powys.............68 E2
Kinnesswood P & K........186 C6
Kinnordy Angus.............196 B5
Kinoulton Notts............102 B6
Kinross P & K................186 B6
Kinrossie P & K.............186 C2
Kinross Services
P & K..........................186 B6
Kinsham Herefs...............69 G2
Kinsham Worcs................71 G7
Kinsley Wakefd..............124 C7
Kinson Bmouth................15 K3
Kintail Highld................200 F2
Kintbury W Berk..............41 G6
Kintessack Moray...........214 B3
Kintillo P & K................186 B4
Kinton Herefs..................83 H8
Kinton Shrops..................98 A8
Kintore Abers................206 E3
Kintour Ag & B................171 H7
Kintra Ag & B.................170 F8
Kintra Ag & B.................180 D3
Kintraw Ag & B..............182 B6
Kintyre Ag & B................161 J2
Kinveachy Highld..........203 L2
Kinver Staffs...................84 E6
Kippax Leeds..................124 C4
Kippen Stirlg..................184 E7
Kippford or Scaur
D & G..........................146 E4
Kipping's Cross Kent......33 H5
Kirbister Ork.................234 b6
Kirby Bedon Norfk...........93 G3
Kirby Bellars Leics.......102 B8
Kirby Cane Norfk.............93 H5
Kirby Cross Essex............62 E4
Kirby Fields Leics............87 G3
Kirby Grindalythe
N York.........................134 D6
Kirby Hill N York............132 F5
Kirby Hill N York............140 E6
Kirby Knowle N York......133 G3
Kirby le Soken Essex.......62 F4
Kirby Misperton
N York.........................134 B4
Kirby Muxloe Leics..........87 G3
Kirby Underdale
E R Yk.........................134 C7
Kirby Wiske N York........132 E3
Kirdford W Susx...............31 G6
Kirk Highld.....................231 K4
Kirkabister Shet............235 d6
Kirkandrews D & G.........146 A5
Kirkandrews upon
Eden Cumb.................148 B4
Kirkbampton Cumb........148 B4
Kirkbean D & G..............147 G3
Kirk Bramwith Donc......124 F7

Kirkbride Cumb.............147 M4
Kirkbuddo Angus...........196 E7
Kirkburn Border............166 D2
Kirkburn E R Yk.............134 F7
Kirkburton Kirk............123 J7
Kirkby Knows................111 L2
Kirkby Lincs..................117 H3
Kirkby N York...............142 C6
Kirkby Fleetham
N York.........................141 G7
Kirkby Green Lincs.......103 H2
Kirkby in Ashfield
Notts..........................101 J2
Kirkby-in-Furness
Cumb..........................128 F3
Kirkby la Thorpe
Lincs...........................103 J4
Kirkby Lonsdale
Cumb..........................130 B4
Kirkby Malham
N York.........................131 G7
Kirkby Mallory Leics.......86 F4
Kirkby Malzeard
N York.........................132 C5
Kirkbymoorside
N York.........................133 L3
Kirkby on Bain Lincs.....118 C8
Kirkby Overblow
N York.........................123 L2
Kirkby Stephen
Cumb..........................139 H5
Kirkby Thore Cumb........138 F3
Kirkby Underwood
Lincs...........................103 H6
Kirkby Wharf N York......124 D3
Kirkcaldy Fife...............186 D8
Kirkcaldy
Crematorium Fife......186 D8
Kirkcambeck Cumb........148 F2
Kirkchrist D & G............146 B5
Kirkcolm D & G..............144 B2
Kirkconnel D & G...........164 E6
Kirkconnell D & G..........147 G2
Kirkcowan D & G............145 G3
Kirkcudbright D & G......146 B5
Kirkdale Lpool...............111 K3
Kirk Deighton N York....124 B1
Kirk Ella E R Yk.............126 C5
Kirkfieldbank S Lans....165 G2
Kirkgunzeon D & G........146 F2
Kirk Hallam Derbys.......101 J4
Kirkham Lancs...............120 F4
Kirkham N York.............134 B6
Kirkhamgate Wakefd.....123 K6
Kirk Hammerton
N York.........................133 G7
Kirkhaugh Nthumb.........149 H5
Kirkheaton Kirk.............123 H6
Kirkheaton Nthumb.......158 C6
Kirkhill Highld...............212 E5
Kirkhope S Lans............165 J7
Kirkibost Highld............199 H2
Kirkinch P & K...............195 L7
Kirkinner D & G..............145 J5
Kirkintilloch E Duns.....175 H4
Kirk Ireton Derbys........100 E3
Kirkland Cumb...............136 E4
Kirkland D & G...............154 E4
Kirkland D & G...............155 H4
Kirkland D & G...............164 E6
Kirk Langley Derbys......100 F5
Kirkleatham R & Cl........142 D3
Kirklevington S on T.....141 K5
Kirkley Suffk...................93 L5
Kirklington N York.........132 D4
Kirklington Notts...........102 B2
Kirklinton Cumb............148 D2
Kirkliston C Edin...........176 F4
Kirkmabreck D & G.........145 K4
Kirkmaiden D & G...........144 D7
Kirk Merrington Dur......141 G2
Kirk Michael IoM...........237 C4
Kirkmichael P & K.........195 H4
Kirkmichael S Ayrs.......163 J7
Kirkmuirhill S Lans......164 F2
Kirknewton Nthumb......168 D4

Kirknewton W Loth 176 F5
Kirkney Abers...............215 L7
Kirk of Shotts N Lans...175 L5
Kirkoswald Cumb...........148 F6
Kirkoswald S Ayrs.........163 G7
Kirkpatrick D & G..........154 F4
Kirkpatrick Durham
D & G..........................154 D7
Kirkpatrick-Fleming
D & G..........................156 B7
Kirk Sandall Donc.........124 F8
Kirksanton Cumb...........128 D4
Kirk Smeaton N York....124 D7
Kirkstall Leeds...............123 K4
Kirkstead Lincs.............103 K1
Kirkstile Abers..............215 L7
Kirkstile D & G..............156 C4
Kirkstyle Highld............231 L2
Kirkthorpe Wakefd........124 B6
Kirkton Abers................206 C1
Kirkton D & G................155 G6
Kirkton Fife...................186 F3
Kirkton Highld..............210 C8
Kirkton Highld..............210 D6
Kirkton P & K................185 K4
Kirkton Manor Border...166 C2
Kirkton of Airlie
Angus.........................195 L6
Kirkton of
Auchterhouse
Angus.........................196 B8
Kirkton of Barevan
Highld.........................213 K5
Kirkton of Collace
P & K..........................186 C2
Kirkton of
Glenbuchat Abers.....205 J3
Kirkton of Logie
Buchan Abers...........217 J7
Kirkton of Menmuir
Angus.........................196 E4
Kirkton of Monikie
Angus.........................196 E8
Kirkton of Rayne
Abers..........................216 D7
Kirkton of Skene
Abers..........................206 F4
Kirkton of
Strathmartine
Angus.........................186 F1
Kirkton of Tealing
Angus.........................196 C8
Kirkton of Tough
Abers..........................206 C3
Kirktown Abers..............217 J2
Kirktown Abers..............217 K4
Kirktown of Alvah
Abers..........................216 D3
Kirktown of Bourtie
Abers..........................206 F1
Kirktown of
Fetteresso Abers......206 F7
Kirktown of
Mortlach Moray........215 H6
Kirktown of Slains
Abers..........................217 K8
Kirkurd Border..............165 M1
Kirkwall Ork..................234 c6
Kirkwall Airport Ork....234 c6
Kirkwhelpington
Nthumb........................158 C5
Kirk Yetholm Border.....168 C4
Kirmington N Linc.........126 D7
Kirmond le Mire Lincs...117 K3
Kirn Ag & B....................173 K3
Kirriemuir Angus...........196 C5
Kirstead Green Norfk......93 G4
Kirtlebridge D & G.........155 M7
Kirtling Cambs.................77 G3
Kirtling Green Cambs.....76 F4
Kirtlington Oxon.............57 J4
Kirtomy Highld..............229 M3
Kirton Lincs...................104 A5
Kirton Notts..................116 B7
Kirton Suffk.....................78 F6
Kirtonhill W Duns.........174 D4

Kirton in Lindsey
N Linc 116 F2
Kirwaugh D & G...........145 J4
Kishorn Highld................210 C6
Kislingbury Nhants 73 K3
Kittisford Somset..........25 G6
Kittybrewster C Aber...207 H4
Kivernoll Herefs.............54 C2
Kiveton Park Rothm...115 J5
Knaith Lincs..................116 D5
Knap Corner Dorset....27 J6
Knaphill Surrey 42 F8
Knapp Somset.................25 L6
Knapton C York 124 E1
Knapton N York.............134 D4
Knapton Norfk...............107 G5
Knapwell Cambs............75 K2
Knaresborough
N York......................132 E7
Knarsdale Nthumb......149 H4
Knaven Abers................217 G5
Knayton N York 132 F2
Knebworth Herts............59 L4
Knedlington E R Yk.....125 H5
Kneesall Notts..............116 B8
Kneesworth Cambs........75 L5
Kneeton Notts..............102 B4
Knelston Swans.............50 F7
Knenhall Staffs...............99 L5
Knightcote Warwks.........72 E4
Knightley Staffs..............99 J7
Knighton C Leic..............87 H4
Knighton Dorset.............14 C1
Knighton Powys..............82 F8
Knighton Somset............25 J3
Knighton Staffs...............99 G4
Knighton Staffs...............99 H6
Knighton on Teme
Worcs........................70 B1
Knightwick Worcs...........70 D4
Knill Herefs.....................68 F3
Knipton Leics...............102 D6
Kniveton Derbys...........100 E3
Knock Cumb..................138 F2
Knock Highld.................199 K4
Knock Moray.................215 L4
Knock W Isls.................232 g2
Knockally Highld...........227 K3
Knockan Highld.............224 F6
Knockando Moray........214 F6
Knockbain Highld.........212 E5
Knockbain Highld.........212 F3
Knock Castle N Ayrs...173 L5
Knockdee Highld..........231 H4
Knockdow Ag & B........173 J4
Knockdown Wilts...........39 J3
Knockeen S Ayrs..........153 G3
Knockenkelly N Ayrs...162 D4
Knockentiber E Ayrs...163 K2
Knockholt Kent..............32 E2
Knockholt Pound
Kent..........................32 E2
Knockin Shrops..............97 M7
Knockinlaw E Ayrs......163 K2
Knocknain D & G..........144 B3
Knockrome Ag & B.......171 K4
Knocksharry IoM..........237 b4
Knocksheen D & G......153 M5
Knockvennie Smithy
D & G.......................154 D7
Knodishall Suffk............79 J3
Knodishall Common
Suffk.........................79 J3
Knole Somset..................26 C6
Knolls Green Ches E...113 J5
Knolton Wrexhm.............98 B5
Knook Wilts.....................27 L3
Knossington Leics..........88 B2
Knott End-on-Sea
Lancs......................120 E2
Knotting Bed.................74 E2
Knotting Green Bed.......74 E3
Knottingley Wakefd.....124 D5
Knotty Ash Lpool.........112 B3
Knowbury Shrops..........83 L7
Knowe D & G...............153 G7

Knowehead D & G........154 A4
Knoweside S Ayrs.........163 G6
Knowle Bristl...................38 E6
Knowle Devon.................11 H5
Knowle Devon.................12 C2
Knowle Devon.................12 D6
Knowle Devon.................23 H4
Knowle Shrops................83 L8
Knowle Solhll..................85 L7
Knowle Somset..............24 E3
Knowlefield Cumb.........148 D4
Knowle Green Lancs...121 J3
Knowle St Giles
Somset......................13 J1
Knowl Hill W & M..........42 D4
Knowsley Knows...........112 C3
Knowsley Safari Park
Knows.....................112 C3
Knowstone Devon..........24 C6
Knox Bridge Kent...........33 K5
Knucklas Powys..............82 F8
Knuston Nhants.............74 D2
Knutsford Ches E..........113 H5
Knutsford Services
Ches E.....................113 G6
Krumlin Calder.............122 F6
Kuggar Cnwll....................3 J7
Kyleakin Highld.............200 B1
Kyle of Lochalsh
Highld......................210 B8
Kylerhea Highld.............200 B2
Kylesku Highld..............224 F2
Kylesmorar Highld........200 C6
Kyles Scalpay W Isls...232 e4
Kylestrome Highld........224 F2
Kynnersley Wrekin.........84 C1
Kyrewood Worcs............69 L2

L

Lacasaigh W Isls.........232 f3
Lacasdal W Isls...........232 f2
Laceby NE Lin..............117 K1
Lacey Green Bucks.......58 D7
Lach Dennis Ches W...113 G6
Lackford Suffk...............77 H1
Lackford Green Suffk....77 H1
Lacock Wilts...................39 K6
Ladbroke Warwks...........72 E3
Laddingford Kent...........33 J4
Ladock Cnwll....................4 D5
Lady Ork.......................234 d4
Ladybank Fife...............186 E5
Ladygill S Lans.............165 H4
Lady Hall Cumb.............128 E3
Ladykirk Border............179 J8
Ladywood Birm..............85 J6
Ladywood Worcs............70 F3
La Fontenelle Guern....236 e1
Lag D & G.....................154 F5
Laga Highld..................190 D4
Lagavulin Ag & B..........160 C1
Lagg N Ayrs..................162 B5
Laggan Highld...............201 L6
Laggan Highld...............202 F6
Lagganlia Highld...........203 K5
La Greve de Lecq
Jersey.....................236 b5
Laid Highld....................228 F4
Laide Highld..................219 L3
Laig Highld....................199 G7
Laigh Clunch E Ayrs....174 E8
Laigh Fenwick E Ayrs..163 L2
Laigh Glenmuir E Ayrs..164 C5
Laighstonehall
S Lans.....................175 J7
Laindon Essex................46 B3
Lairg Highld..................225 M7
Laisterdyke C Brad.......123 J4
Lake IoW........................17 H5
Lake Wilts......................28 C4
Lake District
National Park
Cumb.....................137 H5
Lakenheath Suffk...........91 G6

Lakesend Norfk..............90 D4
Laleston Brdgnd.............36 D4
Lamarsh Essex...............77 K7
Lamas Norfk.................106 F7
Lambden Border...........167 L2
Lamberhurst Kent..........33 H6
Lamberhurst Down
Kent..........................33 H6
Lamberton Border........179 K6
Lambeth Gt Lon.............44 F4
Lambeth
Crematorium
Gt Lon......................44 F5
Lambfair Green Suffk....77 G4
Lambley Notts...............101 M4
Lambley Nthumb...........149 H4
Lambourn W Berk...........40 F5
Lambourne End
Essex........................45 J2
Lambs Green W Susx....31 L4
Lamerton Devon...............6 C1
Lamesley Gatesd...........151 G4
Lamington S Lans..........165 J3
Lamlash N Ayrs.............162 C3
Lamonby Cumb..............148 D7
Lamorna Cnwll..................2 E6
Lamorran Cnwll.................4 D7
Lampeter Cerdgn............66 D5
Lampeter Velfrey
Pembks.....................49 K5
Lamphey Pembks...........49 H7
Lamplugh Cumb.............136 F3
Lamport Nhants..............87 L8
Lamyatt Somset..............26 F4
Lanark S Lans................165 G2
Lancaster Lancs............129 K7
Lancaster &
Morecambe
Crematorium
Lancs.......................129 K6
Lancaster Services
(Forton) Lancs.....121 G1
Lanchester Dur.............150 F5
Lancing W Susx..............19 G5
L'Ancresse Guern.........236 d1
Landbeach Cambs..........76 C2
Landcross Devon............23 G6
Landerberry Abers.......206 E4
Landford Wilts................28 E7
Land-hallow Highld......227 L2
Landican
Crematorium
Wirral......................111 J4
Landimore Swans...........50 F6
Landkey Devon................23 J5
Landore Swans................51 J6
Landrake Cnwll.................6 B4
Land's End Cnwll.............2 C6
Land's End Airport
Cnwll..........................2 C5
Landulph Cnwll................6 C4
Lane Cnwll.......................4 C4
Laneast Cnwll...................9 G7
Lane End Bucks.............42 D3
Lane End Wilts...............27 J3
Lane Ends Derbys........100 E5
Laneham Notts..............116 D6
Lane Head Dur.............140 E5
Lanehead Dur...............149 L6
Langaller Somset...........25 K6
Langar Notts.................102 B5
Langbank Rens.............174 D4
Langbar N York.............123 G1
Langcliffe N York..........130 F6
Langdale End N York...134 E2
Langdown Hants.............16 E2
Langdyke Fife................186 E6
Langenhoe Essex...........62 B4
Langford C Beds............75 H6
Langford Devon..............12 D2
Langford Essex...............61 K6
Langford Notts..............102 D2
Langford Oxon................56 E7
Langford Budville
Somset......................25 H6
Langham Essex..............62 B2

Langham Norfk..............106 B4
Langham Rutlnd.............88 B2
Langham Suffk................77 L1
Langho Lancs................121 K4
Langholm D & G............156 C5
Langlee Border...............167 H3
Langley Hants..................16 F3
Langley Herts..................59 K4
Langley Kent...................33 K3
Langley Nthumb.............149 L3
Langley Slough................43 G5
Langley Somset...............25 G5
Langley W Susx...............30 D5
Langley Warwks..............71 L3
Langley Burrell Wilts.....39 L5
Langley Green Essex......61 L4
Langley Marsh
Somset......................25 G5
Langley Park Dur..........150 F6
Langley Street Norfk......93 H3
Langley Upper Green
Essex........................76 C7
Langney E Susx..............20 D5
Langold Notts................115 L4
Langore Cnwll..................9 J7
Langport Somset............26 B6
Langrick Lincs...............103 L3
Langridge BaNES............39 H6
Langrigg Cumb..............147 K5
Langrish Hants................30 B6
Langsett Barns..............114 E2
Langside P & K..............185 G5
Langstone Hants.............17 K2
Langthorne N York........132 C2
Langthorpe N York........132 F6
Langthwaite N York......140 C6
Langtoft E R Yk..............134 F6
Langtoft Lincs.................89 G2
Langton Dur..................140 F4
Langton Lincs................118 C7
Langton Lincs................118 E7
Langton N York.............134 C6
Langton by Wragby
Lincs.......................117 J6
Langton Green Kent.......32 F5
Langton Herring
Dorset.......................14 C6
Langton Matravers
Dorset.......................15 J6
Langtree Devon..............10 C2
Langwathby Cumb.........148 F7
Langwell House
Highld......................227 K4
Langwith Derbys............115 K7
Langwith Junction
Derbys.....................115 K7
Langworth Lincs............117 H6
Lanhydrock House &
Gardens Cnwll...........5 H3
Lanivet Cnwll....................5 G3
Lanlivery Cnwll.................5 G4
Lanner Cnwll.....................3 J4
Lanreath Cnwll.................5 J4
Lansallos Cnwll................5 J5
Lanteglos Cnwll...............8 E7
Lanteglos Highway
Cnwll..........................5 J5
Lanton Border................167 J5
Lanton Nthumb..............168 D3
Lapford Devon................11 H3
Laphroaig Ag & B.........160 C1
Lapley Staffs...................84 F2
Lapworth Warwks...........71 L1
Larachbeg Highld..........190 E6
Larbert Falk..................176 B3
Largie Abers..................216 B7
Largiemore Ag & B........172 F2
Largoward Fife..............187 H5
Largs N Ayrs..................173 L6
Largybeg N Ayrs...........162 D5
Largymore N Ayrs........162 D4
Larkfield Inver...............173 L4
Larkfield Kent.................33 J2
Larkhall S Lans.............175 K7
Larkhill Wilts...................28 C3
Larling Norfk...................92 B5

La Rocque Jersey 236 e8
Lartington Dur 140 C4
Lasham Hants 30 A3
Lasswade Mdloth 177 J5
Lastingham N York 133 L2
Latchingdon Essex.........61 L7
Latchley Cnwll 6 B2
Lathbury M Keyn.........74 C5
Latheron Highld 227 L2
Latheronwheel
  Highld.........227 L3
Lathones Fife.........187 H5
Latimer Bucks 59 G7
Latteridge S Glos 38 F4
Lattiford Somset.........27 G6
Latton Wilts.........40 C2
Lauder Border.........178 C8
Laugharne Carmth.........50 C4
Laughterton Lincs.........116 D6
Laughton E Susx.........20 A3
Laughton Leics 87 J5
Laughton Lincs.........103 H6
Laughton Lincs.........116 D3
Laughton-en-le-
  Morthen Rothm.....115 K4
Launcells Cnwll.............9 H4
Launceston Cnwll..............9 J7
Launton Oxon.........57 L4
Laurencekirk Abers 197 H3
Laurieston D & G.........146 B3
Laurieston Falk.........176 B3
Lavendon M Keyn.........74 D4
Lavenham Suffk 77 K5
Lavernock V Glam 37 J6
Laversdale Cumb.........148 E3
Laverstock Wilts.........28 D5
Laverstoke Hants.........29 J2
Laverton Gloucs 71 J7
Laverton N York 132 C5
Laverton Somset.........27 H2
La Villette Guern.........236 d4
Lavister Wrexhm.........98 A2
Law S Lans.........175 L7
Lawers P & K.........193 L2
Lawford Essex 62 C2
Lawford Somset.........25 H4
Law Hill S Lans.........175 L7
Lawhitton Cnwll.............9 J7
Lawkland N York 130 E6
Lawns Wood
  Crematorium
  Leeds.........123 K3
Lawrenny Pembks 49 H6
Lawshall Suffk 77 K4
Laxay W Isls.........232 f3
Laxdale W Isls.........232 f2
Laxey IoM.........237 d4
Laxfield Suffk.........93 G8
Laxford Bridge
  Highld.........228 C6
Laxo Shet.........235 d4
Laxton E R Yk.........125 J5
Laxton Nhants.........88 D4
Laxton Notts.........116 B7
Laycock C Brad.........122 F3
Layer Breton Essex.........61 M4
Layer-de-la-Haye
  Essex 62 A4
Layer Marney Essex.........61 L4
Layham Suffk.........78 B6
Laymore Dorset.........13 K2
Laytham E R Yk.........125 H3
Lazonby Cumb.........148 F6
Lea Derbys.........101 G2
Lea Herefs.........54 F4
Lea Lincs.........116 D4
Lea Shrops.........83 G5
Lea Wilts.........39 L3
Leachkin Highld.........212 F5
Leadburn Border.........177 H7
Leadenham Lincs.........102 F3
Leaden Roding Essex 60 F5
Leadgate Dur.........150 E5
Leadhills S Lans.........165 G6
Leafield Oxon.........56 F5
Leagrave Luton.........59 H4

Leake Common Side
  Lincs.........104 C3
Lealholm N York 142 F5
Lealt Highld.........209 H3
Lea Marston Warwks.....86 B5
Leamington Hastings
  Warwks.........72 F2
Leamington Spa
  Warwks.........72 D2
Leap Cross E Susx.........20 C4
Leasgill Cumb.........129 K3
Leasingham Lincs.........103 H3
Leasingthorne Dur 141 G2
Leatherhead Surrey.........31 K1
Leathley N York 123 J2
Leaton Shrops.........98 C8
Leaveland Kent.........34 D4
Leavenheath Suffk 77 L6
Leavening N York 134 C6
Leaves Green Gt Lon.........45 H7
Lebberston N York 135 G3
Le Bourg Guern.........236 c2
Lechlade on Thames
  Gloucs.........56 E7
Lecht Gruinart Ag & B...170 E5
Leck Lancs.........130 C4
Leckbuie P & K.........193 L7
Leckford Hants.........29 G4
Leckhampstead
  Bucks.........73 K6
Leckhampstead
  W Berk.........41 H5
Leckhampstead
  Thicket W Berk.........41 H5
Leckhampton Gloucs.....55 L4
Leckmelm Highld.........220 F4
Leconfield E R Yk.........126 C2
Ledaig Ag & B.........191 H8
Ledburn Bucks.........58 E4
Ledbury Herefs.........70 C6
Ledgemoor Herefs.........69 H4
Ledmore Junction
  Highld.........224 F6
Ledsham Leeds.........124 C4
Ledston Leeds.........124 C5
Ledwell Oxon.........57 H3
Lee Devon.........23 H3
Lee Gt Lon.........45 H5
Leebotwood Shrops.......83 J4
Lee Brockhurst
  Shrops.........98 D6
Leece Cumb.........128 F5
Lee Chapel Essex.........46 B3
Lee Clump Bucks.........58 E6
Leeds Kent.........33 L3
Leeds Leeds.........123 K4
Leeds Bradford
  Airport Leeds.........123 J3
Leeds Castle Kent.........33 L3
Leedstown Cnwll.........3 G4
Leek Staffs.........99 M2
Leek Wootton
  Warwks.........72 C2
Lee Mill Devon.........6 E5
Leeming N York 132 D2
Leeming Bar N York 132 D2
Lee-on-the-Solent
  Hants.........17 G3
Lees Derbys.........100 E5
Lees Oldham.........113 L2
Lees Green Derbys.......100 E5
Leesthorpe Leics.........87 L2
Leeswood Flints.........97 K1
Leetown P & K.........186 C3
Leftwich Ches W 112 F6
Legbourne Lincs.........118 E5
Legerwood Border.........167 J2
Legoland W & M 42 F5
Legsby Lincs.........117 J4
Leicester C Leic.........87 H3
Leicester Forest East
  Leics.........87 G3
Leicester Forest East
  Services Leics.........87 G3
Leigh Dorset.........14 C2
Leigh Gloucs.........55 K3

Leigh Kent.........32 F4
Leigh Surrey.........31 L3
Leigh Wigan.........112 F2
Leigh Wilts.........40 B3
Leigh Worcs.........70 D4
Leigh Beck Essex.........46 D4
Leigh Delamere Wilts 39 K5
Leigh Delamere
  Services Wilts.........39 K5
Leigh Green Kent.........34 B7
Leigh Knoweglass
  S Lans.........175 H7
Leigh-on-Sea Sthend.....46 D3
Leigh Park Dorset.........15 J3
Leigh Sinton Worcs.......70 D4
Leighswood Wsall.........85 J3
Leighterton Gloucs.........39 J3
Leighton Powys.........82 E3
Leighton Shrops.........84 B3
Leighton Bromswold
  Cambs.........89 G7
Leighton Buzzard
  C Beds.........58 F5
Leigh upon Mendip
  Somset.........27 G3
Leigh Woods N Som.....38 E6
Leinthall Earls Herefs....69 J2
Leinthall Starkes
  Herefs.........69 J1
Leintwardine Herefs......83 H8
Leire Leics.........87 G5
Leiston Suffk.........79 J3
Leith C Edin.........177 H3
Leitholm Border.........168 B1
Lelant Cnwll.................2 F4
Lelley E R Yk.........126 F4
Lempitlaw Border.........168 B3
Lemreway W Isls.........232 f3
Lemsford Herts.........59 L5
Lenchwick Worcs.........71 J5
Lendalfoot S Ayrs.........152 D4
Lendrick Stirlg.........184 C6
Lendrum Terrace
  Abers.........217 L6
Lenham Kent.........34 B4
Lenham Heath Kent.......34 B5
Lenie Highld.........202 D1
Lennel Border.........168 C2
Lennox Plunton
  D & G.........146 A5
Lennoxtown E Duns.....175 H3
Lenton C Nott.........101 K5
Lenton Lincs.........103 G6
Lenwade Norfk.........106 D8
Lenzie E Duns.........175 H4
Leochel-Cushnie
  Abers.........205 L4
Leominster Herefs.........69 K3
Leonard Stanley
  Gloucs.........55 J7
Lephin Highld.........208 B4
Leppington N York 134 B7
Lepton Kirk.........123 J7
Lerags Ag & B.........182 B3
L'Eree Guern.........236 b3
Lerryn Cnwll.................5 J4
Lerwick Shet.........235 d6
Lesbury Nthumb.........169 J6
Leslie Abers.........206 B1
Leslie Fife.........186 D6
Lesmahagow S Lans....164 F2
Lesnewth Cnwll.................8 F6
Les Quartiers Guern....236 d2
Les Quennevais
  Jersey.........236 b7
Lessingham Norfk.........107 H6
Lessonhall Cumb.........147 L5
Leswalt D & G.........144 B3
L'Etacq Jersey.........236 a6
Letchmore Heath
  Herts.........43 J2
Letchworth Garden
  City Herts.........59 L3
Letcombe Bassett
  Oxon.........41 G4
Letcombe Regis Oxon...41 G3

Letham Angus 196 E6
Letham Border.........167 K7
Letham Falk.........176 B2
Letham Fife.........186 E4
Letham Grange
  Angus.........197 G7
Lethendy P & K.........195 H7
Lethenty Abers.........206 B2
Lethenty Abers.........216 F6
Letheringham Suffk.......78 F3
Letheringsett Norfk.....106 C5
Letterewe Highld.........219 L7
Letterfearn Highld.........200 D2
Letterfinlay Lodge
  Hotel Highld.........201 K6
Lettermorar Highld.......199 M7
Letters Highld.........220 F4
Lettershaw S Lans.......165 H5
Letterston Pembks.........48 F2
Lettoch Highld.........204 C2
Lettoch Highld.........214 D7
Letton Herefs.........69 G5
Letty Green Herts.........59 M5
Letwell Rothm.........115 K4
Leuchars Fife.........187 G3
Leumrabhagh W Isls....232 f3
Leurbost W Isls.........232 f3
Levedale Staffs.........84 F1
Leven E R Yk.........126 D2
Leven Fife.........186 F7
Levens Cumb.........129 K3
Levens Green Herts.......60 B4
Levenshulme Manch....113 K3
Levenwick Shet.........235 c7
Leverburgh W Isls.........232 d5
Leverington Cambs.........90 C2
Leverstock Green
  Herts.........59 H6
Leverton Lincs.........104 C3
Le Villocq Guern.........236 c2
Levington Suffk.........78 F6
Levisham N York 134 C2
Lew Oxon.........56 F6
Lewannick Cnwll.............9 H8
Lewdown Devon.........10 C7
Lewes E Susx.........19 L4
Leweston Pembks.........48 F3
Lewisham Gt Lon.........45 G5
Lewisham
  Crematorium
  Gt Lon.........45 H5
Lewiston Highld.........212 D8
Lewistown Brdgnd.........36 E3
Lewknor Oxon.........42 B2
Lewson Street Kent.......34 C3
Lewtrenchard Devon.....10 C7
Lexden Essex.........62 A3
Lexworthy Somset.........25 K4
Leybourne Kent.........33 H2
Leyburn N York 131 L2
Leygreen Herts.........59 K3
Ley Hill Bucks.........59 G7
Leyland Lancs.........121 H6
Leylodge Abers.........206 E3
Leys Abers.........217 J4
Leys P & K.........195 K8
Leysdown-on-Sea
  Kent.........47 G6
Leysmill Angus.........196 F6
Leys of Cossans
  Angus.........196 C6
Leysters Herefs.........69 L2
Leyton Gt Lon.........45 G3
Leytonstone Gt Lon.......45 H3
Lezant Cnwll.................5 M1
Lhanbryde Moray.........215 G3
Libanus Powys.........52 F3
Libberton S Lans.........165 J2
Liberton C Edin.........177 J4
Lichfield Staffs.........85 K2
Lickey Worcs.........85 H7
Lickey End Worcs.........85 H8
Lickfold W Susx.........30 F6
Liddesdale Highld.........190 F4
Liddington Swindn.........40 E4
Lidgate Suffk.........77 G3

Lidlington C Beds 74 E6
Liff Angus 186 E2
Lifford Birm. 85 J7
Lifton Devon 9 K7
Liftondown Devon 9 K7
Lighthorne Warwks 72 D4
Lighthorne Heath
    Warwks 72 D4
Lightwater Surrey 42 F7
Lightwater Valley
    Theme Park
    N York. 132 D4
Lilbourne Nhants 87 H7
Lilleshall Wrekin 84 D1
Lilley Herts. 59 J3
Lilliesleaf Border 167 H4
Lillingstone Dayrell
    Bucks 73 K6
Lillingstone Lovell
    Bucks 73 K6
Lillington Dorset 26 F8
Lilliput Poole 15 K4
Lilstock Somset 25 J3
Limbury Luton 59 H3
Limekilnburn S Lans 175 J7
Limekilns Fife 176 E2
Limerigg Falk 176 B4
Limerstone IoW 16 E6
Lime Street Worcs 55 J2
Limington Somset. 26 D6
Limmerhaugh E Ayrs ...164 C4
Limpenhoe Norfk 93 H3
Limpley Stoke Wilts 39 H7
Limpsfield Surrey 32 D3
Limpsfield Chart
    Surrey 32 D3
Linby Notts. 101 K3
Linchmere W Susx 30 E5
Lincluden D & G 155 G6
Lincoln Lincs. 116 F7
Lincoln Crematorium
    Lincs. 117 G7
Lincomb Worcs 70 E2
Lindale Cumb. 129 J4
Lindal in Furness
    Cumb 128 F4
Lindfield W Susx 32 C7
Lindford Hants. 30 D4
Lindley Kirk. 123 G6
Lindridge Worcs 70 C2
Lindsell Essex. 61 G3
Lindsey Suffk 77 L5
Lindsey Tye Suffk 78 B5
Lingdale R & Cl. 142 E4
Lingen Herefs. 69 G2
Lingfield Surrey 32 C4
Lingwood Norfk 93 H2
Linicro Highld. 218 B7
Linkend Worcs 55 J2
Linkenholt Hants. 41 G8
Linkinhorne Cnwll 5 L2
Linktown Fife 177 J1
Linkwood Moray 214 F3
Linley Shrops. 83 G5
Linley Green Herefs 70 C4
Linlithgow W Loth. 176 D3
Linsidemore Highld. 222 D2
Linslade C Beds 58 E3
Linstead Parva Suffk 93 G7
Linstock Cumb 148 D4
Linthurst Worcs 85 H8
Linthwaite Kirk. 123 G7
Lintlaw Border 179 H6
Lintmill Moray 215 L2
Linton Border 168 B4
Linton Cambs. 76 E5
Linton Derbys. 86 C1
Linton Herefs. 54 F3
Linton Kent. 33 K3
Linton Leeds. 124 B2
Linton N York 131 J6
Linton Hill Herefs. 54 F3
Linton-on-Ouse
    N York. 133 G7
Linwood Lincs. 117 J4
Linwood Rens. 174 E5

Lionacleit W Isls 233 b7
Lional W Isls 232 g1
Liphook Hants. 30 D5
Liscard Wirral 111 J3
Liscombe Somset 24 D5
Liskeard Cnwll. 5 K3
Lismore Ag & B 191 G7
Liss Hants. 30 C5
Lissett E R Yk. 135 H7
Lissington Lincs. 117 J5
Lisvane Cardif 37 J4
Liswerry Newpt 37 M3
Litcham Norfk 105 L8
Litchborough Nhants 73 J4
Litchfield Hants. 29 J2
Litherland Sefton 111 K2
Litlington Cambs. 75 K6
Litlington E Susx. 20 B5
Little Abington
    Cambs. 76 D5
Little Addington
    Nhants. 88 D8
Little Airies D & G 145 J5
Little Alne Warwks. 71 K3
Little Altcar Sefton. 111 J1
Little Amwell Herts 60 B5
Little Aston Staffs. 85 K4
Little Ayton N York 142 C5
Little Baddow Essex 61 J6
Little Badminton
    S Glos 39 J4
Little Bampton Cumb ...148 A4
Little Bardfield Essex. 61 G2
Little Barford Bed 75 H3
Little Barningham
    Norfk 106 D5
Little Barrington
    Gloucs 56 D5
Little Barrow Ches W ...112 C7
Little Bavington
    Nthumb 158 C6
Little Bedwyn Wilts. 40 F7
Little Bentley Essex 62 D3
Little Berkhamsted
    Herts. 59 M6
Little Billing Nhants 74 B3
Little Billington
    C Beds 58 F4
Little Birch Herefs. 54 D2
Little Blakenham
    Suffk 78 D5
Little Blencow Cumb 148 E7
Little Bognor W Susx 31 G7
Little Bollington
    Ches E 113 G4
Little Bookham
    Surrey. 31 J1
Littleborough Notts. 116 D5
Littleborough Rochdl. ..122 D7
Littlebourne Kent. 35 G3
Little Bourton Oxon. 72 F5
Little Braxted Essex. 61 K5
Little Brechin Angus. 196 F4
Littlebredy Dorset. 14 B5
Little Brickhill M Keyn. ...58 E2
Little Brington
    Nhants. 73 J2
Little Bromley Essex 62 C3
Little Budworth
    Ches W 112 E7
Littleburn Highld. 212 F4
Little Burstead Essex. 46 A2
Littlebury Essex. 76 D6
Littlebury Green
    Essex. 76 C6
Little Bytham Lincs. 103 G8
Little Carlton Lincs. 118 E4
Little Casterton
    Rutlnd 88 E2
Little Cawthorpe
    Lincs. 118 E5
Little Chalfont Bucks 43 G2
Little Chart Kent. 34 C5
Little Chesterford
    Essex. 76 D6
Little Cheverell Wilts. 27 M2

Little Chishill Cambs 76 B6
Little Clacton Essex. 62 E4
Little Clifton Cumb. 136 E2
Little Comberton
    Worcs 71 G5
Little Common E Susx ...20 E4
Little Compton
    Warwks. 56 E3
Little Cornard Suffk. 77 K6
Little Cowarne Herefs. ...69 L4
Little Coxwell Oxon 40 F2
Little Crakehall
    N York. 132 C2
Little Cressingham
    Norfk. 91 K4
Little Crosby Sefton. 111 K2
Little Cubley Derbys. 100 D5
Little Dalby Leics. 87 L2
Littledean Gloucs. 54 F5
Little Dewchurch
    Herefs. 54 D2
Little Ditton Cambs. 76 F3
Little Downham
    Cambs. 90 D6
Little Driffield E R Yk....134 F7
Little Dunham Norfk. 91 K2
Little Dunkeld P & K. ...195 G7
Little Dunmow Essex. 61 G4
Little Durnford Wilts. 28 C5
Little Easton Essex. 60 F3
Little Eaton Derbys. 101 G4
Little Ellingham Norfk. ...92 B4
Little Everdon Nhants 73 H3
Little Eversden
    Cambs. 75 L4
Little Faringdon Oxon. ...56 E7
Little Fencote N York. ..132 D2
Little Fenton N York 124 D4
Little Fransham
    Norfk. 91 K2
Little Gaddesden
    Herts. 59 G5
Little Glemham Suffk. 79 H3
Little Gorsley Herefs. 55 G3
Little Gransden
    Cambs. 75 J4
Little Green Somset 27 G2
Little Hadham Herts. 60 C4
Little Hale Lincs. 103 J4
Little Hallam Derbys. 101 J4
Little Hallingbury
    Essex 60 D4
Littleham Devon. 12 D6
Littleham Devon. 23 G6
Littlehampton W Susx. ...18 D5
Little Harrowden
    Nhants. 74 C1
Little Haseley Oxon. 57 M7
Little Haven Pembks. 48 E5
Littlehaven W Susx. 31 K5
Little Hay Staffs. 85 K3
Little Haywood Staffs. ..100 A7
Littlehempston
    Devon. 7 J4
Little Hereford Herefs. ...69 K2
Little Horkesley Essex. ...62 A2
Little Hormead Herts. 60 C3
Little Horsted E Susx. 19 M3
Little Horton C Brad. 123 H4
Little Horwood Bucks. 58 C2
Little Houghton
    Barns 115 H1
Little Houghton
    Nhants. 74 B3
Little Hucklow Derbys. ..114 D5
Little Hutton N York. 133 G4
Little Irchester
    Nhants. 74 C2
Little Keyford Somset. 27 H3
Little Kimble Bucks. 58 D6
Little Kineton Warwks 72 D4
Little Kingshill Bucks. 58 E7
Little Knox D & G. 146 E3
Little Langdale Cumb. ..137 J6
Little Langford Wilts. 28 B4
Little Leigh Ches W 112 F6

Little Leighs Essex. 61 H5
Little Lever Bolton. 121 L8
Little Linford M Keyn. 74 B5
Little Load Somset. 26 C6
Little London E Susx 20 C2
Little London Hants. 29 G2
Little London Hants. 41 L8
Little Longstone
    Derbys. 114 D6
Little Maplestead
    Essex. 77 J7
Little Marcle Herefs. 70 C7
Little Marlow Bucks. 42 E3
Little Massingham
    Norfk. 105 J7
Little Melton Norfk. 92 E3
Littlemill Abers. 205 H6
Littlemill Highld. 213 L4
Little Mill Mons. 53 L7
Little Milton Oxon. 57 L7
Little Missenden
    Bucks. 58 F7
Littlemore Oxon. 57 K7
Little Musgrave
    Cumb 139 H5
Little Ness Shrops. 98 B8
Little Newcastle
    Pembks. 49 G2
Little Newsham Dur. 140 E4
Little Norton Somset. 26 C7
Little Oakley Essex. 62 F3
Little Oakley Nhants. 88 C6
Little Orton Cumb. 148 C4
Littleover C Derb. 101 G5
Little Packington
    Warwks 86 B6
Little Paxton Cambs. 75 H3
Little Petherick Cnwll. 4 E2
Little Plumstead
    Norfk. 93 G2
Little Ponton Lincs. 102 F6
Littleport Cambs. 90 E6
Little Preston Nhants. 73 H4
Little Raveley Cambs. 89 J7
Little Reedness E R Yk...125 J6
Little Ribston N York. ...132 F8
Little Rissington
    Gloucs. 56 D4
Little Rollright Oxon. 56 F3
Little Ryburgh Norfk. 106 A6
Little Salkeld Cumb. 148 F7
Little Sampford Essex. 76 F7
Little Saughall
    Ches W. 111 K7
Little Saxham Suffk. 77 H2
Little Scatwell Highld. ...212 B3
Little Shelford Cambs. 76 C4
Little Singleton Lancs. ..120 E3
Little Skipwith N York. ..125 G3
Little Smeaton N York. ..124 D6
Little Snoring Norfk. 106 A6
Little Sodbury S Glos. 39 H4
Little Somborne
    Hants. 29 G5
Little Somerford Wilts. 39 J4
Little Soudley Shrops. 99 G6
Little Stainton Darltn. ...141 J3
Little Stanney Ches W ..112 B6
Little Staughton Bed. 75 G3
Little Steeping Lincs. 118 F8
Little Stoke Staffs. 99 K6
Littlestone-on-Sea
    Kent. 21 L2
Little Stonham Suffk. 78 D3
Little Stretton Leics. 87 J4
Little Stretton Shrops. 83 J5
Little Strickland
    Cumb 138 E4
Little Stukeley Cambs. ...89 H7
Little Sugnall Staffs. 99 J6
Little Swinburne
    Nthumb 158 B6
Little Sypland D & G. ...146 C4
Little Tew Oxon. 57 G3
Little Tey Essex. 61 L4
Little Thetford Cambs. ...90 D7

Little Thorpe Dur 151 K6
Littlethorpe Leics 87 G4
Littlethorpe N York 132 E5
Little Thurlow Suffk......76 F4
Little Thurrock Thurr....45 L4
Littleton Angus..........196 B6
Littleton Ches W........112 C7
Littleton D & G..........146 B4
Littleton Hants............29 J5
Littleton Somset..........26 C5
Littleton Surrey 43 H6
Littleton Drew Wilts 39 J4
Littleton-on-Severn
  S Glos.....................38 E3
Littleton Pannell
  Wilts........................27 M2
Little Torrington
  Devon.....................10 D2
Littletown Dur...........151 H6
Little Town Lancs 121 K4
Little Urswick Cumb.....128 F5
Little Wakering Essex...46 F3
Little Walden Essex......76 D6
Little Waldingfield
  Suffk........................77 K5
Little Walsingham
  Norfk......................105 M5
Little Waltham Essex....61 H5
Little Weighton
  E R Yk.....................126 B4
Little Weldon Nhants....88 D5
Little Wenlock Wrekin ...84 B3
Little Weston Somset 26 F6
Little Whitefield IoW 17 H4
Littlewick Green
  W & M......................42 D4
Little Wilbraham
  Cambs......................76 D3
Little Witcombe
  Gloucs.....................55 K5
Little Witley Worcs.......70 D2
Little Wittenham
  Oxon.......................41 K2
Little Wolford Warwks ...72 C7
Little Woodcote
  Gt Lon......................44 F7
Littleworth Oxon 40 F2
Littleworth Staffs..........99 L7
Littleworth Worcs.........70 F4
Little Wymington
  Bed..........................74 D2
Little Wymondley
  Herts........................59 K3
Little Wyrley Staffs......85 H3
Little Yeldham Essex 77 H6
Littley Green Essex 61 H4
Litton Derbys............114 D6
Litton N York............131 G5
Litton Somset............26 E1
Litton Cheney
  Dorset......................14 A4
Liurbost W Isls...........232 f3
Liverpool Lpool..........111 K4
Liverpool Maritime
  Mercantile City
  Lpool......................111 K4
Liversedge Kirk..........123 J5
Liverton Devon.............7 J2
Liverton R & Cl..........142 F4
Livingston W Loth........176 E5
Livingston Village
  W Loth.....................176 E5
Lixwm Flints..............111 G7
Lizard Cnwll.................3 J8
Llanaelhaearn Gwynd...95 G4
Llanafan Cerdgn..........66 F1
Llanafan-Fawr Powys ...67 L4
Llanallgo IoA.............109 G4
Llanarmon Dyffryn
  Ceiriog Wrexhm.........97 J6
Llanarmon-yn-Ial
  Denbgs......................97 J2
Llanarth Cerdgn 65 L3
Llanarth Mons 54 B5
Llanarthne Carmth 51 G2
Llanasa Flints............110 F5

Llanbadarn Fawr
  Cerdgn.....................80 E7
Llanbadarn Fynydd
  Powys......................82 C7
Llanbadoc Mons 54 B7
Llanbeder Newpt...........38 B3
Llanbedr Gwynd...........95 K7
Llanbedr Powys 53 K4
Llanbedr-Dyffryn-
  Clwyd Denbgs............97 H2
Llanbedrgoch IoA........109 G5
Llanbedrog Gwynd........94 F6
Llanbedr-y-Cennin
  Conwy....................109 L7
Llanberis Gwynd..........95 K1
Llanbethery V Glam.......37 G6
Llanbister Powys..........82 C8
Llanblethian V Glam......36 F5
Llanboidy Carmth 49 L3
Llanbradach Caerph 37 J3
Llanbrynmair Powys......81 J3
Llancadle V Glam..........37 G6
Llancarfan V Glam.........37 G6
Llancloudy Herefs........54 D4
Llandaff Cardif............37 J5
Llandanwg Gwynd........95 K6
Llanddaniel Fab IoA.....109 G7
Llanddarog Carmth 51 G3
Llanddeiniol Cerdgn......66 D1
Llanddeiniolen
  Gwynd.....................109 H7
Llandderfel Gwynd........96 F5
Llanddeusant IoA........108 D4
Llanddew Powys 53 G2
Llanddewi Swans..........50 F7
Llanddewi Brefi
  Cerdgn.....................66 F4
Llanddewi
  Rhydderch Mons 53 M5
Llanddewi Velfrey
  Pembks......................49 K4
Llanddewi
  Ystradenni Powys.......68 C2
Llanddoget Conwy......109 M8
Llanddona IoA............109 H5
Llanddowror Carmth......50 B3
Llanddulas Conwy........110 C6
Llanddwywe Gwynd.......95 K7
Llanddyfnan IoA.........109 G5
Llandefaelog-Tre'r-
  Graig Powys 53 H3
Llandefalle Powys.........68 C7
Llandegfan IoA...........109 H6
Llandegla Denbgs.........97 J3
Llandegley Powys.........68 D2
Llandegveth Mons........37 M2
Llandeilo Carmth..........51 J2
Llandeilo Graban
  Powys......................68 C5
Llandeloy Pembks.........48 E3
Llandenny Mons...........54 B7
Llandevaud Newpt........38 B3
Llandevenny Mons........38 B3
Llandinam Powys..........82 B5
Llandissilio Pembks.......49 J3
Llandogo Mons............54 D7
Llandough V Glam........36 F6
Llandough V Glam........37 J5
Llandovery Carmth.......67 G7
Llandow V Glam..........36 E5
Llandre Carmth............66 F4
Llandre Cerdgn............80 E6
Llandre Isaf Pembks 49 J2
Llandrillo Denbgs.........97 G5
Llandrillo-yn-Rhos
  Conwy....................110 B5
Llandrindod Wells
  Powys......................68 B3
Llandrinio Powys.........97 L8
Llandudno Conwy.......109 L5
Llandudno Junction
  Conwy....................109 M6
Llandulas Powys...........67 J6
Llandwrog Gwynd........95 H2
Llandybie Carmth..........51 J3
Llandyfaelog Carmth 50 E3

Llandyfriog Cerdgn 65 K6
Llandygai Gwynd.........109 H7
Llandygwydd Cerdgn.....65 H5
Llandyrnog Denbgs......110 F8
Llandyssil Powys..........82 E4
Llandysul Cerdgn..........65 L6
Llanedeyrn Cardif.........37 K4
Llaneglwys Powys.........68 B6
Llanegryn Gwynd..........80 D3
Llanegwad Carmth........51 G2
Llaneilian IoA.............108 F3
Llanelian-yn-Rhôs
  Conwy....................110 B6
Llanelidan Denbgs.........97 H3
Llanelieu Powys............68 D7
Llanellen Mons 53 L5
Llanelli Carmth............51 G5
Llanelli Crematorium
  Carmth.....................51 G5
Llanelltyd Gwynd..........96 A8
Llanelwedd Powys.........68 B4
Llanenddwyn Gwynd......95 K7
Llanengan Gwynd..........94 E6
Llanerchymedd IoA......108 E5
Llanerfyl Powys............82 B2
Llanfachraeth IoA........108 D5
Llanfachreth Gwynd 96 B7
Llanfaelog IoA............108 D6
Llanfaelrhys Gwynd.......94 D6
Llanfaethlu IoA...........108 D4
Llanfair Gwynd.............95 K6
Llanfair Caereinion
  Powys......................82 C3
Llanfair Clydogau
  Cerdgn.....................66 E4
Llanfair Dyffryn
  Clwyd Denbgs............97 H2
Llanfairfechan Conwy...109 K6
Llanfair P G IoA..........109 G6
Llanfair Talhaiarn
  Conwy....................110 C7
Llanfair Waterdine
  Shrops.....................82 E7
Llanfairynghornwy
  IoA........................108 D4
Llanfair-yn-Neubwll
  IoA........................108 C6
Llanfallteg Carmth........49 K4
Llanfallteg West
  Carmth.....................49 K4
Llanfarian Cerdgn.........80 D7
Llanfechain Powys........97 J7
Llanfechell IoA...........108 E3
Llanferres Denbgs.........97 J1
Llanfihangel-ar-arth
  Carmth.....................66 B6
Llanfihangel Glyn
  Myfyr Conwy 96 F3
Llanfihangel Nant
  Bran Powys 67 K7
Llanfihangel
  Rhydithon Powys.......68 D2
Llanfihangel Rogiet
  Mons......................38 C3
Llanfihangel-y-
  Creuddyn Cerdgn.......80 F7
Llanfihangel-yng-
  Ngwynfa Powys.........82 C1
Llanfihangel yn
  Nhowyn IoA.............108 D6
Llanfihangel-y-
  traethau Gwynd.........95 K5
Llanfilo Powys.............53 H7
Llanfoist Mons.............53 L5
Llanfor Gwynd.............96 E5
Llanfrechfa Torfn..........37 L2
Llanfrynach Powys........53 G3
Llanfwrog Denbgs.........97 H2
Llanfwrog IoA............108 C5
Llanfyllin Powys...........97 H8
Llanfynydd Carmth........66 D8
Llanfynydd Flints..........97 L2
Llanfyrnach Pembks......49 L2
Llangadfan Powys.........81 L2
Llangadog Carmth 66 F8
Llangadwaladr IoA.......108 E7

Llangaffo IoA.............108 F7
Llangammarch Wells
  Powys......................67 K5
Llangan V Glam 36 E5
Llangarron Herefs........54 D4
Llangathen Carmth........51 H2
Llangattock Powys 53 K4
Llangattock Lingoed
  Mons......................54 A4
Llangedwyn Powys........97 J7
Llangefni IoA.............108 F6
Llangeinor Brdgnd........36 E3
Llangeitho Cerdgn.........66 E3
Llangeler Carmth..........65 L6
Llangelynin Gwynd.......80 D3
Llangendeirne
  Carmth.....................50 F3
Llangennech Carmth......51 H5
Llangennith Swans........50 E7
Llangernyw Conwy......110 B7
Llangian Gwynd............94 E6
Llangloffan Pembks.......64 C7
Llanglydwen Carmth......49 K3
Llangoed IoA.............109 J5
Llangollen Denbgs........97 K4
Llangolman Pembks......49 J3
Llangors Powys............53 H3
Llangower Gwynd.........96 D6
Llangranog Cerdgn 65 K4
Llangristiolus IoA........108 F6
Llangrove Herefs..........54 D4
Llangunllo Powys.........68 E1
Llangunnor Carmth.......50 E2
Llangurig Powys...........81 K7
Llangwm Conwy..........96 E6
Llangwm Mons 54 B7
Llangwm Pembks.........49 G5
Llangwnnadl Gwynd......94 D6
Llangwyryfon Cerdgn....66 D1
Llangybi Cerdgn...........66 E4
Llangybi Gwynd............95 G4
Llangybi Mons 38 A2
Llangynhafal Denbgs ...110 F8
Llangynidr Powys..........53 J4
Llangynin Carmth.........50 B2
Llangynog Carmth.........50 D3
Llangynog Powys..........97 G7
Llangynwyd Brdgnd.......36 D3
Llanhamlach Powys........53 H3
Llanharan Rhondd.........36 F4
Llanharry Rhondd.........36 F4
Llanhennock Mons........38 A2
Llanhilleth Blae G.........53 K7
Llanidloes Powys..........81 K6
Llaniestyn Gwynd..........94 E5
Llanigon Powys............68 E6
Llanilar Cerdgn.............80 E8
Llanilid Rhondd............36 F4
Llanina Cerdgn.............65 L3
Llanishen Cardif...........37 J4
Llanishen Mons............54 C7
Llanllechid Gwynd......109 J7
Llanllowell Mons...........54 B7
Llanllugan Powys..........82 B3
Llanllwch Carmth..........50 E2
Llanllwchaiarn Powys 82 C5
Llanllwni Carmth..........66 C6
Llanllyfni Gwynd...........95 H3
Llanmadoc Swans.........50 F6
Llanmaes V Glam..........36 E5
Llanmartin Newpt.........38 B3
Llanmiloe Carmth.........50 B4
Llannefydd Conwy......110 D7
Llannon Carmth...........51 G4
Llannor Gwynd.............94 F5
Llanon Cerdgn.............66 C2
Llanover Mons.............53 L6
Llanpumsaint Carmth 65 L2
Llanrhaeadr-ym-
  Mochnant Powys........97 H7
Llanrhian Pembks.........48 D2
Llanrhidian Swans.........50 F6
Llanrhychwyn Conwy....96 B1
Llanrhyddlad IoA.........108 D4
Llanrhystud Cerdgn.......66 C1
Llanrug Gwynd...........109 G8

Llanrumney Cardif 37 K4
Llanrwst Conwy 96 C1
Llansadurnen Carmth ...50 C4
Llansadwrn Carmth 66 F7
Llansadwrn IoA 109 H6
Llansaint Carmth 50 E4
Llansamlet Swans 51 K6
Llansanffraid Glan
  Conwy Conwy 109 M6
Llansannan Conwy 110 C7
Llansantffraed Powys ...53 H4
Llansantffraed-
  Cwmdeuddwr
  Powys 67 L2
Llansantffraed-in-
  Elvel Powys 68 C4
Llansantffraid
  Cerdgn 66 C2
Llansantffraid-ym-
  Mechain Powys 97 K7
Llansawel Carmth 66 E7
Llansilin Powys 97 K6
Llansoy Mons 54 C7
Llanspyddid Powys 52 F3
Llanstadwell Pembks 48 F6
Llansteffan Carmth 50 D4
Llantarnam Torfn 37 L2
Llanteg Pembks 49 K5
Llanthewy Skirrid
  Mons 53 M5
Llanthony Mons 53 L3
Llantilio-Crossenny
  Mons 54 B5
Llantilio Pertholey
  Mons 53 L5
Llantrisant Mons 38 B2
Llantrisant Rhondd 37 G4
Llantrithyd V Glam 37 G6
Llantwit Fardre
  Rhondd 37 G3
Llantwit Major V Glam ..36 F6
Llanuwchllyn Gwynd 96 D6
Llanvaches Newpt 38 B3
Llanvair Discoed
  Mons 38 C3
Llanvapley Mons 54 A5
Llanvetherine Mons 54 A5
Llanvihangel
  Crucorney Mons 53 L4
Llanwddyn Powys 96 F8
Llanwenog Cerdgn 66 C5
Llanwern Newpt 38 A3
Llanwinio Carmth 50 C1
Llanwnda Gwynd 95 H2
Llanwnda Pembks 64 C6
Llanwnnen Cerdgn 66 C5
Llanwnog Powys 82 B5
Llanwrda Carmth 66 F7
Llanwrin Powys 81 H3
Llanwrthwl Powys 67 L2
Llanwrtyd Wells
  Powys 67 J5
Llanwyddelan Powys 82 C4
Llanyblodwel Shrops 97 K7
Llanybri Carmth 50 D3
Llanybydder Carmth 66 C5
Llanycefn Pembks 49 J3
Llanychaer Bridge
  Pembks 64 D7
Llanymawddwy
  Gwynd 96 D8
Llanymynech Powys 97 K7
Llanynghenedl IoA 108 D5
Llanynys Denbgs 110 F8
Llanyre Powys 68 B3
Llanystumdwy
  Gwynd 95 H5
Llanywern Powys 53 H3
Llawhaden Pembks 49 H4
Llawryglyn Powys 81 K5
Llay Wrexhm 97 M2
Llechrhyd Caerph 53 H6
Llechryd Cerdgn 65 H5
Lledrod Cerdgn 66 E1
Lleyn Peninsula
  Gwynd 94 E5

Llithfaen Gwynd 94 F4
Lloc Flints 111 G6
Llowes Powys 68 D6
Llwydcoed Rhondd 52 F6
Llwydcoed
  Crematorium
  Rhondd 52 F6
Llwydiarth Powys 82 B1
Llwyncelyn Cerdgn 66 B3
Llwyndafydd Cerdgn 65 L4
Llwyngwril Gwynd 80 D2
Llwynmawr Wrexhm 97 K5
Llwynypia Rhondd 36 F2
Llynclys Shrops 97 L7
Llynfaes IoA 108 E5
Llysfaen Conwy 110 B6
Llyswen Powys 68 C6
Llysworney V Glam 36 E5
Llys-y-frân Pembks 49 H3
Llywel Powys 52 D3
Loan Falk 176 C3
Loanhead Mdloth 177 J5
Loaningfoot D & G 147 G4
Loans S Ayrs 163 J3
Lobhillcross Devon 10 C7
Lochailort Highld 200 B8
Lochaline Highld 190 D7
Lochans D & G 144 C4
Locharbriggs D & G 155 H6
Lochavich Ag & B 182 D4
Lochawe Ag & B 183 G2
Loch Baghasdail
  W Isls 233 C8
Lochboisdale W Isls ...233 c8
Lochbuie Ag & B 181 J3
Lochcarron Highld 210 D6
Lochdon Ag & B 181 L2
Lochdonhead Ag & B 181 L2
Lochead Ag & B 172 D3
Lochearnhead Stirlg ...184 D3
Lochee C Dund 186 F2
Locheilside Station
  Highld 191 K2
Lochend Highld 212 F6
Locheport W Isls 233 c6
Loch Euphoirt W Isls ..233 c6
Lochfoot D & G 154 F7
Lochgair Ag & B 172 F1
Lochgelly Fife 186 C8
Lochgilphead Ag & B ...172 E2
Lochgoilhead Ag & B ...183 H6
Lochieheads Fife 186 D5
Lochill Moray 215 G2
Lochindorb Lodge
  Highld 214 B7
Lochinver Highld 224 D4
Loch Lomond and
  The Trossachs
  National Park 184 A5
Lochluichart Highld ...211 L2
Lochmaben D & G 155 J5
Lochmaddy W Isls 233 c6
Loch Maree Hotel
  Highld 219 L7
Loch nam Madadh
  W Isls 233 c6
Loch Ness Highld 202 E1
Lochore Fife 186 C7
Lochranza N Ayrs 172 F7
Lochside Abers 197 H4
Lochside D & G 155 G6
Lochside D & G 213 J4
Lochslin Highld 223 J5
Lochton S Ayrs 152 F6
Lochty Angus 196 E4
Lochty Fife 187 H5
Lochuisge Highld 190 F5
Lochwinnoch Rens 174 C6
Lochwood D & G 155 J3
Lockengate Cnwll 5 G4
Lockerbie D & G 155 K5
Lockeridge Wilts 40 C6
Lockerley Hants 28 F6
Locking N Som 38 A8
Locking Stumps
  Warrtn 112 F3

Lockington E R Yk 126 B2
Lockleywood Shrops 99 G6
Locksbottom Gt Lon 45 H6
Locks Heath Hants 17 G2
Lockton N York 134 C2
Loddington Leics 87 L3
Loddington Nhants 88 B7
Loddiswell Devon 7 G6
Loddon Norfk 93 H4
Lode Cambs 76 D3
Lode Heath Solhll 85 L7
Loders Dorset 13 L4
Lodge Hill
  Crematorium
  Birm 85 H6
Lodsworth W Susx 30 F6
Lofthouse Leeds 123 L5
Lofthouse N York 131 L5
Lofthouse Gate
  Wakefd 123 L5
Loftus R & Cl 142 F4
Logan E Ayrs 164 C5
Loganlea W Loth 176 C6
Loggerheads Staffs 99 G5
Logie Angus 197 H4
Logie Fife 186 F4
Logie Moray 214 C4
Logie Coldstone
  Abers 205 K4
Logie Newton Abers 216 C6
Logie Pert Angus 197 G4
Logierait P & K 194 F6
Logierieve Abers 217 H8
Login Carmth 49 K3
Lolworth Cambs 75 L2
Lonbain Highld 209 L4
Londesborough
  E R Yk 125 K2
London Gt Lon 44 F4
London Apprentice
  Cnwll 4 F6
London Colney Herts 59 K7
Londonderry N York 132 D3
London Gateway
  Services Gt Lon 44 D2
Londonthorpe Lincs 102 F5
London Zoo ZSL
  Gt Lon 44 F4
Londubh Highld 219 K5
Lonemore Highld 219 J6
Long Ashton N Som 38 D6
Long Bank Worcs 84 D8
Long Bennington
  Lincs 102 D4
Longbenton N Tyne 151 G2
Longborough Gloucs 56 D3
Long Bredy Dorset 14 B4
Longbridge Birm 85 H7
Longbridge Deverill
  Wilts 27 K4
Long Buckby Nhants 73 J2
Longburton Dorset 26 F8
Long Clawson Leics 102 B6
Longcliffe Derbys 100 E2
Longcombe Devon 7 J4
Long Compton Staffs 99 J7
Long Compton
  Warwks 56 F2
Longcot Oxon 40 F3
Long Crendon Bucks 58 B6
Long Crichel Dorset 15 J1
Longden Shrops 83 J3
Long Ditton Surrey 44 D6
Longdon Staffs 85 J2
Longdon Worcs 70 E7
Longdon Green Staffs ...85 J2
Longdon upon Tern
  Wrekin 84 B1
Longdown Devon 11 K6
Longdowns Cnwll 3 J4
Long Duckmanton
  Derbys 115 H7
Long Eaton Derbys 101 J5
Longfield Kent 45 L6
Longford Covtry 86 D6
Longford Derbys 100 E5

Longford Gloucs 55 J4
Longford Shrops 98 F5
Longford Wrekin 99 G8
Longforgan P & K 186 E2
Longformacus
  Border 178 E6
Longframlington
  Nthumb 158 E3
Long Green Ches W 112 C7
Longham Dorset 15 K3
Longham Norfk 91 L1
Long Hanborough
  Oxon 57 H5
Longhaven Abers 217 L6
Longhirst Nthumb 158 E4
Longhope Gloucs 55 G4
Longhope Ork 234 b7
Longhorsley Nthumb 158 E4
Longhoughton
  Nthumb 169 J6
Long Itchington
  Warwks 72 E2
Longlane Derbys 100 E5
Long Lawford
  Warwks 86 F7
Longleat Safari &
  Adventure Park
  Wilts 27 J3
Longlevens Gloucs 55 J4
Longleys P & K 195 L7
Long Load Somset 26 C6
Longmanhill Abers 216 E2
Long Marston Herts 58 E5
Long Marston N York ...124 D1
Long Marston Warwks 71 L5
Long Marton Cumb 138 F3
Long Melford Suffk 77 J5
Longmoor Camp
  Hants 30 C5
Longmorn Moray 214 F3
Longmoss Ches E 113 K6
Long Newton Gloucs 39 K3
Longnewton Border 167 J4
Long Newton S Loth 178 B5
Longnewton S on T 141 J4
Longney Gloucs 55 H5
Longniddry E Loth 177 L3
Longnor Shrops 83 J4
Longnor Staffs 114 C8
Longparish Hants 29 H3
Long Preston N York ...130 F7
Longridge Lancs 121 J3
Longridge W Loth 176 C5
Longriggend N Lans 175 L4
Long Riston E R Yk 126 E3
Longrock Cnwll 2 E5
Longsdon Staffs 99 L3
Longside Abers 217 K5
Longstanton Cambs 76 B2
Longstock Hants 29 G4
Longstowe Cambs 75 K4
Long Stratton Norfk 92 E5
Long Street M Keyn 74 B5
Longstreet Wilts 28 C2
Long Sutton Hants 30 C3
Long Sutton Lincs 104 C7
Long Sutton Somset 26 C6
Longthorpe C Pete 89 H4
Long Thurlow Suffk 78 B2
Longthwaite Cumb 138 B3
Longton C Stke 99 K4
Longton Lancs 121 G5
Longtown Cumb 148 C2
Longtown Herefs 53 L3
Longueville Jersey 236 d7
Longville in the Dale
  Shrops 83 K5
Long Waste Wrekin 84 B1
Long Whatton Leics 101 J7
Longwick Bucks 58 C6
Long Wittenham
  Oxon 41 K2
Longwitton Nthumb 158 D4
Longwood D & G 146 C3
Longworth Oxon 57 G7
Longyester E Loth 178 C5

Lonmay Abers............217 J3
Lonmore Highld........208 D5
Looe Cnwll..................5 K5
Loose Kent.................33 K3
Loosley Row Bucks....58 D7
Lootcherbrae Abers.....216 B4
Lopen Somset..............26 B8
Loppington Shrops......98 C6
Lords Wood Medway....46 C7
Lornty P & K..............195 J6
Loscoe Derbys...........101 H3
Lossiemouth Moray....214 F1
Lostock Gralam
  Ches W...................113 G6
Lostock Green
  Ches W...................113 G6
Lostwithiel Cnwll.........5 H4
Lothbeg Highld..........227 G6
Lothersdale N York....122 E2
Lothmore Highld........227 G6
Loudwater Bucks........42 E3
Loughborough Leics...101 K8
Loughborough
  Crematorium
  Leics.....................101 K8
Loughor Swans............51 H6
Loughton Essex..........45 H2
Loughton M Keyn.........74 B6
Lound Lincs...............103 H8
Lound Notts..............116 B4
Lound Suffk................93 K4
Lount Leics...............101 G8
Louth Lincs...............118 D4
Lovedean Hants...........30 B8
Lover Wilts.................28 E7
Loversall Donc............115 L2
Loves Green Essex.......61 G6
Loveston Pembks.........49 J5
Lovington Somset........26 E5
Low Ackworth
  Wakefd...................124 C6
Low Barbeth D & G.....144 B2
Low Bentham N York....130 C5
Low Biggins Cumb......130 K8
Low Borrowbridge
  Cumb....................138 E6
Low Bradfield Sheff....114 E3
Low Bradley N York....122 F2
Low Burnham N Linc...116 C2
Lowca Cumb...............136 D3
Low Catton E R Yk.....133 L8
Low Crosby Cumb.......148 D3
Lowdham Notts..........102 A3
Low Dinsdale Darltn...141 J5
Lower Aisholt
  Somset....................25 J4
Lower Ansty Dorset......14 E2
Lower Apperley
  Gloucs.....................55 J3
Lower Ashton Devon.....11 J7
Lower Assendon
  Oxon.......................42 C4
Lower Bartle Lancs.....121 G4
Lower Basildon
  W Berk.....................41 L5
Lower Beeding
  W Susx.....................31 L6
Lower Benefield
  Nhants.....................88 E5
Lower Bentley Worcs....71 H2
Lower Boddington
  Nhants.....................72 F4
Lower Bourne Surrey....30 D3
Lower Brailes Warwks...72 C6
Lower Breakish
  Highld....................199 L2
Lower Broadheath
  Worcs......................70 E3
Lower Broxwood
  Herefs......................69 G4
Lower Bullingham
  Herefs......................69 K6
Lower Burgate Hants....28 D7
Lower Caldecote
  C Beds.....................75 H5
Lower Chapel Powys.....68 B7

Lower Chicksgrove
  Wilts.......................27 L5
Lower Chute Wilts........28 F2
Lower Clapton Gt Lon...45 G3
Lower Clent Worcs.......85 G7
Lower Cumberworth
  Kirk.......................123 J8
Lower Dean Bed..........74 F2
Lower Diabaig Highld...210 C3
Lower Dicker E Susx.....20 B4
Lower Down Shrops......83 G6
Lower Dunsforth
  N York....................133 G6
Lower Egleton Herefs....70 B5
Lower End M Keyn........74 D6
Lower Eythorne Kent.....35 H5
Lower Failand N Som.....38 D5
Lower Farringdon
  Hants......................30 B4
Lower Feltham
  Gt Lon.....................43 H6
Lower Froyle Hants.......30 C3
Lower Gabwell Devon.....7 L2
Lower Gledfield
  Highld....................222 D4
Lower Godney
  Somset....................26 C3
Lower Gravenhurst
  C Beds.....................75 G7
Lower Green Kent........32 F5
Lower Green Kent........33 G5
Lower Halliford
  Surrey.....................43 H6
Lower Halstow Kent.....46 E6
Lower Hamworthy
  Poole......................15 J4
Lower Hardres Kent.....34 F4
Lower Hartwell Bucks...58 C5
Lower Hergest Herefs....68 F4
Lower Heyford Oxon.....57 J3
Lower Houses Kirk.....123 H7
Lower Irlam Salfd......113 G3
Lower Killeyan Ag & B..160 A2
Lower Langford
  N Som.....................38 C7
Lower Largo Fife.......187 G6
Lower Leigh Staffs....100 A5
Lower Loxhore
  Devon......................23 K4
Lower Lydbrook
  Gloucs.....................54 E5
Lower Lye Herefs........69 H2
Lower Machen
  Newpt......................37 K3
Lower Merridge
  Somset....................25 J4
Lower Middleton
  Cheney Nhants..........73 G6
Lower Moor Worcs.......71 H5
Lower Morton S Glos.....38 F3
Lower Nazeing Essex....60 C6
Lower Penarth
  V Glam.....................37 J6
Lower Penn Staffs.......84 F4
Lower Peover Ches E...113 H6
Lower Quinton
  Warwks....................71 L5
Lower Raydon Suffk.....78 C6
Lower Roadwater
  Somset....................25 G4
Lower Seagry Wilts......39 L4
Lower Shelton C Beds...74 E6
Lower Shiplake Oxon....42 C4
Lower Shuckburgh
  Warwks....................72 F3
Lower Slaughter
  Gloucs.....................56 D4
Lower Standen Kent.....35 H6
Lower Stanton St
  Quintin Wilts............39 L4
Lower Stoke Medway....46 D5
Lower Stone Gloucs......38 F2
Lower Stow Bedon
  Norfk......................91 L5
Lower Street Norfk....106 F5
Lower Street Suffk......78 D4

Lower Swanwick
  Hants......................16 F1
Lower Swell Gloucs......56 D3
Lower Tean Staffs......100 A5
Lower Town Devon.........7 G2
Lower Town Pembks......64 D6
Lower Upcott Devon......11 K8
Lower Upham Hants......29 K7
Lower Weare Somset.....26 B2
Lower Welson Herefs....68 F4
Lower Westmancote
  Worcs......................71 G6
Lower Whatley
  Somset....................27 H3
Lower Whitley
  Ches W...................112 E5
Lower Wield Hants.......29 M4
Lower Willingham
  E Susx.....................20 C5
Lower Withington
  Ches E....................113 J7
Lower Woodford
  Wilts.......................28 C4
Lower Wraxhall
  Dorset......................14 B3
Lowesby Leics............87 K3
Lowestoft Suffk...........93 L5
Loweswater Cumb......137 G3
Low Fell Gatesd........151 G3
Lowfield Heath
  W Susx.....................31 L4
Low Gartachorrans
  Stirlg.....................174 E2
Low Grantley N York...132 C5
Low Ham Somset.........26 B5
Low Harrogate
  N York....................132 D7
Low Hesket Cumb.......148 E5
Low Hutton N York.....134 B6
Lowick Nhants............88 E7
Lowick Nthumb.........168 F2
Lowick Green Cumb....129 G3
Low Lorton Cumb.......137 G3
Low Marnham Notts...116 D7
Low Mill N York.........142 E7
Low Moorsley Sundld..151 H5
Low Moresby Cumb.....136 D3
Low Newton Cumb.....129 J3
Low Row Cumb..........149 G3
Low Row N York........140 B7
Low Salchrie D & G....144 B2
Low Santon N Linc....125 L7
Lowsonford Warwks.....71 L2
Low Tharston Norfk.....92 E4
Lowther Cumb...........138 D3
Lowthorpe E R Yk.....135 G7
Lowton Somset...........25 J7
Low Torry Fife..........176 D2
Low Worsall N York....141 J5
Low Wray Cumb.........137 K6
Loxbeare Devon..........11 L2
Loxhill Surrey.............31 G4
Loxhore Devon............23 K4
Loxley Warwks............72 C4
Loxton N Som.............26 A11
Loxwood W Susx..........31 H5
Loyal Lodge Highld.....229 J6
Lubenham Leics..........87 K6
Luccombe Somset.......24 E3
Luccombe Village
  IoW........................17 H6
Lucker Nthumb.........169 H4
Luckett Cnwll..............6 B7
Lucking Street Essex....77 J7
Luckington Wilts........39 J4
Lucklawhill Fife.......187 G3
Luckwell Bridge
  Somset....................24 E4
Lucton Herefs............69 J2
Ludag N Isls.............233 b9
Ludborough Lincs.....118 D3
Ludbrook Devon...........6 F5
Ludchurch Pembks......49 K5
Luddenden Calder.....122 F5
Luddenden Foot
  Calder...................122 F5

Luddesdown Kent........46 A6
Luddington N Linc.....125 J7
Luddington Warwks.....71 L4
Luddington in the
  Brook Nhants............89 G6
Ludford Lincs............117 K4
Ludford Shrops...........83 K8
Ludgershall Bucks......58 A4
Ludgershall Wilts........28 E2
Ludgvan Cnwll..............2 E5
Ludham Norfk...........107 H8
Ludlow Shrops............83 K7
Ludney Somset...........26 B8
Ludwell Wilts.............27 K6
Ludworth Dur............151 J6
Luffness E Loth........178 B3
Lugar E Ayrs..............164 C5
Luggate Burn E Loth...178 D4
Luggiebank N Lans....175 K4
Lugton E Ayrs...........174 D7
Lugwardine Herefs......69 K6
Luib Highld..............209 J8
Luing Ag & B............181 L5
Lulham Herefs............69 H6
Lullington Derbys........86 B2
Lullington Somset.......27 H2
Lulsgate Bottom
  N Som.....................38 D7
Lulsley Worcs.............70 D4
Lumb Calder.............122 F6
Lumby N York...........124 D4
Lumloch E Duns........175 H4
Lumphanan Abers.....206 B4
Lumphinnans Fife.....186 C8
Lumsden Abers.........205 K2
Lunan Angus............197 H6
Lunanhead Angus.....196 D6
Luncarty P & K.........186 A2
Lund E R Yk..............126 B2
Lund N York.............125 G4
Lundie Angus...........186 E1
Lundin Links Fife.....187 G6
Lundin Mill Fife.......187 G6
Lundy Devon..............22 B3
Lunga Ag & B............181 L5
Lunna Shet..............235 d4
Lunsford Kent............33 J2
Lunsford's Cross
  E Susx.....................20 E4
Lunt Sefton.............111 K2
Luppitt Devon............12 F2
Lupset Wakefd..........123 L6
Lupton Cumb............129 L4
Lurgashall W Susx.......30 F6
Lurley Devon..............11 L2
Luscombe Devon..........7 J4
Luss Ag & B.............183 L8
Lussagiven Ag & B....171 L2
Lusta Highld............208 D3
Lustleigh Devon..........11 H8
Luston Herefs............69 J2
Luthermuir Abers.....197 G3
Luthrie Fife.............186 E4
Luton Devon................7 K1
Luton Devon..............12 D2
Luton Luton...............59 H4
Luton Medway............46 C6
Luton Airport Luton.....59 J4
Lutterworth Leics.......87 G6
Lutton Devon...............6 E4
Lutton Devon...............7 G4
Lutton Lincs............104 C7
Lutton Nhants............89 G6
Luxborough Somset.....24 F4
Luxulyan Cnwll............5 G4
Luxulyan Valley Cnwll...5 G4
Lybster Highld..........231 J7
Lydbury North Shrops...83 G6
Lydd Kent.................21 K2
Lydd Airport Kent.......21 L2
Lydden Kent...............35 H5
Lydden Kent...............35 K2
Lyddington Rutlnd.......88 C4
Lydeard St Lawrence
  Somset....................25 H5
Lydford Devon............10 D7

Lydford on Fosse
Somset 26 E5
Lydgate Calder............122 D5
Lydham Shrops.............83 G5
Lydiard Millicent Wilts 40 C3
Lydiard Tregoze
Swindn 40 C4
Lydiate Sefton 111 K2
Lydiate Ash Worcs.........85 H7
Lydlinch Dorset............27 H8
Lydney Gloucs 54 F7
Lydstep Pembks 49 J7
Lye Dudley 85 G6
Lye Green E Susx 32 F6
Lye Green Warwks 71 L2
Lye's Green Wilts 27 J3
Lyford Oxon 41 H2
Lymbridge Green
Kent 34 F6
Lyme Regis Dorset 13 J4
Lyminge Kent...............34 F6
Lymington Hants............16 C4
Lyminster W Susx 18 D5
Lymm Warrtn 113 G4
Lympne Kent................34 F7
Lympsham Somset 25 M1
Lympstone Devon 12 C5
Lynchat Highld............203 J5
Lynch Green Norfk..........92 D3
Lyndhurst Hants............16 C2
Lyndon Rutlnd 88 C3
Lyne Border...............166 B2
Lyne Surrey 43 G7
Lyneal Shrops...............98 C6
Lyneham Oxon 56 F4
Lyneham Wilts 40 A5
Lynemouth Nthumb........159 H4
Lyne of Skene Abers 206 E4
Lyness Ork 234 b7
Lyng Norfk 106 C8
Lyng Somset 25 M5
Lynmouth Devon 23 L2
Lynsted Kent...............34 C3
Lynton Devon 23 L2
Lyon's Gate Dorset 14 C2
Lyonshall Herefs............69 G4
Lytchett Matravers
Dorset 15 H4
Lytchett Minster
Dorset 15 H4
Lyth Highld...............231 K3
Lytham Lancs 120 E5
Lytham St Anne's
Lancs 120 D5
Lythe N York 143 H5
Lythmore Highld 230 F3

M

Mabe Burnthouse
Cnwll..........................3 K4
Mablethorpe Lincs 119 G4
Macclesfield Ches E 113 K6
Macclesfield
Crematorium
Ches E 113 K6
Macduff Abers 216 D2
Macharioch Ag & B........161 J7
Machrie N Ayrs............162 A3
Machrihanish Ag & B.....161 G5
Machrins Ag & B..........180 E8
Machynlleth Powys 81 G4
Machynys Carmth...........51 G5
Mackworth Derbys 100 F5
Macmerry E Loth..........177 L4
Madderty P & K 185 K3
Maddiston Falk............176 D3
Madeley Staffs 99 H4
Madeley Wrekin 84 C3
Madingley Cambs...........76 B3
Madley Herefs...............69 H6
Madresfield Worcs..........70 E5
Madron Cnwll................2 E5
Maenclochog Pembks......49 J3

Maendy V Glam............36 F5
Maentwrog Gwynd 95 L4
Maen-y-groes Cerdgn 65 L3
Maer Staffs 99 H5
Maerdy Rhondd..............36 F2
Maesbrook Shrops..........97 L7
Maesbury Shrops...........97 L7
Maesbury Marsh
Shrops 97 L7
Maesllyn Cerdgn 65 K5
Maesteg Brdgnd............36 D3
Maesybont Carmth..........51 H3
Maesycwmmer
Caerph........................37 J2
Maggieknockater
Moray 215 H5
Magham Down
E Susx 20 C4
Maghull Sefton 111 K2
Magna Park Leics 87 G6
Magor Mons 38 B3
Magor Services Mons 38 B3
Maidenbower W Susx.......32 B6
Maiden Bradley Wilts 27 J4
Maidencombe Torbay........7 L3
Maidenhayne Devon 13 H4
Maiden Head N Som........38 E6
Maidenhead W & M 42 E4
Maiden Newton
Dorset 14 B3
Maidens S Ayrs............163 G7
Maiden's Green
Br For 42 E5
Maiden Wells Pembks......49 G7
Maidford Nhants 73 H4
Maids Moreton Bucks......73 K7
Maidstone Kent.............33 K3
Maidstone Services
Kent 33 L3
Maidwell Nhants 87 L7
Mail Shet...................235 d6
Maindee Newpt 37 L3
Mainland Ork 234 c6
Mainland Shet 235 c5
Mainsforth Dur 141 H2
Mains of Balhall
Angus 196 E4
Mains of Balnakettle
Abers 197 G2
Mains of Dalvey
Highld 214 D7
Mains of Haulkerton
Abers 197 H2
Mains of Lesmoir
Abers 215 K8
Mains of Melgunds
Angus 196 E5
Mainsriddle D & G 147 G4
Mainstone Shrops 82 F6
Maisemore Gloucs..........55 J4
Malborough Devon...........7 G7
Maldon Essex 61 K6
Malham N York 131 G6
Maligar Highld.............209 G2
Mallaig Highld.............199 L6
Mallaigvaig Highld 199 L5
Malleny Mills C Edin......177 G5
Malltraeth IoA 108 E7
Mallwyd Gwynd 81 J2
Malmesbury Wilts 39 L3
Malmsmead Devon 24 C2
Malpas Ches W 98 C3
Malpas Cnwll..................4 D7
Malpas Newpt...............37 L3
Maltby Rothm...............115 K3
Maltby S on T 141 L5
Maltby le Marsh Lincs 118 F5
Maltman's Hill Kent 34 B6
Malton N York 134 C5
Malvern Hills 70 D5
Malvern Link Worcs 70 E5
Malvern Wells Worcs 70 D6
Mamble Worcs 70 C1
Mamhilad Mons.............53 L7
Manaccan Cnwll..............3 K6
Manafon Powys.............82 C3

Manais W Isls..............232 d5
Manaton Devon..............11 H8
Manby Lincs 118 E4
Mancetter Warwks 86 D4
Manchester Manch 113 J3
Manchester Airport
Manch 113 J5
Manchester
Cathedral Salfd.......113 J2
Mancot Flints 111 K7
Mandally Highld 201 L5
Manea Cambs 90 C5
Maney Birm..................85 K4
Manfield N York 140 F4
Mangotsfield S Glos........38 F5
Manish W Isls 232 d5
Manley Ches W 112 D7
Manmoel Caerph............53 J7
Mannel Ag & B 188 C7
Manningford
Bohune Wilts...........40 C8
Manningford Bruce
Wilts 40 C8
Manningham C Brad.......123 H4
Manning's Heath
W Susx 31 K5
Mannington Dorset 15 K2
Manningtree Essex..........62 D2
Mannofield C Aber........207 H4
Manorbier Pembks 49 H7
Manorbier Newton
Pembks 49 H7
Manorhill Border...........167 K3
Manorowen Pembks 64 C7
Manor Park Gt Lon..........45 H3
Manor Park
Crematorium
Gt Lon 45 H3
Mansell Gamage
Herefs 69 H5
Mansell Lacy Herefs........69 H5
Mansfield E Ayrs 164 C6
Mansfield Notts...........101 K1
Mansfield & District
Crematorium
Notts 101 K2
Mansfield
Woodhouse Notts ...115 K8
Manston Dorset..............27 J7
Manston Kent 35 J2
Manston Leeds.............124 B4
Manswood Dorset 15 J2
Manthorpe Lincs 88 F1
Manton N Linc 116 F2
Manton Rutlnd 88 C3
Manton Wilts 40 D6
Manuden Essex 60 D3
Maperton Somset 26 F6
Maplebeck Notts...........102 B1
Mapledurham Oxon 42 A5
Mapledurwell Hants.........30 B2
Maplehurst W Susx 31 K6
Maplescombe Kent..........45 K7
Mapleton Derbys 100 D3
Mapperley Derbys..........101 H4
Mapperley Park
C Nott 101 L4
Mapperton Dorset 13 L3
Mappleborough
Green Warwks 71 J2
Mappleton E R Yk..........126 F2
Mapplewell Barns 123 L7
Mappowder Dorset 14 E2
Marazanvose Cnwll 4 C5
Marazion Cnwll................2 F5
Marbury Ches E 98 E4
March Cambs 90 B4
March S Lans................165 J6
Marcham Oxon 41 J2
Marchamley Shrops 98 E6
Marchington Staffs........100 C6
Marchros Gwynd 94 F7
Marchwiel Wrexhm..........98 A3
Marchwood Hants...........16 D1
Marcross V Glam............36 E6
Marden Herefs...............69 K5

Marden Kent 33 J4
Marden Wilts 40 C8
Marden Thorn Kent 33 K5
Mardy Mons 53 L5
Mareham le Fen Lincs 103 L1
Mareham on the Hill
Lincs 118 C7
Marehill W Susx 18 E3
Maresfield E Susx 19 M2
Marfleet C KuH 126 E5
Marford Wrexhm.............98 A2
Margam Neath 36 B3
Margam
Crematorium
Neath 36 C4
Margaret Marsh
Dorset 27 J7
Margaretting Essex 61 G7
Margaretting Tye
Essex 61 G7
Margate Kent................35 K1
Margnaheglish N Ayrs....162 D3
Margrie D & G 145 M5
Margrove Park R & Cl....142 E4
Marham Norfk 91 G2
Marhamchurch Cnwll........9 G4
Marholm C Pete 89 G3
Mariansleigh Devon 24 B6
Marine Town Kent 46 F5
Marionburgh Abers 206 D4
Marishader Highld 209 H2
Maristow Devon 6 C3
Marjoriebanks D & G 155 J5
Mark Somset 26 B2
Markbeech Kent 32 E5
Markby Lincs 119 G5
Mark Cross E Susx 33 G6
Markeaton
Crematorium
C Derb 100 F5
Market Bosworth
Leics 86 E3
Market Deeping Lincs 89 G2
Market Drayton
Shrops 98 F5
Market Harborough
Leics 87 K6
Market Lavington
Wilts 28 A1
Market Overton
Rutlnd 88 C1
Market Rasen Lincs 117 J4
Market Stainton Lincs 118 C5
Market Warsop Notts......115 K7
Market Weighton
E R Yk 125 K3
Market Weston Suffk 92 B7
Markfield Leics 86 F2
Markham Caerph 53 J7
Markham Moor Notts......116 B6
Markinch Fife 186 E6
Markington N York.........132 D6
Markle E Loth..............178 C3
Marksbury BaNES...........38 F7
Marks Tey Essex............61 L4
Markyate Herts 59 H5
Marlborough Wilts 40 D6
Marlcliff Warwks 71 K4
Marldon Devon................7 K3
Marlesford Suffk 79 G3
Marlingford Norfk 92 D2
Marloes Pembks 48 D5
Marlow Bucks 42 D3
Marlow Bottom
Bucks 42 D3
Marlpit Hill Kent 32 D4
Marnhull Dorset.............27 H7
Marple Stockp.............113 L4
Marr Donc 115 K1
Marrick N York.............140 D7
Marsden Kirk 122 F7
Marsden S Tyne...........151 J3
Marshalswick Herts 59 K6
Marsham Norfk 106 E7
Marsh Baldon Oxon 57 K7
Marshborough Kent.........35 J3

Marshbrook Shrops 83 J5
Marshchapel Lincs 118 E2
Marsh Farm Luton 59 H3
Marshfield Newpt 37 K4
Marshfield S Glos............39 H5
Marshgate Cnwll 8 F6
Marsh Gibbon Bucks.......57 M4
Marsh Green Devon........12 D4
Marsh Green Kent...........32 D4
Marshland St James
   Norfk 90 D2
Marsh Lane Derbys 115 H5
Marsh Street Somset.......24 F3
Marshwood Dorset.........13 J3
Marske N York...............140 D6
Marske-by-the-Sea
   R & CI 142 D3
Marston Herefs...............69 G3
Marston Lincs 102 E4
Marston Oxon.................57 K6
Marston Staffs.................99 L6
Marston Wilts..................27 L1
Marston Green Solhll......85 L6
Marston Magna
   Somset 26 E6
Marston Meysey Wilts....40 C2
Marston
   Montgomery
   Derbys 100 C5
Marston Moretaine
   C Beds 74 E6
Marston on Dove
   Derbys 100 E6
Marston St Lawrence
   Nhants............................73 G6
Marston Trussell
   Nhants............................87 K6
Marstow Herefs...............54 D4
Marsworth Bucks............58 F5
Marten Wilts....................40 F7
Martham Norfk 107 J8
Martin Hants...................28 B7
Martin Kent.....................35 J5
Martin Lincs...................103 J1
Martinhoe Devon............23 L2
Martin Hussingtree
   Worcs..............................70 F3
Martinstown Dorset 14 C5
Martlesham Suffk 78 F5
Martlesham Heath
   Suffk................................78 F5
Martletwy Pembks 49 H5
Martley Worcs 70 D3
Martock Somset...............26 C7
Marton Ches E................113 J7
Marton E R Yk 126 F3
Marton Lincs 116 D5
Marton Middsb 142 B4
Marton N York................132 F6
Marton N York................134 B3
Marton Shrops.................82 F3
Marton Warwks...............72 E2
Marton-le-Moor
   N York...........................132 E5
Martyr Worthy Hants 29 K5
Marwell Wildlife
   Hants 29 J6
Marwick Ork 234 b5
Marwood Devon 23 H4
Marybank Highld..........212 D4
Maryburgh Highld........212 E3
Maryculter Abers 207 G5
Marygold Border 179 G6
Maryhill C Glas 175 G4
Maryhill
   Crematorium
   C Glas 175 G4
Marykirk Abers 197 H3
Marylebone Gt Lon 44 F4
Marylebone Wigan........121 H8
Marypark Moray.............214 F6
Maryport Cumb 147 H7
Maryport D & G 144 D7
Marystow Devon.............10 C7
Mary Tavy Devon 6 D1
Maryton Angus..............197 H5

Marywell Abers 206 B6
Marywell Abers 207 H1
Marywell Angus 197 G7
Masham N York 132 C4
Masongill N York 130 C4
Masonhill
   Crematorium
   S Ayrs 163 J5
Mastin Moor Derbys 115 J6
Matching Green
   Essex 60 E5
Matching Tye Essex 60 E5
Matfen Nthumb 158 C7
Matfield Kent...................33 H5
Mathern Mons.................38 D3
Mathon Herefs.................70 D5
Mathry Pembks 48 E2
Matlask Norfk 106 D5
Matlock Derbys..............100 F1
Matlock Bath Derbys.....100 F2
Matson Gloucs 55 J5
Mattersey Notts.............116 B4
Mattingley Hants 42 B8
Mattishall Norfk 92 C2
Mattishall Burgh
   Norfk 92 C2
Mauchline E Ayrs 163 L4
Maud Abers 217 H5
Maufant Jersey 236 d6
Maugersbury Gloucs 56 D3
Maughold IoM 237 e3
Mauld Highld 212 C6
Maulden C Beds...............74 F6
Maulds Meaburn
   Cumb 138 F4
Maunby N York 132 E3
Maundown Somset 25 G5
Mautby Norfk 93 K2
Mavesyn Ridware
   Staffs 85 J1
Mavis Enderby Lincs 118 E7
Mawbray Cumb 147 J5
Mawdesley Lancs 121 G7
Mawdlam Brdgnd 36 C4
Mawgan Cnwll 3 J6
Mawgan Porth Cnwll........4 D3
Mawla Cnwll 3 J3
Mawnan Cnwll 3 K5
Mawnan Smith Cnwll 3 K5
Mawsley Nhants..............88 B7
Maxey C Pete..................89 G2
Maxstoke Warwks 86 B6
Maxton Border 167 J4
Maxton Kent 35 J6
Maxwell Town D & G 155 G6
Maxworthy Cnwll..............9 H6
Maybole S Ayrs 163 H7
Maybury Surrey 43 G8
Mayfield E Susx 25 G7
Mayfield Mdloth 177 K5
Mayfield Staffs...............100 D4
Mayford Surrey 31 G1
May Hill Gloucs 55 G4
Mayland Essex 61 L7
Maylandsea Essex 61 L7
Maynard's Green
   E Susx 20 C3
Maypole Green Norfk......93 J4
Maypole Green Suffk.......77 K3
Meadgate BaNES 39 G8
Meadle Bucks 58 D6
Meadowfield Dur...........151 G6
Meadwell Devon 9 K8
Meanwood Leeds...........123 K3
Meare Somset..................26 C3
Meare Green Somset 25 L6
Meare Green Somset 25 M6
Mearns E Rens 174 F7
Mears Ashby Nhants......74 B2
Measham Leics 86 D2
Meathop Cumb 129 J4
Meavy Devon 6 D3
Medbourne Leics.............88 B5
Meddon Devon 9 H2
Meden Vale Notts 115 L7

Medmenham Bucks........42 D4
Medomsley Dur..............150 E4
Medstead Hants 30 A4
Medway
   Crematorium
   Kent 46 C7
Medway Services
   Medway 46 D7
Meerbrook Staffs 99 M1
Meesden Herts 60 C2
Meeth Devon 10 E3
Meeting House Hill
   Norfk 107 G6
Meidrim Carmth 50 C2
Meifod Powys 82 D2
Meigle P & K 195 L7
Meikle Carco D & G 164 F6
Meikle Earnock
   S Lans 175 J7
Meikle Kilmory
   Ag & B 173 H6
Meikle Obney P & K 195 G8
Meikleour P & K 195 J7
Meikle Wartle Abers 216 D7
Meinciau Carmth.............50 F4
Meir C Stke 99 L4
Melbourn Cambs.............75 L5
Melbourne Derbys 101 G7
Melbourne E R Yk..........125 H2
Melbury Abbas
   Dorset 27 K7
Melbury Bubb Dorset 14 B2
Melbury Osmond
   Dorset 14 B2
Melchbourne Bed 74 E2
Melcombe Bingham
   Dorset 14 E2
Meldon Devon 10 E6
Meldon Nthumb 158 E5
Meldreth Cambs..............75 L5
Meldrum Stirlg 184 F7
Melfort Ag & B 182 B5
Meliden Denbgs.............110 E5
Melin-y-wig Denbgs........97 G3
Melkinthorpe Cumb.......138 D3
Melkridge Nthumb 149 J3
Melksham Wilts...............39 K7
Melling Lancs 130 B5
Melling Sefton 111 L2
Mellis Suffk 92 C8
Mellon Charles Highld ..219 K3
Mellon Udrigle Highld...219 K3
Mellor Lancs 121 J4
Mellor Stockp 113 M4
Mellor Brook Lancs 121 J4
Mells Somset 27 G2
Melmerby Cumb 149 G7
Melmerby N York 131 K3
Melmerby N York 132 E4
Melness Highld 229 J3
Melplash Dorset 13 L3
Melrose Border 167 H3
Melsetter Ork.................234 b7
Melsonby N York 140 F5
Meltham Kirk 123 G7
Melton E R Yk 126 B5
Melton Suffk 79 G4
Melton Constable
   Norfk 106 C6
Melton Mowbray
   Leics 102 C8
Melton Ross N Linc 126 D7
Melvaig Highld 219 H4
Melverley Shrops 83 G1
Melvich Highld 230 C3
Membury Devon 13 H2
Membury Services
   W Berk.............................40 F5
Memsie Abers 217 H2
Memus Angus 196 C5
Menai Bridge IoA 109 H6
Mendham Suffk 92 F6
Mendip Crematorium
   Somset 26 E3
Mendip Hills Somset 26 D2
Mendlesham Suffk..........78 D2

Mendlesham Green
   Suffk................................78 D2
Menheniot Cnwll...............5 L4
Mennock D & G 164 F7
Menston C Brad.............123 H2
Menstrie Clacks.............185 H7
Mentmore Bucks.............58 E4
Meoble Highld................200 C7
Meole Brace Shrops.......83 J2
Meonstoke Hants............29 L1
Meopham Kent.................45 M6
Mepal Cambs...................90 B7
Meppershall C Beds.......75 G7
Mere Ches E....................113 G5
Mere Wilts........................27 J5
Mere Brow Lancs 120 F6
Mereclough Lancs 122 C4
Mereworth Kent..............33 H3
Meriden Solhll.................86 B6
Merkadale Highld...........208 F7
Merley Poole....................15 J3
Merrion Pembks 48 F7
Merriott Somset 26 C8
Merrow Surrey..................31 G2
Merry Hill Herts 43 J2
Merryhill Wolves 84 F4
Merrymeet Cnwll...............5 L3
Mersea Island Essex......62 B5
Mersham Kent..................34 E6
Merstham Surrey.............32 B3
Merston W Susx 18 B5
Merstone IoW 17 G5
Merthyr Cynog
   Powys 67 L6
Merthyr Mawr
   Brdgnd 36 D5
Merthyr Tydfil Myr Td.....53 G6
Merthyr Vale Myr Td......53 G7
Merton Devon 10 D3
Merton Gt Lon..................44 E6
Merton Norfk 91 K4
Merton Oxon....................57 L4
Meshaw Devon 24 B7
Messing Essex 61 L4
Messingham N Linc.......116 E2
Metfield Suffk 93 G7
Metherell Cnwll.................6 B3
Metheringham Lincs 103 H1
Methil Fife......................186 F7
Methilhill Fife.................186 F7
Methlick Abers...............217 G6
Methven P & K 185 L3
Methwold Norfk..............91 G4
Methwold Hythe
   Norfk 91 G4
Mettingham Suffk...........93 H5
Metton Norfk..................106 E5
Mevagissey Cnwll.............4 F6
Mexborough Donc 115 J2
Mey Highld.....................231 K2
Meyllteyrn Gwynd...........94 D6
Meysey Hampton
   Gloucs 56 C7
Miabhig W Isls 232 d2
Miavaig W Isls 232 d2
Michaelchurch Herefs...54 D3
Michaelchurch
   Escley Herefs 69 G7
Michaelstone-y-
   Fedw Newpt...................37 K4
Michaelston-le-Pit
   V Glam 37 J5
Michaelstow Cnwll...........5 G1
Michaelwood
   Services Gloucs............39 G2
Micheldever Hants..........29 K4
Micheldever Station
   Hants 29 K5
Michelmersh Hants.........29 G6
Mickfield Suffk.................78 D3
Mickle Bridge Donc.......115 K3
Mickleby N York.............143 G5
Micklefield Leeds 124 C4
Mickleham Surrey...........31 K2
Mickleover C Derb 100 F5
Mickleton Dur................140 B3

Mickleton Gloucs.............71 L5
Mickletown Leeds.........124 B5
Mickle Trafford
  Ches W.......................112 C7
Mickley N York...............132 C4
Mickley Square
  Nthumb......................150 D3
Mid Ardlaw Abers.........217 H2
Midbea Ork....................234 C4
Mid Beltie Abers............206 C5
Mid Calder W Loth.........176 E5
Mid Clyth Highld............231 K7
Mid Culbeuchly Abers...216 C3
Middle Aston Oxon..........57 J3
Middle Barton Oxon........57 H3
Middlebie D & G.............155 L6
Middlebridge P & K........194 D3
Middle Chinnock
  Somset........................26 C8
Middle Claydon Bucks....58 B3
Middleham N York..........131 L3
Middle Handley
  Derbys.......................115 H6
Middlehill Wilts................39 J6
Middlehope Shrops..........83 K5
Middle Kames Ag & B....172 F1
Middle Littleton
  Worcs...........................71 J5
Middlemarsh Dorset........14 C2
Middle Mayfield
  Staffs........................100 C4
Middle Rasen Lincs.......117 H4
Middle Rocombe
  Devon...........................7 K2
Middlesbrough
  Middsb.......................141 L4
Middleshaw Cumb.........129 L2
Middlesmoor N York......131 K5
Middle Stoke Medway......46 D5
Middlestone Dur............141 G2
Middlestown Wakefd....123 K6
Middlethird Border.........167 K2
Middleton Ag & B...........188 B7
Middleton Derbys...........100 F2
Middleton Derbys...........114 D8
Middleton Essex..............77 K6
Middleton Hants..............29 H3
Middleton Herefs.............69 K1
Middleton Leeds............123 L5
Middleton N York...........123 G2
Middleton N York...........134 B3
Middleton Nhants............88 B5
Middleton Norfk...............90 F1
Middleton Nthumb.........158 D5
Middleton P & K............186 B6
Middleton Rochdl...........113 K1
Middleton Shrops............83 K7
Middleton Suffk...............79 J2
Middleton Swans............50 E7
Middleton Warwks..........85 L4
Middleton Cheney
  Nhants.........................73 G6
Middleton
  Crematorium
  Rochdl.......................113 K1
Middleton-in-
  Teesdale Dur.............139 L3
Middleton Moor Suffk....79 J2
Middleton One Row
  Darltn........................141 J5
Middleton-on-Sea
  W Susx........................18 C5
Middleton on the Hill
  Herefs..........................69 K2
Middleton on the
  Wolds E R Yk.............125 L2
Middleton Park
  C Aber.......................207 H3
Middleton
  Quernhow N York.....132 E4
Middleton St George
  Darltn........................141 J5
Middleton Scriven
  Shrops.........................84 C6
Middleton Stoney
  Oxon............................57 K4

Middleton Tyas
  N York........................141 G6
Middle Town IoS................2 a2
Middletown Powys...........82 F2
Middle Tysoe Warwks......72 D5
Middle Wallop Hants........28 F4
Middlewich Ches E.........113 G7
Middle Winterslow
  Wilts............................28 E5
Middlewood Cnwll.............5 L2
Middle Woodford
  Wilts............................28 C4
Middlewood Green
  Suffk............................78 D3
Middleyard E Ayrs.........163 M3
Middlezoy Somset...........26 B5
Midford BaNES................39 H7
Midgham W Berk.............41 K6
Midgley Calder..............122 F5
Midgley Wakefd.............123 K7
Midhopestones Sheff....114 E2
Midhurst W Susx.............30 E6
Mid Lavant W Susx..........18 B4
Midlem Border...............167 H4
Mid Mains Highld...........212 C6
Midpark Ag & B..............173 H6
Midsomer Norton
  BaNES..........................26 F1
Midtown Highld.............229 J4
Mid Warwickshire
  Crematorium
  Warwks........................72 C3
Mid Yell Shet................235 d3
Migvie Abers.................205 K4
Milborne Port Somset.....26 F7
Milborne St Andrew
  Dorset.........................14 F3
Milborne Wick
  Somset........................26 F7
Milbourne Nthumb........158 E6
Milbourne Wilts..............39 L3
Milburn Cumb................138 F2
Milbury Heath S Glos......38 F3
Milby N York..................132 F6
Milcombe Oxon...............72 E7
Milden Suffk....................77 L5
Mildenhall Suffk..............91 G8
Mildenhall Wilts..............40 E6
Mileham Norfk...............105 L8
Mile Oak Br & H...............19 H4
Milesmark Fife...............176 E2
Miles Platting
  Manch........................113 J2
Mile Town Kent...............46 F5
Milfield Nthumb.............168 D3
Milford Derbys...............101 G4
Milford Devon..................22 C6
Milford Staffs..................99 L7
Milford Surrey.................30 F3
Milford Haven
  Pembks.......................48 F6
Milford on Sea Hants......16 C4
Milkwall Gloucs..............54 E6
Milland W Susx...............30 D5
Mill Bank Calder............122 F6
Millbreck Abers.............217 J3
Millbridge Surrey............30 D3
Millbrook C Beds.............74 E6
Millbrook C Sotn.............29 G8
Millbrook Cnwll.................6 B5
Millbrook Jersey............236 C7
Mill Brow Stockp...........113 L4
Millbuie Abers...............206 F4
Millbuie Highld..............212 E4
Millcorner E Susx............21 G2
Millcraig Highld.............222 E7
Milldale Staffs...............100 C2
Mill End Bucks................42 C4
Mill End Herts.................60 B2
Millerhill Mdloth............177 J4
Miller's Dale Derbys.....114 C6
Millerston C Glas...........175 H5
Mill Green Cambs...........76 F5
Mill Green Essex.............61 G7
Mill Green Lincs............103 L7
Mill Green Suffk..............77 L6

Mill Green Suffk..............78 B3
Mill Green Suffk..............78 D3
Millhalf Herefs................68 F5
Millheugh S Lans...........175 K7
Mill Hill Gt Lon................44 E2
Millhouse Ag & B...........173 G4
Millhousebridge
  D & G.........................155 K5
Millhouse Green
  Barns........................114 E2
Millhouses Sheff...........115 G5
Milliken Park Rens........174 D6
Millington E R Yk...........125 J1
Millmeece Staffs.............99 J5
Mill of Drummond
  P & K.........................185 H4
Mill of Haldane
  W Duns......................174 D2
Millom Cumb.................128 E4
Millport N Ayrs..............173 K7
Mill Street Suffk..............78 C1
Millthrop Cumb.............130 C2
Milltimber C Aber..........207 G5
Milltown Abers...............205 G4
Milltown Abers...............205 K3
Milltown D & G..............156 C6
Milltown Devon...............23 J4
Milltown of
  Campfield Abers......206 C5
Milltown of Edinvillie
  Moray.........................215 G6
Milltown of Learney
  Abers.........................206 C5
Milnathort P & K............186 B6
Milngavie E Duns..........175 G4
Milnrow Rochdl.............122 D7
Milnthorpe Cumb...........129 K3
Milovaig Highld.............208 B4
Milson Shrops.................84 B8
Milstead Kent..................34 B3
Milston Wilts...................28 D3
Milthorpe Nhants............73 H5
Milton Cambs..................76 C2
Milton Cumb..................148 F3
Milton D & G.................144 F4
Milton D & G.................154 E7
Milton Derbys...............100 F7
Milton Highld.................209 L5
Milton Highld.................212 D7
Milton Highld.................212 E4
Milton Highld.................223 G6
Milton Highld.................231 L5
Milton Inver..................174 C5
Milton Kent.....................46 A5
Milton Moray................204 E2
Milton Moray................215 L2
Milton N Som...................37 M7
Milton Notts..................116 B6
Milton Oxon.....................41 J3
Milton Oxon.....................72 F7
Milton P & K.................195 G4
Milton Pembks................49 H6
Milton Somset.................26 C6
Milton Stirlg..................184 B6
Milton W Duns...............174 D4
Milton Abbas Dorset......14 F3
Milton Abbot Devon.........9 K8
Milton Bridge Mdloth....177 H5
Milton Bryan C Beds.......58 F3
Milton Clevedon
  Somset........................26 F4
Milton Combe Devon........6 D3
Milton Damerel
  Devon...........................9 K3
Milton Ernest Bed..........74 E4
Milton Green Ches W......98 C2
Milton Hill Oxon..............41 J3
Milton Keynes M Keyn...74 C6
Milton Lilbourne Wilts...40 D7
Milton Malsor Nhants.....73 K4
Milton Morenish
  P & K.........................184 D1
Milton of
  Auchinhove Abers...206 B5
Milton of Balgonie
  Fife............................186 E7

Milton of Buchanan
  Stirlg.........................174 E1
Milton of Campsie
  E Duns.......................175 H3
Milton of Leys Highld...213 G6
Milton of Murtle
  C Aber.......................207 G5
Milton of Tullich
  Abers.........................205 J6
Milton on Stour
  Dorset.........................27 J5
Milton Regis Kent............46 E6
Milton-under-
  Wychwood Oxon........56 E4
Milverton Somset............25 H6
Milverton Warwks...........72 C2
Milwich Staffs.................99 L6
Minard Ag & B...............182 D7
Minchinhampton
  Gloucs.........................55 K7
Minehead Somset...........24 F3
Minera Wrexhm...............97 L3
Minety Wilts....................40 A3
Minffordd Gwynd............95 K5
Mingarrypark Highld....190 D3
Miningsby Lincs.............118 D8
Minions Cnwll....................5 L2
Minishant S Ayrs...........163 J6
Minllyn Gwynd................81 J2
Minnigaff D & G............145 J2
Minnonie Abers.............216 E3
Minskip N York..............132 F6
Minstead Hants...............16 C1
Minsted W Susx..............30 D7
Minster Kent...................35 J2
Minster Kent...................46 F5
Minsterley Shrops...........83 G3
Minster Lovell Oxon........56 F5
Minsterworth Gloucs......55 H5
Minterne Magna
  Dorset.........................14 C2
Minting Lincs.................117 K6
Mintlaw Abers...............217 J5
Mintlyn
  Crematorium
  Norfk.........................105 G8
Minto Border.................167 H5
Minton Shrops.................83 H5
Mirehouse Cumb............136 D4
Mireland Highld.............231 K4
Mirfield Kirk..................123 J6
Miserden Gloucs.............55 L6
Miskin Rhondd................37 G4
Misson Notts..................116 B3
Misterton Leics...............87 G6
Misterton Notts..............116 C3
Misterton Somset............13 L2
Mistley Essex...................62 D2
Mitcham Gt Lon...............44 F6
Mitcheldean Gloucs........54 F4
Mitchell Cnwll...................4 D5
Mitchellslacks D & G.....155 G3
Mitchel Troy Mons...........54 C6
Mitford Nthumb.............158 F5
Mithian Cnwll....................3 J2
Mixbury Oxon..................73 H7
Mobberley Ches E.........113 H5
Mobberley Staffs...........100 A4
Mochdre Powys...............82 B5
Mochrum D & G.............145 H5
Mockbeggar Kent...........33 J4
Mockerkin Cumb............136 F3
Modbury Devon................6 F5
Moddershall Staffs..........99 L5
Moelfre IoA....................109 G4
Moelfre Powys.................97 J6
Moffat D & G.................155 J2
Moggerhanger
  C Beds.........................75 G5
Moira Leics.....................86 C1
Molash Kent....................34 D4
Mol-chlach Highld.........199 G3
Mold Flints....................111 H8
Moldgreen Kirk..............123 H7
Molehill Green Essex......60 E3
Molescroft E R Yk.........126 C3

Molesworth Cambs 88 F7
Molland Devon 24 C5
Mollington Ches W.....111 L7
Mollington Oxon 72 F5
Mollinsburn N Lans.....175 J4
Mondynes Abers 197 J1
Monewden Suffk..........78 F3
Moneydie P & K 185 M2
Moniaive D & G..........154 D4
Monifieth Angus 187 H2
Monikie Angus............196 E8
Monimail Fife..............186 E5
Monken Hadley
  Gt Lon.......................44 E1
Monk Fryston N York ...124 D5
Monkhide Herefs..........70 B5
Monkhill Cumb............148 C3
Monkhopton Shrops......84 B5
Monkland Herefs...........69 J3
Monkleigh Devon..........23 G7
Monknash V Glam.........36 E6
Monkokehampton
  Devon.......................10 E4
Monkseaton N Tyne.....159 H7
Monks Eleigh Suffk.......77 L5
Monk's Gate W Susx.....31 K6
Monks Heath Ches E.....113 J6
Monk Sherborne
  Hants........................29 L1
Monksilver Somset.......25 G4
Monks Kirby Warwks.....86 F6
Monk Soham Suffk.......78 E2
Monks Risborough
  Bucks.......................58 D6
Monksthorpe Lincs......118 F7
Monk Street Essex 60 F3
Monkswood Mons.........53 M7
Monkton Devon............12 F2
Monkton Kent...............47 M6
Monkton S Ayrs...........163 J4
Monkton S Tyne...........151 H3
Monkton Combe
  BaNES.......................39 H7
Monkton Deverill
  Wilts.........................27 J4
Monkton Farleigh
  Wilts.........................39 J7
Monkton Heathfield
  Somset......................25 K6
Monkton Wyld Dorset...13 J3
Monkwearmouth
  Sundld......................151 J4
Monkwood Hants 30 A5
Monmore Green
  Wolves.......................85 G4
Monmouth Mons..........54 D5
Monnington on Wye
  Herefs........................69 G5
Monreith D & G...........145 H6
Montacute Somset........26 D7
Montford Shrops...........83 H1
Montford Bridge
  Shrops.......................83 H1
Montgarrie Abers..........206 B2
Montgomery Powys........82 E4
Montrose Angus...........197 H5
Mont Saint Guern........236 b3
Monxton Hants.............28 F3
Monyash Derbys...........114 D7
Monymusk Abers..........206 D3
Monzie P & K..............185 H3
Moodiesburn N Lans.....175 J4
Moonzie Fife................186 E4
Moor Allerton Leeds.....123 L3
Moorby Lincs...............118 D8
Moor Crichel Dorset.....15 J2
Moordown Bmouth........15 K4
Moore Halton...............112 E5
Moor End Calder..........122 F5
Moorends Donc............125 G7
Moorhead C Brad.........123 H3
Moorhouse Cumb..........148 B4
Moorhouse Notts..........116 C7
Moorhouse Bank
  Surrey........................32 D3
Moorlinch Somset..........26 B4

Moor Monkton
  N York........................133 H7
Moorsholm R & Cl 142 E4
Moorside Dorset............27 H7
Moorswater Cnwll...........5 K3
Moorthorpe Wakefd......124 C7
Moortown Leeds...........123 K3
Moortown Lincs...........117 H2
Morangie Highld..........223 G5
Morar Highld...............199 L6
Moray Crematorium
  Moray.......................215 J3
Morborne Cambs..........89 G5
Morchard Bishop
  Devon.......................11 H4
Morcombelake
  Dorset.......................13 K4
Morcott Rutlnd.............88 D4
Morda Shrops................97 L6
Morden Dorset.............15 H4
Morden Gt Lon.............44 E6
Mordiford Herefs...........69 L6
Mordon Dur.................141 H2
More Shrops.................83 G5
Morebath Devon...........24 E6
Morebattle Border........168 B4
Morecambe Lancs.........129 J6
Moredon Swindn...........40 C3
Morefield Highld..........220 E3
Morehall Kent...............35 G7
Moreleigh Devon............7 H5
Morenish P & K............184 D1
Morestead Hants............29 K6
Moreton Dorset............14 F4
Moreton Essex...............60 E6
Moreton Herefs.............69 K2
Moreton Oxon...............58 B6
Moreton Wirral.............111 J4
Moreton Corbet
  Shrops.......................98 E7
Moretonhampstead
  Devon.......................11 H7
Moreton-in-Marsh
  Gloucs......................56 D2
Moreton Jeffries
  Herefs........................69 L5
Moreton Morrell
  Warwks......................72 C4
Moreton on Lugg
  Herefs........................69 K5
Moreton Pinkney
  Nhants.......................73 H5
Moreton Say Shrops......98 F5
Moreton Valence
  Gloucs......................55 H6
Morfa Nefyn Gwynd......94 E4
Morham E Loth.............178 C4
Morland Cumb.............138 E3
Morley Ches E.............113 J5
Morley Derbys.............101 H4
Morley Leeds...............123 K5
Morley Green Ches E....113 J5
Morley St Botolph
  Norfk.........................92 C4
Morningside C Edin......177 H4
Morningside N Lans......175 L2
Morningthorpe Norfk.....92 F5
Morpeth Nthumb..........158 F5
Morphie Abers.............197 H4
Morrey Staffs...............100 C8
Morriston Swans...........51 J6
Morston Norfk.............106 B4
Mortehoe Devon...........23 G3
Morthen Rothm............115 J4
Mortimer W Berk...........41 M7
Mortimer West End
  Hants........................41 M7
Mortlake Gt Lon............44 E5
Mortlake
  Crematorium
  Gt Lon.......................44 D5
Morton Cumb..............148 C4
Morton Derbys.............101 H1
Morton Lincs...............103 H7
Morton Lincs...............116 D3
Morton Notts...............102 B3

Morton Shrops..............97 L7
Mortonhall
  Crematorium
  C Edin.......................177 H5
Morton-on-Swale
  N York........................132 E2
Morton on the Hill
  Norfk.........................92 D1
Morvah Cnwll.................2 D4
Morvich Highld............200 E2
Morville Shrops.............84 C5
Morwenstow Cnwll..........9 G2
Mosborough Sheff........115 H5
Moscow E Ayrs............163 L2
Moseley Birm................85 J4
Moseley Wolves............85 G4
Moseley Worcs.............70 E3
Moss Ag & B...............188 B7
Moss Donc..................124 F7
Mossat Abers..............205 K2
Mossbank Shet.............235 d4
Moss Bank St Hel.........112 D3
Mossbay Cumb............136 D2
Mossblown S Ayrs........163 K4
Mossburnford Border.....167 K6
Mossdale D & G............154 B7
Mossdale E Ayrs...........153 K2
Moss Edge Lancs.........120 F2
Mossend N Lans...........175 K6
Mossley Tamesd...........113 L2
Mosspaul Hotel
  Border.......................156 D3
Moss-side Highld..........213 K4
Mosstodloch Moray.......215 H3
Mossyard D & G...........145 L5
Mossy Lea Lancs.........121 H7
Mosterton Dorset..........13 L2
Moston Manch.............113 K2
Mostyn Flints...............111 G5
Motcombe Dorset..........27 J6
Mothecombe Devon........6 F6
Motherby Cumb............138 B2
Motherwell N Lans........175 K6
Motspur Park Gt Lon.....44 E6
Mottingham Gt Lon........45 H5
Mottisfont Hants...........28 F6
Mottistone IoW.............16 E5
Mottram in
  Longdendale
  Tamesd.....................113 M3
Mottram St Andrew
  Ches E......................113 K5
Mouldsworth Ches W.....112 D7
Moulin P & K...............194 E4
Moulsecoomb Br & H.....19 J4
Moulsford Oxon............41 L4
Moulsoe M Keyn...........74 C6
Moultavie Highld..........222 E7
Moulton Ches W...........112 F7
Moulton Lincs..............104 A7
Moulton N York............141 G6
Moulton Nhants............73 L2
Moulton Suffk...............77 G2
Moulton V Glam............37 G6
Moulton Chapel Lincs....103 M8
Moulton St Mary
  Norfk.........................93 H3
Moulton Seas End
  Lincs........................104 A6
Mount Cnwll..................5 J3
Mountain C Brad..........123 G4
Mountain Ash
  Rhondd.......................53 G7
Mountain Cross
  Border.......................176 F8
Mount Ambrose
  Cnwll..........................3 J3
Mount Bures Essex.......61 L2
Mountfield E Susx.........20 E2
Mountgerald House
  Highld.......................212 E3
Mount Hawke Cnwll........3 J2
Mountjoy Cnwll..............4 D4
Mount Lothian
  Mdloth......................177 H6
Mountnessing Essex......60 F8

Mounton Mons.............38 D2
Mount Pleasant
  Derbys......................101 G3
Mount Pleasant Suffk....77 G5
Mountsett
  Crematorium Dur....150 E4
Mountsorrel Leics..........87 H2
Mount Tabor Calder......122 F5
Mousehill Surrey...........30 F3
Mousehole Cnwll............2 E6
Mouswald D & G...........155 J7
Mow Cop Ches E...........99 J2
Mowhaugh Border.........168 B5
Mowsley Leics..............87 J5
Moy Highld.................202 C8
Moy Highld.................213 J7
Moyle Highld...............200 D2
Moylegrove Pembks.......64 F5
Muasdale Ag & B..........161 H2
Muchalls Abers.............207 G6
Much Birch Herefs.........54 D3
Much Cowarne
  Herefs........................70 B5
Much Dewchurch
  Herefs........................54 C2
Muchelney Somset........26 B6
Muchelney Ham
  Somset......................26 C6
Much Hadham Herts......60 C4
Much Hoole Lancs........120 F6
Muchlarnick Cnwll..........5 K5
Much Marcle Herefs.......54 F2
Much Wenlock
  Shrops.......................84 B4
Muck Highld................189 K1
Mucklebrugh
  Collection Norfk........106 D4
Mucklestone Staffs........99 G5
Muckton Lincs.............118 E5
Muddiford Devon...........23 J4
Muddles Green E Susx...20 B3
Mudford Dorset.............16 A4
Mudford Somset...........26 E7
Mudford Sock
  Somset......................26 E7
Mugdock Stirlg.............175 G3
Mugeary Highld............209 G6
Mugginton Derbys........100 F4
Muirden Abers.............216 D4
Muirdrum Angus...........196 F8
Muiresk Abers..............216 D5
Muirhead Angus...........186 E1
Muirhead Fife..............186 E6
Muirhead N Lans..........175 J4
Muirkirk E Ayrs............164 D4
Muirmill Stirlg.............175 J2
Muir of Fowlis Abers.....206 B3
Muir of Miltonduff
  Moray.......................214 E3
Muir of Ord Highld.......212 E4
Muirshearlich Highld.....192 B1
Muirtack Abers.............217 J6
Muirton P & K.............185 J5
Muirton Mains Highld....212 C4
Muirton of Ardblair
  P & K........................195 J7
Muker N York..............139 K7
Mulbarton Norfk...........92 E4
Mulben Moray..............215 H4
Mull Ag & B................181 J1
Mullion Cnwll................3 H7
Mullion Cove Cnwll........3 H7
Mumby Lincs...............119 G6
Munderfield Row
  Herefs........................70 B4
Munderfield Stocks
  Herefs........................70 B4
Mundesley Norfk..........107 G5
Mundford Norfk............91 H5
Mundham Norfk............93 G4
Mundon Hill Essex.........61 K7
Mungrisdale Cumb........137 K2
Munlochy Highld...........213 G4
Munnoch N Ayrs...........174 B8
Munsley Herefs.............70 B6
Munslow Shrops............83 K6

Murchington Devon 11 G7
Murcott Oxon 57 L5
Murkle Highld 231 H2
Murlaggan Highld 200 F6
Murroes Angus 187 G1
Murrow Cambs...............89 L3
Mursley Bucks.................58 D3
Murthill Angus 196 D5
Murthly P & K 195 H8
Murton C York................133 K8
Murton Cumb 139 G3
Murton Dur 151 J5
Murton Nthumb 179 K8
Musbury Devon 13 H4
Musselburgh E Loth......177 K4
Muston Leics 102 D5
Muston N York 135 H4
Muswell Hill Gt Lon 44 F3
Mutehill D & G 146 C5
Mutford Suffk..................93 K6
Muthill P & K 185 H4
Mybster Highld 231 H5
Myddfai Carmth 52 B3
Myddle Shrops................98 C7
Mydroilyn Cerdgn 66 B4
Mylor Cnwll 4 C8
Mylor Bridge Cnwll 4 C8
Mynachlog ddu
 Pembks 49 K2
Mynydd-bach Mons 38 C2
Mynydd-Bach Swans 51 J6
Mynyddgarreg
 Carmth 50 E4
Mynydd Isa Flints..........111 J8
Myrebird Abers...............206 E6
Myredykes Border 157 G3
Mytchett Surrey 30 E1
Mytholm Calder.............122 F6
Mytholmroyd Calder.....122 F5
Myton-on-Swale
 N York 132 F6

N

Naast Highld..................219 J5
Na Buirgh W Isls............232 d4
Naburn C York...............124 F2
Nab Wood
 Crematorium
 C Brad........................123 H3
Nackington Kent..............34 F4
Nacton Suffk....................78 F6
Nafferton E R Yk............135 G7
Nailsbourne Somset 25 K5
Nailsea N Som................38 C6
Nailstone Leics................86 E3
Nailsworth Gloucs...........55 J7
Nairn Highld 213 K3
Nannerch Flints.............111 G7
Nanpantan Leics 87 G1
Nanpean Cnwll 4 F5
Nanstallon Cnwll 5 G3
Nanternis Cerdgn.............65 L3
Nantgaredig Carmth 50 F2
Nantglyn Denbgs.............96 F1
Nantmel Powys................68 B2
Nantmor Gwynd...............95 K4
Nant Peris Gwynd............95 K2
Nantwich Ches E.............98 F3
Nantyglo Blae G...............53 J6
Nant-y-moel Brdgnd........36 E2
Naphill Bucks...................42 D2
Napton on the Hill
 Warwks 72 F3
Narberth Pembks.............49 J4
Narborough Leics.............87 G4
Narborough Norfk............91 H2
Nasareth Gwynd..............95 H3
Naseby Nhants.................87 K7
Nash Bucks......................73 L7
Nash Newpt......................37 M4
Nash Shrops.....................69 L1
Nassington Nhants..........88 F4
Nateby Cumb.................139 H6
Nateby Lancs 120 F2

National Memorial
 Arboretum Staffs 85 L1
National Motor
 Museum
 (Beaulieu) Hants.....16 E2
National Space
 Science Centre
 C Leic.........................87 H3
Natland Cumb...............129 L2
Naughton Suffk................78 B5
Naunton Gloucs...............56 C4
Naunton Worcs................70 F6
Naunton Beauchamp
 Worcs 71 G4
Navenby Lincs 103 G2
Navestock Essex..............45 K1
Navestock Side Essex....60 E8
Navidale House
 Hotel Highld..............227 J5
Navity Highld 213 J2
Nawton N York 133 K3
Nayland Suffk 77 L7
Nazeing Essex.................60 C6
Neap Shet......................235 d5
Near Cotton Staffs........100 B4
Near Sawrey Cumb 137 K7
Neasden Gt Lon 44 E3
Neasham Darltn.............141 H5
Neath Neath.....................51 L6
Neatham Hants................30 C4
Neatishead Norfk...........107 H7
Nebo Cerdgn....................66 D2
Nebo Conwy.....................96 C2
Nebo Gwynd.....................95 H3
Nebo IoA.........................108 F4
Necton Norfk....................91 K2
Nedd Highld...................224 D3
Nedging Suffk...................78 B5
Nedging Tye Suffk...........78 B4
Needham Norfk................92 F6
Needham Lake &
 Nature Reserve
 Suffk...........................78 C4
Needham Market
 Suffk...........................78 C4
Needingworth Cambs.....75 L1
Neen Savage Shrops......84 C7
Neen Sollars Shrops.......84 B8
Neenton Shrops...............84 B6
Nefyn Gwynd....................94 E4
Neilston E Rens..............174 E6
Nelson Caerph.................37 H2
Nelson Lancs 122 C3
Nemphlar S Lans...........165 G1
Nempnett Thrubwell
 BaNES 38 D7
Nenthall Cumb...............149 K6
Nenthorn Border............167 K2
Nercwys Flints.................97 K1
Nereabolls Ag & B.........170 E7
Nerston S Lans 175 H6
Nesbit Nthumb...............168 E3
Nesfield N York..............123 G1
Nesscliffe Shrops.............98 B8
Neston Ches W..............111 J6
Neston Wilts....................39 K6
Netchwood Shrops..........84 B5
Nether Alderley
 Ches E 113 J6
Netheravon Wilts.............28 D2
Nether Blainslie
 Border 167 H2
Nether Broughton
 Leics..........................102 B7
Netherburn S Lans 175 L8
Netherbury Dorset..........13 L3
Netherby N York.............123 L2
Nether Cerne Dorset......14 C3
Nethercleuch D & G......155 K5
Nether Compton
 Dorset 26 E7
Nether Crimond
 Abers 206 F2
Nether Dallachy
 Moray.........................215 H2

Netherend Gloucs............54 E7
Netherfield E Susx 20 E2
Nether Fingland
 S Lans.......................165 H7
Netherhampton Wilts.......28 C5
Nether Handwick
 Angus........................196 B7
Nether Haugh Rothm.....115 H3
Netherhay Dorset............13 K2
Nether Headon Notts....116 C6
Nether Heage Derbys....101 G3
Nether Heyford
 Nhants.........................73 J3
Nether Howcleugh
 S Lans.......................165 K6
Nether Kellet Lancs......129 K6
Nether Kinmundy
 Abers 217 K5
Nether Langwith
 Notts..........................115 K7
Netherlaw D & G 146 C6
Netherley Abers.............207 G6
Nethermill D & G 155 H5
Nethermuir Abers...........217 G5
Netherne-on-the-Hill
 Surrey 32 B3
Netheroyd Hill Kirk........123 H6
Nether Padley Derbys....114 E6
Netherplace E Rens.......174 F7
Nether Poppleton
 C York 133 J8
Netherseal Derbys..........86 C2
Nether Silton N York.....133 G2
Nether Stowey
 Somset.........................25 J4
Netherthong Kirk...........123 H8
Netherton Angus...........196 E5
Netherton Devon 7 K2
Netherton Dudley............85 G6
Netherton Kirk...............123 H7
Netherton N Lans..........175 K7
Netherton Nthumb.........168 E7
Netherton P & K............195 J6
Netherton Stirlg.............175 G3
Netherton Wakefd.........123 K6
Nethertown Cumb..........136 D5
Nethertown Highld........231 L1
Nethertown Staffs.........100 C8
Netherurd Border..........165 L1
Nether Wallop Hants.......28 F4
Nether Wasdale
 Cumb.........................136 F6
Nether Westcote
 Gloucs 56 E4
Nether Whitacre
 Warwks 86 B5
Nether Whitecleuch
 S Lans.......................165 G5
Nether Winchendon
 Bucks...........................58 B5
Netherwitton
 Nthumb......................158 D4
Nethy Bridge Highld.....204 B2
Netley Hants....................16 F2
Netley Marsh Hants........29 G8
Nettlebed Oxon...............42 B3
Nettlebridge Somset......26 F2
Nettlecombe Dorset.......13 M4
Nettleden Herts...............59 G6
Nettleham Lincs.............117 G6
Nettlestead Kent.............33 H3
Nettlestead Green
 Kent............................33 H3
Nettlestone IoW...............17 H4
Nettlesworth Dur...........151 G5
Nettleton Lincs...............117 J2
Nettleton Wilts.................39 J5
Netton Wilts.....................28 C4
Nevern Pembks...............64 F6
Nevill Holt Leics..............88 B5
New Abbey D & G..........147 G2
New Addington
 Gt Lon 45 G7
Newall Leeds.................123 J2
New Alresford Hants.......29 L5

Netherend Gloucs............54 E7
New Alyth P & K............195 K6
Newark Ork....................234 e4
Newark-on-Trent
 Notts..........................102 D2
Newarthill N Lans..........175 K6
New Ash Green Kent.......45 L6
New Balderton Notts.....102 D3
New Barn Kent.................45 L6
New Barnet Gt Lon 44 F2
Newbattle Mdloth...........177 J5
New Bewick Nthumb......169 G5
Newbie D & G 147 L3
Newbiggin Cumb............138 C2
Newbiggin Cumb............138 F2
Newbiggin Cumb............148 F5
Newbiggin Dur...............139 K2
Newbiggin N York..........131 J3
Newbiggin-by-the-
 Sea Nthumb..............159 H5
Newbigging Angus.........187 H1
Newbigging Angus.........195 L7
Newbigging Angus.........196 C8
Newbigging S Lans.......165 K1
Newbiggin-on-Lune
 Cumb.........................139 G6
New Bilton Warwks.........86 F7
Newbold Derbys.............115 G6
Newbold on Avon
 Warwks 86 F7
Newbold on Stour
 Warwks 72 B5
Newbold Pacey
 Warwks 72 C3
Newbold Verdon
 Leics............................86 F3
New Bolingbroke
 Lincs..........................104 A2
Newborough C Pete.......89 H3
Newborough IoA............108 E7
Newborough Staffs.......100 C7
New Boultham Lincs......116 F7
Newbourne Suffk.............78 F6
New Bradwell M Keyn....74 B6
New Brampton
 Derbys.......................115 G7
New Brancepeth Dur.....151 G6
Newbridge C Edin..........176 F4
Newbridge Caerph..........37 K2
Newbridge Cnwll...............2 D5
Newbridge D & G 155 G6
Newbridge Hants.............28 F7
Newbridge IoW................16 E5
Newbridge Green
 Worcs 70 E6
Newbridge on Wye
 Powys.........................67 L3
New Brighton Wirral......111 J3
Newbrough Nthumb.......149 L2
New Buckenham
 Norfk............................92 C5
Newbuildings Devon 11 J4
Newburgh Abers............207 J1
Newburgh Abers............217 H3
Newburgh Fife...............186 D4
Newburgh Lancs............121 G7
Newburgh Priory
 N York 133 H4
Newburn N u Ty..............150 F2
Newbury Somset.............27 G2
Newbury W Berk..............41 J6
Newbury Park Gt Lon 45 J3
Newby Cumb..................138 E3
Newby Lancs 122 B2
Newby N York................130 D5
Newby N York................142 B5
Newby Bridge Cumb 129 H3
Newby East Cumb.........148 E4
New Byth Abers.............216 F4
Newby West Cumb........148 C4
Newcastle Mons..............54 C5
Newcastle Shrops............82 E6
Newcastle Airport
 Nthumb......................158 F7
Newcastle Emlyn
 Carmth 65 J6
Newcastleton Border....156 E5

Newcastle-under-
  Lyme Staffs..................99 J4
Newcastle upon
  Tyne N u Ty................151 G3
Newchapel Pembks.......65 H6
Newchapel Surrey............32 C5
Newchurch IoW 17 G5
Newchurch Kent..............34 E7
Newchurch Mons.............38 C2
Newchurch Powys...........68 E4
Newchurch Staffs 100 D7
New Costessey Norfk....92 E2
Newcraighall C Edin 177 J4
New Crofton Wakefd...124 B6
New Cross Gt Lon...........45 G5
New Cross Somset 26 B7
New Cumnock E Ayrs..164 C6
New Deer Abers 217 G5
New Denham Bucks 43 H4
Newdigate Surrey............31 K3
New Duston Nhants 73 K3
New Earswick C York...133 J7
New Edlington Donc....115 K2
New Elgin Moray..........214 F3
New Ellerby E R Yk......126 E3
Newell Green Br For 42 E6
New Eltham Gt Lon.........45 H5
New End Worcs 71 J3
Newenden Kent 33 L7
New England C Pete......89 H4
Newent Gloucs 55 G3
Newfield Dur 150 F7
Newfield Highld...........223 H6
New Fletton C Pete 89 H4
New Forest
  National Park 16 C2
Newgale Pembks 48 E3
New Galloway D & G...154 B6
Newgate Street Herts ...59 M6
New Gilston Fife...........187 G5
New Grimsby IoS..............2 a1
Newhall Ches E...............98 E4
New Hartley
  Nthumb 159 H6
Newhaven C Edin..........177 H3
Newhaven E Susx...........19 L5
New Haw Surrey...............43 H7
New Hedges Pembks......49 J6
New Holland N Linc 126 D5
Newholm N York 143 H5
New Houghton
  Derbys 115 J7
New Houghton Norfk ..105 J6
Newhouse N Lans 175 L6
New Hutton Cumb 130 B2
Newick E Susx................19 L2
Newington Kent............35 G7
Newington Kent.............46 E6
Newington Oxon...........41 L2
New Inn Carmth 66 B6
New Inn Torfn................53 L7
New Invention
  Shrops 82 F7
New Lakenham Norfk ...92 F3
New Lanark S Lans 165 G2
New Lanark Village
  S Lans 165 G2
Newland C KuH............126 D4
Newland Gloucs............54 D6
Newland N York 125 G5
Newland Somset 24 C4
Newland Worcs 70 E5
Newlandrig Mdloth.....177 K6
Newlands Border 156 K4
Newlands Nthumb........150 D4
Newlands of
  Dundurcas Moray 215 G4
New Langholm D & G..156 C5
New Leake Lincs 104 C2
New Leeds Abers..........217 J4
New Lodge Barns.........123 L8
New Longton Lancs 121 G5
New Luce D & G 144 E3
Newlyn Cnwll 2 E5
Newlyn East Cnwll 4 C5
Newmachar Abers 207 G2

Newmains N Lans..........175 L6
New Malden Gt Lon......44 E6
Newman's Green
  Suffk 77 K5
Newmarket Suffk...........76 F2
Newmarket W Isls 232 f2
New Marske R & Cl.....142 D3
New Marston Oxon........57 K6
New Mill Abers 206 E8
Newmill Border............167 G7
New Mill Cnwll 2 E4
New Mill Kirk 123 H8
Newmill Moray.............215 K4
Newmillerdam
  Wakefd 123 L7
Newmill of Inshewan
  Angus 196 C4
Newmills C Edin...........177 J4
New Mills Derbys 113 M4
Newmills Fife..............176 D2
Newmills Mons 54 D6
New Mills Powys...........82 C4
Newmiln P & K 186 B2
Newmilns E Ayrs..........164 B2
New Milton Hants 16 B4
New Mistley Essex.........62 D2
New Moat Pembks.........49 H3
Newney Green Essex....61 G6
Newnham Gloucs 55 G5
Newnham Hants 30 B2
Newnham Herts 75 J6
Newnham Kent 34 C3
Newnham Nhants 73 H3
Newnham Worcs............70 B2
New Ollerton Notts 116 A7
New Pitsligo Abers 217 G3
Newport Cnwll..................9 J7
Newport E R Yk...........125 K4
Newport Essex 76 D7
Newport Gloucs.............39 G2
Newport Highld...........227 K4
Newport IoW 16 F5
Newport Newpt 37 L3
Newport Pembks 64 E6
Newport Wrekin............99 H8
Newport-on-Tay Fife ..187 G2
Newport Pagnell
  M Keyn 74 C5
Newport Pagnell
  Services M Keyn 74 C5
New Prestwick S Ayrs...163 J4
New Quay Cerdgn...........65 L3
Newquay Cnwll 4 C4
Newquay Airport
  Cnwll................................4 D3
New Rackheath
  Norfk 93 G2
New Radnor Powys.......68 E3
New Ridley Nthumb....150 D3
New Romney Kent..........21 L2
New Rossington
  Donc...........................115 L2
New Sauchie Clacks 185 J7
Newseat Abers 216 D7
Newsham Lancs 121 G4
Newsham N York 132 E3
Newsham N York 140 E5
Newsham Nthumb 159 H6
New Sharlston
  Wakefd 124 B6
Newsholme E R Yk......125 H5
New Silksworth
  Sundld........................151 J4
Newsome Kirk 123 H7
New Somerby Lincs 102 F5
New Southgate
  Crematorium
  Gt Lon..........................44 F2
Newstead Border 167 H3
Newstead Notts 101 K3
Newstead Nthumb 169 H4
New Stevenston
  N Lans........................175 K6
Newthorpe Notts.........101 J4
Newton Ag & B 182 F7
Newton Border 167 J5

Newton Brdgnd.............36 C5
Newton C Beds..............75 J5
Newton Cambs...............76 B5
Newton Cambs...............90 B1
Newton Ches W.............76 B1
Newton Ches W...........112 B7
Newton Cumb 128 F5
Newton Derbys............101 H2
Newton Herefs 53 M2
Newton Herefs 69 K4
Newton Highld.............212 F4
Newton Highld.............213 H5
Newton Highld.............213 J2
Newton Highld.............231 L5
Newton Lincs 103 H5
Newton Mdloth............177 J4
Newton Moray.............214 E2
Newton Moray.............215 H2
Newton Nhants 88 C6
Newton Notts 102 B4
Newton Nthumb...........150 C3
Newton S Lans 165 H3
Newton S Lans 175 H6
Newton Staffs 100 B7
Newton Suffk.................77 K6
Newton W Loth 176 E3
Newton Warwks............87 G7
Newton Abbot Devon 7 K2
Newton Arlosh Cumb ..147 L4
Newton Aycliffe Dur...141 G3
Newton Bewley
  Hartpl 141 K2
Newton Blossomville
  M Keyn 74 D4
Newton Bromswold
  Nhants 74 E2
Newton Burgoland
  Leics 86 D2
Newton-by-the-Sea
  Nthumb 169 J4
Newton by Toft Lincs ...117 H4
Newton Ferrers Cnwll......6 A3
Newton Ferrers
  Devon 6 E6
Newton Ferry W Isls 232 c5
Newton Flotman
  Norfk 92 E4
Newtongrange
  Mdloth.......................177 J5
Newton Green Mons....38 D3
Newton Harcourt
  Leics 87 J4
Newton Heath Manch ..113 K2
Newtonhill Abers 207 G6
Newton-in-Bowland
  Lancs 121 K1
Newton Kyme N York...124 C2
Newton-le-Willows
  N York........................132 C2
Newton-le-Willows
  St Hel 112 E3
Newtonloan Mdloth ...177 J5
Newton Longville
  Bucks...........................58 D2
Newton Mearns
  E Rens 174 F7
Newtonmill Angus 196 F4
Newtonmore Highld...203 H5
Newton Morrell
  N York........................141 G5
Newton of
  Balcanquhal P & K..186 B5
Newton of Balcormo
  Fife 187 H6
Newton on Ouse
  N York........................133 H7
Newton-on-
  Rawcliffe N York 134 C2
Newton-on-the-
  Moor Nthumb 158 F2
Newton on Trent
  Lincs 116 D6
Newton Poppleford
  Devon 12 E4
Newton Purcell Oxon...57 L3

Newton Regis
  Warwks 86 C3
Newton Reigny
  Cumb.........................138 C2
Newton St Cyres
  Devon 11 K5
Newton St Faith
  Norfk 92 F1
Newton St Loe BaNES...39 G7
Newton St Petrock
  Devon 9 K3
Newton Solney
  Derbys.......................100 F7
Newton Stacey Hants ...29 H4
Newton Stewart
  D & G 145 J3
Newton Tony Wilts......28 E4
Newton Tracey
  Devon 23 H6
Newton under
  Roseberry R & Cl....142 C5
Newton upon
  Derwent E R Yk......125 H2
Newton Valence
  Hants 30 B5
Newton Wamphray
  D & G 155 K3
Newton with Scales
  Lancs 120 F4
Newtown Cumb............147 L3
Newtown Cumb...........148 E3
Newtown D & G...........164 F7
Newtown Devon............12 D3
Newtown Devon............24 B6
New Town Dorset 27 L7
New Town Dorset 27 M7
New Town E Susx.........19 M2
Newtown Gloucs...........54 F7
Newtown Hants 29 L8
Newtown Herefs............70 B5
Newtown Herefs............70 C6
Newtown Highld.........202 B4
Newtown IoW 16 E4
Newtown Nthumb........168 F4
Newtown Poole.............15 K4
Newtown Powys...........82 C5
Newtown Shrops...........98 B7
Newtown Shrops...........98 C6
Newtown Somset 25 L8
Newtown Staffs 99 K1
Newtown Wigan..........112 E1
Newtown Worcs............70 F4
Newtown Linford
  Leics 87 G2
Newtown of
  Beltrees Rens 174 D6
Newtown St
  Boswells Border 167 J3
New Tredegar Caerph....53 H7
New Trows S Lans 164 F2
Newtyle Angus.............195 L7
New Walsoken
  Cambs..........................90 C2
New Waltham
  NE Lin 118 C1
New Winton E Loth.....177 L4
Newyork Ag & B 182 D5
New York Lincs 103 L2
Neyland Pembks 49 G6
Nicholashayne Devon ...25 H7
Nicholaston Swans........51 G7
Nidd N York 132 D7
Nigg C Aber 207 H5
Nigg Highld.................223 H6
Nigg Ferry Highld........223 H7
Ninebanks Nthumb 149 K4
Nine Elms Swindn........40 C3
Ninfield E Susx..............20 E3
Ningwood IoW 16 E5
Nisbet Border 167 K4
Nisbet Hill Border 179 G7
Niton IoW 17 F6
Nitshill C Glas..............174 F6
Nocton Lincs 117 H8
Noke Oxon......................57 K5
Nolton Pembks 48 E4

Nolton Haven
Pembks 48 E4
No Man's Heath
Ches W 98 D3
No Man's Heath
Warwks 86 C2
Nomansland Devon 11 J3
Nomansland Wilts 28 E7
Noneley Shrops 98 C6
Nonington Kent 35 H4
Nook Cumb 129 L3
Norbiton Gt Lon 44 D6
Norbury Ches E 98 E3
Norbury Derbys 100 C4
Norbury Gt Lon 44 F6
Norbury Shrops 83 G5
Norbury Staffs 99 H7
Norchard Worcs 70 F2
Nordelph Norfk 90 D4
Nordley Shrops 84 C4
Norfolk Broads 93 K2
Norham Nthumb 179 J8
Norley Ches W 112 E6
Norleywood Hants 16 D3
Normanby Lincs 117 G4
Normanby N Linc 125 K7
Normanby N York 134 B3
Normanby R & Cl 142 C4
Normanby le Wold
Lincs 117 J3
Normandy Surrey 30 F2
Norman's Green
Devon 12 D2
Normanton C Derb 101 G5
Normanton Leics 102 D4
Normanton Lincs 102 F4
Normanton Notts 102 B2
Normanton Wakefd 124 B6
Normanton le Heath
Leics 86 D2
Normanton on Soar
Notts 101 K7
Normanton on the
Wolds Notts 101 L6
Normanton on Trent
Notts 116 C7
Norris Green Lpool 111 L3
Norris Hill Leics 86 D1
Norristhorpe Kirk 123 J6
Northall Bucks 58 F4
Northallerton N York ..141 J7
Northam C Sotn 29 H8
Northam Devon 23 G5
Northampton Nhants 73 L3
Northampton Worcs 70 E2
Northampton
Services Nhants 73 K3
North Anston Rothm ..115 K5
North Ascot Br For 42 E6
North Aston Oxon 57 J3
Northaw Herts 59 L7
Northay Somset 13 H1
North Baddesley
Hants 29 H7
North Ballachulish
Highld 191 L4
North Barrow
Somset 26 E5
North Barsham Norfk ..105 L6
North Benfleet Essex 46 C3
North Bersted W Susx ..18 C5
North Berwick E Loth ..178 C2
North Boarhunt
Hants 17 H1
Northborough C Pete ...89 H3
Northbourne Kent 35 J4
North Bovey Devon 11 H7
North Bradley Wilts 27 J1
North Brentor Devon 10 C8
North Brewham
Somset 27 G4
Northbrook Hants 29 K4
North Buckland
Devon 23 H4
North Burlingham
Norfk 93 H2

North Cadbury
Somset 26 F6
North Carlton Lincs 116 F6
North Carlton Notts 115 L4
North Cave E R Yk 125 K4
North Cerney Gloucs 56 A6
North Chailey E Susx 19 K2
Northchapel W Susx 30 F5
North Charford Hants ..28 D7
North Charlton
Nthumb 169 H5
North Cheam Gt Lon 44 E6
North Cheriton
Somset 27 G6
North Chideock
Dorset 13 K4
Northchurch Herts 58 F6
North Cliffe E R Yk 125 K3
North Clifton Notts 116 D6
North Cockerington
Lincs 118 E4
North Connel Ag & B ..182 C1
North Cornelly
Brdgnd 36 C4
North Cotes Lincs 118 E2
Northcott Devon 9 J6
Northcourt Oxon 57 J7
North Cove Suffk 93 K5
North Cowton N York ..141 G6
North Crawley
M Keyn 74 D5
North Creake Norfk 105 K5
North Curry Somset 25 L6
North Dalton E R Yk 125 L1
North Deighton
N York 124 B1
North Devon
Crematorium
Devon 23 H5
Northdown Kent 35 K2
North Downs 34 B4
North Duffield N York ..125 G3
North Duntulm
Highld 218 C6
North East Surrey
Crematorium
Gt Lon 44 E6
North Elmham Norfk 106 B7
North Elmsall Wakefd ..124 D7
North End C Port 17 J3
North End Essex 61 G4
North End Hants 28 C7
North End Nhants 74 D2
North End W Susx 18 D5
Northend Warwks 72 E4
Northenden Manch 113 J4
North Erradale Highld ..219 H5
North Evington C Leic ..87 J3
North Fambridge
Essex 61 K7
North Ferriby E R Yk 126 B5
Northfield Birm 85 H7
Northfield C Aber 207 G4
Northfield E R Yk 126 C5
Northfields Lincs 88 E2
Northfleet Kent 45 M5
North Frodingham
E R Yk 135 H8
North Gorley Hants 15 M1
North Green Suffk 79 G3
North Greetwell Lincs ..117 G6
North Grimston
N York 134 C6
North Hayling Hants 17 K2
North Hill Cnwll 5 L1
North Hillingdon
Gt Lon 43 H4
North Hinksey
Village Oxon 57 J6
North Holmwood
Surrey 31 K3
North Huish Devon 7 G5
North Hykeham Lincs ..116 F7
Northiam E Susx 21 G2
Northill C Beds 75 G5
Northington Hants 29 K4

North Kelsey Lincs 117 H2
North Kessock Highld ..213 G5
North Killingholme
N Linc 126 E6
North Kilvington
N York 132 F3
North Kilworth Leics 87 H6
North Kyme Lincs 103 J3
North Landing E R Yk ..135 K5
Northlands Lincs 104 B2
Northleach Gloucs 56 C5
North Lee Bucks 58 D6
Northleigh Devon 12 F3
North Leigh Oxon 57 H5
North Leverton with
Habblesthorpe
Notts 116 C5
Northlew Devon 10 D5
North Littleton Worcs ..71 J5
North Lopham Norfk 92 C6
North Luffenham
Rutlnd 88 D3
North Marden W Susx ..30 D7
North Marston Bucks 58 C4
North Middleton
Mdloth 177 K6
North Millbrex Abers ..216 F5
North Milmain D & G ..144 C4
North Molton Devon 24 B5
Northmoor Oxon 57 H7
North Moreton Oxon 41 K3
Northmuir Angus 196 C5
North Mundham
W Susx 18 B5
North Muskham
Notts 102 D2
North Newbald E R Yk ..125 L3
North Newington
Oxon 72 E6
North Newnton Wilts 40 C8
North Newton
Somset 25 L5
Northney Hants 17 K2
North Nibley Gloucs 39 H2
Northolt Gt Lon 43 J4
Northop Flints 111 H7
Northop Hall Flints 111 J7
North Ormesby
Middsb 142 B4
North Ormsby Lincs 118 C3
Northorpe Kirk 123 J6
Northorpe Lincs 103 K5
Northorpe Lincs 116 E3
North Otterington
N York 132 E2
North Owersby Lincs ..117 H3
Northowram Calder 123 G5
North Perrott Somset 13 L1
North Petherton
Somset 25 L5
North Petherwin
Cnwll 9 H6
North Pickenham
Norfk 91 J3
North Piddle Worcs 71 G4
North Poorton
Dorset 13 M3
Northport Dorset 15 H5
North Queensferry
Fife 176 F3
North Rauceby Lincs ..103 G3
Northrepps Norfk 106 F5
North Reston Lincs 118 E5
North Rigton N York 123 K1
North Rode Ches E 113 K7
North Ronaldsay Ork ..234 e3
North Ronaldsay
Airport Ork 234 e3
North Runcton Norfk 90 F1
North Scarle Lincs 116 D7
North Shian Ag & B 191 H7
North Shields N Tyne ..151 J2
North Shoebury
Sthend 46 F3
North Shore Bpool 120 D3
North Side C Pete 89 K4

North Somercotes
Lincs 118 F3
North Stainley
N York 132 D4
North Stifford Thurr 45 L4
North Stoke BaNES 39 G6
North Stoke Oxon 41 L3
North Stoke W Susx 18 D4
North Street Kent 34 D3
North Street W Berk 41 M6
North Sunderland
Nthumb 169 J3
North Tamerton
Cnwll 9 J5
North Tawton Devon 10 F4
North Third Stirlg 175 K1
North Thoresby Lincs ..118 D2
Northton W Isls 232 d5
North Town Devon 10 D3
North Town Somset 26 E3
North Town W & M 42 E4
North Tuddenham
Norfk 92 C2
North Uist W Isls 233 b6
Northumberland
National Park
Nthumb 157 L3
North Walsham Norfk ..107 G6
North Waltham Hants ..29 K3
North Warnborough
Hants 30 B2
North Weald Bassett
Essex 60 D7
North Wheatley
Notts 116 C4
Northwich Ches W 112 F6
Northwick Worcs 70 E3
North Widcombe
BaNES 38 E8
North Willingham
Lincs 117 K4
North Wingfield
Derbys 115 H8
North Witham Lincs 102 F7
Northwold Norfk 91 H4
Northwood Gt Lon 43 H3
Northwood IoW 16 F4
Northwood Shrops 98 C6
Northwood Green
Gloucs 55 G5
North Wootton
Dorset 26 F8
North Wootton Norfk ..105 G7
North Wootton
Somset 26 E3
North Wraxall Wilts 39 J5
North York Moors
National Park 142 F6
Norton Donc 124 E7
Norton E Susx 19 M5
Norton Gloucs 55 J3
Norton Halton 112 D5
Norton N York 134 C5
Norton Nhants 73 H2
Norton Notts 115 L6
Norton Powys 68 F2
Norton S on T 141 K3
Norton Shrops 84 D4
Norton Suffk 77 L2
Norton W Susx 18 C4
Norton Wilts 39 K4
Norton Worcs 70 F4
Norton Worcs 71 J5
Norton Bavant Wilts 27 K3
Norton Bridge Staffs 99 K6
Norton Canes Staffs 85 H2
Norton Canes
Services Staffs 85 H3
Norton Canon Herefs ..69 H5
Norton Disney Lincs ..102 F2
Norton Fitzwarren
Somset 25 J6
Norton Green IoW 16 D5
Norton Hawkfield
BaNES 38 E7
Norton Heath Essex 60 F6

Norton in Hales
Shrops.................99 G5
Norton-Juxta-
Twycross Leics...........86 D3
Norton-le-Clay N York ..132 F5
Norton Lindsey
Warwks 72 B2
Norton Little Green
Suffk 77 L2
Norton Malreward
BaNES...................38 E7
Norton St Philip
Somset 27 H1
Norton Subcourse
Norfk 93 J4
Norton sub Hamdon
Somset 26 C7
Norwell Notts 102 C1
Norwell Woodhouse
Notts 116 B8
Norwich Norfk..............92 F2
Norwich Airport Norfk 92 E2
Norwich (St Faith)
Crematorium
Norfk 92 F1
Norwick Shet 235 e1
Norwood Clacks 185 J8
Norwood Green
Gt Lon 43 J5
Norwood Hill Surrey 31 L3
Noss Mayo Devon 6 E6
Nosterfield N York 132 D4
Nostie Highld 210 D8
Notgrove Gloucs 56 C4
Nottage Brdgnd 36 C5
Nottingham C Nott.......101 L5
Notton Wakefd 123 L7
Notton Wilts 39 K6
Noutard's Green
Worcs 70 E2
Nuffield Oxon 42 A3
Nunburnholme
E R Yk 125 K2
Nuneaton Warwks........86 D5
Nunhead Gt Lon 45 G5
Nun Monkton N York 133 H7
Nunney Somset 27 G3
Nunnington N York.......133 K4
Nunsthorpe NE Lin.......127 G8
Nunthorpe C York 124 F1
Nunthorpe Middsb........142 C4
Nunthorpe Village
Middsb 142 C5
Nunton Wilts 28 D6
Nunwick N York 132 E5
Nursling Hants 29 G7
Nutbourne W Susx........17 L2
Nutbourne W Susx........18 E3
Nutfield Surrey 32 B3
Nuthall Notts 101 K4
Nuthampstead Herts 76 B7
Nuthurst W Susx...........31 K6
Nutley E Susx 32 D7
Nuttall Bury 122 B7
Nybster Highld 231 L3
Nyetimber W Susx........18 B6
Nyewood W Susx 30 D6
Nymans W Susx 31 L5
Nymet Rowland
Devon 11 G4
Nymet Tracey Devon......11 G5
Nympsfield Gloucs........55 J7
Nynehead Somset.........25 H6
Nyton W Susx 18 C5

Oadby Leics 87 J4
Oad Street Kent...........34 B3
Oakamoor Staffs 100 B4
Oakbank W Loth.........176 E5
Oak Cross Devon 10 D5
Oakdale Caerph 37 J2
Oake Somset 25 J6
Oaken Staffs 84 F3

Oakenclough Lancs 121 H2
Oakengates Wrekin.......84 C2
Oakenshaw Dur..........150 F7
Oakenshaw Kirk 123 H5
Oakford Cerdgn 66 B3
Oakford Devon 24 E6
Oakham Rutlnd 88 C2
Oakhanger Hants 30 C4
Oakhill Somset 26 F3
Oakington Cambs 76 B2
Oakle Street Gloucs......55 H4
Oakley Bed 74 E4
Oakley Bucks 57 M5
Oakley Fife 176 D1
Oakley Hants 29 K2
Oakley Suffk 92 E7
Oakridge Gloucs 55 K7
Oaksey Wilts 39 M2
Oakthorpe Leics 86 D2
Oakwood C Derb.........101 G5
Oakworth C Brad 122 F3
Oare Kent 34 D3
Oare Somset 24 C3
Oare Wilts 40 D7
Oasby Lincs 103 G5
Oath Somset 26 B6
Oathlaw Angus...........196 D5
Oatlands Park Surrey 43 H7
Oban Ag & B................182 B2
Oban Airport Ag & B........182 C1
Obley Shrops...............83 G7
Obney P & K 195 G8
Oborne Dorset 26 F7
Occold Suffk 78 D1
Occumster Highld 231 J7
Ochiltree E Ayrs 163 L4
Ockbrook Derbys 101 H5
Ockham Surrey 31 H1
Ockle Highld 190 B3
Ockley Surrey 31 J4
Ocle Pychard Herefs......69 L5
Odcombe Somset..........26 D7
Odd Down BaNES..........39 H7
Oddingley Worcs 71 G3
Oddington Gloucs........56 E3
Oddington Oxon 57 K5
Odell Bed 74 D3
Odiham Hants 30 C2
Odsal C Brad 123 H5
Odsey Cambs 75 K6
Odstock Wilts 28 D6
Odstone Leics 86 E3
Offchurch Warwks........72 D2
Offenham Worcs 71 J5
Offerton Stockp.........113 K4
Offham E Susx 19 L3
Offham Kent 33 H2
Offham W Susx 18 D4
Offord Cluny Cambs......75 J2
Offord D'Arcy Cambs.....75 J2
Offton Suffk 78 C5
Offwell Devon 12 F3
Ogbourne Maizey
Wilts 40 D6
Ogbourne St Andrew
Wilts 40 D6
Ogbourne St George
Wilts 40 D5
Ogle Nthumb 158 E6
Oglet Lpool 112 C5
Ogmore V Glam 36 D5
Ogmore-by-Sea
V Glam 36 D5
Ogmore Vale Brdgnd.....36 E3
Okeford Fitzpaine
Dorset 14 F1
Okehampton Devon......10 E5
Oker Side Derbys........100 F1
Okewood Hill Surrey.....31 J4
Old Nhants 87 L8
Old Aberdeen C Aber ...207 H4
Old Alresford Hants......29 L5
Oldany Highld 224 D2
Old Auchenbrack
D & G 154 D3
Old Basford C Nott 101 K4

Old Basing Hants..........30 A2
Old Beetley Norfk.......106 A8
Oldberrow Warwks........71 K2
Old Bewick Nthumb 169 G5
Old Bolingbroke Lincs ..118 E8
Old Bramhope Leeds 123 J2
Old Brampton Derbys..115 G6
Old Bridge of Urr
D & G 146 D2
Old Buckenham
Norfk 92 C5
Old Burghclere Hants 41 J8
Oldbury Sandw 85 H5
Oldbury Shrops.............84 C5
Oldbury Warwks 86 C5
Oldbury-on-Severn
S Glos 38 E2
Oldbury on the Hill
Gloucs...................39 J3
Old Byland N York 133 H3
Old Cantley Donc 115 L2
Oldcastle Mons...........53 L3
Old Catton Norfk..........92 F2
Old Clee NE Lin...........127 G8
Old Cleeve Somset 25 G3
Old Clipstone Notts 115 L8
Old Colwyn Conwy.......110 B6
Oldcotes Notts 115 L4
Old Dailly S Ayrs.........152 F3
Old Dalby Leics 102 A7
Old Deer Abers............217 J5
Old Edlington Donc 115 K3
Old Ellerby E R Yk.......126 E3
Old Felixstowe Suffk 79 G7
Oldfield Worcs 70 E2
Old Fletton C Pete........89 H4
Oldford Somset 27 H2
Old Forge Herefs 54 E4
Old Grimsby IoS............2 a1
Old Hall Green Herts......60 B4
Oldham Oldham..........113 L1
Oldhamstocks E Loth ...178 F4
Old Harlow Essex 60 D5
Old Hunstanton
Norfk 105 G4
Old Hurst Cambs 89 K7
Old Hutton Cumb........130 B2
Old Kilpatrick W Duns...174 E4
Old Knebworth Herts.....59 L4
Old Lakenham Norfk......92 F3
Oldland S Glos.............38 F6
Old Langho Lancs 121 K4
Old Leake Lincs 104 C3
Old Malton N York 134 C5
Oldmeldrum Abers.......216 F8
Oldmill Cnwll 6 B2
Old Milverton Warwks ...72 C2
Oldmixon N Som 37 M8
Old Newton Suffk.........78 C3
Old Radnor Powys 68 E3
Old Rayne Abers..........216 D8
Old Romney Kent..........21 K2
Old Shoreham W Susx ...19 G4
Oldshoremore Highld...228 C4
Old Sodbury S Glos........39 H4
Old Somerby Lincs.......102 F5
Oldstead N York 133 H4
Old Stratford Nhants.....73 L6
Old Struan P & K.........194 C4
Old Swinford Dudley 84 F6
Old Thirsk N York 132 F3
Old Town Cumb...........130 B3
Old Town E Susx 20 C5
Old Town IoS................2 b2
Old Trafford Traffd 113 J3
Oldwall Cumb 148 E3
Oldwalls Swans 50 F6
Old Warden C Beds........75 G5
Old Weston Cambs........89 G7
Old Wick Highld 231 L5
Old Windsor W & M 43 G5
Old Wives Lees Kent......34 E4
Old Woking Surrey 43 G8
Olgrinmore Highld.......231 G5
Olive Green Staffs.......100 C8
Oliver's Battery Hants ...29 J6

Ollaberry Shet 235 C3
Ollach Highld 209 H6
Ollerton Ches E 113 H6
Ollerton Notts.............116 A7
Ollerton Shrops............98 F7
Olney M Keyn 74 C4
Olrig House Highld 231 H3
Olton Solhll 85 K6
Olveston S Glos............38 E3
Ombersley Worcs..........70 E2
Ompton Notts 116 B7
Onchan IoM 237 d5
Onecote Staffs 100 B2
Onibury Shrops............83 J7
Onich Highld 191 K4
Onllwyn Neath............52 C6
Onneley Staffs 99 H4
Onslow Green Essex......61 G4
Onslow Village Surrey....31 G2
Onston Ches W 112 E6
Opinan Highld 219 H6
Orbliston Moray..........215 G3
Orbost Highld 208 D5
Orby Lincs 119 G7
Orchard Portman
Somset 25 K6
Orcheston Wilts 28 B3
Orcop Herefs...............54 C3
Orcop Hill Herefs 54 C3
Ord Abers 216 C3
Ordhead Abers 206 C3
Ordie Abers 205 K5
Ordiequish Moray........215 H3
Ordsall Notts..............116 B5
Ore E Susx 21 G4
Orford Suffk 79 J4
Orford Warrtn 112 E4
Organford Dorset 15 H4
Orkney Islands Ork 234 c6
Orkney, Heart of
Neolithic Ork............234 b6
Orlestone Kent 34 D7
Orleton Herefs.............69 J2
Orleton Worcs.............70 C2
Orlingbury Nhants 74 C1
Ormesby R & Cl..........142 C4
Ormesby St
Margaret Norfk 93 K1
Ormesby St Michael
Norfk 93 K1
Ormiscaig Highld........219 K4
Ormiston E Loth 177 L4
Ormsaigmore Highld....189 L4
Ormsary Ag & B...........172 C4
Ormskirk Lancs 120 F8
Oronsay Ag & B 171 G2
Orphir Ork 234 b6
Orpington Gt Lon 45 J6
Orrell Sefton 111 K3
Orrell Wigan 112 D2
Orroland D & G 146 D5
Orsett Thurr 45 M4
Orslow Staffs...............84 E1
Orston Notts 102 C4
Orton Cumb 138 F5
Orton Nhants 88 B7
Orton Staffs 84 F4
Orton Longueville
C Pete...................89 H4
Orton-on-the-Hill
Leics......................86 C3
Orton Waterville
C Pete...................89 H4
Orwell Cambs 75 L4
Osbaldeston Lancs 121 J4
Osbaldwick C York 124 F1
Osbaston Leics 86 E3
Osbaston Shrops 97 L7
Osborne House IoW......17 G4
Osbournby Lincs 103 H5
Oscroft Ches W 112 D7
Ose Highld 208 E6
Osgathorpe Leics 101 H8
Osgodby Lincs 117 H3
Osgodby N York...........124 F4
Osgodby N York...........135 G3

Oskaig Highld 209 H6
Oskamull Ag & B 189 L7
Osmaston Derbys 100 D4
Osmington Dorset 14 D5
Osmington Mills
  Dorset 14 E6
Osmondthorpe Leeds .. 123 L4
Osmotherley N York 141 K7
Osney Oxon 57 J6
Ospringe Kent 34 D3
Ossett Wakefd 123 K6
Ossington Notts 116 C8
Osterley Gt Lon 44 D5
Oswaldkirk N York 133 K4
Oswaldtwistle Lancs 121 L5
Oswestry Shrops 97 L6
Otford Kent 32 F2
Otham Kent 33 K3
Othery Somset 26 B5
Otley Leeds 123 J4
Otley Suffk 78 E4
Otterbourne Hants 29 J6
Otterburn N York 131 G7
Otterburn Nthumb 157 M4
Otter Ferry Ag & B 172 F2
Otterham Cnwll 8 F6
Otterhampton
  Somset 25 K3
Otternish W Isls 232 c5
Ottershaw Surrey 43 G7
Otterswick Shet 235 d3
Otterton Devon 12 E5
Ottery St Mary Devon ... 12 E4
Ottinge Kent 34 F6
Ottringham E R Yk 127 G5
Oughterside Cumb 147 K6
Oughtibridge Sheff 114 F3
Oughtrington Warrtn .. 113 G4
Oulston N York 133 H5
Oulton Cumb 147 M5
Oulton Norfk 106 D6
Oulton Staffs 99 K5
Oulton Suffk 93 L5
Oulton Broad Suffk 93 L5
Oulton Street Norfk 106 D6
Oundle Nhants 88 F6
Ounsdale Staffs 84 F5
Our Dynamic Earth
  C Edin 177 H4
Ousby Cumb 149 G7
Ousden Suffk 77 G3
Ousefleet E R Yk 125 K6
Ouston Dur 151 G4
Outgate Cumb 137 K7
Outhgill Cumb 139 H6
Outhill Warwks 71 K2
Outlane Kirk 123 G6
Out Rawcliffe Lancs 120 E3
Outwell Norfk 90 D3
Outwood Surrey 32 B4
Outwoods Staffs 99 H8
Ouzlewell Green
  Leeds 123 L5
Over Cambs 75 L1
Overbury Worcs 71 G6
Overcombe Dorset 14 D6
Over Compton Dorset .. 26 E7
Overdale
  Crematorium
  Bolton 121 K8
Over Haddon Derbys .. 114 D7
Over Kellet Lancs 129 L5
Over Kiddington
  Oxon 57 H4
Overleigh Somset 26 C4
Over Norton Oxon 56 F3
Over Peover Ches E 113 H6
Overpool Ches W 111 L6
Overscaig Hotel
  Highld 225 J4
Overseal Derbys 86 C1
Over Silton N York 133 G2
Oversland Kent 34 E3
Overstone Nhants 74 B2
Over Stowey Somset 25 J4
Overstrand Norfk 106 F4

Over Stratton
  Somset 26 B7
Overthorpe Nhants 72 F6
Overton C Aber 207 G3
Overton Hants 29 K2
Overton Lancs 129 J7
Overton N York 133 H7
Overton Shrops 69 K1
Overton Swans 50 F7
Overton Wakefd 123 K7
Overton Wrexhm 98 A4
Overtown N Lans 175 L7
Over Wallop Hants 28 F4
Over Whitacre
  Warwks 86 B5
Over Worton Oxon 57 H3
Oving Bucks 58 C4
Oving W Susx 18 B5
Ovingdean Br & H 19 K5
Ovingham Nthumb 150 D3
Ovington Dur 140 E4
Ovington Essex 77 H6
Ovington Hants 29 K5
Ovington Norfk 91 K3
Ovington Nthumb 150 D3
Ower Hants 28 F7
Owermoigne Dorset 14 E5
Owlerton Sheff 115 G4
Owlsmoor Br For 42 D7
Owlswick Bucks 58 C6
Owmby Lincs 117 G4
Owmby Lincs 117 H1
Owslebury Hants 29 K6
Owston Donc 124 E7
Owston Leics 87 L3
Owston Ferry N Linc ... 116 D2
Owstwick E R Yk 127 G4
Owthorne E R Yk 127 H5
Owthorpe Notts 102 A5
Owton Manor Hartpl ... 141 L2
Oxborough Norfk 91 G3
Oxcombe Lincs 118 D6
Oxenholme Cumb 129 L2
Oxenhope C Brad 122 F4
Oxen Park Cumb 129 G3
Oxenpill Somset 26 C3
Oxenton Gloucs 55 L2
Oxenwood Wilts 40 F8
Oxford Oxon 57 K6
Oxford Airport Oxon 57 J5
Oxford Crematorium
  Oxon 57 K6
Oxford Services Oxon .. 57 L6
Oxhey Herts 43 J2
Oxhill Warwks 72 C5
Oxley Wolves 84 F3
Oxley Green Essex 61 L5
Oxlode Cambs 90 C6
Oxnam Border 167 L5
Oxnead Norfk 106 F7
Oxshott Surrey 43 J7
Oxspring Barns 114 F2
Oxted Surrey 32 C3
Oxton Border 178 B7
Oxton N York 124 D2
Oxton Notts 101 M3
Oxwich Swans 51 G7
Oxwich Green Swans 50 F7
Oykel Bridge Hotel
  Highld 221 K2
Oyne Abers 206 D1
Oystermouth Swans 51 H7

P

Pabail W Isls 232 g2
Packington Leics 86 D1
Padanaram Angus 196 C6
Padbury Bucks 58 B2
Paddington Gt Lon 44 F4
Paddlesworth Kent 35 G6
Paddlesworth Kent 46 B7
Paddock Wood Kent 33 H4
Padiham Lancs 122 B4
Padside N York 132 B7

Padstow Cnwll 4 E2
Padworth W Berk 41 L7
Pagham W Susx 18 B6
Paglesham Essex 46 F2
Paignton Torbay 7 K4
Pailton Warwks 86 F6
Painscastle Powys 68 D5
Painshawfield
  Nthumb 150 D3
Painsthorpe E R Yk 134 C7
Painswick Gloucs 55 K6
Painter's Forstal
  Kent 34 D3
Paisley Rens 174 E5
Paisley Woodside
  Crematorium
  Rens 174 E5
Pakefield Suffk 93 L5
Pakenham Suffk 77 L2
Paley Street W & M 42 E5
Palfrey Wsall 85 H4
Palgrave Suffk 92 D7
Pallington Dorset 14 E4
Palmerston E Ayrs 163 L5
Palnackie D & G 146 E4
Palnure D & G 145 J3
Palterton Derbys 115 J7
Pamber End Hants 41 L8
Pamber Green Hants 41 L8
Pamber Heath Hants 41 L7
Pamington Gloucs 55 L2
Pamphill Dorset 15 J3
Pampisford Cambs 76 C5
Panbride Angus 187 J1
Pancrasweek Devon 9 H4
Pandy Mons 53 M4
Pandy Tudur Conwy 110 B8
Panfield Essex 61 H3
Pangbourne W Berk 41 M5
Pangdean W Susx 19 J4
Pannal N York 123 L1
Pannal Ash N York 132 D8
Pannanich Wells
  Hotel Abers 205 J6
Pant Shrops 97 L7
Pantasaph Flints 111 G6
Pant-ffrwyth Brdgnd 36 E4
Pant Glas Gwynd 95 H3
Pantglas Powys 81 G4
Panton Lincs 117 K5
Pant-y-dwr Powys 81 L8
Pant-y-mwyn Flints 111 H8
Panxworth Norfk 93 H2
Papa Westray Airport
  Ork 234 c3
Papcastle Cumb 136 F2
Papigoe Highld 231 L5
Papple E Loth 178 D4
Papplewick Notts 101 K3
Papworth Everard
  Cambs 75 K3
Papworth St Agnes
  Cambs 75 J2
Par Cnwll 5 G5
Parbold Lancs 121 G7
Parbrook Somset 26 E4
Parc Gwynd 96 D5
Parc Gwyn
  Crematorium
  Pembks 49 K5
Parc Seymour Newpt 38 B3
Pardshaw Cumb 136 F3
Parham Suffk 79 G3
Park D & G 154 F4
Park Nthumb 149 H3
Park Corner Oxon 42 B3
Park Crematorium
  Lancs 120 E5
Parkend Gloucs 54 E6
Parkers Green Kent 33 G4
Park Farm Kent 34 D6
Parkgate Ches W 111 J6
Parkgate D & G 155 H4
Park Gate Hants 17 G2
Park Gate Leeds 123 J3
Parkgate Surrey 31 K3

Parkgrove
  Crematorium
  Angus 196 F6
Parkhall W Duns 174 E4
Parkham Devon 22 F6
Parkmill Swans 51 G7
Park Royal Gt Lon 44 D4
Parkside Dur 151 K5
Parkside N Lans 175 L7
Parkstone Poole 15 J4
Park Street Herts 59 J6
Park Wood
  Crematorium
  Calder 123 G6
Parndon Essex 60 C6
Parndon Wood
  Crematorium
  Essex 60 C6
Parracombe Devon 23 L3
Parson Drove Cambs 89 L2
Parson's Heath Essex ... 62 B3
Partick C Glas 174 F5
Partington Traffd 113 G3
Partney Lincs 118 F7
Parton Cumb 136 D3
Partridge Green
  W Susx 19 G2
Parwich Derbys 100 D2
Passenham Nhants 73 L6
Paston Norfk 107 G5
Patcham Br & H 19 J4
Patching W Susx 18 E4
Patchway S Glos 38 E4
Pateley Bridge N York . 132 B6
Pathhead Fife 186 E8
Pathhead Mdloth 177 K5
Path of Condie P & K ... 185 M5
Patna E Ayrs 163 K7
Patney Wilts 40 B8
Patrick IoM 237 b5
Patrick Brompton
  N York 132 C2
Patricroft Salfd 113 H2
Patrington E R Yk 127 H6
Patrington Haven
  E R Yk 127 H6
Patrixbourne Kent 35 G4
Patterdale Cumb 137 L4
Pattingham Staffs 84 E4
Pattishall Nhants 73 J4
Pattiswick Green
  Essex 61 K3
Paul Cnwll 2 E5
Paulerspury Nhants 73 K5
Paull E R Yk 126 E5
Paul's Dene Wilts 28 C5
Paulton BaNES 26 F1
Pauperhaugh
  Nthumb 158 D3
Pavenham Bed 74 E4
Pawlett Somset 25 L3
Paxford Gloucs 71 L6
Paxton Border 179 J7
Payhembury Devon 12 E3
Paythorne Lancs 122 C1
Peacehaven E Susx 19 L5
Peak District
  National Park 114 D3
Peak Forest Derbys 114 C5
Peakirk C Pete 89 H3
Peasedown St John
  BaNES 39 G8
Peaseland Green
  Norfk 92 C1
Peasemore W Berk 41 J5
Peasenhall Suffk 79 H2
Pease Pottage
  W Susx 31 L5
Peaslake Surrey 31 H3
Peasley Cross St Hel ... 112 D3
Peasmarsh E Susx 21 H2
Peathill Abers 217 H2
Peat Inn Fife 187 G5
Peatling Magna Leics ... 87 H5
Peatling Parva Leics 87 H5
Pebmarsh Essex 77 J7

Pebworth Worcs 71 K5
Pecket Well Calder 122 E5
Peckforton Ches E 98 D2
Peckham Gt Lon 45 G5
Peckleton Leics 86 F4
Pedlinge Kent 34 F7
Pedmore Dudley 85 G6
Pedwell Somset 26 B4
Peebles Border 166 C2
Peel IoM 237 b4
Peene Kent 35 G6
Pegsdon C Beds 59 J2
Pegswood Nthumb 159 G5
Pegwell Kent 35 K2
Peinchorran Highld 209 H7
Peinlich Highld 208 F3
Peldon Essex 62 B5
Pelsall Wsall 85 H3
Pelton Dur 151 G4
Pelynt Cnwll 5 K5
Pemberton Carmth 51 G5
Pemberton Wigan 112 D2
Pembrey Carmth 50 E5
Pembridge Herefs 69 H3
Pembroke Pembks 49 G7
Pembroke Dock
   Pembks 49 G6
Pembrokeshire Coast
   National Park
   Pembks 48 E4
Pembury Kent 33 G5
Pen-allt Herefs 54 E3
Penallt Mons 54 D6
Penally Pembks 49 J7
Penarth V Glam 37 J6
Pen-bont
   Rhydybeddau
   Cerdgn 80 F6
Penbryn Cerdgn 65 J4
Pencader Carmth 66 B7
Pencaitland E Loth 177 L5
Pencarnisiog IoA 108 D6
Pencarreg Carmth 66 C5
Pencelli Powys 53 H3
Penclawdd Swans 51 G6
Pencoed Brdgnd 36 E4
Pencombe Herefs 69 L4
Pencraig Herefs 54 E4
Pencraig Powys 97 G6
Pendeen Cnwll 2 C4
Penderyn Rhondd 52 E6
Pendine Carmth 50 B4
Pendlebury Salfd 113 H2
Pendleton Lancs 121 L3
Pendock Worcs 55 H2
Pendoggett Cnwll 8 D8
Pendomer Somset 13 M1
Pendoylan V Glam 37 G5
Penegoes Powys 81 G4
Pen-ffordd Pembks 49 J3
Pengam Caerph 37 J2
Pengam Cardif 37 K5
Penge Gt Lon 45 G6
Pengelly Cnwll 8 E7
Penhallow Cnwll 3 K2
Penhalvean Cnwll 3 J4
Penhill Swindn 40 D3
Penhow Newpt 38 B3
Penicuik Mdloth 177 H6
Peniel Carmth 66 B6
Penifiler Highld 209 G6
Peninver Ag & B 161 J4
Penistone Barns 114 E2
Penkill S Ayrs 152 F3
Penkridge Staffs 85 G2
Penley Wrexhm 98 B4
Penllyn V Glam 36 F5
Penmachno Conwy 96 C3
Penmaen Caerph 37 J2
Penmaen Swans 51 G7
Penmaenmawr
   Conwy 109 K6
Penmaenpool Gwynd 95 M8
Penmark V Glam 37 G6
Penmount
   Crematorium
   Cnwll 4 C6

Penmynydd IoA 109 G6
Penn Bucks 42 F2
Pennal Gwynd 80 F4
Pennan Abers 216 F2
Pennant Powys 81 J4
Pennerley Shrops 83 G4
Pennines 122 E4
Pennington Cumb 128 F4
Pennorth Powys 53 H3
Penn Street Bucks 42 F2
Penny Bridge Cumb 129 G3
Pennycross Ag & B 181 G3
Pennyghael Ag & B 181 H3
Pennyglen S Ayrs 163 H7
Pennymoor Devon 11 K3
Pennywell Sundld 151 J4
Penparc Cerdgn 65 H5
Penperlleni Mons 53 L6
Penpoll Cnwll 5 J5
Penponds Cnwll 3 H4
Penpont D & G 154 E4
Pen-rhiw Pembks 65 H6
Penrhiwceiber
   Rhondd 37 G2
Pen Rhiwfawr Neath 51 L4
Penrhiw-llan Cerdgn 65 K6
Penrhiw-pal Cerdgn 65 K5
Penrhos Gwynd 94 F5
Penrhos Mons 54 B5
Penrhyn Bay Conwy 110 A5
Penrhyndeudraeth
   Gwynd 95 K5
Penrice Swans 50 F7
Penrioch N Ayrs 161 L1
Penrith Cumb 138 D2
Penrose Cnwll 4 D2
Penruddock Cumb 138 B2
Penryn Cnwll 3 K4
Pensarn Conwy 110 C5
Pensax Worcs 70 C2
Penselwood Somset 27 H5
Pensford BaNES 38 F7
Pensham Worcs 71 G5
Penshaw Sundld 151 H4
Penshurst Kent 32 F4
Pensilva Cnwll 5 L2
Pentewan Cnwll 4 F6
Pentir Gwynd 109 H7
Pentire Cnwll 4 C4
Pentlow Essex 77 J5
Pentney Norfk 91 G2
Pentonbridge Cumb 156 D6
Penton Mewsey
   Hants 29 G3
Pentraeth IoA 109 G5
Pentre Mons 54 B7
Pentre Rhondd 36 F2
Pentre Shrops 98 A8
Pentrebach Myr Td 53 G7
Pentre-bach Powys 52 E2
Pentre Berw IoA 108 F6
Pentrebychan
   Crematorium
   Wrexhm 97 L3
Pentre-celyn Denbgs 97 J2
Pentre-celyn Powys 81 J3
Pentre-chwyth
   Swans 51 J6
Pentre-cwrt Carmth 65 L6
Pentredwr Denbgs 97 J3
Pentrefelin Gwynd 95 J5
Pentrefoelas Conwy 96 D3
Pentregat Cerdgn 65 K4
Pentre-Gwenlais
   Carmth 51 H3
Pentre Hodrey
   Shrops 83 G7
Pentre Llanrhaeadr
   Denbgs 110 F8
Pentre Meyrick
   V Glam 36 E5
Pentre-tafarn-y-
   fedw Conwy 96 C1
Pentrich Derbys 101 H3
Pentridge Dorset 28 B7
Pen-twyn Mons 54 D6

Pentwynmaur
   Caerph 37 J2
Pentyrch Cardif 37 H4
Penwithick Cnwll 5 G5
Penybanc Carmth 51 H2
Penybont Powys 68 C2
Pen-y-bont Powys 97 K7
Pen-y-bont-fawr
   Powys 97 G7
Pen-y-bryn Pembks 65 G6
Penycae Wrexhm 97 L4
Pen-y-clawdd Mons 54 C6
Pen-y-coedcae
   Rhondd 37 G3
Pen-y-cwn Pembks 48 E3
Pen-y-felin Flints 111 G7
Penyffordd Flints 97 L1
Pen-y-Garnedd
   Powys 97 H7
Pen-y-graig Gwynd 94 D5
Penygraig Rhondd 36 F3
Penygroes Carmth 51 H3
Penygroes Gwynd 95 H2
Pen-y-Mynydd
   Carmth 50 F5
Penymynydd Flints 97 L1
Penysarn IoA 108 F4
Pen-y-stryt Denbgs 97 J3
Penywaun Rhondd 52 F6
Penzance Cnwll 2 E5
Peopleton Worcs 71 G4
Peplow Shrops 98 F7
Perceton N Ayrs 163 J2
Percyhorner Abers 217 H2
Perham Down Wilts 28 E2
Periton Somset 24 E3
Perivale Gt Lon 44 D4
Perkins Village Devon ... 12 D4
Perlethorpe Notts 115 M7
Perranarworthal
   Cnwll 3 K4
Perranporth Cnwll 3 K1
Perranuthnoe Cnwll 2 F5
Perranwell Cnwll 3 K4
Perranzabuloe Cnwll 3 K2
Perry Barr Birm 85 J5
Perry Barr
   Crematorium
   Birm 85 J5
Perry Green Wilts 39 L3
Pershall Staffs 99 J6
Pershore Worcs 71 G5
Pertenhall Bed 74 F2
Perth P & K 186 B3
Perth Crematorium
   P & K 186 A3
Perthy Shrops 98 A5
Perton Herefs 69 L6
Perton Staffs 84 F4
Peterborough C Pete 89 H4
Peterborough
   Crematorium
   C Pete 89 H3
Peterborough
   Services Cambs 89 G5
Peterchurch Herefs 69 G6
Peterculter C Aber 206 F5
Peterhead Abers 217 L5
Peterlee Dur 151 K6
Petersfield Hants 30 C5
Peter's Green Herts 59 J4
Petersham Gt Lon 44 D5
Peters Marland
   Devon 10 C3
Peterstone
   Wentlooge Newpt 37 K4
Peterston-super-Ely
   V Glam 37 G5
Peterstow Herefs 54 E3
Peter Tavy Devon 6 D1
Petham Kent 34 F4
Petherwin Gate Cnwll 9 H6
Petrockstow Devon 10 D3
Pett E Susx 21 H3
Pettaugh Suffk 78 E3
Petterden Angus 196 C7

Pettinain S Lans 165 J2
Pettistree Suffk 79 G4
Petton Devon 24 F6
Petts Wood Gt Lon 45 J6
Pettycur Fife 177 H2
Pettymuk Abers 207 G1
Petworth W Susx 31 G6
Pevensey E Susx 20 D5
Pevensey Bay E Susx 20 D5
Pewsey Wilts 40 D7
Phepson Worcs 71 G3
Philham Devon 22 D6
Philiphaugh Border 166 F4
Phillack Cnwll 2 F4
Philleigh Cnwll 4 D7
Philpstoun W Loth 176 E3
Phoenix Green Hants 30 C1
Phones Highld 203 G6
Pibsbury Somset 26 C6
Pickburn Donc 115 K1
Pickering N York 134 C3
Pickford Covtry 86 C6
Pickhill N York 132 E3
Picklescott Shrops 83 J4
Pickmere Ches E 113 G6
Pickney Somset 25 J5
Pickwell Leics 87 L2
Pickworth Lincs 103 H5
Pickworth Rutlnd 88 E2
Picton Ches W 112 B7
Picton N York 141 K5
Piddinghoe E Susx 19 L5
Piddington Nhants 74 B4
Piddington Oxon 57 M5
Piddlehinton Dorset 14 D3
Piddletrenthide
   Dorset 14 D3
Pidley Cambs 89 K7
Piercebridge Darltn 140 F4
Pierowall Ork 234 C3
Pilgrims Hatch Essex 45 L2
Pilham Lincs 116 E3
Pillaton Cnwll 6 A3
Pillerton Hersey
   Warwks 72 C5
Pillerton Priors
   Warwks 72 C5
Pilley Barns 115 G2
Pilley Hants 16 D3
Pilling Lancs 120 E2
Pilning S Glos 38 D4
Pilsbury Derbys 114 C8
Pilsdon Dorset 13 K3
Pilsley Derbys 101 H1
Pilsley Derbys 114 E7
Pilson Green Norfk 93 H2
Piltdown E Susx 19 L2
Pilton Devon 23 J5
Pilton Nhants 88 E6
Pilton Rutlnd 88 D3
Pilton Somset 26 E3
Pimperne Dorset 15 G1
Pinchbeck Lincs 103 L7
Pin Green Herts 59 L3
Pinhoe Devon 12 C4
Pinley Green Warwks 72 B2
Pinminnoch S Ayrs 152 E4
Pinmore S Ayrs 152 E4
Pinn Devon 12 E5
Pinner Gt Lon 43 J3
Pinner Green Gt Lon 43 J3
Pinvin Worcs 71 G5
Pinwherry S Ayrs 152 E5
Pinxton Derbys 101 J2
Pipe and Lyde Herefs 69 K5
Pipe Aston Herefs 69 J1
Pipe Gate Shrops 99 G4
Piperhill Highld 213 K4
Pipewell Nhants 88 B6
Pirbright Surrey 30 F1
Pirnie Border 167 K4
Pirnmill N Ayrs 161 L1
Pirton Herts 59 J2
Pishill Oxon 42 B3
Pistyll Gwynd 94 F4
Pitagowan P & K 194 C3

Pitblae Abers 217 J2
Pitcairngreen P & K 185 M3
Pitcalnie Highld 223 H6
Pitcaple Abers 206 D1
Pitcarity Angus 196 B4
Pitchcombe Gloucs 55 J6
Pitchcott Bucks 58 C4
Pitchford Shrops 83 K3
Pitch Green Bucks 58 C7
Pitchroy Moray 214 E6
Pitcombe Somset 26 F5
Pitcox E Loth 178 E4
Pitfichie Abers 206 D3
Pitglassie Abers 216 D5
Pitgrudy Highld 223 H3
Pitlessie Fife 186 E5
Pitlochry P & K 194 E5
Pitmachie Abers 216 C8
Pitmain Highld 203 H5
Pitmedden Abers 217 G8
Pitmedden Garden
    Abers 217 G8
Pitminster Somset 25 K7
Pitmuies Angus 196 F6
Pitmunie Abers 206 C3
Pitney Somset 26 C5
Pitroddie P & K 186 C3
Pitscottie Fife 187 G5
Pitsea Essex 46 C3
Pitsford Nhants 73 L2
Pitstone Bucks 58 F5
Pittarrow Abers 197 H2
Pittenweem Fife 187 J6
Pitteuchar Fife 186 D7
Pittington Dur 151 H6
Pittodrie House
    Hotel Abers 206 D1
Pitton Wilts 28 E5
Pittulie Abers 217 H2
Pity Me Dur 151 G5
Pixham Surrey 31 K2
Plains N Lans 175 L5
Plaish Shrops 83 K4
Plaistow Gt Lon 45 H4
Plaistow W Susx 31 G5
Plaitford Hants 28 F7
Platt Kent 33 G2
Plawsworth Dur 151 G5
Plaxtol Kent 33 G3
Playden E Susx 21 H2
Playford Suffk 78 F5
Play Hatch Oxon 42 C5
Playing Place Cnwll 4 C7
Playley Green Gloucs 55 H2
Plealey Shrops 83 H3
Plean Stirlg 175 L2
Pleasance Fife 186 D5
Pleasington Bl w D 121 J5
Pleasington
    Crematorium
    Bl w D 121 J5
Pleasley Derbys 115 J8
Plemstall Ches W 112 C7
Pleshey Essex 61 G5
Plockton Highld 210 C7
Plowden Shrops 83 H6
Pluckley Kent 34 B5
Pluckley Thorne Kent 34 B5
Plumbland Cumb 147 K6
Plumley Ches E 113 G6
Plumpton Cumb 148 E7
Plumpton E Susx 19 K3
Plumpton Nhants 73 H5
Plumpton Green
    E Susx 19 K3
Plumstead Gt Lon 45 J4
Plumstead Norfk 106 D5
Plumtree Notts 101 L6
Plungar Leics 102 C5
Plurenden Kent 34 C7
Plush Dorset 14 D3
Plwmp Cerdgn 65 K4
Plymouth C Plym 6 C5
Plymouth Airport
    C Plym 6 D4
Plympton C Plym 6 D5

Plymstock C Plym 6 D5
Plymtree Devon 12 D2
Pockley N York 133 K3
Pocklington E R Yk 125 J2
Podimore Somset 26 D6
Podington Bed 74 D3
Podmore Staffs 99 H5
Pointon Lincs 103 J6
Pokesdown Bmouth 15 L4
Polbain Highld 224 B6
Polbathic Cnwll 6 A4
Polbeth W Loth 176 D5
Poldark Mine Cnwll 3 H5
Polebrook Nhants 88 F6
Polegate E Susx 20 C5
Polesden Lacey
    Surrey 31 J2
Polesworth Warwks 86 C3
Polglass Highld 224 C6
Polgooth Cnwll 4 F5
Polgown D & G 154 C2
Poling W Susx 18 E5
Poling Corner W Susx 18 E5
Polkerris Cnwll 5 H5
Pollington E R Yk 124 F6
Polloch Highld 190 F3
Pollokshaws C Glas 175 G6
Pollokshields C Glas 175 G5
Polmassick Cnwll 4 F6
Polmont Falk 176 C3
Polnish Highld 200 B8
Polperro Cnwll 5 K5
Polruan Cnwll 5 H5
Polstead Suffk 78 B6
Poltalloch Ag & B 182 B7
Poltimore Devon 12 C3
Polton Mdloth 177 J5
Polwarth Border 178 F7
Polyphant Cnwll 9 H7
Polzeath Cnwll 4 E1
Pomathorn Mdloth 177 H6
Pondersbridge
    Cambs 89 J5
Ponders End Gt Lon 45 G2
Ponsanooth Cnwll 3 K4
Ponsworthy Devon 7 G2
Pont Abraham
    Services Carmth 51 H4
Pontantwn Carmth 50 F3
Pontardawe Neath 51 K5
Pontarddulais Swans 51 H5
Pont-ar-gothi Carmth 51 G2
Pontarsais Carmth 66 B8
Pontblyddyn Flints 97 L1
Pontcysyllte
    Aqueduct
    Wrexhm 97 L4
Pontefract Wakefd 124 C6
Pontefract
    Crematorium
    Wakefd 124 C6
Ponteland Nthumb 158 F7
Ponterwyd Cerdgn 81 G7
Pontesbury Shrops 83 H3
Pontesford Shrops 83 H3
Pontfadog Wrexhm 97 K5
Pontfaen Pembks 64 E7
Pont-faen Powys 67 L7
Pontgarreg Cerdgn 65 K4
Ponthenry Carmth 50 F4
Ponthir Torfn 37 M2
Ponthirwaun Cerdgn 65 J5
Pontllanfraith Caerph 37 J2
Pontlliw Swans 51 H5
Pontlottyn Caerph 53 H6
Pontlyfni Gwynd 95 G3
Pontneddfechan
    Neath 52 D6
Pontnewydd Torfn 37 L2
Pontrhydfendigaid
    Cerdgn 67 G2
Pont-rhyd-y-fen
    Neath 36 C2
Pontrhydygroes
    Cerdgn 81 G8
Pontrilas Herefs 54 B3

Pont Robert Powys 82 C2
Pontshaen Cerdgn 66 B5
Pontsticill Myr Td 53 G5
Pontwelly Carmth 65 L6
Pontyates Carmth 50 F4
Pontyberem Carmth 51 G4
Pontybodkin Flints 97 L2
Pontyclun Rhondd 37 G4
Pontycymer Brdgnd 36 D3
Pont-y-pant Conwy 96 B2
Pontypool Torfn 53 L7
Pontypridd Rhondd 37 G3
Pontywaun Caerph 37 K2
Pool Cnwll 3 H3
Pool Leeds 123 J2
Poole Poole 15 J4
Poole Crematorium
    Poole 15 J3
Poole Keynes Gloucs 39 M2
Poolewe Highld 219 K5
Pooley Bridge Cumb 138 C3
Poolfold Staffs 99 K1
Poolhill Gloucs 55 G3
Pool of Muckhart
    Clacks 185 L7
Pool Street Essex 77 H6
Poplar Gt Lon 45 G4
Porchfield IoW 16 F4
Poringland Norfk 92 F3
Porkellis Cnwll 3 J5
Porlock Somset 24 D3
Porlock Weir Somset 24 D2
Portachoillan Ag & B 172 C6
Port-an-Eorna Highld 210 B7
Port Appin Ag & B 191 H7
Port Askaig Ag & B 171 H5
Portavadie Ag & B 172 F4
Port Bannatyne
    Ag & B 173 J5
Portbury N Som 38 D5
Port Carlisle Cumb 147 M3
Port Charlotte Ag & B 170 B6
Portchester Hants 17 H2
Portchester
    Crematorium
    Hants 17 H2
Port Driseach Ag & B 173 G4
Port Ellen Ag & B 160 C1
Port Elphinstone
    Abers 206 E2
Portencalzie D & G 152 B7
Portencross N Ayrs 173 K8
Port Erin IoM 237 a6
Portesham Dorset 14 B5
Portessie Moray 215 K2
Port Eynon Swans 50 F7
Portfield Gate
    Pembks 48 F4
Portgate Devon 10 B7
Port Gaverne Cnwll 8 D8
Port Glasgow Inver 174 C4
Portgordon Moray 215 J2
Portgower Highld 227 H5
Porth Cnwll 4 C4
Porth Rhondd 36 F3
Porthallow Cnwll 3 K6
Porthallow Cnwll 5 K5
Porthcawl Brdgnd 36 C5
Porthcothan Cnwll 4 D2
Porthcurno Cnwll 2 C6
Port Henderson
    Highld 219 H6
Porthgain Pembks 64 A7
Porthgwarra Cnwll 2 C6
Porthkerry V Glam 37 G6
Porthleven Cnwll 3 H6
Porthmadog Gwynd 95 K5
Porth Navas Cnwll 3 K5
Porthoustock Cnwll 3 L6
Porthpean Cnwll 5 G5
Porthtowan Cnwll 3 H3
Porthyrhyd Carmth 51 G3
Portincaple Ag & B 183 J8
Portington E R Yk 125 J4
Portinnisherrich
    Ag & B 182 D5

Portinscale Cumb 137 H3
Port Isaac Cnwll 8 D8
Portishead N Som 38 C5
Portknockie Moray 215 K2
Portland Dorset 14 D7
Portlethen Abers 207 H6
Portling D & G 146 F4
Portloe Cnwll 4 E7
Port Logan D & G 144 D6
Portmahomack
    Highld 223 K5
Portmeirion Gwynd 95 K5
Portmellon Cnwll 4 F6
Port Mor Highld 189 K1
Portnacroish Ag & B 191 H6
Portnaguran W Isls 232 g2
Portnahaven Ag & B 170 B7
Portnalong Highld 208 E7
Port nan Giuran
    W Isls 232 g2
Port nan Long W Isls 232 c5
Port Nis W Isls 232 g1
Portobello C Edin 177 J4
Portobello Wolves 85 G4
Port of Menteith
    Stirlg 184 D6
Port of Ness W Isls 232 g1
Porton Wilts 28 D4
Portpatrick D & G 144 B4
Port Quin Cnwll 8 C8
Port Ramsay Ag & B 191 H7
Portreath Cnwll 3 H3
Portreath Harbour
    Cnwll 3 H3
Portree Highld 209 G5
Port St Mary IoM 237 b7
Portscatho Cnwll 4 D8
Portsea C Port 17 J3
Portskerra Highld 230 C3
Portskewett Mons 38 D3
Portslade Br & H 19 H4
Portslade-by-Sea
    Br & H 19 H5
Portslogan D & G 144 B3
Portsmouth C Port 17 J3
Portsmouth Calder 122 D5
Port Soderick IoM 237 c6
Portsonachan Hotel
    Ag & B 182 F3
Portsoy Abers 216 B2
Port Sunlight Wirral 111 K5
Portswood C Sotn 29 H8
Port Talbot Neath 36 B3
Portuairk Highld 189 K3
Portway Worcs 85 J8
Port Wemyss Ag & B 170 D2
Port William D & G 145 H6
Portwrinkle Cnwll 6 A5
Poslingford Suffk 77 H5
Posso Border 166 B3
Postbridge Devon 10 F8
Postcombe Oxon 58 B7
Postling Kent 34 F6
Postwick Norfk 93 G2
Potarch Abers 206 B6
Potten End Herts 59 G6
Potter Brompton
    N York 134 F4
Potterhanworth
    Lincs 117 H7
Potterhanworth
    Booths Lincs 117 H7
Potter Heigham
    Norfk 107 J8
Potterne Wilts 39 M8
Potterne Wick Wilts 39 M8
Potters Bar Herts 59 L7
Potters Crouch Herts 59 J6
Potters Green Covtry 86 D6
Potters Marston Leics 87 G4
Potterspury Nhants 73 L6
Potterton Abers 207 H3
Potto N York 141 L6
Potton C Beds 75 J5
Pott Shrigley Ches E 113 L5

Poughill Cnwll.................9 G4
Poughill Devon..............11 K3
Poulner Hants.................15 M2
Poulshot Wilts.................39 L7
Poulton Gloucs...............56 C7
Poulton-le-Fylde
  Lancs......................120 D3
Poundbury Dorset........14 D4
Poundffald Swans.........51 H6
Pound Green E Susx.....20 B2
Pound Green Suffk.......77 G4
Pound Hill W Susx.........32 B5
Poundon Bucks..............57 M3
Poundsgate Devon..........7 G2
Poundstock Cnwll............9 G5
Pouton D & G................145 K5
Povey Cross Surrey.......31 L3
Powburn Nthumb........168 F6
Powderham Devon.......12 C5
Powerstock Dorset.......13 M3
Powfoot D & G...............147 K2
Powick Worcs................70 E4
Powmill P & K...............185 L7
Poxwell Dorset..............14 E5
Poyle Slough.................43 G5
Poynings W Susx............19 H4
Poyntington Dorset......26 F7
Poynton Ches E............113 L5
Poynton Green
  Wrekin.....................98 E8
Praa Sands Cnwll............3 G5
Pratt's Bottom Gt Lon...45 J7
Praze-an-Beeble
  Cnwll........................3 H4
Prees Shrops.................98 D5
Preesall Lancs..............120 E2
Prees Green Shrops.......98 E6
Prees Heath Shrops......98 E5
Prees Higher Heath
  Shrops.....................98 E5
Pren-gwyn Cerdgn.......65 L5
Prenteg Gwynd.............95 K4
Prescot Knows.............112 C3
Prescott Devon............25 H8
Presnerb Angus...........195 J3
Prestatyn Denbgs.......110 E5
Prestbury Ches E.........113 K6
Prestbury Gloucs.........55 L4
Presteigne Powys.........69 G2
Prestleigh Somset.......26 F4
Preston Border...........179 G6
Preston Br & H..............19 J4
Preston Devon................7 K2
Preston Dorset.............14 D5
Preston E R Yk.............126 F4
Preston Gloucs.............56 B7
Preston Herts..............59 K3
Preston Kent................34 D3
Preston Kent................35 H3
Preston Lancs.............121 H4
Preston Nthumb.........169 H4
Preston Rutlnd............88 C3
Preston Somset...........25 H4
Preston Suffk..............77 L4
Preston Torbay..............7 K4
Preston Wilts...............40 B5
Preston Bagot
  Warwks.....................71 L2
Preston Bissett
  Bucks.......................58 A3
Preston Bowyer
  Somset....................25 H6
Preston Brockhurst
  Shrops.....................98 D7
Preston Brook Halton ..112 E5
Preston Candover
  Hants.......................29 L3
Preston Capes
  Nhants.....................73 H4
Preston
  Crematorium
  Lancs.....................121 H4
Preston Green
  Warwks.....................71 L2
Preston Gubbals
  Shrops.....................98 C8

Preston on Stour
  Warwks.....................72 B4
Preston on the Hill
  Halton....................112 E5
Preston on Wye
  Herefs......................69 H6
Prestonpans E Loth....177 K4
Preston Patrick
  Cumb......................129 L3
Preston Plucknett
  Somset....................26 D7
Preston-under-Scar
  N York....................131 K2
Preston upon the
  Weald Moors
  Wrekin.....................84 C1
Preston Wynne
  Herefs......................69 L5
Prestwich Bury...........113 J1
Prestwick S Ayrs........163 J4
Prestwick Airport
  S Ayrs....................163 J4
Prestwood Bucks.........58 E7
Prickwillow Cambs.......90 E6
Priddy Somset..............26 D2
Priest Hutton Lancs....129 L5
Priestland E Ayrs........164 B2
Priest Weston
  Shrops.....................82 F4
Primrosehill Border....179 G6
Primsidemill Border...168 B4
Princes Risborough
  Bucks.......................58 D7
Princethorpe Warwks..72 E1
Princetown Devon..........6 E2
Priors Hardwick
  Warwks.....................72 F3
Priorslee Wrekin.........84 C2
Priors Marston
  Warwks.....................72 F3
Priors Norton Gloucs...55 K3
Priory Vale Swindn......40 C3
Priston BaNES..............39 G7
Prittlewell Sthend.......46 E3
Privett Hants................30 B6
Prixford Devon.............23 J4
Probus Cnwll..................4 E6
Prora E Loth...............178 C3
Prospect Cumb...........147 K6
Prospidnick Cnwll..........3 H5
Protstonhill Abers.....216 F2
Prudhoe Nthumb.......150 D3
Publow BaNES..............38 F7
Puckeridge Herts.........60 C4
Puckington Somset......26 B7
Pucklechurch S Glos....39 G5
Puddington Ches W....111 K6
Puddington Devon.......11 J3
Puddletown Dorset......14 E4
Pudsey Leeds..............123 J4
Pulborough W Susx......18 E3
Pulford Ches W.............98 A2
Pulham Dorset.............14 D2
Pulham Market
  Norfk.......................92 E6
Pulham St Mary
  Norfk.......................92 E6
Pulloxhill C Beds..........74 F7
Pumpherston W Loth..176 E4
Pumsaint Carmth..........66 E6
Punchestone Pembks...49 G2
Puncknowle Dorset......14 A5
Punnett's Town
  E Susx.....................20 C2
Purbrook Hants............17 J2
Purfleet Thurr.............45 K4
Puriton Somset............25 L3
Purleigh Essex.............61 K7
Purley Gt Lon...............44 F7
Purley W Berk..............42 A5
Purse Caundle Dorset...27 G7
Purtington Somset......13 K2
Purton Gloucs..............54 F6
Purton Gloucs..............55 G7
Purton Wilts................40 C3
Purton Stoke Wilts.......40 C3

Pury End Nhants...........73 K5
Pusey Oxon...................41 G2
Putley Herefs................70 B6
Putley Green Herefs......70 B6
Putney Gt Lon...............44 E5
Putney Vale
  Crematorium
  Gt Lon.....................44 E5
Puttenham Surrey........30 F2
Puxley Nhants...............73 L6
Puxton N Som..............38 B7
Pwll Carmth.................50 F5
Pwll-glâs Denbgs..........97 H2
Pwllgloyw Powys..........68 B7
Pwllheli Gwynd.............94 F5
Pwllmeyric Mons..........38 D2
Pwll Trap Carmth..........50 C3
Pwll-y-glaw Neath........36 C2
Pye Bridge Derbys......101 H3
Pyecombe W Susx........19 J3
Pyle Brdgnd..................36 C4
Pyleigh Somset............25 H5
Pylle Somset................26 E4
Pymoor Cambs..............90 C6
Pymore Dorset.............13 L4
Pyrford Surrey.............43 H8
Pyrton Oxon.................42 B2
Pytchley Nhants...........88 C8
Pyworthy Devon............9 J4

R

Raasay Highld..............209 J5
Rachan Mill Border....165 L3
Rachub Gwynd.............109 J7
Rackenford Devon........24 D7
Rackham W Susx...........18 E3
Rackheath Norfk..........93 G1
Racks D & G................155 H7
Rackwick Ork..............234 a7
Radbourne Derbys......100 F5
Radcliffe Bury.............113 H1
Radcliffe on Trent
  Notts......................101 M5
Radclive Bucks.............73 J7
Raddery Highld...........213 H3
Radernie Fife..............187 G5
Radford Covtry.............86 D7
Radford Semele
  Warwks.....................72 D2
Radlett Herts...............59 K7
Radley Oxon.................57 K7
Radley Green Essex......60 F6
Radnage Bucks.............42 C2
Radstock BaNES...........27 G1
Radstone Nhants..........73 H6
Radway Warwks...........72 D5
Radwell Bed.................74 E3
Radwell Herts...............75 J7
Radwinter Essex..........76 E6
Radyr Cardif................37 H4
Rafford Moray............214 D3
RAF Museum
  Cosford Shrops........84 E3
Ragdale Leics.............102 A8
Raglan Mons.................54 B6
Ragnall Notts.............116 D6
Raigbeg Highld..........213 J8
Rainbow Hill Worcs......70 F4
Rainford St Hel..........112 C2
Rainham Gt Lon...........45 K4
Rainham Medway.........46 D6
Rainhill St Hel.............112 C4
Rainhill Stoops
  St Hel.....................112 D4
Rainow Ches E............113 L6
Rainsbrook
  Crematorium
  Warwks.....................87 G8
Rainton N York...........132 E4
Rainworth Notts.........101 L2
Rait P & K..................186 D3
Raithby Lincs..............118 D5
Raithby Lincs..............118 E7
Rake Hants..................30 D5
Ralia Highld...............203 H5
Ramasaig Highld.......208 B5
Rame Cnwll....................3 J4
Rame Cnwll....................6 B6
Rampisham Dorset......14 B3
Rampside Cumb..........128 F6
Rampton Cambs...........76 B2
Rampton Notts...........116 D5
Ramsbottom Bury.......122 B6
Ramsbury Wilts............40 F6
Ramscraigs Highld.....227 K3
Ramsdean Hants..........30 B6
Ramsdell Hants............41 L8
Ramsden Oxon.............57 G5
Ramsden Bellhouse
  Essex......................46 B2
Ramsey Cambs.............89 K6
Ramsey Essex...............62 E2
Ramsey IoM.................237 e3
Ramsey Forty Foot
  Cambs......................89 K6
Ramsey Heights
  Cambs......................89 J6
Ramsey Island Essex...61 M6
Ramsey Island
  Pembks.....................48 B3
Ramsey Mereside
  Cambs......................89 K5

Ramsey St Mary's
Cambs 89 J6
Ramsgate Kent............ 35 K2
Ramsgill N York 131 L5
Ramshope Nthumb 157 J2
Ramshorn Staffs.......... 100 B4
Ramsnest Common
Surrey 30 F5
Ranby Lincs 118 B5
Ranby Notts 116 A5
Rand Lincs 117 J5
Randalls Park
Crematorium
Surrey 44 D8
Randwick Gloucs......... 55 J6
Ranfurly Rens............. 174 D5
Rangemore Staffs........ 100 D7
Rangeworthy S Glos 39 G3
Rankinston E Ayrs........ 163 L6
Rannoch Station
P & K...................... 193 G5
Ranscombe Somset... 24 E3
Ranskill Notts 116 A4
Ranton Staffs............... 99 J7
Ranton Green Staffs 99 J7
Ranworth Norfk........... 93 H1
Raploch Stirlg 185 G7
Rapness Ork.............. 234 c4
Rascarrel D & G.......... 146 D5
Rashfield Ag & B.......... 173 K2
Rashwood Worcs 71 G2
Raskelf N York 133 G5
Rastrick Calder 123 H6
Ratagan Highld............ 200 E2
Ratby Leics 87 G3
Ratcliffe Culey Leics ...86 D4
Ratcliffe on Soar
Notts 101 J6
Ratcliffe on the
Wreake Leics 87 J1
Rathen Abers............. 217 J3
Rathillet Fife.............. 186 F3
Rathmell N York 130 F7
Ratho C Edin 176 F4
Ratho Station C Edin ... 176 F4
Rathven Moray........... 215 K2
Ratley Warwks 72 E5
Ratling Kent................ 35 H4
Ratlinghope Shrops...... 83 H4
Rattar Highld 231 J2
Rattery Devon 7 H4
Rattlesden Suffk 77 L3
Rattray P & K 195 J7
Raunds Nhants 88 E8
Ravenfield Rothm....... 115 J3
Ravenglass Cumb 136 F7
Raveningham Norfk...... 93 H4
Ravenscar N York 143 K6
Ravenscraig N Lans 175 K6
Ravensden Bed 74 F4
Ravenshead Notts 101 K2
Ravensthorpe Kirk...... 123 J6
Ravensthorpe Nhants.... 73 J1
Ravenstone Leics 86 E2
Ravenstone M Keyn...... 74 B4
Ravenstonedale
Cumb 139 G6
Ravensthruther S Lans.. 165 H1
Ravensworth N York.... 140 E5
Rawcliffe C York 133 J8
Rawcliffe E R Yk 125 G6
Rawdon Leeds 123 J3
Rawdon
Crematorium
Leeds 123 J3
Rawling Street Kent ... 34 B3
Rawmarsh Rothm....... 115 H3
Rawreth Essex............ 46 C2
Rawridge Devon 12 F2
Rawtenstall Lancs...... 122 B6
Raydon Suffk 78 C6
Rayleigh Essex............ 46 D2
Rayne Essex................ 61 H4
Raynes Park Gt Lon 44 E6
Reach Cambs............. 76 E2

Read Lancs 122 B4
Reading Readg 42 B5
Reading
Crematorium
Readg 42 B5
Reading Services
W Berk 42 A6
Reading Street Kent.... 34 B8
Reading Street Kent.... 35 K2
Reagill Cumb 138 E4
Realwa Cnwll 3 G4
Rearquhar Highld....... 223 G3
Rearsby Leics 87 J2
Reay Highld 230 D3
Reculver Kent............. 47 L6
Red Ball Devon 25 H7
Redberth Pembks 49 J6
Redbourn Herts........... 59 J5
Redbourne N Linc 116 F2
Redbrook Gloucs......... 54 D6
Redbrook Wrexhm....... 98 D4
Redbrook Street Kent... 34 C7
Redburn Highld......... 213 L5
Redcar R & Cl 142 D3
Redcastle D & G 146 E2
Redcastle Highld 212 E4
Redding Falk 176 C3
Reddingmuirhead
Falk 176 C3
Redditch Worcs 71 J2
Redditch
Crematorium
Worcs 71 J2
Rede Suffk 77 J4
Redenhall Norfk......... 92 F6
Redesmouth Nthumb... 157 L5
Redford Abers 197 J3
Redford Angus 196 F7
Redford W Susx........... 30 E6
Redfordgreen Border .. 166 E6
Redgorton P & K 186 A2
Redgrave Suffk............ 92 C7
Redhill Abers............ 206 E4
Red Hill Bmouth 15 K4
Redhill Herts 59 M2
Redhill N Som............. 38 D7
Redhill Surrey.............. 32 B3
Redisham Suffk 93 J6
Redland Bristl 38 E5
Redland Ork 234 b5
Redlingfield Suffk....... 78 E1
Redlingfield Green
Suffk 78 E1
Red Lodge Suffk.......... 77 G1
Redlynch Somset 27 G5
Redlynch Wilts........... 28 D7
Redmarley Worcs........ 70 D2
Redmarley D'Abitot
Gloucs 55 H2
Redmarshall S on T..... 141 J3
Redmile Leics 102 D5
Redmire N York 131 K2
Redmyre Abers.......... 197 J2
Rednal Shrops............ 98 A6
Redpath Border 167 J3
Redpoint Highld 219 H7
Red Roses Carmth....... 49 L5
Red Row Nthumb 159 G3
Redruth Cnwll.............. 3 J3
Redstone P & K 186 C1
Red Wharf Bay IoA.... 109 G5
Redwick Newpt.......... 38 B4
Redwick S Glos 38 D3
Redworth Darltn....... 141 G3
Reed Herts 75 L7
Reedham Norfk........... 93 J3
Reedness E R Yk 125 J6
Reeds Holme Lancs 122 B5
Reepham Lincs 117 H6
Reepham Norfk.......... 106 D7
Reeth N York 140 C7
Reeves Green Solhll.... 86 C7
Regil N Som................ 38 D7
Reiff Highld 224 B5
Reigate Surrey............ 31 L2
Reighton N York....... 135 H4

Reisque Abers............ 207 G2
Reiss Highld.............. 231 L5
Relubbus Cnwll.............. 2 F5
Relugas Moray........... 214 B5
Remenham Wokham..... 42 C4
Remenham Hill
Wokham 42 C4
Rempstone Notts 101 L7
Rendcomb Gloucs 56 A6
Rendham Suffk............ 79 H2
Rendlesham Suffk........ 79 H4
Renfrew Rens............ 174 F5
Renhold Bed............... 74 F4
Renishaw Derbys 115 J6
Rennington Nthumb.... 169 J5
Renton W Duns......... 174 D3
Renwick Cumb 149 G6
Repps Norfk................ 93 J1
Repton Derbys 100 F6
Resaurie Highld 213 H5
Resipole Highld 190 E4
Reskadinnick Cnwll........ 3 H3
Resolis Highld 213 G2
Resolven Neath 52 C7
Rest and be thankful
Ag & B 183 J6
Reston Border 179 H6
Reswallie Angus........ 196 E6
Retford Notts 116 B5
Rettendon Essex.......... 61 J7
Revesby Lincs 103 M1
Rewe Devon 12 B3
Rew Street IoW 16 F4
Reydon Suffk.............. 93 K7
Reymerston Norfk....... 92 B3
Reynalton Pembks....... 49 J5
Reynoldston Swans...... 50 F7
Rezare Cnwll................ 6 A1
Rhandirmwyn
Carmth.................. 67 H5
Rhayader Powys 67 L2
Rheindown Highld 212 D5
Rhes-y-cae Flints 111 G7
Rhewl Denbgs............. 97 H1
Rhewl Denbgs............. 97 J4
Rhicarn Highld 224 D4
Rhiconich Highld 228 C5
Rhicullen Highld 222 F6
Rhigos Rhondd............ 52 E6
Rhireavach Highld 220 D3
Rhives Highld 223 H2
Rhiwbina Cardif.......... 37 J4
Rhiwderyn Newpt........ 37 K3
Rhiwlas Gwynd......... 109 H7
Rhoden Green Kent...... 33 H4
Rhodes Minnis Kent..... 34 F6
Rhodiad-y-brenin
Pembks.................. 48 C3
Rhonehouse D & G...... 146 C3
Rhoose V Glam........... 37 G6
Rhos Carmth 65 L7
Rhos Neath................. 51 L5
Rhoscolyn IoA........... 108 C6
Rhoscrowther
Pembks.................. 48 F6
Rhosesmor Flints 111 H7
Rhosgoch Powys.......... 68 D5
Rhoshill Pembks 65 H6
Rhoshirwaun Gwynd... 94 D6
Rhoslefain Gwynd....... 80 D3
Rhosllanerchrugog
Wrexhm.................. 97 L3
Rhosmeirch IoA......... 108 F6
Rhosneigr IoA........... 108 D6
Rhosnesni Wrexhm..... 97 M3
Rhôs-on-Sea Conwy ... 110 B5
Rhossili Swans........... 50 E7
Rhostryfan Gwynd....... 95 H2
Rhostyllen Wrexhm..... 97 L3
Rhosybol IoA............ 108 F4
Rhos-y-gwaliau
Gwynd 96 E5
Rhosymedre Wrexhm.... 97 L4
Rhu Ag & B 174 B2
Rhuallt Denbgs......... 110 F6
Rhubodach Ag & B..... 173 H4

Rhuddlan Denbgs........ 110 E6
Rhunahaorine Ag & B..172 C8
Rhyd Gwynd.............. 95 L4
Rhydargaeau Carmth....50 F1
Rhydcymerau
Carmth.................. 66 D6
Rhyd-Ddu Gwynd........ 95 K3
Rhydlewis Cerdgn........ 65 K5
Rhydowen Cerdgn........ 66 B5
Rhyd-uchaf Gwynd...... 96 D5
Rhyd-y-clafdy Gwynd... 94 F5
Rhyd-y-foel Conwy 110 C6
Rhydyfro Neath 51 K4
Rhyd-y-groes Gwynd...109 H7
Rhyd-y pennau
Cerdgn 80 E6
Rhyl Denbgs.............. 110 D5
Rhymney Caerph 53 H6
Rhynd P & K 186 B4
Rhynie Abers............ 215 L8
Rhynie Highld 223 J5
Ribbesford Worcs........ 84 D8
Ribbleton Lancs 121 H4
Ribchester Lancs 121 J4
Riby Lincs 126 F8
Riccall N York 124 F3
Riccarton Border....... 156 F3
Riccarton E Ayrs........ 163 K3
Richards Castle
Herefs.................... 69 J1
Richmond Gt Lon........ 44 D5
Richmond N York 140 F6
Richmond Sheff 115 H4
Rickerscote Staffs 99 L7
Rickford N Som........... 38 C8
Rickham Devon 7 H7
Rickinghall Suffk........ 92 C7
Rickling Green Essex.... 60 E3
Rickmansworth Herts.... 43 H2
Riddell Border 167 H4
Riddlecombe Devon.... 10 F3
Riddlesden C Brad...... 123 G3
Ridge Dorset 15 H5
Ridge Herts 59 K7
Ridge Wilts 27 L5
Ridge Lane Warwks...... 86 C4
Ridgeway Derbys 115 H5
Ridgewell Essex........... 77 G6
Ridgewood E Susx 19 M2
Ridgmont C Beds 74 E7
Riding Mill Nthumb.... 150 C3
Ridlington Norfk....... 107 H6
Ridlington Rutlnd....... 88 B3
Ridsdale Nthumb...... 158 A5
Rievaulx N York 133 J3
Rigg D & G 148 B2
Riggend N Lans......... 175 K4
Righoul Highld 213 K4
Rigsby Lincs 118 F6
Rigside S Lans.......... 165 G3
Riley Green Lancs 121 J5
Rilla Mill Cnwll............. 5 L2
Rillington N York....... 134 D5
Rimington Lancs 122 B2
Rimpton Somset 26 E6
Rimswell E R Yk 127 H5
Rinaston Pembks 49 G3
Rindleford Shrops....... 84 D4
Ringford D & G 146 C4
Ringland Norfk........... 92 D2
Ringmer E Susx........... 19 L3
Ringmore Devon 6 F6
Ringmore Devon 7 L2
Ringorm Moray......... 215 G5
Ringsfield Suffk........... 93 J5
Ringsfield Corner
Suffk 93 J6
Ringshall Herts 59 G5
Ringshall Suffk........... 78 C4
Ringshall Stocks
Suffk 78 C4
Ringstead Nhants........ 88 E7
Ringstead Norfk........ 105 H4
Ringwood Hants 15 L2
Ringwould Kent.......... 35 K5
Ripe E Susx 20 B4

Ripley Derbys 101 H3
Ripley Hants 15 M3
Ripley N York 132 D7
Ripley Surrey 31 H1
Riplington Hants 30 A6
Ripon N York 132 D5
Rippingale Lincs 103 H6
Ripple Kent 35 J5
Ripple Worcs 70 F6
Ripponden Calder 122 F6
Risabus Ag & B 160 B2
Risbury Herefs 69 K4
Risby Suffk 77 H2
Risca Caerph 37 K3
Rise E R Yk 126 E3
Risegate Lincs 103 K6
Riseley Bed 74 F3
Riseley Wokham 42 B7
Rishangles Suffk 78 E2
Rishton Lancs 121 L4
Rishworth Calder 122 F6
Risley Derbys 101 J5
Risley Warrtn 112 F3
Risplith N York 132 C5
River Kent 35 J6
River W Susx 30 F6
Riverford Highld 212 E4
Riverhead Kent 32 F3
Rivington Lancs 121 J7
Rivington Services
  Lancs 121 J7
Roade Nhants 73 L4
Roadmeetings
  S Lans 176 B7
Roadside E Ayrs 164 B5
Roadside Highld 231 H4
Roadwater Somset 25 G4
Roag Highld 208 D5
Roan of Craigoch
  S Ayrs 153 G2
Roath Cardif 37 J5
Roberton Border 166 F6
Roberton S Lans 165 H4
Robertsbridge E Susx 20 E2
Roberttown Kirk 123 J6
Robeston Wathen
  Pembks 49 J4
Robgill Tower D & G 155 M7
Robin Hood
  Crematorium
  Solhll 85 K7
Robin Hood
  Doncaster
  Sheffield Airport
  Donc 115 M2
Robin Hood's Bay
  N York 143 K6
Roborough Devon 6 D4
Roborough Devon 10 E2
Roby Knows 112 B4
Rocester Staffs 100 C5
Roch Pembks 48 E3
Rochdale Rochdl 122 D7
Rochdale
  Crematorium
  Rochdl 122 C7
Roche Cnwll 4 F4
Rochester Medway 46 C6
Rochester Nthumb 157 L3
Rochford Essex 46 E3
Rochford Worcs 70 B2
Rock Cnwll 4 E2
Rock Nthumb 169 J5
Rock Worcs 70 D1
Rockbeare Devon 12 C4
Rockbourne Hants 28 C7
Rockcliffe Cumb 148 C3
Rockcliffe D & G 146 E4
Rockend Torbay 7 L4
Rock Ferry Wirral 111 K4
Rockfield Highld 223 K5
Rockfield Mons 54 C5
Rockford Devon 24 B2
Rockhampton S Glos 38 F2
Rockhill Shrops 82 F7
Rockingham Nhants 88 C5

Rockland All Saints
  Norfk 92 B4
Rockland St Mary
  Norfk 93 G3
Rockland St Peter
  Norfk 92 B4
Rockley Notts 116 B6
Rockville Ag & B 173 L1
Rockwell End Bucks 42 D3
Rodborough Gloucs 55 J6
Rodbourne Swindn 40 C4
Rodbourne Wilts 39 L4
Rodden Dorset 14 B5
Rode Somset 27 J2
Rode Heath Ches E 99 J2
Rodel W Isls 232 d5
Roden Wrekin 83 L1
Rodhuish Somset 24 F4
Rodington Wrekin 83 L1
Rodington Heath
  Wrekin 83 L1
Rodley Gloucs 55 H5
Rodmarton Gloucs 39 L2
Rodmell E Susx 19 L4
Rodmersham Kent 34 B3
Rodmersham Green
  Kent 34 B3
Rodney Stoke Somset 26 C2
Rodsley Derbys 100 D4
Roecliffe N York 132 E6
Roe Green Herts 59 K6
Roe Green Herts 75 K7
Roehampton Gt Lon 44 E5
Roffey W Susx 31 K5
Rogart Highld 226 C7
Rogate W Susx 30 D6
Rogerstone Newpt 37 L3
Roghadal W Isls 232 d5
Rogiet Mons 38 C3
Roke Oxon 41 L2
Roker Sundld 151 J3
Rollesby Norfk 93 J1
Rolleston Leics 87 K4
Rolleston Notts 102 C3
Rolleston on Dove
  Staffs 100 E6
Rolston E R Yk 126 F2
Rolvenden Kent 33 L6
Rolvenden Layne
  Kent 33 L7
Romaldkirk Dur 140 C3
Romanby N York 132 E2
Romanno Bridge
  Border 177 G8
Romansleigh Devon 24 B7
Romesdal Highld 208 F4
Romford Dorset 15 K1
Romford Gt Lon 45 K3
Romiley Stockp 113 L4
Romsey Hants 29 G6
Romsley Shrops 84 D6
Romsley Worcs 85 G7
Rona Highld 209 K3
Ronachan Ag & B 172 C7
Rookhope Dur 150 B6
Rookley IoW 17 G5
Rooks Bridge Somset 26 A2
Rooks Nest Somset 25 H5
Rookwith N York 132 C3
Roos E R Yk 127 G4
Roothams Green Bed 75 G3
Ropley Hants 29 M5
Ropley Dean Hants 29 L5
Ropsley Lincs 103 G5
Rora Abers 217 K4
Rorrington Shrops 82 F4
Rosarie Moray 215 J4
Rose Cnwll 3 K1
Rose Ash Devon 24 C6
Rosebank S Lans 175 L7
Rosebush Pembks 49 J2
Rosedale Abbey
  N York 142 F7
Rose Green Essex 61 L3
Rose Green Suffk 77 L5
Rose Green Suffk 77 L6

Rose Green W Susx 18 B5
Rosehall Highld 225 K7
Rosehearty Abers 217 H2
Rose Hill Lancs 122 C4
Roseisle Moray 214 E2
Roselands E Susx 20 C5
Rosemarket Pembks 49 G5
Rosemarkie Highld 213 H3
Rosemary Lane
  Devon 25 J7
Rosemount P & K 195 J7
Rosenannon Cnwll 4 E3
Rosewell Mdloth 177 J6
Roseworth S on T 141 K3
Rosgill Cumb 138 D4
Roskhill Highld 208 D5
Rosley Cumb 148 B6
Roslin Mdloth 177 H5
Rosliston Derbys 86 B1
Rosneath Ag & B 174 B2
Ross D & G 146 B6
Rossett Wrexhm 98 A2
Rossett Green N York 132 D8
Rossington Donc 115 L3
Rossland Rens 174 E4
Ross-on-Wye Herefs 54 E4
Roster Highld 231 J7
Rostherne Ches E 113 H5
Rosthwaite Cumb 137 H4
Roston Derbys 100 C4
Rosyth Fife 176 F2
Rothbury Nthumb 158 D2
Rotherby Leics 87 J1
Rotherfield E Susx 32 F7
Rotherfield Greys
  Oxon 42 B4
Rotherfield Peppard
  Oxon 42 B4
Rotherham Rothm 115 H3
Rotherham
  Crematorium
  Rothm 115 J3
Rothersthorpe
  Nhants 73 K3
Rotherwick Hants 30 B1
Rothes Moray 215 G4
Rothesay Ag & B 173 J5
Rothiebrisbane Abers 216 E6
Rothiemay Moray 215 M5
Rothiemurchus
  Lodge Highld 204 B4
Rothiemurchus
  Visitor Centre
  Highld 203 L3
Rothienorman Abers 216 D7
Rothley Leics 87 H2
Rothmaise Abers 216 D7
Rothwell Leeds 123 L5
Rothwell Lincs 117 J2
Rothwell Nhants 88 B7
Rottal Lodge Angus 196 B3
Rottingdean Br & H 19 K5
Rottington Cumb 136 D5
Roucan D & G 155 H6
Roucan Loch
  Crematorium
  D & G 155 H6
Rough Common Kent 34 F3
Roughpark Abers 205 H3
Roughton Lincs 118 C8
Roughton Norfk 106 F5
Roughton Shrops 84 D5
Roundbush Green
  Essex 60 F5
Round Green Luton 59 J4
Roundham Somset 13 K1
Roundhay Leeds 123 L3
Roundway Wilts 40 A7
Roundyhill Angus 196 C6
Rousay Ork 234 c4
Rousdon Devon 13 H4
Rousham Oxon 57 J3
Rous Lench Worcs 71 H4

Routenburn N Ayrs 173 L6
Routh E R Yk 126 D3
Row Cumb 129 K2
Rowanburn D & G 156 D6
Rowardennan Stirlg 183 L7
Rowarth Derbys 114 A4
Rowberrow Somset 38 C8
Rowde Wilts 39 L7
Rowen Conwy 109 L6
Rowfoot Nthumb 149 H3
Rowhedge Essex 62 B4
Rowington Warwks 72 B2
Rowland Derbys 114 E6
Rowland's Castle
  Hants 17 K1
Rowland's Gill Gatesd 150 E4
Rowledge Surrey 30 D3
Rowley Dur 150 D5
Rowley Regis Sandw 85 H6
Rowley Regis
  Crematorium
  Sandw 85 G6
Rowlstone Herefs 54 A3
Rowly Surrey 31 H4
Rowner Hants 17 H3
Rowney Green Worcs 71 J1
Rownhams Hants 29 G7
Rownhams Services
  Hants 29 H7
Rowrah Cumb 136 E4
Rowsham Bucks 58 D4
Rowsley Derbys 114 E7
Rowston Lincs 103 H2
Rowton Ches W 112 C4
Rowton Wrekin 98 E8
Roxburgh Border 167 L4
Roxby N Linc 125 L6
Roxton Bed 75 G4
Roxwell Essex 61 G6
Royal Leamington
  Spa Warwks 72 D2
Royal Tunbridge
  Wells Kent 33 G5
Royal Wootton
  Bassett Wilts 40 B4
Royal Yacht
  Britannia C Edin 177 H3
Roy Bridge Highld 192 D1
Roydon Essex 60 C6
Roydon Norfk 92 D7
Roydon Norfk 105 H7
Roydon Hamlet Essex 60 C6
Royston Barns 124 B7
Royston Herts 75 L6
Royton Oldham 122 D8
Rozel Jersey 236 e6
Ruabon Wrexhm 97 L4
Ruaig Ag & B 188 D6
Ruan Lanihorne Cnwll 4 D7
Ruan Major Cnwll 3 J7
Ruan Minor Cnwll 3 J7
Ruardean Gloucs 54 F4
Ruardean Hill Gloucs 54 F5
Ruardean Woodside
  Gloucs 54 F5
Rubery Birm 85 H7
Rubha Ban W Isls 233 c9
Ruckhall Herefs 69 J6
Ruckinge Kent 34 D7
Ruckley Shrops 83 K4
Rudby N York 141 L6
Rudchester Nthumb 150 E2
Ruddington Notts 101 L6
Rudge Somset 27 J2
Rudgeway S Glos 38 F3
Rudgwick W Susx 31 H5
Rudheath Ches W 112 F6
Rudley Green Essex 61 K7
Rudloe Wilts 39 J6
Rudry Caerph 37 J3
Rudston E R Yk 135 H6
Rudyard Staffs 99 L2
Ruecastle Border 167 J5
Rufford Lancs 120 F7
Rufford Abbey Notts 115 M8
Rufforth C York 124 D1

Rugby Warwks 87 G7
Rugeley Staffs 100 B8
Ruishton Somset 25 K6
Ruislip Gt Lon 43 H3
Rùm Highld 198 F5
Rumbach Moray 215 J4
Rumbling Bridge
  P & K 185 L7
Rumburgh Suffk 93 H7
Rumford Cnwll 4 D2
Rumford Falk 176 C3
Rumney Cardif 37 K5
Runcorn Halton 112 D5
Runcton W Susx 18 B5
Runcton Holme Norfk 90 E2
Runfold Surrey 30 E3
Runhall Norfk 92 C3
Runham Norfk 93 K2
Runnington Somset 25 H6
Runswick N York 143 G4
Runtaleave Angus 195 L3
Runway Visitor Park
  Manch 113 J5
Runwell Essex 46 C2
Ruscombe Wokham 42 D5
Rushall Herefs 70 B7
Rushall Norfk 92 E6
Rushall Wilts 28 C1
Rushbrooke Suffk 77 K3
Rushbury Shrops 83 K5
Rushden Herts 60 A2
Rushden Nhants 74 D2
Rushenden Kent 46 E5
Rushford Norfk 91 K7
Rush Green Essex 62 E5
Rush Green Gt Lon 45 K3
Rush Green Warrtn 113 G4
Rushlake Green
  E Susx 20 D3
Rushmere Suffk 93 K6
Rushmoor Surrey 30 E4
Rushock Worcs 70 F1
Rusholme Manch 113 J3
Rushton Nhants 88 B6
Rushton Spencer
  Staffs 113 L8
Rushwick Worcs 70 E4
Rushyford Dur 141 G2
Ruskie Stirlg 184 D7
Ruskington Lincs 103 H3
Rusland Cross Cumb 129 H2
Rusper W Susx 31 K4
Ruspidge Gloucs 54 F5
Russell's Water Oxon 42 B3
Russ Hill Surrey 31 L4
Rusthall Kent 32 F5
Rustington W Susx 18 E5
Ruston N York 134 E3
Ruston Parva E R Yk ... 135 G6
Ruswarp N York 143 H5
Rutherford Border 167 K4
Rutherglen S Lans 175 H6
Ruthernbridge Cnwll 4 F3
Ruthin Denbgs 97 H2
Ruthrieston C Aber 207 H4
Ruthven Abers 215 L5
Ruthven Angus 195 L6
Ruthven Highld 203 H5
Ruthvoes Cnwll 4 E4
Ruthwell D & G 147 J2
Ruyton-XI-Towns
  Shrops 98 B7
Ryal Nthumb 158 C7
Ryall Dorset 13 K4
Ryall Worcs 70 F6
Ryarsh Kent 33 H2
Rydal Cumb 137 K6
Ryde IoW 17 H4
Rye E Susx 21 H2
Rye Foreign E Susx 21 H2
Rye Street Worcs 70 D7
Ryhall Rutlnd 88 F2
Ryhill Wakefd 124 B7
Ryhope Sundld 151 K4
Ryland Lincs 117 G5
Rylands Notts 101 K5

Rylstone N York 131 H7
Ryme Intrinseca
  Dorset 14 B1
Ryther N York 124 E3
Ryton Gatesd 150 E3
Ryton Shrops 84 D3
Ryton-on-Dunsmore
  Warwks 86 E8

S

Sabden Lancs 122 B3
Sacombe Herts 60 B4
Sacriston Dur 151 G5
Sadberge Darltn 141 H4
Saddell Ag & B 161 K3
Saddington Leics 87 J5
Saddle Bow Norfk 90 E1
Saddlescombe
  W Susx 19 H4
Saffron Walden Essex ... 76 D6
Sageston Pembks 49 H6
Saham Hills Norfk 91 K3
Saham Toney Norfk 91 K3
Saighton Ches W 98 C1
St Abbs Border 179 J5
St Agnes Border 178 E5
St Agnes Cnwll 3 J2
St Agnes IoS 2 a2
St Agnes Mining
  District Cnwll 3 J2
St Albans Herts 59 J4
St Allen Cnwll 4 C5
St Andrew Guern 236 c3
St Andrews Fife 187 H4
St Andrews Botanic
  Garden Fife 187 H4
St Andrew's Major
  V Glam 37 H6
St Andrews Well
  Dorset 13 L4
St Anne's Lancs 120 D5
St Ann's D & G 155 J4
St Ann's Chapel Cnwll 6 B2
St Ann's Chapel
  Devon 6 F6
St Anthony Cnwll 3 K6
St Anthony's Hill
  E Susx 20 D5
St Arvans Mons 38 D2
St Asaph Denbgs 110 E6
St Athan V Glam 36 F6
St Aubin Jersey 236 b7
St Austell Cnwll 4 F5
St Bees Cumb 136 D5
St Blazey Cnwll 5 G5
St Boswells Border 167 J3
St Brelade Jersey 236 b7
St Brelade's Bay
  Jersey 236 b7
St Breock Cnwll 4 F2
St Breward Cnwll 5 H1
St Briavels Gloucs 54 E6
St Bride's Major
  V Glam 36 D5
St Brides super-Ely
  V Glam 37 H5
St Brides Wentlooge
  Newpt 37 L4
St Budeaux C Plym 6 C4
Saintbury Gloucs 71 K6
St Buryan Cnwll 2 D6
St Catherines Ag & B .. 183 G6
St Chloe Gloucs 55 J7
St Clears Carmth 50 C3
St Cleer Cnwll 5 K3
St Clement Cnwll 4 D5
St Clement Jersey 236 e8
St Clether Cnwll 9 G7
St Colmac Ag & B 173 H5
St Columb Major
  Cnwll 4 E3
St Columb Minor
  Cnwll 4 D4
St Columb Road Cnwll 4 E4

St Combs Abers 217 K2
St Cross South
  Elmham Suffk 93 G6
St Cyrus Abers 197 J4
St David's P & K 185 K4
St Davids Pembks 48 C3
St David's Cathedral
  Pembks 48 C3
St Day Cnwll 3 J3
St Dennis Cnwll 4 E4
St Dogmaels Pembks 65 G5
St Dominick Cnwll 6 B3
St Donats V Glam 36 E6
St Endellion Cnwll 4 F1
St Enoder Cnwll 4 D4
St Erme Cnwll 4 D6
St Erney Cnwll 6 B4
St Erth Cnwll 2 F4
St Erth Praze Cnwll 3 G4
St Ervan Cnwll 4 D2
St Eval Cnwll 4 D3
St Ewe Cnwll 4 F6
St Fagans Cardif 37 H5
St Fagans: National
  History Museum
  Cardif 37 H5
St Fergus Abers 217 K4
St Fillans P & K 184 F3
St Florence Pembks 49 J7
St Gennys Cnwll 8 F5
St George Conwy 110 D6
St Georges N Som 38 B7
St George's V Glam 37 H5
St Germans Cnwll 6 A4
St Giles in the Wood
  Devon 23 H7
St Giles-on-the-
  Heath Devon 9 K6
St Harmon Powys 81 L8
St Helen Auckland
  Dur 140 F2
St Helens IoW 17 J5
St Helens St Hel 112 D3
St Helens
  Crematorium
  St Hel 112 C3
St Helier Gt Lon 44 E6
St Helier Jersey 236 d7
St Hilary Cnwll 2 F5
St Hilary V Glam 36 F5
St Ippollitts Herts 59 K3
St Ishmael's Pembks 48 E6
St Issey Cnwll 4 E2
St Ive Cnwll 5 L3
St Ives Cambs 75 K1
St Ives Cnwll 2 F3
St James's End
  Nhants 73 L3
St James South
  Elmham Suffk 93 G7
St Jidgey Cnwll 4 E3
St John Cnwll 6 B5
St John Jersey 236 c5
St John's IoM 237 b5
St Johns Kent 32 F3
St Johns Surrey 43 G8
St Johns Worcs 70 E4
St John's Chapel
  Devon 23 H5
St John's Chapel Dur .. 149 M7
St John's Fen End
  Norfk 90 D2
St John's Kirk S Lans .. 165 J3
St John's Town of
  Dalry D & G 154 B6
St John's Wood
  Gt Lon 44 F4
St Jude's IoM 237 d3
St Just Cnwll 2 C5
St Just-in-Roseland
  Cnwll 4 D8
St Just Mining
  District Cnwll 2 D5
St Katherines Abers 216 E7
St Keverne Cnwll 3 K6
St Kew Cnwll 5 G1

St Kew Highway
  Cnwll 5 G2
St Keyne Cnwll 5 K4
St Lawrence Essex 46 A6
St Lawrence IoW 17 G6
St Lawrence Jersey 236 c6
St Lawrence Kent 35 K2
St Leonards Bucks 58 E6
St Leonards Dorset 15 L2
St Leonards E Susx 20 F4
St Levan Cnwll 2 C6
St Lythans V Glam 37 H6
St Mabyn Cnwll 5 G2
St Madoes P & K 186 C3
St Margarets Herefs 69 G7
St Margarets Herts 60 B5
St Margaret's at
  Cliffe Kent 35 K5
St Margaret's Hope
  Ork 234 c7
St Margaret South
  Elmham Suffk 93 G6
St Marks IoM 237 c6
St Martin Cnwll 3 J6
St Martin Cnwll 5 K5
St Martin Guern 236 d3
St Martin Jersey 236 e6
St Martin's IoS 2 b1
St Martin's P & K 186 B2
St Martins Shrops 97 L5
St Mary Jersey 236 b6
St Mary Bourne Hants .. 29 H2
St Marychurch Torbay 7 L3
St Mary Church
  V Glam 36 F6
St Mary Cray Gt Lon 45 J6
St Mary in the Marsh
  Kent 21 L1
St Marylebone
  Crematorium
  Gt Lon 44 E3
St Mary's IoS 2 b1
St Mary's Ork 234 c6
St Mary's Bay Kent 21 L1
St Mary's Hoo
  Medway 46 D5
St Maughans Green
  Mons 54 C5
St Mawes Cnwll 3 L5
St Mawgan Cnwll 4 D3
St Mellion Cnwll 6 B3
St Mellons Cardif 37 K4
St Merryn Cnwll 4 D2
St Michael Caerhays
  Cnwll 4 F7
St Michael Church
  Somset 25 L5
St Michael Penkevil
  Cnwll 4 D7
St Michaels Kent 34 B7
St Michaels Worcs 69 L2
St Michael's Mount
  Cnwll 2 F5
St Michael's on Wyre
  Lancs 120 F3
St Minver Cnwll 4 F1
St Monans Fife 187 H6
St Neot Cnwll 5 J3
St Neots Cambs 75 H3
St Nicholas Pembks 64 C7
St Nicholas V Glam 37 H5
St Nicholas at Wade
  Kent 47 L6
St Ninians Stirlg 185 G8
St Olaves Norfk 93 J4
St Osyth Essex 62 D5
St Ouen Jersey 236 b6
St Owens Cross
  Herefs 54 D3
St Pauls Cray Gt Lon 45 J6
St Paul's Walden
  Herts 59 K4
St Peter Jersey 236 b6
St Peter Port Guern ... 236 d3
St Peter's Guern 236 b3
St Peter's Kent 35 K2

St Pinnock Cnwll 5 J3
St Quivox S Ayrs............163 J5
St Sampson Guern 236 d2
St Saviour Guern 236 c3
St Saviour Jersey.........236 d7
St Stephen Cnwll 4 E5
St Stephens Cnwll 6 B4
St Stephens Cnwll 9 J7
St Teath Cnwll 8 E8
St Tudy Cnwll 5 G1
St Twynnells Pembks...48 F7
St Veep Cnwll 5 J5
St Vigeans Angus 197 G7
St Wenn Cnwll..................4 F3
St Weonards Herefs.....54 D3
Salcey Forest 74 B4
Salcombe Devon 7 H7
Salcombe Regis
    Devon.......................12 F5
Salcott-cum-Virley
    Essex 61 M5
Sale Traffd 113 H3
Saleby Lincs..................118 F5
Sale Green Worcs 71 G3
Salem Cerdgn 80 F6
Salen Ag & B................190 C7
Salen Highld 190 D4
Salford C Beds 74 D6
Salford Oxon.................56 F3
Salford Salfd 113 J2
Salford Priors Warwks...71 J4
Salfords Surrey 32 B4
Salhouse Norfk 93 G1
Saline Fife....................185 L8
Salisbury Wilts 28 C5
Salisbury
    Crematorium
    Wilts 28 D5
Salisbury Plain Wilts 28 B3
Salkeld Dykes Cumb....148 F7
Salle Norfk...................106 D7
Salmonby Lincs 118 D6
Salperton Gloucs 56 B4
Salsburgh N Lans 175 L5
Salt Staffs.....................99 L6
Saltaire C Brad 123 H3
Saltaire C Brad 123 H3
Saltash Cnwll...................6 B4
Saltburn Highld 223 G7
Saltburn-by-the-Sea
    R & Cl......................142 E3
Saltby Leics 102 D7
Saltcoats N Ayrs...........163 G2
Saltdean Br & H 19 K5
Salterbeck Cumb 136 D3
Salterforth Lancs 122 D2
Salterton Wilts 28 C4
Saltfleet Lincs 118 F3
Saltfleetby All Saints
    Lincs.......................118 F4
Saltfleetby St
    Clement Lincs 118 F3
Saltfleetby St Peter
    Lincs.......................118 F4
Saltford BaNES 39 G6
Salthouse Norfk 106 C4
Saltmarshe E R Yk 125 J5
Saltney Flints 111 L8
Salton N York 133 L4
Saltrens Devon 23 G6
Saltwell
    Crematorium
    Gatesd 151 G3
Saltwood Kent...............34 F7
Salvington W Susx 18 F5
Salwarpe Worcs 70 F3
Salway Ash Dorset.........13 L3
Sambourne Warwks.......71 J3
Sambrook Wrekin 99 G7
Sampford Arundel
    Somset......................25 H7
Sampford Brett
    Somset......................25 G3
Sampford Courtenay
    Devon.......................10 F5

Sampford Moor
    Somset......................25 H7
Sampford Peverell
    Devon.......................25 G8
Sampford Spiney
    Devon.........................6 D2
Samsonlane Ork...........234 d5
Samuelston E Loth........178 B4
Sanaigmore Ag & B......170 E4
Sancreed Cnwll 2 D5
Sancton E R Yk............125 L3
Sandaig Highld 199 L5
Sandal Magna
    Wakefd 123 L6
Sandavore Highld 199 G7
Sanday Ork..................234 d4
Sanday Airport Ork......234 d4
Sandbach Ches E..........99 H1
Sandbach Services
*   Ches E........................99 H1*
Sandbank Ag & B 173 K3
Sandbanks Poole 15 K5
Sandend Abers 216 B2
Sanderstead Gt Lon 45 G7
Sandford Cumb............139 G4
Sandford Devon.............11 J4
Sandford Dorset............15 H5
Sandford Hants.............15 M3
Sandford IoW 17 G6
Sandford N Som............38 B8
Sandford S Lans...........164 E2
Sandford-on-Thames
    Oxon........................57 K7
Sandford Orcas
    Dorset......................26 F7
Sandford St Martin
    Oxon........................57 H3
Sandgate Kent...............35 G7
Sandhaven Abers.........217 H2
Sandhead D & G 144 D5
Sand Hills Leeds 124 B3
Sandhills Oxon...............57 K6
Sandhills Surrey............30 F4
Sandhoe Nthumb.........150 B2
Sandhole Ag & B..........182 E7
Sand Hole E R Yk 125 J3
Sandholme E R Yk........125 J4
Sandhurst Br For...........42 D7
Sandhurst Gloucs 55 J4
Sandhurst Kent.............33 K7
Sandhutton N York 132 F3
Sand Hutton N York......133 L7
Sandiacre Derbys 101 J5
Sandilands Lincs 119 G5
Sandleheath Hants........28 C7
Sandleigh Oxon.............57 J7
Sandley Dorset.............27 H6
Sandness Shet 235 b5
Sandon Essex...............61 H6
Sandon Herts................75 K7
Sandon Staffs................99 L6
Sandon Bank Staffs 99 L6
Sandown IoW 17 H5
Sandplace Cnwll 5 L6
Sandridge Herts.............59 K6
Sandringham Norfk......105 H6
Sandsend N York 143 H5
Sandtoft N Linc 125 H8
Sandway Kent...............34 B5
Sandwich Kent...............35 J3
Sandwick Shet.............235 c7
Sandwick W Isls 232 g2
Sandwith Cumb............136 D4
Sandy C Beds 75 H5
Sandyford D & G 155 L4
Sandygate Devon 7 K2
Sandygate IoM 237 d3
Sandyhills D & G..........146 F4
Sandylands Lancs.........129 J6
Sandy Lane Wilts 39 L6
Sandy Park Devon 11 G6
Sangobeg Highld 228 F3
Sangomore Highld 228 F3
Sankyn's Green
    Worcs.......................70 E2
Sanna Bay Highld.........189 K3

Sanndabhaig W Isls......232 g2
Sannox N Ayrs..............162 C1
Sanquhar D & G 164 F7
Santon Bridge Cumb...136 F6
Santon Downham
    Suffk 91 J6
Sapcote Leics 86 F5
Sapey Common
    Herefs......................70 C2
Sapiston Suffk 91 K7
Sapperton Gloucs 55 L7
Sapperton Lincs 103 G5
Saracen's Head Lincs...104 B6
Sarclet Highld 231 L6
Sarisbury Hants 17 G2
Sarn Gwynd 94 D6
Sarn Powys...................81 K4
Sarn Powys...................82 E5
Sarnau Cerdgn 65 K4
Sarnau Powys................82 E1
Sarn Park Services
*   Brdgnd 36 D4*
Saron Carmth................51 H3
Saron Gwynd 109 G7
Sarratt Herts.................59 H7
Sarre Kent 47 L6
Sarsden Oxon 56 F4
Satley Dur...................150 E6
Satterleigh Devon..........23 L6
Satterthwaite Cumb.....129 H2
Sauchen Abers.............206 D3
Saucher P & K 186 C2
Sauchieburn Abers.......197 G3
Saul Gloucs...................55 H6
Saundby Notts 116 C4
Saundersfoot
    Pembks.....................49 K6
Saunderton Bucks 58 C7
Saunton Devon 23 G4
Sausthorpe Lincs.........118 E7
Savile Town Kirk 123 K6
Sawbridge Warwks 73 G2
Sawbridgeworth
    Herts 60 D5
Sawdon N York 134 E3
Sawley Lancs 122 B2
Sawley N York 132 C6
Sawston Cambs............76 C5
Sawtry Cambs 89 H6
Saxby Leics 102 D8
Saxby Lincs 117 G4
Saxby All Saints
    N Linc 126 B7
Saxelbye Leics 102 B7
Saxham Street Suffk 78 C3
Saxilby Lincs 116 E6
Saxlingham Norfk........106 B5
Saxlingham Green
    Norfk 92 F4
Saxlingham
    Nethergate Norfk..92 F4
Saxlingham Thorpe
    Norfk 92 E4
Saxmundham Suffk.......79 H2
Saxondale Notts..........102 B4
Saxon Street Cambs 76 F3
Saxtead Suffk 78 F2
Saxtead Green Suffk......78 F2
Saxtead Little Green
    Suffk 78 F2
Saxthorpe Norfk 106 D6
Saxton N York 124 D3
Sayers Common
    W Susx......................19 H3
Scackleton N York 133 K5
Scafell Pike Cumb........137 H5
Scaftworth Notts..........116 A3
Scagglethorpe N York ..134 C5
Scalasaig Ag & B..........180 E8
Scalby E R Yk...............125 K5
Scalby N York 134 F2
Scaldwell Nhants 73 L1
Scaleby Cumb..............148 D3
Scalebyhill Cumb.........148 D3
Scales Cumb 129 G5
Scales Cumb 137 K2

Scalford Leics..............102 C7
Scaling N York 142 F4
Scalloway Shet............235 c6
Scalpay Highld 209 J7
Scamblesby Lincs........118 C5
Scamodale Highld 191 G2
Scampston N York 134 D4
Scampton Lincs 116 F5
Scaniport Highld 212 F6
Scapegoat Hill Kirk......123 G7
Scarba Ag & B..............181 K6
Scarborough N York 135 G2
Scarcewater Cnwll 4 E5
Scarcliffe Derbys 115 J7
Scarcroft Leeds 124 B3
Scarfskerry Highld 231 J2
Scarinish Ag & B 188 D7
Scarisbrick Lancs 120 E7
Scarning Norfk 91 L2
Scarrington Notts.........102 B4
Scartho NE Lin.............118 C1
Scatsta Airport Shet....235 c4
Scawby N Linc 116 F1
Scawsby Donc 115 K1
Scawthorpe Donc.........115 K1
Scawton N York 133 H3
Scayne's Hill W Susx.....19 K2
Scethrog Powys.............53 H3
Scholar Green Ches E....99 J2
Scholemoor
    Crematorium
    C Brad......................123 H4
Scholes Kirk.................123 H8
Scholes Leeds 124 B3
Scholes Rothm 115 H3
Scholes Wigan.............112 E1
Scissett Kirk.................123 K7
Scleddau Pembks..........64 C7
Scofton Notts 115 L5
Scole Norfk....................92 D7
Scone P & K 186 B3
Sconser Highld 209 H7
Scoonie Fife................186 F6
Scopwick Lincs 103 H2
Scoraig Highld 220 C3
Scorborough E R Yk 126 C2
Scorrier Cnwll 3 J3
Scorton Lancs 121 G2
Scorton N York 141 G7
Scotby Cumb...............148 D4
Scotch Corner N York ...140 F6
Scotforth Lancs 129 K7
Scothern Lincs.............117 G6
Scotlandwell P & K 186 C6
Scotscalder Station
    Highld 231 G4
Scot's Gap Nthumb......158 C5
Scotsmill Abers............206 B2
Scotstoun C Glas 174 F5
Scotswood N u Ty........150 F3
Scotter Lincs 116 E2
Scotterthorpe Lincs......116 E2
Scottish Seabird
    Centre E Loth..........178 C2
Scottish Wool Centre
    Stirlg.......................184 C7
Scotton Lincs 116 E2
Scotton N York 132 E7
Scotton N York 140 F7
Scoulton Norfk 92 B4
Scourie Highld 228 B6
Scourie More Highld 228 B6
Scousburgh Shet 235 c7
Scrabster Highld 231 G2
Scraesburgh Border 167 K5
Scrane End Lincs 104 C4
Scraptoft Leics 87 J3
Scratby Norfk.................93 K1
Scrayingham N York.....133 L7
Scredington Lincs 103 H4
Scremby Lincs 118 F7
Scremerston Nthumb....179 L8
Screveton Notts...........102 B4
Scriven N York 132 E7
Scrooby Notts 115 M4
Scropton Derbys 100 D6

Scrub Hill Lincs.............. 103 L2
Scruton N York 132 D2
Scullomie Highld 229 J4
Sculthorpe Norfk 105 L6
Scunthorpe N Linc 125 K7
Seaborough Dorset 13 K2
Seabrook Kent............... 35 G7
Seaburn Sundld............ 151 J3
Seacroft Leeds.............. 124 B4
Seafield Highld 209 G5
Seafield W Loth 176 D5
Seafield
  Crematorium
  C Edin.................... 177 J4
Seaford E Susx............... 20 A6
Seaforth Sefton............ 111 K3
Seagrave Leics............. 101 L8
Seaham Dur................ 151 K5
Seahouses Nthumb...... 169 J3
Seal Kent..................... 32 F2
Sealand Flints.............. 111 K7
Seale Surrey 30 E2
Seamer N York 134 F3
Seamer N York 142 B5
Seamill N Ayrs 173 L8
Sea Palling Norfk 107 J6
Searby Lincs 117 H1
Seasalter Kent............... 47 H6
Seascale Cumb............ 136 E6
Seathwaite Cumb......... 137 H7
Seatoller Cumb............ 137 H4
Seaton Cnwll 5 L5
Seaton Cumb............... 136 E2
Seaton Devon............... 13 G4
Seaton E R Yk.............. 126 E2
Seaton Kent................. 35 G3
Seaton Nthumb............ 159 H6
Seaton Rutlnd................ 88 C4
Seaton Carew Hartpl ... 142 B2
Seaton Delaval
  Nthumb.................. 159 H6
Seaton Ross E R Yk 125 J3
Seaton Sluice
  Nthumb.................. 159 H6
Seatown Dorset 13 K4
Seave Green N York 142 C7
Seaview IoW 17 J4
Seaville Cumb.............. 147 K4
Seavington St Mary
  Somset.................... 26 B7
Seavington St
  Michael Somset....... 26 B7
Sebergham Cumb......... 148 C6
Seckington Warwks 86 C3
Sedbergh Cumb............ 130 C2
Sedbury Gloucs............. 38 D2
Sedbusk N York 131 G2
Sedgeberrow Worcs....... 71 H6
Sedgebrook Lincs 102 D5
Sedgefield Dur............ 141 J2
Sedgeford Norfk 105 H5
Sedgehill Wilts.............. 27 K5
Sedgemoor Services
  Somset.................... 26 A2
Sedgley Dudley............. 85 G5
Sedgwick Cumb........... 129 L3
Sedlescombe E Susx...... 20 F3
Sedrup Bucks................ 58 D5
Seend Wilts................... 39 L7
Seend Cleeve Wilts......... 39 L7
Seer Green Bucks 42 F3
Seething Norfk 93 G4
Sefton Sefton 111 K2
Seighford Staffs............. 99 K7
Seion Gwynd 109 H7
Seisdon Staffs............... 84 E4
Selattyn Shrops............. 97 K5
Selborne Hants.............. 30 C5
Selby N York 124 F4
Selham W Susx.............. 30 F7
Selhurst Gt Lon............. 45 G6
Selkirk Border 167 G4
Sellack Herefs................ 54 E3
Sellafirth Shet............. 235 d2
Sellindge Kent............... 34 E6
Selling Kent.................. 34 D4

Sells Green Wilts 39 L7
Selly Oak Birm................. 85 J6
Selmeston E Susx 20 B4
Selsdon Gt Lon............... 45 G7
Selsey Gloucs................ 55 J7
Selsey W Susx................ 18 B6
Selside N York 130 E4
Selsted Kent.................. 35 G5
Selston Notts............... 101 J2
Selworthy Somset 24 E3
Semer Suffk................... 78 B5
Semington Wilts............. 39 K7
Semley Wilts.................. 27 K6
Send Surrey 31 G1
Senghenydd Caerph 37 H3
Sennen Cnwll 2 C6
Sennen Cove Cnwll 2 C6
Sennybridge Powys......... 52 E3
Sessay N York.............. 133 G4
Setchey Norfk................ 90 F2
Seton Mains E Loth 177 L4
Settle N York 130 F6
Settrington N York....... 134 C5
Sevenhampton
  Gloucs..................... 56 B4
Sevenhampton
  Swindn................... 40 E3
Seven Hills
  Crematorium
  Suffk....................... 78 F6
Seven Kings Gt Lon........ 45 J3
Sevenoaks Kent.............. 32 F3
Sevenoaks Weald
  Kent........................ 32 F3
Seven Sisters Neath........ 52 C6
Seven Star Green
  Essex...................... 61 M3
Severn Beach S Glos....... 38 D4
Severn Stoke Worcs 70 F5
Severn View Services
  S Glos..................... 38 E3
Sevington Kent.............. 34 D6
Sewards End Essex......... 76 E6
Sewell C Beds................ 59 G4
Sewerby E R Yk............ 135 J5
Seworgan Cnwll 3 J5
Sewstern Leics............. 102 E7
Sgiogarstaigh W Isls 232 g1
Shabbington Bucks......... 58 A6
Shackerstone Leics........ 86 D3
Shackleford Surrey......... 30 F3
Shader W Isls............... 232 f1
Shadforth Dur.............. 151 H6
Shadingfield Suffk.......... 93 J6
Shadoxhurst Kent........... 34 C7
Shadwell Norfk.............. 91 L6
Shaftenhoe End
  Herts...................... 76 B6
Shaftesbury Dorset 27 K6
Shafton Barns.............. 124 B7
Shakerley Wigan 113 G2
Shalbourne Wilts........... 40 F7
Shalden Hants................ 30 B3
Shaldon Devon 7 L2
Shalfleet IoW 16 E5
Shalford Essex.............. 61 H3
Shalford Surrey............. 31 G3
Shalford Green Essex..... 61 H3
Shalmsford Street
  Kent........................ 34 E4
Shalstone Bucks............ 73 J7
Shamley Green
  Surrey..................... 31 G3
Shandford Angus.......... 196 D4
Shandon Ag & B 174 B2
Shandwick Highld 223 J6
Shangton Leics.............. 87 K4
Shanklin IoW................. 17 H6
Shap Cumb.................. 138 E4
Shapinsay Ork.............. 234 c5
Shapwick Dorset............ 15 H3
Shapwick Somset........... 26 B4
Shardlow Derbys........... 101 H6
Shareshill Staffs............. 85 G3
Sharlston Wakefd......... 124 B6
Sharnbrook Bed............. 74 E3

Sharnford Leics.............. 86 F5
Sharoe Green Lancs...... 121 G4
Sharow N York............. 132 E5
Sharpenhoe C Beds........ 59 H2
Sharperton Nthumb...... 158 B2
Sharpness Gloucs........... 54 F7
Sharrington Norfk 106 C5
Shatterford Worcs.......... 84 E7
Shaugh Prior Devon......... 6 D3
Shavington Ches E.......... 99 G3
Shaw Oldham............... 122 D8
Shaw W Berk................ 41 J6
Shaw Wilts................... 39 K7
Shawbirch Wrekin........... 84 B2
Shawbost W Isls........... 232 e2
Shawbury Shrops........... 98 E7
Shawell Leics................. 87 G7
Shawford Hants............. 29 J6
Shawhead D & G.......... 154 F6
Shaw Mills N York........ 132 C6
Shawsburn S Lans........ 175 K7
Shearington D & G....... 147 H2
Shearsby Leics............... 87 J5
Shearston Somset........... 25 L5
Shebbear Devon............. 10 C3
Shebdon Staffs.............. 99 H7
Shebster Highld........... 230 E3
Sheddens E Rens.......... 175 G6
Shedfield Hants............. 29 K8
Sheen Staffs................ 100 C1
Sheepridge Kirk........... 123 H6
Sheepscar Leeds........... 123 L4
Sheepscombe
  Gloucs..................... 55 K6
Sheepstor Devon............. 6 E3
Sheepwash Devon.......... 10 C4
Sheepy Magna Leics....... 86 D3
Sheepy Parva Leics........ 86 D3
Sheering Essex.............. 60 E5
Sheerness Kent.............. 46 F5
Sheerwater Surrey.......... 43 H7
Sheet Hants.................. 30 C6
Sheffield Sheff............. 115 G4
Sheffield City Road
  Crematorium
  Sheff...................... 115 G4
Sheffield Park E Susx..... 19 L2
Shefford C Beds............ 75 G6
Sheigra Highld............ 228 B4
Sheinton Shrops............ 83 L3
Shelderton Shrops......... 83 H7
Sheldon Birm................ 85 L6
Sheldon Derbys........... 114 D7
Sheldon Devon.............. 12 E2
Sheldwich Kent.............. 34 D4
Shelfanger Norfk........... 92 D6
Shelford Notts............. 102 A4
Shelley Kirk................. 123 J7
Shelley Suffk................. 78 B6
Shellingford Oxon.......... 40 F2
Shellow Bowells
  Essex...................... 60 F6
Shelsley Beauchamp
  Worcs..................... 70 D2
Shelsley Walsh Worcs.... 70 C2
Shelton Bed................. 74 F2
Shelton Norfk............... 92 F5
Shelton Notts............. 102 C4
Shelton Under
  Harley Staffs............ 99 J5
Shelve Shrops............... 83 G4
Shelwick Herefs............. 69 K6
Shenfield Essex............. 45 L2
Shenington Oxon.......... 72 D6
Shenley Herts............... 59 K7
Shenley Brook End
  M Keyn................... 74 B7
Shenley Church End
  M Keyn................... 74 B7
Shenmore Herefs........... 69 H6
Shennanton D & G...... 145 H3
Shenstone Staffs............ 85 K3
Shenstone Worcs........... 84 F8
Shenton Leics............... 86 E4
Shenval Moray............. 214 F7
Shephall Herts.............. 59 L4

Shepherd's Bush
  Gt Lon.................... 44 E4
Shepherdswell Kent........ 35 H5
Shepley Kirk............... 123 J8
Shepperton Surrey......... 43 H6
Shepreth Cambs............. 76 B5
Shepshed Leics............ 101 J8
Shepton Beauchamp
  Somset.................... 26 B7
Shepton Mallet
  Somset.................... 26 F3
Shepton Montague
  Somset.................... 27 G5
Shepway Kent............... 33 K3
Sheraton Dur.............. 151 K7
Sherborne Dorset........... 26 F7
Sherborne Gloucs........... 56 D5
Sherborne Somset.......... 26 E1
Sherborne St John
  Hants...................... 29 L1
Sherbourne Warwks 72 C3
Sherburn Dur.............. 151 H6
Sherburn N York.......... 134 E4
Sherburn Hill Dur........ 151 H6
Sherburn in Elmet
  N York.................... 124 D4
Shere Surrey................. 31 H2
Shereford Norfk........... 105 L6
Sherfield English
  Hants...................... 28 F6
Sherfield on Loddon
  Hants...................... 42 B8
Sherford Devon.............. 7 H6
Sheriffhales Shrops........ 84 D2
Sheriff Hutton N York... 133 K6
Sheringham Norfk........ 106 E4
Sherington M Keyn........ 74 C5
Shernborne Norfk......... 105 H6
Sherrington Wilts........... 27 L4
Sherston Wilts.............. 39 J3
Sherwood C Nott......... 101 K4
Sherwood Forest
  Notts...................... 101 L2
Sherwood Forest
  Crematorium
  Notts...................... 116 A7
Shetland Islands Shet ... 235 C5
Shettleston C Glas........ 175 H5
Shevington Wigan 121 H8
Sheviock Cnwll 6 B5
Shibden Head C Brad.... 123 G5
Shide IoW..................... 16 F5
Shidlaw Nthumb.......... 168 B2
Shiel Bridge Highld 200 E2
Shieldaig Highld........... 210 C4
Shieldhill D & G 155 H5
Shieldhill Falk............. 176 B3
Shieldhill House
  Hotel S Lans............ 165 J2
Shields S Lans............. 175 K7
Shielfoot Highld.......... 190 D3
Shielhill Angus............ 196 C5
Shielhill Inver............. 173 L4
Shifnal Shrops.............. 84 D2
Shilbottle Nthumb........ 169 J7
Shildon Dur................ 141 G3
Shillford E Rens........... 174 E6
Shillingford Devon......... 24 F6
Shillingford Oxon.......... 41 L2
Shillingford Abbot
  Devon..................... 11 K6
Shillingford St
  George Devon........... 11 K7
Shillingstone Dorset...... 14 F1
Shillington C Beds......... 75 G7
Shilton Oxon................ 56 E6
Shilton Warwks............. 86 E6
Shimpling Norfk............ 92 D6
Shimpling Suffk............. 77 J4
Shimpling Street
  Suffk...................... 77 K4
Shincliffe Dur.............. 151 H6
Shiney Row Sundld...... 151 H4
Shinfield Wokham.......... 42 B6
Shinness Highld........... 225 L5
Shipbourne Kent........... 33 G3

Shipdham Norfk.............91 L3
Shipham Somset..........38 C8
Shiphay Torbay...............7 K3
Shiplake Oxon.............42 C5
Shipley C Brad..........123 H3
Shipley W Susx............31 J6
Shipley Bridge Surrey...32 B5
Shipmeadow Suffk.......93 H5
Shippon Oxon...............41 J2
Shipston-on-Stour
  Warwks.....................72 B6
Shipton Gloucs.............56 B4
Shipton N York..........133 H7
Shipton Shrops.............83 L5
Shipton Bellinger
  Hants........................28 E3
Shipton Gorge Dorset...13 L4
Shipton Green W Susx...17 L3
Shipton Moyne
  Gloucs......................39 K3
Shipton-on-Cherwell
  Oxon........................57 J5
Shiptonthorpe E R Yk..125 K2
Shipton-under-
  Wychwood Oxon....56 F4
Shirburn Oxon.............42 B2
Shirdley Hill Lancs.....120 E7
Shirebrook Derbys.....115 K7
Shiregreen Sheff........115 G3
Shirehampton Bristl....38 D5
Shiremoor N Tyne......159 H7
Shirenewton Mons......38 C2
Shireoaks Notts.........115 K5
Shirland Derbys.........101 H2
Shirley C Sotn.............29 H8
Shirley Derbys...........100 E4
Shirley Gt Lon.............45 G6
Shirley Solhll..............85 K7
Shirrell Heath Hants....29 L8
Shirvan Ag & B.........172 E2
Shirwell Devon............23 J4
Shiskine N Ayrs.........162 B4
Shobdon Herefs..........69 H3
Shobrooke Devon........11 K5
Shoby Leics...............102 B7
Shocklach Ches W.......98 C3
Shoeburyness Sthend...46 F3
Sholden Kent..............35 K4
Sholing C Sotn............16 F1
Shop Cnwll....................9 G2
Shoreditch Gt Lon.......45 G4
Shoreditch Somset......25 K6
Shoreham Kent............45 K7
Shoreham Airport
  W Susx.....................19 G5
Shoreham-by-Sea
  W Susx.....................19 H5
Shorley Hants.............29 L6
Shorne Kent................46 B6
Shortgate E Susx.........20 A3
Shortlanesend Cnwll......4 C6
Shortlees E Ayrs.......163 K3
Shortstown Bed...........74 F5
Shorwell IoW...............16 F5
Shoscombe BaNES.......27 G1
Shotesham Norfk.........92 F4
Shotgate Essex...........46 C2
Shotley Suffk...............78 F7
Shotley Bridge Dur...150 D4
Shotley Gate Suffk.......78 F7
Shotley Street Suffk....78 F7
Shottenden Kent..........34 D4
Shottery Warwks.........71 L4
Shotteswell Warwks....72 E5
Shottisham Suffk.........79 G5
Shottlegate Derbys....100 F3
Shotton Dur...............151 K6
Shotton Flints............111 J7
Shotton Colliery Dur..151 J6
Shotts N Lans............176 B6
Shotwick Ches W........111 K6
Shougle Moray...........214 F4
Shouldham Norfk.........90 F2
Shouldham Thorpe
  Norfk........................90 F2
Shoulton Worcs...........70 E3

Shrawardine Shrops......83 H1
Shrawley Worcs...........70 E2
Shrewley Warwks........72 B2
Shrewsbury Shrops.....83 J2
Shrewton Wilts............28 B3
Shripney W Susx.........18 C5
Shrivenham Oxon.......40 E3
Shropham Norfk..........92 B5
Shucknall Herefs.........69 L6
Shudy Camps Cambs...76 E5
Shuna Ag & B...........181 M5
Shurdington Gloucs.....55 L4
Shurlock Row W & M...42 D5
Shurrery Highld..........230 F4
Shurrery Lodge
  Highld......................230 F4
Shurton Somset...........25 J3
Shustoke Warwks........86 B5
Shute Devon................11 K5
Shute Devon................13 G3
Shutford Oxon.............72 E6
Shut Heath Staffs........99 K1
Shuthonger Gloucs......70 F7
Shutlanger Nhants.......73 K4
Shuttington Warwks....86 B3
Shuttlewood Derbys...115 J6
Shuttleworth Bury.....122 B6
Siabost W Isls............232 e2
Siadar W Isls.............232 f1
Sibbertoft Nhants........87 K6
Sibford Ferris Oxon.....72 D6
Sibford Gower Oxon....72 D6
Sible Hedingham
  Essex.......................77 H7
Sibley's Green Essex...60 F3
Sibsey Lincs..............104 B3
Sibson Cambs.............89 G4
Sibson Leics...............86 D4
Sibster Highld...........231 K5
Sibthorpe Notts.........102 C4
Sibthorpe Notts.........116 B6
Sibton Suffk................79 H1
Sicklesmere Suffk.......77 K3
Sicklinghall N York....124 B2
Sidbury Devon.............12 E4
Sidbury Shrops............84 C5
Sidcot N Som..............38 B8
Sidcup Gt Lon.............45 J5
Siddington Ches E......113 J7
Siddington Gloucs........56 B7
Sidestrand Norfk.......106 F4
Sidford Devon.............12 E4
Sidlesham W Susx.......18 B6
Sidley E Susx.............20 E4
Sidmouth Devon..........12 E5
Sigglesthorne E R Yk...126 E2
Sigingstone V Glam......36 F6
Silchester Hants..........41 L7
Sileby Leics................87 H1
Silecroft Cumb..........128 D3
Silfield Norfk...............92 D4
Silkstone Barns.........114 F1
Silkstone Common
  Barns......................114 F1
Silk Willoughby Lincs..103 H4
Silloth Cumb..............147 K6
Silpho N York............134 E2
Silsden C Brad..........122 F2
Silsoe C Beds.............74 F7
Silton Dorset...............27 H5
Silverburn Mdloth.....177 G6
Silverdale Lancs........129 K4
Silverdale Staffs.........99 J3
Silver End Essex.........61 K4
Silverford Abers........216 E2
Silverstone Nhants......73 J5
Silverton Devon..........12 B2
Silvington Shrops.......84 B7
Simonburn Nthumb...157 L7
Simonsbath Somset.....24 B4
Simonstone Lancs.....122 B4
Simprim Border.........168 C1
Simpson M Keyn.........74 C7
Simpson Cross
  Pembks.....................48 F4
Sinclair's Hill Border..179 G7

Sinclairston E Ayrs....163 L6
Sinderby N York........132 E3
Sinderland Green
  Traffd......................113 G4
Sindlesham Wokham...42 C6
Sinfin C Derb............101 G5
Singleton Kent............34 D6
Singleton Lancs........120 E3
Singleton W Susx........18 B3
Singlewell Kent...........46 A6
Sinnarhard Abers......205 K3
Sinnington N York.....134 B3
Sinton Worcs...............70 E3
Sinton Worcs...............70 F2
Sinton Green Worcs.....70 E3
Sissinghurst Kent........33 K5
Siston S Glos..............39 G5
Sithney Cnwll................3 H5
Sittingbourne Kent.....34 B3
Six Ashes Shrops........84 E5
Sixhills Lincs.............117 K4
Six Mile Bottom
  Cambs......................76 E3
Sixpenny Handley
  Dorset......................27 M7
Skaill Ork..................234 d6
Skara Brae Ork.........234 b5
Skares E Ayrs............164 B6
Skateraw Abers........207 G6
Skateraw E Loth........178 F4
Skeabost Highld........208 F5
Skeeby N York...........140 F6
Skeffington Leics........87 L3
Skeffling E R Yk........127 J6
Skegby Notts.............101 J1
Skegby Notts.............116 C7
Skegness Lincs.........119 H8
Skelbo Highld...........223 H3
Skelbo Street Highld..223 H3
Skelbrooke Donc.......124 D7
Skeldyke Lincs..........104 B5
Skellingthorpe Lincs...116 F6
Skellow Donc...........124 E7
Skelmanthorpe Kirk...123 J7
Skelmersdale Lancs..112 C1
Skelmorlie N Ayrs.....173 L5
Skelpick Highld.........229 L4
Skelston D & G..........154 E5
Skelton C York..........133 J7
Skelton Cumb............148 D7
Skelton E R Yk..........125 H5
Skelton N York..........132 E5
Skelton R & Cl..........142 E4
Skelwith Bridge
  Cumb......................137 K6
Skendleby Lincs........118 F7
Skene House Abers....206 E4
Skenfrith Mons...........54 C4
Skerne E R Yk...........135 G7
Skerray Highld..........229 K3
Skerricha Highld.......228 C5
Skerton Lancs...........129 K6
Sketchley Leics..........86 E5
Sketty Swans..............51 J6
Skewen Neath.............51 K6
Skewsby N York.........133 K5
Skiall Highld.............230 E3
Skidby E R Yk...........126 C4
Skigersta W Isls........232 g1
Skilgate Somset..........24 F6
Skillington Lincs.......102 E7
Skinburness Cumb.....147 K4
Skinflats Falk............176 B2
Skinidin Highld.........208 C5
Skipness Ag & B.......172 F6
Skipper's Bridge
  D & G......................156 C5
Skipsea E R Yk..........135 J8
Skipton N York..........122 E1
Skipton-on-Swale
  N York......................132 E4
Skipwith N York........125 G3
Skirlaugh E R Yk......126 E3
Skirling Border.........165 L2
Skirmett Bucks...........42 C3
Skirpenbeck E R Yk...134 B7

Skirwith Cumb...........149 G7
Skirza Highld............231 L2
Skokholm Island
  Pembks.....................48 C6
Skomer Island
  Pembks.....................48 C5
Skulamus Highld.......199 K2
Skye Green Essex.......61 L4
Skye of Curr Highld...204 B1
Slack Calder.............122 E5
Slacks of Cairnbanno
  Abers......................216 F5
Slad Gloucs................55 K6
Slade Devon...............23 H3
Slade Green Gt Lon.....45 K5
Slade Hooton Rothm..115 K4
Slaggyford Nthumb...149 H4
Slaidburn Lancs........130 D8
Slaithwaite Kirk........123 G7
Slaley Nthumb..........150 B4
Slamannan Falk........176 B4
Slapton Bucks............58 F4
Slapton Devon..............7 J6
Slapton Nhants...........73 J5
Slaugham W Susx.......31 L5
Slaughterford Wilts....39 J5
Slawston Leics...........87 L5
Sleaford Hants............30 D4
Sleaford Lincs...........103 H4
Sleagill Cumb...........138 E4
Sleapford Wrekin........84 B1
Sleasdairidh Highld...222 E3
Sledmere E R Yk.......134 E6
Sleetbeck Cumb........156 E6
Sleights N York.........143 H5
Slickly Highld...........231 K3
Sliddery N Ayrs........162 B5
Sligachan Highld.......209 G7
Sligrachan Ag & B....173 K1
Slimbridge Gloucs......55 H7
Slimbridge Wetland
  Centre Gloucs.......55 G6
Slindon Staffs............99 J6
Slindon W Susx..........18 C4
Slinfold W Susx..........31 J5
Slingsby N York........133 L4
Slip End C Beds..........59 H4
Slip End Herts............75 K6
Slipton Nhants...........88 D7
Slitting Mill Staffs....100 B8
Slockavullin Ag & B..182 B7
Sloncombe Devon.......11 H7
Sloothby Lincs...........119 G7
Slough Slough............43 G4
Slough Crematorium
  Bucks......................43 G4
Slough Green Somset..25 L7
Slumbay Highld........210 D6
Slyne Lancs..............129 K6
Smailholm Border.....167 K3
Smallburgh Norfk.....107 G7
Small Dole W Susx.....19 G3
Smalley Derbys.........101 H4
Smallfield Surrey........32 B5
Small Heath Birm.......85 K6
Small Hythe Kent.......34 B8
Smallridge Devon.......13 H3
Smallworth Norfk.......92 B7
Smannell Hants..........29 G2
Smarden Kent............34 B6
Smarden Bell Kent......34 B6
Smart's Hill Kent.......32 F5
Smearisary Highld....190 D2
Smeatharpe Devon.....12 F1
Smeeth Kent..............34 E6
Smeeton Westerby
  Leics........................87 K5
Smerral Highld.........227 L2
Smestow Staffs..........84 F5
Smethwick Sandw......85 H6
Smisby Derbys.........101 G8
Smithfield Cumb.......148 D2
Smith's Green Essex...76 F6
Smithstown Highld...219 J6
Smithton Highld.......213 H5
Smoo Highld.............228 F3

Smythe's Green Essex 61   L4
Snade D & G 154   E5
Snailbeach Shrops 83   G3
Snailwell Cambs 76   F2
Snainton N York 134   E3
Snaith E R Yk 124   F6
Snape N York 132   D3
Snape Suffk 79   H3
Snape Street Suffk 79   H3
Snaresbrook Gt Lon 45   H3
Snarestone Leics 86   D2
Snarford Lincs 117   H5
Snargate Kent 34   D8
Snave Kent 34   D8
Sneaton N York 143   J5
Snelland Lincs 117   H5
Snelston Derbys 100   D4
Snetterton Norfk 92   B5
Snettisham Norfk 105   G5
Snitter Nthumb 158   C2
Snitterby Lincs 117   G3
Snitterfield Warwks 72   B3
Snitton Shrops 83   L7
Snodland Kent 46   B7
Snowdon Gwynd 95   K2
Snowdonia
    National Park............ 96   C6
Snow End Herts............. 60   C2
Snowshill Gloucs 71   K7
Soake Hants 17   J1
Soay Highld 199   G3
Soberton Hants 29   L7
Soberton Heath
    Hants....................... 29   L8
Sockburn Darltn 141   J5
Soham Cambs 90   E8
Solas W Isls 232   C5
Soldridge Hants 29   M4
Sole Street Kent 34   E5
Sole Street Kent 46   A6
Solihull Solhll 85   L7
Sollers Dilwyn Herefs ... 69   H4
Sollers Hope Herefs 54   E2
Solva Pembks 48   D3
Solwaybank D & G 156   B6
Somerby Leics 87   L2
Somerby Lincs 117   H1
Somercotes Derbys 101   H2
Somerford Dorset........... 15   M4
Somerford Keynes
    Gloucs...................... 40   A2
Somerley W Susx 17   M3
Somerleyton Suffk 93   K4
Somersal Herbert
    Derbys.................... 100   C5
Somersby Lincs 118   D6
Somersham Cambs......... 89   L7
Somersham Suffk 78   C5
Somerton Oxon 57   J3
Somerton Somset 26   C5
Somerton Suffk 77   J4
Sompting W Susx 19   G5
Sonning Wokham 42   C5
Sonning Common
    Oxon........................ 42   B4
Sopley Hants 15   M3
Sopworth Wilts 39   J3
Sorbie D & G 145   J5
Sordale Highld 231   G3
Sorisdale Ag & B 189   H4
Sorn E Ayrs 164   B4
Sortat Highld 231   K3
Sotby Lincs 117   K5
Sotterley Suffk 93   J6
Soughton Flints 111   H7
Soulbury Bucks 58   E3
Soulby Cumb 139   H5
Souldern Oxon.............. 57   K2
Souldrop Bed................. 74   E3
Sound Ches E 98   F3
Sound Muir Moray....... 215   H4
Soundwell S Glos........... 38   F5
Sourton Devon 10   D6
Soutergate Cumb 128   F3
South Acre Norfk 91   J2
South Alkham Kent 35   H6

Southall Gt Lon............. 43   J4
South Allington
    Devon......................... 7   J7
South Alloa Falk 185   J8
Southam Gloucs 55   L3
Southam Warwks 72   E3
South Ambersham
    W Susx...................... 30   E7
Southampton C Sotn 29   H8
Southampton Airport
    Hants........................ 29   J7
Southampton
    Crematorium
    Hants........................ 29   H7
South Anston Rothm ... 115   K5
South Ashford Kent....... 34   D6
South Baddesley
    Hants........................ 16   D3
South Ballachulish
    Highld..................... 191   K5
South Bank C York 124   F1
South Barrow
    Somset...................... 26   E5
South Beddington
    Gt Lon...................... 44   F7
South Benfleet Essex 46   C3
South Bersted W Susx ... 18   C5
Southborough Gt Lon ... 45   H6
Southborough Kent........ 33   G5
Southbourne Bmouth..... 15   L4
Southbourne W Susx..... 17   L2
South Bramwith
    Donc....................... 124   F7
South Brent Devon 7   G4
South Brewham
    Somset...................... 27   G4
South Bristol
    Crematorium
    Bristl........................ 38   E6
South Broomhill
    Nthumb................... 159   G3
Southburgh Norfk 92   B3
South Burlingham
    Norfk........................ 93   H3
Southburn E R Yk 134   F8
South Cadbury
    Somset...................... 26   F6
South Carlton Lincs 116   F6
South Carlton Notts 115   L5
South Cave E R Yk 125   L4
South Cerney Gloucs 40   B2
South Chailey E Susx 19   K3
South Charlton
    Nthumb................... 169   H5
South Cheriton
    Somset...................... 27   G6
South Church Dur 140   F2
Southchurch Sthend...... 46   E3
South Cliffe E R Yk 125   K4
South Clifton Notts 116   D7
South Cockerington
    Lincs....................... 118   E4
South Cornelly
    Brdgnd...................... 36   C4
Southcott Cnwll 9   G5
Southcott Devon............ 11   H8
Southcourt Bucks 58   D5
South Cove Suffk 93   K7
South Creake Norfk 105   K5
South Croxton Leics 87   K2
South Dalton E R Yk ... 126   B2
South Darenth Kent 45   K6
South Downs
    National Park............ 19   K4
South Duffield N York . 125   G4
Southease E Susx 19   L5
South Elkington Lincs . 118   D4
South Elmsall Wakefd . 124   D7
Southend Ag & B 161   H7
Southend Airport
    Essex........................ 46   E3
Southend
    Crematorium
    Sthend...................... 46   E3
Southend-on-Sea
    Sthend...................... 46   E3

Southerndown
    V Glam...................... 36   D5
Southerness D & G 147   G4
South Erradale Highld . 219   H7
Southerton Devon 12   D4
Southery Norfk 90   E5
South Essex
    Crematorium
    Gt Lon...................... 45   L3
South Fambridge
    Essex........................ 46   E2
South Ferriby N Linc... 126   B6
South Field E R Yk 126   C5
Southfield Falk 175   L4
Southfleet Kent.............. 45   L5
Southgate Gt Lon 44   F2
Southgate Swans 51   G7
South Gorley Hants........ 15   M1
South Gosforth
    N u Ty..................... 151   G2
South Green Essex 46   B2
South Green Kent 33   L2
South Green Norfk........ 92   C2
South Gyle C Edin....... 177   G4
South Hanningfield
    Essex........................ 61   H8
South Harting W Susx ... 30   C7
South Hayling Hants..... 17   K3
South Heath Bucks 58   E7
South Heighton
    E Susx....................... 19   L5
South Hetton Dur........ 151   J6
South Hiendley
    Wakefd.................... 124   B7
South Hill Cnwll 5   M2
South Hinksey Oxon....... 57   K7
South Holmwood
    Surrey....................... 31   K3
South Hornchurch
    Gt Lon...................... 45   K4
South Huish Devon 7   G7
South Hykeham Lincs . 116   F8
South Hylton Sundld ... 151   J4
Southill C Beds............. 75   H6
Southington Hants 29   J2
South Kelsey Lincs 117   H2
South Kessock
    Highld..................... 213   G5
South Killingholme
    N Linc...................... 126   E7
South Kilvington
    N York..................... 132   F3
South Kilworth Leics ... 87   H6
South Kirkby Wakefd... 124   C7
South Kyme Lincs 103   K3
South Lanarkshire
    Crematorium
    S Lans...................... 175   J7
Southleigh Devon 12   F4
South Leigh Oxon 57   H6
South Leverton Notts.. 116   C5
South Littleton Worcs... 71   J5
South London
    Crematorium
    Gt Lon...................... 44   F6
South Lopham Norfk.... 92   C7
South Luffenham
    Rutlnd....................... 88   D3
South Malling E Susx.... 19   L4
South Marston
    Swindn...................... 40   D3
South Merstham
    Surrey....................... 32   B3
South Milford N York.. 124   D7
South Milton Devon......... 7   G7
South Mimms Herts....... 59   L7
South Mimms
    Services Herts............ 59   L7
Southminster Essex....... 62   A7
South Molton Devon 23   L6
South Moor Dur 150   F5
Southmoor Oxon 41   H2
South Moreton Oxon 41   K3
Southmuir Angus......... 196   C5
South Mundham
    W Susx...................... 18   B5

South Newbald
    E R Yk.................... 125   L4
South Newington
    Oxon........................ 57   H2
South Newton Wilts 28   C4
South Normanton
    Derbys.................... 101   H2
South Norwood
    Gt Lon...................... 45   G6
South Ockendon
    Thurr........................ 45   L4
Southoe Cambs 75   H2
Southolt Suffk 78   E2
South Ormsby Lincs..... 118   E6
Southorpe C Pete 88   F3
South Otterington
    N York..................... 132   E3
Southover Dorset 14   C4
South Owersby Lincs... 117   H3
Southowram Calder 123   G5
South Park Surrey 31   L2
South Perrott Dorset 13   L2
South Petherton
    Somset...................... 26   B7
South Petherwin
    Cnwll.......................... 9   J8
South Pickenham
    Norfk........................ 91   J3
South Pill Cnwll............... 6   B4
South Pool Devon 7   H7
South Poorton
    Dorset....................... 13   M3
Southport Sefton 120   D6
Southport
    Crematorium
    Lancs...................... 120   E7
South Queensferry
    C Edin..................... 176   F3
South Rauceby Lincs ... 103   G4
South Raynham
    Norfk....................... 105   L7
Southrepps Norfk 106   F5
South Reston Lincs 118   E5
Southrey Lincs 117   J7
South Ronaldsay Ork . 234   c7
Southrop Gloucs 56   D7
Southrope Hants............ 30   A3
South Runcton Norfk.... 90   F2
South Scarle Notts 116   D8
Southsea C Port 17   J3
South Shian Ag & B ... 191   H7
South Shields S Tyne... 151   J2
South Shields
    Crematorium
    S Tyne..................... 151   J3
South Shore Bpool...... 120   D4
Southside Dur 140   E2
South Stainley N York. 132   D6
South Stoke BaNES 39   H7
South Stoke Oxon......... 41   L4
South Stoke W Susx 18   D4
South Street Kent 34   E3
South Street Kent 47   J6
South Tarbrax S Lans.. 176   D7
South Tawton Devon 10   F6
South Tehidy Cnwll 3   H3
South Thoresby Lincs.. 118   E6
Southtown Norfk........... 93   L3
South Uist W Isls 233   c8
Southwaite Cumb 148   D6
Southwaite Services
    Cumb...................... 148   D6
South Walsham
    Norfk........................ 93   H2
Southwark Gt Lon........ 44   F4
South Warnborough
    Hants........................ 30   B3
Southwater W Susx 31   J6
South Weald Essex......... 45   L2
Southwell Notts 102   B2
South West
    Middlesex
    Crematorium
    Gt Lon...................... 43   J5
South Weston Oxon....... 42   B2
Southwick Hants........... 17   J2

Southwick Nhants 88 E5
Southwick Sundld........151 J4
Southwick W Susx......19 H5
Southwick Wilts 27 J1
South Widcombe
  BaNES...........................38 E8
South Wigston Leics 87 H4
South Willesborough
  Kent..............................34 D6
South Willingham
  Lincs 117 K5
South Wingfield
  Derbys.........................101 G2
South Witham Lincs 102 F8
Southwold Suffk 93 K7
South Woodham
  Ferrers Essex 61 J7
South Wootton Norfk...105 G7
South Wraxall Wilts 39 J7
South Zeal Devon..........10 F6
Sowerby Calder...........122 F6
Sowerby N York...........132 F4
Sowerby Bridge
  Calder 122 F5
Sowood Calder 123 G6
Sowton Devon 6 D3
Sowton Devon 12 C4
Soyland Town Calder....122 F6
Spain's End Essex..........76 F6
Spalding Lincs 103 L7
Spaldington E R Yk......125 H4
Spaldwick Cambs...........89 G8
Spalford Notts...............116 D7
Spanby Lincs 103 H5
Sparham Norfk..............106 C8
Spark Bridge Cumb......129 G3
Sparkford Somset...........26 E6
Sparkhill Birm................85 K6
Sparkwell Devon...............6 E4
Sparrowpit Derbys........114 C5
Sparrows Green
  E Susx...........................33 H6
Sparsholt Hants.............29 H5
Sparsholt Oxon..............41 G3
Spaunton N York...........133 L2
Spaxton Somset.............25 K4
Spean Bridge Highld....201 K8
Spearywell Hants...........28 F6
Speen Bucks...................58 D7
Speen W Berk.................41 J6
Speeton N York.............135 J5
Speke Lpool.................112 C5
Speldhurst Kent.............32 F5
Spellbrook Herts............60 D4
Spencers Wood
  Wokham........................42 B6
Spen Green Ches E........99 J1
Spennithorne N York....131 L2
Spennymoor Dur..........151 G7
Spetchley Worcs.............70 F4
Spetisbury Dorset..........15 G3
Spexhall Suffk................93 H7
Spey Bay Moray...........215 H2
Speybridge Highld........204 C1
Speyview Moray...........215 G6
Spilsby Lincs.................118 E7
Spinkhill Derbys...........115 J5
Spinningdale Highld....222 F4
Spital Hill Donc...........115 L3
Spittal E Loth...............178 B3
Spittal Highld...............231 H5
Spittal Nthumb............179 L7
Spittal Pembks...............49 G3
Spittalfield P & K.........195 H7
Spittal of Glenmuick
  Abers..........................205 G7
Spittal of Glenshee
  P & K..........................195 H3
Spittal-on-Rule
  Border..........................167 J5
Spixworth Norfk............92 F1
Splatt Devon..................10 E4
Splayne's Green
  E Susx...........................19 L2
Splottlands Cardif.........37 K5
Spofforth N York..........124 B1

Spondon C Derb...........101 H5
Spooner Row Norfk......92 D4
Sporle Norfk..................91 J2
Spott E Loth................178 E4
Spottiswoode Border...178 D7
Spratton Nhants............73 K1
Spreakley Surrey...........30 D3
Spreyton Devon.............11 G5
Spriddlestone Devon........6 D5
Spridlington Lincs........117 G5
Springburn C Glas........175 G5
Springfield D & G.........148 B2
Springfield Essex...........61 H6
Springfield Fife............186 E5
Springholm D & G........154 E7
Springside N Ayrs........163 J2
Springthorpe Lincs.......116 E4
Springwell Sundld........151 H4
Springwood
  Crematorium
  Lpool..........................112 B4
Sproatley E R Yk..........126 F4
Sproston Green
  Ches W.........................113 G7
Sprotbrough Donc.......115 K2
Sproughton Suffk..........78 D5
Sprouston Border........168 A3
Sprowston Norfk...........92 F2
Sproxton Leics.............102 D7
Sproxton N York...........133 J3
Spurstow Ches E............98 D2
Spyway Dorset...............14 A4
Stableford Shrops...........84 D4
Stacey Bank Sheff.........114 F4
Stackhouse N York........130 F6
Stackpole Pembks...........49 G7
Staddiscombe C Plym......6 D5
Stadhampton Oxon........57 L7
Stadhlaigearraidh
  W Isls...........................233 b7
Staffield Cumb.............148 F6
Staffin Highld...............218 D7
Stafford Staffs................99 L7
Stafford
  Crematorium
  Staffs.............................99 L7
Stafford Services
  (northbound)
  Staffs.............................99 K6
Stafford Services
  (southbound)
  Staffs.............................99 K6
Stagsden Bed.................74 E5
Stainburn Cumb...........136 E2
Stainby Lincs................102 E7
Staincross Barns...........123 L7
Staindrop Dur..............140 E3
Staines-upon-
  Thames Surrey...........43 G6
Stainforth Donc...........124 F7
Stainforth N York..........130 F6
Staining Lancs..............120 D4
Stainland Calder..........123 G6
Stainsacre N York.........143 J5
Stainton Cumb..............129 L3
Stainton Cumb..............138 C2
Stainton Donc..............115 K3
Stainton Dur................140 D4
Stainton Middsb..........141 L4
Stainton by
  Langworth Lincs......117 H6
Staintondale N York....143 K7
Stainton le Vale Lincs....117 K3
Stainton with
  Adgarley Cumb.........128 F5
Stair E Ayrs.................163 K5
Stairhaven D & G.........144 E4
Staithes N York............143 G4
Stakeford Nthumb.......159 G5
Stakes Hants..................17 K2
Stalbridge Dorset..........27 G7
Stalbridge Weston
  Dorset 27 G7
Stalham Norfk..............107 H7
Stalisfield Green Kent....34 C4
Stallen Dorset................26 E7

Stallingborough
  NE Lin.........................126 F7
Stalmine Lancs............120 E2
Stalybridge Tamesd.....113 L2
Stambourne Essex.........77 G6
Stambourne Green
  Essex.............................77 G6
Stamford Lincs..............88 E3
Stamford Nthumb........169 J5
Stamford Bridge
  Ches W.........................112 C7
Stamford Bridge
  E R Yk..........................133 L7
Stamfordham
  Nthumb.......................158 D7
Stamford Hill Gt Lon....45 G3
Stanbridge C Beds.........58 F3
Stanbury C Brad...........122 F3
Stand N Lans.................175 K5
Standburn Falk..............176 C4
Standeford Staffs...........85 G3
Standen Kent..................33 L5
Standerwick Somset.......27 J2
Standford Hants.............30 D4
Standingstone Cumb....147 J7
Standish Wigan............121 H7
Standlake Oxon..............57 H7
Standon Hants................29 H6
Standon Herts................60 C4
Standon Staffs................99 J5
Stane N Lans................176 B6
Stanfield Norfk............105 M7
Stanford C Beds.............75 H6
Stanford Kent................34 F6
Stanford Bishop
  Herefs...........................70 C4
Stanford Bridge
  Worcs............................70 C2
Stanford Dingley
  W Berk...........................41 L6
Stanford in the Vale
  Oxon.............................41 G2
Stanford le Hope
  Thurr.............................46 B4
Stanford on Avon
  Nhants...........................87 H7
Stanford on Soar
  Notts...........................101 K7
Stanford on Teme
  Worcs............................70 C2
Stanfree Derbys...........115 J6
Stanghow R & Cl..........142 E4
Stanground C Pete.........89 H4
Stanhoe Norfk..............105 J5
Stanhope Border..........165 L4
Stanhope Dur...............150 C6
Stanhope Kent...............34 D6
Stanion Nhants..............88 D6
Stanley Derbys.............101 H4
Stanley Dur..................150 F4
Stanley P & K...............186 B2
Stanley Staffs.................99 L3
Stanley Crook Dur.......150 E7
Stanley Pontlarge
  Gloucs...........................55 M3
Stanmer Br & H..............19 K4
Stanmore Gt Lon...........44 D2
Stanmore Hants.............29 J5
Stannersburn
  Nthumb.......................157 J5
Stanningfield Suffk........77 K3
Stannington Nthumb....158 F6
Stannington Sheff........114 F4
Stannington Station
  Nthumb.......................158 F5
Stansbatch Herefs.........69 G3
Stansfield Suffk..............77 H4
Stanstead Suffk..............77 J5
Stanstead Abbotts
  Herts.............................60 C5
Stansted Kent................45 L7
Stansted Airport
  Essex.............................60 E4
Stansted
  Mountfitchet
  Essex.............................60 E3

Stanton Gloucs..............71 J7
Stanton Nthumb..........158 E4
Stanton Staffs..............100 C4
Stanton Suffk................91 L8
Stanton by Bridge
  Derbys.........................101 G6
Stanton by Dale
  Derbys.........................101 J5
Stanton Drew BaNES....38 E7
Stanton Fitzwarren
  Swindn..........................40 D3
Stanton Harcourt
  Oxon.............................57 H6
Stanton in Peak
  Derbys.........................114 E8
Stanton Lacy Shrops......83 K7
Stanton Lees Derbys....114 E8
Stanton Long Shrops......83 L5
Stanton on the
  Wolds Notts..............101 M6
Stanton Prior BaNES.....39 G7
Stanton St Bernard
  Wilts..............................40 C7
Stanton St John Oxon....57 L6
Stanton St Quintin
  Wilts..............................39 K4
Stanton Street Suffk......77 L2
Stanton under
  Bardon Leics...............86 F2
Stanton upon Hine
  Heath Shrops..............98 E7
Stanton Wick BaNES.....38 E7
Stanway Essex................61 M3
Stanway Gloucs..............56 B2
Stanwell Surrey.............43 H5
Stanwick Nhants............74 E1
Stanwix Cumb.............148 D4
Staoinebrig W Isls........233 b8
Stape N York................143 G7
Stapeley Ches E.............99 G3
Stapenhill Staffs...........100 E7
Staple Kent....................35 H4
Staple Cross Devon........25 C7
Staple Cross E Susx.......20 F2
Staplefield W Susx.........32 B7
Staple Fitzpaine
  Somset...........................25 K7
Stapleford Cambs..........76 C4
Stapleford Herts............60 A5
Stapleford Leics...........102 D8
Stapleford Lincs...........102 E2
Stapleford Notts...........101 J5
Stapleford Wilts.............28 B4
Stapleford Abbotts
  Essex.............................45 K2
Staplegrove Somset........25 K6
Staplehay Somset...........25 K6
Staplehurst Kent............33 K5
Staplestreet Kent............34 E3
Stapleton Herefs............69 G2
Stapleton Leics..............86 E4
Stapleton N York..........141 G5
Stapleton Shrops...........83 J3
Stapleton Somset...........26 C7
Stapley Somset...............25 J8
Staploe Bed....................75 G3
Staplow Herefs...............70 C6
Star Fife.......................186 E6
Star Pembks...................65 H7
Star Somset....................38 C8
Starbeck N York...........132 E7
Starbotton N York........131 H5
Starcross Devon.............12 C6
Stareton Warwks...........72 D1
Starlings Green Essex....60 D2
Starston Norfk................92 F6
Startforth Dur..............140 D4
Startley Wilts.................39 L4
Statenborough Kent.......35 J4
Statham Warrtn.............112 F4
Stathe Somset................26 A5
Stathern Leics..............102 C6
Staughton Green
  Cambs...........................75 G2
Staunton Gloucs............54 D5
Staunton Gloucs............55 H3

Staunton on Arrow
Herefs..........................69 G3
Staunton on Wye
Herefs..........................69 G5
Staveley Cumb.............129 H3
Staveley Cumb.............138 C7
Staveley Derbys............115 H6
Staveley N York.............132 E6
Staverton Devon................7 J3
Staverton Gloucs.............55 K4
Staverton Nhants............73 G3
Staverton Wilts................39 J7
Stawell Somset.................26 A4
Stawley Somset.................25 G6
Staxigoe Highld............231 L5
Staxton N York.............134 F4
Staynall Lancs...............120 E2
Stean N York................131 K5
Stearsby N York.............133 J5
Steart Somset.................25 L3
Stebbing Essex...............61 G3
Stedham W Susx..............30 E6
Steelend Fife................185 L8
Steele Road Border........156 F4
Steen's Bridge Herefs......69 K3
Steep Hants...................30 C6
Steep Lane Calder...........122 F5
Steeple Essex................61 M7
Steeple Ashton Wilts........27 K1
Steeple Aston Oxon..........57 J3
Steeple Bumpstead
Essex..........................76 F6
Steeple Claydon
Bucks..........................58 B3
Steeple Gidding
Cambs..........................89 G7
Steeple Langford
Wilts..........................28 B4
Steeple Morden
Cambs..........................75 K6
Steeton C Brad..............122 F2
Stein Highld.................208 D3
Stelling Minnis Kent.........34 F5
Stembridge Somset..........26 B7
Stenalees Cnwll................4 F4
Stenhouse D & G............154 D4
Stenhousemuir Falk........176 B2
Stenscholl Highld...........218 D7
Stenson Fields Derbys....101 G6
Stenton E Loth..............178 D4
Steornabhagh W Isls.....232 f2
Stepaside Pembks............49 K6
Stepford D & G..............154 E5
Stepney Gt Lon................45 G4
Steppingley C Beds...........74 E7
Stepps N Lans...............175 H5
Sternfield Suffk...............79 H3
Stert Wilts.....................40 B8
Stetchworth Cambs..........76 F3
Stevenage Herts...............59 L3
Stevenston N Ayrs.........163 H2
Steventon Hants..............29 K2
Steventon Oxon..............41 J3
Steventon End Essex........76 E6
Stevington Bed...............74 E4
Stewartby Bed................74 E6
Stewartfield S Lans........175 H7
Stewarton E Ayrs...........163 K1
Stewkley Bucks...............58 D3
Stewley Somset................25 L7
Steyning W Susx..............19 G4
Steynton Pembks..............48 F6
Stibb Cnwll......................9 G3
Stibbard Norfk...............106 B6
Stibb Cross Devon............10 C2
Stibb Green Wilts.............40 E7
Stibbington Cambs............88 F4
Stichill Border...............167 L2
Sticker Cnwll.....................4 F5
Stickford Lincs...............104 B1
Sticklepath Devon............10 F6
Stickney Lincs...............104 B2
Stiffkey Norfk................106 A4
Stilligarry W Isls...........233 b7
Stillingfleet N York.........124 F3
Stillington N York...........133 J6

Stillington S on T..........141 J3
Stilton Cambs.................89 H5
Stinchcombe Gloucs..........55 G7
Stinsford Dorset..............14 D4
Stiperstones Shrops..........83 G4
Stirchley Wrekin...............84 C3
Stirling Abers...............217 L6
Stirling Stirlg...............185 G8
Stirling Castle Stirlg.......185 G8
Stirling Services
Stirlg.........................175 L2
Stirtloe Cambs................75 H2
Stirton N York...............131 H8
Stisted Essex..................61 J3
Stithians Cnwll.................3 J4
Stivichall Covtry..............86 D7
Stixwould Lincs.............117 K7
Stoak Ches W................112 B6
Stobo Border................166 B2
Stoborough Dorset...........15 H5
Stobs Castle Border.........167 G7
Stobswood Nthumb.........158 F3
Stock Essex....................61 H7
Stock N Som....................38 C7
Stockbridge Hants............29 G4
Stockbriggs S Lans.........164 F3
Stockbury Kent.................46 D7
Stockcross W Berk............41 H6
Stockerston Leics.............88 B4
Stock Green Worcs...........71 H3
Stocking Herefs................54 F2
Stockingford Warwks.........86 D5
Stocking Pelham
Herts..........................60 D3
Stockland Devon...............13 G2
Stockland Bristol
Somset.........................25 K3
Stockleigh English
Devon..........................11 K4
Stockleigh Pomeroy
Devon..........................11 K4
Stockley Wilts................39 M6
Stocklinch Somset.............26 B7
Stockport Stockp............113 K4
Stockport
Crematorium
Stockp........................113 K4
Stocksbridge Sheff..........114 E2
Stocksfield Nthumb.........150 D3
Stockton Herefs...............69 K3
Stockton Norfk................93 H5
Stockton Shrops...............84 C4
Stockton Warwks...............72 E2
Stockton Wilts................27 M4
Stockton Wrekin...............84 D1
Stockton Heath
Warrtn........................112 E4
Stockton-on-Tees
S on T.........................141 K4
Stockton on Teme
Worcs...........................70 C2
Stockton on the
Forest C York..............133 K7
Stockwood Bristl..............38 F6
Stockwood Dorset.............14 B2
Stock Wood Worcs.............71 H3
Stodmarsh Kent................35 G3
Stody Norfk...................106 C5
Stoer Highld.................224 C3
Stoford Somset................26 E8
Stoford Wilts..................28 B4
Stogumber Somset............25 H4
Stogursey Somset..............25 J3
Stoke Covtry...................86 D7
Stoke Devon....................22 C6
Stoke Hants....................17 K3
Stoke Hants....................29 H2
Stoke Medway..................46 D5
Stoke Abbott Dorset..........13 L3
Stoke Albany Nhants..........88 B5
Stoke Ash Suffk................78 D1
Stoke Bardolph Notts......101 M4
Stoke Bliss Worcs.............70 B2
Stoke Bruerne
Nhants.........................73 L4
Stoke by Clare Suffk.........77 G5

Stoke-by-Nayland
Suffk...........................78 B7
Stoke Canon Devon...........12 B3
Stoke Charity Hants..........29 J4
Stoke Climsland Cnwll.........6 A2
Stoke Cross Herefs...........70 B4
Stoke D'Abernon
Surrey..........................43 J8
Stoke Doyle Nhants...........88 E6
Stoke Dry Rutlnd..............88 C4
Stoke Edith Herefs............69 L6
Stoke Farthing Wilts..........28 B6
Stoke Ferry Norfk.............91 G4
Stoke Fleming Devon...........7 K6
Stokeford Dorset..............15 G5
Stoke Gabriel Devon............7 J4
Stoke Gifford S Glos..........38 F4
Stoke Golding Leics...........86 E4
Stoke Goldington
M Keyn.........................74 B5
Stokeham Notts...............116 C6
Stoke Hammond
Bucks..........................58 E3
Stoke Holy Cross
Norfk...........................92 F3
Stokeinteignhead
Devon...........................7 L2
Stoke Lacy Herefs............70 B5
Stoke Lyne Oxon..............57 K3
Stoke Mandeville
Bucks..........................58 D6
Stokenchurch Bucks..........42 C2
Stoke Newington
Gt Lon.........................45 G3
Stokenham Devon...............7 J7
Stoke-on-Trent C Stke........99 K3
Stoke Orchard Gloucs.........55 K3
Stoke Poges Bucks............42 F4
Stoke Prior Herefs............69 K3
Stoke Prior Worcs.............71 G2
Stoke Rivers Devon............23 K4
Stoke Rochford Lincs.......102 F6
Stoke Row Oxon................42 B4
Stoke St Gregory
Somset.........................25 M6
Stoke St Mary Somset.......25 K6
Stoke St Michael
Somset.........................26 F3
Stoke St Milborough
Shrops.........................83 L6
Stokesby Norfk................93 J2
Stokesley N York.............142 B5
Stoke sub Hamdon
Somset.........................26 C7
Stoke Talmage Oxon...........58 B7
Stoke Trister Somset.........27 H5
Stoke upon Tern
Shrops.........................98 F6
Stoke-upon-Trent
C Stke.........................99 K4
Stolford Somset...............25 K3
Stondon Massey
Essex..........................60 F7
Stone Bucks....................58 C5
Stone Gloucs...................39 G2
Stone Rothm...................115 K4
Stone Staffs...................99 K5
Stone Worcs....................84 D7
Stone Allerton
Somset.........................26 B2
Ston Easton Somset..........26 F2
Stonebridge N Som............38 B7
Stonebridge Warwks..........86 B6
Stonebroom Derbys..........101 H2
Stone Cross Kent..............35 J4
Stonecrouch Kent..............33 J6
Stoneferry C KuH.............126 D4
Stonefield Castle
Hotel & B....................172 E4
Stonegate E Susx..............33 H7
Stonegrave N York...........133 K4
Stonehaven Abers...........207 G7
Stonehenge Wilts.............28 C3
Stonehouse C Plym.............6 C5
Stonehouse Gloucs............55 J6
Stonehouse S Lans...........175 K8

Stone in Oxney Kent..........21 J1
Stoneleigh Warwks............86 D8
Stonesby Leics...............102 D7
Stonesfield Oxon..............57 H4
Stones Green Essex...........62 E3
Stone Street Kent.............33 G3
Stone Street Suffk............93 H6
Stonewells Moray............215 G2
Stoneybridge W Isls........233 b8
Stoneyburn W Loth..........176 D5
Stoneygate C Leic.............87 H3
Stoneykirk D & G............144 C4
Stoney Middleton
Derbys........................114 E6
Stoney Stanton Leics.........86 F4
Stoney Stoke Somset..........27 G5
Stoney Stratton
Somset.........................26 F4
Stoneywood C Aber.........207 G3
Stoneywood Falk............175 L2
Stonham Aspal Suffk.........78 D3
Stonnall Staffs................85 J3
Stonor Oxon....................42 B3
Stonton Wyville Leics........87 K4
Stony Houghton
Derbys........................115 J7
Stony Stratford
M Keyn.........................73 L6
Stoodleigh Devon..............23 K5
Stoodleigh Devon..............24 E7
Stop 24 Services Kent........34 F7
Stopham W Susx...............18 D2
Stopsley Luton.................59 J3
Stornoway W Isls...........232 f2
Stornoway Airport
W Isls........................232 g2
Storrington W Susx...........18 E3
Storth Cumb..................129 K4
Storwood E R Yk.............125 H2
Stotfield Moray..............214 F1
Stotfold C Beds................75 J7
Stottesdon Shrops.............84 C6
Stoughton Leics...............87 J3
Stoughton Surrey.............31 G2
Stoughton W Susx.............17 L1
Stoulton Worcs.................70 F4
Stourbridge Dudley...........84 F6
Stourbridge
Crematorium
Dudley........................84 F6
Stourhead Wilts...............27 H5
Stourpaine Dorset.............15 G1
Stourport-on-Severn
Worcs...........................70 E1
Stour Provost Dorset..........27 H6
Stour Row Dorset..............27 J7
Stourton Staffs................84 F6
Stourton Warwks...............72 C6
Stourton Wilts.................27 H5
Stourton Caundle
Dorset.........................27 G7
Stove Shet....................235 C7
Stoven Suffk....................93 J6
Stow Border...................167 G1
Stow Lincs....................116 E5
Stow Bardolph Norfk..........90 F3
Stow Bedon Norfk..............91 L4
Stowbridge Norfk..............90 E3
Stow-cum-Quy
Cambs..........................76 D3
Stowe Shrops...................82 F8
Stowe by Chartley
Staffs........................100 A6
Stowell Somset................27 G6
Stowey BaNES..................38 E7
Stowford Devon................10 C7
Stowlangtoft Suffk.............77 L2
Stow Longa Cambs............75 G1
Stow Maries Essex............61 K7
Stowmarket Suffk..............78 C3
Stow-on-the-Wold
Gloucs.........................56 D3
Stowting Kent..................34 F6
Stowting Common
Kent...........................34 F6
Stowupland Suffk..............78 C3

Straanruie - Swanley Village

Straanruie Highld..........204 B3
Strachan Abers...........206 D6
Strachur Ag & B...........182 F6
Stradbroke Suffk............92 F8
Stradishall Suffk...........77 H4
Stradsett Norfk.............90 F3
Stragglethorpe Lincs....102 E3
Straiton Mdloth...........177 H5
Straiton S Ayrs............153 H2
Straloch Abers.............207 G2
Straloch P & K..............195 G4
Stramshall Staffs..........100 B5
Strang IoM..................237 c5
Strangeways Salfd........113 J2
Strangford Herefs..........54 E3
Stranraer D & G...........144 C3
Stratfield Mortimer
      W Berk...................42 A7
Stratfield Saye Hants...42 B7
Stratfield Turgis
      Hants......................42 B7
Stratford Gt Lon............45 H3
Stratford St Andrew
      Suffk......................79 H3
Stratford St Mary
      Suffk......................78 C7
Stratford Tony Wilts.....28 C6
Stratford-upon-Avon
      Warwks..................72 B4
Strath Highld...............219 J5
Strathan Highld............224 D4
Strathan Highld............229 J3
Strathaven S Lans........164 D1
Strathblane Stirlg........175 G3
Strathcanaird Highld....222 D7
Strathcarron Highld.....210 E6
Strathcoil Ag & B..........181 K2
Strathdon Abers...........205 H3
Strathkinness Fife.......187 G4
Strathloanhead
      W Loth....................176 C4
Strathmashie House
      Highld....................202 F6
Strathmiglo Fife...........186 C5
Strathpeffer Highld.....212 D3
Strathtay P & K...........194 E5
Strathwhillan N Ayrs...162 D3
Strathy Highld.............230 B3
Strathy Inn Highld........230 B3
Strathyre Stirlg...........184 C4
Stratton Cnwll................9 G4
Stratton Dorset.............14 C4
Stratton Gloucs.............56 A7
Stratton Audley Oxon....57 L3
Stratton-on-the-
      Fosse Somset...........26 F2
Stratton St Margaret
      Swindn....................40 D3
Stratton St Michael
      Norfk......................92 E5
Stratton Strawless
      Norfk....................106 F7
Streat E Susx................19 K3
Streatham Gt Lon...........44 F5
Streatley C Beds............59 H3
Streatley W Berk............41 L4
Street Devon.................12 F5
Street Somset...............26 C4
Street Ashton Warwks....86 F6
Street Dinas Shrops.......97 M5
Street End Kent.............34 F4
Street End W Susx.........18 A5
Streethay Staffs.............85 K2
Streetlam N York.........141 H7
Streetly
      Crematorium
      Wsall.......................85 J4
Streetly End Cambs.......76 E5
Street on the Fosse
      Somset...................26 F4
Strelitz P & K...............186 C1
Strelley Notts..............101 K4
Strensall C York...........133 K7
Strensham Services
      (northbound)
      Worcs.....................70 F6

Strensham Services
      (southbound)
      Worcs.....................70 F6
Stretcholt Somset.........25 L3
Strete Devon....................7 J6
Stretford Traffd...........113 H3
Strethall Essex.............76 C6
Stretham Cambs............90 D8
Strettington W Susx......18 B4
Stretton Derbys...........101 H1
Stretton Rutlnd.............88 D1
Stretton Staffs..............84 F2
Stretton Staffs............100 E7
Stretton Warrtn...........112 F5
Stretton Grandison
      Herefs....................70 B5
Stretton-on-
      Dunsmore Warwks..86 E8
Stretton on Fosse
      Warwks..................72 B6
Stretton Sugwas
      Herefs....................69 J6
Stretton under Fosse
      Warwks..................86 F7
Stretton Westwood
      Shrops....................83 L4
Strichen Abers.............217 H4
Stringston Somset........25 J3
Strixton Nhants............74 C3
Stroat Gloucs................38 E2
Stroma Highld.............231 L1
Stromeferry Highld......210 D7
Stromness Ork.............234 b6
Stronachlachar Stirlg...183 L5
Stronafian Ag & B.........173 H3
Stronchrubie Highld.....224 F5
Strone Ag & B...............173 L3
Strone Highld................192 B1
Strone Highld................212 E8
Stronenaba Highld.......201 J8
Stronmilchan Ag & B...183 G2
Stronsay Ork................234 d5
Stronsay Airport Ork....234 d5
Strontian Highld..........191 G4
Strood Medway..............46 B6
Stroud Gloucs................55 J6
Stroud Hants.................30 B6
Stroud Green Gloucs.....55 J6
Stroxton Lincs.............102 E6
Struan Highld..............208 E6
Struan P & K................194 C4
Strumpshaw Norfk.........93 H3
Strutherhill S Lans......175 K7
Struthers Fife.............186 F5
Struy Highld................212 B6
Stuartfield Abers.........217 H5
Stubbington Hants.........17 G2
Stubbins Lancs............122 B6
Stubton Lincs..............102 E3
Stuckton Hants.............28 D8
Studham C Beds............59 G5
Studland Dorset............15 J6
Studley Warwks.............71 J2
Studley Wilts................39 L6
Studley Roger N York...132 D5
Studley Royal N York...132 D5
Studley Royal Park &
      Fountains Abbey
      N York..................132 D5
Stuntney Cambs............90 D7
Sturmer Essex..............77 G5
Sturminster
      Common Dorset........27 H8
Sturminster Marshall
      Dorset....................15 H3
Sturminster Newton
      Dorset....................27 H8
Sturry Kent..................35 G3
Sturton N Linc..............116 F2
Sturton by Stow
      Lincs.....................116 E5
Sturton le Steeple
      Notts.....................116 C5
Stuston Suffk................92 D7
Stutton N York............124 D3
Stutton Suffk................78 D7

Styal Ches E................113 J5
Stynie Moray...............215 H3
Styrrup Notts..............115 L4
Succoth Ag & B.............183 K6
Suckley Worcs...............70 C4
Sudborough Nhants........88 D6
Sudbourne Suffk............79 J4
Sudbrook Lincs............102 F4
Sudbrook Mons.............38 D3
Sudbrooke Lincs..........117 G6
Sudbury Derbys...........100 D6
Sudbury Gt Lon.............44 D3
Sudbury Suffk...............77 K6
Suffield N York............134 F2
Suffield Norfk..............106 F6
Sugnall Staffs...............99 H6
Sugwas Pool Herefs......69 J6
Suisnish Highld...........199 J3
Sulby IoM....................237 d3
Sulgrave Nhants............73 G5
Sulham W Berk..............41 M5
Sulhamstead W Berk.....41 M6
Sullom Shet.................235 c4
Sullom Voe Shet...........235 c4
Sully V Glam..................37 J6
Sumburgh Airport
      Shet.....................235 c8
Summerbridge
      N York..................132 C6
Summercourt Cnwll........4 D5
Summerfield Norfk.......105 J5
Summerhill Pembks........49 K6
Summerhouse Darltn...140 F4
Summersdale W Susx....18 B4
Summerseat Bury.........122 B7
Summertown Oxon.........57 K6
Sunbury-on-Thames
      Surrey....................43 J6
Sundaywell D & G.........154 E5
Sunderland Ag & B.......170 E5
Sunderland Cumb.........147 L7
Sunderland Lancs.........129 J7
Sunderland Sundld.......151 J4
Sunderland Bridge
      Dur.......................151 G7
Sunderland
      Crematorium
      Sundld...................151 J4
Sundhope Border.........166 E4
Sundon Park Luton........59 H3
Sundridge Kent.............32 E3
Sunningdale W & M........42 F6
Sunninghill W & M.........42 F6
Sunningwell Oxon..........57 J7
Sunniside Dur..............150 E7
Sunniside Gatesd.........150 F3
Sunnyhill C Derb..........101 G6
Sunnyhurst Bl w D.......121 K6
Sunnylaw Stirlg...........185 G7
Sunnymead Oxon...........57 J6
Surbiton Gt Lon.............44 D6
Surfleet Lincs.............103 L6
Surlingham Norfk..........93 G3
Surrex Essex.................61 L4
Surrey & Sussex
      Crematorium
      W Susx....................32 B5
Sustead Norfk..............106 E5
Susworth Lincs............116 D2
Sutcombe Devon.............9 J3
Sutcombemill Devon.......9 J3
Sutterby Lincs.............118 E6
Sutterton Lincs...........103 M5
Sutton C Beds...............75 J5
Sutton C Pete...............89 G4
Sutton Cambs................90 C7
Sutton Devon..................7 G7
Sutton E Susx...............20 A5
Sutton Gt Lon................44 E7
Sutton Kent..................35 J5
Sutton N York..............124 D5
Sutton Norfk................107 H7
Sutton Notts................102 C5
Sutton Oxon.................57 H6
Sutton Shrops...............84 D6
Sutton Staffs................99 H7

Sutton Suffk..................79 G5
Sutton W Susx...............18 D3
Sutton at Hone Kent.....45 K6
Sutton Bassett
      Nhants....................87 L5
Sutton Benger Wilts......39 L5
Sutton Bonington
      Notts....................101 K7
Sutton Bridge Lincs....104 D7
Sutton Cheney Leics......86 E4
Sutton Coldfield
      Birm.......................85 K4
Sutton Coldfield
      Crematorium
      Birm.......................85 K4
Sutton Courtenay
      Oxon......................41 J2
Sutton cum Lound
      Notts....................116 B5
Sutton Green Surrey.....31 G1
Sutton Howgrave
      N York..................132 D4
Sutton in Ashfield
      Notts....................101 J2
Sutton-in-Craven
      N York..................122 F2
Sutton Maddock
      Shrops....................84 C3
Sutton Mallet Somset...26 A4
Sutton Mandeville
      Wilts......................27 M5
Sutton Montis
      Somset...................26 F6
Sutton-on-Hull C KuH...126 E4
Sutton on Sea Lincs....119 G5
Sutton-on-the-
      Forest N York........133 J6
Sutton on the Hill
      Derbys..................100 E5
Sutton on Trent
      Notts....................116 D7
Sutton St Edmund
      Lincs......................89 L2
Sutton St James Lincs..104 C8
Sutton St Nicholas
      Herefs....................69 K5
Sutton Scotney Hants....29 J4
Sutton-under-Brailes
      Warwks..................72 C6
Sutton-under-
      Whitestonecliffe
      N York..................133 G3
Sutton upon
      Derwent E R Yk......125 G2
Sutton Valence Kent.....33 L4
Sutton Veny Wilts..........27 K3
Sutton Waldron
      Dorset....................27 K7
Sutton Weaver
      Ches W...................112 D5
Sutton Wick BaNES........38 E8
Sutton Wick Oxon..........41 J2
Swaby Lincs.................118 E6
Swadlincote Derbys.....100 F8
Swaffham Norfk.............91 J2
Swaffham Bulbeck
      Cambs....................76 D3
Swaffham Prior
      Cambs....................76 E2
Swafield Norfk............107 G6
Swainby N York...........141 L6
Swainsthorpe Norfk......92 F4
Swainswick BaNES........39 H6
Swalcliffe Oxon............72 E6
Swalecliffe Kent...........47 J5
Swallow Lincs..............117 K2
Swallow Beck Lincs.....116 F7
Swallowcliffe Wilts.......27 L6
Swallowfield
      Wokham...................42 B7
Swanage Dorset............15 J4
Swanbourne Bucks.........58 D3
Swan Green Ches W......113 G6
Swanland E R Yk..........126 B5
Swanley Kent................45 K6
Swanley Village Kent....45 K6

Swanmore Hants 29 L7
Swannington Leics 86 E1
Swannington Norfk......106 D8
Swanpool Garden
  Suburb Lincs............116 F7
Swanscombe Kent.........45 L5
Swansea Swans 51 J6
Swansea Airport
  Swans 51 H7
Swansea
  Crematorium
  Swans 51 J5
Swansea West
  Services Swans 51 J5
Swanton Abbot
  Norfk......................106 F7
Swanton Morley
  Norfk........................92 B1
Swanton Novers
  Norfk......................106 B6
Swanwick Derbys......101 H2
Swanwick Hants.........17 G1
Swarby Lincs..............103 H4
Swardeston Norfk.......92 E3
Swarkestone Derbys...101 G6
Swarland Nthumb 158 F2
Swarraton Hants 29 K4
Swarthmoor Cumb 129 G4
Swaton Lincs..............103 J5
Swavesey Cambs 75 L2
Sway Hants 16 C3
Swayfield Lincs...........103 G7
Swaythling C Sotn 29 H7
Sweetham Devon 11 K5
Sweethaws E Susx 32 E7
Sweets Cnwll................8 F5
Sweetshouse Cnwll........5 H4
Swefling Suffk..............79 H2
Swepstone Leics 86 D2
Swerford Oxon.............57 G2
Swettenham Ches E....113 J7
Swilland Suffk...............78 E4
Swillington Leeds........124 B4
Swimbridge Devon 23 K5
Swimbridge
  Newland Devon........23 J5
Swinbrook Oxon..........56 F5
Swincliffe N York........132 C7
Swinderby Lincs.........116 E8
Swindon Gloucs............55 L3
Swindon Staffs.............84 F5
Swindon Swindn...........40 D4
Swine E R Yk..............126 E4
Swinefleet E R Yk.......125 H6
Swineshead Bed..........74 F2
Swineshead Lincs........103 L4
Swiney Highld............227 M2
Swinford Leics.............87 H7
Swingfield Minnis
  Kent........................35 G6
Swingfield Street
  Kent........................35 H6
Swingleton Green
  Suffk.......................77 L5
Swinhoe Nthumb........169 J4
Swinithwaite N York...131 K2
Swinside Cumb...........137 H3
Swinstead Lincs.........103 G7
Swinton Border..........179 H8
Swinton N York..........132 C4
Swinton N York..........134 B5
Swinton Rothm..........115 J2
Swinton Salfd............113 H2
Swithland Leics...........87 G2
Swordale Highld.........212 E2
Swordland Highld.......200 B6
Swordly Highld...........229 M3
Swynnerton Staffs.......99 J5
Swyre Dorset...............13 M5
Sychtyn Powys............81 L3
Syde Gloucs.................55 L5
Sydenham Gt Lon.........45 G5
Sydenham Oxon...........58 B7
Sydenham Damerel
  Devon........................6 B2
Syderstone Norfk........105 K6

Sydling St Nicholas
  Dorset 14 C3
Sydmonton Hants.........41 J8
Syerston Notts............102 C3
Sykehouse Donc.........124 F6
Symbister Shet...........235 d4
Symington S Ayrs.......163 J3
Symington S Lans.......165 J3
Symondsbury Dorset 13 K4
Symonds Yat Herefs 54 E5
Syre Highld................229 L6
Syreford Gloucs...........56 B4
Syresham Nhants 73 J6
Syston Leics................87 J2
Syston Lincs...............102 F4
Sytchampton Worcs......70 E2
Sywell Nhants..............74 B2

T

Tackley Oxon...............57 J4
Tacolneston Norfk........92 D4
Tadcaster N York.........124 D2
Taddington Derbys......114 C7
Tadley Hants................41 L7
Tadlow Cambs.............75 K5
Tadmarton Oxon..........72 E6
Tadworth Surrey..........44 E8
Taff's Well Rhondd........37 H4
Taibach Neath..............36 B3
Tain Highld.................223 G5
Tain Highld.................231 J3
Tairbeart W Isls.........232 e4
Takeley Essex..............60 F4
Takeley Street Essex....60 E4
Talaton Devon..............12 D3
Talbenny Pembks.........48 E5
Taleford Devon.............12 E3
Talerddig Powys...........81 K4
Talgarreg Cerdgn.........65 L4
Talgarth Powys............68 D7
Talisker Highld...........208 E7
Talke Staffs.................99 J2
Talkin Cumb...............148 F4
Talla Linnfoots
  Border 165 M5
Tallaminnock S Ayrs...153 J3
Tallarn Green
  Wrexhm....................98 C4
Tallentire Cumb.........147 K7
Talley Carmth..............66 E7
Tallington Lincs...........88 F2
Talmine Highld...........229 J3
Talog Carmth...............50 D1
Talsarn Cerdgn............66 D4
Talsarnau Gwynd..........95 K5
Talskiddy Cnwll.............4 E3
Talwrn IoA.................109 G6
Tal-y-bont Cerdgn........80 E5
Tal-y-bont Conwy.......109 L7
Tal-y-bont Gwynd.........95 K7
Tal-y-bont Gwynd.......109 J7
Talybont-on-Usk
  Powys......................53 H4
Tal-y-Cafn Conwy......109 M7
Tal-y-coed Mons..........54 B5
Talysarn Gwynd...........95 H2
Tamar Valley Mining
  District Devon............6 C3
Tamerton Foliot
  C Plym......................6 C4
Tamworth Staffs..........86 B3
Tamworth Services
  Warwks.....................86 B4
Tandridge Surrey..........32 C3
Tanfield Dur...............150 F4
Tanfield Lea Dur.........150 F4
Tangley Hants..............28 F2
Tangmere W Susx........18 B4
Tangusdale W Isls......233 b9
Tankerness Ork..........234 c6
Tankersley Barns.......115 G2
Tankerton Kent............47 J6
Tannach Highld..........231 K6

Tannachie Abers.........206 E8
Tannadice Angus........196 D5
Tanner's Green Worcs....85 J8
Tannington Suffk.........78 F2
Tannochside N Lans...175 J6
Tansley Derbys...........100 F1
Tansor Nhants..............88 F5
Tantobie Dur..............150 F4
Tanworth in Arden
  Warwks.....................71 K1
Tan-y-groes Cerdgn......65 J3
Taobh Tuath W Isls.....232 d5
Taplow Bucks..............42 E4
Tarbert Ag & B............172 B7
Tarbert Ag & B............172 E5
Tarbert W Isls............232 e4
Tarbet Ag & B............183 K6
Tarbet Highld.............200 B6
Tarbet Highld.............228 B5
Tarbolton S Ayrs.........163 K4
Tarbrax S Lans............176 D7
Tardebigge Worcs........71 H2
Tarfside Angus...........196 D1
Tarland Abers.............205 K4
Tarleton Lancs............120 F6
Tarlton Gloucs..............55 L7
Tarnock Somset............26 B2
Tarporley Ches W.......112 D8
Tarrant Crawford
  Dorset 15 H2
Tarrant Gunville
  Dorset 27 L8
Tarrant Hinton Dorset....15 H1
Tarrant Keyneston
  Dorset 15 H2
Tarrant Launceston
  Dorset 15 H1
Tarrant Monkton
  Dorset 15 H2
Tarrant Rawston
  Dorset 15 H2
Tarrant Rushton
  Dorset 15 H2
Tarring Neville E Susx....19 L5
Tarrington Herefs.........70 B6
Tarskavaig Highld.......199 J4
Tarves Abers...............217 G2
Tarvin Ches W............112 C7
Tasburgh Norfk............92 E4
Tatenhill Staffs...........100 D7
Tathwell Lincs............118 D5
Tatsfield Surrey............32 D2
Tattenhall Ches W........98 C2
Tatterford Norfk.........105 K6
Tattersett Norfk..........105 K6
Tattershall Lincs.........103 K2
Tattershall Thorpe
  Lincs......................103 L1
Tattingstone Suffk........78 D6
Tattingstone White
  Horse Suffk...............78 D6
Tatton Park Ches E.....113 H5
Tatworth Somset..........13 J2
Tauchers Moray..........215 J4
Taunton Somset...........25 K6
Taunton Deane
  Crematorium
  Somset.....................25 J6
Taunton Deane
  Services Somset.......25 J7
Taverham Norfk............92 E2
Tavernspite Pembks.....49 K5
Tavistock Devon............6 C2
Taw Green Devon.........10 F5
Tawstock Devon...........23 J5
Taxal Derbys...............114 A5
Taychreggan Hotel
  Ag & B....................182 F3
Tay Forest Park P & K..194 C4
Tayinloan Ag & B.......161 H1
Taynton Gloucs............55 G4
Taynton Oxon..............56 E5
Taynuilt Ag & B...........182 E2
Tayport Fife...............187 G2
Tayvallich Ag & B........172 C2

Tealby Lincs...............117 J4
Tealing Angus............196 C8
Team Valley Gatesd...151 G3
Teangue Highld..........199 K4
Teanord Highld...........212 F2
Tebay Cumb...............138 E6
Tebay Services Cumb..138 E6
Tebworth C Beds..........59 G3
Tedburn St Mary
  Devon.......................11 J6
Teddington Gloucs........55 L2
Teddington Gt Lon........44 D6
Tedstone Delamere
  Herefs.......................70 C3
Tedstone Wafer
  Herefs.......................70 C3
Teesside
  Crematorium
  Middsb....................141 L4
Teeton Nhants..............73 K1
Teffont Evias Wilts.......27 M5
Teffont Magna Wilts.....27 M5
Tegryn Pembks.............65 H7
Teigh Rutlnd................88 C1
Teigngrace Devon...........7 K2
Teignmouth Devon........12 B7
Teindside Border.........166 F7
Telford Wrekin.............84 C2
Telford Crematorium
  Wrekin......................84 D2
Telford Services
  Shrops......................84 D2
Tellisford Somset.........27 J1
Telscombe E Susx........19 L5
Tempar P & K.............193 L5
Templand D & G..........155 J5
Temple Cnwll................5 J2
Temple Mdloth...........177 J6
Temple Bar Cerdgn......66 C3
Temple Cloud BaNES....38 F8
Templecombe
  Somset......................27 G6
Temple Ewell Kent.......35 H5
Temple Grafton
  Warwks.....................71 K4
Temple Guiting
  Gloucs......................56 C3
Temple Hirst N York....124 F5
Temple Normanton
  Derbys....................115 H7
Temple of Fiddes
  Abers.....................197 K1
Temple Sowerby
  Cumb......................138 E2
Templeton Devon.........11 K3
Templeton Pembks.......49 J5
Templetown Dur........150 E5
Tempsford C Beds........75 H4
Tenbury Wells Worcs....69 L2
Tenby Pembks..............49 J7
Tendring Essex.............62 D3
Tendring Green Essex....62 D3
Tendring Heath Essex....62 D3
Ten Mile Bank Norfk......90 E4
Tenterden Kent............34 B7
Terling Essex...............61 J5
Ternhill Shrops............98 F6
Terregles D & G..........155 G6
Terrington N York.......133 K5
Terrington St
  Clement Norfk.........104 E7
Terrington St John
  Norfk........................90 D2
Teston Kent.................33 J3
Testwood Hants............29 G8
Tetbury Gloucs.............39 K2
Tetchill Shrops.............98 B6
Tetcott Devon................9 J5
Tetford Lincs..............118 D6
Tetney Lincs...............118 D2
Tetsworth Oxon............58 B7
Tettenhall Wolves.........84 F4
Teversal Notts............101 J1
Teversham Cambs........76 C3
Teviothead Border......156 D2
Tewin Herts.................59 L5

Tewkesbury Gloucs........55 K2
Teynham Kent..............34 C3
Thackley C Brad........123 H3
Thakeham W Susx.........18 F3
Thame Oxon................58 B6
Thames Ditton Surrey ...44 D6
Thamesmead Gt Lon.....45 J4
Thanet Crematorium
　Kent........................35 K2
Thanington Kent...........34 F4
Thankerton S Lans......165 J3
Tharston Norfk.............92 E5
Thatcham W Berk..........41 K6
Thaxted Essex..............60 F2
Theakston N York........132 D3
Thealby N Linc...........125 K6
Theale Somset.............26 C3
Theale W Berk.............41 M6
Thearne E R Yk..........126 D3
The Beeches Gloucs......56 B7
Theberton Suffk...........79 J2
The Braes Highld........209 H7
The Brunt E Loth.......178 E4
The Bungalow IoM.......237 d4
The Burf Worcs............70 E2
The Butts Gloucs..........55 K5
The City Bucks.............42 C2
The Common Wilts........28 E5
The Counties
　Crematorium
　Nhants......................73 K3
Theddingworth Leics.....87 J6
Theddlethorpe All
　Saints Lincs............118 F4
Theddlethorpe St
　Helen Lincs.............119 G4
The Den N Ayrs..........174 C7
The Forest of Dean
　Crematorium
　Gloucs.....................54 F5
The Forstal Kent..........34 D6
The Garden of
　England
　Crematorium
　Kent........................46 E6
The Green Cumb.........128 E3
The Green Essex..........61 J4
The Green N York.......143 G6
The Green Wilts...........27 K5
The Headland Hartpl...151 M7
The Hill Cumb............128 E3
The Lee Bucks.............58 E6
The Lhen IoM.............237 d2
The Linn
　Crematorium
　E Rens...................175 G6
Thelnetham Suffk........92 B7
The Lochs Moray........215 G2
Thelveton Norfk...........92 E7
Thelwall Warrtn.........112 F4
The Manchester
　Crematorium
　Manch....................113 J3
Themelthorpe Norfk....106 C7
The Moor Kent............33 K7
The Mumbles Swans.....51 J7
The Murray S Lans.....175 H7
The Neuk Abers..........206 D5
Thenford Nhants..........73 G6
The Park
　Crematorium
　Hants.....................30 E2
The Reddings Gloucs.....55 K4
Therfield Herts............75 L6
The Rose Hill
　Crematorium
　Donc.....................115 L2
The Ross P & K.........185 G3
The Stocks Kent..........21 H1
The Strand Wilts..........39 L8
Thetford Norfk.............91 K6
Thetford Forest Park 91 J5
The Vale
　Crematorium
　Luton.....................59 J3
Theydon Bois Essex......60 D7

Thickwood Wilts..........39 J5
Thimbleby Lincs.........118 C7
Thimbleby N York......141 K7
Thingwall Wirral.........111 J5
Thirkleby N York.......133 G4
Thirlby N York...........133 G3
Thirlestane Border......178 C8
Thirn N York.............132 C3
Thirsk N York............132 F3
Thistleton Lancs.........120 E3
Thistleton Rutlnd.......102 E8
Thistley Green Suffk.....90 F7
Thixendale N York......134 C7
Thockrington
　Nthumb.................158 B6
Tholomas Drove
　Cambs....................90 B3
Tholthorpe N York.....133 G6
Thomastown Abers......216 B6
Thompson Norfk..........91 K4
Thoralby N York.........131 J3
Thoresway Lincs.........117 K3
Thorganby Lincs.........117 K3
Thorganby N York......125 G3
Thorgill N York..........142 E7
Thorington Suffk..........93 J8
Thorington Street
　Suffk......................78 B7
Thorlby N York..........131 H8
Thorley Herts..............60 D4
Thorley Street IoW.......16 D5
Thormanby N York......133 G5
Thornaby-on-Tees
　S on T...................141 K4
Thornage Norfk.........106 C5
Thornborough Bucks 73 L7
Thornborough N York..132 D4
Thornbury C Brad......123 J4
Thornbury Devon..........9 K3
Thornbury Herefs........70 B3
Thornbury S Glos........38 F3
Thornby Nhants..........87 J7
Thorncliff Staffs.........100 A2
Thorncliffe
　Crematorium
　Cumb....................128 E5
Thorncombe Dorset......13 J2
Thorndon Suffk...........78 D1
Thorndon Cross
　Devon.....................10 D6
Thorne Donc..............125 G7
Thorner Leeds...........124 B3
Thorne St Margaret
　Somset....................25 H7
Thorney C Pete...........89 K3
Thorney Notts...........116 E6
Thorney Somset..........26 B6
Thorney Hill Hants.......16 A3
Thorney Island
　W Susx...................17 L2
Thornfalcon Somset......25 L6
Thornford Dorset.........26 E8
Thorngrafton
　Nthumb.................149 K2
Thorngumbald E R Yk .126 F5
Thornham Norfk.........105 H4
Thornham Magna
　Suffk......................78 D1
Thornham Parva
　Suffk......................92 D8
Thornhaugh C Pete......88 F4
Thornhill C Sotn..........29 J8
Thornhill Cumb..........136 D5
Thornhill D & G.........154 F3
Thornhill Derbys........114 D5
Thornhill Kirk...........123 K6
Thornhill Stirlg.........184 E7
Thornhill
　Crematorium
　Cardif.....................37 J4
Thornholme E R Yk ...135 H6
Thornicombe Dorset.....15 G2
Thornington Nthumb...168 D3
Thornley Dur............150 E7
Thornley Dur............151 J6
Thornliebank E Rens...174 F6

Thorns Suffk...............77 G4
Thornsett Derbys.......114 A4
Thornthwaite Cumb....137 H3
Thornthwaite N York..132 B7
Thornton Angus.........196 C6
Thornton Bucks...........73 L7
Thornton C Brad........123 G4
Thornton E R Yk.......125 H2
Thornton Fife............178 E7
Thornton Lancs..........120 D3
Thornton Leics...........86 F3
Thornton Middsb......141 L4
Thornton Nthumb......179 K8
Thornton Curtis
　N Linc...................126 D6
Thornton Garden
　of Rest
　Crematorium
　Sefton....................111 K2
Thorntonhall S Lans...175 G7
Thornton Heath
　Gt Lon....................44 F6
Thornton Hough
　Wirral....................111 J5
Thornton-in-Craven
　N York...................122 D2
Thornton in Lonsdale
　N York...................130 D5
Thornton-le-Beans
　N York...................132 F2
Thornton-le-Clay
　N York...................133 L6
Thornton le Dale
　N York...................134 C3
Thornton le Moor
　Lincs.....................117 H3
Thornton-le-Moor
　N York...................132 F2
Thornton-le-Moors
　Ches W..................112 C6
Thornton-le-Street
　N York...................132 F3
Thorntonloch E Loth..178 F4
Thornton Rust N York .131 H2
Thornton Steward
　N York...................132 B3
Thornton Watlass
　N York...................132 C3
Thornydykes Border...178 D8
Thornythwaite Cumb...137 L3
Thoroton Notts.........102 C4
Thorp Arch Leeds......124 C2
Thorpe Derbys...........100 D3
Thorpe E R Yk..........126 B2
Thorpe N York...........131 J6
Thorpe Notts............102 C3
Thorpe Surrey............43 G6
Thorpe Abbotts
　Norfk......................92 E7
Thorpe Arnold Leics...102 C7
Thorpe Audlin
　Wakefd..................124 D7
Thorpe Bassett
　N York...................134 D5
Thorpe Bay Sthend......46 E3
Thorpe by Water
　Rutlnd....................88 C4
Thorpe Constantine
　Staffs......................86 C2
Thorpe End Norfk........93 G2
Thorpe Green Essex......62 E4
Thorpe Green Suffk......77 L4
Thorpe Hesley Rothm ..115 G3
Thorpe in Balne Donc .124 F7
Thorpe Langton Leics...87 L5
Thorpe Lea Surrey.......43 G6
Thorpe-le-Soken
　Essex.....................62 E4
Thorpe le Street
　E R Yk..................125 K2
Thorpe Malsor
　Nhants....................88 B7
Thorpe Mandeville
　Nhants....................73 G5
Thorpe Market Norfk ..106 F5
Thorpe Marriot Norfk...92 E1

Thorpe Morieux Suffk ...77 L4
Thorpeness Suffk.........79 K3
Thorpe on the Hill
　Lincs.....................116 E7
Thorpe Park Surrey.....43 G6
Thorpe St Andrew
　Norfk......................92 F2
Thorpe St Peter Lincs...104 D7
Thorpe Salvin Rothm ..115 K5
Thorpe Satchville
　Leics.......................87 K2
Thorpe Thewles
　S on T...................141 J3
Thorpe Tilney Lincs....103 J2
Thorpe Underwood
　N York...................133 G7
Thorpe Waterville
　Nhants....................88 E7
Thorpe Willoughby
　N York...................124 E4
Thorrington Essex........62 C4
Thorverton Devon........11 L4
Thrandeston Suffk........92 D7
Thrapston Nhants.........88 E7
Threapwood Ches W.....98 C8
Threapwood Staffs.....100 B4
Threave S Ayrs..........163 J7
Three Bridges W Susx ..32 B5
Three Chimneys Kent....33 L5
Three Cocks Powys......68 D6
Three Counties
　Crematorium
　Essex.....................61 J3
Three Crosses Swans 51 H6
Three Cups Corner
　E Susx....................20 D2
Threekingham Lincs...103 H5
Three Leg Cross
　E Susx....................33 H6
Three Legged Cross
　Dorset....................15 K2
Three Mile Cross
　Wokham...................42 B6
Threemilestone Cnwll.....3 K3
Three Miletown
　W Loth..................176 E3
Three Oaks E Susx.......21 G3
Threlkeld Cumb.........137 J3
Threshers Bush Essex...60 D6
Threshfield N York.....131 J6
Thrigby Norfk.............93 K2
Thringstone Leics......101 H8
Thrintoft N York........132 D2
Thriplow Cambs..........76 B5
Throcking Herts..........60 B3
Throckley N u Ty......150 E2
Throckmorton Worcs....71 H4
Throop Bmouth...........15 L4
Thropton Nthumb......158 C2
Throsk Stirlg..............176 B1
Throughgate D & G...154 F5
Throwleigh Devon........11 G6
Throwley Forstal
　Kent........................34 C4
Thrumpton Notts.......101 J6
Thrumster Highld......231 L6
Thrunscoe NE Lin......127 H8
Thrupp Gloucs............55 K7
Thrussington Leics......87 J1
Thruxton Hants...........28 F3
Thruxton Herefs..........69 J7
Thrybergh Rothm......115 J3
Thulston Derbys........101 H6
Thundersley Essex.......46 C3
Thurcaston Leics.........87 H2
Thurcroft Rothm.......115 J4
Thurgarton Norfk......106 E5
Thurgarton Notts......102 B3
Thurgoland Barns......114 F2
Thurlaston Leics..........87 G4
Thurlaston Warwks......72 F1
Thurlbear Somset.........25 K7
Thurlby Lincs.............89 G1
Thurlby Lincs...........102 E1
Thurlby Lincs...........119 G6
Thurleigh Bed............74 F3

Thurlestone Devon..........7 G7
Thurloxton Somset.........25 L5
Thurlstone Barns.........114 E2
Thurlton Norfk............93 J4
Thurmaston Leics..........87 H2
Thurnby Leics.............87 J3
Thurne Norfk..............93 J1
Thurnham Kent.............33 K2
Thurning Nhants...........88 F6
Thurning Norfk...........106 C6
Thurnscoe Barns..........115 J1
Thurrock Services
 Thurr....................45 L4
Thursby Cumb.............148 B5
Thursford Norfk..........106 B5
Thursley Surrey...........30 E4
Thurso Highld............231 G2
Thurstaston Wirral.......111 H5
Thurston Suffk............77 L2
Thurstonfield Cumb.......148 B4
Thurstonland Kirk........123 H7
Thurton Norfk.............93 G4
Thurvaston Derbys........100 E5
Thuxton Norfk.............92 B3
Thwaite N York...........139 K7
Thwaite Suffk.............78 D2
Thwaite Head Cumb........129 H2
Thwaite St Mary
 Norfk....................93 G4
Thwing E R Yk............135 G5
Tibbermore P & K..........85 L3
Tibbers D & G............154 E3
Tibberton Gloucs..........55 H4
Tibberton Worcs...........70 F3
Tibberton Wrekin..........99 G7
Tibbie Shiels Inn
 Border..................166 C5
Tibenham Norfk............92 D5
Tibshelf Derbys..........101 H1
Tibshelf Services
 Derbys..................101 H1
Tibthorpe E R Yk.........134 E7
Ticehurst E Susx..........33 H7
Tichborne Hants...........29 L5
Tickencote Rutlnd.........88 E2
Tickenham N Som...........38 C6
Tickhill Donc............115 L3
Ticklerton Shrops.........83 J5
Ticknall Derbys..........101 G7
Tickton E R Yk...........126 D3
Tidcombe Wilts............40 F8
Tiddington Oxon...........57 M6
Tiddington Warwks.........72 B4
Tidebrook E Susx..........33 G7
Tideford Cnwll.............6 A4
Tidenham Gloucs...........38 E2
Tideswell Derbys.........114 D6
Tidmarsh W Berk...........41 M5
Tidmington Warwks.........72 C6
Tidworth Wilts............28 E2
Tiers Cross Pembks........48 F5
Tiffield Nhants...........73 K4
Tigerton Angus...........196 E4
Tigh a Ghearraidh
 W Isls..................233 b6
Tigharry W Isls..........233 b6
Tighnabruaich Ag & B.....173 G4
Tigley Devon...............7 H4
Tilbrook Cambs............74 F2
Tilbury Thurr.............45 M5
Tile Hill Covtry..........86 C7
Tilehurst Readg...........42 A5
Tilford Surrey............30 E3
Tilgate W Susx............31 L4
Tilham Street Somset......26 E4
Tillicoultry Clacks......185 J7
Tillietudlem S Lans......164 F1
Tillingham Essex..........62 B7
Tillington Herefs.........69 J5
Tillington W Susx.........30 F6
Tillington Common
 Herefs...................69 J5
Tillybirloch Abers.......206 D4
Tillyfourie Abers........206 C3
Tillygreig Abers.........207 G2
Tillyrie P & K...........186 B6

Tilmanstone Kent..........35 J4
Tilney All Saints Norfk..104 F8
Tilney High End Norfk....104 E8
Tilney St Lawrence
 Norfk....................90 D2
Tilshead Wilts............28 B2
Tilstock Shrops...........98 D5
Tilston Ches W............98 C3
Tilstone Fearnall
 Ches W...................98 E1
Tilsworth C Beds..........59 G3
Tilton on the Hill Leics..87 L3
Tiltups End Gloucs........39 J2
Timberland Lincs.........103 J2
Timbersbrook Ches E......113 K8
Timberscombe Somset.......24 E3
Timble N York............132 B8
Timpanheck D & G.........156 B7
Timperley Traffd.........113 H4
Timsbury BaNES............38 F8
Timsbury Hants............29 G6
Timsgarry W Isls.........232 d2
Timsgearraidh W Isls.....232 d2
Timworth Suffk............77 J2
Timworth Green
 Suffk....................77 J2
Tincleton Dorset..........14 E4
Tindale Cumb.............149 G3
Tindale Crescent Dur.....140 F2
Tingewick Bucks...........58 A2
Tingrith C Beds...........59 G2
Tingwall Airport Shet....235 c6
Tingwell Ork.............234 c5
Tinhay Devon...............9 K7
Tinsley Sheff............115 H4
Tinsley Green W Susx......32 B5
Tintagel Cnwll.............8 E7
Tintern Parva Mons........54 D7
Tintinhull Somset.........26 D7
Tintwistle Derbys........114 A3
Tinwald D & G............155 H5
Tinwell Rutlnd............88 E3
Tipton Sandw..............85 G5
Tipton St John Devon......12 E4
Tiptree Essex.............61 L5
Tiptree Heath Essex.......61 L5
Tirabad Powys.............67 J6
Tiree Ag & B.............188 D7
Tiree Airport Ag & B.....188 C7
Tiretigan Ag & B.........172 C6
Tirley Gloucs.............55 J3
Tirphil Caerph............53 H7
Tirril Cumb..............138 D2
Tisbury Wilts.............27 L5
Tissington Derbys........100 D3
Titchberry Devon..........22 C6
Titchfield Hants..........17 G2
Titchmarsh Nhants.........88 E7
Titchwell Norfk..........105 J4
Tithby Notts.............102 B5
Titley Herefs.............69 G3
Titsey Surrey.............32 D3
Titson Cnwll...............9 H5
Tittensor Staffs..........99 K5
Tittleshall Norfk........105 L7
Titton Worcs..............70 E1
Tiverton Ches W...........98 D1
Tiverton Devon............24 E8
Tivetshall St
  Margaret Norfk..........92 E6
Tivetshall St Mary
  Norfk...................92 E6
Tixall Staffs.............99 L7
Tixover Rutlnd............88 E4
Toab Shet................235 c8
Tobermory Ag & B.........189 L5
Toberonochy Ag & B.......181 L5
Tobha Mor W Isls.........233 b7
Tocher Abers.............216 D7
Tochieneal Moray.........215 L2
Tockenham Wilts...........40 B4
Tockholes Bl w D.........121 K6
Tockington S Glos.........38 E3
Tockwith N York..........133 G8
Todber Dorset.............27 J7
Toddington C Beds.........59 G3

Toddington Gloucs.........56 B2
Toddington Services
  C Beds..................59 G3
Todenham Gloucs...........72 B7
Todhills Angus...........196 C8
Todhills Services
  Cumb...................148 C3
Todmorden Calder.........122 D5
Todwick Rothm............115 J5
Toft Cambs................75 L4
Toft Lincs................88 F1
Toft Shet................235 c3
Toft Hill Dur............140 E2
Toft Monks Norfk..........93 J4
Toft next Newton
  Lincs..................117 H4
Toftrees Norfk...........105 L6
Togston Nthumb...........159 G2
Tokavaig Highld..........199 J3
Tokers Green Oxon.........42 B5
Tolastadh W Isls.........232 g2
Tolland Somset............25 H5
Tollard Royal Wilts.......27 L7
Toll Bar Donc............124 E8
Toller Fratrum Dorset.....14 B3
Toller Porcorum
  Dorset..................14 B3
Tollerton N York.........133 H6
Tollerton Notts..........101 L5
Tollesbury Essex..........62 A6
Tolleshunt D'Arcy
  Essex...................61 L5
Tolleshunt Knights
  Essex...................61 L5
Tolleshunt Major Essex....61 L5
Tolpuddle Dorset..........14 E4
Tolsta W Isls............232 g2
Tolworth Gt Lon...........44 D6
Tomatin Highld...........213 J8
Tomchrasky Highld........201 K3
Tomdoun Highld...........201 H5
Tomich Highld............211 L8
Tomich Highld............212 E5
Tomich Highld............222 F7
Tomich Highld............226 A7
Tomintoul Moray..........204 E2
Tomnacross Highld........212 D6
Tomnavoulin Moray........204 F1
Tonbridge Kent............33 G4
Tondu Brdgnd..............36 D4
Tonedale Somset...........25 H6
Tong C Brad..............123 J4
Tong Kent.................34 C4
Tong Shrops...............84 E3
Tonge Leics..............101 H7
Tongham Surrey............30 E3
Tongland D & G...........146 C4
Tong Norton Shrops........84 E2
Tongue Highld............229 J4
Tongwynlais Cardif........37 H4
Tonmawr Neath.............36 C2
Tonna Neath...............52 B7
Tonwell Herts.............60 B5
Tonypandy Rhondd..........36 F3
Tonyrefail Rhondd.........36 F3
Toot Baldon Oxon..........57 K7
Toot Hill Essex...........60 E7
Toothill Swindn...........40 C4
Tooting Gt Lon............44 F5
Tooting Bec Gt Lon........44 F5
Topcliffe N York.........132 F4
Topcroft Norfk............92 F5
Topcroft Street Norfk.....92 F5
Toppesfield Essex.........77 G6
Toprow Norfk..............92 E4
Topsham Devon.............12 C5
Torbeg N Ayrs............162 A4
Torboll Highld...........223 J2
Torbreck Highld..........213 G6
Torbryan Devon.............7 J3
Torcastle Highld.........192 B2
Torcross Devon.............7 J7
Tore Highld..............212 F4
Torinturk Ag & B.........172 D5
Torksey Lincs............116 D5
Tormarton S Glos..........39 H5

Tormore N Ayrs...........161 M3
Tornagrain Highld........213 J4
Tornaveen Abers..........206 C4
Torness Highld...........212 E8
Toronto Dur..............140 F2
Torpenhow Cumb...........147 L6
Torphichen W Loth........176 C4
Torphins Abers...........206 C5
Torpoint Cnwll.............6 C5
Torquay Torbay.............7 L3
Torquay
  Crematorium
    Torbay...............7 K3
Torquhan Border..........177 L8
Torran Highld............209 J5
Torrance E Duns..........175 H4
Torranyard N Ayrs........163 J1
Torridon Highld..........210 D3
Torridon House
  Highld.................210 D3
Torrin Highld............199 J2
Torrisdale Ag & B........161 K3
Torrisdale Highld........229 K3
Torrish Highld...........227 G5
Torrisholme Lancs........129 K6
Torrobull Highld.........226 A7
Torry C Aber.............207 H4
Torryburn Fife...........176 D2
Torteval Guern...........236 b4
Torthorwald D & G........155 H6
Tortington W Susx.........18 D5
Torton Worcs..............84 E8
Tortworth S Glos..........39 G2
Torvaig Highld...........209 H5
Torver Cumb..............137 J7
Torwood Falk.............175 L2
Torwoodlee Border........167 G2
Torworth Notts...........116 A4
Toscaig Highld...........209 L6
Toseland Cambs............75 J3
Tosside Lancs............130 E7
Tostock Suffk.............77 L2
Totaig Highld............208 C4
Tote Highld..............208 F5
Tote Highld..............209 H3
Totland IoW...............16 D5
Totley Sheff.............114 F5
Totnes Devon...............7 J4
Toton Notts..............101 J5
Totronald Ag & B.........188 F5
Totscore Highld..........208 F2
Tottenham Gt Lon..........45 G3
Tottenhill Norfk..........90 F2
Totteridge Gt Lon.........44 E2
Totternhoe C Beds.........59 G4
Tottington Bury..........122 B7
Totton Hants..............29 G8
Toulston Somset...........25 J5
Toulvaddie Highld........223 J5
Tovil Kent................33 K3
Toward Ag & B............173 K5
Toward Quay Ag & B.......173 J5
Towcester Nhants..........73 K5
Towednack Cnwll............2 E4
Tower of London
  Gt Lon..................45 G4
Towersey Oxon.............58 B6
Towie Abers..............205 K3
Tow Law Dur..............150 E6
Town End Cambs............90 B4
Townend W Duns...........174 D3
Townhead Barns...........114 D2
Townhead D & G...........155 H4
Townhead of
  Greenlaw D & G.........146 C3
Townhill Fife............176 F1
Town Littleworth
  E Susx..................19 L3
Towns End Hants...........41 K8
Townshend Cnwll............3 G5
Town Street Suffk.........91 H6
Town Yetholm Border......168 B4
Towthorpe C York.........133 K7
Towton N York............124 D3
Towyn Conwy..............110 D5
Toxteth Lpool............111 K4

Toynton All Saints
Lincs 118 E8
Toy's Hill Kent 32 K5
Trabboch E Ayrs............163 K5
Trabbochburn E Ayrs....163 L5
Tradespark Highld........213 K3
Trallong Powys................52 E3
Tranent E Loth................177 L4
Tranmere Wirral..............111 J4
Trantelbeg Highld........230 C5
Trantlemore Highld 230 C5
Trapp Carmth...................51 J2
Traprain E Loth..............178 D4
Traquair Border............166 E3
Trawden Lancs..............122 D3
Trawsfynydd Gwynd......96 A5
Trealaw Rhondd..............36 F3
Treales Lancs.................120 F4
Trearddur Bay IoA........108 C5
Treaslane Highld..........208 F4
Trebetherick Cnwll..........4 E1
Treborough Somset........24 F4
Trebullett Cnwll................5 M1
Treburley Cnwll................6 A1
Trecastle Powys..............52 D3
Trecwn Pembks...............64 D7
Trecynon Rhondd............52 F7
Tredegar Blae G..............53 H6
Tredington Gloucs..........55 K3
Tredington Warwks..........72 C5
Tredunnock Mons............38 B2
Treen Cnwll.........................2 D6
Treeton Rothm...............115 H4
Trefasser Pembks...........64 C6
Trefecca Powys................53 H2
Trefeglwys Powys............81 L5
Treffgarne Pembks........49 G3
Treffgarne Owen
Pembks........................48 E3
Trefforest Rhondd..........37 G3
Trefilan Cerdgn..............66 D3
Trefin Pembks..................64 B7
Trefnant Denbgs..........110 E7
Trefonen Shrops.............97 K6
Trefor Gwynd...................94 F4
Trefriw Conwy................109 L8
Tregadillett Cnwll............9 H7
Tregare Mons...................54 B6
Tregaron Cerdgn.............66 F3
Tregarth Gwynd............109 H7
Tregeare Cnwll..................9 H7
Tregeiriog Wrexhm.........97 J5
Tregele IoA....................108 D3
Treglemais Pembks........48 D2
Tregonetha Cnwll..............4 E3
Tregonning &
Gwinear Mining
District Cnwll...............3 G5
Tregony Cnwll....................4 E6
Tregorrick Cnwll...............4 F5
Tregoyd Powys.................68 E6
Tre-groes Cerdgn............65 L5
Tregynon Powys...............82 C4
Tre-gynwr Carmth...........50 E2
Trehafod Rhondd.............37 G3
Trehan Cnwll......................6 B4
Treharris Myr Td..............37 H2
Treherbert Rhondd.........52 E7
Trekenner Cnwll................6 A1
Treknow Cnwll...................8 D7
Trelawnyd Flints...........110 F5
Trelech Carmth................65 J7
Treleddyd-fawr
Pembks........................48 C2
Trelewis Myr Td...............37 H2
Trelights Cnwll..................8 C8
Trelill Cnwll..........................5 G1
Trellech Mons..................54 D6
Trelogan Flints..............110 F5
Tremadog Gwynd............95 K4
Tremail Cnwll.....................8 F7
Tremain Cerdgn...............65 H5
Tremaine Cnwll..................9 G6
Tremar Cnwll......................5 K3
Trematon Cnwll.................6 B4
Tremeirchion Denbgs...110 F6

Trenance Cnwll..................4 D3
Trenance Cnwll..................4 E2
Trench Wrekin..................84 C2
Trenear Cnwll....................3 H5
Treneglos Cnwll................9 G7
Trent Dorset......................26 E7
Trentham C Stke..............99 K4
Trentishoe Devon............23 K2
Treoes V Glam..................36 E5
Treorchy Rhondd............36 E2
Trequite Cnwll...................5 G1
Trerhyngyll V Glam..........36 F5
Trerulefoot Cnwll...............5 M4
Tresaith Cerdgn...............65 J4
Tresco IoS...........................2 a1
Trescowe Cnwll.................3 G5
Tresean Cnwll....................4 C4
Tresham Gloucs...............39 H3
Treshnish Isles Ag & B ..189 G7
Tresillian Cnwll..................4 D6
Treskinnick Cross
Cnwll.............................9 G5
Tresmeer Cnwll.................9 G7
Tresparrett Cnwll.............8 F6
Tressait P & K.................194 C4
Tresta Shet.......................235 c5
Tresta Shet.......................235 e3
Treswell Notts.................116 C5
Treswithian Downs
Crematorium
Cnwll.............................3 H3
Tre Taliesin Cerdgn........80 E5
Trethevey Cnwll................8 E6
Trethewey Cnwll...............2 C6
Trethurgy Cnwll.................5 G5
Tretire Herefs...................54 D4
Tretower Powys................53 J4
Treuddyn Flints................97 K2
Trevalga Cnwll...................8 E6
Trevalyn Wrexhm.............98 B2
Trevarrian Cnwll..............4 D3
Treveal Cnwll......................4 C4
Treveighan Cnwll...............8 E8
Trevellas Downs
Cnwll.............................3 J2
Trevelmond Cnwll.............5 K3
Treverva Cnwll...................3 K5
Trevescan Cnwll...............2 C6
Treviscoe Cnwll................4 E5
Trevone Cnwll....................4 D2
Trevor Wrexhm.................97 L4
Trewalder Cnwll................8 E7
Trewarmett Cnwll.............8 E7
Trewavas Mining
District Cnwll..................3 G6
Trewen Cnwll......................9 H7
Trewint Cnwll......................9 G8
Trewithian Cnwll...............4 D7
Trewoon Cnwll....................4 F5
Treyford W Susx..............30 D7
Trimdon Dur....................151 J7
Trimdon Colliery Dur....151 J7
Trimdon Grange Dur....151 J7
Trimingham Norfk.........107 G5
Trimley St Martin
Suffk...........................78 F6
Trimley St Mary Suffk....79 G7
Trimsaran Carmth...........50 F5
Trimstone Devon.............23 H3
Trinafour P & K...............194 B4
Tring Herts........................58 F5
Trinity Angus....................196 F4
Trinity Jersey...................236 d6
Trinity Gask P & K..........185 K4
Triscombe Somset..........25 J4
Trislaig Highld................191 L2
Trispen Cnwll.....................4 D5
Tritlington Nthumb........158 F4
Trochry P & K...................194 F7
Troedyraur Cerdgn...........65 K5
Troedyrhiw Myr Td..........53 G7
Troon Cnwll.........................3 H4
Troon S Ayrs....................163 H3
Tropical World
Roundhay Park
Leeds.........................123 L3

Trossachs Stirlg.............184 B5
Trossachs Pier Stirlg 184 B6
Troston Suffk....................91 K8
Trotshill Worcs.................70 F4
Trottiscliffe Kent.............33 H2
Trotton W Susx.................30 D6
Troutbeck Cumb.............137 L6
Troutbeck Bridge
Cumb..........................137 L7
Troway Derbys................115 H5
Trowbridge Wilts.............39 J8
Trowell Notts...................101 J4
Trowell Services
Notts..........................101 J4
Trowse Newton
Norfk...........................92 F3
Trudoxhill Somset..........27 H3
Trull Somset......................25 K6
Trumpan Highld..............208 C3
Trumpet Herefs................70 B6
Trumpington Cambs........76 C4
Trunch Norfk...................107 G5
Truro Cnwll.........................4 C6
Trusham Devon.................11 K7
Trusley Derbys................100 E5
Trusthorpe Lincs............119 G3
Trysull Staffs....................84 F5
Tubney Oxon.....................57 H7
Tuckenhay Devon...............7 J5
Tuckhill Shrops.................84 E6
Tuckingmill Cnwll..............3 H3
Tuckingmill Wilts.............27 L5
Tuckton Bmouth................15 L4
Tuddenham Suffk.............77 G1
Tuddenham Suffk.............78 E5
Tudeley Kent.....................33 G4
Tudhoe Dur.....................151 G7
Tudweiliog Gwynd............94 D5
Tuffley Gloucs...................55 J5
Tufton Hants......................29 J3
Tufton Pembks..................49 H2
Tugby Leics.......................87 L4
Tugford Shrops.................83 L6
Tughall Nthumb...............169 J4
Tullibody Clacks.............185 H7
Tullich Highld...................212 F8
Tullich Highld...................223 J6
Tulliemet P & K................194 F5
Tulloch Abers..................216 F7
Tullochgorm Ag & B.......182 D7
Tulloch Station
Highld........................192 F1
Tullymurdoch P & K........195 J5
Tullynessle Abers...........206 B2
Tulse Hill Gt Lon..............44 F5
Tumble Carmth.................51 G3
Tumby Lincs....................103 L1
Tumby Woodside
Lincs.........................103 L2
Tummel Bridge P & K 194 B5
Tunbridge Wells Kent.....33 G5
Tundergarth D & G.........155 L6
Tunley BaNES...................39 G8
Tunstall C Stke.................99 K3
Tunstall E R Yk................127 H4
Tunstall Kent.....................34 B3
Tunstall Lancs.................130 B5
Tunstall N York................140 F7
Tunstall Norfk....................93 J2
Tunstall Staffs...................99 H6
Tunstall Suffk....................79 H4
Tunstall Sundld...............151 J4
Tunstead Derbys.............114 C6
Tunstead Norfk...............107 G7
Tunstead Milton
Derbys.......................114 B5
Turgis Green Hants.........42 B8
Turkdean Gloucs..............56 C4
Tur Langton Leics...........87 K5
Turleigh Wilts....................39 J7
Turnastone Herefs..........69 G7
Turnberry S Ayrs............152 E2
Turnditch Derbys............100 F3
Turner's Hill W Susx.......32 C6
Turnhouse C Edin..........177 G4
Turnworth Dorset............14 C2

Turriff Abers...................216 D4
Turton Bottoms
Bl w D.........................121 L7
Turves Cambs...................89 L4
Turvey Bed........................74 D4
Turville Bucks....................42 C3
Turweston Bucks..............73 H6
Tushielaw Inn Border 166 D5
Tutbury Staffs.................100 E6
Tutshill Gloucs.................38 D2
Tuttington Norfk.............106 F6
Tuxford Notts...................116 C7
Twatt Ork.........................234 b5
Twatt Shet........................235 c5
Twechar E Duns...............175 J3
Tweedbank Border.........167 H3
Tweedmouth
Nthumb......................179 K7
Tweedsmuir Border........165 L4
Twelveheads Cnwll...........3 K3
Twemlow Green
Ches E........................113 H7
Twenty Lincs....................103 J7
Twerton BaNES.................39 G7
Twickenham Gt Lon.........44 D5
Twigworth Gloucs............55 J4
Twineham W Susx............19 H2
Twinstead Essex..............77 J6
Twitchen Devon................24 C5
Two Dales Derbys..........114 F8
Two Gates Staffs.............86 B4
Twycross Leics.................86 D3
Twycross Zoo Leics........86 C3
Twyford Bucks..................58 A3
Twyford Hants..................29 J6
Twyford Leics....................87 K2
Twyford Norfk.................106 B7
Twyford Wokham.............42 C5
Twynholm D & G.............146 B4
Twyning Green
Gloucs.........................70 F6
Twynllanan Carmth..........51 L2
Twywell Nhants.................88 D7
Tyberton Herefs................69 H6
Tycroes Carmth................51 H4
Tycrwyn Powys.................97 H8
Tydd Gote Lincs..............104 D8
Tydd St Giles Cambs.......90 B1
Tydd St Mary Lincs.........104 C8
Tye Green Essex..............76 E7
Tyldesley Wigan.............113 G2
Tyler Hill Kent...................34 F3
Tylorstown Rhondd..........36 F2
Ty-nant Conwy..................96 F4
Tyndrum Stirlg................183 K2
Ty'n-dwr Denbgs..............97 K4
Tynemouth N Tyne..........151 J2
Tynemouth
Crematorium
N Tyne.......................151 J2
Tyninghame E Loth........178 D3
Tynron D & G...................154 E4
Tynygraig Cerdgn............66 F1
Ty'n-y-Groes Conwy......109 L7
Tyn-y-nant Rhondd..........37 G4
Tyringham M Keyn...........74 C5
Tythegston Brdgnd.........36 D5
Tytherington Ches E.......113 K6
Tytherington S Glos........38 F3
Tytherington Wilts...........27 K3
Tytherleigh Devon...........13 H2
Tytherton Lucas Wilts.....39 L5
Tywardreath Cnwll............5 H5
Tywyn Gwynd....................80 D4

U

Ubbeston Green
Suffk...........................79 G1
Ubley BaNES.....................38 D8
Uckfield E Susx................19 M2
Uckinghall Worcs.............70 F6
Uckington Gloucs.............55 K3
Uddingston S Lans.........175 J6
Uddington S Lans..........165 G3

Udimore E Susx 21 H2
Udny Green Abers.......207 G1
Udny Station Abers 207 G1
Uffculme Devon 25 G8
Uffington Lincs.............88 F3
Uffington Oxon 40 F3
Uffington Shrops 83 K2
Ufford C Pete...............89 G3
Ufford Suffk 79 G4
Ufton Warwks 72 E3
Ufton Nervet W Berk ...41 M6
Ugadale Ag & B.........161 K4
Ugborough Devon 7 G5
Uggeshall Suffk 93 J7
Ugglebarnby N York ...143 H5
Ughill Sheff................114 E4
Ugley Essex 60 E3
Ugley Green Essex 60 E3
Ugthorpe N York 143 G5
Uibhist A Deas W Isls...233 c8
Uibhist A Tuath W Isls .233 b6
Uig Ag & B................188 F5
Uig Highld 208 C4
Uig Highld 208 F2
Uig W Isls 232 d2
Uigshader Highld 209 G5
Uisken Ag & B 180 E4
Ulbster Highld 231 K7
Ulceby Lincs 118 F6
Ulceby N Linc 126 D7
Ulceby Skitter N Linc .126 E7
Ulcombe Kent..............33 L4
Uldale Cumb 147 M7
Uley Gloucs.................55 H7
Ulgham Nthumb 159 G4
Ullapool Highld 220 E3
Ullenhall Warwks 71 K2
Ulleskelf N York 124 D3
Ullesthorpe Leics 87 G6
Ulley Rothm 115 J4
Ullingswick Herefs 69 L4
Ullinish Lodge Hotel
    Highld 208 E6
Ullock Cumb 136 E3
Ullswater Cumb 138 B3
Ullswater Steamers
    Cumb 137 L4
Ulpha Cumb 128 E2
Ulrome E R Yk 135 J7
Ulsta Shet 235 d3
Ulva Ag & B...............189 K7
Ulverston Cumb..........129 G4
Ulwell Dorset 15 J6
Ulzieside D & G 164 F7
Umberleigh Devon........23 J6
Unapool Highld...........224 F2
Underbarrow Cumb......129 K2
Under Burnmouth
    Border 156 E5
Undercliffe C Brad.......123 J4
Underdale Shrops 83 K2
Under River Kent 32 F3
Underwood Notts.........101 J3
Undy Mons 38 C3
Union Mills IoM 237 c5
Unst Shet 235 d1
Unstone Derbys 115 G6
Upavon Wilts................28 C1
Upchurch Kent 46 D6
Upcott Devon 24 B5
Up Exe Devon 12 B2
Upgate Norfk 106 D8
Uphall Dorset 14 B2
Uphall W Loth 176 E4
Upham Devon 11 K3
Upham Hants 29 K7
Uphampton Herefs 69 H2
Uphampton Worcs 70 E2
Uphill N Som................37 L8
Up Holland Lancs 112 D1
Uplawmoor E Rens 174 E7
Upleadon Gloucs 55 H3
Upleatham R & Cl........142 D4
Uploders Dorset 13 L4
Uplowman Devon 24 F7
Uplyme Devon 13 H4

Up Marden W Susx........30 D8
Upminster Gt Lon 45 K3
Up Mudford Somset 26 E7
Up Nately Hants 30 B2
Upottery Devon 12 F2
Upper Affcot Shrops.....83 J6
Upper Ardchronie
    Highld 222 E4
Upper Arley Worcs.......84 D7
Upper Basildon
    W Berk 41 L5
Upper Beeding
    W Susx 19 G4
Upper Benefield
    Nhants 88 E5
Upper Bentley Worcs 71 H2
Upper Bighouse
    Highld 230 C4
Upper Boddington
    Nhants 72 F4
Upper Brailes Warwks ...72 C6
Upper Breakish
    Highld 199 L2
Upper Broadheath
    Worcs 70 E4
Upper Broughton
    Notts 102 B7
Upper Bucklebury
    W Berk 41 K6
Upper Burgate Hants ...28 D7
Upperby Cumb 148 D4
Upper Caldecote
    C Beds 75 H5
Upper Chapel Powys 67 L6
Upper Chicksgrove
    Wilts 27 L5
Upper Chute Wilts 28 F2
Upper Clapton Gt Lon ...45 G3
Upper Clatford Hants ...29 G3
Upper Cound Shrops 83 K3
Upper Cumberworth
    Kirk 123 J8
Upper Dallachy
    Moray 215 H2
Upper Deal Kent 35 K4
Upper Dean Bed 74 F2
Upper Denby Kirk 114 E1
Upper Dicker E Susx 20 B4
Upper Dounreay
    Highld 230 E3
Upper Dovercourt
    Essex 62 F2
Upper Drumbane
    Stirlg 184 E6
Upper Dunsforth
    N York 133 G6
Upper Eashing Surrey ...30 F3
Upper Eathie Highld 213 J2
Upper Egleton Herefs ...70 B5
Upper Elkstone Staffs ..100 B2
Upper Ellastone
    Staffs 100 C4
Upper Farringdon
    Hants 30 B4
Upper Framilode
    Gloucs 55 H6
Upper Froyle Hants 30 C3
Upperglen Highld 208 E4
Upper Godney
    Somset 26 C3
Upper Gravenhurst
    C Beds 75 G7
Upper Green W Berk 41 G7
Upper Grove
    Common Herefs 54 E3
Upper Hale Surrey 30 D2
Upper Halliford
    Surrey 43 H6
Upper Hambleton
    Rutlnd 88 C3
Upper Harbledown
    Kent 34 F3
Upper Hartfield
    E Susx 32 E6
Upper Hatherley
    Gloucs 55 L4

Upper Heaton Kirk 123 H6
Upper Helmsley
    N York 133 L7
Upper Hergest Herefs ...68 F4
Upper Heyford
    Nhants 73 J3
Upper Heyford Oxon 57 J3
Upper Hill Herefs 69 J4
Upper Hopton Kirk 123 J6
Upper Hulme Staffs 100 A1
Upper Inglesham
    Swindn 40 D2
Upper Killay Swans 51 H6
Upper Kinchrackine
    Ag & B 183 G2
Upper Lambourn
    W Berk 40 F4
Upper Landywood
    Staffs 85 H3
Upper Langford
    N Som 38 C7
Upper Langwith
    Derbys 115 K7
Upper Largo Fife........187 G6
Upper Leigh Staffs 100 A5
Upper Lochton Abers ..206 D6
Upper Longdon
    Staffs 85 J2
Upper & Lower
    Stondon C Beds 75 H7
Upper Lybster Highld ..231 J7
Upper Lydbrook
    Gloucs 54 E5
Upper Lye Herefs 69 H2
Uppermill Oldham 113 M1
Upper Milton Worcs.....84 E8
Upper Minety Wilts 40 A3
Upper Mulben Moray ..215 H4
Upper Netchwood
    Shrops 83 L5
Upper Nobut Staffs 100 B5
Upper Norwood
    W Susx 18 C3
Upper Poppleton
    C York 133 H8
Upper Ratley Hants 28 F6
Upper Rissington
    Gloucs 56 D4
Upper Rochford
    Worcs 70 B2
Upper Ruscoe D & G ...145 L3
Upper Sapey Herefs.....70 C2
Upper Seagry Wilts 39 L4
Upper Shelton C Beds ..74 E5
Upper Sheringham
    Norfk 106 D4
Upper Skelmorlie
    N Ayrs 173 L5
Upper Slaughter
    Gloucs 56 D4
Upper Soudley Gloucs ...54 F6
Upper Standen Kent 35 H6
Upper Stoke Norfk 92 F3
Upper Stowe Nhants 73 J3
Upper Street Hants 28 D7
Upper Street Norfk 93 H1
Upper Street Norfk 107 G8
Upper Street Suffk 77 H4
Upper Street Suffk 78 D4
Upper Sundon C Beds ..59 H3
Upper Swell Gloucs 56 D3
Upper Tasburgh
    Norfk 92 E4
Upper Tean Staffs 100 A5
Upperthong Kirk 123 H8
Upperton W Susx 30 F6
Upper Town Herefs 69 L5
Uppertown Highld 231 L1
Upper Town N Som 38 D7
Upper Town Suffk 77 K2
Upper Tumble
    Carmth 51 G3
Upper Tysoe Warwks....72 D5
Upper Victoria Angus...187 J1
Upper Wardington
    Oxon 72 F5

Upper Welland Worcs...70 D6
Upper Wellingham
    E Susx 19 L3
Upper Weybread
    Suffk 92 F7
Upper Wield Hants 29 L4
Upper Winchendon
    Bucks 58 C5
Upper Woodford
    Wilts 28 C4
Upper Wraxall Wilts 39 J5
Uppingham Rutlnd.......88 C4
Uppington Shrops........83 L2
Upsall N York 133 G3
Upsettlington
    Border 168 C1
Upshire Essex 60 C7
Up Somborne Hants 29 H5
Upstreet Kent 35 G3
Upton Bucks................58 C5
Upton C Pete 89 G4
Upton Cambs 89 H7
Upton Ches W 112 B7
Upton Cnwll 5 L2
Upton Devon 7 G7
Upton Devon 12 E2
Upton Dorset 14 E5
Upton Dorset 15 J4
Upton Halton 112 C4
Upton Hants 29 G1
Upton Hants 29 G7
Upton Leics 86 D4
Upton Lincs 116 E4
Upton Norfk 93 H2
Upton Notts 102 B2
Upton Notts 116 C6
Upton Oxon 41 K3
Upton Slough 43 G5
Upton Somset 24 F5
Upton Somset 26 C6
Upton Wakefd 124 D7
Upton Wirral 111 J4
Upton Bishop
    Herefs 54 F3
Upton Cheyney
    S Glos 39 G6
Upton Cressett
    Shrops 84 B5
Upton Grey Hants 30 B2
Upton Hellions Devon ...11 J4
Upton Lovell Wilts 27 L4
Upton Magna Shrops 83 K2
Upton Noble Somset 27 G4
Upton Pyne Devon 11 L5
Upton St Leonards
    Gloucs 55 K5
Upton Scudamore
    Wilts 27 K2
Upton Snodsbury
    Worcs 71 G4
Upton-upon-Severn
    Worcs 70 F6
Upton Warren Worcs.....71 G2
Upwaltham W Susx.......18 C3
Upwell Norfk 90 C3
Upwood Cambs 89 J6
Urchfont Wilts 40 B8
Urmston Traffd 113 H3
Urquhart Moray 215 G2
Urquhart Castle
    Highld 212 E8
Urra N York 142 C6
Urray Highld 212 D4
Usan Angus 197 H5
Ushaw Moor Dur 151 G6
Usk Mons 54 B7
Usselby Lincs 117 H3
Usworth Sundld 151 H4
Utkinton Ches W 112 D7
Utley C Brad 122 F3
Uton Devon 11 J5
Utterby Lincs 118 D3
Uttoxeter Staffs 100 C5
Uxbridge Gt Lon 43 H4
Uyeasound Shet 235 d2
Uzmaston Pembks 49 G5

V

Vale Guern 236 d2
Vale of Glamorgan
 Crematorium
  V Glam 37 H6
Valley IoA 108 C5
Valtos Highld 209 H2
Valtos W Isls 232 d2
Vange Essex 46 B3
Vatsetter Shet 235 d3
Vatten Highld 208 D5
Vaynor Myr Td 53 G6
Veensgarth Shet 235 c6
Velindre Powys 68 D7
Venngreen Devon 9 K3
Venn Ottery Devon 12 D4
Ventnor IoW 17 G6
Venton Devon 6 E4
Vernham Dean Hants 29 G1
Vernham Street
 Hants 41 G8
Verwood Dorset 15 K2
Veryan Cnwll 4 E7
Vickerstown Cumb 128 E5
Victoria Cnwll 4 F4
Vidlin Shet 235 d4
Viewfield Moray 215 G2
Viewpark N Lans 175 J6
Vigo Kent 45 M7
Village de Putron
 Guern 236 d3
Vines Cross E Susx 20 C3
Vinters Park
 Crematorium
  Kent 33 K2
Virginia Water Surrey 43 G6
Virginstow Devon 9 K6
Vobster Somset 27 G2
Voe Shet 235 C4
Vowchurch Herefs 69 G7

W

Waberthwaite Cumb 128 D2
Wackerfield Dur 140 E3
Wacton Norfk 92 E5
Wadborough Worcs 70 F5
Waddesdon Bucks 58 C5
Waddesdon Manor
 Bucks 58 B5
Waddeton Devon 7 K4
Waddingham Lincs 117 G3
Waddington Lancs 121 L2
Waddington Lincs 116 F8
Wadebridge Cnwll 4 F2
Wadeford Somset 13 H1
Wadenhoe Nhants 88 E6
Wadesmill Herts 60 B4
Wadhurst E Susx 33 H6
Wadshelf Derbys 114 F7
Wadworth Donc 115 K3
Wainfleet All Saints
 Lincs 104 D2
Wainfleet St Mary
 Lincs 104 D2
Wainhouse Corner
 Cnwll 9 G5
Wainscott Medway 46 C6
Wainstalls Calder 122 F5
Waitby Cumb 139 H5
Waithe Lincs 118 C2
Wakefield Wakefd 123 L6
Wakefield
 Crematorium
  Wakefd 123 L7
Wakehurst Place
 W Susx 32 C6
Wakerley Nhants 88 D4
Wakes Colne Essex 61 L3
Walberswick Suffk 93 K8
Walberton W Susx 18 C4
Walbutt D & G 146 D2
Walcombe Somset 26 D3

Walcot Lincs 103 H5
Walcot Shrops 83 L2
Walcot Swindn 40 D4
Walcote Leics 87 H6
Walcot Green Norfk 92 D7
Walcott Lincs 103 J2
Walcott Norfk 107 H6
Walden Stubbs
 N York 124 E6
Walderslade Medway 46 C7
Walderton W Susx 17 L1
Walditch Dorset 13 L4
Waldridge Dur 151 G5
Waldringfield Suffk 79 G5
Waldron E Susx 20 B2
Wales Rothm 115 J5
Wales Somset 26 E6
Walesby Lincs 117 J3
Walesby Notts 116 B7
Wales Millennium
 Centre Cardif 37 J5
Walford Herefs 54 E4
Walford Herefs 83 H8
Walford Heath
 Shrops 98 C8
Walgherton Ches E 99 G3
Walgrave Nhants 74 B1
Walkden Salfd 113 G2
Walker N u Ty 151 H3
Walkerburn Border 166 E3
Walkeringham Notts 116 C3
Walkerith Lincs 116 C3
Walkern Herts 59 M3
Walkerton Fife 186 D6
Walkford Dorset 16 B4
Walkhampton Devon 6 D2
Walkington E R Yk 126 B3
Walkley Sheff 115 G4
Walk Mill Lancs 122 C5
Walkwood Worcs 71 J2
Wall Nthumb 150 A2
Wall Staffs 85 K3
Wallacetown S Ayrs 153 G2
Wallacetown S Ayrs 163 J5
Wallands Park
 E Susx 19 L4
Wallasey Wirral 111 J3
Wallingford Oxon 41 L3
Wallington Gt Lon 44 F6
Wallington Hants 17 H2
Wallington Herts 75 K7
Wallisdown Poole 15 K4
Walls Shet 235 b5
Wallsend N Tyne 151 H2
Wallyford E Loth 177 K4
Walmer Kent 35 K5
Walmer Bridge Lancs 121 G5
Walmley Birm 85 K5
Walpole Suffk 93 H8
Walpole Cross Keys
 Norfk 104 E8
Walpole Highway
 Norfk 90 D2
Walpole St Andrew
 Norfk 104 D8
Walpole St Peter
 Norfk 90 C1
Walsall Wsall 85 H4
Walsden Calder 122 D6
Walsgrave on Sowe
 Covtry 86 E7
Walsham le Willows
 Suffk 78 B1
Walshford N York 132 F8
Walsoken Norfk 90 C2
Walston S Lans 165 K1
Walsworth Herts 59 K3
Walter's Ash Bucks 42 D2
Waltham Kent 34 E5
Waltham NE Lin 118 C2
Waltham Abbey
 Essex 60 C7
Waltham Chase Hants 29 K7
Waltham Cross Herts 60 B7
Waltham on the
 Wolds Leics 102 D7

Waltham St
 Lawrence W & M 42 D5
Walthamstow Gt Lon 45 G3
Walton Cumb 148 F3
Walton Derbys 115 G7
Walton Leeds 124 C2
Walton Leics 87 H6
Walton M Keyn 74 C7
Walton Powys 68 F3
Walton Somset 26 C4
Walton Suffk 79 G7
Walton W Susx 17 M2
Walton Wakefd 123 L6
Walton Wrekin 98 E8
Walton Cardiff
 Gloucs 55 K2
Walton East Pembks 49 H3
Walton-in-Gordano
 N Som 38 B5
Walton Lea
 Crematorium
  Warrtn 112 E4
Walton-le-Dale Lancs 121 H5
Walton-on-Thames
 Surrey 43 J6
Walton-on-the-Hill
 Staffs 99 L7
Walton on the Hill
 Surrey 31 L1
Walton on the Naze
 Essex 62 F4
Walton on the Wolds
 Leics 101 L8
Walton-on-Trent
 Derbys 100 E8
Walton Park N Som 38 B6
Walton West Pembks 48 E5
Waltonwrays
 Crematorium
  N York 122 E1
Walworth Darltn 141 G4
Walworth Gt Lon 45 G4
Walwyn's Castle
 Pembks 48 E5
Wambrook Somset 13 H2
Wanborough Surrey 30 F2
Wanborough Swindn 40 E4
Wandsworth Gt Lon 44 E5
Wangford Suffk 93 K7
Wanlip Leics 87 H2
Wanlockhead D & G 165 G6
Wannock E Susx 20 C5
Wansford C Pete 88 F4
Wansford E R Yk 135 G7
Wanshurst Green
 Kent 33 K4
Wanstead Gt Lon 45 H3
Wanstrow Somset 27 G3
Wanswell Gloucs 55 G7
Wantage Oxon 41 H3
Wapenbury Warwks 72 E2
Wappenham Nhants 73 J3
Warbleton E Susx 20 C3
Warborough Oxon 41 L2
Warboys Cambs 89 K7
Warbreck Bpool 120 D3
Warbstow Cnwll 9 G6
Warburton Traffd 113 G4
Warcop Cumb 139 H4
Warden Nthumb 150 A2
Wardington Oxon 72 F5
Wardle Ches E 98 E2
Wardle Rochdl 122 D6
Wardley Gatesd 151 H3
Wardley Rutlnd 88 B4
Wardlow Derbys 114 D6
Wardy Hill Cambs 90 C6
Ware Herts 60 B5
Wareham Dorset 15 H5
Warehorne Kent 34 D7
Warenford Nthumb 169 H4
Wareside Herts 60 C5
Waresley Cambs 75 J4
Warfield Br For 42 E6
Warfleet Devon 7 K6
Wargrave Wokham 42 C5

Warham All Saints
 Norfk 105 M4
Warham St Mary
 Norfk 105 M4
Wark Nthumb 157 L6
Wark Nthumb 168 C2
Warkleigh Devon 23 K6
Warkton Nhants 88 C7
Warkworth Nhants 72 F6
Warkworth Nthumb 159 G2
Warlaby N York 132 E2
Warleggan Cnwll 5 J3
Warley Town Calder 122 F5
Warlingham Surrey 32 C2
Warmfield Wakefd 124 B6
Warmingham Ches E 99 G1
Warmington Nhants 88 F5
Warmington Warwks 72 E5
Warminster Wilts 27 K3
Warmley S Glos 38 F5
Warmsworth Donc 115 K2
Warmwell Dorset 14 E5
Warner Bros Studio
 Tour Herts 59 H7
Warnford Hants 29 L6
Warnham W Susx 31 J5
Warningcamp W Susx 18 D4
Warninglid W Susx 31 L6
Warren Ches E 113 K7
Warren Pembks 48 F7
Warrenhill S Lans 165 J2
Warren Row W & M 42 D4
Warren Street Kent 34 C4
Warrington M Keyn 74 C4
Warrington Warrtn 112 E4
Warriston C Edin 177 H4
Warriston
 Crematorium
  C Edin 177 H3
Warsash Hants 16 F2
Warslow Staffs 100 C2
Warter E R Yk 125 K1
Warthermaske N York 132 C4
Warthill N York 133 K7
Wartling E Susx 20 D4
Wartnaby Leics 102 B7
Warton Lancs 120 E5
Warton Lancs 129 K5
Warton Warwks 86 C3
Warwick Warwks 72 C2
Warwick Bridge
 Cumb 148 E4
Warwick Castle
 Warwks 72 C2
Warwick Services
 Warwks 72 D3
Wasbister Ork 234 c4
Wasdale Head Cumb 137 G5
Washaway Cnwll 5 G2
Washbourne Devon 7 J5
Washbrook Suffk 78 D6
Washfield Devon 11 L2
Washford Somset 25 G3
Washford Pyne
 Devon 11 J3
Washingborough
 Lincs 117 G7
Washington Sundld 151 H4
Washington W Susx 18 F3
Washington Services
 Gatesd 151 G4
Wasperton Warwks 72 C3
Wass N York 133 H4
Watchet Somset 25 G3
Watchfield Oxon 40 E3
Watchgate Cumb 138 D7
Water Devon 11 H8
Waterbeach Cambs 76 C2
Waterbeach W Susx 18 B4
Waterbeck D & G 155 M6
Water End E R Yk 125 J3
Waterfall Staffs 100 B3
Waterfoot E Rens 175 G7
Waterford Herts 60 A5
Waterheads Border 177 H7
Waterhouses Staffs 100 B3

Wateringbury Kent........33 H3
Waterloo Highld 199 K2
Waterloo N Lans.........175 L7
Waterloo P & K.............195 G8
Waterloo Pembks..........49 G6
Waterloo Sefton............111 K2
Waterlooville Hants......17 J1
Watermillock Cumb.......138 C3
Water Newton
 Cambs 89 G4
Water Orton Warwks....85 L5
Waterperry Oxon...........57 L6
Waterrow Somset..........25 G6
Watersfield W Susx......18 D3
Waterside Bl w D..........121 K5
Waterside E Ayrs.........163 K7
Waterside E Ayrs.........163 L2
Waterside E Duns........175 J4
Waterstein Highld.........208 B5
Waterstock Oxon...........57 M6
Waterston Pembks........48 F6
Water Stratford
 Bucks.............................73 J7
Waters Upton Wrekin....98 F8
Watford Herts.................43 J2
Watford Nhants............73 H2
Watford Gap
 Services Nhants.............73 H2
Wath N York..................132 B6
Wath N York..................132 E4
Wath upon Dearne
 Rothm...........................115 H2
Watlington Norfk...........90 E2
Watlington Oxon............42 B2
Watten Highld................231 J5
Wattisfield Suffk..........92 B8
Wattisham Suffk...........78 B4
Watton Dorset...............13 L4
Watton E R Yk..............126 C1
Watton Norfk.................91 K4
Watton-at-Stone
 Herts.............................60 A4
Wattston N Lans..........175 L4
Wattsville Caerph...........37 J3
Waulkmill Abers...........206 C6
Waunarlwydd Swans.....51 H6
Waunfawr Cerdgn...........80 E6
Waunfawr Gwynd............95 J2
Wavendon M Keyn..........74 C6
Waverbridge Cumb........147 L5
Waverton Ches W.........112 C8
Waverton Cumb............147 L5
Wawne E R Yk..............126 D3
Waxham Norfk...............107 J7
Wayford Somset............13 K2
Waytown Dorset............13 L3
Way Village Devon..........11 K3
Weacombe Somset.........25 H4
Weald Oxon....................56 F7
Wealdstone Gt Lon.........44 D3
Weardley Leeds............123 K2
Weare Somset................26 B2
Weare Giffard Devon.....23 G6
Wearhead Dur...............149 L6
Wearne Somset..............26 B5
Wear Valley
 Crematorium Dur........141 G2
Weasenham All
 Saints Norfk...............105 K7
Weasenham St Peter
 Norfk...........................105 K7
Weaste Salfd................113 J2
Weaverham Ches W.....112 E6
Weaverthorpe N York...134 E5
Webheath Worcs...........71 H2
Wedderlairs Abers........216 F7
Weddington Warwks......86 D5
Wedhampton Wilts........40 B8
Wedmore Somset..........26 C2
Wednesbury Sandw.......85 H4
Wednesfield Wolves......85 G4
Weedon Bucks...............58 D4
Weedon Nhants.............73 J3
Weedon Lois Nhants......73 H5
Weeford Staffs..............85 K3
Weeke Hants.................29 J5

Weekley Nhants............88 C7
Week St Mary Cnwll........9 H5
Weel E R Yk..................126 D3
Weeley Essex................62 D4
Weeley Crematorium
 Essex...........................62 D4
Weeley Heath Essex......62 D4
Weem P & K.................194 D6
Weethley Warwks..........71 J4
Weeting Norfk................91 H5
Weeton E R Yk..............127 H6
Weeton Lancs................120 E4
Weeton N York..............123 K2
Weetwood Leeds..........123 K3
Weir Lancs....................122 C5
Weir Quay Devon.............6 C3
Weisdale Shet..............235 C5
Welborne Norfk..............92 C2
Welbourn Lincs.............102 F2
Welburn N York.............133 L6
Welbury N York.............141 J6
Welby Lincs..................102 F5
Welcombe Devon...........22 C7
Welford Nhants.............87 J7
Welford W Berk.............41 H5
Welford-on-Avon
 Warwks.........................71 K4
Welham Leics................87 L5
Welham Notts................116 B5
Welham Green Herts.....59 L6
Well Hants.....................30 C3
Well Lincs....................118 F6
Well N York..................132 D3
Welland Worcs...............70 E6
Wellbank Angus...........196 D8
Wellesbourne
 Warwks.........................72 C4
Well Head Herts.............59 K3
Welling Gt Lon...............45 J5
Wellingborough
 Nhants..........................74 C2
Wellingham Norfk.........105 L7
Wellingore Lincs...........103 G3
Wellington Cumb..........136 F6
Wellington Herefs..........69 K5
Wellington Somset.........25 H7
Wellington Wrekin.........84 B2
Wellington Heath
 Herefs...........................70 C6
Wellow BaNES...............39 H8
Wellow IoW....................16 E5
Wellow Notts.................116 A7
Wells Somset.................26 D3
Wells-next-the-sea
 Norfk...........................105 L4
Wellstye Green Essex....61 G4
Welltree P & K..............185 K3
Wellwood Fife...............176 E2
Welney Norfk..................90 D5
Welshampton Shrops....98 C5
Welsh Frankton
 Shrops..........................98 A6
Welsh Newton Herefs....54 D4
Welshpool Powys..........82 E3
Welsh St Donats
 V Glam..........................36 F5
Welton Cumb................148 C6
Welton E R Yk..............126 B5
Welton Lincs.................117 G5
Welton Nhants...............73 H2
Welton le Marsh
 Lincs............................119 G7
Welton le Wold Lincs....118 C4
Welwick E R Yk............127 H6
Welwyn Herts.................59 L5
Welwyn Garden City
 Herts.............................59 L5
Wem Shrops..................98 D6
Wembdon Somset..........25 L4
Wembley Gt Lon............44 D3
Wembury Devon...............6 D6
Wembworthy Devon.......10 F3
Wemyss Bay Inver.......173 L4
Wendens Ambo Essex...76 D7
Wendlebury Oxon...........57 K4
Wendling Norfk..............91 L2

Wendover Bucks............58 E6
Wendover Woods
 Bucks............................58 E6
Wendron Cnwll................3 H5
Wendron Mining
 District Cnwll..................3 J5
Wendy Cambs................75 K5
Wenhaston Suffk...........93 J7
Wennington Cambs........89 J7
Wennington Gt Lon........45 K4
Wennington Lancs........130 C5
Wensley Derbys............100 E1
Wensley N York............131 K2
Wentbridge Wakefd......124 D6
Wentnor Shrops............83 H5
Wentworth Cambs..........90 C7
Wentworth Rothm........115 G2
Wenvoe V Glam..............37 H6
Weobley Herefs.............69 H4
Wepham W Susx...........18 E4
Wereham Norfk..............90 F3
Werrington C Pete.........89 H3
Werrington Cnwll.............9 J7
Wervin Ches W.............112 B6
Wesham Lancs.............120 F4
Wessex Vale
 Crematorium
 Hants............................29 J7
Wessington Derbys......101 G2
West Acre Norfk.............91 H1
West Alvington
 Devon..............................7 G6
West Anstey Devon........24 D6
West Ashby Lincs.........118 C6
West Ashling W Susx.....17 M2
West Ashton Wilts.........27 K1
West Auckland Dur.......140 F3
West Ayton N York........134 F3
West Bagborough
 Somset.........................25 J5
West Bank Halton.........112 D5
West Barkwith Lincs.....117 K5
West Barnby N York.....143 G5
West Barns E Loth......178 E3
West Barsham Norfk....105 L5
West Bay Dorset...........13 L4
West Beckham Norfk....106 D5
West Bedfont Surrey.....43 H5
Westbere Kent...............35 G3
West Bergholt Essex......62 A3
West Berkshire
 Crematorium
 W Berk..........................41 K6
West Bexington
 Dorset...........................14 A5
West Bilney Norfk..........91 G1
West Blatchington
 Br & H............................19 J4
West Boldon S Tyne.....151 J3
Westborough Lincs.......102 D4
Westbourne Bmouth......15 K4
Westbourne W Susx.......17 L2
West Bowling C Brad...123 H4
West Bradenham
 Norfk............................91 K2
West Bradford Lancs....121 L2
West Bradley Somset.....26 E4
West Bretton Wakefd...123 K7
West Bridgford Notts....101 L5
West Bromwich
 Sandw...........................85 H5
West Bromwich
 Crematorium
 Sandw...........................85 H5
Westbrook Kent.............35 J2
Westbrook W Berk.........41 H6
West Buckland Devon....23 K5
West Buckland
 Somset.........................25 J7
West Burton N York......131 J3
Westbury Bucks.............73 J7
Westbury Shrops............83 G2
Westbury Wilts..............27 K2
Westbury Leigh Wilts.....27 K2
Westbury on Severn
 Gloucs..........................55 G5

Westbury-on-Trym
 Bristl.............................38 E5
Westbury-sub-
 Mendip Somset............26 D2
West Butterwick
 N Linc..........................116 D1
Westby Lancs................120 E4
West Byfleet Surrey.......43 H7
West Cairngaan D & G..144 D8
West Caister Norfk.........93 K2
West Calder W Loth......176 D5
West Camel Somset.......26 E6
West Chaldon Dorset.....14 E5
West Challow Oxon........41 G3
West Charleton
 Devon..............................7 H7
West Chiltington
 W Susx..........................18 E3
West Chinnock
 Somset.........................26 C8
West Clandon Surrey.....31 H2
West Cliffe Kent............35 J5
Westcliff-on-Sea
 Sthend...........................46 E3
West Coker Somset........26 D8
Westcombe Somset........27 G4
West Compton
 Somset.........................26 E3
West Compton
 Abbas Dorset...............14 B4
Westcote Gloucs............56 E4
Westcote Barton
 Oxon.............................57 H3
Westcott Bucks.............58 B5
Westcott Devon.............12 D2
Westcott Surrey............31 J2
West Cottingwith
 N York.........................125 G3
Westcourt Wilts.............40 E7
West Cowick E R Yk.....124 F6
West Cross Swans........51 H7
West Curthwaite
 Cumb...........................148 B5
Westdean E Susx..........20 B5
West Dean W Susx.......18 B3
West Dean Wilts............28 E6
West Deeping Lincs.......89 G2
West Derby Lpool.........111 L3
West Dereham Norfk......90 F4
West Down Devon..........23 H3
Westdowns Cnwll............8 E7
West Drayton Gt Lon.....43 H4
West Drayton Notts......116 B6
West Dunnet Highld.....231 J2
West Ella E R Yk..........126 C5
West End Bed...............74 E4
West End Hants.............29 J8
West End N Som...........38 C6
West End Norfk..............93 K2
West End Surrey............42 F7
West End Wilts..............27 M6
West End Green
 Hants............................42 A7
Westerdale Highld........231 G5
Westerdale N York........142 E6
Westerfield Suffk...........78 E5
Westergate W Susx.......18 C5
Westerham Kent............32 D3
Westerhope N u Ty.......150 F2
Westerland Devon............7 K4
Westerleigh S Glos.......39 G4
Westerleigh
 Crematorium
 S Glos...........................39 G5
Western Isles W Isls....232 d5
Wester Ochiltree
 W Loth.........................176 D4
Wester Pitkierie Fife....187 J6
Wester Ross Highld.....220 C2
Westerton of Rossie
 Angus..........................197 G5
Westerwick Shet..........235 c6
West Farleigh Kent........33 J3
West Farndon Nhants....73 G4
West Felton Shrops........97 M7
Westfield BaNES...........26 F2

Westfield Cumb 136 D2
Westfield E Susx.............21 G3
Westfield Highld............230 F3
Westfield N Lans.........175 J4
Westfield Norfk...............92 B2
Westfield W Loth 176 C4
Westfields of Rattray
P & K.....................195 J6
Westgate Dur 150 A7
Westgate N Linc 125 J8
Westgate on Sea
Kent...........................35 J2
West Grafton Wilts..........40 E7
West Green Hants 30 C1
West Grimstead Wilts 28 E6
West Grinstead
W Susx......................31 K6
West Haddlesey
N York......................124 E5
West Haddon Nhants 73 J1
West Hagbourne
Oxon 41 K3
West Hagley Worcs.........84 F7
Westhall Suffk................93 J7
West Hallam Derbys....101 H4
West Halton N Linc 125 L6
Westham Dorset 14 C6
Westham E Susx..............20 D5
West Ham Gt Lon..........45 H4
Westham Somset 26 B3
Westhampnett
W Susx......................18 B4
West Handley Derbys 115 H6
West Hanney Oxon 41 H2
West Hanningfield
Essex 61 H7
West Harnham Wilts....28 C5
West Harptree BaNES....38 E8
West Harting W Susx....30 C2
West Hatch Somset 25 L7
West Hatch Wilts...........27 L5
West Haven Angus.......187 J1
Westhay Somset 26 C3
West Heath Birm...........85 J7
West Helmsdale
Highld.....................227 H5
West Hendred Oxon 41 H3
West Hertfordshire
Crematorium
Herts 59 J7
West Heslerton
N York......................134 E4
West Hewish N Som 38 B7
Westhide Herefs.............69 L5
Westhill Abers...............206 F4
West Hill Devon 12 D4
West Hoathly W Susx....32 C6
West Holme Dorset 15 G5
Westhope Herefs 69 J4
Westhope Shrops...........83 J6
West Horndon Essex 45 M3
Westhorpe Lincs...........103 L6
Westhorpe Suffk............78 C2
West Horrington
Somset 26 E3
West Horsley Surrey 31 H2
West Hougham Kent......35 H6
Westhoughton
Bolton 112 F1
Westhouse N York........130 D5
Westhouses Derbys 101 H2
West Howe Bmouth 15 K4
Westhumble Surrey 31 K2
West Huntingtower
P & K......................185 M3
West Huntspill
Somset 25 L3
West Hythe Kent 34 F7
West Ilsley W Berk.........41 J4
West Itchenor W Susx....17 L3
West Kennett Wilts........40 C6
West Kilbride N Ayrs....173 L8
West Kingsdown
Kent...........................45 L7
West Kington Wilts........39 J5
West Kirby Wirral.......111 H4

West Knapton N York....134 D4
West Knighton
Dorset 14 D5
West Knoyle Wilts...........27 K5
Westlake Devon 6 F5
West Lambrook
Somset 26 B7
West Langdon Kent 35 J5
West Lavington
W Susx......................30 E7
West Lavington Wilts 28 A2
West Layton N York 140 E5
West Leake Notts..........101 K7
Westleigh Devon 23 G5
Westleigh Devon 25 G7
West Leigh Somset 25 H5
Westleton Suffk...............79 J2
West Lexham Norfk........91 J1
Westley Suffk.................77 J2
Westley Waterless
Cambs 76 E3
West Lilling N York 133 K6
Westlington Bucks..........58 C6
West Linton Border.......176 F7
Westlinton Cumb..........148 D3
West Littleton S Glos 39 H5
West Lockinge Oxon.......41 H3
West London
Crematorium
Gt Lon......................44 E4
West Lulworth Dorset....14 F6
West Lutton N York......134 E5
West Lydford Somset......26 E5
West Lyng Somset...........25 L5
West Lynn Norfk...........104 F7
West Malling Kent..........33 H2
West Malvern Worcs.......70 D5
West Marden W Susx......30 C8
West Markham Notts....116 B6
Westmarsh Kent.............35 H3
West Marsh NE Lin 127 G8
West Marton N York 122 D1
West Melbury Dorset......27 K7
West Meon Hants...........29 M6
West Mersea Essex 62 B5
Westmeston E Susx 19 K3
West Midland Safari
Park Worcs................84 E7
Westmill Herts..............60 B3
West Milton Dorset........13 L3
Westminster Gt Lon......44 F4
West Minster Kent.........46 E5
*Westminster Abbey
& Palace* Gt Lon 44 F4
West Molesey Surrey 43 J6
West Monkton
Somset 25 K5
West Moors Dorset 15 K2
West Morden Dorset 15 G4
West Morriston
Border 167 J2
West Mudford
Somset 26 E7
Westmuir Angus...........196 B5
West Ness N York 133 L4
Westnewton Cumb......147 K6
West Newton E R Yk....126 F3
West Newton Norfk......105 H6
West Newton Somset.....25 L5
West Norwood
Gt Lon......................44 F5
West Norwood
Crematorium
Gt Lon......................44 F5
Westoe S Tyne..............151 J2
West Ogwell Devon 7 J2
Weston BaNES...............39 G6
Weston Ches E...............99 G3
Weston Devon 12 E3
Weston Devon 12 F5
Weston Hants 30 B6
Weston Herts 59 L3
Weston Lincs.................103 M7
Weston N York 123 H2
Weston Nhants...............73 H5
Weston Notts.................116 C7

Weston Shrops 83 L5
Weston Shrops 97 L6
Weston Staffs.................99 L6
Weston W Berk 41 H5
Weston Beggard
Herefs 69 L6
Westonbirt Gloucs 39 J3
Weston by Welland
Nhants 87 L5
Weston Colville
Cambs 76 E4
Weston Corbett
Hants 30 B3
Weston Coyney
C Stke 99 L4
Weston Favell Nhants 73 L3
Weston Green Cambs.....76 F4
Weston Heath Shrops 84 D2
Westoning C Beds...........59 G2
Weston-in-Gordano
N Som 38 C5
Weston Jones Staffs 99 H7
Weston Longville
Norfk 92 D1
Weston Lullingfields
Shrops 98 B7
Weston Mill
Crematorium
C Plym 6 C4
Weston-on-the-
Green Oxon 57 K4
Weston Park Staffs 84 E2
Weston Patrick Hants 30 B3
Weston Rhyn Shrops.....97 L5
Weston-sub-Edge
Gloucs 71 K6
Weston-super-Mare
N Som 37 L7
Weston-super-Mare
Crematorium
N Som 38 A7
Weston Turville Bucks....58 D6
Weston-under-Lizard
Staffs 84 E2
Weston under
Penyard Herefs 54 F4
Weston-under-
Redcastle Shrops 98 E6
Weston under
Wetherley Warwks 72 D1
Weston Underwood
Derbys 100 F4
Weston Underwood
M Keyn 74 C4
Weston-upon-Trent
Derbys 101 H6
Westonzoyland
Somset 25 M4
West Orchard Dorset......27 J7
West Overton Wilts........40 C6
Westow N York 134 B6
West Park Abers 206 E5
West Parley Dorset.........15 K3
West Peckham Kent........33 H3
West Pelton Dur...........151 G4
West Pennard
Somset 26 D4
West Pentire Cnwll 4 B4
West Perry Cambs 75 G2
West Porlock Somset 24 D3
Westport Somset 26 B7
West Putford Devon..........9 K2
West Quantoxhead
Somset 25 H3
Westquarter Falk 176 B3
West Rainton Dur........151 H5
West Rasen Lincs.........117 H4
Westray Ork 234 c3
Westray Airport Ork 234 c3
West Raynham Norfk....105 L7
Westrigg W Loth..........176 B5
West Road
Crematorium
N u Ty 150 F2
Westrop Swindn 40 D2
West Rounton N York ...141 K6

West Row Suffk 90 F7
West Rudham Norfk....105 K6
West Runton Norfk.......106 E4
Westruther Border 178 D7
Westry Cambs.................90 B4
West Saltoun E Loth 178 B5
West Sandford Devon....11 J4
West Sandwick Shet....235 d3
West Scrafton N York...131 K3
West Stafford Dorset 14 D4
West Stockwith
Notts.......................116 C3
West Stoke W Susx........17 M2
West Stour Dorset...........27 H6
West Stourmouth
Kent...........................35 H3
West Stow Suffk.............77 J1
West Stowell Wilts..........40 C7
West Street Suffk............78 B1
West Suffolk
Crematorium
Suffk..........................77 J2
West Tanfield N York 132 D4
West Taphouse Cnwll 5 J3
West Tarbert Ag & B 172 E5
West Tarring W Susx 18 F5
West Thirston
Nthumb....................158 F3
West Thorney W Susx....17 L3
West Thorpe Notts 101 L7
West Thurrock Thurr 45 L4
West Tilbury Thurr.........46 A4
West Tisted Hants 29 M5
West Torrington Lincs ..117 J5
West Town Hants 17 K3
West Town N Som..........38 C6
West Tytherley Hants....28 F5
West Walton Norfk.........90 C2
West Walton
Highway Norfk..........90 C2
Westward Cumb..........148 B6
Westward Ho! Devon 23 G5
Westwell Kent 34 D5
Westwell Oxon 56 E6
Westwell Leacon
Kent...........................34 C5
West Wellow Hants........28 F7
West Wembury
Devon 6 D6
West Wemyss Fife 186 E7
Westwick Cambs............76 B2
West Wickham
Cambs 76 E5
West Wickham Gt Lon....45 G6
West Williamston
Pembks 49 H6
West Wiltshire
Crematorium
Wilts...........................39 K7
West Winch Norfk..........90 F1
West Winterslow
Wilts...........................28 E5
West Wittering
W Susx......................17 L3
West Witton N York 131 K2
Westwood Devon 12 C3
Westwood Kent 35 K2
Westwood Wilts 39 J8
West Woodburn
Nthumb....................157 M5
West Woodhay
W Berk......................41 H7
Westwoodside
N Linc 116 C2
West Worldham
Hants 30 C4
West Worthing
W Susx......................18 F5
West Wratting Cambs ...76 E4
Wetheral Cumb 148 E4
Wetherby Leeds 124 B2
Wetherby Services
N York......................124 C1
Wetherden Suffk............78 B3
Wetheringsett Suffk......78 D2
Wethersfield Essex 61 H2

Wetherup Street
Suff 78 D2
Wetley Rocks Staffs 99 L3
Wettenhall Ches E.............98 F1
Wetton Staffs..................100 C2
Wetwang E R Yk 134 E7
Wetwood Staffs................99 H5
Wexcombe Wilts 40 F8
Weybourne Norfk 106 D4
Weybourne Surrey 30 D2
Weybread Suffk.................92 F7
Weybread Street
Suff 92 F7
Weybridge Surrey 43 H7
Weycroft Devon 13 H3
Weydale Highld 231 H3
Weyhill Hants 28 F3
Weymouth Dorset 14 D6
Weymouth
Crematorium
Dorset 14 C6
Whaddon Bucks 74 B7
Whaddon Cambs 75 L5
Whaddon Gloucs 55 J5
Whaddon Wilts 28 D6
Whaddon Wilts 39 K7
Whaley Derbys 115 K7
Whaley Bridge
Derbys 114 A5
Whaley Thorns
Derbys 115 K7
Whaligoe Highld 231 K7
Whalley Lancs 121 L4
Whalsay Shet..................235 d4
Whalton Nthumb 158 E6
Whaplode Lincs 104 A7
Whaplode Drove
Lincs 89 K2
Wharf Warwks 72 E4
Wharfe N York 130 E5
Wharles Lancs 120 F4
Wharley End C Beds 74 D5
Wharncliffe Side
Sheff 114 F3
Wharram-le-Street
N York 134 D6
Wharton Herefs................69 K4
Whashton N York 140 E6
Whasset Cumb 129 L4
Whatcote Warwks 72 C5
Whateley Warwks 86 B4
Whatfield Suffk 78 B5
Whatley Somset 13 J2
Whatley Somset 27 G3
Whatlington E Susx 20 F3
Whatton Notts 102 C5
Whauphill D & G 145 J5
Wheal Peevor Cnwll 3 J3
Wheatacre Norfk 93 K5
Wheathampstead
Herts 59 K5
Wheatley Hants 30 C4
Wheatley Oxon 57 L6
Wheatley Hill Dur 151 J6
Wheatley Hills Donc 115 L1
Wheaton Aston Staffs 84 F2
Wheddon Cross
Somset 24 E4
Wheelock Ches E..............99 H2
Wheelton Lancs 121 J6
Wheldrake C York 125 G2
Whelford Gloucs 56 D7
Whelpley Hill Bucks 59 G6
Whempstead Herts 60 A4
Whenby N York 133 K5
Whepstead Suffk 77 J3
Wherstead Suffk 78 E6
Wherwell Hants 29 H3
Wheston Derbys 114 C6
Whetsted Kent 33 H4
Whetstone Leics 87 G4
Whicham Cumb 128 D3
Whichford Warwks 72 C7
Whickham Gatesd 150 F3
Whiddon Down
Devon 11 G6

Whigstreet Angus 196 D7
Whilton Nhants 73 J2
Whimple Devon 12 D3
Whimpwell Green
Norfk 107 H6
Whinburgh Norfk 92 B2
Whinnie Liggate
D & G 146 C4
Whinnyfold Abers 217 K7
Whippingham IoW 17 G4
Whipsnade C Beds 59 G4
Whipsnade Zoo ZSL
C Beds 59 G4
Whipton Devon 12 B4
Whisby Lincs 116 E7
Whissendine Rutlnd 88 B2
Whissonsett Norfk 105 L7
Whistlefield Ag & B........183 J8
Whistlefield Inn
Ag & B 183 G8
Whistley Green
Wokham 42 C5
Whiston Knows 112 C3
Whiston Nhants 74 B3
Whiston Rothm 115 H4
Whiston Staffs 84 F2
Whiston Staffs 100 B3
Whitbeck Cumb 128 D3
Whitbourne Herefs 70 D3
Whitburn S Tyne 151 J3
Whitburn W Loth 176 C5
Whitby N York 143 J5
Whitchester Border 178 F6
Whitchurch BaNES...........38 F6
Whitchurch Bucks 58 D4
Whitchurch Cardif 37 J4
Whitchurch Devon 6 D2
Whitchurch Hants 29 J2
Whitchurch Herefs 54 D4
Whitchurch Oxon 41 M5
Whitchurch Pembks 48 D3
Whitchurch Shrops 98 D4
Whitchurch
Canonicorum
Dorset 13 K4
Whitchurch Hill Oxon 41 M5
Whitcombe Dorset 14 D5
Whitcot Shrops 83 H5
Whitcott Keysett
Shrops 82 F6
Whiteacre Heath
Warwks 86 B5
White Ball Somset 25 H7
Whitebridge Highld 202 D3
Whitebrook Mons 54 D6
Whitecairns Abers 207 H2
Whitechapel Gt Lon 45 G4
White Chapel Lancs 121 H3
Whitecliffe Gloucs 54 E6
White Colne Essex...........61 L3
Whitecraig E Loth 177 K4
Whitecrook D & G 144 E4
White Cross Cnwll 3 H6
Whitecross Falk 176 C3
Whiteface Highld 222 F4
Whitefarland N Ayrs 161 L2
Whitefaulds S Ayrs 163 H7
Whitefield Bury 113 J1
Whitefield Somset 25 G5
Whiteford Abers 206 D1
Whitegate Ches W 112 F7
Whitehall Ork 234 d5
Whitehaven Cumb 136 D4
Whitehill and Bordon
Hants 30 C5
Whitehills Abers 216 C2
Whitehouse Abers 206 C3
Whitehouse Ag & B.........172 D6
Whitekirk E Loth 178 D3
White Lackington
Dorset 14 D3
Whitelackington
Somset 26 B7
White Ladies Aston
Worcs 71 G4
Whiteleaf Bucks 58 D6

Whiteley Hants 17 G1
Whiteley Bank IoW 17 G6
Whitemire Moray 214 B4
Whitemoor C Nott 101 K4
Whitemoor Cnwll 4 F4
Whiteness Shet 235 c6
White Notley Essex 61 J4
Whiteparish Wilts 28 E6
White Pit Lincs 118 E6
Whiterashes Abers 206 F2
White Roding Essex..........60 E5
Whiterow Highld 231 L5
Whiterow Moray 214 C3
Whiteshill Gloucs 55 J6
Whitesmith E Susx 20 B3
Whitestaunton
Somset 13 H1
Whitestone Cross
Devon 11 K6
White Waltham
W & M 42 D5
Whitewell Lancs 121 K2
Whitfield C Dund 187 G2
Whitfield Kent 35 J5
Whitfield Nhants 73 H6
Whitfield Nthumb 149 K4
Whitfield S Glos 38 F3
Whitford Devon 13 G4
Whitford Flints 111 G5
Whitgift E R Yk 125 J6
Whitgreave Staffs 99 K6
Whithorn D & G 145 J6
Whiting Bay N Ayrs 162 D4
Whitkirk Leeds 124 B4
Whitland Carmth...............49 L4
Whitlaw Border 167 G6
Whitletts S Ayrs 163 J5
Whitley N York 124 E6
Whitley Readg 42 B6
Whitley Sheff 115 G3
Whitley Wilts 39 K6
Whitley Bay N Tyne 159 J7
Whitley Bay
Crematorium
N Tyne 159 H7
Whitley Chapel
Nthumb 150 B4
Whitley Lower Kirk 123 J6
Whitminster Gloucs 55 H6
Whitmore Staffs 99 J4
Whitnage Devon 25 G7
Whitnash Warwks 72 D2
Whitney-on-Wye
Herefs 68 F5
Whitsbury Hants 28 C7
Whitsome Border 179 H7
Whitson Newpt 38 B4
Whitstable Kent 47 J6
Whitstone Cnwll 9 H5
Whittingham
Nthumb 168 F6
Whittingslow Shrops 83 H5
Whittington Derbys 115 G6
Whittington Gloucs 56 A4
Whittington Lancs 130 B4
Whittington Norfk 91 G4
Whittington Shrops 97 L6
Whittington Staffs 84 F6
Whittington Staffs 85 J2
Whittington Warwks 86 C4
Whittington Worcs 70 F4
Whittlebury Nhants 73 K5
Whittle-le-Woods
Lancs 121 H6
Whittlesey Cambs 89 J4
Whittlesford Cambs 76 C5
Whitton N Linc 125 L5
Whitton Nthumb 158 D3
Whitton Powys 68 F2
Whitton S on T 141 J3
Whitton Shrops 83 L8
Whittonstall Nthumb 150 D4
Whitway Hants 41 J8
Whitwell Derbys 115 K6
Whitwell Herts 59 K4
Whitwell IoW 17 G6

Whitwell N York 141 G7
Whitwell Rutlnd 88 D2
Whitwell-on-the-Hill
N York 133 L6
Whitwell Street
Norfk 106 D7
Whitwick Leics 86 E1
Whitworth Lancs 122 D6
Whixall Shrops 98 D5
Whixley N York 133 G7
Whorlton Dur 140 E4
Whyle Herefs 69 L3
Whyteleafe Surrey 32 C2
Wibsey C Brad 123 H4
Wibtoft Warwks 86 F6
Wichenford Worcs 70 D3
Wichling Kent 34 B4
Wick Bmouth 15 L4
Wick Highld 231 L5
Wick S Glos 39 G5
Wick V Glam 36 C4
Wick W Susx 18 D5
Wick Worcs 71 J4
Wicken Cambs 76 E1
Wicken Nhants 73 L6
Wicken Bonhunt
Essex 60 D2
Wickenby Lincs 117 H5
Wicken Green Village
Norfk 105 K6
Wickersley Rothm 115 J3
Wicker Street Green
Suffk 77 L6
Wickford Essex..................46 C2
Wickham Hants 17 H1
Wickham W Berk 41 H6
Wickham Bishops
Essex 61 K5
Wickhambreaux Kent 35 G3
Wickhambrook Suffk 77 H4
Wickhamford Worcs 71 J6
Wickham Green Suffk 78 D2
Wickham Market
Suffk 79 G4
Wickhampton Norfk 93 J3
Wickham St Paul
Essex 77 J7
Wickham Skeith Suffk 78 C2
Wickham Street Suffk 78 C1
Wick John o' Groats
Airport Highld 231 L5
Wicklewood Norfk 92 C3
Wickmere Norfk 106 E5
Wick St Lawrence
N Som 38 A7
Wicksteed Park
Nhants 88 C7
Wickwar S Glos 39 G3
Widdington Essex..............60 E2
Widdrington Nthumb 159 G3
Widdrington Station
Nthumb 159 G4
Widecombe in the
Moor Devon 7 G1
Widegates Cnwll 5 L4
Widemouth Bay
Cnwll 9 G4
Wide Open N Tyne 159 G7
Widford Essex....................61 H6
Widford Herts 60 C5
Widmer End Bucks 42 E2
Widmerpool Notts 101 M6
Widmore Gt Lon 45 H6
Widnes Halton 112 D5
Widnes Crematorium
Halton 112 D4
Widworthy Devon 13 G3
Wigan Wigan 112 E1
Wigan Crematorium
Wigan 112 E2
Wigborough Somset 26 C7
Wiggaton Devon 12 E4
Wiggenhall St
Germans Norfk 90 E2
Wiggenhall St Mary
Magdalen Norfk 90 E2

Wiggenhall St Mary
  the Virgin Norfk 90 E2
Wigginton C York 133 J7
Wigginton Herts............58 F6
Wigginton Oxon.............57 H2
Wigginton Staffs..........86 B3
Wigglesworth N York 130 F7
Wiggonby Cumb............148 B4
Wighill N York.............124 D2
Wighton Norfk 105 M4
Wightwick Wolves.........84 F4
Wigley Hants................29 G7
Wigmore Herefs............69 H2
Wigmore Medway 46 D6
Wigsley Notts 116 E7
Wigsthorpe Nhants 88 F6
Wigston Leics...............87 H4
Wigston Parva Leics 86 F5
Wigthorpe Notts...........115 L5
Wigtoft Lincs 103 L5
Wigton Cumb 148 A5
Wigtown D & G.............145 J4
Wike Leeds 123 L3
Wilbarston Nhants........88 B5
Wilberfoss E R Yk 125 H1
Wilburton Cambs............90 C7
Wilby Nhants................74 C2
Wilby Norfk 92 B5
Wilby Suffk 78 F1
Wilcot Wilts 40 C7
Wilcott Shrops 98 B8
Wildboarclough
  Ches E 113 M7
Wilden Bed...................75 G4
Wilden Worcs 84 E8
Wildmanbridge
  S Lans 175 L7
Wildmoor Worcs............85 G7
Wildsworth Lincs 116 D3
Wilford Hill
  Crematorium
  Notts 101 L5
Wilkesley Ches E...........98 F4
Wilkhaven Highld.........223 K4
Wilkieston W Loth 176 F5
Willand Devon...............12 D1
Willaston Ches E...........99 G3
Willaston Ches W 111 K6
Willen M Keyn...............74 C6
Willenhall Covtry...........86 D7
Willenhall Wsall............85 H4
Willerby E R Yk............126 C4
Willerby N York...........134 F4
Willersey Gloucs............71 K6
Willersley Herefs...........68 F5
Willesborough Kent 34 D6
Willesborough Lees
  Kent......................34 D6
Willesden Gt Lon 44 E3
Willesley Wilts..............39 J3
Willett Somset...............25 H5
Willey Shrops 84 C4
Willey Warwks 86 F6
Willey Green Surrey 30 F2
Williamscot Oxon...........72 F5
Willian Herts.................59 L2
Willingale Essex............60 F6
Willingdon E Susx..........20 C5
Willingham Cambs.........76 B1
Willingham by Stow
  Lincs 116 E6
Willington Bed...............75 G4
Willington Derbys.........100 F6
Willington Dur.............150 F7
Willington Kent.............33 K3
Willington Warwks 72 C6
Willington Quay
  N Tyne 151 H2
Willitoft E R Yk 125 H4
Williton Somset.............25 H4
Willoughby Lincs 119 G6
Willoughby Warwks 73 G2
Willoughby-on-the-
  Wolds Notts 101 M7
Willoughby
  Waterleys Leics 87 H5

Willoughton Lincs 116 F3
Willows Green Essex.......61 H4
Willtown Somset............26 B6
Wilmcote Warwks 71 L3
Wilmington Devon..........13 G3
Wilmington E Susx..........20 B5
Wilmington Kent............45 K5
Wilmslow Ches E..........113 J5
Wilpshire Lancs............121 K4
Wilsden C Brad 123 G3
Wilsford Lincs 103 G4
Wilsford Wilts 28 C4
Wilsford Wilts 40 C8
Wilshaw Kirk 123 G8
Wilsill N York...............132 B6
Wilson Leics.................101 H7
Wilsontown S Lans 176 C7
Wilstead Bed 74 F5
Wilsthorpe Lincs............88 F2
Wilstone Herts...............58 E5
Wilton Herefs 54 E3
Wilton N York..............134 D3
Wilton R & Cl 142 C4
Wilton Wilts 28 C5
Wilton Wilts 40 E7
Wilton Dean Border 167 G6
Wimbish Green Essex......76 E7
Wimbledon Gt Lon 44 E6
Wimblington Cambs........90 B5
Wimboldsley Ches W 113 G8
Wimborne Minster
  Dorset 15 J3
Wimborne St Giles
  Dorset 28 B8
Wimbotsham Norfk........90 E3
Wimpole Cambs.............75 L4
Wimpstone Warwks........72 B5
Wincanton Somset..........27 G5
Winchburgh W Loth 176 E4
Winchcombe Gloucs........56 A3
Winchelsea E Susx 21 H3
Winchester Hants 29 J5
Winchester Services
  Hants 29 K4
Winchet Hill Kent 33 J5
Winchfield Hants...........30 C1
Winchmore Hill Bucks 42 F2
Winchmore Hill
  Gt Lon 44 F2
Wincle Ches E 113 L7
Wincobank Sheff 115 G3
Windermere Cumb........137 L7
Windermere
  Steamboats &
  Museum Cumb........137 L7
Winderton Warwks.........72 D6
Windhill Highld............212 E5
Windlesham Surrey.........42 F7
Windmill Cnwll...............4 D2
Windmill Hill E Susx.......20 D4
Windmill Hill Somset......25 L7
Windrush Gloucs............56 D5
Windsole Abers 216 B3
Windsor W & M.............42 F5
Windsor Castle W & M....42 F5
Windsoredge Gloucs 55 J7
Windsor Green Suffk 77 K4
Windy Arbour
  Warwks 72 C1
Windygates Fife...........186 E7
Wineham W Susx...........31 L7
Winestead E R Yk.........127 G5
Winfarthing Norfk 92 D6
Winford IoW 17 G5
Winford N Som...............38 D7
Winforton Herefs...........68 F5
Winfrith Newburgh
  Dorset 14 F5
Wing Bucks 58 E4
Wing Rutlnd 88 C3
Wingate Dur 151 J7
Wingerworth Derbys......115 G7
Wingfield C Beds...........59 G3
Wingfield Suffk 92 F7
Wingfield Wilts 27 J1
Wingham Kent 35 H3

Wingrave Bucks 58 E4
Winkburn Notts 102 B2
Winkfield Br For 42 E6
Winkfield Row
  Br For 42 E6
Winkhill Staffs............100 B3
Winkleigh Devon...........10 F4
Winksley N York..........132 C5
Winlaton Gatesd..........150 F3
Winless Highld............231 K5
Winmarleigh Lancs 120 F2
Winnall Hants................29 J5
Winnersh Wokham.........42 C6
Winnington Ches W......112 F6
Winscombe N Som.........38 B8
Winsford Ches W.........112 F7
Winsford Somset 24 E4
Winsham Somset 13 J2
Winshill Staffs.............100 F7
Winshwen Swans 51 K6
Winskill Cumb..............149 G7
Winsley Wilts 39 J7
Winslow Bucks 58 C3
Winson Gloucs...............56 C6
Winsor Hants 28 F8
Winster Cumb..............129 J2
Winster Derbys 100 E1
Winston Dur 140 E4
Winston Suffk 78 E3
Winstone Gloucs 55 L6
Winswell Devon.............10 D3
Winterborne Came
  Dorset 14 D5
Winterborne
  Clenston Dorset 14 F2
Winterborne
  Houghton Dorset......14 F2
Winterborne
  Kingston Dorset 15 G3
Winterborne
  Monkton Dorset......14 D5
Winterborne
  Stickland Dorset......14 F2
Winterborne
  Whitechurch
  Dorset 14 F3
Winterborne Zelston
  Dorset 15 G3
Winterbourne S Glos 38 F4
Winterbourne W Berk ...41 J6
Winterbourne Abbas
  Dorset 14 C4
Winterbourne
  Bassett Wilts 40 C5
Winterbourne
  Dauntsey Wilts 28 D4
Winterbourne Earls
  Wilts......................28 D5
Winterbourne
  Gunner Wilts 28 D4
Winterbourne
  Monkton Wilts 40 C6
Winterbourne
  Steepleton Dorset ...14 C4
Winterbourne Stoke
  Wilts......................28 B3
Winterburn N York.......131 H7
Winteringham N Linc ...125 L6
Winterley Ches E 99 H2
Winterslow Wilts 28 E5
Winterton N Linc.........125 L6
Winterton-on-Sea
  Norfk 107 K8
Winthorpe Notts.........102 D2
Winton Bmouth.............15 K4
Winton Cumb 139 H5
Wintringham N York.....134 D5
Winwick Cambs.............89 G7
Winwick Nhants 87 J8
Winwick Warrtn...........112 E3
Wirksworth Derbys......100 F2
Wirral Wirral 111 J4
Wirswall Ches E 98 D4
Wisbech Cambs.............90 C2
Wisbech St Mary
  Cambs 90 B2

Wisborough Green
  W Susx 31 H6
Wiseman's Bridge
  Pembks 49 K6
Wiseton Notts 116 B4
Wishaw N Lans 175 L7
Wishaw Warwks 85 L5
Wisley Garden RHS
  Surrey 43 H8
Wispington Lincs 117 K6
Wissett Suffk 93 H7
Wissington Suffk 62 A2
Wistanstow Shrops........83 H6
Wistanswick Shrops.......98 F6
Wistaston Ches E 99 G2
Wiston Pembks 49 H4
Wiston S Lans 165 J3
Wiston W Susx 18 F3
Wistow Cambs...............89 K7
Wistow N York.............124 F4
Wiswell Lancs...............121 L3
Witcham Cambs.............90 C7
Witchampton Dorset 15 J2
Witchford Cambs...........90 C7
Witcombe Somset 26 C6
Witham Essex 61 K5
Witham Friary
  Somset 27 H3
Witham on the Hill
  Lincs 88 F1
Withcall Lincs 118 C5
Withdean Br & H 19 J4
Witherenden Hill
  E Susx 33 H7
Witheridge Devon..........11 J3
Witherley Leics 86 D4
Withern Lincs 118 F5
Withernsea E R Yk 127 H5
Withernwick E R Yk 126 F3
Withersdale Street
  Suffk 92 F7
Withersfield Suffk..........76 F5
Witherslack Cumb.........129 J3
Withiel Cnwll 4 F3
Withiel Florey Somset....24 F5
Withington Gloucs 56 B5
Withington Herefs 69 L5
Withington Manch.........113 J3
Withington Shrops 83 L2
Withington Staffs.........100 B5
Withleigh Devon............11 K3
Withnell Lancs 121 J6
Withybed Green
  Worcs.....................85 H8
Withybrook Warwks 86 E6
Withycombe
  Somset 24 F3
Withyham E Susx 32 E6
Withypool Somset 24 D4
Withywood Bristl............38 E6
Witley Surrey.................30 F4
Witnesham Suffk 78 E4
Witney Oxon 57 G6
Wittering C Pete 88 F3
Wittersham Kent 21 H1
Witton Birm 85 J5
Witton Norfk 93 G2
Witton Norfk 107 H6
Witton Gilbert Dur.......151 G5
Witton le Wear Dur......140 E2
Witton Park Dur 140 F2
Wiveliscombe Somset....25 G5
Wivelrod Hants 30 A4
Wivelsfield E Susx 19 K2
Wivelsfield Green
  E Susx 19 K2
Wivenhoe Essex............62 C4
Wiveton Norfk 106 C4
Wix Essex 62 E3
Wixford Warwks 71 K4
Wixoe Suffk 77 G6
Woburn C Beds..............58 F2
Woburn Abbey
  C Beds....................58 F2
Woburn Sands
  M Keyn 74 D7

Woking Surrey 43 G8
Woking
  Crematorium
   Surrey 42 F8
Wokingham Wokham 42 D6
Woldingham Surrey 32 C3
Wold Newton E R Yk.... 135 G5
Wold Newton NE Lin...... 118 C3
Wolfclyde S Lans 165 K3
Wolferton Norfk........... 105 G6
Wolfhill P & K 186 B2
Wolf's Castle Pembks 49 G3
Wolfsdale Pembks 48 F3
Wollaston Dudley 84 F6
Wollaston Nhants.......... 74 C2
Wollaston Shrops 83 C3
Wollaton C Nott 101 K4
Wollaton Hall & Park
  C Nott...................... 101 K5
Wollerton Shrops 98 F6
Wollescote Dudley 85 G6
Wolseley Bridge
  Staffs 100 A7
Wolsingham Dur 150 D7
Wolstanton Staffs 99 J3
Wolston Warwks............ 86 E7
Wolvercote Oxon 57 J6
Wolverhampton
  Wolves 85 G4
Wolverhampton
  Halfpenny Green
  Airport Staffs............ 84 E5
Wolverley Worcs 84 E7
Wolverton Hants 41 K8
Wolverton M Keyn 74 B6
Wolverton Warwks......... 72 B3
Wolverton Wilts............. 27 H5
Wolvesnewton Mons 54 C7
Wolvey Warwks............. 86 E6
Wolvey Heath
  Warwks 86 E5
Wolviston S on T 141 K3
Wombleton N York 133 K3
Wombourne Staffs......... 84 F5
Wombwell Barns 115 H2
Womenswold Kent......... 35 G5
Womersley N York 124 E6
Wonersh Surrey............ 31 G3
Wonford Devon.............. 12 B4
Wonston Dorset............ 14 E2
Wonston Hants............. 29 J4
Wooburn Bucks............. 42 E3
Wooburn Green Bucks.... 42 E3
Woodacott Devon........... 9 K4
Woodall Rothm 115 J5
Woodall Services
  Rothm...................... 115 J5
Woodbastwick Norfk...... 93 G1
Wood Bevington
  Warwks 71 J4
Woodborough Notts..... 101 M3
Woodborough Wilts....... 40 C7
Woodbridge Suffk......... 78 F5
Woodbury Devon........... 12 C5
Woodbury Salterton
  Devon 12 C5
Woodchester Gloucs 55 J7
Woodchurch Kent.......... 34 C7
Woodcombe Somset....... 24 E3
Woodcote Gt Lon 44 F7
Woodcote Oxon 41 M4
Woodcote Wrekin........... 84 D1
Woodcroft Gloucs.......... 38 D2
Wood Dalling Norfk...... 106 C6
Woodditton Cambs 76 F3
Woodeaton Oxon........... 57 K5
Wood End Gt Lon 43 J4
Wood End Herts............ 60 B3
Woodend Highld 190 F4
Woodend Nhants........... 73 H5
Woodend W Loth 176 C4
Woodend W Susx 17 M2
Wood End Warwks......... 71 K1
Woodfalls Wilts............ 28 D7
Woodford Cnwll 9 G3

Woodford Gloucs 39 G2
Woodford Gt Lon 45 H2
Woodford Nhants.......... 88 D7
Woodford Stockp.......... 113 K5
Woodford Bridge
  Gt Lon 45 H2
Woodford Halse
  Nhants....................... 73 G4
Woodford Wells
  Gt Lon 45 H2
Woodgate Birm............. 85 H6
Woodgate Devon............ 25 H7
Woodgate W Susx.......... 18 C5
Woodgate Worcs 71 H2
Wood Green Gt Lon 44 F2
Woodgreen Hants.......... 28 D7
Woodhall N York........... 131 J2
Woodhall Spa Lincs...... 117 K8
Woodham Bucks............ 58 B4
Woodham Surrey........... 43 H7
Woodham Ferrers
  Essex 61 J7
Woodham Mortimer
  Essex 61 K6
Woodham Walter
  Essex 61 K6
Wood Hayes Wolves 85 G3
Woodhead Abers 216 E6
Woodhill Shrops 84 D6
Woodhill Somset........... 26 A6
Woodhorn Nthumb 159 H4
Woodhouse Leeds 123 K4
Woodhouse Leics 87 G1
Woodhouse Sheff 115 H4
Woodhouse Wakefd 124 B6
Woodhouse Eaves
  Leics 87 G2
Woodhouselee
  Mdloth 177 H5
Woodhouselees
  D & G 156 D6
Woodhouses Staffs...... 100 D8
Woodhurst Cambs 89 K7
Woodingdean Br & H..... 19 K5
Woodkirk Leeds 123 K5
Woodland Abers 207 G2
Woodland Devon............ 6 F5
Woodland Devon............ 7 J3
Woodland Dur 140 D2
Woodland S Ayrs 152 E3
Woodlands Abers 206 E6
Woodlands Donc......... 124 E8
Woodlands Dorset......... 15 K2
Woodlands Hants.......... 16 C1
Woodlands N York 132 E8
Woodlands (Coleshill)
  Crematorium
   Warwks 85 L5
Woodlands Park
  W & M 42 E5
Woodlands
  (Scarborough)
  Crematorium
   N York 134 F3
Woodlands
  (Scunthorpe)
  Crematorium
   N Linc 125 K7
Woodleigh Devon........... 7 H6
Woodley Wokham 42 C5
Woodmancote
  Gloucs 39 H2
Woodmancote
  Gloucs 55 L3
Woodmancote
  Gloucs 56 A6
Woodmancote
  W Susx 17 L2
Woodmancote
  W Susx 19 H3
Woodmancott Hants...... 29 K3
Woodmansey E R Yk.... 126 C3
Woodmansgreen
  W Susx 30 E6
Woodmansterne
  Surrey 32 B2

Woodmanton Devon...... 12 C5
Woodnesborough
  Kent......................... 35 J4
Woodnewton Nhants.... 88 F5
Wood Norton Norfk.... 106 B6
Woodplumpton
  Lancs 121 G4
Woodrising Norfk.......... 92 B3
Wood's Corner E Susx ... 20 D2
Woodseaves Staffs 99 H7
Woodsetts Rothm........ 115 K5
Woodsford Dorset......... 14 E4
Wood's Green E Susx..... 20 D3
Woodside Br For 42 F6
Woodside Fife 187 G5
Woodside Gt Lon 45 G6
Woodside P & K 195 K8
Woodstock Oxon 57 H5
Woodston C Pete 89 H4
Wood Street Norfk...... 107 H7
Wood Street Village
  Surrey 30 F2
Woodton Norfk............. 93 G5
Woodtown Devon........... 22 F6
Woodvale
  Crematorium
   Br & H 19 J4
Wood Walton Cambs...... 89 J7
Woofferton Shrops......... 69 K2
Wookey Somset 26 D3
Wookey Hole Somset...... 26 D2
Wool Dorset 14 F5
Woolacombe Devon....... 23 G3
Woolage Green Kent...... 35 H5
Woolaston Gloucs 54 E7
Woolaston Common
  Gloucs 54 E7
Woolavington
  Somset 25 M3
Woolbeding W Susx 30 E6
Woolbrook Devon.......... 12 E3
Wooler Nthumb.......... 168 E4
Woolfardisworthy
  Devon 11 J3
Woolfardisworthy
  Devon 22 E7
Woolfords S Lans 176 D6
Woolhampton
  W Berk 41 L6
Woolhope Herefs 69 L7
Woolland Dorset........... 14 E2
Woolley BaNES............. 39 H6
Woolley Cambs............. 89 G8
Woolley Wakefd 123 L7
Woolley Edge
  Services Wakefd 123 K7
Woolmere Green
  Worcs 71 G2
Woolmer Green Herts 59 L4
Woolminstone
  Somset 13 K2
Woolpit Suffk............... 77 L3
Woolstaston Shrops....... 83 J4
Woolsthorpe Lincs...... 102 D5
Woolsthorpe-by-
  Colsterworth
   Lincs 102 F7
Woolston C Sotn 16 E1
Woolston Shrops........... 97 L7
Woolston Somset........... 25 H4
Woolston Somset........... 26 F5
Woolston Warrtn........ 112 F4
Woolstone Gloucs 55 L3
Woolstone M Keyn 74 C6
Woolstone Oxon 40 F3
Woolston Green
  Devon 7 H3
Woolton L'pool 112 B4
Woolton Hill Hants........ 41 H7
Woolverstone Suffk....... 78 E6
Woolverton Somset........ 27 H2
Woolwich Gt Lon 45 H4
Woonton Herefs 69 G4
Woore Shrops 99 G4
Wootten Green Suffk..... 92 F8
Wootton Bed................ 74 E5

Wootton Kent................ 35 G5
Wootton N Linc 126 D7
Wootton Nhants........... 73 L3
Wootton Oxon.............. 57 H4
Wootton Oxon.............. 57 J7
Wootton Staffs 100 C4
Wootton Bassett
  Wilts 40 B4
Wootton Bridge IoW 17 G4
Wootton Courtenay
  Somset 24 E3
Wootton Fitzpaine
  Dorset 13 J4
Wootton Rivers Wilts..... 40 D7
Wootton St
  Lawrence Hants 29 L2
Wootton Wawen
  Warwks 71 L2
Worcester Worcs........... 70 F4
Worcester Park
  Gt Lon 44 E6
Wordsley Dudley 84 F6
Worfield Shrops............. 84 D4
Workington Cumb....... 136 D2
Worksop Notts............ 115 L5
Worlaby N Linc 126 C7
Worlds End Hants........ 29 M8
Worlds End W Susx 19 J2
Worle N Som................ 38 A7
Worleston Ches E.......... 98 F2
Worlingham Suffk......... 93 J5
Worlington Devon......... 11 H3
Worlington Suffk.......... 91 G8
Worlingworth Suffk....... 78 F2
Wormbridge Herefs....... 54 B2
Wormegay Norfk........... 90 F2
Wormelow Tump
  Herefs 54 C3
Wormhill Derbys......... 114 C6
Wormingford Essex....... 61 M2
Worminghall Bucks........ 57 M6
Wormington Gloucs....... 71 J7
Wormit Fife 186 F3
Wormleighton
  Warwks 72 F4
Wormley Herts 60 B6
Wormley Surrey............ 30 F4
Wormshill Kent............. 34 B3
Wormsley Herefs........... 69 H5
Worplesdon Surrey........ 30 F2
Worrall Sheff 114 F3
Worsbrough Barns....... 115 G2
Worsbrough Bridge
  Barns 115 G2
Worsbrough Dale
  Barns 115 G2
Worsley Salfd 113 H2
Worstead Norfk.......... 107 G7
Worsthorne Lancs....... 122 C4
Worston Devon.............. 6 E5
Worston Lancs............ 122 B3
Worth Kent.................. 35 J4
Wortham Suffk............. 92 C7
Worthen Shrops........... 83 G3
Worthenbury
  Wrexhm...................... 98 B4
Worthing Norfk.......... 106 B8
Worthing W Susx.......... 18 F5
Worthing
  Crematorium
   W Susx 18 F4
Worthington Leics 101 H7
Worth Matravers
  Dorset 15 H6
Wortley Barns............ 114 F2
Wortley Leeds............ 123 K4
Worton N York........... 131 H2
Worton Wilts................ 39 L8
Wortwell Norfk............. 92 F6
Wotton-under-Edge
  Gloucs 39 H2
Wotton Underwood
  Bucks 58 B5
Woughton on the
  Green M Keyn............ 74 C6
Wouldham Kent........... 46 B7

Wrabness Essex..............62 E2
Wrafton Devon..............23 H4
Wragby Lincs..............117 J6
Wragby Wakefd............124 C6
Wrangaton Devon............7 G4
Wrangle Lincs..............104 C3
Wrangway Somset..........25 H7
Wrantage Somset............25 L6
Wrawby N Linc..............126 C8
Wraxall N Som..............38 C6
Wraxall Somset..............26 E4
Wray Lancs..............130 B6
Wraysbury W & M..........43 G5
Wrayton Lancs..............130 C5
Wrea Green Lancs..........120 E4
Wreay Cumb..............148 D5
Wrecclesham Surrey..........30 D3
Wrekenton Gatesd..........151 G3
Wrelton N York..............134 B3
Wrenbury Ches E..............98 C3
Wreningham Norfk..........92 E4
Wrentham Suffk..............93 K6
Wrentnall Shrops..............83 H3
Wressle E R Yk..............125 G4
Wressle N Linc..............126 B8
Wrestlingworth
   C Beds..............75 J5
Wretton Norfk..............91 G4
Wrexham Wrexhm............97 M3
Wribbenhall Worcs..........84 E7
Wrinehill Staffs..............99 H3
Wrington N Som..............38 C7
Writhlington BaNES..........27 G1
Writtle Essex..............61 G6
Wrockwardine
   Wrekin..............84 B2
Wroot N Linc..............116 B2
Wrose C Brad..............123 H3
Wrotham Kent..............33 G2
Wroughton Swindn..........40 C4
Wroxall IoW..............17 G6
Wroxall Warwks..............72 B1
Wroxeter Shrops..............83 L2
Wroxham Norfk..............107 G8
Wroxham Barns
   Norfk..............107 G7
Wroxton Oxon..............72 E6
Wyaston Derbys..............100 D4
Wyberton East Lincs..........104 B4
Wyboston Bed..............75 H3
Wybunbury Ches E..............99 G3
Wychbold Worcs..............71 G2
Wychnor Staffs..............85 L1
Wyck Rissington
   Gloucs..............56 D4
Wycliffe Dur..............140 E4
Wycoller Lancs..............122 D3
Wycomb Leics..............102 C7
Wycombe Marsh
   Bucks..............42 E3
Wyddial Herts..............60 B2
Wye Kent..............34 E5
Wyke C Brad..............123 H5
Wyke Dorset..............27 H6
Wyke Champflower
   Somset..............26 F4
Wykeham N York..............134 E3
Wyken Covtry..............86 D7
Wyken Shrops..............84 D4
Wyke Regis Dorset..........14 C6
Wykey Shrops..............98 B7
Wylam Nthumb..............150 E3
Wylde Green Birm..........85 K5
Wylye Wilts..............28 A4
Wymeswold Leics..........101 L7
Wymington Bed..............74 D2
Wymondham Leics..........102 D8
Wymondham Norfk..........92 D3
Wynford Eagle
   Dorset..............14 B3
Wyre Forest
   Crematorium
   Worcs..............84 E8
Wyre Piddle Worcs..........71 G5
Wysall Notts..............101 L6
Wythall Worcs..............85 J7

Wytham Oxon..............57 J6
Wythenshawe Manch....113 J4
Wyton Cambs..............89 K8
Wyton E R Yk..............126 E4
Wyverstone Suffk..........78 C2
Wyverstone Street
   Suffk..............78 B2

Y

Yaddlethorpe N Linc.....116 E1
Yafforth N York..............141 H7
Yalberton Torbay..............7 K4
Yalding Kent..............33 J3
Yanwath Cumb..............138 D2
Yanworth Gloucs..............56 B5
Yapham E R Yk..............125 J1
Yapton W Susx..............18 D5
Yarborough N Som..........38 B8
Yarburgh Lincs..............118 E3
Yarcombe Devon..............13 G2
Yard Devon..............24 B6
Yardley Birm..............85 K6
Yardley
   Crematorium
   Birm..............85 K6
Yardley Gobion
   Nhants..............73 L5
Yardley Hastings
   Nhants..............74 C3
Yardley Wood Birm..........85 K7
Yarkhill Herefs..............69 L6
Yarley Somset..............26 D3
Yarlington Somset..........26 F5
Yarm S on T..............141 K5
Yarmouth IoW..............16 D4
Yarnbrook Wilts..............27 K1
Yarnfield Staffs..............99 K6
Yarnscombe Devon..........23 J6
Yarnton Oxon..............57 J5
Yarpole Herefs..............69 J2
Yarrow Border..............166 E4
Yarrow Feus Border.....166 E4
Yarrowford Border..........166 F4
Yarwell Nhants..............88 F4
Yate S Glos..............39 G4
Yateley Hants..............42 D7
Yatesbury Wilts..............40 B6
Yattendon W Berk..........41 K5
Yatton Herefs..............69 H2
Yatton N Som..............38 B7
Yatton Keynell Wilts.....39 K5
Yaverland IoW..............17 H5
Yaxham Norfk..............92 B2
Yaxley Cambs..............89 H5
Yaxley Suffk..............92 D8
Yazor Herefs..............69 H5
Yeading Gt Lon..............43 J4
Yeadon Leeds..............123 J3
Yealand Conyers
   Lancs..............129 K5
Yealand Redmayne
   Lancs..............129 K4
Yealmpton Devon..........6 E5
Yearsley N York..............133 J5
Yeaton Shrops..............98 B8
Yeaveley Derbys..............100 D4
Yeavering Nthumb........168 D4
Yedingham N York........134 D4
Yelford Oxon..............57 G6
Yell Shet..............235 d3
Yelling Cambs..............75 J3
Yelvertoft Nhants..........87 H7
Yelverton Devon..............6 D3
Yelverton Norfk..............93 G3
Yenston Somset..............27 G7
Yeoford Devon..............11 H5
Yeolmbridge Cnwll..........9 J7
Yeovil Somset..............26 D7
Yeovil Crematorium
   Somset..............26 D7
Yeovil Marsh Somset....26 D7
Yeovilton Somset..........26 D6
Yesnaby Ork..............234 b5
Yetminster Dorset..........14 B1

Yettington Devon..........12 D5
Yetts o'Muckhart
   Clacks..............185 L6
Yew Tree Sandw..............85 H4
Y Felinheli Gwynd........109 G7
Y Ferwig Cerdgn..............65 G5
Y Ffor Gwynd..............95 G5
Y Cyffylliog Denbgs........97 G2
Yielden Bed..............74 E2
Yieldshields S Lans......176 B7
Yiewsley Gt Lon..............43 H4
Y Maerdy Conwy..............96 F4
Ynysboeth Rhondd..........37 G2
Ynysddu Caerph..............37 J2
Ynyshir Rhondd..............36 F3
Ynystawe Swans..............51 K5
Ynysybwl Rhondd..........37 G2
Yockleton Shrops..............83 H2
Yokefleet E R Yk..........125 J5
Yoker C Glas..............174 F5
York C York..............124 F1
York City
   Crematorium
   C York..............124 F2
Yorkletts Kent..............34 E3
Yorkley Gloucs..............54 F6
York Minster C York.....124 F1
Yorkshire Dales
   National Park..........131 G4
York Town Surrey..........42 E7
Youlgreave Derbys......114 E8
Youlthorpe E R Yk........134 B7
Youlton N York..............133 G6
Yoxall Staffs..............100 C8
Yoxford Suffk..............79 H2
Y Rhiw Gwynd..............94 D6
Ysbyty Ifan Conwy..........96 C3
Ysbyty Ystwyth
   Cerdgn..............67 G1
Ysceifiog Flints..............111 G7
Ystalyfera Neath..............52 B6
Ystrad Rhondd..............36 F2
Ystrad Aeron Cerdgn....66 C4
Ystradfellte Powys..........52 S5
Ystradgynlais Powys......52 C6
Ystrad Meurig
   Cerdgn..............66 F2
Ystrad Mynach
   Caerph..............37 H2
Ystradowen V Glam........36 F5
Ythanbank Abers..........217 G7
Ythanwells Abers..........216 C6
Ythsie Abers..............217 G7

Z

Zeal Monachorum
   Devon..............11 G4
Zeals Wilts..............27 H5
Zelah Cnwll..............4 C5
Zennor Cnwll..............2 E4
Zouch Notts..............101 J7
ZSL London Zoo
   Gt Lon..............44 F4
ZSL Whipsnade Zoo
   C Beds..............59 G4

Ireland

Troon (Mar–Oct)
Cairnryan
Douglas (Apr–Sept) Cairnryan
Liverpool (Birkenhead)
Rathlin Island
Malin Head
Toraigh
Tory Island
Árainn Mhór
Aran Island
DONEGAL
An Clochán Liath
Dunglow
Letterkenny
Ballybofey
CITY OF DERRY
LONDONDERRY
DERRY
Strabane
Portrush
Ballycastle
Coleraine
Limavady
Ballymena
Larne
Maghera
SPERRIN MTS
NORTHERN IRELAND
Antrim
BELFAST INTERNATIONAL
BELFAST
GEORGE BEST BELFAST CITY
Bangor
Newtownards
Cookstown
Dungannon
Omagh
Donegal
NORTH ATLANTIC OCEAN
Ballyshannon
Donegal Bay
Bundoran
Portaferry
Portadown
Armagh
Downpatrick
Enniskillen
Newcastle
Monaghan
Newry
MOURNE MTS
Béal an Mhuirthead
Belmullet
Sligo
Castleblayney
Bangor
Ballina
OX MTS
Dundalk
IRISH SEA
Carrickmacross
Oileán Acla
Achill Island
Charlestown
Cavan
Foxford
Boyle
Carrick-on-Shannon
Douglas (Apr–Sept) Holyhead
Castlebar
IRELAND WEST AIRPORT KNOCK
Virginia
Knock
Slane
Drogheda
Clare Island
Westport
Castlerea
Kells
Longford
Navan
Claremorris
Inishturk
Balbriggan
REPUBLIC OF IRELAND
Roscommon
Inishbofin
DUBLIN
Mullingar
Kinnegad
Lambay
Tuam
Clifden
Athlone
Liverpool Holyhead
DUBLIN
Dún Laoghaire
Oughterard
Tullamore
GALWAY
Garumna
Gorumna Island
Kildare
Naas
Bray
Oranmore
Loughrea
Galway Bay
Blessington
Holyhead (Apr–Sept)
Oileáin Árann
Aran Islands
Birr
SLIEVE BLOOM MTS
Portumna
Gort
Wicklow
Portlaoise
Roscrea
WICKLOW MTS
Ennistymon
Carlow
Tullow
Arklow
Ennis
Newmarket-on-Fergus
Nenagh
Gorey
SHANNON
Thurles
Kilkenny
Kilkee
LIMERICK
Kilrush
Enniscorthy
Loop Head
Adare
Cashel
Tipperary
Wexford
GALTY MTS
Clonmel
New Ross
Abbeyfeale
Cahir
Rosslare
KNOCKMEALDOWN MTS
Charleville
Rosslare Harbour
Tralee
WATERFORD
Carnsore Point
Castleisland
Mitchelstown
Lismore
Fishguard Pembroke
An Daingean
Dingle
KERRY
Mallow
Fermoy
An Blascaod Mór
Great Blasket Island
Killorglin
Killarney
BOGGERAGH MTS
Dungarvan
Dingle Bay
CORK
Youghal
Celtic Sea
Cahersiveen
Macroom
Parknasilla
Kenmare
Ringaskiddy
An Coireán
Waterville
Glengarriff
Cherbourg Roscoff (May–Sept)
Kinsale
Bantry
Clonakilty
Dursey Island
Bantry Bay
Skibbereen
Mizen Head
Clear Island
Roscoff (Mar–Oct)
0 20 40 miles
0 20 40 60 kilometres

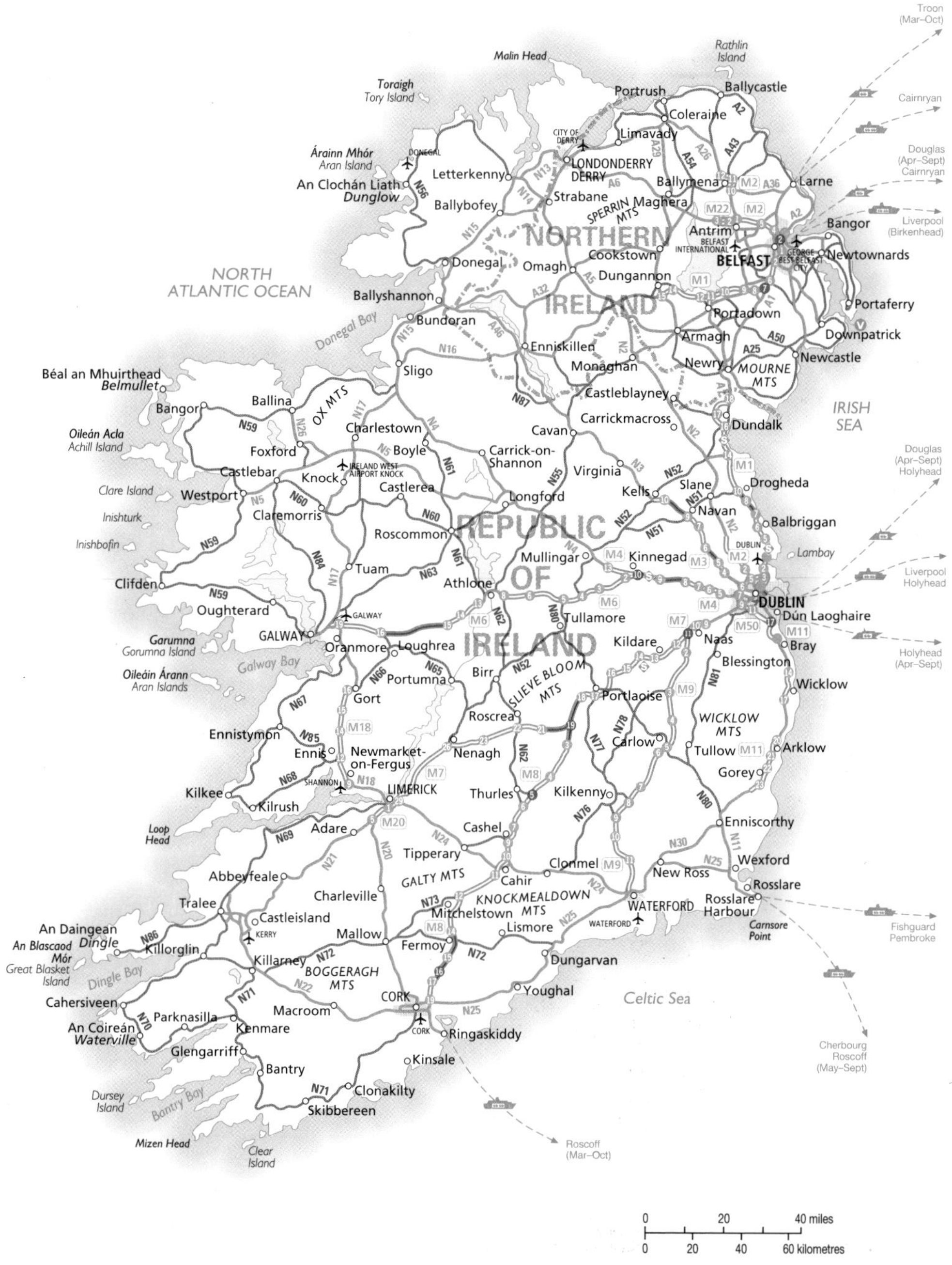

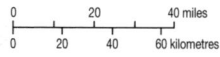

Map pages north

HOSTELS.

BEVERLEY 0845 371 9004.

YORK   01904 413 693

WHITBY   0845 371 9049
          0845 371 9504
          0845 371 9128

DURHAM   0191 334 3358

BARDON MILL 0845 371 9753

WOOLER   01668 216358

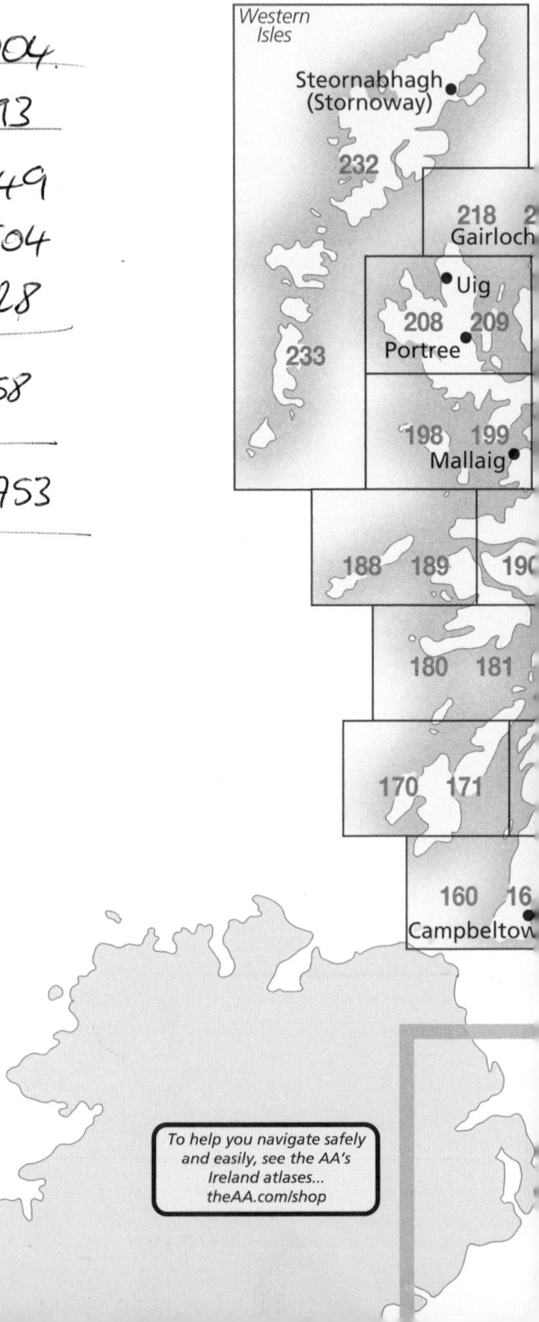

Western Isles

Steornabhagh
(Stornoway)

232

218 2
Gairloch

Uig

208 209
Portree

233

198 199
Mallaig

188 189 190

180 181

170 171

160 16
Campbeltow